RULES FOR CATEGORICAL SYLLOGISMS

Rule 1: *The middle term must be distributed at least once.*
Fallacy: Undistributed middle.

Rule 2: *If a term is distributed in the conclusion, then it must be distributed in the premise.*
Fallacy: Illicit major; illicit minor.

Rule 3: *Two negative premises are not allowed.*
Fallacy: Exclusive premises.

Rule 4: *A negative premise requires a negative conclusion, and a negative conclusion requires a negative premise.*
Fallacy: Drawing an affirmative conclusion from a negative premise; drawing a negative conclusion from affirmative premises.

Rule 5: *If both premises are universal, the conclusion cannot be particular.*
Fallacy: Existential fallacy.

(NOTE: If only Rule 5 is broken, the syllogism is conditionally valid, that is, valid on condition that certain terms denote actually existing things.)

TRUTH TABLES FOR THE PROPOSITIONAL CONNECTIVES

$\sim p$		$p \cdot q$			$p \vee q$			$p \supset q$			$p \equiv q$		
F	T	T	T	T	T	T	T	T	T	T	T	T	T
T	F	T	F	F	T	T	F	T	F	F	T	F	F
		F	F	T	F	T	T	F	T	T	F	F	T
		F	F	F	F	F	F	F	T	F	F	T	F

RULES FOR THE PROBABILITY CALCULUS

1. $P(A \text{ or not } A) = 1$
2. $P(A \text{ and not } A) = 0$
3. $P(A \text{ and } B) = P(A) \times P(B)$ (when A and B are independent)
4. $P(A \text{ and } B) = P(A) \times P(B \text{ given } A)$
5. $P(A \text{ or } B) = P(A) + P(B)$ (when A and B are mutually exclusive)
6. $P(A \text{ or } B) = P(A) + P(B) - P(A \text{ and } B)$
7. $P(A) = 1 - P(\text{not } A)$

A CONCISE INTRODUCTION TO LOGIC

Third Edition

A CONCISE INTRODUCTION TO LOGIC

Third Edition

PATRICK J. HURLEY
University of San Diego

Wadsworth Publishing Company
Belmont, California

A division of Wadsworth, Inc.

Philosophy Editor: Kenneth King
Production: Del Mar Associates
Designer: Richard Carter
Copy Editor: Jackie Estrada

Printed in the United States of America

2 3 4 5 6 7 8 9 10—92 91 90 89 88

ISBN 0-534-08928-3

Library of Congress Cataloging-in-Publication Data

Hurley, Patrick J., 1942-
   A concise introduction to logic.

   Includes index.
   1. Logic.   I. Title.
BC108.H83   1988   160   87-22994
ISBN 0-534-08928-3

To: *Mary*
    Heidi
    John
    Stephen
    Maggie

"Oh, send him somewhere where they will teach him to think for himself!" Mrs. Shelley answered: "Teach him to think for himself? Oh, my God, teach him rather to think like other people!"

Matthew Arnold, Essays in Criticism

PREFACE

The most immediate benefit derived from the study of logic is the skill needed to construct sound arguments of one's own and to evaluate the arguments of others. In accomplishing this goal, logic instills a sensitivity for the formal component in language, a thorough command of which is indispensable to clear, effective, and meaningful communication. On a broader scale, by focusing attention on the requirement for reasons or evidence to support our views, logic provides a fundamental defense against the prejudiced and uncivilized attitudes that threaten the foundations of our democratic society. Finally, through its analysis of inconsistency as a fatal flaw in any theory or point of view, logic proves a useful device in disclosing ill-conceived policies in the political sphere, and, ultimately, in distinguishing the rational from the irrational, the sane from the insane.

To realize the benefits offered by the study of logic, one must thoroughly understand the central concepts of the subject and be able to apply them in actual situations. To promote the achievement of these goals, this text presents the central concepts of logic clearly and simply. Examples are used extensively, key terms are introduced in boldface type and defined in the glossary/index, and major points are illustrated in graphic boxes. Furthermore, to ensure sufficient practice in applying the basic principles, the text includes nearly 2,000 exercise problems and questions selected to illustrate the main points and guard against the most typical mistakes. In most cases, every third exercise is answered in the back of the book.

New to the Third Edition

This third edition preserves the basic format of its predecessors. The principal changes are in the examples and exercises and in Chapter 3, which has been reorganized. Throughout the text, hundreds of examples and exercises have been replaced with new ones having a more real life flavor and by selections taken from such sources as editorials and letters to the editor of newspapers and magazines. The reorganization of Chapter 3 has involved the addition of a new fallacy classification called "Fallacies of Weak Induction" and the assignment of the previously treated fallacies to more easily manageable groups. In addition, the sections dealing with the red herring, straw man, and appeal to authority fallacies have been rewritten. Other changes include the rewriting of numerous paragraphs throughout the first six chapters, the simplification of Section 1.6 (extended arguments), the expansion of Section 4.7 to allow the application of Venn diagrams to immediate inferences, and the addition of more exercise answers in the back of the book. A complete list of changes is included in the instructor's manual.

Robert Burch has updated his study guide, which accompanies this text, and I am confident that students will continue to find it useful as a supplementary source of exercises and a review for examinations. In addition, commencing with this edition, Susan and Michael Anderson, of the University of Connecticut, have produced computer software titled *Proofreader +*, which covers the areas of syllogistic logic, truth tables, and natural deduction. This software provides an excellent opportunity for student practice and is available to adopters of this text free of charge from Wadsworth Publishing Co.

Ways of Using the Text

Depending on the instructor's preferences, this text can be approached in several different ways. The following chart presents three possible approaches for three different kinds of course.

TYPE OF COURSE

	Traditional logic course	Informal logic course, critical reasoning course	Course emphasizing modern formal logic
Recommended material	Chapter 1 Chapter 3 Chapter 4 Chapter 5 Chapter 6 Sections 7.1–7.4	Chapter 1 Chapter 2 Chapter 3 Sections 4.1–4.3 Sections 4.6–4.8 Sections 5.1–5.3 Sections 5.5–5.6 Sections 6.1–6.5 Sections 9.3–9.4	Chapter 1 Chapter 6 (except Section 6.4) Chapter 7 Sections 4.1–4.3 Sections 4.5–4.6 Section 4.8 Chapter 8

	Traditional logic course	Informal logic course, critical reasoning course	Course emphasizing modern formal logic
Optional material	Chapter 2 Chapter 9	Sections 4.4–4.5 Section 5.4 Section 5.7 Section 6.6 Sections 9.1–9.2	Chapter 3 Section 4.7 Sections 5.1–5.2 Section 5.7 Section 6.4

In general, the material in each chapter is arranged so that certain later sections can be skipped without affecting subsequent chapters. For example, those wishing a brief treatment of syllogistic logic could skip Sections 4.4, 4.7, and 4.8 and then cover only the first three sections of Chapter 5. Analogously, those wishing a brief treatment of natural deduction in both propositional and predicate logic may want to skip the last three sections of Chapter 7 and the last three (or even four) sections of Chapter 8. Chapter 2 can be skipped altogether, although some may want to cover the first section of that chapter as an introduction to Chapter 3. Finally, the four sections of Chapter 9 depend only slightly on earlier chapters, so these sections can be treated in any order one chooses.

Acknowledgments

For their reviews and comments leading to the changes in this third edition, I want to thank William Carroll, Coppin State University; James Baley, Mary Washington College; Robert McKay, Norwich University; John Bender, Ohio University, Athens; Victor Grassian, Los Angeles Harbor College; David Ring, Southern Methodist University; Robert Burch, Texas A & M University; Richard W. and Beverly R. Doss, Orange Coast College; Keith Burgess-Jackson, University of Arizona; Kenneth R. Merrill, University of Oklahoma; and John D. Mullen, Dowling College. Of course, any errors or omissions that may remain in the text are the result of my own oversight.

Those who made comments regarding the two previous editions, and to whom I want to express my continued thanks, are Thomas H. Franks, Eastern Michigan University; William Uzgalis, Oregon State University; Paul A. Roth, University of Missouri, Saint Louis; Ralph W. Clarke, West Virginia University; Paul Santelli, Siena College; Paul DeVries, Wheaton College; Bangs Tapscott, University of Utah; Thomas Michaud, Mount Saint Mary's College; James Campbell, University of Toledo; David Weinburger, Stockton State College; Lewis S. Ford, Old Dominion University; Gray Prince, West Los Angeles College; Gary Jones, University of San Diego; Lenore Erikson, Cuesta College; Gary

Foulk, Indiana State University, Terre Haute; Nani Rankin, Indiana University at Kokomo; Robert Burch, Texas A & M University; Donald Cress, Northern Illinois University, DeKalb; George Gale, University of Missouri, Kansas City; John R. Bosworth, Oklahoma State University; William F. Cooper, Baylor University; Evan Fales, University of Iowa; Glen Kessler, University of Virginia; John Mize, Long Beach City College; Larry D. Mayhew, Western Kentucky University; R. Puligandla, University of Toledo; Daniel Rothbart, George Mason University; Lynne Spellman, University of Arkansas; John Sweigart, James Madison University; and Victor Balowitz, State University College at Buffalo.

Finally, it has again been a pleasure working with production supervisor Nancy Sjoberg and copy editor Jackie Estrada, and I am grateful to Ken King, philosophy editor at Wadsworth, for his continued support and helpful suggestions.

CONTENTS

A CONCISE INTRODUCTION TO LOGIC

Third Edition

1
BASIC CONCEPTS

1.1 ARGUMENTS, PREMISES, AND CONCLUSIONS

Logic may be defined as the science that evaluates arguments. All of us encounter arguments in our day-to-day experience. We read them in books and newspapers, hear them on television, and formulate them when communicating with friends and associates. The aim of logic is to develop a system of methods and principles that we may use as criteria for evaluating the arguments of others and as guides in constructing arguments of our own. Among the benefits to be expected from the study of logic is an increase in confidence that we are making sense when we criticize the arguments of others and when we advance arguments of our own.

An **argument,** as it occurs in logic, is a group of statements, one or more of which (the premises) are claimed to provide support for, or reasons to believe, one of the others (the conclusion). In other words, one of the statements (the conclusion) is claimed to follow from the others (the premises). All arguments may be placed in one of two basic groups: those in which the premises really do support the conclusion and those in which they do not, even though they are claimed to. The former are said to be good arguments, the latter bad arguments. The purpose of logic, as the science that evaluates arguments, is thus to develop methods and techniques that allow us to distinguish good arguments from bad.

As is apparent from the above definition, the term "argument" has a very specific meaning in logic. It does not mean, for example, a mere verbal fight, as one might have with one's parent, spouse, or friend. Let us examine the features of this definition in greater detail. First of all, an argument is a group of statements. A **statement** is a sentence that is either true or false; in other words, typically a declarative sentence. The following sentences are statements:

> Aluminum is attacked by hydrochloric acid.
> Broccoli is a good source of vitamin A.
> The *Lusitania* was sunk by the British Navy.
> *The Scarlet Letter* was written by Melville.

The first two are true, the second two false. Truth and falsity are called the two possible **truth values** of the statement. Thus, the truth value of the first two statements is true, and the truth value of the second two is false.

Unlike statements, many sentences cannot be said to be either true or false. Questions, proposals, suggestions, commands, and exclamations usually cannot, and so are not usually classified as statements. The following sentences are not statements:

> What is the atomic weight of carbon?   (question)
> Let's go to the park today.   (proposal)
> We suggest that you travel by bus.   (suggestion)
> Turn to the left at the next corner.   (command)
> Right on!   (exclamation)

The statements that make up an argument are divided into one or more premises and one and only one conclusion. The **premises** are the statements that set forth the reasons or evidence, and the **conclusion** is the statement that is claimed to follow from the reasons or evidence. Here is an example of an argument:

> All crimes are violations of the law.
> Theft is a crime.
> Therefore, theft is a violation of the law.

The first two statements are the premises; the third is the conclusion. The claim that the conclusion follows from the premises is indicated by the word "therefore." In this argument the conclusion really does follow from the premises (i.e., the premises really do support the conclusion), and so the argument is a good one. But consider this argument:

> Some crimes are misdemeanors.
> Murder is a crime.
> Therefore, murder is a misdemeanor.

A CONCISE INTRODUCTION TO LOGIC

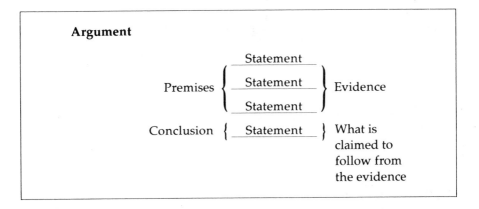

Argument

Premises $\left\{\begin{array}{l}\underline{\text{Statement}} \\ \underline{\text{Statement}} \\ \underline{\text{Statement}}\end{array}\right\}$ Evidence

Conclusion $\left\{\underline{\text{Statement}}\right\}$ What is claimed to follow from the evidence

In this argument the conclusion does not in fact follow from the premises, even though it is claimed to, and so the argument is not a good one.

One of the most important tasks in the analysis of arguments is being able to distinguish premises from conclusion. If what is thought to be a conclusion is really a premise, and vice versa, the subsequent analysis cannot possibly be correct. Frequently, arguments contain certain indicator words that provide clues in identifying premises and conclusion. Some typical **conclusion indicators** are:

therefore	hence	whence
wherefore	thus	so
accordingly	consequently	it follows that
we may conclude	we may infer	implies that
entails that	it must be that	as a result

[handwritten annotation: For this reason]

Whenever a statement follows one of these indicators, it can usually be identified as the conclusion. By process of elimination the other statements in the argument are the premises. Example:

> Corporate raiders leave their target corporation with a heavy debt burden and no increase in productive capacity. Consequently, corporate raiders are bad for the business community.

The conclusion of this argument is "Corporate raiders are bad for the business community," and the premise is "Corporate raiders leave their target corporation with a heavy debt burden and no increase in productive capacity."

If an argument does not contain a conclusion indicator, it may contain a premise indicator. Some typical **premise indicators** are:

since	in that	seeing that
as indicated by	may be inferred from	for the reason that

because	as	inasmuch as
for	given that	owing to

Any statement following one of these indicators can usually be identified as a premise. Example:

> Expectant mothers should never use recreational drugs, since the use of these drugs can jeopardize the development of the fetus.

The premise of this argument is "The use of these drugs can jeopardize the development of the fetus," and the conclusion is "Expectant mothers should never use recreational drugs."

One premise indicator not included in the above list is "for this reason." This indicator is special in that it comes immediately *after* the premise that it indicates. "For this reason" means for the reason (premise) that was just given. In other words, the premise is the statement that occurs immediately *before* "for this reason." One should be careful not to confuse "for this reason" with "for the reason that."

Sometimes a single indicator can be used to identify more than one premise. Consider the following argument:

> The development of high-temperature superconducting materials is technologically justified, for such materials will allow electricity to be transmitted without loss over great distances, and they will pave the way for trains that levitate magnetically.

The premise indicator "for" goes with both "Such materials will allow electricity to be transmitted without loss over great distances" and "They will pave the way for trains that levitate magnetically." These are the premises. By process of elimination, "The development of high-temperature superconducting materials is technologically justified" is the conclusion.

Sometimes an argument contains no indicators. When this occurs, the reader/listener must ask himself or herself such questions as: What single statement is claimed (implicitly) to follow from the others? What is the arguer trying to prove? What is the main point in the passage? The answers to these questions should point to the conclusion. Example:

> The space program deserves increased expenditures in the years ahead. Not only does the national defense depend upon it, but the program will more than pay for itself in terms of technological spinoffs. Furthermore, at current funding levels the program cannot fulfill its anticipated potential.

The main point of this argument is that the space program deserves increased expenditures in the years ahead. All the other statements provide support for this statement. Accordingly, the argument is analyzed as follows:

P₁: The national defense is dependent upon the space program.

P₂: The space program will more than pay for itself in terms of technological spinoffs.

P₃: At current funding levels the space program cannot fulfill its anticipated potential.

C: The space program deserves increased expenditures in the years ahead.

When restructuring arguments such as this, one should remain as close as possible to the original version, while at the same time attending to the requirement that premises and conclusion be complete sentences that are meaningful in the order in which they are listed.

Note that the first two premises are included within the scope of a single statement in the original argument. For the purposes of this text, compound arrangements of statements in which the various components are all claimed to be true will be considered as separate statements.

Passages that contain arguments sometimes contain statements that are neither premises nor conclusion. Only statements that are actually intended to support the conclusion should be included in the list of premises. If a statement has nothing to do with the conclusion or, for example, simply makes a passing comment, it should not be included within the context of the argument. Example:

> Socialized medicine is not recommended because it would result in a reduction in the overall quality of medical care available to the average citizen. In addition, it might very well bankrupt the federal treasury. This is the whole case against socialized medicine in a nutshell.

The conclusion of this argument is "Socialized medicine is not recommended," and the two statements following the word "because" are the premises. The last statement makes only a passing comment about the argument itself and is therefore neither a premise nor a conclusion.

Closely related to the concepts of argument and statement are those of inference and proposition. An **inference,** in the technical sense of the term, is the reasoning process expressed by an argument. As we will see in the next section, inferences may be expressed not only through arguments but through conditional statements as well. In the loose sense of the term, "argument" and "inference" are used interchangeably.

A **proposition,** in the technical sense, is the meaning or information content of a statement. Because information may be expressed in different ways, the same proposition may be expressed by different statements. Conversely, because the meaning of a statement sometimes depends on the context in which it is used, a single statement may express more than one proposition. For the purposes of this text, however, "proposition" and "statement" will be used interchangeably.

Note on the History of Logic

The person who is generally credited with the title Father of Logic is the ancient Greek philosopher Aristotle (384–322 B.C.). Aristotle's predecessors had been interested in the art of constructing persuasive arguments and in techniques for refuting the arguments of others, but it was Aristotle who first devised systematic criteria for analyzing and evaluating arguments. Aristotle's logic is called **syllogistic logic** and includes much of what is treated in Chapters 4 and 5 of this text. The fundamental elements in this logic are terms, and arguments are evaluated as good or bad depending on how the terms are arranged in the argument. In addition to his development of syllogistic logic, Aristotle cataloged a number of informal fallacies, a topic treated in Chapter 3 of this text.

After Aristotle's death, another Greek philosopher, Chrysippus (279–206 B.C.), one of the founders of the Stoic school, developed a logic in which the fundamental elements were whole propositions. Chrysippus treated every proposition as either true or false and developed rules for determining the truth or falsity of compound propositions from the truth or falsity of their components. In the course of doing so, he laid the foundation for the truth functional interpretation of the logical connectives presented in Chapter 6 of this text and introduced the notion of natural deduction, treated in Chapter 7.

For thirteen hundred years after the death of Chrysippus, relatively little creative work was done in logic. The physician Galen (A.D. 129–c. 199) developed the theory of the compound categorical syllogism, but for the most part philosophers confined themselves to writing commentaries on the works of Aristotle and Chrysippus. Boethius (c. 480–524) is a noteworthy example.

The first major logician of the Middle Ages was Peter Abelard (1079–1142). Abelard reconstructed and refined the logic of Aristotle and Chrysippus as communicated by Boethius, and he originated a theory of universals that traced the universal character of general terms to concepts in the mind rather than to "natures" existing outside the mind, as Aristotle had held. In addition, Abelard distinguished arguments that are valid because of their form from those that are valid because of their content, but he held that only formal validity was the "perfect" or conclusive variety. The present text follows Abelard on this point.

After Abelard, the study of logic during the Middle Ages blossomed and flourished through the work of numerous philosophers. It attained its final expression in the writings of the Oxford philosopher William of Occam (c. 1285–1349). Occam devoted much of his attention to **modal** logic, a kind of logic that involves such notions as possibility, necessity, belief, and doubt. He also conducted an exhaustive study of forms of valid and invalid syllogisms and contributed to the development of the concept of a metalanguage, that is, a higher-level language used to discuss linguistic entities such as words, terms, propositions, and so on.

Toward the middle of the fifteenth century, a reaction set in against the logic of the Middle Ages. Rhetoric largely displaced logic as the primary focus of attention; the logic of Chrysippus, which had already begun to lose its unique identity in the Middle Ages, was ignored altogether, and the logic of Aristotle was studied only in highly simplistic presentations. A reawakening did not occur until two hundred years later through the work of Gottfried Wilhelm Leibniz (1646–1716).

Leibniz was a genius who attempted to develop a symbolic language or "calculus" that could be used to settle all forms of disputes, whether they be in theology, philosophy, or international relations. As a result of this work, Leibniz is sometimes credited with being the father of symbolic logic. Leibniz's efforts to symbolize logic were carried into the nineteenth century by Bernard Bolzano (1781–1848).

With the arrival of the middle of the nineteenth century, logic commenced an extremely rapid period of development that has continued to this day. Work in symbolic logic was done by a number of philosophers and mathematicians, including Augustus DeMorgan (1806–1871), George Boole (1815–1864), William Stanley Jevons (1835–1882), and John Venn (1834–1923), some of whom are popularly known today by the logical theorems and techniques that bear their names. At the same time, a revival in inductive logic was initiated by the British philosopher John Stuart Mill (1806–1873), whose methods of induction are presented in Chapter 9 of this text.

Toward the end of the nineteenth century, the foundations of modern mathematical logic were laid by Gottlob Frege (1848–1925). His *Begriffsschrift* sets forth the theory of quantification presented in Chapter 8 of this text. Frege's work was continued into the twentieth century by Alfred North Whitehead (1861–1947) and Bertrand Russell (1872–1970), whose monumental *Principia Mathematica* attempted to reduce the whole of pure mathematics to logic. The *Principia* is the source of much of the symbolism that appears in Chapters 6, 7, and 8 of this text.

During the twentieth century, much of the work in logic has focused on the formalization of logical systems and on questions dealing with the completeness and consistency of such systems. A now-famous theorem proved by Kurt Goedel (1906–1978) states that in any formal system adequate for number theory there exists an undecidable formula—that is, a formula such that neither it nor its negation is derivable from the axioms of the system. Other developments include multivalued logics and the formalization of modal logic. Most recently, logic has made a major contribution to technology by providing the conceptual foundation for the electronic circuitry of digital computers.

EXERCISE 1.1

I. Each of the following passages contains a single argument. Using the letters "P" and "C," identify the premises and conclusion of each argument, writing premises first and conclusion last. List the premises in the order in which they make the most sense, and write both premises and conclusion in the form of separate declarative sentences. Indicator words may be eliminated once premises and conclusion have been appropriately labeled. The exercises marked with a star are answered in the back of the text.

★1. Titanium combines readily with oxygen, nitrogen, and hydrogen, all of which have an adverse affect on its mechanical properties. As a result, titanium must be processed in their absence.

(*Illustrated World of Science Encyclopedia*)

2. Since the good, according to Plato, is that which furthers a person's real interests, it follows that in any given case when the good is known, men will seek it.

(Avrum Stroll and Richard Popkin, *Philosophy and the Human Spirit*)

3. As the denial or perversion of justice by the sentences of courts, as well as in any other manner, is with reason classed among the just causes of war, it will follow that the federal judiciary ought to have cognizance of all causes in which the citizens of other countries are concerned.

(Alexander Hamilton, *Federalist Papers*, No. 80)

★4. When individuals voluntarily abandon property, they forfeit any expectation of privacy in it that they might have had. Therefore, a warrantless search or seizure of abandoned property is not unreasonable under the Fourth Amendment.

(Judge Stephanie Kulp Seymour, *United States v. Jones*)

5. Artists and poets look at the world and seek relationships and order. But they translate their ideas to canvas, or to marble, or into poetic images. Scientists try to find relationships between different objects and events. To express the order they find, they create hypotheses and theories. Thus the great scientific theories are easily compared to great art and great literature.

(Douglas C. Giancoli, *The Ideas of Physics*, 3rd edition)

6. The psychological impact and crisis created by birth of a defective infant is devastating. Not only is the mother denied the normal tension release from the stress of pregnancy, but both parents feel a crushing blow to their dignity, self-esteem, and self-confidence. In a very short time, they feel grief for the loss of the normal expected child, anger at fate, numbness, disgust, waves of helplessness and disbelief.

(John A. Robertson, "Involuntary Euthanasia of Defective Newborns")

★7. The measurement of time has two different aspects. For civil and for some scientific purposes, we want to know the time of day so that we can order events in sequence. In most scientific work, we want to know how long an event lasts. Thus any time standard must be able to answer the question "What time is it?" and the question "How long does it last?"

(David Halliday and Robert Resnick, *Fundamentals of Physics*)

8. Like a flame or the wake of a boat, the form of a plant changes slowly but the components are in continual flux. The motion of the components can therefore be analyzed in terms of fluid flow.

(Ralph O. Erickson and Wendy Kuhn Silk, "The Kinematics of Plant Growth")

9. Some split-brain experiments have revealed surprising differences between the two hemispheres. The left side of the brain tends to specialize in active speech events such as talking and writing. If we present a word to the left side of the brain by placing it in the right visual field, the split-brain subject can read it and say it aloud. If the same word is presented to the right side of the brain (placed in the left visual field) the patient cannot say it aloud.

(John P. Houston, Helen Bee, and David C. Rimm, *Essentials of Psychology*, 2nd edition)

★10. Punishment, when speedy and specific, may suppress undesirable behavior, but it cannot teach or encourage desirable alternatives. Therefore, it is crucial to use positive techniques to model and reinforce appropriate behavior that the person can use in place of the unacceptable response that has to be suppressed.

(Walter Mischel and Harriet Mischel, *Essentials of Psychology*)

11. Since the drive for profits underlies the very existence of business organizations, it follows that a most important function of an accounting system is to provide information about the profitability of a business.

(Walter B. Meigs and Robert F. Meigs, *Accounting*)

12. Since private property helps people define themselves, since it frees people from mundane cares of daily subsistence, and since it is finite, no individual should accumulate so much property that others are prevented from accumulating the necessities of life.

(Leon P. Baradat, *Political Ideologies, Their Origins and Impact*)

★13. To every existing thing God wills some good. Hence, since to love any thing is nothing else than to will good to that thing, it is manifest that God loves everything that exists.

(Thomas Aquinas, *Summa Theologica*)

14. Women of the working class, especially wage workers, should not have more than two children at most. The average working man can support no more and the average working woman can take care of no more in decent fashion.

(Margaret Sanger, *Family Limitations*)

15. Every art and every inquiry, and similarly every action and pursuit, is

thought to aim at some good; and for this reason the good has rightly
been declared to be that at which all things aim.

(Aristotle, *Nicomachean Ethics*)

★16. Poverty offers numerous benefits to the nonpoor. Antipoverty programs
provide jobs for middle-class professionals in social work, penology and
public health. Such workers' future advancement is tied to the continued
growth of bureaucracies dependent on the existence of poverty.

(J. John Palen, *Social Problems*)

17. Corn is an annual crop. Butcher's meat, a crop which requires four or
five years to grow. As an acre of land, therefore, will produce a much
smaller quantity of the one species of food than the other, the inferiority
of the quantity must be compensated by the superiority of the price.

(Adam Smith, *The Wealth of Nations*)

18. Neither a borrower nor lender be
For loan oft loses both itself and friend,
And borrowing dulls the edge of husbandry.

(William Shakespeare, *Hamlet* I, 3)

★19. All over the world the close of the sixteenth century saw monarchy prevailing and tending towards absolutism. Germany and Italy were patchworks of autocratic princely dominions, Spain was practically autocratic,
the throne had never been so powerful in England, and as the seventeenth century drew on, the French monarchy gradually became the
grandest and most consolidated power in Europe.

(H. G. Wells, *The Outline of History*)

20. Contrary to the tales of some scuba divers, the toothsome, gaping grin
on the mouth of an approaching shark is not necessarily anticipatory. It
is generally accepted that by constantly swimming with its mouth
open, the shark is simply avoiding suffocation. This assures a continu-
ous flow of oxygen-laden water into their mouths, over their gills, and
out through the gill slits.

(Robert A. Wallace et al., *Biology: The Science of Life*)

21. Not only is the sky blue [as a result of scattering], but light coming
from it is also partially polarized. You can readily observe this by placing a piece of Polaroid (for example, one lens of a pair of Polaroid
sunglasses) in front of your eye and rotating it as you look at the sky
on a clear day. You will notice a change in light intensity with the or-
ientation of the Polaroid.

(Frank J. Blatt, *Principles of Physics*, 2nd ed.)

★22. Anyone familiar with our prison system knows that there are some inmates who behave little better than brute beasts. But the very fact that
these prisoners exist is a telling argument against the efficacy of capital
punishment as a deterrent. If the death penalty had been truly effective
as a deterrent, such prisoners would long ago have vanished.

("The Injustice of the Death Penalty," *America*)

23. Since the secondary light [from the moon] does not inherently belong
to the moon, and is not received from any star or from the sun, and

since in the whole universe there is no other body left but the earth, what must we conclude? What is to be proposed? Surely we must assert that the lunar body (or any other dark and sunless orb) is illuminated by the earth.

(Galileo Galilei, *The Starry Messenger*)

24. Though it is possible that REM sleep and dreaming are not necessary in the adult, REM deprivation studies seem to suggest otherwise. Why would REM pressure increase with deprivation if the system is unimportant in the adult?

(Herbert L. Petri, *Motivation: Theory and Research,* 2nd ed.)

★25. World government and the balance of power are in many ways opposites. World government means one central authority, a permanent standing world police force, and clearly defined conditions under which this force will go into action. A balance of power system has many sovereign authorities, each controlling its own army, combining only when they feel like it to control aggression. To most people world government now seems unattainable.

(David W. Ziegler, *War, Peace, and International Politics*, 4th ed.)

II. The following arguments were taken from magazine and newspaper editorials and letters to the editor. In most instances the main conclusion must be rephrased to capture the full intent of the author. Write out what you interpret the main conclusion to be.

★1. Has anyone noticed that in the current U.S.-Soviet disarmament negotiations at Geneva, so central to the future of humanity, women are conspicuous by their absence from both delegations? Given the established masculine propensity for mayhem (see any set of violent crime statistics), and the contrasting feminine impulse toward peaceful nurturing, isn't this a little odd—not to say stupid?

(Ted Berkman, Letter to the Editor)

2. In a nation of immigrants, people of diverse ethnic backgrounds must have a common bond through which to exchange ideas. How can this bond be accomplished if there is no common language? It is those who shelter the immigrant from learning English by encouraging the development of a multilingual society who are creating a xenophobic atmosphere. They allow the immigrant to surround himself with a cocoon of language from which he cannot escape and which others cannot penetrate.

(Rita Toften, Letter to the Editor)

3. The health and fitness of our children has become a problem partly because of our attitude toward athletics. The purpose of sports, especially for children, should be to make healthy people healthier. The concept of team sports has failed to do this. Rather than learning to interact and cooperate with others, youngsters are taught to compete. Team sports have only reinforced the notion that the team on top is the winner, and all others are losers. This approach does not make sports appealing to

many children, and some, especially among the less fit, burn out by the time they are twelve.

(Mark I. Pitman, "Young Jocks")

★4. College is the time in which a young mind is supposed to mature and acquire wisdom, and one can only do this by experiencing as much diverse intellectual stimuli as possible. A business student may be a whiz at accounting, but has he or she ever experienced the beauty of a Shakespearean sonnet or the boundless events composing Hebrew history? Most likely not. While many of these neoconservatives will probably go on to be financially successful, they are robbing themselves of the true purpose of collegiate academics, a sacrifice that outweighs the future salary checks.

(Robert S. Griffith, "Conservative College Press")

5. It would, of course, be best if, under nuclear attack, Soviet warheads exploded high in space, rather than at their targets, but nuclear explosions in space are not without consequences. The electromagnetic pulse from even a single weapon can knock out the electric power grid of half a continent. We cannot even speculate on the immensity of the damage to electrical and electronic systems that dozens or hundreds of near-simultaneous bursts would inflict. In any event, the first few explosions might well cripple the rest of the U.S. defense system and allow the remaining Soviet attack to get through.

(Peter D. Zimmerman, "Through the Holes in 'Star Wars' ")

6. History has shown repeatedly that you cannot legislate morality, nor does anyone have a right to. The real problem is the people who have a vested interest in sustaining the multibillion-dollar drug industry created by the laws against drugs. The legalization of drugs would remove the thrill of breaking the law; it would end the suffering caused by unmetered doses, impurities and substandard paraphernalia. A huge segment of the underground and extralegal economy would move into a legitimate economy, taking money away from criminals, eliminating crime and violence, and restoring many talented people to useful endeavor.

(Thomas L. Wayburn, Letter to the Editor)

★7. Roughly 20 years ago, the Berkeley free speech movement reached its crescendo. It was the first spark of student protest in modern America, a spark that ignited a nationwide flame in which college students distinguished themselves as leaders in the national search for social justice. Today the campuses are inert. Except for one. At Illinois State University students protesting town rules against large parties attacked officers and smashed windows at City Hall before state police drove them away with tear gas. Students chanting "We want beer!" stopped traffic, tore down street signs, vandalized university property, and threw beer bottles, eggs and rocks at police and passing cars. The irony of this protest on the 20th anniversary of the Berkeley protests is hard to miss.

(Paul Mattson, "State of Student Protests—20 Years After Berkeley")

8. The United States stands alone among Western nations in its continued use of capital punishment. Israel has executed no one since Adolf Eichmann, the Nazi war criminal. Britain, France, and Germany do not resort to capital punishment. Britain's Parliament overwhelmingly rejected a proposal to reinstate the death penalty in 1983. France, the last European nation to execute its criminals, abolished the death penalty in 1981. West Germany's constitution forbids capital punishment. Sweden abolished the death penalty as far back as 1920. The United States is out of step with the very countries whose basic values are most similar to ours.

(Maygene Giari, "What Russia, South Africa, and U.S. Have in Common")

9. After six years of college, Los Angeles teachers start at $20,600 a year. After six weeks of training, people without a high school diploma are hired as school district locksmiths starting at $31,532. When the locksmith leaves work he goes home and spends time with his wife and kids. When I leave work I go home and grade papers from 190 students. On Saturday and Sunday, while the locksmith is at the park or beach with his wife and kids, I'm grading more papers and making lesson plans for the coming week's classes. The kid's lockers all open and the teachers' filing cabinets don't jam, but kids are graduating who can't read or write. Gee, I wonder why?

(Lou Cohan, "Locksmiths and Teachers")

★10. At a time when our religious impulses might help heal the pains and strains in our society, today's television pulpiteers preach intolerance, censure and discrimination. They package a "believer life-style," and rail against everyone who doesn't fit it—homosexuals, communists, Jews and other non-Christians, sex educators and so on. Such intolerance threatens to undermine the pluralism that marks our heritage. The packaging of that intolerance in slick Hollywood programming or under the guise of patriotic fervor is skillfully accomplished on many fronts. That, however, does not make it right.

(Peter G. Kreitler, "TV Preachers' Religious Intolerance")

III. Define the following terms:

logic	conclusion	inference
argument	conclusion indicator	proposition
statement	premise indicator	truth value
premise		

IV. Answer "true" or "false" to the following statements:

1. The purpose of the premise or premises is to set forth the reasons or evidence given in support of the conclusion.

2. Some arguments have more than one conclusion.

3. All arguments must have more than one premise.

4. The words "therefore," "hence," "so," "since," and "thus" are all conclusion indicators.

5. The words "for," "because," "as," and "for the reason that" are all premise indicators.

6. In the strict sense of the term, "inference" and "argument" have exactly the same meaning.

7. In the strict sense of the term, "proposition" and "statement" have exactly the same meaning.

8. Any sentence that is either true or false is a statement.

9. Every statement has a truth value.

10. The person usually credited with being the Father of Logic is Aristotle.

1.2 RECOGNIZING ARGUMENTS

Not all passages contain arguments. Because logic deals with arguments, it is important to be able to distinguish passages that contain arguments from those that do not. In general, a passage contains an argument if it purports to prove something; if it does not do so, it does not contain an argument. Two conditions must be fulfilled for a passage to purport to prove something:

1. At least one of the statements in the passage must present evidence (or reasons for something).

2. There must be a claim that the evidence (or reasons) supports something.

As we have seen, the statement or statements that present the evidence (or reasons) are the premises, and the statement the premises claim to support is the conclusion. It is not necessary, of course, that the premises *actually* support the conclusion—the argument may not be a good argument; nor is it necessary that the claim be explicit—an implicit claim is sufficient. But at the very least there must be some kind of evidence (or reasons) and some kind of claim that something follows from the evidence.

The existence of an *explicit* claim that something follows from evidence is usually indicated by the occurrence of premise or conclusion indicator words ("thus," "since," "because," "hence," "therefore," etc.). Example:

> The human eye can see a source of light that is as faint as an ordinary candle from a distance of 27 kilometers, through a nonabsorbing atmosphere. Thus, a powerful searchlight directed from a new moon should be visible on earth with the naked eye.
>
> (Diane E. Papalia and Sally Wendkos Olds, *Psychology*)

The word "thus" expresses the claim that something is being proved, so the passage is an argument. Whenever the reader or listener encounters such indicator words, he or she should be on the lookout for an argument. But the mere fact that such words occur in a passage does not guarantee the presence of an argument. As we will see shortly, these words are often used for purposes other than to indicate the occurrence of a premise or conclusion. Thus, when indicator words are encountered, one must make certain that they are actually being used to indicate the occurrence of premises and conclusion before deciding that an argument exists.

Even if a passage contains no indicator words, an argument may be present if there is the *implicit* claim that something follows from evidence. Example:

> The price reduction [seen with the electronic calculator] is the result of a technological revolution. The calculator of the 1960s used integrated electronic circuits that contained about a dozen transistors or similar components on a single chip. Today, mass-produced chips, only a few millimeters square, contain several thousand such components.
> (Robert S. Boikess and Edward Edelson, *Chemical Principles*)

The inferential relationship between the first statement and the other two constitutes an implicit claim that something follows from evidence, so we are justified in calling the passage an argument. The first statement is the conclusion, and the other two are the premises.

Thus, in deciding whether there is a claim that something follows from evidence, the evaluator should keep an eye out for (1) indicator words and (2) the presence of an inferential relationship between the statements. But even then, the existence of such a claim is often far from obvious. In borderline cases the decision may amount to an arbitrary choice by the evaluator to interpret the passage in such a way that it either contains or does not contain the requisite claim. Once the decision is made that a passage is an argument, however, it should be clear which statements are the premises and which is the conclusion.

Additional help in distinguishing arguments from nonarguments is provided by familiarity with typical kinds of nonarguments. Some that we will now discuss are warnings, pieces of advice, statements of belief or opinion, descriptions, reports, expository passages, illustrations, conditional statements, and explanations.

Warnings (such as "Watch out that you don't slip on the ice") and **pieces of advice** (such as "I suggest you take accounting during your first semester") are kinds of discourse aimed at modifying someone's behavior. If no evidence or reason is given to prove that someone should do something or avoid doing something, then there is no argument.

Statements of belief or **opinion** are expressions of what someone happens to believe or think at a certain time. Example:

> I think a nation such as ours, with its high moral traditions and commitments, has a further responsibility to know how we became drawn into this conflict, and to learn the lessons it has to teach us for the future.
>
> (Alfred Hassler, *Saigon, U.S.A.*)

Because no evidence or reason is given to prove that what the author thinks is in fact true, there is no argument.

A **description** consists of one or more statements that, taken together, cause a certain picture to appear in the mind of the reader or listener. Example:

> At Rajghat, a few hundred feet from the river, a fresh pyre had been built of stone, brick and earth. It was eight feet square and about two feet high. Long, thin sandalwood logs sprinkled with incense were stacked on it. Mahatma Gandhi's body lay on the pyre with his head to the north. In that position Buddha had met his end.
>
> (Louis Fischer, *Gandhi: His Life and Message for the World*)

Because no claim is made that anything follows from evidence, there is no argument.

A **report,** which may be similar in many ways to a description, is a group of statements that conveys information about some situation or event. Like descriptions, reports do not claim to prove anything. The following is an item clipped from a newspaper:

> The Soviet Union joined the West in denouncing the tiny Mediterranean island state of Malta for blocking final accord at the 35-nation European security conference in Madrid. Malta is holding up the formal conclusion of the conference to press its demand for a follow-up meeting on security in the Mediterranean.

Again, nothing is claimed to follow from anything, so no argument exists.

One must be careful, though, with reports *about* arguments. Here is another newspaper clipping:

> 56,000 curies of radioactive tritium were accidentally released from the Savanna River nuclear weapons plant in South Carolina. A spokesman for the plant said that the radiation posed "no health hazard to the public" since it was "equivalent to the amount that would be received on a 30-minute jet flight at 36,000 feet."

Properly speaking, this passage is not an argument, because the author of the passage does not claim that anything follows from evidence. Rather, the author *reports* the claim by the plant spokesman that something follows from evidence. If such passages are interpreted as "containing" arguments, it must be made clear that the argument is not the author's but one made by someone about whom the author is reporting.

Caution must also be exercised with certain types of ordinary **expository passages.** It often happens that an author will begin a paragraph with a topic sentence and then go on to develop it. The author's aim is not to *prove* the topic sentence, but merely to *expand* it or *develop* it. Example:

> There is a stylized relation of artist to mass audience in the sports, especially in baseball. Each player develops a style of his own—the swagger as he steps to the plate, the unique windup a pitcher has, the clean-swinging and hard-driving hits, the precision quickness and grace of infield and outfield, the sense of surplus power behind whatever is done.
>
> (Max Lerner, *America as a Civilization*)

The aim of this passage is not so much to prove that the first statement is true as it is to "flesh out" the notion of a "stylized relation" to a mass audience. Passages such as this, however, come very close to being arguments and, depending on the circumstances, one might want to take them as such.

An **illustration** consists of a statement about a certain subject combined with a reference to one or more specific instances intended to exemplify that statement. Illustrations are often confused with arguments because many of them contain indicator words such as "thus." Example:

> Chemical elements, as well as compounds, can be represented by molecular formulas. Thus, oxygen is represented by "O_2," sodium chloride by "$NaCl$," and sulfuric acid by "H_2SO_4."

This passage is not an argument because there is no claim that anything follows from evidence. The purpose of the word "thus" is not to indicate that something is being proved but merely to show how something is done (i.e., how chemical elements and compounds can be represented by formulas).

Nevertheless, as with expository passages, there are many illustrations that can also be interpreted as arguments. Example:

> Water is an excellent solvent. It can dissolve a wide range of materials that will not dissolve in other liquids. For example, salts do not dissolve in most common solvents, such as gasoline, kerosene, turpentine and cleaning fluids. But many salts dissolve readily in water. So do a variety of nonionic organic substances, such as sugars and alcohols of low molecular weight.
>
> (Robert S. Boikess and Edward Edelson, *Chemical Principles*)

Here the examples that are cited can correctly be interpreted as proving that water is an excellent solvent. Thus, the passage may be considered an argument.

Two kinds of nonargument that require more extensive treatment are conditional statements and explanations.

Conditional Statements

A **conditional statement** is an "if . . . then . . ." statement; for example:

> If air is removed from a solid closed container, then the container will weigh less than it did.

Every conditional statement is made up of two component statements. The component statement immediately following the "if" is called the **antecedent,** and the one following the "then" is called the **consequent.** (Occasionally, the word "then" is left out, and occasionally the order of antecedent and consequent is reversed.) In the above example the antecedent is "Air is removed from a solid closed container," and the consequent is "The container will weigh less than it did." This example asserts a causal connection between the air being removed and the container weighing less. However, not all conditional statements express causal connections. The statement "If yellow fever is an infectuous disease, then the Dallas Cowboys are a football team" is just as much a conditional statement as the one about the closed container.

Conditional statements are not arguments for the following reason. In an argument the premises are asserted to be true (at least hypothetically), and the conclusion, because it is claimed to follow from the premises, is also asserted to be true. In a conditional statement, on the other hand, neither the antecedent nor the consequent is asserted to be true. What is asserted is that *if* the antecedent is true, then the consequent is true. For example, the conditional statement "If yellow fever is an infectious disease, then the Dallas Cowboys are a football team" does not assert that yellow fever *is* an infectious disease. It merely asserts that *if* it is, then the Dallas Cowboys are a football team. Because

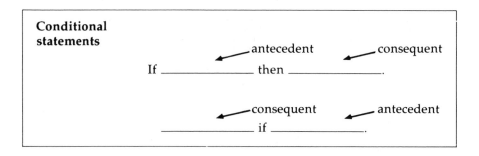

neither the antecedent nor the consequent is asserted to be true, conditional statements are not arguments.

Some conditional statements are similar to arguments, however, because they express inferences, or reasoning processes, just as arguments do. Consider the following:

> If both Saturn and Uranus have rings, then Saturn has rings.
>
> If iron is less dense than mercury, then it will float in mercury.

The consequent of these conditional statements is inferentially linked to the antecedent, much in the way that the conclusion of an argument is inferentially linked to the premises. Nevertheless, these conditional statements are not arguments.* An argument expresses an inference in a special way, in terms of one or more premises that present evidence and a conclusion that is claimed to follow from that evidence. Because the antecedent of a conditional statement is not asserted to be true, it presents no evidence; and because it presents no evidence, a conditional statement is not an argument, even though it may express an inference.

The inferences expressed in conditional statements such as these may, however, be reexpressed in the form of arguments:

> Both Saturn and Uranus have rings.
> Therefore, Saturn has rings.
>
> Iron is less dense than mercury.
> Therefore, iron will float in mercury.

Finally, while no single conditional statement is an argument, a conditional statement may serve as either the premise or the conclusion (or both) of an argument, as the following examples illustrate:

> If cigarette companies publish warning labels, then smokers assume the risk of smoking.
> Cigarette companies do publish warning lablels.
> Therefore, smokers assume the risk of smoking.
>
> If banks make bad loans, then they will be threatened with collapse.
> If banks are threatened with collapse, then the taxpayer will come to the rescue.
> Therefore, if banks make bad loans, then the taxpayer will come to the rescue.

---

*In saying this we are temporarily ignoring the possibility of these statements being enthymemes. As we will see in Chapter 5, an enthymeme is an argument in which a premise or conclusion (or both) is implied but not stated. If, to the second example, we add the premise, "Iron is less dense than mercury," and the conclusion, "Therefore, iron will float in mercury," we have a complete argument. To decide whether a conditional statement is an enthymeme, we must be familiar with the context in which it occurs.

The relation between conditional statements and arguments may now be summarized as follows:

1. A single conditional statement is not an argument.
2. A conditional statement may serve as either the premise or the conclusion (or both) of an argument.
3. The inferential content of a conditional statement may be reexpressed in the form of an argument.

The first two rules are especially pertinent to the recognition of arguments. According to the first rule, if a passage consists of a single conditional statement, it is not an argument. But if it consists of a conditional statement together with some other statement, then, by the second rule, it *may* be an argument, depending on such factors as the presence of indicator words and the relation of the statements to each other.

Conditional statements are very important in logic because they are used to express the relationship between necessary and sufficient conditions. An event A is said to be the **sufficient condition** for an event B whenever the occurrence of A is all that is required for the occurrence of B. For example, a sufficient condition for increasing one's heart rate is running 1,000 yards. Running 1,000 yards is sufficient to the job, but other ways are equally effective, such as lifting weights, swimming, taking certain drugs, and so on.

On the other hand, an event B is said to be a **necessary condition** for an event A whenever A cannot occur without the occurrence of B. For example, a necessary condition for watching television is opening your eyes. Without opening your eyes, you cannot watch television; opening your eyes is necessary. But there are other things equally necessary: the television must be turned on, electricity must be supplied, a program must be transmitted, and so on.

Combining the two notions of sufficient and necessary conditions, running 1,000 yards is sufficient, but not necessary, to increase one's heart rate; and opening one's eyes is necessary, but not sufficient, to watch television.

Sufficient and necessary conditions may be expressed in terms of conditional statements by placing the sufficient condition in the antecedent and the necessary condition in the consequent. The examples just given are expressed as follows:

If a person runs 1,000 yards, then that person's heart rate will increase.
If a person watches television, then that person must open his or her eyes.

The first statement asserts that running 1,000 yards is *sufficient* to increase heart rate, and the second asserts that opening one's eyes is *necessary* for watching television. Once these conditions are expressed in terms of conditional statements, it becomes clear how *each* statement expresses *both* a necessary *and* a sufficient condition. Since the antecedent of each statement expresses a sufficient condition and the consequent expresses a necessary condition, the first statement also says that an increased heart rate is a *necessary* result of running 1,000 yards, and the second says that watching television is *sufficient* to guarantee that one's eyes are open. These concepts of sufficient and necessary conditions will be used in later chapters to explain other logical concepts.

Explanations

Now that we have seen how arguments differ from conditional statements, let us turn to the question of **explanations.** Here are some examples:

> The Challenger spacecraft exploded after liftoff because an O-ring failed in one of the booster rockets.
>
> The sky appears blue from the earth's surface because light rays from the sun are scattered by particles in the atmosphere.
>
> Cows can digest grass, while humans cannot, because their digestive systems contain enzymes not found in humans.

Every explanation is composed of two distinct components: the explanandum and the explanans. The **explanandum** is the statement that describes the event or phenomenon to be explained, and the **explanans** is the statement or group of statements that purport to do the explaining. In the first example above, the explanandum is the statement "The Challenger spacecraft exploded after liftoff," and the explanans is "An O-ring failed in one of the booster rockets."

Explanations are sometimes mistaken for arguments because they often contain the indicator word "because." Yet explanations are not arguments for the following reason: In an explanation, the explanans is intended to show *why* something is the case, whereas in an argument the premises are intended to prove *that* something is the case. In the first example above, the fact that the Challenger spacecraft exploded is known to everyone. The statement that an O-ring failed in one of the booster rockets is not intended to prove *that* the spacecraft exploded but rather to show *why* it exploded. In the second example, the fact that the sky is blue is readily apparent. The intention of the passage is to explain *why* it appears blue—not to prove *that* it appears blue. Similarly, in the third example, virtually everyone knows that people cannot digest grass. The intention of the passage is to explain *why* this is true.

Explanations bear a similarity to arguments in that, like certain conditional statements, they express inferences. But this fact is not sufficient to make them arguments. An argument is a special kind of expression of an inference, one that attempts to prove something on the basis of evidence. Because explanations do not attempt to prove anything, they are not arguments.

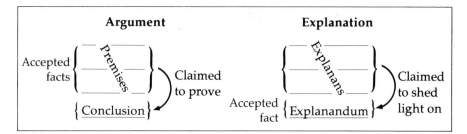

The inferences expressed in many explanations may, however, be reexpressed in the form of arguments. This is particularly true of the explanations found in science. For example, the inference expressed in the blue sky example may be reexpressed in the following argument:

> Light rays from the sun are scattered by particles in the atmosphere. Therefore, the sky appears blue from the earth's surface.

In distinguishing explanations from arguments, first identify the statement that is either the conclusion or the explanandum (this is often the statement that occurs before the word "because"). Then ask the question: Is the event described in this statement something that is an accepted fact? If the answer is "yes," then ask: Is the remainder of the passage intended to shed light on this event? If the answer is again "yes," the passage in question is an explanation.

While a basic distinction exists between arguments and explanations, some passages may be interpreted as being either arguments or explanations (or both). Consider the following:

> The patient shows a reduced leukocyte count today because radiation treatments were recently commenced.

The purpose of this passage may be either to prove *that* the leukocyte (white blood cell) count is down, or to explain *why* it is down, or both. Thus, the passage may be interpreted as being either an argument, an explanation, or both.

Our analysis of illustrations and explanations points up the fact that many indicator words, especially the words "because" and "thus," can have a twofold meaning. Sometimes "because" indicates a premise, sometimes an explanans; and sometimes "thus" indicates an illustration

A CONCISE INTRODUCTION TO LOGIC

and sometimes a conclusion. Another indicator that readily admits of a double meaning is the word "since," as exemplified by the following passages:

> Since Edison invented the phonograph there have been many technological developments.
>
> Since Edison invented the phonograph he deserves credit for a major technological development.

In the first passage (which is *not* an argument) "since" means "from the time that." This is the *temporal* meaning of the word. The second passage (which *is* an argument) expresses the *logical* meaning of "since."

EXERCISE 1.2

I. Determine which of the following passages are arguments. For those that are, identify the conclusion. For those that are not, attempt to determine whether they are warnings, pieces of advice, statements of belief or opinion, descriptions, reports, expository passages, illustrations, conditional statements, or explanations.

★1. The price of gold increased yesterday because of increased tensions in the Middle East.

2. If public education fails to improve the quality of instruction in both primary and secondary schools, then it is likely that it will lose additional students to the private sector in the years ahead.

3. Freedom of the press is the most important of our constitutionally guaranteed freedoms. Without it, our other freedoms would be immediately threatened. Furthermore, it provides the fulcrum for the advancement of new freedoms.

★4. The Swiss Alps contain a number of very high peaks. Thus, the Weisshorn, Matterhorn, and Nadelhorn are all over 14,000 feet.

5. It is strongly recommended that you have your house inspected for termite damage at the earliest possible opportunity.

6. Shut the cage door, you fool! The lions are escaping into the streets!

★7. If the earth's magnetic field disappears, then the Van Allen radiation belt will be destroyed. If the Van Allen radiation belt is destroyed, then intense cosmic rays will bombard the earth. Therefore, if the earth's magnetic field disappears, then intense cosmic rays will bombard the earth.

8. Fictional characters behave according to the same psychological probabilities as real people. But the characters of fiction are found in exotic dilemmas that real people hardly encounter. Consequently, fiction provides us with the opportunity to ponder how people react in uncommon

situations, and to deduce moral lessons, psychological principles, and philosophical insights from their behavior.

(J.R. McCuen and A.C. Winkler, *Readings for Writers*, 4th edition)

opinion

9. I believe that it must be the policy of the United States to support free peoples who are resisting attempted subjugation by armed minorities or by outside pressures. I believe that we must assist free peoples to work out their own destinies in their own way. I believe that our help should be primarily through economic and financial aid, which is essential to economic stability and orderly political processes.

(President Truman, Address to Congress, 1947)

report

★10. Mexican workers at a recently opened Ford Motor Co. assembly plant in Hermosillo went on strike, demanding a 70 percent pay raise. The 1400 workers, who are non-union and the lowest paid at the plant, earn the peso equivalent of $105 to $116 a month. Mexico's minimum wage is about $91 a month.

(Newspaper clipping)

argument

11. In every insurance contract there is an implied covenant of good faith and fair dealing. The duty to so act is imminent in the contract whether the company is attending to the claims of third persons against the insured or the claims of the insured itself. Accordingly, when the insurer unreasonably and in bad faith withholds payment of the claim of its insured, it is subject to liability in tort.

(Justice Sullivan, *Gruenberg* v. *Aetna Insurance Co.*)

exposit

12. The pace of reading, clearly, depends entirely upon the reader. He may read as slowly or as rapidly as he can or wishes to read. If he does not understand something, he may stop and reread it, or go in search of elucidation before continuing. The reader can accelerate his pace when the material is easy or less than interesting, and can slow down when it is difficult or enthralling. If what he reads is moving he can put down the book for a few moments and cope with his emotions without fear of losing anything.

(Marie Winn, *The Plug-In Drug*)

descrip

★13. The central rotunda [of the John G. Shedd Aquarium] is surmounted by a low octagonal tower roofed by a pyramidal skylight. The soft diffused light that descends through this skylight onto the circular pool and vine-covered island below forms one of the pleasing features of the aquarium.

(*Chicago's Famous Buildings*, ed. Ira J. Bach)

report contain ing argu ment

14. Israeli doctors have discovered that nation's first known heterosexual transmission of the AIDs virus. The Jerusalem Post said the wife of a drug addict tested positive for the antibodies of the virus. Since the woman is not a drug addict or the recipient of a blood transfusion, she probably was infected through heterosexual relations with her husband, doctors said.

(Newspaper clipping)

15. Economics is of practical value in business. An understanding of the overall operation of the economic system puts the business executive in a better position to formulate policies. The executive who understands the

causes and consequences of inflation is better equipped during inflationary periods to make more intelligent decisions than otherwise.

(Campbell R. McConnell, *Economics*, 8th edition)

★16. Bear one thing in mind before you begin to write your paper: Famous literary works, especially works regarded as classics, have been thoroughly studied to the point where prevailing opinion on them has assumed the character of orthodoxy.

(J.R. McCuen and A.C. Winkler, *Readings for Writers*, 4th edition)

17. Young people at universities study to achieve knowledge and not to learn a trade. We must all learn how to support ourselves, but we must also learn how to live. We need a lot of engineers in the modern world, but we do not want a world of modern engineers.

(Winston Churchill, *A Churchill Reader*, ed. Colin R. Coote)

18. No business concern wants to sell on credit to a customer who will prove unable or unwilling to pay his or her account. Consequently, most business organizations include a credit department which must reach a decision on the credit worthiness of each prospective customer.

(Walter B. Meigs and Robert F. Meigs, *Accounting*)

★19. Behavior evoked by brain stimulation is sensitive to environmental changes, even in animals. Gibbons attacked their cage mates in a Yale laboratory when their brains were stimulated. The same animals, moved to Bermuda and placed in a large corral, did not behave aggressively at all in response to the same stimulation.

(Walter Mischel and Harriet Mischel, *Essentials of Psychology*)

20. Since the time of the ancient Greeks, two distinct types of motion have seemed central to an understanding of the universe: the motion of the celestial bodies and the motion of objects on earth. These two kinds of motion were considered as separate matters until the works of Galileo and Newton.

(Douglas C. Giancoli, *The Ideas of Physics*)

21. Dachshunds are ideal dogs for small children, as they are already stretched and pulled to such a length that the child cannot do much harm one way or the other.

(Robert Benchley, quoted in *Cold Noses and Warm Hearts*)

★22. Atoms are the basic building blocks of all matter. They can combine to form molecules, whose properties are generally very different from those of the constituent atoms. Table salt, for example, a simple chemical compound formed from chlorine and sodium, resembles neither the poisonous gas nor the highly reactive metal.

(Frank J. Blatt, *Principles of Physics*, 2nd ed.)

23. The coarsest type of humor is the *practical joke*: pulling away the chair from the dignitary's lowered bottom. The victim is perceived first as a person of consequence, then suddenly as an inert body subject to the laws of physics: authority is debunked by gravity, mind by matter; man is degraded to a mechanism.

(Arthur Koestler, *Janus: A Summing Up*)

24. If we place a solid homogeneous mass, having the form of a sphere or cube, in a medium maintained at a constant temperature, and if it remains immersed for a very long time, it will acquire at all points a temperature differing very little from that of the fluid.

(Joseph Fourier, *Analytical Theory of Heat*)

★25. Silver, mercury, and all the other metals except iron and zinc, are insoluble in diluted sulfuric acid, because they have not sufficient affinity with oxygen to draw it off from its combination either with the sulfur, the sulfurous acid, or the hydrogen.

(Antoine Lavoisier, *Elements of Chemistry*)

26. Words are slippery customers. The full meaning of a word does not appear until it is placed in its context. . . . And even then the meaning will depend upon the listener, upon the speaker, upon their entire experience of the language, upon their knowledge of one another, and upon the whole situation.

(C. Cherry, *On Human Communication*)

27. Anything a doctor does that requires cutting, jabbing, or injecting is a "procedure." Anything a doctor does that requires thinking, talking, or counseling of patients is "cognitive services." Procedures pay much better than cognitive services.

(Gregg Easterbrook, "The Revolution in Medicine," *Newsweek*)

★28. A person never becomes truly self-reliant. Even though he deals effectively with things, he is necessarily dependent upon those who have taught him to do so. They have selected the things he is dependent upon and determined the kinds and degrees of dependencies.

(B. F. Skinner, *Beyond Freedom and Dignity*)

29. There is no doubt that some businessmen conspire to shorten the useful life of their products in order to guarantee replacement sales. There is, similarly, no doubt that many of the annual model changes with which American (and other) consumers are increasingly familiar are not technologically substantive.

(Alvin Toffler, *Future Shock*)

30. If one knows the plant life of an area, certain assumptions can be made about the climate and the animals that will be found there. For example, in grasslands the animal life typically includes large mammalian herbivores, insects, and birds.

(King, Saunders, and Wallace, *Biology: The Science of life*)

★31. Almost all living things act to free themselves from harmful contacts. . . . A person sneezes and frees his respiratory passages from irritating substances. He vomits and frees his stomach from indigestible or poisonous food. He pulls back his hand and frees it from a sharp or hot object.

(B. F. Skinner, *Beyond Freedom and Dignity*)

32. Men are less likely to develop osteoporosis until later in life than women and seldom suffer as severely because they have 30 percent more bone mass on the average and don't undergo the sudden drop in estrogen that occurs with menopause.

(Matt Clark, "The Calcium Craze," *Newsweek*)

33. What seems to be one of the simplest proposals for preventing war turns out on closer examination to be one of the most complex. Defining *disarmament* is not hard; it means the reduction or elimination of weapons. As a means of preventing war it is logically unassailable. Without the means to fight you cannot have a war, any more than you can have highway accidents without vehicles. The problem comes when you try to describe precisely what weapons you want states to eliminate.

(David W. Ziegler, *War, Peace, and International Politics*, 4th ed.)

★34. Four hundred French medical students protesting proposed university reforms burned their white lab coats in Marseille, then marched to the docks and threw a police officer into the sea. The officer was rescued by a fisherman. About three hundred law students staged a similar protest in Lyons, and authorities said there were minor injuries in clashes with police. Six students were arrested.

(newspaper clipping)

35. Although the plane mirror is perhaps the oldest optical instrument known to man, it remains an important element in the modern arsenal of sophisticated optical devices. For example, the earth-moon laser-ranging experiments, initiated in 1969, rely on high-quality reflectors.

(Frank J. Blatt, *Principles of Physics*, 2nd ed.)

II. The following selections were originally submitted as letters to the editor of newspapers and magazines. Determine which of them can, with good reason, be considered arguments. In those that can, identify the conclusion.

★1. What this country needs is a return to the concept of swift and certain justice. If we need more courts, judges and prisons, then so be it. And as for capital punishment, I say let the punishment fit the crime. When criminals behave more like humans, then we can start to treat them more humanely. In the meantime, I would like to see the Night Stalkers of our society swiftly executed rather than coddled by our courts and prisons.

(John Pearson)

2. At the risk of proselytizing for vegetarianism and thus invoking the wrath of my fellow mad-for-meat Texans, I must add one observation of my own. Meat eating is not only hypocritical, it is immoral. Many if not most of the world's people are starving. It has been estimated that for every pound of meat protein consumed, approximately 20 pounds of vegetable protein are lost, having been consumed by the animal that is later converted into meat.

(James M. Martin)

3. Shelters and the relocation of city populations are outmoded concepts, suitable only for the more limited wars of the past rather than the international extinction our world leaders have been preparing. Civil "defense" goals should be directed toward moving our millions of citizens promptly into the most likely target areas so that transition into a possible next dimension will take the fewest possible seconds.

(Evan Lodge)

★4. After reading your cover story, I find that cable TV has simply flooded our airwaves with more sex, violence and teen-age punk junk. Now our children can spend even less time studying and we can spend more time in blank-space stares at the idiot box. Cable would be fine with more educational channels—and fewer cheap thrills aimed at narrow-minded bubble brains.

(Jacqueline Murray)

5. In opposing obligatory prayer in the public schools, I am not deserting my God (and I would like to think of myself as a Christian). On the contrary, it is perfectly possible that I am thus serving my god, who I believe wants his children to pray to him of their own free will and not because some legislator, who may or may not be motivated by truly religious considerations, forces them to.

(Philip D. Walker)

6. Americans think more of their automobiles than they do of educating their children. When I had my car serviced the other day, I saw a sign that said the labor charge for working on an automobile is $34 an hour. If teachers were paid this much, they would make $54,400 a year. This is about twice what the highest paid teacher in Los Angeles earns.

(Walter O. Harris)

★7. The poor quality of parenting and the lack in continuity of adult care provided to many U.S. children contribute to a passivity and a sense of helplessness that hobbles individuals for the remainder of their lives. Their subsequent unemployment, lack of education, and inability to make necessary life-style changes such as quitting an addiction can be attributed, in large part, to the helplessness they learned from childhood.

(William J. McCarthy)

8. The difference [between the mean starting salaries of men and women in executive positions] is less than $300—a difference that is not statistically significant and could be due to chance. After working for ten years, however, women's salaries are $9,334 lower than men's—no longer a chance probability. Thus, while women make 99 percent of male starting salaries in entry-level positions, when they are ten years into their careers they are making 81 percent of what men with identical backgrounds and training earn.

(Mary Anne Devanna)

9. The suggestion by sociobiologists that stepparent child abuse has evolutionary advantages is superficial. If there were evolutionary advantages to harming one's mate's offspring of a different parent, then by now there probably wouldn't be loving and generous stepparents around— and there are plenty. I know. I have a loving stepparent and am one.

(Ronald Cohen)

★10. It disturbs me to no end that 700,000 demonstrators gathered in New York's Central Park to protest the nuclear arms race and to urge disarmament. A number of other demonstrations were held in other parts of this country as well.

I am firmly convinced that there is an element of conspiracy in this country. It isn't all just innocent, democratic, happy-as-a-lark, spontaneous protest.

There are enemies of America, and I'm convinced even some KGB agents are trying to use these demonstrations to bring America down.

(Mrs. William J. Ufer)

III. Define the following terms:

conditional statement	necessary condition
antecedent	explanation
consequent	explanandum
sufficient condition	explanans

IV. Answer "true" or "false" to the following statements:

1. Any passage that contains an argument must contain a claim that something follows from evidence or reasons.

2. In an argument, the claim that something follows from evidence or reasons is always explicit.

3. Passages that contain indicator words such as "thus," "since," and "because" are always arguments.

4. In deciding whether a passage contains an argument, we should always keep an eye out for indicator words and the presence of an inferential relationship between the statements.

5. Expository passages can never be correctly interpreted as arguments.

6. Many illustrations are correctly interpreted as arguments.

7. Some conditional statements express inferences.

8. Explanations are never correctly interpreted as arguments.

9. In an explanation, the explanandum usually describes an accepted matter of fact.

10. In an explanation, the explanans is the statement or group of statements that does the explaining.

11. Explanations are never correctly interpreted as arguments.

12. Drinking a pint of gin in an hour is a necessary condition for becoming intoxicated.

13. Having water present is a necessary condition for plant life.

14. Getting into a fistfight is a sufficient condition for someone being injured.

15. Having legs is a sufficient condition for walking.

V. Page through a book, magazine, or newspaper and find two arguments, one with indicator words, the other without. Copy the arguments as written, giving the appropriate reference. Then identify the premises and conclusion of each.

1.3 DEDUCTION AND INDUCTION

Arguments can be divided into two groups: deductive and inductive. A **deductive argument** is an argument in which we expect the conclusion to follow *necessarily* from the premises; in other words, we expect the premises to support the conclusion in such a way that if they are assumed true, it is impossible that the conclusion be false. On the other hand, an **inductive argument** is an argument in which we expect the conclusion to follow only *probably* from the premises; in other words, we expect the premises to support the conclusion in such a way that if they are assumed true, then, based on that assumption, it is only probable that the conclusion be true.

While the distinction between inductive and deductive derives from the expectations we have for an argument, this does not mean that the distinction is purely subjective. Our expectations must be grounded in good reasons. Three factors that bear upon the evaluation of an argument as inductive or deductive are (1) the occurrence of special indicator words, (2) the nature of the inferential link between premises and conclusion, and (3) the character or form of argumentation the arguer uses.

First, if in drawing a conclusion the arguer uses words such as "probable," "improbable," "plausible," "implausible," "likely," "unlikely," or "reasonable to conclude," the evaluator may want to take such indicators as reason for considering the argument inductive. On the other hand, if the arguer uses words such as "necessarily," "certainly," "absolutely," or "definitely," the evaluator may want to consider the argument deductive. (Note that the phrase "must happen that" in an argument is ambiguous; "must" can imply either probability or necessity.) Examples:

> If a substance is a noble gas, it is inert. Therefore, since argon is a noble gas, it necessarily follows that it is inert.

> Neon has unstable isotopes. Therefore, since argon is similar in many ways to neon, it probably follows that argon has unstable isotopes, too.

The first example is best interpreted as deductive and the second as inductive.

Inductive and deductive indicator words can usually be depended on to suggest the correct interpretation. However, if they suggest an interpretation that conflicts with one of the other criteria (discussed shortly), the evaluator will probably want to ignore them. Arguers often use phrases such as "it certainly follows that" for rhetorical purposes to add impact to their conclusion and not to suggest that the argument be taken as deductive. Similarly, some arguers, not knowing the distinction between inductive and deductive, will claim to "deduce" a conclusion when their argument is more correctly interpreted as inductive.

The second factor to be taken into account in distinguishing inductive from deductive arguments is the nature of the inferential link between premises and conclusion. If this link is such that the conclusion follows necessarily from the premises, the argument is clearly deductive. When we say that the conclusion follows "necessarily," we mean that the premises support the conclusion in such a way that if they are assumed true, it is absolutely impossible that the conclusion be false. On the other hand, if the conclusion does not follow necessarily from the premises but does follow probably, it is usually best to consider the argument inductive. Examples:

> All saleswomen are extroverts.
> Tova Borgnine is a saleswoman.
> Therefore, Tova Borgnine is an extrovert.

> The vast majority of saleswomen are extroverts.
> Tova Borgnine is a saleswoman.
> Therefore, Tova Borgnine is an extrovert.

In the first example the conclusion follows necessarily from the premises, and so the argument is deductive. If we assume that all saleswomen are extroverts and that Tova Borgnine is a saleswoman, it is absolutely impossible that Tova Borgnine not be an extrovert. In the second example, the conclusion does not follow necessarily from the premises, but it does follow probably. In other words, if the premises are assumed true, it is probable, based on that assumption, that the conclusion be true. Thus, the argument is best considered inductive.

Sometimes it happens that an argument contains no indicator words and that the conclusion follows neither necessarily nor probably from the premises (i.e., the premises provide no support for the conclusion). This situation points up the need for the third factor to be taken into account, which is the character or form of argumentation the arguer uses. Five such types of argumentation that are typically deductive are arguments based on mathematics, arguments from definition, and categorical, hypothetical, and disjunctive syllogisms. Additional ones will be studied in later chapters.

An **argument based on mathematics** is an argument in which the conclusion depends on some purely arithmetic or geometric computation or measurement. For example, a shopper might place two apples and three oranges into a paper bag and then conclude that the bag contains five pieces of fruit. Or a surveyor might measure a square piece of land and, after determining that it is 100 feet on each side, conclude that it contains 10,000 square feet. Since all arguments in pure mathematics are deductive, we can usually consider arguments that depend on mathematics to be deductive as well. A noteworthy exception, however, is arguments that depend on statistics. As we will see shortly, such arguments are usually best interpreted as inductive.

An **argument from definition** is an argument in which the conclusion is claimed to depend merely upon the definition of some word or phrase used in the premise or conclusion. For example, someone might argue that because Claudia is mendacious, it follows that she tells lies, or that because a certain paragraph is prolix, it follows that it is excessively wordy. These arguments are deductive because their conclusions follow with necessity from the definitions of "mendacious" and "prolix."

A syllogism, in general, is an argument consisting of exactly two premises and one conclusion. Categorical syllogisms will be treated in greater depth in Chapter 5, but for now we will say that a **categorical syllogism** is a syllogism in which each statement begins with one of the words "all," "no," or "some." Example:

> All lasers are optical devices.
> Some lasers are surgical instruments.
> Therefore, some optical devices are surgical instruments.

Arguments such as these are nearly always best treated as deductive.

A **hypothetical syllogism** is a syllogism having a conditional statement for one or both of its premises. Examples:

> If electricity flows through a conductor, then a magnetic field is produced.
> If a magnetic field is produced, then a nearby compass will be deflected.
> Therefore, if electricity flows through a conductor, then a nearby compass will be deflected.

> If quartz scratches glass, then quartz is harder than glass.
> Quartz scratches glass.
> Therefore, quartz is harder than glass.

Although certain forms of such arguments can sometimes be interpreted inductively, the deductive interpretation is usually the most appropriate.

A **disjunctive syllogism** is a syllogism having a disjunctive statement (i.e., an "either ... or ..." statement) for one or both of its premises. Example:

> Either breach of contract is a crime or it is not punishable by the state.
> Breach of contract is not a crime.
> Therefore, it is not punishable by the state.

As with hypothetical syllogisms, such arguments are usually best taken as deductive. Hypothetical and disjunctive syllogisms will be treated in greater depth in Chapter 6.

Now let us consider some typically inductive forms of argumentation. In general, inductive arguments are such that the content of the conclusion is in some way intended to "go beyond" the content of the premises. The premises of such an argument typically deal with some subject that is relatively familiar, and the conclusion then moves beyond this to a subject that is less familiar or that little is known about. Such an argument may take any of several forms: predictions about the future, arguments from analogy, inductive generalizations, arguments from authority, arguments based on signs, and causal inferences, to name just a few.

In a **prediction,** the premises deal with some known event in the present or past, and the conclusion moves beyond this event to some event in the relative future. For example, someone might argue that because certain meteorological phenomena have been observed to develop over a certain region of central Missouri, a storm will occur there in six hours. Or again, one might argue that because certain fluctuations occurred in the prime interest rate on Friday, the value of the dollar will decrease against foreign currencies on Monday. Nearly everyone realizes that the future cannot be known with certainty; thus, whenever an argument makes a prediction about the future, one is usually justified in considering the argument inductive.

An **argument from analogy** is an argument that depends on the existence of an analogy, or similarity, between two things or states of affairs. Because of the existence of this analogy, a certain condition that affects the better-known thing or situation is concluded to affect the similar, lesser-known thing or situation. For example, someone might argue that because Christina's Porsche is a great handling car, it follows that Angela's Porsche must also be a great handling car. The argument depends on the existence of a similarity, or analogy, between the two cars. The certitude attending such an inference is obviously probabilistic at best.

An **inductive generalization** is an argument that proceeds from the knowledge of a selected sample to some claim about the whole group. Because the members of the sample have a certain characteristic, it is argued that all the members of the group have that same characteristic. For example, one might argue that because three oranges selected from a certain crate were especially tasty and juicy, all the oranges from that crate are especially tasty and juicy. Or again, one might argue that because six out of a total of nine members sampled from a certain labor union intend to vote for Johnson for union president, two-thirds of the entire membership intend to vote for Johnson. These examples illustrate the use of statistics in inductive argumentation.

An **argument from authority** is an argument in which the conclusion rests upon a statement made by some presumed authority or witness. For example, a person might argue that earnings for Texas Instruments

Corporation will be up in the coming quarter because of a statement to that effect by an investment counselor. Or a lawyer might argue that Mack the Knife committed the murder because an eyewitness testified to that effect under oath. Because the investment counselor and the eyewitness could be either mistaken or lying, such arguments are essentially probabilistic.

An **argument based on signs** is an argument that proceeds from the knowledge of a certain sign to a knowledge of the thing or situation that the sign symbolizes. For example, when driving on an unfamiliar highway one might see a sign indicating that the road makes several sharp turns one mile ahead. Based on this information, one might argue that the road does indeed make several sharp turns one mile ahead. Because the sign might be misplaced or in error about the turns, the conclusion is only probable.

A **causal inference** underlies arguments that proceed from knowledge of a cause to knowledge of the effect, or, conversely, from knowledge of an effect to knowledge of a cause. For example, from the knowledge that a bottle of wine had been accidentally left in the freezer overnight, someone might conclude that it had frozen (cause to effect). Conversely, after tasting a piece of chicken and finding it dry and crunchy, one might conclude that it had been overcooked (effect to cause). Because specific instances of cause and effect can never be known with absolute certainty, one may usually interpret such arguments as inductive.

Arguments from effect to cause are sometimes confused with arguments based on signs because an effect can sometimes be interpreted as a "sign" of the cause. For example, a symptom is sometimes viewed as a sign of a disease. This mistake can be avoided if one remembers that a sign, in the sense in which we are using it here, is not produced *by* the thing it signifies. An effect, on the other hand, is always produced by its correlative cause.

Another mistake that is sometimes made is to confuse arguments in geometry, which are always deductive, with arguments from analogy or inductive generalizations. For example, an argument that concludes that a triangle has a certain attribute (such as a right angle) because another triangle, with which it is congruent, also has that attribute, might be mistaken for an argument from analogy. Similarly, an argument that concludes that all triangles have a certain attribute (such as angles totaling two right angles) because any particular triangle has that attribute, might be mistaken for an inductive generalization. Arguments such as these, however, are always deductive because the conclusion follows necessarily and with complete certainty from the premises.

A final point needs to be made about the distinction between inductive and deductive arguments. There is a tradition extending back to the time of Aristotle which holds that inductive arguments are those that proceed from the particular to the general, while deductive arguments are those that proceed from the general to the particular. (A **particular statement** is one that makes a claim about one or more particular members of a class, while a **general statement** makes a claim about *all* the members of a class.) It is true, of course, that many inductive and deductive arguments do work in this way; but this fact should not be used as a criterion for distinguishing induction from deduction. As a matter of fact, there are deductive arguments that proceed from the general to the general, from the particular to the particular, and from the particular to the general, as well as from the general to the particular; and there are inductive arguments that do the same. For example, here is a deductive argument that proceeds from the particular to the general:

> One is a prime number.
> Three is a prime number.
> Five is a prime number.
> Seven is a prime number.
> Therefore, all odd numbers between zero and eight are prime numbers.

And here is one that proceeds from the particular to the particular:

> Gabriel is a wolf.
> Gabriel has a tail.
> Therefore, Gabriel's tail is the tail of a wolf.

Here is an inductive argument that proceeds from the general to the particular:

> All emeralds previously found have been green.
> Therefore, the next emerald to be found will be green.

The other varieties are easy to construct. The point is that the criterion for distinguishing inductive from deductive arguments arises, in general, not from the kinds of statements in the argument but from such factors as the nature of the link between premises and conclusion, the occurrence of special indicator words, and the form of argumentation the arguer uses.

EXERCISE 1.3

I. Determine whether the following arguments are best interpreted as being inductive or deductive. Also state the criteria you use in reaching your decision (*i.e.*, the presence of indicator words, the nature of the inferential link between premises and conclusion, or the character or form of argumentation).

★1. Because triangle A is congruent with triangle B, and triangle A is isosceles, it follows that triangle B is isosceles.

2. The plaque on the leaning tower of Pisa says that Galileo performed experiments there with falling objects. It must be the case that Galileo did indeed perform those experiments there.

3. The rainfall in Seattle has been more than 15 inches every year for the past thirty years. Therefore, the rainfall next year will probably be more than 15 inches.

★4. All street gangs are organizations involved in crime, and some street gangs are not clans shrouded in romance. Therefore, some organizations involved in crime are not clans shrouded in romance.

5. Amoco, Exxon, and Texaco are all listed on the New York Stock Exchange. It must be the case that all major American oil companies are listed on the New York Stock Exchange.

6. The longer a pendulum is, the longer it takes to swing. Therefore, when the pendulum of a clock is lengthened, the clock will slow down.

★7. Paying off terrorists in exchange for hostages is not a wise policy, since such action will only lead them to take more hostages in the future.

8. The Matterhorn is higher than Mount Whitney, and Mount Whitney is higher than Mount Rainier. The obvious conclusion is that the Matterhorn is higher than Mount Rainier.

9. Although both front and rear doors were found open after the burglary, there were pry marks around the lock on the rear door and deposits of mud near the threshold. It must be the case that the thief entered through the rear door and left through the front.

★10. The *Encylopaedia Britannica* has an article on symbiosis. The *Encyclopedia Americana*, like the *Britannica*, is an excellent reference work. Therefore, the *Americana* probably also has an article on symbiosis.

11. Cholesterol is endogenous with humans. Therefore, it is manufactured inside the human body.

12. Either the bumps on people's heads are indicators of personality characteristics, or phrenology is a fraud. The bumps on people's heads are not indicators of personality characteristics. Therefore, phrenology is a fraud.

★13. Investment banker Felix G. Rohatyn has stated that the integrity and safety of the securities markets are in jeopardy, and to preserve them new legislation is needed controlling junk bonds, arbitrage, greenmail, takeover bids, and takeover defenses. In view of Rohatyn's credentials, we may conclude that such legislation is indeed needed.

14. If cigarette smoking costs $65 billion annually in health care and lost productivity, then cigarette taxes should be raised to reflect this cost. But cigarette smoking does cost $65 billion annually in health care and lost productivity. Therefore, cigarette taxes should be raised to reflect this cost.

15. It seems likely that young people will be at war with old people in an-

other 15 or 20 years. You can see it coming in the numbers. In 1900 only one percent of the population was older than 75. Today four percent of all Americans are more than 75 years old, and in a few years it's going to be five percent . . . 13 million people.

(newspaper editorial)

★16. Each element, such as hydrogen and iron, has a set of gaps—wavelengths that it absorbs rather than radiates. So if those wavelengths are missing from the spectrum, you know that that element is present in the star you are observing.

(Rick Gore, "Eyes of Science")

17. Because the apparent daily movement which is common to both the planets and the fixed stars is seen to travel from the east to the west, but the far slower single movements of the single planets travel in the opposite direction from west to east, it is therefore certain that these movements cannot depend on the common movement of the world but should be assigned to the planets themselves.

(Johannes Kepler, *Epitomy of Copernican Astronomy*)

18. Reserves of coal in the United States have an energy equivalent 33 times that of oil and natural gas. On a world-wide basis the multiple is about 10. By shifting to a coal-based economy, we could satisfy our energy requirements for at least a century, probably longer.

(William L. Masterson and Emil J. Slowinski, *Principles of Chemistry*)

★19. Probably most of human behavior operates on the basis of inference. Most of the time we just do not have the facts on which to base our behavior. Yet to make sense of what we do and to anticipate what we should do in the future, we must make assumptions, draw conclusions.

(F. S. Sathre-Eldon et al., *Let's Talk*)

20. The graphical method for solving a system of equations is an approximation, since reading the point of intersection depends on the accuracy with which the lines are drawn and on the ability to interpret the coordinates of the point.

(Karl J. Smith and Patrick J. Boyle, *Intermediate Algebra for College Students*)

21. That [the moons of Jupiter] revolve in unequal circles is manifestly deduced from the fact that at the longest elongation from Jupiter it is never possible to see two of these moons in conjunction, whereas in the vicinity of Jupiter they are found united two, three, and sometimes all four together.

(Galileo Galilei, *The Starry Messenger*)

★22. Lenses function by refracting light at their surfaces. Consequently, their action depends not only on the shape of the lens surfaces, but also on the indices of refraction of the lens material and the surrounding medium.

(Frank J. Blatt, *Principles of Physics*, 2nd ed.)

23. Given present growth rates in underdeveloped countries, the limited practice of birth control, and the difficulty of slowing the current growth momentum, it can be said with virtual certainty that none of the people now reading this book will ever live in a world where the population is not growing.

(J. John Palen, *Social Problems*)

24. The interpretation of the laws is the proper and peculiar province of the courts. A constitution is, in fact, and must be regarded by the judges, as a fundamental law. It therefore belongs to them to ascertain its meaning, as well as the meaning of any particular act proceeding from the legislative body.

(Alexander Hamilton, *Federalist Papers*, No. 78)

★25. The Simpson incident had shown me that a dog was kept in the stables, and yet, though someone had been in and had fetched out a horse, he had not barked enough to arouse the two lads in the loft. Obviously the midnight visitor was someone whom the dog knew well.

(A. Conan Doyle, *Memoirs of Sherlock Holmes*)

26. Eternity is simultaneously whole. But time has a before and an after. Therefore time and eternity are not the same thing.

(Thomas Aquinas, *Summa Theologica*)

27. Ordinary things that we encounter every day are electrically neutral. Therefore, since negatively charged electrons are a part of everything, positively charged particles must also exist in all matter.

(James E. Brady and Gerard E. Humiston, *General Chemistry*)

★28. In consequence of the division of labor, the whole of every man's attention comes naturally to be directed towards some one very simple object. It is naturally to be expected, therefore, that some one or other of those who are employed in each particular branch of labor should soon find out easier and readier methods of performing their own particular work.

(Adam Smith, *The Wealth of Nations*)

29. [Psychologists] Wirtshafter and Davis noted that the glycerol content of the blood is related to the size of the fat cells [in the body]. Since the size of the fat cells would indicate something about the amount of stored fats, increases in blood glycerol should indicate increases in body weight.

(Herbert L. Petri, *Motivation: Theory and Research*, 2nd ed.)

30. Because the moon moves relative to the earth so that it returns to the same position overhead after about 25 hours, there are two high and two low tides at any point every 25 hours.

(Douglas C. Giancoli, *The Ideas of Physics*, 3rd ed.)

II. Define the following terms:

deductive argument   argument from analogy
inductive argument   inductive generalization

argument based on mathematics	prediction
argument from definition	argument from authority
categorical syllogism	argument based on signs
hypothetical syllogism	causal inference — *noun couse and effect*
disjunctive syllogism	particular statement
	general statement

III. Answer "true" or "false" to the following statements:

F 1. In an inductive argument, it is intended that the conclusion contain information not contained in the premises.

2. In a deductive argument, the conclusion is not supposed to contain information not contained in the premises.

T 3. The form of argumentation the arguer uses may allow one to determine whether an argument is inductive or deductive.

T 4. The nature of the link between premises and conclusion may allow one to determine whether an argument is inductive or deductive.

F 5. A geometrical proof is an example of an inductive argument.

F 6. Most arguments based on statistical reasoning are deductive.

7. If the conclusion of an argument follows merely from the definition of a word used in a premise, the argument is deductive.

8. An argument that draws a conclusion about a thing based on that thing's similarity to something else is a deductive argument.

9. An argument that draws a conclusion that something is true because someone has said that it is, is a deductive argument.

10. An argument that presents two alternatives and eliminates one, leaving the other as the conclusion, is an inductive argument.

11. An argument that proceeds from knowledge of a cause to knowledge of an effect is an inductive argument.

12. If an argument contains the phrase "it definitely follows that," then we know for certain that the argument is deductive.

13. An argument that predicts what will happen in the future, based upon what has happened in the past, is an inductive argument.

14. Inductive arguments always proceed from the particular to the general.

15. Deductive arguments always proceed from the general to the particular.

IV. Page through a book, magazine, or newspaper and find two arguments, one inductive and the other deductive. Copy the arguments as written, giving the appropriate reference. Then identify the premises and conclusion of each.

1.4 VALIDITY, TRUTH, SOUNDNESS, STRENGTH, COGENCY

In the previous section we defined a deductive argument as an argument in which we *expect* the conclusion to follow necessarily from the premises. If the conclusion does in fact follow necessarily from the premises, the argument is said to be valid. In other words, a **valid deductive argument** is an argument in which the premises support the conclusion in such a way that if they are assumed true, it is impossible that the conclusion be false. Conversely, an **invalid deductive argument** is a deductive argument in which the conclusion does not follow necessarily from the premises; in other words, a deductive argument such that if the premises are assumed true, it is possible that the conclusion be false.

Two immediate consequences follow from these definitions. The first is that there is no middle ground between valid and invalid. There are no arguments that are "almost" valid or "almost" invalid. If the conclusion does follow necessarily, the argument is valid; if not, it is invalid.

The second consequence is that there is only an indirect relation between validity and truth. For an argument to be valid, it is not necessary that either the premises or the conclusion be true, but merely that *if* the premises are *assumed* true, it is impossible that the conclusion be false. Here is an example of a valid argument having false premises and a false conclusion:

> All auto makers are computer manufacturers.
> Union Carbide is an auto maker.
> Therefore, Union Carbide is a computer manufacturer.

To see that this argument is valid one must ignore the fact that the premises are false and attempt to determine what *would* be true if the premises *were* true. Clearly, if the premises were true, it would follow necessarily that Union Carbide is a computer manufacturer. Thus, the argument is valid.

Just as the occurrence of false premises and a false conclusion does not prevent an argument from being valid, so the occurrence of true premises and a true conclusion does not guarantee validity. Here is an example of an invalid argument having true premises and a true conclusion:

> All banks are financial organizations.
> Wells Fargo is a financial organization.
> Therefore, Wells Fargo is a bank.

The question is not whether the premises and conclusion are true, but whether the premises support the conclusion in such a way that if they are assumed true, it is impossible that the conclusion be false. In the above argument, if we assume that banks are included in one part of the group of financial organizations and that Wells Fargo is included in another part, then Wells Fargo would *not* be a bank. That is, if we assume that the premises are true, it is possible for the conclusion to be false, and so the argument is invalid.

Examples of deductive arguments illustrating the various possibilities of truth and falsity in the premises and conclusion are presented in Table 1.1. When examining this table, note that the only combination of truth and falsity that does not allow for *both* valid and invalid arguments is true premises and false conclusion. In other words, the truth or falsity of premises and conclusion is irrelevant to the question of validity except in that one case. Any deductive argument having true premises and a false conclusion is necessarily invalid. This is perhaps the most important fact in all of deductive logic. The entire system of deductive logic would be quite useless if it accepted as valid any inferential process by which a person could start with truth in the premises and arrive at falsity in the conclusion.

Table 1.1

	Valid	Invalid
True premises **True conclusion**	All wines are beverages. Chardonnay is a wine. Therefore, chardonnay is a beverage. [sound]	All wines are beverages. Chardonnay is a beverage. Therefore, chardonnay is a wine. [unsound]
True premises **False conclusion**	None exist	All wines are beverages. Ginger ale is a beverage. Therefore, ginger ale is a wine. [unsound]
False premises **True conclusion**	All wines are soft drinks. Ginger ale is a wine. Therefore, ginger ale is a soft drink. [unsound]	All wines are whiskeys. Chardonnay is a whiskey. Therefore, chardonnay is a wine. [unsound]
False premises **False conclusion**	All wines are whiskeys. Ginger ale is a wine. Therefore, ginger ale is a whiskey. [unsound]	All wines are whiskeys. Ginger ale is a whiskey. Therefore, ginger ale is a wine. [unsound]

The relationship between the validity of a deductive argument and the truth or falsity of its premises and conclusion, as illustrated in Table 1.1, is summarized as follows:

Premises	Conclusion	Validity
T	T	?
T	F	Invalid
F	T	?
F	F	?

A **sound argument** is a deductive argument that is *valid* and has *true premises*. Both conditions must be met for an argument to be sound, and if either is missing the argument is *unsound*. The qualification that the premises must be true means that *all* the premises must be true. Because a valid argument is one such that if the premises are true it necessarily follows that the conclusion is true, and because a sound argument does in fact have true premises, it follows that every sound argument, by definition, will have a true conclusion as well. A sound argument, therefore, is what is meant by a "good" deductive argument in the fullest sense of the term.

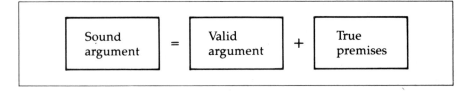

Let us now consider inductive arguments. In the previous section we defined an inductive argument as an argument in which we *expect* the conclusion to follow only probably from the premises. If the conclusion does in fact follow probably from the premises, the argument is said to be strong. In other words, a **strong inductive argument** is an inductive argument such that if the premises are assumed true, then, based on that assumption, it is probable that the conclusion be true. On the other hand, a **weak inductive argument** is an inductive argument in which the conclusion does not follow probably from the premises; in other words, an inductive argument such that if the premises are assumed true, then, based on that assumption, it is not probable that the conclusion be true.

Here are two examples of inductive arguments. The first is weak, the second strong:

> This barrel contains one hundred apples.
> Three apples selected at random were found to be ripe.
> Therefore, probably all one hundred apples are ripe.

> This barrel contains one hundred apples.
> Eighty apples selected at random were found to be ripe.
> Therefore, probably all one hundred apples are ripe.

As is evident from these examples, strength and weakness, unlike validity and invalidity, generally admit of degrees. The first argument is not absolutely weak nor the second absolutely strong. Both arguments would be strengthened or weakened by the random selection of a larger or smaller sample. The incorporation of additional premises into an inductive argument will also generally tend to strengthen or weaken it. For example, if the premise "One unripe apple that had been found earlier was removed" were added to the second argument, the argument would presumably be weakened.

As with validity and invalidity, strength and weakness are only indirectly related to truth and falsity. The central question in determining strength or weakness is whether the conclusion would probably be true if the premises are assumed true. Here is an example of a strong inductive argument having a false premise and a probably false conclusion:

> All meteorites found to this day have contained gold. Therefore, probably the next meteorite to be found will contain gold.

In fact, few, if any, meteorites contain any gold. But if it were assumed that all of the ones found to this day did contain gold, it would follow with high probability that the next one found would also.

Conversely, the fact that the premises of an inductive argument are true and the conclusion probably true does not make the argument strong. Here is an example of a weak inductive argument having a true premise and a probably true conclusion:

> During the past 50 years, inflation has consistently reduced the value of the American dollar. Therefore, industrial productivity will probably increase in the years ahead.

Even though the premise is true and the conclusion probably true, the premise does not provide probabilistic support for the conclusion—there is no direct connection between inflation and increased industrial productivity.

Examples of inductive arguments illustrating the various possibilities of truth and falsity in the premises and conclusion are presented in Table 1.2. As with deductive arguments, truth and falsity (or probable truth/falsity) are irrelevant to the question of strength except in the case of true premises and a probably false conclusion. Any inductive argument having true premises and a probably false conclusion is always weak. Inductive logic would be useless if it accepted as strong any inductive argument having true premises and a probably false conclusion.

Table 1.2

	Strong	Weak
True premise **Probably true conclusion**	All previous American presidents were men. Therefore, probably the next American president will be a man. [cogent]	A few American presidents were Federalists. Therefore, probably the next American president will be a man. [uncogent]
True premise **Probably false conclusion**	None exist	A few American presidents were Federalists. Therefore, probably the next American president will be a Federalist. [uncogent]
False premise **Probably true conclusion**	All previous American presidents were television debaters. Therefore, probably the next American president will be a television debater. [uncogent]	A few American presidents were Libertarians. Therefore, probably the next American president will be a television debater. [uncogent]
False premise **Probably false conclusion**	All previous American presidents were women. Therefore, probably the next American president will be a woman. [uncogent]	A few American presidents were Libertarians. Therefore, probably the next American president will be a Libertarian. [uncogent]

The relationship between the strength of an inductive argument and the truth or falsity of its premises and conclusion, as illustrated in Table 1.2, is summarized as follows:

Premises	Conclusion	Strength
T	prob. T	?
T	prob. F	Weak
F	prob. T	?
F	prob. F	?

A **cogent argument** is an inductive argument that is *strong* and has *true premises,* and if either condition is missing the argument is *uncogent.* A cogent argument is the inductive analogue of a sound deductive argument and is what is meant by a "good" inductive argument without qualification. Because the conclusion of a cogent argument is genuinely supported by true premises, it follows that the conclusion of every cogent argument is probably true.

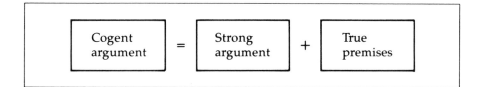

In summary, whether an argument is inductive or deductive, there are basically two separate questions that are involved in its evaluation:

1. Do the premises support the conclusion?
2. Are the premises true?

The answer to the first question determines whether a deductive argument is valid or invalid and whether an inductive argument is strong or weak. Then, assuming the argument is valid or strong, the answer to the second question determines whether a deductive argument is sound or unsound and whether an inductive argument is cogent or uncogent.

The various alternatives open to statements and arguments may be diagramed as follows. Note that in logic one never speaks of an argument as being "true" or "false," and one never speaks of a statement as being "valid," "invalid," "strong," or "weak."

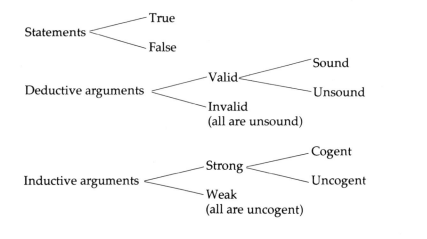

EXERCISE 1.4

I. The following arguments are deductive. Determine whether each is valid or invalid and note the relationship between your answer and the truth or falsity of the premises and conclusion. Finally, determine whether the argument is sound or unsound.

★1. Since *Moby Dick* was written by Shakespeare, and *Moby Dick* is a science fiction novel, it follows that Shakespeare wrote a science fiction novel.

2. If George Washington was beheaded, then George Washington died. George Washington died. Therefore, George Washington was beheaded.

3. Since some fruits are green, and some fruits are apples, it follows that some fruits are green apples.

★4. Since the Spanish American War occurred before the American Civil War, and the American Civil War occurred after the Korean War, it follows that the Spanish American War occurred before the Korean War.

5. The United States Congress has more members than there are days in the year. Therefore, at least two members of Congress have the same birthday.

6. Since Winston Churchill was English, and Winston Churchill was a famous statesman, we may conclude that at least one Englishman was a famous statesman.

★7. Chicago is a city in Canada and Canada is part of the United States. Therefore, Chicago is a city in the United States.

8. Since the Department of Defense Building in Washington, D.C. has the shape of a hexagon, it follows that it has seven sides.

II. The following inductive arguments involve rolling a single plastic die. In each case assume that the die is a fair one with sides numbered 1 through 6. The premise of each argument may or may not tell the truth about this die. Determine whether each argument is strong or weak and note the relationship between your answer and the truth or falsity of the premise and conclusion. Finally, determine whether each argument is cogent or uncogent.

★1. This die is marked with numbers 1 through 6. Therefore, probably the next roll will turn up a 6.

2. This die is marked with numbers 1 through 6. Therefore, probably the next roll will turn up a number less than 6.

3. This die is made of plastic. Therefore, probably the next roll will turn up a number less than 6.

★4. This die is marked with a 1 and five 6s. Therefore, probably the next roll will turn up a 6.

5. This die is marked with a 1 and five 6s. Therefore, probably the next roll will turn up a number less than 6.

6. This die is marked with numbers 1 through 6. Therefore, probably the next roll will turn up a number greater than 1.

★7. This die is marked with numbers 1 through 4 and two 6s. Therefore, probably the next roll will turn up a 4.

8. This die is marked with numbers 1 through 4 and two 6s. Therefore, probably the next roll will turn up a number greater than 1.

III. Determine whether the following arguments are inductive or deductive. If inductive, determine whether strong or weak. If deductive, determine whether valid or invalid.

★1. Since Agatha is the mother of Raquel and the sister of Tom, it follows that Tom is the uncle of Raquel.

2. Hydrogen is a tasteless, odorless gas that is both lighter than air and combustible. Helium, like hydrogen, is also a tasteless, odorless gas that is lighter than air. Therefore, helium must be combustible, too.

3. The sign on the highway leading into Denver, Colorado says that the city's elevation is 5280 feet. It must be the case that Denver is 1 mile high.

★4. Since Christmas is always on a Thursday, it follows that the day after Christmas is always a Friday.

5. This figure is a Euclidean triangle. Therefore, the sum of its angles is equal to two right angles.

6. By accident Karen baked her brownies two hours longer than she should have. Therefore, they have probably been ruined.

★7. After taking LSD, Alice said she saw a flying saucer land in the shopping center parking lot. Since Alice has a reputation for always telling the truth, we must conclude that a flying saucer really did land there.

8. Since Phyllis is the cousin of Denise, and Denise is the cousin of Harriet, it follows necessarily that Harriet is the cousin of Phyllis.

9. The picnic scheduled in the park for tomorrow will most likely be cancelled. It's been snowing for six days straight.

★10. Circle A has exactly twice the diameter of circle B. From this we may conclude that circle A has exactly twice the area of circle B.

11. Robert has lost consistently at blackjack every day for the past several days. Therefore, it is very likely that he will win today.

12. Since John loves Nancy and Nancy loves Peter, it follows necessarily that John loves Peter.

★13. This cash register drawer contains over 100 coins. Three coins selected at random were found to have dates earlier than 1945. Therefore, probably all of the coins in the drawer have dates earlier than 1945.

14. The Japanese attack on Pearl Harbor happened in either 1941 or 1951. But it didn't happen in 1941. Therefore, it happened in 1951.

15. Harry will never be able to solve that difficult problem in advanced calculus in the limited time allowed. He has never studied anything beyond algebra, and in that he earned only a C−.

★16. Since $x + y = 10$, and $x = 7$, it follows that $y = 4$.

17. Joe's birthday is exactly one week after Mark's, and Mark's is on May 10. Hence, Joe's is on May 17.

18. If taxes increase, there will be budgetary cutbacks. If there are budgetary cutbacks, a funding drive will be initiated. Therefore, if taxes increase, a funding drive will be initiated.

★19. Statistics reveal that 86 percent of those who receive flu shots do not get the flu. Jack received a flu shot one month ago. Therefore, he should be immune, even though the flu is going around now.

20. Since Michael is a Pisces, it necessarily follows that he was born in March.

IV. Define the following terms:

valid argument	strong argument
invalid argument	weak argument
sound argument	cogent argument
unsound argument	uncogent argument

V. Answer "true" or "false" to the following statements:

1. Some arguments, while not completely valid, are almost valid.

2. Inductive arguments admit of varying degrees of strength and weakness.

3. Invalid deductive arguments are basically the same as inductive arguments.

4. If a deductive argument has true premises and a false conclusion, it is necessarily invalid.

5. A valid argument may have a false premise and a false conclusion.

6. A valid argument may have a false premise and a true conclusion.

7. A sound argument may be invalid.

8. A sound argument may have a false conclusion.

9. A strong argument may have false premises and a probably false conclusion.

10. A strong argument may have true premises and a probably false conclusion.

11. A cogent argument may have a probably false conclusion.

12. A cogent argument must be inductively strong.

13. If an argument has true premises and a true conclusion, we know that it is a perfectly good argument.

14. A statement may legitimately be spoken of as "valid" or "invalid."

15. An argument may legitimately be spoken of as "true" or "false."

1.5 ARGUMENT FORMS: PROVING INVALIDITY

In the previous section we saw that a valid deductive argument is one in which if the premises are assumed true, it necessarily follows that the conclusion is true. Let us analyze this concept of validity a little further. For these purposes the following argument will prove instructive:

> All adlers are bobkins.
> All bobkins are crockers
> Therefore, all adlers are crockers.

Because the words "adlers," "bobkins," and "crockers" are meaningless, we do not know whether any of the statements in this argument are true or false. Yet, we do know that if we *assume* that the premises are true, it necessarily follows that the conclusion is true. That is, if we assume that the adlers, whatever they might be, are included in the bobkins, and the bobkins in the crockers, then we must accept the conclusion that the adlers are included in the crockers. By definition, therefore, the argument is valid.

This fact is important for understanding the nature of validity because it shows that the validity of an argument has nothing to do with its specific subject matter. Even though we know nothing about adlers, bobkins, and crockers, we still know that the argument is valid. Rather, the validity of an argument arises from the *form* or *structure* of the argument. The argument above is valid because of the way in which the terms "adlers," "bobkins," and "crockers" are arranged in the statements. If we represent these terms by their first letters, we obtain the following argument form:

> All *A* are *B*.
> All *B* are *C*.
> Therefore, all *A* are *C*.

This is a valid argument form. Its validity rests purely upon the arrangement of the letters within the statements, and it has nothing to do with what the letters might stand for. In light of this fact, we can substitute any terms we choose in place of *A*, *B*, and *C*, and as long as we are consistent, we will obtain a valid argument. For example, we might substitute "daisies" for *A*, "flowers" for *B*, and "plants" for *C* and obtain a valid argument.

Depending on what words we substitute, the premises and conclusion will sometimes turn out to be true and sometimes false. But whatever arrangement of truth and falsity we obtain, it will always be the case that if we *assume* that the premises are true, the conclusion will be true on the basis of that assumption. The following arguments have been produced by substituting various terms in place of the letters in the valid argument form above. All of them, therefore, are valid. Notice the various arrangements of truth and falsity in the premises and conclusion:

All tigers are mammals.	True premises
All mammals are animals.	
Therefore, all tigers are animals.	True conclusion
All pigs are fish.	False premises
All fish are birds.	
Therefore, all pigs are birds.	False conclusion
All rabbits are fish.	False premises
All fish are mammals.	
Therefore, all rabbits are mammals.	True conclusion

The only arrangement of truth and falsity missing here is true premises and false conclusion. Try as we may, we can never produce an argument having true premises and a false conclusion from a valid form. By definition, such an argument would be invalid and would therefore have an invalid form, instead of the valid form from which it was produced.

Let us turn now to the concept of invalidity. Consider the following argument:

> All adlers are bobkins.
> All crockers are bobkins.
> Therefore, all adlers are crockers.

As with the previous argument, we do not know whether the premises and conclusion of this argument are true or false. But if we assume that the premises are true, it is not *necessarily* the case that the conclusion is true. It might be the case, for example, that the adlers make up one part of the bobkins, that the crockers make up another part, and that the adlers and the crockers are completely separate from one another. In this case the premises would be true and the conclusion false. The argument is therefore invalid. If we represent the terms in this argument by their first letters, we obtain the following argument form:

> All *A* are *B*.
> All *C* are *B*.
> Therefore, all *A* are *C*.

This is an invalid form. Accordingly, since invalidity, like validity, has nothing to do with the specific subject matter of an argument, we may substitute any terms we choose in place of the letters and obtain an invalid argument. It is important only that we make the substitution in such a way that the resulting argument, when best interpreted, has a form identical to the given form.* The following arguments were produced in this way and are therefore invalid. Notice the various arrangements of truth and falsity in the premises and conclusion:

All tigers are animals.
All mammals are animals.   True premises
Therefore, all tigers are mammals.   True conclusion

All cats are animals.
All dogs are animals.   True premises
Therefore, all cats are dogs.   False conclusion

All pigs are fish.
All birds are fish.   False premises
Therefore, all pigs are birds.   False conclusion

All rabbits are fish.
All mammals are fish.   False premises
Therefore, all rabbits are mammals.   True conclusion

These four arguments, like the previous three, are called **substitution instances** of their respective form. If we compare this group of invalid arguments with the group of valid ones we will notice one distinguishing characteristic: The invalid form has a substitution instance in which the premises are true and the conclusion false. This fact provides the basis for an alternate definition of **invalidity**: *An argument is invalid if and only if its form allows for a substitution instance having true premises and a false conclusion.* That this definition correctly characterizes invalid arguments may be seen as follows. If an argument is invalid, it has an invalid form. But if the form is invalid, there is at least one substitution instance having true premises and a false conclusion; otherwise, every substitution instance having true premises would have a true conclusion, and by definition the form would be valid. Conversely, if a substitution instance exists having true premises and a false conclusion, the substitution instance is clearly invalid and thus has an invalid form. But since

---

*The problem with invalid argument forms is that most, if not all, of them are susceptible to having substitution instances that are valid. For example, the argument

All black cats are animals.
All black animals are animals.
Therefore, all black cats are black animals.

appears to be a substitution instance of the form discussed above. But if the argument is interpreted in such a way that the conclusion follows from the tacitly true premise "All cats are animals," the argument is valid. Accordingly, if valid, it has in fact a valid argument form. Thus, we adopt the convention that an argument is best interpreted as having an invalid form only if it is not susceptible to being interpreted as having a valid form.

this form is identical to that of the original argument, the existence of this substitution instance proves the original argument invalid.

This alternate definition of invalidity leads directly to a method for *proving* invalidity. If a deductive argument is known to be invalid in the first place, it may be proven invalid by isolating the form of the argument and then constructing a substitution instance having true premises and a false conclusion. We will call this method for proving invalidity the **counterexample method.** Let us apply it to the following categorical syllogism:

> Since some employees are not social climbers and all vice-presidents are employees, we may conclude that some vice-presidents are not social climbers.

This argument is invalid because the employees who are not social climbers might not be vice-presidents. According, we can *prove* the argument invalid by constructing a substitution instance of its form. The form of the argument is as follows:

> Some E are not S.
> All V are E.
> Therefore, some V are not S.

Let us now make the following substitution:

> E = animals
> S = mammals
> V = dogs

The resulting substitution instance is:

> Some animals are not mammals.
> All dogs are animals.
> Therefore, some dogs are not mammals.

The substitution instance has true premises and a false conclusion and is therefore, by definition, invalid. Since it has the same form as the original argument, it constitutes proof that the original argument is invalid.

Not all deductive arguments, of course, are of the same general type as the one above. Consider the following hypothetical syllogism:

> If the government imposes import restrictions, the price of automobiles will rise. Therefore, since the government will not impose import restrictions, it follows that the price of automobiles will not rise.

A CONCISE INTRODUCTION TO LOGIC

This argument is invalid because the price of automobiles might rise even though import restrictions are not imposed. It has the following form:

> If G, then P.
> Not G.
> Therefore, not P.

This form differs from the previous one in that its letters stand for complete statements. G, for example, stands for "The government imposes import restrictions." If we make the substitution

> G = Abraham Lincoln committed suicide.
> P = Abraham Lincoln is dead.

we obtain the following substitution instance:

> If Abraham Lincoln committed suicide, then Abraham Lincoln is dead.
> Abraham Lincoln did not commit suicide.
> Therefore, Abraham Lincoln is not dead.

Since the premises are true and the conclusion false, the substitution instance is clearly invalid. Thus, it constitutes proof that the original argument is invalid.

When applying the counterexample method to an argument having a conditional statement as a premise (such as the one above), it is recommended that the statement substituted in place of the conditional statement express some kind of necessary connection. In the example above, the first premise asserts the necessary connection between suicide and death. There can be no doubt about the truth of such a statement.

Using the counterexample method to prove arguments invalid requires a little ingenuity because there is no rule that will automatically produce the required term or statement to be substituted. Any term or statement will work, of course, provided that it yields a substitution instance that has premises that are indisputably true and a conclusion that is indisputably false. Ideally, the truth value of these statements should be known to the average individual; otherwise, the substitution instance cannot be depended upon to prove anything. If, for example, P in the above argument form had been replaced by the statement "George Wilson is dead," the substitution instance would be useless, because nobody knows whether this statement is true or false.

The counterexample method is useful only for proving arguments invalid, because, as we saw earlier, the only arrangement of truth and falsity that proves anything is true premises and false conclusion. If a substitution instance is produced having true premises and a true conclusion, it does *not* prove that the argument is valid. Furthermore, the method is only useful for deductive arguments because the strength and weakness of inductive arguments is only partially dependent on the form of the argument. Accordingly, no method that relates exclusively to the form of an inductive argument can be used to prove the argument weak.

One final comment is needed regarding the form of an argument. It often happens that the form is not explicit and that making it explicit requires an analysis of the meaning of the language. Many of the arguments in Exercise 1.4 were of this sort. Consider the following example:

> This figure is a square.
> Therefore, this figure has four sides.

The conclusion follows necessarily from the premise because every square, by definition, has four sides. To make the form of the argument explicit, a premise must be added stating this fact:

> This figure is a square.
> All squares have four sides.
> Therefore, this figure has four sides.

As this example illustrates, the statement at the beginning of this section that the validity of an argument is concerned not with the subject matter but rather with the form of an argument needs qualification. When the form of an argument is immediately clear, the subject matter is irrelevant to the question of validity. But when the form is not clear, the subject matter may have to be analyzed to determine what the form is.

EXERCISE 1.5

I. Use the counterexample method to prove each of the following arguments invalid. To do this, isolate the form of each argument, using letters to represent the terms. Then select three new terms to replace the letters, yielding a substitution instance having true premises and a false conclusion. Select these three terms from the following list of five: "cats," "dogs," "mammals," "fish," and "animals." A few of the arguments involve the word "some." In logic "some" always means "at least one." For example, the statement "Some dogs are animals" means "At least one dog is an animal"—which is true. This statement does not imply that some dogs are not animals.

★1. All galaxies are structures that contain black holes in the center, so all galaxies are quasars, since all quasars are structures that contain black holes in the center.

2. Some evolutionists are not persons who believe in the Bible, for no creationists are evolutionists, and some persons who believe in the Bible are not creationists.

3. No patents are measures that discourage research and development, and all patents are regulations that protect intellectual property. Thus, no measures that discourage research and development are regulations that protect intellectual property.

★4. Some farm workers are not persons who are paid decent wages, because no illegal aliens are persons who are paid decent wages, and some illegal aliens are not farm workers.

5. Some politicians are persons who will stop at nothing to win an election, and no persons who will stop at nothing to win an election are true statesmen. Hence, no politicians are true statesmen.

6. All veterans exposed to Agent Orange are persons with a higher than average risk of cancer, for all individuals whose blood contains dioxin are persons with a higher than average risk of cancer, and all individuals whose blood contains dioxin are veterans exposed to Agent Orange.

★7. No members of the African National Congress are supporters of apartheid. Consequently, no members of the African National Congress are members of the Labor Party, since no members of the Labor Party are supporters of apartheid.

8. Some toxic dumps are sites that emit hazardous wastes, and some sites that emit hazardous wastes are undesirable places to live near. Thus, some toxic dumps are undesirable places to live near.

9. All persons who assist others in suicide are persons guilty of murder. Accordingly, some individuals motivated by compassion are not persons guilty of murder, inasmuch as some persons who assist others in suicide are individuals motivated by compassion.

★10. Some school boards are not groups that oppose values clarification because some school boards are not organizations with vision, and some groups that oppose values clarification are not organizations with vision.

II. Use the counterexample method to prove each of the following arguments invalid.

★1. If animal species are fixed and immutable, then evolution is a myth. Therefore, evolution is not a myth, since animal species are not fixed and immutable.

2. If carbon dioxide is present in the atmosphere, then plants have a source of carbon. Hence, since plants have a source of carbon, carbon dioxide is present in the atmosphere.

3. If gene splicing is successful, then disease-resistant livestock will be produced. If genetic defects can be eliminated, then disease-resistant livestock will be produced. Thus, if gene splicing is successful, then genetic defects can be eliminated.

★4. Some diplomats are clever spies, since some diplomats are clever and some diplomats are spies.

5. All swift runners are fine athletes. Therefore, all runners are athletes.

1.6 EXTENDED ARGUMENTS

The logical analysis of extended arguments, such as those found in editorials, essays, and lengthy letters to newspaper editors, involves numerous difficulties. Such arguments are often mixed together with fragments of reports, pieces of expository writing, illustrations, explanations, and statements of opinion. Proper analysis involves weeding out the extraneous material and isolating premises and conclusions. Another problem stems from the fact that lengthy arguments often involve complex arrangements of subarguments that feed into the main argument in various ways. Distinguishing one subargument from another is often a complicated task. And then there are some argumentative passages that involve completely separate strands of argumentation leading to separate conclusions. Again, distinguishing the strands and assigning premises to the right conclusion is not only problematic but often involves an element of creativity on the part of the analyst.

To facilitate the analysis of extended arguments we will assign numerals to the various statements in the passage and use arrows to represent the inferential links. Example:

> ① The contamination of underground aquifers represents a pollution problem of catastrophic proportions. ② Half the nation's drinking water, which comes from these aquifers, is being poisoned by chemical wastes dumped into the soil for generations.

This argument is diagramed as follows:

$$
\begin{array}{c}
② \\
\downarrow \\
①
\end{array}
$$

The diagram says that statement ② supports statement ①.

In extended arguments we can identify two distinct patterns of argumentation, which we will name the vertical pattern and the horizontal pattern. The *vertical pattern* consists of a series of arguments in which a conclusion of a logically prior argument becomes a premise of a subsequent argument. Example:

① The selling of human organs, such as hearts, kidneys, and corneas, should be outlawed. ② Allowing human organs to be sold will inevitably lead to a situation in which only the rich will be able to afford transplants. ③ This is so because whenever something scarce is bought and sold as a commodity, the price always goes up. ④ The law of supply and demand requires it.

This argument is diagramed as follows:

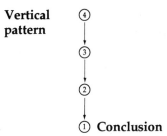

Vertical pattern

The diagram says that statement ④ supports ③, which in turn supports ②, which in turn supports ①.

The *horizontal pattern* consists of a single argument in which a single conclusion is supported by two or more premises. Example:

① The selling of human organs, such as hearts, kidneys, and corneas, should be outlawed. ② If this practice is allowed to get a foothold, people in desperate financial straits will start selling their own organs to pay their bills. ③ Alternately, those with a criminal bent will take to killing healthy young people and selling their organs on the black market. ④ In the final analysis, the buying and selling of human organs comes just too close to the buying and selling of life itself.

The diagram for this argument is as follows:

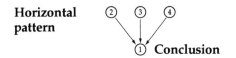

Horizontal pattern

This diagram says that statements ②, ③, and ④ support ① independently.

Two variations on the horizontal and vertical patterns occur when premises support a conclusion *conjointly* and when a set of premises supports *multiple* conclusions. For both variations we use braces to keep the requisite statements together. The following argument illustrates the first variation:

> ① The development of weapons for use in outer space will increase the threat of accidental nuclear war. ② The primary target of such weapons would be the world-wide network of communications satellites. ③ And the satellite network deters accidental war by detecting and evaluating the strength of a potential nuclear attack.

Statement ① is the conclusion. Taken separately, statements ② and ③ provide little or no support for ①, but taken together they do provide support. That is, ② and ③ support ① *conjointly*. This relationship between the premises is illustrated by the use of the brace in the following diagram:

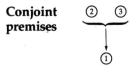

The next example illustrates the occurrence of a multiple conclusion:

> ① The development of weapons for use in outer space opens the door to an unlimited theater of war fraught with gargantuan technological difficulties. ② Therefore, the development of such weapons will undoubtedly expand the arms race between the superpowers. ③ Additionally, it will cost the competitors hundreds of billions of dollars that might otherwise be spent for more humane purposes.

In this passage statement ① supports both ② and ③. Since no single argument can have more than one conclusion, the passage is correctly evaluated as consisting of two arguments. For present purposes, however, we will treat it as if it were a single argument by joining the two conclusions with a brace:

At this point our symbolism is sufficiently developed to handle most editorial-length arguments. The next example illustrates the horizontal pattern combined with the vertical pattern and includes both variations just discussed. We will call such an argument pattern a *composite pattern*:

> ① Economic sanctions against Soviet Bloc countries to accomplish political goals are not effective in today's economy. ② In many instances they are even counterproductive. ③ Agricultural embargoes provide a case in point. ④ The 1979 grain embargo did not prevent the Soviets from obtaining grain from other sources. ⑤ Concurrently, American farmers suffered from a reduced market. ⑥ Restrictions on oil technology have met with similar results. ⑦ The embargo against the trans-Siberian gas pipeline did not interrupt construction. ⑧ And, as with the grain embargo, the American economy suffered. ⑨ Orders for pipe-laying equipment that would have gone to Caterpillar Tractor Co. went instead to Japan's Komatsu. ⑩ The needs of the semiconductor industry point up a third consideration. ⑪ To support the constant demands of research and development, American firms must depend heavily on exports. ⑫ But if exports are allowed, there can be no guarantee that high-tech American products will not wind up in the Soviet Bloc.

This argument is diagramed as follows:

Composite pattern

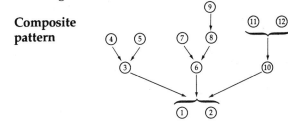

The argument has a multiple conclusion, and statements ⑪ and ⑫ support ⑩ conjointly.

EXERCISE 1.6

I. The following arguments were abstracted from newspaper articles, editorials, and letters to the editor. Use the method presented in this section to diagram them. If a statement either is redundant or does not play a role in the argument, it should not be included in the diagram.

★1. ① There is virtually no difference between the amount of care given the poor by for-profit hospital chains and by nonprofit hospitals. ② According to the American Hospital Association, for-profit hospitals' devoted 4.3 percent of their total costs to "unsponsored care" in 1984. ③ The figure for nonprofits was 4.6 percent.

(Gregg Easterbrook, "The Revolution in Medicine")

2. ① The development of carbon-embedded plastics, otherwise called "composits," is an important new technology because ② it holds the

key for new aircraft and spacecraft designs. ③ This is so because these composits are not only stronger than steel but lighter than aluminum.
(Thomas H. Maugh II, "Composits—The Lightweight Champs of Aircraft Industry")

3. ① Homework stifles the thrill of learning in the mind of the student. ② It instills an oppressive learn-or-else discipline. ③ It quenches the desire for knowledge and the love of truth. ④ For these reasons homework should never be assigned.
(Colman McCarthy, "Homework's Tyranny Hobbles Promising Minds")

★4. ① When parents become old and destitute, the obligation of caring for them should be imposed on their children. ② Clearly, children owe a debt to their parents. ③ Their parents brought them into the world and cared for them when they were unable to care for themselves. ④ This debt could be appropriately discharged by having grown children care for their parents.
(Gary Jones, "The Responsibility of Parents")

5. ① Many people believe that the crime of bribery cannot extend to campaign contributions. ② From a legal standpoint, however, countless campaign contributions are in fact bribes. ③ A bribe is anything of value or advantage given with the intent to unlawfully influence the person to whom it is given in his official capacity. ④ A campaign contribution is certainly something of value or advantage. ⑤ Furthermore, every contribution from a lobbyist or special interest group is given with the intent to influence voting, and ⑥ thousands of such contributions are made in every important election.
(Daniel Hays Lowenstein, "Can Candidates Run for Political Office Without Taking Bribes?")

6. ① The United States will shrink as a world power in the years ahead. ② The same can be said for the Soviet Union. ③ Both countries are stuck on the idea that power is tied to military strength. ④ In fact, power in today's world is directly tied to economic strength. ⑤ Japan, with its incredible economic influence, is really the most powerful nation in the world today.
(Betty Cuniberti, "A Report on the State of the World")

★7. ① Society values white lives more than black lives. ② This is clear from the fact that killers of whites are much more likely to be sentenced to death than killers of blacks. ③ Of the 1788 people currently on death row, 1713 were convicted of killing a white person. ④ Yet blacks are six times more likely to be murder victims than whites are. ⑤ In Florida, no one has ever been executed for murdering a black person, ⑥ but dozens have been executed for murdering white people.
(*Los Angeles Times* editorial, "Death and Race")

8. ① Powerful new particle accelerators are important in high energy physics and ② they are worth their cost because ③ they will allow scientists to produce and capture significant quantities of Z particles. ④ Z particles result from the collision of positrons and electrons, and ⑤ particle

accelerators are needed to achieve significant numbers of these collisions. ⑥ Z particles are thought to be the bearers of the weak nuclear
force, and ⑦
learning the nature of this force may lead to the development of entirely new sources of energy.

(Lee Dye, "Linear Collider: Bold Gamble in Atomic Physics")

9. ① All men crave material success because ② it serves as an insurance
policy against sexual rejection. This is true because ③ women love men
who are successful. ④ Both men and women want power, and ⑤ success is the form of power women feel most deprived of. ⑥ Thus,
women try to achieve it vicariously through men. ⑦ As the 5-foot 6-
inch Dustin Hoffman once put it, "When I was in high school, women
wouldn't touch me with a 10-foot pole. Now I can't keep them away
with a 10-foot pole."

(Warren Farrell, "Success Story: From Frog to Prince")

★10. ① Cigarette consumption could be easily reduced by simply outlawing
tailor-made cigarettes. ② The manufacture of tailor-made cigarettes to
American standards is a high-tech industry. ③ It cannot be done in
small illicit labs like the processing of PCP, cocaine or heroin. ④ The
availability of quality tobacco for hand-rolling would discourage the development of an illegal tailor-made market. ⑤ Most people would not
pay the premium prices demanded by an illicit market for a product of
unknown quality. ⑥ They could roll a high quality product for themselves. ⑦ Truly addicted persons would continue to smoke no matter
how inconvenient. ⑧ But most would give it up as too much bother
before it became a deeply ingrained habit.

(Richard Sand, "An Easy Way to Reduce Cigarette Consumption")

11. ① Flesh food is not a necessity in the human diet, as ② nutritionally
adequate alternatives are readily available. ③ Many people in the world
thrive on a non-meat diet. ④ Indeed, vegetarian Seventh-day Adven-
tists in this country live an average of six years longer than their meat-
eating counterparts. ⑤ The National Academy of Science warns that
our fat-laden diet is directly responsible for much of the heart disease
and cancer that afflict so many. ⑥ At a time when people are starving
in certain parts of the world, it should be noted that a steer must con-
sume sixteen pounds of grain and soy to produce one pound of meat.
⑦ The grain and soybeans we feed our meat-producing animals would
feed every hungry mouth in the world many times over. ⑧ Cattle are
competing with humans for food. ⑨ Clearly, a reassessment of the
whole concept of killing and eating animals is in order.

(Suzanne Sutton, "Killing Animals for Food—Time for a Second Look")

12. ① The argument has been made that to cut down on teenage drunk
driving we should increase the federal excise tax on beer. ② Such a
measure, however, would almost certainly fail to achieve its intended
result. ③
Teenagers are notoriously insensitive to cost. ④ They gladly accept premium prices for the latest style in clothes or the most popular record
albums. ⑤ And then, those who drink and drive already risk arrest and

loss of driving privileges. ⑥ They would not think twice about paying a little more for a six-pack. ⑦ Finally, the situation is not as bleak as it has been made to appear. ⑧ The fatality rate for teenage drivers is lower today than it has been in years.

(James C. Sanders, "Increased U.S. Tax on Beer")

★13. ① It has been widely acknowledged that the quality of undergraduate education in this country is diminishing. ② An often unrecognized cause of this malady is the exploitative way that universities as employers treat their part-time and temporary faculty members. ③ In many universities there are no formal guidelines for evaluating the work of these instructors. ④ As a result, poor instructors who solicit the favor of the department chairman are often retained over better ones who do not. ⑤ Another factor is the low pay given to these instructors. ⑥ In order to survive, many of them must accept heavy teaching loads spread out over three or four institutions. ⑦ The quality of instruction can only suffer when faculty members stretch themselves so thin. ⑧ Lastly, because part-time and temporary faculty are rarely members of the faculty senate, ⑨ they have no voice in university governance. ⑩ But without a voice, the shoddy conditions under which they work are never brought to light.

(Michael Schwalbe, "Part-Time Faculty Members Deserve a Break")

14. ① A manned trip to Mars is a justified scientific goal ② because it affords a unique opportunity to explore the origins of the solar system and the emergence of life. ③ However, from a scientific standpoint, an initial landing on the tiny Martian moons, Phobos and Deimos, would be more rewarding than a landing on the planet itself. ④ Because the Martian terrain is rugged, ⑤ humans would not be able to venture far, ⑥ nor could they operate a robot vehicle without the use of a satellite, ⑦ since Mars's mountains would block their view. ⑧ Explorers on Phobos and Deimos could easily send robot vehicles to the planet's surface. ⑨ Using Mars's moons as a base would also be better than unmanned exploration directed from the Houston space center. ⑩ Because the distance is so great, ⑪ radio signals to and from Mars can take as long as an hour. ⑫ Thus, driving an unmanned rover from Earth, step by step, would be a time-consuming operation. ⑬ Sample returns to Earth would take months instead of hours, and ⑭ follow-on missions would be years apart instead of days, further slowing the process of exploration.

(S. Fred Singer, "The Case for Going to Mars")

15. ① There are lots of problems with the U.S. airline system, ② but deregulation isn't one of them. ③ Airline deregulation has delivered most of what it promised when enacted in 1978. ④ It has held down fares, ⑤ increased competition, ⑥ and raised the industry's efficiency. ⑦ Despite claims to the contrary, airline safety has not suffered. ⑧ And, with some exceptions, service to some cities and towns has improved. ⑨ On average, fares are lower today than in 1980. ⑩ Morrison and Winston estimate that fares are 20% to 30% below what they would be under regulation. ⑪ Competition has increased ⑫ because prior to de-

regulation airlines had protected routes. ⑬ After deregulation this changed. ⑭ Efficiency has also improved. ⑮ After deregulation the percentage of occupied seats jumped by 10% and miles traveled by 32%. ⑯ Despite fears that airlines would cut unprofitable service to small communities, most smaller cities and towns experienced a 20% to 30% increase in flight frequency. ⑰ Lastly, travel on U.S. airlines remains among the safest forms of transportation. ⑱ Between 1975 and 1985, deaths resulting from crashes totaled fewer than 3000.

(Robert J. Samuelson, "Let's not Regulate the Deregulated Airlines")

II. The following three selections are nearly complete editorials. Use the method presented in this section to diagram the arguments.

★1. **The Fed's Independence Should Be Maintained**
Sherman J. Maisel
① For more than 70 years, debates have raged over the relationship of the Federal Reserve with the Treasury and the White House. ② Most analysts have concluded that the Fed's present "independent," semi-autonomous position is preferable to anything else that has been proposed.

③ Contrary to some opinions, making the Fed an adjunct of the Treasury would not increase the Administration's ability to obtain a monetary policy consistent with its economic goals. ④ The President already has the necessary power. ⑤ If the President requires a particular monetary policy, the Federal Reserve *must* accept his views. ⑥ If conflicts become serious, resignation of governors may be necessary, but institutional opposition cannot long continue. ⑦ This derives from the President's duties and constitutional powers, and is so recognized by the Fed, as well as in laws that affect the economy.

⑧ More ominous, if the Treasury controlled the Fed, the money supply might be manipulated for partisan political purposes.

⑨ Throughout history, cheap money has had a siren appeal, and the separation of the Fed makes it easier to escape such enticements.

⑩ While monetary policy must adjust to the President's desires, the ability of the central bank to demand that instructions be in the open—and subject to public and congressional scrutiny—reduces the danger that money will be created strictly for partisan purposes.

⑪ Finally, the Federal Reserve has been valuable as a source of specialized knowledge about money, the financial system, the economy and their interrelationships. ⑫ Such analysis currently reflects the combined judgment of skilled men and women devoting full time to it.

⑬ In the Treasury, money growth would depend on the (frequently erroneous) views of short-term political appointees. ⑭ These appointees are often fresh from the banking industry with strong opinions but faulty knowledge about how the system operates. ⑮ And because their other tasks are difficult, ⑯ they have too little time and knowledge to control money.

⑰ Clearly, the present arrangement remains better than the alternatives.

2. We Need Fairer Standards for College Admissions
Jess Bravin

① College admission officers are regularly quoted criticizing high-school students' tendency to take only the minimum number of academic courses needed for graduation and college admission, at the lowest levels of complexity available, while filling the hours left in the school day with electives like Beginning Chorus. ② While I dislike generalizations made about students by educators, I must admit that this one is true. ③ And why not? ④ Any student would be foolish to take a course schedule more demanding than absolutely necessary under current grading and admission policies.

⑤ Public universities now judge a student's proficiency exclusively by the grade-point average of courses completed in high school, plus scores on standardized tests that may be required. ⑥ The flaw in this system is that the GPA presents all academic or elective courses as equal, while in practice they vary in complexity, challenge and workload. ⑦ When Introductory Algebra counts the same as Advance-Placement Calculus, the student is rewarded for playing safe. Consider:

⑧ Student A, moderately above-average in English skills, takes three required courses—10th-grade English, Advanced Composition, and Advance-Placement English—earning an A, a B and a C. ⑨ He also takes two rigorous electives—Appreciation and Interpretation of Poetry and Literary Analysis/Expository Writing, earning an A and a B. ⑩ His GPA In English is 3.2.

⑪ Student B, with the same skills and ability, takes the same 10th-grade English course, earning an A, then splits the 11th-grade school year with two courses less rigorous than Advanced Composition, earning an A in one, a B in the other. ⑫ In senior year, she takes one semester of a required course, Practical Writing, and a semester of an elective, Books for Pleasure, earning a B in each. ⑬ Her GPA computes at 3.5.

⑭ All else being equal, the 0.3 point difference gives Student B a better chance of admission to the campus of her choice.

⑮ Students are well aware of this anomaly, ⑯ and since most college-bound students intend to go to state universities, which determine admissions on a combination of GPA and SAT (Scholastic Aptitude Test) scores alone, ⑰ they are unwilling to damage their chances by taking challenging courses in high school.

⑱ A further complaint is that the A–through–F marking system prevalent in public schools does not accurately represent most students' abilities. ⑲ This complaint is heard on both sides: College admission officers criticize "grade inflation"; students criticize unfair or arbitrary marks from teachers. ⑳ While truly outstanding and clearly failing students do not suffer under this system—they get A's or F's consistently—the great majority of students are in the middle, the B-to-C category. ㉑ When college admission may hang on one-tenth of a point, this is a critical distinction.

22 It does seem ridiculous to think that five classifications can accurately describe a student's abilities or accomplishments.

3. **What Price Competition?**
   Robert J. Samuelson

① Everyone favors competition's economic benefits—consumer choice, price rivalry. ② But no one likes the disruptive effects. ③ All protected markets create vested interests. ④ People and firms adjust to existing rules. ⑤ Once markets open up, rules change and those who prospered under the old may suffer under the new.

Item: ⑥ Although deregulation has helped railroads, it has hurt some shippers. ⑦ The railroads now have freedom to close weak branch lines, ⑧ but this has deprived some Midwestern grain elevators of freight service. ⑨ Farmers now have to truck their grain to more distant elevators for consolidation into larger, more efficient trains.

Item: ⑩ For years the Federal Communications Commission propped up long-distance telephone rates to subsidize residential rates. ⑪ The average basic cost of residential service is about $28 a customer, but the monthly charge totals roughly $11. ⑫ Thus, the removal of regulations will mean higher monthly service charges but lower long-distance rates.

Item: ⑬ In the past, regulation of the banking industry provided cheap loans for most sectors of the economy. ⑭ Government interest-rate ceilings on savings accounts forced many depositors to accept low rates. ⑮ The removal of these restrictions means higher returns for savers but adds to the burdens of debt-laden farmers, firms and consumers.

Item: ⑯ Since trucking deregulation in 1980, price competition among truckers has dramatically intensified, but high-cost trucking companies with well-paid union drivers have lost business to low-cost, non-union operators. ⑰ The Teamsters' Union estimates that the number of workers under its National Freight Agreement has declined roughly one-third from 300,000 in 1979. ⑱ Simultaneously, independent pricing actions have increased by a factor of eight.

III. Turn to the editorial pages of a newspaper and select an editorial that contains an argument. Keep in mind that some editorials are really reports and contain no arguments at all. Also, few editorials are as neat and straightforward as the selections presented in parts I and II of this exercise. Guest editorials on the Op Ed page (the page opposite the editorial page) are often better written than those on the editorial page. Analyze the argument (or arguments) according to the method presented in this section. Begin by placing a numeral at the beginning of each statement. Compound statements having components that are claimed to be true may be broken up into parts and the parts enumerated accordingly. Numerals should usually be placed in front of genuine premise and conclusion indicators even when they occur in the middle of a statement. Do *not*, however, break up conditional statements into antecedent and consequent. Proceed to identify the main conclusion (or conclusions) and determine how the other statements provide support. Any statement that does not play a direct role in the argument should be left out of the final argument pattern.

2
LANGUAGE: MEANING AND DEFINITION

2.1 COGNITIVE MEANING AND EMOTIVE MEANING

Ordinary language, as most of us are at least vaguely aware, serves various functions in our day-to-day lives. The contemporary philosopher Ludwig Wittgenstein thought the number of these functions virtually unlimited. Thus, among other things, language is used to

ask questions	tell jokes
tell stories	flirt with someone
tell lies	give directions
guess at answers	sing songs
form hypotheses	issue commands
launch verbal assaults	greet someone

and so on.

For our purpose there are two linguistic functions that are particularly important. These are: (1) to convey information and (2) to express or evoke feelings. Consider, for example, the following statements:

The Russian revolution, which occurred in March, 1917, was caused in part by the defeat of the Russian army at the hands of the Germans and by the subsequent collapse of the Russian economy.

> The Russians, a nation of savage, paranoid barbarians, pursue
> their insane dream of world-wide dominion without the slight-
> est regard for even the most basic of human rights.

The first statement is intended primarily to convey information and the second to express or evoke feelings. These statements fulfill their respective functions through the distinct kinds of terminology in which they are phrased. Terminology that conveys information is said to have a *cognitive* meaning, whereas terminology that expresses or evokes feelings has an *emotive* meaning. For example, words such as "house," "tree," "bird," and "book" have primarily a cognitive meaning, whereas words such as "liar," "fool," "charlatan," and "holocaust" have an emotive as well as a cognitive meaning. (Few, if any, words have a purely emotive meaning.)

Words with emotive meaning give language vitality and eloquence. Without such words there would be little poetry and few great speeches. But from the standpoint of argument evaluation such words involve a certain element of danger. The reason is that evidence, pure and simple, is conveyed through words that have a cognitive meaning. Without the presentation of solid evidence no argument can be a good one. Many arguments in ordinary language, however, are expressed in words having an emotive as well as a cognitive meaning. The emotive component tends to convey the illusion that evidence is being presented when in fact it is not and the illusion that evidence, when it is presented, is stronger (or weaker) than it actually is. For these reasons the occurrence of emotive terminology can fool us into thinking that a passage contains an argument when in fact it does not or that an argument is strong when in fact it is weak. This effect is especially likely to occur when we happen to agree with the position taken by the arguer.

Consider the following letter to the editor of a newspaper:

> The atomic bomb may be the greatest peacekeeper ever devised
> by man. In years gone by, most any place in the world, a hand-
> ful of militant old men sitting in safe, comfortable seats, could
> send tens of thousands of peaceable young men and boys to
> fight and kill and be killed. But safe no more. No doubt poten-
> tial war declarers realize that in an up-to-date nuclear conflict
> they could very well end up among the clobbered.

The conclusion of this argument is that nuclear weapons are a great peacekeeper. The premise is that nuclear weapons have placed the people who start wars in a position of vulnerability, therefore rendering them less belligerent. Stripped of its emotive terminology, this argument is at best only marginally persuasive. In fact the atomic bomb is the most horrifying and destructive form of weaponry ever devised. But as the argument stands, the emotive language reinforces the argument's persuasive power. The words and phrases that convey the emotive impact are "peacekeeper," "militant old men," "safe, comfortable seats," and "peaceable young men and boys" who are sent to "kill and be killed." By calling the atomic bomb a peacekeeper, by aligning this peacekeeper with peaceable young men and boys who would otherwise be forced to fight and die, and by placing it in opposition to the militant old men who, sitting in their comfortable seats, initiate and manage the wars, the author makes his conclusion much more palatable than it would otherwise be.

Military spokesmen, political officials, advertisers, corporate officials, and certain religious leaders have elevated the manipulation of emotively laden terminology to the level of a fine art. In the case of the military, the task usually involves inventing terms having favorable, or at least neutral, overtones to depict the horrors of war. Here is a small sampling with translations on the right:

pre-emptive strike	sneak attack
enhanced radiation device	neutron bomb
to pacify	to lay waste or destroy
selective ordnance or soft ordnance	napalm
incontinent ordnance	bombs dropped on friendly troops by mistake
an adjustment on the front	a retreat
an overflight	a flight over enemy territory for the purpose of espionage
a police action	a war
surgical strike	precision bombing
pacification center	concentration camp
to terminate with prejudice	to murder

Obviously it sounds better for a commanding officer to issue the report that troops were killed by soft incontinent ordnance than to report that one's own troops were incinerated alive by napalm dropped from one's own planes by some stupid mistake.

In advertising the use of emotively charged terminology is a virtual precondition for acceptability. Practically everything these days is "new," "improved," "different," "alive," "exclusive," "pure," "safe," or "natural." Korbel Champagne is "magic," and Budweiser Beer is a "tradition." Beefeater gin is "the crown jewel of England," and Merit cigarettes present a "challenge" to the smoker. BMW cars have "sensual lines, sculptured chrome, and the omnipresent scent of leather," while Vanity Fair magazine is "legendary, vibrant, adventurous, innovative, and irreverent." Minolta cameras are "programmed to make creative decisions," Bank of America is the "bank that goes the extra mile," and the American Express Gold Card is "intended for those who like to speak softly and carry a big stick."

The Stevens Corporation, manufacturers of sheets and towels, ran a series of full-page ads in the *New York Times Magazine* that bore the captions:

> The Impact of High Voltage Color
> A Bravura Sweep of Plaid
> The Simplicity of Pure Luxury
> A Dash of Solid Versatility
> The Drama of Bold Design

One would be hard pressed to find language more florid for an item so common as a sheet or a towel.

A short time ago, probably to counteract the image of an impersonal corporate monolith, many companies began using the word "people" in their ads. Digital Corporation became "people changing the way people work," 3M became "the copier people," and Roche Industries, "people who care." Kelly Services became "The Kelly Girl people," and Sperry Univac, "the computer people who listen." The Boeing Company was "getting people together," Weyerhaeuser became "the tree growing people," and General Motors, "people building transportation to serve people." We have yet to see defense contractors, such as Rockwell International or General Dynamics, proclaim themselves "the people-killing people"—but perhaps we can look forward to that.

The language of advertising is relevant to logic because most ads, although not arguments as such, can be restructured in the form of arguments. For example, American Telephone and Telegraph's ad, which calls its phone products "Genuine Bell," might be converted into an argument as follows:

> Only AT&T phones are "Genuine Bell" phones. "Genuine Bell" means engineered by Western Electric Corp. Western Electric phones are better than all other phones. Therefore, AT&T phones are better than all other phones.

The soundness of this argument rests on the questionable truth of the third premise. But before the restructuring is done, the ad persuades through the use of the emotively charged word "genuine." After all, whatever is genuine must be better than whatever is not genuine. This task of restructuring ads as arguments will be taken up again in Chapter 5.

Unlike the language of advertising, which concentrates primarily on terminology that conveys a positive impact, the language of politics involves emotive terminology that is both positive and negative.

Depending on the views of the speaker or writer, a supporter of the women's movement is either a "campaigner for equal rights" or a "fem libber"; a person concerned with the pollution problem is either an "environmentalist" or an "ecofreak"; and practically any South American country of one's choice is either a "pinnacle of stability" or an "autocratic dictatorship that suppresses human rights." Supporters of the U.S. involvement in Nicaragua speak of the U.S. presence as "a moral duty and a solemn responsibility," whereas opponents call it "another Vietnam." Analogously, supporters of a recent California Supreme Court decision blocking an initiative to reapportion the legislative districts along lines more favorable to the Republican party hailed the decision as "a great victory for constitutional democracy," whereas detractors branded the same decision "an unconscionable obstruction of the people's right to vote." Here are some additional pairs of emotively charged phrases used in politics:

Favorable	Unfavorable
right to work	closed shop
freedom fighter	communist guerrilla
emergent nation	backward nation
aid to the needy	welfare
law and order	social and political oppression
undocumented worker	illegal alien *or* wetback
intelligence agent	spy
liberal	commie *or* pinko
conservative	fascist
liquidation	mass murder
patriot	flag waver
disarmament advocate	peacenik
public servant	bureaucrat

Emotively charged language used in business, like military language, is often calculated to make illicit or undesirable events or activities appear in a favorable or at least neutral light. The term "earnings statement" long ago replaced "profit and loss statement": it is never a good idea to allude even to the possibility of losses. Here are some others: stockbrokers are now called "account executives," the term "back engineering" refers to the procedure of dismantling a competitor's product for the purpose of copying it, the "department of competitive intelligence" is the department of corporate spying, a "finder's fee" is a nice name for a bribe, and a strike is otherwise termed an "industrial action."

In earlier years emotively charged language was used within the corporate structure to dehumanize the employees and facilitate their manipulation by management. To correct for this and promote employee loyalty, many of today's managerial experts are urging changes. Instead of "hiring" people we employ them, instead of "sending them through a training tube" we expose them to our beliefs and standards, and in place of the personnel department we now have the department of human resources.

Perhaps the purest, most undiluted form of emotively charged language occurs within the context of religion. The following selection was taken from a full-page religious advertisement run in various newspapers by Tony Alamo, pastor of a church in Alma, Arkansas:

> [Our] bulldozing, bully, antichrist government regime says homosexuality is a third sexual preference, and that it should be taught in school. God says that homosexuality is a demon possession and one of the things that he despises most and that we must not associate ourselves with it or support it. I repeat, God says that it is a demon possession, not a third sexual preference. God hated those lewd, unrepentant, disgusting, vile creatures so much that he destroyed them in the city of Sodom. This satanic one-world government now has the audacity to say that we must allow our children to be taught by homosexuals (perverts, those whom God despises), and are saying it is now lawful to teach our children that homosexuality is a third sexual choice. They want to make homosexuals out of our children and gain more revolutionists that our children and us may be destroyed with them. Misery loves company.

The emotively charged words in this selection are almost too numerous to count. Those who agree with Alamo's position are liable to consider this passage a highly persuasive argument against homosexuality. In fact, the selection is, properly speaking, not an argument at all, but merely a diatribe.

Regardless of our occupation or profession, our day-to-day language is charged with emotive impact. This fact is fairly obvious with words such as "idiot," "blockhead," "sweetheart," and "darling," but it also extends to apparently neutral words such as "in," "the," and "it." Alligator shoes might be "in" this year, Stolichnaya vodka is advertised as "the" vodka, and a few years ago we were all told that Coke is "it." Innocent phrases such as "thanks a lot" can be loaded with negative feelings, and otherwise complimentary words such as "moderate" can convey just the opposite emotional impact. When Adlai Stevenson was accused of being too moderate on civil rights, he responded by asking whether he should be immoderate instead. The problem with emotively charged terminology is that it tends to short-circuit our thought processes. It prompts us into leaping to unjustified conclusions without thinking. Accordingly, anyone who wants to prevent this from happening had best be aware of the impact of emotive terminology and on guard against its use.

EXERCISE 2.1

I. The following passage is an excerpt from President Ronald Reagan's statement following the landing of U.S. troops on Grenada. Identify the emotively charged language and write a paragraph explaining how it affects the impact of the speech.

> Ladies and gentlemen, on Sunday, Oct. 23, the United States received an urgent formal request from the five member nations of the Organization of Eastern Caribbean States to assist in a joint effort to restore order and democracy on the island of Grenada. . . .
>
> Early this morning, forces from six Caribbean democracies and the United States began a landing or landings on the island of Grenada in the eastern Caribbean.
>
> We have taken this decisive action for three reasons.
>
> First, and of overriding importance, to protect innocent lives, including up to 1,000 Americans, whose personal safety is of course my paramount concern.
>
> Second, to forestall further chaos.
>
> And third to assist in the restoration of conditions of law and order and of governmental institutions to the island of Grenada, where a brutal group of leftist thugs violently seized power, killing the prime minister, three Cabinet members, two labor leaders and other civilians, including children.
>
> Let there be no misunderstanding, this collective action has been forced on us by events that have no precedent in the eastern Caribbean and no place in any civilized society.

II. The following selections appeared as letters to the editor of newspapers. Restructure each in the form of an argument using only emotively neutral language.

★1. The creationists have no right to impose their mistaken, ignorant, superstitious beliefs on others. They claim the constitutional right to the free exercise of religion. How about the rights of the majority of people who want their children taught the scientific truth about evolution—not fallacious myths and superstitions from primitive societies?

(Andrew M. Underhill Jr.)

2. God, guts, and guns made this great country of ours free, and you can bet your buns it will take more of the same to keep it that way. One of the very last things in this world we need is handgun control.

(R. Kinzie)

3. Until now, the protest against the holocaust in our own nation has been vocal but far too small. The massacre of an unwanted generation through abortion and infanticide has sounded an alarm that should wake up every Christian. Helpless and guiltless little infants are mercilessly butchered daily in hospitals and clinics across our land. For the love of God, let us all urge the passage of the Human Life Bill, now before Congress.

(Jim Key)

III. The following advertisements may be interpreted as expressing arguments. Restructure each in the form of an argument.

★1. Marithé and François Girbaud: Finally, clothing as intelligently designed as you are.

2. Gucci cologne for men: Nobody is born successful. One becomes successful.

3. International Telephone and Telegraph (ITT): The best ideas are the ideas that help people.

4. Solgar vitamins: Health is your most precious asset. Guard it with Solgar.

5. Honeywell: Together we can find the answers.

IV. The following selection is taken from a speech delivered by George C. Wallace, former Governor of Alabama, on July 4, 1964. In this speech Wallace attacked Lyndon Johnson's signing of The Civil Rights bill. The speech is liberally sprinkled with emotive terminology. Make a list of what you consider to be the fifteen most highly charged words or phrases.

> We come here today in deference to the memory of those Stalwart patriots who on July 4, 1776, pledged their lives, their fortunes, and their sacred honor to establish and defend the proposition that governments are created by the people, empowered by the people, derive their just powers from the consent of the people, and must forever remain subservient to the will of the people.
>
> Today, 188 years later, we celebrate that occasion and find inspiration and determination and courage to preserve and protect the great principles of freedom enunciated in the Declaration of Independence.
>
> It is therefore a cruel irony that the President of the United States has only yesterday signed into law the most monstrous piece of legislation ever enacted by the United States Congress.
>
> It is a fraud, a sham, and a hoax.
>
> This bill will live in infamy. To sign it into law at any time is tragic. To do so upon the eve of the celebration of our independence insults the intelligence of the American people.
>
> It dishonors the memory of countless thousands of our dead who offered up their very lives in defense of principles which this bill destroys.
>
> Never before in the history of this nation have so many human and property rights been destroyed by a single enactment of the Congress. It is an act of tyranny. It is the assassin's knife stuck in the back of liberty.
>
> With this assassin's knife and a blackjack in the hand of the federal force-cult, the left-wing liberals will try to force us back into bondage. Bondage to a tyranny more brutal than that imposed by the British Monarchy which claimed power to rule over the lives of our forefathers under sanction of the omnipotent black-robed despots who sit on the bench of the United States Supreme Court.
>
> This bill is fraudulent in intent, in design and in execution.

It is misnamed. Each and every provision is mistitled. It was rammed through the Congress on the wave of ballyhoo, promotions, and publicity stunts reminiscent of P.T. Barnum.

It was enacted in an atmosphere of pressure, intimidation, and even cowardice, as demonstrated by the refusal of the United States Senate to adopt an amendment to submit the bill to a vote of the people.

To illustrate the fraud—it is not a civil rights bill. It is a federal penal code. It creates federal crimes which would take volumes to list and years to tabulate because it affects the lives of 192 million American citizens. Every person in every walk and station of life and every aspect of our daily lives become subject to the criminal provisions of this bill.

It threatens our freedom of speech, of assembly, of association, and makes the exercise of these freedoms a federal crime under certain conditions.

It affects our political rights, our right to trial by jury, our right to the full use and enjoyment of our private property, the freedom from search and seizure of our private property and possessions, the freedom from harassment by federal police and, in short, all the rights of individuals inherent in a society of free men.

Ministers, lawyers, teachers, newspapers, and every private citizen must guard his speech and watch his actions to avoid the deliberately imposed booby traps put into this bill. It is designed to make federal crimes of our customs, beliefs, and traditions. Therefore, under the fantastic powers of the federal judiciary to punish for contempt of court and under their fantastic powers to regulate our most intimate aspects of our lives by injunction, every American citizen is in jeopardy and must stand guard against these despots.

2.2 THE INTENSION AND EXTENSION OF TERMS

Although the primary aim of logic is the analysis and evaluation of arguments, the interrelated topics of meaning and definition have long occupied a prominent position within the discipline, for a number of reasons. Among them, arguments are composed of statements, statements are made up of words, words have meanings, and meanings are conveyed through definitions. In addition, logic, especially formal logic, is heavily dependent on definitions to attribute highly specific meanings to its technical terminology.

The basic units of any ordinary language are *words*. Our main concern in this chapter, however, is not with words in general but with terms. A **term** is any word or arrangement of words that may serve as the subject of a statement. Terms consist of proper names, common names, and descriptive phrases. Here are some examples:

Proper names	Common names	Descriptive phrases
Napoleon	animal	first president of the United States
North Dakota	restitution	
The United States Senate	house	author of *Hamlet*
	activity	books in my library
Gore Vidal	person	officers in the Swiss Navy
Robinson Crusoe		
		blue things
		those who study hard

Words that are not terms include verbs, nonsubstantive adjectives, adverbs, prepositions, conjunctions, and all nonsyntactic arrangements of words. The following words or phrases are not terms; none can serve as the subject of a statement:

dictatorial	moreover
runs quickly	craves
above and beyond	cabbages into again the forest

The last example is a nonsyntactic arrangement.

At this point it is important to distinguish the *use* of a word from the *mention* of a word. Without this distinction any word can be imagined to serve as the subject of a statement and, therefore, to count as a term. The word "wherever," for example, is not a term, but "wherever" (in quotes) can serve as the subject of a statement, such as " 'Wherever' is an eight-letter word." But in this statement, it is not the word itself that is the subject but rather the *quoted* word. The word is said to be *mentioned*—not *used.* On the other hand, "wherever" is *used* in this statement: "I will follow you wherever you go." In distinguishing terms from nonterms one must be sure that the word or group of words can be *used* as the subject of a statement.

Words are usually considered to be symbols, and the entities they symbolize are usually called **meanings.** Terms, being made up of words, are also symbols, but the meanings they symbolize are of two kinds: intensional and extensional. The **intensional meaning** consists of the qualities or attributes that the term "connotes," and the **extensional meaning** consists of the members of the class that the term "denotes." These two kinds of meaning will provide the basis for the definitional techniques developed in Section 2.3.

The intensional meaning is otherwise known as the **intension** or **connotation,** and the extensional meaning is known as the **extension** or **denotation.** Thus, for example, the intension (or connotation) of the

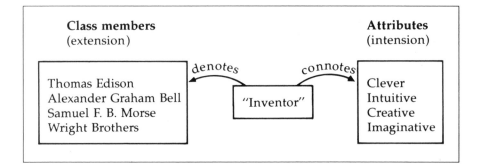

term "cat" consists of the attributes of being furry, of having four legs, of moving in a certain way, of emitting certain sounds, and so on, and the extension (or denotation) consists of the cats themselves—all the cats in the universe. As this example illustrates, logic uses the terms "connotation" and "denotation" differently from the way they are used in grammar. In grammar, "connotation" refers to the subtle nuances of a word, whereas "denotation" refers to the word's direct and specific meaning.

Because terms symbolize meanings to individual persons, it is inevitable for subjective elements to invade the notion of connotation. For example, to a cat lover, the connotation of the word "cat" might include the attributes of being cuddly and adorable, while to one who hates cats it might include those of being obnoxious and disgusting. Because these subjective elements inevitably lead to confusion when it comes to identifying the connotation of specific terms, logicians typically restrict the meaning of "connotation" to what may be called conventional connotation. The **conventional connotation** of a term consists of the properties or attributes that the term commonly connotes to the members of the community who speak the language in question. Under this interpretation, the connotation of a term remains more or less the same from person to person and from time to time.

The denotation of a term also typically remains the same from person to person, but it may change with the passage of time. The denotation of "presently living cat," for example, is constantly fluctuating as some cats die and others are born. The denotation of the term "cat," on the other hand, is presumably constant because it denotes all cats, past, present, and future.

Sometimes the denotation of a term can change radically with the passage of time. The terms "presently living dodo bird" and "present king of France," for example, at one time denoted actually existing entities, but today all such entities have perished. Accordingly, these terms now have what is called **empty extension.** They are said to denote the empty (or "null") class, the class that has no members. Other terms

A CONCISE INTRODUCTION TO LOGIC

with empty extension include "unicorn," "leprechaun," "gnome," "elf," and "griffin." While these terms have empty extension, however, they do not have empty intension. "Presently living dodo bird" and "present king of France," as well as "unicorn," "elf," and "griffin," connote a variety of intelligible attributes.

The fact that some terms have empty extension leads us to an important connection between extension and intension; namely, that *intension determines extension*. The intensional meaning of a term serves as the criterion for deciding what the extension consists of. Because we know the attributes connoted by the term "unicorn," for example, we know that the term has empty extension. That is, we know that there are no four-legged mammals having a single straight horn projecting from their forehead. Similarly, the intension of the word "cat" serves as the criterion for determining what is and what is not a member of the class of cats.

Apart from such meaningless terms as "adlers," "bobkins," and "crockers" used in the previous chapter to demonstrate the formal nature of validity, we will say that there are no terms having empty intension. A term with empty intension would connote nothing at all. Furthermore, since intension determines extension, there would be no way of identifying the class that such a term might denote. Thus, no term used in any kind of meaningful communication can be said to have empty intension.

The distinction between intension and extension may be further illustrated by comparing the way in which these concepts can be used to give order to random sequences of terms. Terms may be put in the order of increasing intension, increasing extension, decreasing intension, and decreasing extension. A series of terms is in the order of **increasing intension** when each term in the series (except the first) connotes more attributes than the one preceding it. In other words, each term in the series (except the first) is *more specific* than the one preceding it. (A term is specific to the degree that it connotes more attributes.) The order of **decreasing intension** is the reverse of that of increasing intension.

A series of terms is in the order of **increasing extension** when each term in the series (except the first) denotes a class having more members than the class denoted by the term preceding it. In other words, the class size gets larger with each successive term. **Decreasing extension** is, of course, the reverse of this order. Examples:

increasing intension:	animal, mammal, feline, tiger
increasing extension:	tiger, feline, mammal, animal
decreasing intension:	tiger, feline, mammal, animal
decreasing extension:	animal, mammal, feline, tiger

These examples illustrate a fact pertaining to most such series: the order of increasing intension is usually the same as that of decreasing extension. Conversely, the order of decreasing intension is usually the same as that of increasing extension. There are some exceptions, however. Consider the following series:

> unicorn; unicorn with blue eyes; unicorn with blue eyes and green horn; unicorn with blue eyes, green horn, and a weight of over 400 pounds

Each term in this series has empty extension; so, while the series exhibits the order of increasing intension, it does not exhibit the order of decreasing extension. Here is another, slightly different, example:

> living human being; living human being with a genetic code; living human being with a genetic code and a brain; living human being with a genetic code, a brain, and a height of less than 100 feet

In this series none of the terms has empty extension, but each term has exactly the *same* extension as the others. Thus, while the intension increases with each successive term, once again the extension does not decrease.

EXERCISE 2.2

I. The following exercises deal with words and terms.

1. Determine which of the following words or groups of words are terms and which are nonterms.

extortion	Thomas Jefferson
laborious	Empire State Building
cunningly	annoy
practitioner	render satisfactory
seriousness	graceful dancer
forever	wake up
whoever studies	not only
interestingly impassive	tallest man on the squad
scarlet	mountaintop
reinvestment	between
therefore	since

2. Name some of the attributes connoted by the following terms. Express your answer with adjectives or adjectival phrases. Example: The term "elephant" connotes the attributes of being large, having tusks, having a trunk.

drum	wolf	fanatic	riot
politician	Mona Lisa	carrot	piano
devil	Statue of Liberty		

3. Name three items denoted by the terms in the left-hand column below and all items denoted by the terms in the right-hand column.

newspaper	tallest mountain on earth
scientist	prime number less than 10
manufacturer	Governor of New York
river	language of Switzerland
opera	Scandinavian country

4. Put the following sequences of terms in the order of increasing intension:

    ★a. conifer, Sitka spruce, tree, spruce, plant
    b. Italian sports car, car, vehicle, Maserati, sports car
    c. Doctor of Medicine, person, brain surgeon, professional person, surgeon
    d. wallaby, marsupial, mammal, animal, kangaroo
    e. parallelogram, polygon, square, rectangle, quadrilateral

5. Construct a series of four terms that exhibits increasing intension but non-decreasing extension.

II. Answer "true" or "false" to the following statements:

1. All words have an intensional meaning and an extensional meaning.
2. The intensional meaning of a term consists of the attributes connoted by the term.
3. The extensional meaning of a term consists of the members of the class denoted by the term.
4. The extension of a term always remains the same with the passage of time.
5. Some terms have empty intension.
6. Some terms have empty extension.
7. The intension of a term determines the extension.
8. The intension of a term determines how specific the term is.
9. The order of increasing intension is always the same as that of decreasing extension.
10. "Leprechaun" and "unicorn" have the same extension.

2.3 DEFINITIONS AND THEIR PURPOSES

Over the years philosophers have held various conflicting views about the purpose of definitions. For Plato, to mention just one, definitions were intended to explicate the meaning of certain eternal essences or forms, such as justice, piety, and virtue. For most logicians today, however, definitions are intended exclusively to explicate the meaning of *words*. In conformity with this latter position, we may define **definition** as a group of words that assigns a meaning to some word or group of words. Accordingly, every definition consists of two parts: the definiendum and the definiens. The **definiendum** is the word or group of words that is supposed to be defined, and the **definiens** is the word or group of words that does the defining. For example, in the definition " 'Tiger' means a large, striped, ferocious feline indigenous to the jungles of India and Asia," the word "tiger" is the definiendum, and everything after the word "means" is the definiens. The definiens is not itself the meaning of the definiendum; rather, it is the group of words that symbolizes (or that is supposed to symbolize) the *same* meaning as the definiendum. Because we presumably know in advance what the definiens symbolizes, we are led, via the definition, to understand what the definiendum symbolizes. It is in this way that the definition "assigns" a meaning to its definiendum.

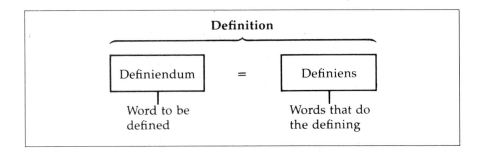

Once it has been decided that definitions explicate the meaning of words, other disagreements emerge among the philosophers. Some argue that since a definition is merely a rule that allows one set of words (the definiens) to be used in place of another set (the definiendum), definitions communicate no information at all about the subject matter of the definiendum. Others take the opposite tack and argue that since definitions result in a clarification of language, they provide a means for the discovery of deeper philosophical truths. It seems, however, that neither of these approaches is able to make good sense of all the various kinds of definitions that are actually employed in ordinary usage. As a result, instead of beginning their analysis of definitions with a set of a priori criteria, many logicians take a pragmatic approach and begin with a survey of the various kinds of definitions that are actually used and of the functions that they actually serve. This is the approach taken here.

Stipulative Definitions

A **stipulative definition** assigns a meaning to a word for the first time. This may involve either coining a new word or giving a new meaning to an old word. The purpose of a stipulative definition is usually to replace a more complex expression with a simpler one.

The need for a stipulative definition is often occasioned by some new phenomenon or development. For example, a few years ago the attempt was made at a certain zoo to crossbreed tigers and lions. Because of the genetic similarity of the two species, the attempt succeeded. Offspring were produced from a male tiger and a female lion and from a male lion and a female tiger. When the offspring were born, it became appropriate to give them names. Of course, the names "offspring of male tiger and female lion" and "offspring of male lion and female tiger" could have been used, but these names were hardly convenient. Instead, the names "tigon" and "liger" were selected. Any two new words would have sufficed equally well for naming the offspring—"topar" and "largine" for example—but "tigon" and "liger" were considered more appropriate, for obvious reasons. "Tigon" was taken to mean the offspring of a male tiger and a female lion, and "liger" the offspring of a male lion and a female tiger. These assignments of meanings were accomplished through stipulative definitions.

Because people are continually coming up with new creations, whether it be new food concoctions, new inventions, new modes of behavior, new kinds of apparel, new dances, or whatever, stipulative definitions are continually being used to introduce names for these things. Sometimes these definitions are only implicit and amount to little more than the spontaneous association of the word with some action—as was probably the case when the words "bop," "twist," "jerk," and "chicken" came to be known as names of dances a few years ago. At other times, they are definitely explicit, as when the word "penicillin" was selected as the name for an antibacterial substance produced by certain *Penicillium* molds, or when the symbol "10^5" was chosen as a simple substitute for "$10 \times 10 \times 10 \times 10 \times 10$."

Because a stipulative definition is a completely arbitrary assignment of a meaning to a word for the first time, there can be no such thing as a "true" or "false" stipulative definition. Furthermore, for the same reason, a stipulative definition cannot provide any new information about the subject matter of the definiendum. The fact that the word "tigon" was selected to replace "offspring of a male tiger and a female lion" tells us nothing new about the nature of the animal in question. One stipulative definition may, however, be more or less convenient or more or less appropriate than another.

Stipulative definitions are misused in verbal disputes when one person covertly uses a word in a peculiar way and then proceeds to assume that everyone else uses that word in the same way. Under these circumstances that person is said to be using the word "stipulatively." In such cases the assumption that other persons use the word in the same way is rarely justified.

Lexical Definitions

A **lexical definition** is used to report the meaning that a word already has in a language. Dictionary definitions are all instances of lexical definitions. Thus, in contrast with a stipulative definition, which assigns a meaning to a word for the first time, a lexical definition may be true or false depending on whether it does or does not report the way a word is actually used. Because words are frequently used in more than one way, lexical definitions have the further purpose of eliminating the ambiguity that would otherwise arise if one of these meanings were to be confused with another.

At this point, it is useful to distinguish ambiguity from vagueness. A word is **vague** if it lacks clarity; that is, if its meaning is blurred or fuzzy around the edges. For example, words such as "love," "happiness," "peace," "excessive," "fresh," "rich," "poor," "normal," "conservative," and "polluted" are vague. We can rarely tell with any degree of precision whether they apply to a given situation. A word is **ambiguous,** on the other hand, when it can be interpreted as having two or more clearly distinct meanings in a given context. Many commonly used words have two or more relatively precise meanings. When, in a given context, it is uncertain which of these meanings is intended, ambiguity results. Some words that are subject to ambiguous usage are "light," "bank," "sound," "right," and "race." "Light" can mean, among other things, light in weight or radiant energy; "bank" can mean a financial institution or the slope bordering a river; and so on.

Because a lexical definition lists the various meanings that a word can have, a person who consults such a definition is better prepared to avoid ambiguous constructions of his or her own and to detect those of others. The undetected ambiguity causes the most trouble. In many cases the problem lies not with the obvious differences in meaning that words such as "light" and "bank" may have but with the subtle shadings of meaning that are more likely to be confused with one another. For example, if a woman is described as "nice," any number of things could be intended. She could be fastidious, refined, modest, pleasant, attractive, or even lewd. A good lexical definition will distinguish these various shadings and thereby guard against the possibility that two such meanings will be unconsciously jumbled together into one.

Precising Definitions

The purpose of a **precising definition** is to reduce the vagueness of a word. Once the vagueness has been reduced, one can reach a decision as to the applicability of the word to a specific situation. We have noted that the word "poor" is vague. If legislation were ever introduced to give direct financial assistance to the poor, a precising definition would have to be supplied specifying exactly who is poor and who is not. The definition " 'Poor' means having an annual income of less than $4,000 and a net worth of less than $20,000" is an example of a precising definition.

Whenever words are taken from ordinary usage and employed in a highly systematic context such as science, mathematics, medicine, or law, they must always be clarified by means of a precising definition. The terms "force," "energy," "acid," "element," "number," "equality," "contract," and "agent" have all been given precising definitions by specific disciplines.

Sometimes the substance of a court trial may revolve around the precise usage of a term. A recent trial in California addressed the question of whether a man who had driven a bicycle while intoxicated violated the motor vehicle code. The question concerned whether, for these purposes, a bicycle could be considered a "vehicle." The court decided in the negative, and the decision amounted to an incremental extension of an already existent precising definition of the word "vehicle."

Another example involves the practice of surgical transplantation of vital organs. Before a heart transplant can be conducted, the donor must be dead; otherwise the surgeon will be accused of murder. If the donor is dead for too long, however, the success of the transplant will be imperiled. But exactly when is a person considered to be dead? Is it when the heart stops beating, when the person stops breathing, when rigor mortis sets in, or some other time? The question involves the meaning of the term "moment of death." The courts have decided that "moment of death" should be taken to mean the moment the brain stops functioning, as measured by an electroencephalograph. This decision amounts to the acceptance of a precising definition for "moment of death."

A precising definition differs from a stipulative definition in that the latter involves a purely arbitrary assignment of meaning, whereas the assignment of meaning in a precising definition is not at all arbitrary. A great deal of care must be taken to insure that the assignment of meaning in a precising definition is appropriate and legitimate for the context within which the term is to be employed.

Theoretical Definitions

A **theoretical definition** provides a theoretical picture or characterization of the entity or entities denoted by the definiendum. In other words, it provides a way of viewing or conceiving these entities that suggests deductive consequences, further investigation (experimental or otherwise), and whatever else would be entailed by the acceptance of a theory governing these entities. The definition of the term "heat" found in texts dealing with the kinetic theory of heat provides a good example: " 'heat' means the energy associated with the random motion of the molecules of a substance." This definition does more than merely assign a meaning to a word; it provides a way of conceiving the physical phenomenon that is heat. In so doing, it suggests the deductive consequence that as the molecules of a substance speed up, the temperature of the substance increases. In addition, it suggests a number of experiments—experiments investigating the relationship between molecular velocity and the phenomena of radiation, gas pressure, molecular elasticity, and molecular configuration. In short, this definition of "heat" provides the impetus for an entire theory about heat.

Other examples of theoretical definitions are the definition of "light" as a form of electromagnetic radiation, and the definition of "force," "mass," and "acceleration" in Newton's second law of motion as expressed in the equation "$F = MA$." The latter is a kind of contextual definition in which each term is defined in terms of the other two. Both definitions entail numerous deductive consequences about the phenomena involved and suggest numerous avenues of experimental investigation.

Not all theoretical definitions are associated with science. Many terms in philosophy, such as "substance," "form," "cause," "change," "idea," "good," "mind," and "God," have been given theoretical definitions. In fact, most of the major philosophers in history have given these terms their own peculiar theoretical definitions, and this fact accounts in part for the unique character of their respective philosophies. For example, Leibniz's definition of "substance" in terms of what he called "monads" laid the foundation for his metaphysical theory and John Stuart Mill's definition of "good" as the greatest happiness of the greatest number provided the underpinnings for his utilitarian theory of ethics.

Like stipulative definitions, theoretical definitions are neither true nor false, strictly speaking. They may, however, be more or less interesting or more or less fruitful, depending on the deductive consequences they entail and on the outcome of the experiments they suggest.

Persuasive Definitions

The purpose of a **persuasive definition** is to engender a favorable or unfavorable attitude toward what is denoted by the definiendum. This purpose is accomplished by assigning an emotionally charged or value-laden meaning to a word while making it appear that the word really has (or ought to have) that meaning in the language in which it is used. Thus, persuasive definitions amount to a certain synthesis of stipulative, lexical, and, possibly, theoretical definitions backed by the rhetorical motive to engender a certain attitude. As a result of this synthesis, a persuasive definition masquerades as an honest assignment of meaning to a term while condemning or blessing with approval the subject matter of the definiendum. Here are some examples of opposing pairs of persuasive definitions:

"Abortion" means the ruthless murdering of innocent human beings.
"Abortion" means a safe and established surgical procedure whereby a woman is relieved of an unwanted burden.

"Liberal" means a drippy-eyed do-gooder obsessed with giving away other people's money.
"Liberal" means a genuine humanitarian committed to the goals of adequate housing and health care and of equal opportunity for all of our citizens.

"Capitalism" means the economic system in which individuals are afforded the God-given freedom to own property and conduct business as they choose.
"Capitalism" means the economic system in which humanity is sacrificed to the wanton quest for money, and mutual understanding and respect are replaced by alienation, greed, and selfishness.

"Taxation" means the procedure by means of which our commonwealth is preserved and sustained.
"Taxation" means the procedure used by bureaucrats to rip off the people who elected them.

The objective of a persuasive definition is to influence the attitudes of the reader or listener; thus, such definitions may be used with considerable effectiveness in political speeches and editorial columns. While persuasive definitions may, like lexical definitions, be evaluated as either true or false, the primary issue is neither truth or falsity but the effectiveness of such definitions as instruments of persuasion.

EXERCISE 2.3

I. Determine whether the following definitions are stipulative, lexical, precising, theoretical, or persuasive.

★1. "Blind" means, for federal income tax purposes, either the inability to see better than 20/200 in the better eye with glasses, or having a field of vision of 20 degrees or less.

2. "Football" means a sport in which modern-day gladiators brutalize one another while trying to move a ridiculously shaped "ball" from one end of the playing field to the other.

3. "Wristovision" means a miniature television set that can be worn on the wrist.

★4. "Diffident" means lacking confidence in oneself; characterized by modest reserve.

5. "Magnetism" means a property of certain substances such as iron, cobalt, and nickel that arises from the spin of the electrons in the unfilled inner shell of the atoms that compose the substance.

6. "Fiduciary" means having to do with a confidence or trust; a person who holds something in trust.

★7. "Politician" means a person of unquestioned honesty and integrity whom the people, in their collective wisdom, have duly elected to guide the ship of state and protect it from the reefs and shoals that threaten it on every side.

8. "Intoxicated," for purposes of driving a car in many states, means having a blood–alcohol ratio of 1 to .001 or greater.

9. "Gweed" means a thoroughly immature person who feigns intellectual prowess; a total loser.

★10. "Sound" means a compression wave in air or some other elastic medium having a frequency ranging (for humans) from 20 to 20,000 vibrations per second.

11. "Radioactive area" means, for purposes of the U.S. Nuclear Regulatory Commission, any area, accessible to individuals, in which there exists radiation at such levels that a major portion of the body could receive in any one hour a dose in excess of 5 millirems, or in any five consecutive days a dose in excess of 100 millirems.

12. "Neurosis" means a chronic emotional disturbance that arises from suppressed or forgotten emotional stress (such as resentment, hostility, aggression, or guilt) experienced in early childhood.

★13. "Scaling" means a sport in which people race four-wheel drive vehicles up the face of boulder-strewn hillsides.

14. "Smoker" means a rude and disgusting individual who callously emits noxious tobacco fumes into the air, threatening the health and comfort of everyone in the vicinity.

15. "Diadem" means an ornamental headband worn as a badge of royalty; a crown.

★16. "Psychiatry" means the fortuitous melding of modern medicine with psychology that promises relief to thousands of poor, desperate souls who suffer the pains of emotional disorder.

17. "Gene" means the hereditary unit that occupies a fixed chromosomal locus, which through transcription has a specific effect on phenotype and which can mutate to various allelic forms.

18. "Subgression" means moving oneself and one's family to a subterranean bomb shelter for the purpose of escaping nuclear attack.

★19. "Intractable" means not easily governed; obstinate; unruly; not disposed to be taught.

20. "Recession" means, for purposes of the National Bureau of Economic Research, two consecutive quarters of negative growth in real GNP or in aggregate output for the entire economy.

21. "Gravity" means a force that results from the universal attraction that every particle of matter has for every other particle, and which varies directly with the mass of the particles and inversely with the square of the distance between them.

★22. "Assault" means, for legal purposes, the intentional and unprivileged affliction of the apprehension of an immediate harmful or offensive contact.

23. "Television" means the electronic medium that keeps an entire nation of viewers in a state of seminarcosis by feeding them a steady stream of inane drivel.

24. "Obelisk" means an upright, four-sided pillar that terminates in a pyramid; a dagger.

★25. "Aereomobile" means a vehicle that is normally driven on the ground but that has the capability of flying through the air to avoid traffic congestion.

II. Constructing definitions.

1. Invent stipulative definitions for two new words that you wish to introduce into the language for the first time.

2. Construct lexical definitions for "peace" and "pawn." Interpret both words as nouns, and indicate two different meanings for each.

3. Construct precising definitions for "middle-aged" and "alcoholic." Interpret both words as relating to people and specify the purpose for which the definitions are to be used.

4. Construct theoretical definitions for "energy" and "atom."

5. Construct opposing pairs of persuasive definitions for "conservative" and "socialism."

III. Answer "true" or "false" to the following statements:

1. From the standpoint of logic, many definitions are concerned not with words but with things.

2. The definiendum is the word or term that is supposed to be defined.

3. The definiens is the word or group of words that assigns a meaning to the word being defined.

4. A stipulative definition is either true or false.

5. A lexical definition reports the way a word is actually used in a language.

6. One of the purposes of a lexical definition is to guard against the ambiguous use of a word.

7. The meaning given to a word by a precising definition is completely arbitrary.

8. Theoretical definitions are either true or false, just as are lexical definitions.

9. Theoretical definitions provide a theoretical characterization of the entity or entities denoted by the word being defined.

10. The purpose of a persuasive definition is to influence attitudes.

2.4 DEFINITIONAL TECHNIQUES

In the last section we presented a survey of some of the kinds of definitions actually in use and the functions they are intended to serve. In this section we will investigate some of the techniques used to produce these definitions. These techniques may be classified in terms of the two kinds of meaning, intensional and extensional, discussed in Section 2.1.

Extensional (Denotative) Definitions

An **extensional definition** is one that assigns a meaning to a term by indicating the members of the class that the definiendum denotes. There are at least three ways of indicating the members of a class: pointing to them, naming them individually, and naming them in groups. The three kinds of definitions that result are called, respectively, demonstrative or ostensive definition, enumerative definition, and definition by subclass.

Demonstrative (ostensive) definitions are probably the most primitive form of definition. All one need know to understand such a definition is the meaning of pointing. As the following examples illustrate, such definitions may be either partial or complete, depending upon whether all or only some of the members of the class denoted by the definiendum are pointed to:

> "Chair" means this and this and this—as you point to a number of chairs, one after the other.

> "Washington Monument" means that—as you point to it.

If you were attempting to teach a foreigner your own native language, and neither of you understood a word of each other's language, demonstrative definition would almost certainly be one of the methods you would use.

Because demonstrative definitions are the most primitive, they are also the most limited. In addition to the limitations affecting all extensional definitions (which will be discussed shortly), there is the obvious limitation that the required objects be available for being pointed at. For example, if one wishes to define the word "sun" and it happens to be nighttime, or the word "dog" and none happen to be in the vicinity, a demonstrative definition cannot be used.

Demonstrative definitions differ from the other kinds of definitions in that the definiens is constituted at least in part by a gesture—the gesture of pointing. Since the definiens in any definition is a group of words, however, a gesture, such as pointing, must count as a word. While this conclusion may appear strange at first, it is supported by the fact that the "words" in many sign languages consist exclusively of gestures.

Enumerative definitions assign a meaning to a term by naming the members of the class the term denotes. Like demonstrative definitions, they may also be either partial or complete. Examples:

> "Actor" means a person such as Gregory Peck, Rod Steiger, or Jack Lemmon.

> "Planet" means one of the following: Mercury, Venus, Earth, Mars, Saturn, Jupiter, Neptune, Uranus, or Pluto.

Complete enumerative definitions are usually more satisfying than partial ones because they identify the definiendum with greater assurance. Relatively few classes, however, can be completely enumerated. Many classes, for example the class of real numbers greater than 1 but less than 2, have an infinite number of members. Others, for example the class of stars and the class of persons, while not infinite, have still too many members to enumerate. Therefore, anything approximating a complete enumerative definition of terms denoting these classes is clearly impossible. Then there are others—the class of insects and the class of trees, for example—the vast majority of whose members have no names. For terms that denote these classes, either a demonstrative definition or a definition by subclass is the more appropriate choice.

A **definition by subclass** assigns a meaning to a term by naming subclasses of the class denoted by the term. Such a definition, too, may be either partial or complete, depending on whether the subclasses named, when taken together, include all the members of the class or only some of them. Examples:

> "Tree" means an oak, pine, elm, spruce, maple, and the like.

> "Flower" means a rose, lily, daisy, geranium, zinnia, and the like.

"Cetacean" means either a whale, dolphin, or a porpoise.

"Fictional work" means either a poem, a play, a novel, or a short story.

The first two are partial, the second two complete. As with definitions by enumeration, complete definitions by subclass are more satisfying than partial ones; but because relatively few terms denote classes that admit of a conveniently small number of subclasses, complete definitions by subclass are often difficult, if not impossible, to provide.

Extensional definitions are chiefly used as techniques for producing lexical and stipulative definitions. Lexical definitions are aimed at communicating how a word is actually used, and one of the ways of doing so is by identifying the members of the class that the word denotes. Dictionaries frequently include references to the individual members (or to the subclasses) of the class denoted by the word being defined. Sometimes they even include a kind of demonstrative definition when they provide a picture of the object that the word denotes. Not all lexical definitions have to occur in dictionaries, however. A lexical definition can just as well be spoken, as when one person attempts to explain orally to another how a word is used in a language. Such attempts, incidentally, often have recourse to all three kinds of extensional definition.

Stipulative definitions are used to assign a meaning to a word for the first time. This task may be accomplished by all three kinds of extensional definition. For example, a biologist engaged in naming and classifying types of fish might assign names to the specific varieties by pointing to their respective tanks (demonstrative definition), and then he might assign a class name to the whole group by referring to the names of the specific varieties (definition by subclass). An astronomer might point via his telescope to a newly discovered comet and announce, "That comet will henceforth be known as 'Henderson's Comet' " (demonstrative definition). The organizer of a children's game might make the stipulation: "John, Mary, and Billy will be called 'Buccaneers,' and Judy, George, and Nancy will be 'Pirates' " (enumerative definition).

Although it is conceivable that extensional definitions could also serve as techniques for theoretical and persuasive definitions (though this would be highly unusual), extensional definitions by themselves cannot properly serve as precising definitions for the following reason. The function of a precising definition is to clarify a vague word, and vagueness is a problem affecting intensional meaning. Because the intension is imprecise, the extension is indefinite. To attempt to render the intension precise by exactly specifying the extension (as with an extensional definition) would be tantamount to having extension determine intension—which cannot be done.

The principle that intension determines extension, whereas the converse is not true, underlies the fact that all extensional definitions suffer serious deficiencies. For example, in the case of the demonstrative definition of the word "chair," if all the chairs pointed to are made of wood, the listener might get the idea that "chair" means "wood," instead of something to sit on. Similarly, he might get the idea that "Washington Monument" means "tall," or "pointed," or any of a number of other things. From the definition of "actor" he might think that "actor" means "famous man"—which would include Albert Einstein and Winston Churchill. From the definition of "tree" the listener might get the idea that "tree" means "firmly planted in the ground," which would also include the pilings of a building. And he might think that "cetacean" means "fast swimmer" instead of "aquatic mammal." In other words, it makes no difference how many individuals or subclasses are named in an extensional definition, there is no assurance that the listener or reader will get the *intensional* meaning. Extensions can *suggest* intensions, but they cannot *determine* them.

Intensional (Connotative) Definitions

An **intensional definition** is one that assigns a meaning to a word by indicating the qualities or attributes that the word connotes. Because at least three strategies may be used to indicate the attributes a word connotes, there are at least three kinds of intensional definitions: synonymous definition, operational definition, and definition by genus and difference.

A **synonymous definition** is one in which the definiens is a single word that connotes the same attributes as the definiendum. In other words, the definiens is a synonym of the word being defined. Examples:

> "Physician" means doctor.
> "Intentional" means willfull.
> "Voracious" means ravenous.
> "Observe" means see.

When a single word can be found that has the same intensional meaning as the word being defined, a synonymous definition is a highly concise way of assigning a meaning. Many words, however, have subtle shades of meaning that are not connoted by any other single word. For example, the word "wisdom" is not exactly synonymous with either "knowledge," "understanding," or "sense"; and "envious" is not exactly synonymous with either "jealous" or "covetous."

An **operational definition** assigns a meaning to a word by specifying certain experimental procedures that determine whether or not the word applies to a certain thing. Examples:

> One substance is "harder than" another if and only if one scratches the other when the two are rubbed together.

> A subject has "brain activity" if and only if an electroencephalograph shows oscillations when attached to the subject's head.

> A "potential difference" exists between two conductors if and only if a voltmeter shows a reading when connected to the two conductors.

> A solution is an "acid" if and only if litmus paper turns red when dipped into it.

Each of these definitions prescribes an operation to be performed. The first prescribes that the two substances in question be rubbed together, the second that the electroencephalograph be connected to the patient's head and observed for oscillations, the third that the voltmeter be connected to the two conductors and observed for deflection, and the fourth that the litmus paper be placed in the solution and observed for color change. Unless it specifies such an operation, a definition cannot be an operational definition. For example, the definition "A solution is an 'acid' if and only if it has a pH of less than 7," while good in other respects, is not an operational definition because it prescribes no operation.

Operational definitions were invented for the purpose of tying down relatively abstract concepts to the solid ground of empirical reality. In this they succeed fairly well; yet, from the standpoint of ordinary language usage, they involve certain deficiencies. One of these deficiencies concerns the fact that operational definitions usually convey only *part* of the intensional meaning of a term. Certainly "brain activity" means more than oscillations on an electroencephalograph, just as "acid" means more than blue litmus paper turning red. This deficiency becomes more acute when one attempts to apply operational definitions to terms outside the framework of science. For example, no adequate operational definition could be given for such words as "love," "respect," "freedom," and "dignity."

A **definition by genus and difference** assigns a meaning to a term by identifying a genus term and one or more difference words that, when combined, convey the meaning of the term being defined. Definition by genus and difference is more generally applicable and achieves more adequate results than any of the other kinds of intensional definition. To explain how it works, we must first explain the meanings of the terms "genus," "species," and "specific difference."

In logic, "genus" and "species" have a somewhat different meaning than they have in biology. In logic, "genus" simply means a relatively larger class, and "species" means a relatively smaller subclass of the genus. For example, we may speak of the genus animal and the species mammal, or of the genus mammal and the species feline, or of the genus feline and the species tiger, or the genus tiger and the species Bengal tiger. In other words, genus and species are merely relative classifications.

The "specific difference," or "difference," for short, is the attribute or attributes that distinguish the various species within a genus. For example, the specific difference that distinguishes tigers from other species in the genus feline would include the attributes of being large, striped, ferocious, and so on. Because the specific difference is what distinguishes the species, when a genus is qualified by a specific difference a species is identified. Definition by genus and difference is based upon this fact. It consists in combining a term denoting a genus with a word or group of words connoting a specific difference so that the combination identifies the meaning of the term denoting the species.

Let us construct a definition by genus and difference for the word "ice." The first step is to identify a genus of which ice is the species. The required genus is water. Next we must identify a specific difference (attribute) that makes ice a special form of water. The required difference is frozen. The completed definition may now be written out:

"Ice" means frozen water.　　ice = species
　　　　　　　　　　　　　　　water = genus
　　　　　　　　　　　　　　　frozen = difference

A definition by genus and difference is easy to construct. Simply select a term that is more general than the term to be defined, then narrow it down so that it means the same thing as the term being defined. Examples:

Species		Difference	Genus
"Daughter"	means a	female	offspring.
"Husband"	means a	married	man.
"Doe"	means a	female	deer.
"Fawn"	means a	very young	deer.
"Skyscraper"	means a	very tall	building.

Other examples are more sophisticated:

"Tent" means a collapsible shelter made of canvas or other material that is stretched and sustained by poles.

"Tent" is the species, "shelter" is the genus, and "collapsible" and "made of canvas . . ." the difference.

Definition by genus and difference is the most effective of the intensional definitions for producing the five kinds of definition discussed in Section 2.2. Stipulative, lexical, precising, theoretical, and persuasive definitions can all be constructed according to the method of genus and difference. Lexical definitions are typically definitions of this type. Operational definition can serve as the method for constructing stipulative, lexical, precising, and persuasive definitions, but because of the limitations we have noted, it typically could not be used to produce a *complete* lexical definition. Other techniques would have to be used in addition. Synonymous definition may be used to produce only lexical definitions. Since, in a synonymous definition, the definiendum must have a meaning before a synonym can be found, this technique cannot be used to produce stipulative definitions, and the fact that the definiens of such a definition contains no more information than the definiendum prohibits its use in constructing precising, theoretical, and persuasive definitions.

EXERCISE 2.4

I. Determine whether the following are demonstrative definitions, enumerative definitions, definitions by subclass, synonymous definitions, operational definitions, or definitions by genus and difference.

★1. "Plant" means something such as a tree, a flower, a vine, or a cactus.

2. "Hammer" means a tool used for pounding.

3. A triangle is "equilateral" if and only if a compass, when placed sequentially on two vertices and properly adjusted, strikes through the other two vertices.

★4. "State" means something such as Ohio, Arkansas, Minnesota, and Tennessee.

5. "Neophyte" means beginner.

6. "Painting" means something like da Vinci's *Mona Lisa,* van Gogh's *Starry Night,* Botticelli's *Birth of Venus,* or Rembrandt's *Night Watch.*

★7. "House" means this:

8. "Hot" means, for an electric iron, that your wetted finger sizzles when placed momentarily in contact with it.

9. "Dessert" means something such as pie, cake, cookies, or ice cream sundaes.

★10. "Hurricane" means a storm having winds of at least 73 miles per hour that originates at sea.

11. "Mountain" means something such as Everest, Rainier, Whitney, or McKinley.

12. A substance is "translucent" if and only if when held up to a strong light some of the light comes through.

★13. "Insect" means something such as a fly, an ant, a wasp, or a caterpillar.

14. "Facade" means face.

15. "Prime number" means a number that is divisible only by itself and one.

★16. "Language" means something such as French, German, Spanish, English, and so on.

17. "Tree" means this, and this, and this (as you point to a number of trees).

18. "Oak" means a tree that bears acorns.

★19. An "electric current" flows in a circuit if and only if an ammeter connected in series with the circuit shows a reading.

20. "Philosopher" means someone such as Plato, Aristotle, Descartes, or Kant.

21. "Professional person" means a person such as a doctor, a lawyer, a professor, or an architect.

★22. "Error" means mistake.

23. "Musical composition" means something such as a symphony, a concerto, a sonata, or a toccata.

24. "Truck" means a vehicle used for hauling.

★25. "Done" means, in reference to a baking cake, that a wooden toothpick poked into the center comes out clean.

II. Constructing definitions.

1. Construct a partial enumerative definition for the following terms by naming three members of the class the term denotes. Then find a nonsynonymous term that these members serve equally well to define. Example: "Poet" means a person such as Wordsworth, Coleridge, or Shelley. A nonsynonymous term is "Englishman."

  ★a. skyscraper
   b. corporation
   c. island
   d. composer
   e. novel

2. Construct a complete enumerative definition for the following terms:

  a. ocean
  b. continent

3. Construct a definition by subclass for the following terms by naming three subclasses of the class the term denotes. Then find a nonsynonymous term that these subclasses serve equally well to define.

  ★a. animal
   b. fish
   c. vehicle
   d. gemstone
   e. polygon

4. Construct a complete definition by subclass for the following terms:

   a. quadrilateral
   b. circulating American coin

5. Construct synonymous definitions for the following terms:

  ★a. intersection
   b. fabric
   c. nucleus
   d. abode
   e. wedlock
   f. cellar
   g. summit
   h. apparel

6. Construct operational definitions for the following words:

  ★a. genius
   b. ferromagnetic
   c. fluorescent
   d. alkaline
   e. polarized (light)

7. Construct definitions by genus and difference for the following terms. In each definition identify the genus term.

  ★a. drake
   b. biologist
   c. felony
   d. widow
   e. library

III. Answer "true" or "false" to the following statements:

1. The technique of extensional definition may be used to produce precising definitions.

2. The technique of extensional definition may be used to produce stipulative and lexical definitions.

3. Most extensional definitions convey the precise intensional meaning of a term.

4. An intensional definition conveys the meaning of a term by indicating the members of the class the term denotes.

5. In a synonymous definition the definiens must be a single word.

6. The technique of synonymous definition may be used to construct precising definitions.

7. Operational definitions typically convey the entire intensional meaning of a word.

8. The species is a subclass of the genus.

9. The specific difference is an attribute or set of attributes that identifies a species.

10. Definition by genus and difference may be used to produce stipulative, lexical, precising, theoretical, and persuasive definitions.

2.5 CRITERIA FOR LEXICAL DEFINITIONS

Because the function of a lexical definition is to report the way a word is actually used in a language, lexical definitions are the ones we most frequently encounter and are what most people mean when they speak of the "definition" of a word. Accordingly, it is appropriate that we have a set of rules that we may use in constructing lexical definitions of our own and in evaluating the lexical definitions of others. Since the rules presented here are intended specifically for lexical definitions, it is only natural that many of them do not apply to the other kinds of definition. The unique functions that are served by stipulative, precising, theoretical, and persuasive definitions prescribe different sets of criteria.

> Rule 1: A lexical definition should conform to the standards of proper grammar.

A definition, like any other form of expression, should be grammatically correct. Examples of definitions that are grammatically *incorrect* are as follows:

> Vacation is when you don't have to go to work or school.
> Furious means if you're angry at someone.
> Cardiac is like something to do with the heart.

The corrected versions are:

> "Vacation" means a period during which activity is suspended from work or school.
> "Furious" means a condition of being angry.
> "Cardiac" means pertaining to, situated near, or acting on the heart.

Technically the definiendum should be put in quotation marks, but this convention is not always followed.

> Rule 2: A lexical definition should convey the essential meaning of the word being defined.

The word "man" is occasionally defined as "featherless biped." Such a definition fails to convey the essential meaning of "man" as the word is used in ordinary English. It says nothing about the important attributes that distinguish man from the other animals, namely, the capacity to reason and to use language on a sophisticated level. A more adequate definition would be " 'man' means the animal that has the capacity to reason and to speak."

If a lexical definition is to be given in terms of an operational definition or in terms of any of the forms of extensional definition, it should usually be supplemented by one of the other forms of intensional definition, preferably definition by genus and difference. As we have noted, from the standpoint of ordinary language usage an operational definition often conveys only part of the intensional meaning of a word, and this part frequently misses the essential meaning altogether. As for extensional definitions, at best they can only *suggest* the essential meaning of a word; they cannot *determine* it precisely. As a result, no adequate lexical definition can consist exclusively of extensional definitions.

> Rule 3: A lexical definition should be neither too broad nor too narrow.

If a definition is too broad, the definiens includes too much; if it is too narrow, the definiens includes too little. If, for example, "bird" were defined as "any warm-blooded animal having wings," the definition would be too broad because it would include bats, and bats are not birds. If, on the other hand, "bird" were defined as "any warm-blooded, feathered animal that can fly," the definition would be too narrow because it would exclude ostriches, which cannot fly.

The only types of lexical definitions that tend to be susceptible to either of these deficiencies are synonymous definitions and definitions by genus and difference. With synonymous definitions, one must be careful that the definiens really is a synonym of the definiendum. For example, the definition " 'king' means ruler" is too broad because many rulers are not kings. "Ruler" is not genuinely synonymous with "king." As for definitions by genus and difference, one must insure that the specific difference narrows the genus in exactly the right way. Both of the above definitions of "bird" are definitions by genus and difference in which the specific difference fails to restrict the genus in exactly the right manner.

Rule 4:   A lexical definition should not be circular.

Sometimes the problem of circularity appears in connection with *pairs* of definitions. The following pair is circular:

"Science" means the activity engaged in by scientists.
"Scientist" means anyone who engages in science.

At other times a definition may be intrinsically circular. Of the following, the first is a synonymous definition, the second a definition by genus and difference:

"Quiet" means quietude.
"Silence" means the state of being silent.

Certain operational definitions also run the risk of circularity:

"Time" means whatever is measured by a clock.

Surely a person would have to know what "time" means before he could understand the purpose of a clock.

Rule 5:   A lexical definition should not be negative when it can be affirmative.

Of the following two definitions, the first is affirmative, the second negative:

"Concord" means harmony.
"Concord" means the absence of discord.

Some words, however, are intrinsically negative. For them, a negative definition is quite appropriate. Examples:

"Bald" means the absence of hair.
"Darkness" means the absence of light.

Rule 6:   A lexical definition should not be expressed in figurative, obscure, vague, or ambiguous language.

A definition is *figurative* if it involves metaphors or tends to paint a picture instead of exposing the essential meaning of a term. Examples:

"Architecture" means frozen music.
"Camel" means a ship of the desert.

A definition is *obscure* if its meaning is hidden. One source of obscurity is overly technical language. Compare these two definitions:

> "Bunny" means a mammalian of the family Leporidae of the order Lagomorpha whose young are born furless and blind.

> "Bunny" means a rabbit.

The problem lies not with technical language as such but with *needlessly* technical language. Because "bunny" is very much a nontechnical term, no technical definition is needed. On the other hand, some words are intrinsically technical, and for them only a technical definition will suffice. Example:

> "Neutrino" means a quasi-massless lepton obeying Fermi-Dirac statistics and having one-half quantum unit of spin.

A definition is *vague* if its meaning is blurred. Example:

> "Democracy" means a kind of government where the people are in control.

This definition fails to identify the people who are in control, how they exercise their control, and what they are in control of.

A definition is *ambiguous* if it lends itself to more than one distinct interpretation. Example:

> "Triangle" means a figure composed of three straight lines in which all the angles are equal to 180°.

Does this mean that each angle separately is equal to 180° or that the angles taken together are equal to 180°? Either interpretation is possible given the ambiguous meaning of "all the angles are equal to 180°."

Rule 7:   A lexical definition should avoid affective terminology.

Affective terminology is any kind of word usage that plays upon the emotions of the reader or listener. It includes sarcastic and facetious language and any other kind of language that is liable to influence attitudes. Examples:

> "Communism" means that "brilliant" invention of Karl Marx and other foolish political visionaries in which the national wealth is supposed to be held in common by the people.

> "Theism" means belief in that great Santa Claus in the sky.

The second example also violates Rule 5 because it contains a metaphor.

> Rule 8: A lexical definition should indicate the context to which the definiens pertains.

This rule applies to any definition in which the context of the definiens is important to the meaning of the definiendum. For example, the definition " 'Deuce' means a tie in points toward a game or in games toward a set" is practically meaningless without any reference to tennis. Whenever the definiendum is a word that means different things in different contexts, a reference to the context is important. Examples:

> "Strike" means (in baseball) a pitch at which a batter swings and misses.

> "Strike" means (in bowling) the act of knocking down all the pins with the first ball of a frame.

> "Strike" means (in fishing) a pull on a line made by a fish in taking the bait.

It is not always necessary to make *explicit* reference to the context, but at least the phraseology of the definiens should indicate what the context is.

EXERCISE 2.5

Criticize the following definitions in light of the eight rules for lexical definitions:

★1. A sculpture is a three-dimensional image made of marble.

2. "Elusory" means elusive.

3. "Develop" means to transform by the action of chemicals.

★4. A cynic is a person who knows the price of everything and the value of nothing.

(Oscar Wilde)

5. "Semantics" is when somebody studies words.

6. A slide rule is a device made of wood, plastic, or metal that consists of a sliding piece that moves between two mutually attached stationary pieces.

★7. A theist is anyone who is not an atheist or an agnostic.

8. "Intelligence" means whatever is measured by an IQ test.

9. A symphony is a musical piece written for full orchestra.

$\star$10. Feminism is a militant movement originated by a group of deviant women for the purpose of undermining the natural distinction between the sexes.

11. A radio is an electronic device consisting of an antenna, variable-frequency oscillator, and mixer circuitry operating in conjunction with RF, IF, and AF amplification stages, the last of which feeds an AF transducer.

12. Logic is the study of arguments including definitions.

$\star$13. "Truculent" is if you're cruel or fierce.

14. A house is a structure made of wood or stone intended for human habitation.

15. Satire is a kind of glass, wherein beholders do generally discover everybody's face but their own.

(Jonathan Swift)

$\star$16. A carpenter's square is a square used by a carpenter.

17. "Safety" means a play in which a player grounds the ball behind his own goal line when the ball was caused to cross the goal line by his own team.

18. Puberty: the time in life in which the two sexes begin first to be acquainted.

(Johnson's Dictionary)

$\star$19. "Normal" means an attribute possessed by people who are able to get on in the world.

20. An organic substance is any substance that is not inorganic.

21. Faith is the bird that sings when the dawn is still dark.

(Rabindranath Tagore)

$\star$22. "Schooner" means sort of like a sailboat.

23. "Faith" means reason succumbing to insecurity.

24. "Gammon" means, in backgammon, a victory in which one player defeats another before he can remove any of his men from the board.

$\star$25. A cello is a stringed musical instrument played with a bow.

26. Tobacco is a plant grown in the southeastern United States that, when enjoyed in the form of cigars and cigarettes, produces a most delightful and satisfying taste and aroma.

27. History is the unfolding of miscalculations.

(Barbara Tuchman)

$\star$28. "Camera" means a device for taking photographs.

29. "Photograph" means an image produced by the combined action of electromagnetic radiation in the range of 4000 to 7000 Angstroms and certain organic reducing agents such as diaminophenol hydrochloride on silver halide particles affixed to a backing material of high alpha cellulose content.

30. Mackerel: a sea-fish.

(Johnson's Dictionary)

★31. "Anchor person" means an electronic media guru who has great looks but less than average intelligence and who brings canned news to people incapable of reading a newspaper.

32. "Diet" means like when you cut back on your calories.

33. Animal: a living creature corporeal, distinct, on the one side, from pure spirit, on the other, from pure matter.

(Johnson's Dictionary)

★34. "Pen" means an instrument used for writing on paper.

35. Wine is an alcoholic beverage made from grapes.

3

INFORMAL FALLACIES

3.1 FALLACIES IN GENERAL

A **fallacy** is a certain kind of defect in an argument. One way that an argument can be defective is by having one or more false premises. Another way is by containing a fallacy. Both deductive and inductive arguments may be affected by fallacies; if either kind contains a fallacy, it is either unsound or uncogent, depending on the kind of argument.

Fallacies are usually divided into two groups: formal and informal. A **formal fallacy** is one that may be identified through mere inspection of the form or structure of an argument. Here is an example of a deductive argument that contains a formal fallacy:

> All tigers are animals.
> All mammals are animals.
> Therefore, all tigers are mammals.

This argument has the following form:

> All *A* are *B*.
> All *C* are *B*.
> Therefore, all *A* are *C*.

Through mere inspection of this form, one can see that the argument is invalid. The fact that *A*, *B*, and *C* stand respectively for "tigers," "animals," and "mammals" is irrelevant in detecting the fallacy. The problem may be traced to the second premise. If the letters *C* and *B* are interchanged, the form becomes valid, and the original argument, with the same change introduced, also becomes valid (but unsound). This particular fallacy, together with certain others, will be discussed in later chapters.

Informal fallacies are those that can be detected only through analysis of the content of the argument. Consider the following example:

(homonym)
2 diff meaning of some word

> All factories are plants.
> All plants are things that contain chlorophyll
> Therefore, all factories are things that contain chlorophyll.

A cursory inspection of this argument might lead one to think that it has the following form:

> All *A* are *B*.   *not*
> All *B* are *C*.
> All *A* are *C*.

Since this form is valid, one might conclude that the argument itself is valid. Yet the argument is clearly invalid because it has true premises and a false conclusion. An analysis of the content, that is, the meaning of the words, reveals the source of the trouble. The word "plants" is used in two different senses. In the first premise it means a building where something is manufactured, and in the second it means a life form. Thus, the argument really has the following invalid form:

, but

> All *A* are *B*.
> All *C* are *D*.
> All *A* are *D*.

Precisely how the informal fallacies accomplish their purpose varies from case to case. Sometimes, as in the example above, they obscure the form of the argument so that the reader or listener is deluded into thinking that the argument is valid when in fact it is not. In other cases they tend to prevent the reader or listener from acknowledging a missing premise that, if acknowledged, would be clearly seen to be false (or at least questionable). And then, in some cases (such as begging the question), they delude the reader or listener into thinking that an acknowledged premise is true when it is either false or questionable. In any event, the effect of an informal fallacy is to make a bad argument *appear* good. In fact, some fallacious arguments may appear to be even better than some arguments that commit no fallacies.

Informal fallacies are frequently backed by some motive on the part of the arguer to deceive the reader or listener. The arguer may not have sufficient evidence to support a certain conclusion and as a result may attempt to win its acceptance by resorting to a trick. Sometimes the trick fools even the arguer. The arguer may delude himself into thinking that he is presenting genuine evidence when in fact he is not. By studying some of the typical ways in which arguers deceive both themselves and others, one is less likely to be fooled by the fallacious arguments posed by others and is less likely to stumble blindly into fallacies when constructing arguments for one's own use.

Since the time of Aristotle, logicians have attempted to classify the various informal fallacies. Aristotle himself identified thirteen and separated them into two groups. The work of subsequent logicians has produced dozens more, which has rendered the task of classifying them even more difficult. The presentation that follows divides twenty-two informal fallacies into five groups: fallacies of relevance, fallacies of weak induction, fallacies of presumption, fallacies of ambiguity, and fallacies of grammatical analogy. The final section of the chapter considers some of the problems that arise when fallacies are encountered in the context of ordinary language.

EXERCISE 3.1

Determine whether the fallacies committed by the following arguments are formal fallacies or informal fallacies.

★1. If Laetril is as good as it's supposed to be, then it will cure cancer. Laetril is not as good as it's supposed to be. Therefore, Laetril will not cure cancer.

2. Everything that runs has feet. The Columbia River runs very swiftly. Therefore, the Columbia River has feet.

3. All persons who believe we create our own reality are persons who lack social responsibility. All persons governed by selfish motives are persons who lack social responsibility. Therefore, all persons who believe we create our own reality are persons governed by selfish motives.

★4. The ship of state is like a ship at sea. No sailor is ever allowed to protest orders from the captain. For the same reason, no citizen should ever be allowed to protest presidential policies.

5. Renowned violinist Pinchas Zukerman has said, "When it comes to vodka, Smirnoff plays second fiddle to none." We must therefore conclude that Smirnoff is the best vodka available.

6. If the Golan Heights properly belong to Syria, then the Israelis are trespassers. The Israelis are indeed trespassers. Therefore, the Golan Heights properly belong to Syria.

★7. Ed Asner, Gregory Peck, and Jane Fonda are Democrats. Therefore, it must be the case that all Hollywood stars are Democrats.

8. Lynne Cheney, Chairwoman of the National Endowment for the Humanities, has argued persuasively for a return to liberal arts education. Cheney's arguments should hardly be taken seriously, however, because as the director of this organization she is obviously biased in favor of the liberal arts.

9. If plastic guns are sold to the public, then terrorists will carry them aboard airliners undetected. If plastic guns are sold to the public, then airline hijackings will increase. Therefore, if terrorists carry plastic guns aboard airliners undetected, then airline hijackings will increase.

★10. Some prenuptial agreements are contracts that allow one partner full freedom when the other partner is out of town. Some contracts that allow one partner full freedom when the other partner is out of town are arrangements detrimental to a successful marriage. Therefore, some prenuptial agreements are arrangements detrimental to a successful marriage.

3.2 FALLACIES OF RELEVANCE

The **fallacies of relevance** share the common characteristic that the arguments in which they occur have premises that are *logically* irrelevant to the conclusion. Yet the premises are relevant *psychologically*, so the conclusion may *seem* to follow from the premises, even though it does not follow logically. In a good argument the premises provide genuine evidence in support of the conclusion. In an argument that commits a fallacy of relevance, on the other hand, the connection between premises and conclusion is emotional. To identify a fallacy of relevance, therefore, one must be able to distinguish genuine evidence from various forms of emotional appeal.

1. Appeal to Force (*Argumentum ad Baculum*: Appeal to the "Stick")

The fallacy of **appeal to force** occurs whenever an arguer poses a conclusion to another person and tells that person either implicitly or explicitly that some harm will come to him or her if he or she does not accept the conclusion. The fallacy always involves a threat by the arguer to the physical or psychological well-being of the listener or reader, who may be either a single person or a group of persons. Obviously, such a threat is logically irrelevant to the subject matter of the conclu-

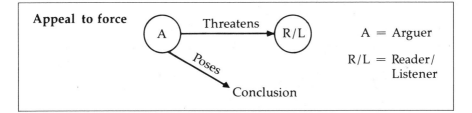

sion, so any argument based on such a procedure is fallacious. The *ad baculum* fallacy often occurs when children argue with one another:

> *Child to playmate:* "Mister Rogers" is the best show on TV; and if you don't believe it, I'm going to call my big brother over here and he's going to beat you up.

But it occurs among adults as well:

> *Secretary to boss:* I'm sure you'll want to raise my salary for the coming year. After all, you know how friendly I am with your wife, and I'm sure you wouldn't want her to find out what's been going on between you and that sexpot client of yours.

The first example involves a physical threat, the second a psychological threat. While neither threat provides any genuine evidence that the conclusion is true, both provide evidence that someone might be injured. If the two types of evidence are confused with each other, both arguer and listener may be deluded into thinking that the conclusion is supported by evidence, when in fact it is not.

The appeal to force fallacy usually accomplishes its purpose by psychologically impeding the reader or listener from acknowledging a missing premise that, if acknowledged, would be seen to be false or at least questionable. The two examples just given can be interpreted as concealing the following premises, both of which are most likely false:

> If my brother forces you to admit that Mister Rogers is the best show on TV, then Mister Rogers is in fact the best show.

> If I succeed in threatening you, then you will want to raise my salary.

The conclusion of the first argument is that Mister Rogers is the best show on TV. But just because someone is forced into saying that it is does not mean that such is the case. Similarly, the conclusion of the second argument is that the boss will *want* to raise the secretary's salary. But if the boss is threatened into raising the secretary's salary, this does not mean that he does it because he wants to. Many of the other informal fallacies can be interpreted as accomplishing their purpose in this way.

2. Appeal to Pity (*Argumentum ad Misericordiam*)

The fallacy of **appeal to pity** occurs whenever an arguer poses a conclusion and then attempts to evoke pity from the reader or listener in an effort to get him or her to accept the conclusion. Example:

> *Taxpayer to judge:* Your Honor, I admit that I declared thirteen children as dependents on my tax return, even though I have only two, and I realize that this was wrong. But if you find me

guilty of tax evasion, my reputation will be ruined. I'll probably lose my job, my poor wife will not be able to have the operation that she desperately needs, and my kids will starve. Surely you will find me not guilty.

The conclusion of this argument is, "Surely you will find me not guilty." Obviously, the conclusion is not *logically* relevant to the arguer's set of pathetic circumstances, although it *is* *psychologically* relevant. If the arguer succeeds in evoking pity from the listener or reader, the latter is liable to exercise his or her desire to help the arguer by accepting the argument. In this way the reader or listener may be fooled into accepting a conclusion that is not supported by any evidence. The appeal to pity is quite common and is frequently used by students on their instructors at exam time and by lawyers on behalf of their clients before judges and juries.

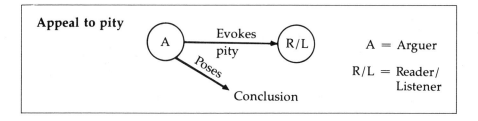

3. Appeal to the People (*Argumentum ad Populum*)

Nearly everyone wants to be loved, esteemed, admired, valued, recognized, and accepted by others. The **appeal to the people** uses these desires to get the reader or listener to accept a conclusion. Two approaches are involved, one of them direct, the other indirect.

The *direct approach* occurs when an arguer, addressing a large group of people, excites the emotions and enthusiasm of the crowd to win acceptance for his conclusion. The objective is to arouse a kind of mob mentality. This is the strategy used by nearly every propagandist and demagogue. Adolf Hitler was a master of the technique, but it is also used with some measure of success by speechmakers at Democratic and Republican national conventions. Waving flags and blaring music add to the overall effect. Because the individuals in the audience want to share in the camaraderie, the euphoria, and the excitement, they find themselves accepting any number of conclusions with ever-increasing fervor.

The direct approach is not limited to verbal argumentation, of course; a similar effect can be accomplished in writing. By employing such emotionally charged phraseology as "fighter of communism" "champion of the free enterprise system," and "defender of the working man," a polemicist can awaken the same kind of mob mentality as he would if he were speaking.

In the *indirect approach* the arguer directs his appeal not to the crowd as a whole but to one or more individuals separately, focusing upon some aspect of their relationship to the crowd. The indirect approach includes such specific forms as the bandwagon argument, the appeal to vanity, and the appeal to snobbery. All are standard techniques of the advertising industry. Here is an example of the **bandwagon argument:**

> Of course you want to buy Zest toothpaste. Why, 90 percent of America brushes with Zest.

The idea is that you will be left behind or left out of the group if you do not use the product.

The **appeal to vanity** often associates the product with a certain celebrity who is admired and pursued, the idea being that you, too, will be admired and pursued if you use it. Example:

> Only the ultimate in fashion could complement the face of Bianca Jagger. Spectrum sunglasses—for the beautiful people in the jet set.

And here is an example of the **appeal to snobbery:**

> A Rolls Royce is not for everyone, If you qualify as one of the select few, this distinguished classic may be seen and driven at British Motor Cars, Ltd. (By appointment only, please).

Needless to say, the indirect approach is used by others besides advertisers:

> *Mother to child:* You want to grow up and be just like Wonder Woman, don't you? Then eat your liver and carrots.

Both the direct and indirect approaches of the *ad populum* fallacy have the same basic structure:

> You want to be accepted/included in the group/loved/esteemed. . . . Therefore, you should accept XYZ as true.

In the direct approach the arousal of a mob mentality produces an immediate feeling of belonging for each person in the crowd. Each person feels united with the crowd, which evokes a sense of strength and security. When the crowd roars its approval of the conclusions that are then offered, anyone who does not accept them automatically cuts himself or herself off from the crowd and risks the loss of his or her security, strength, and acceptance. The same thing happens in the indirect approach, but the context and technique are somewhat subtler.

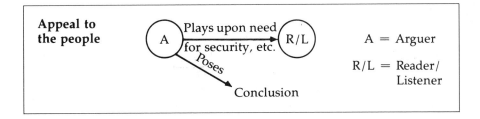

4. Argument Against the Person (Argumentum ad Hominem)

This fallacy always involves two arguers. One of them advances (either directly or implicitly) a certain argument, and the other then responds by directing his or her attention not to the first person's argument but to the first person *himself*. When this occurs, the second person is said to commit an **argument against the person.**

The argument against the person occurs in three forms: the *ad hominem* abusive, *ad hominem* circumstantial, and the *tu quoque*. In the **ad hominem abusive,** the second person responds to the first person's argument by verbally abusing the first person. Example:

> Poet Allen Ginsberg has argued in favor of abolishing censorship of pornographic literature. But Ginsberg's arguments are nothing but trash. Ginsberg, you know, is a marijuana-smoking homosexual and a thoroughgoing advocate of the drug culture.

Because Ginsberg's (behaviors) being a marijuana-smoking homosexual and advocate of the drug culture has no bearing on his ability to construct good arguments, this argument is fallacious.

The **ad hominem circumstantial** begins the same way as the *ad hominem* abusive, but instead of heaping verbal abuse on his or her opponent, the respondent attempts to discredit the opponent's argument by alluding to certain circumstances that (affect) the opponent. By doing so the respondent hopes to show that the opponent is predisposed to argue the way he or she does and should therefore not be taken seriously. Here is an example:

> Economist Milton Friedman has argued in favor of reducing federal income taxes. But Friedman's argument should be discounted. Friedman is a millionaire who would benefit greatly from a reduction in taxes. Also, Friedman has no need for the government social programs that higher taxes provide for.

The author of this argument ignores the substance of Friedman's argument for reducing taxes and attempts instead to discredit it by calling attention to certain circumstances that affect Friedman, namely, the fact that he is a millionaire and the fact that he has no need for government social programs. The *ad hominem* circumstantial is easy to recognize because it always takes this form: "Of course Mr. X argues this way; just look at the circumstances that affect him." Merely because a person happens to be affected by certain circumstances is not sufficient reason to think that the person is incapable of arguing logically. Any attempt to discredit such an argument in this way therefore involves a fallacy.

The **tu quoque** ("you, too") fallacy begins the same way as the other two varieties of the *ad hominem* except that the first person's argument causes the respondent to appear guilty. The respondent then replies by attempting to shift the burden of guilt back to the first person. The response usually takes the form, "Your argument cannot be taken seriously because you are no better than I." Example:

> A parent admonishes his or her child for having stolen candy from the corner store. The child responds: "Your argument is no good. You told me yourself just a week ago that you, too, stole candy when you were a kid."

The *tu quoque* is sometimes called the "two wrongs make a right" fallacy. Obviously, two wrongs do not make a right. Whether the parent stole candy when he or she was a child is irrelevant to whether the child should steal candy.

The three forms of the *ad hominem* fallacy are often convincing because they catch the immediate attention of the reader or listener and they do introduce some kind of evidence into the picture. The fact that Ginsberg is a marijuana-smoking homosexual is eyecatching, and it does constitute evidence in support of some conclusion about Ginsberg's lifestyle. But it is totally irrelevant to the conclusion of the argument. If the reader or listener is not careful to distinguish relevant evidence from irrelevant evidence, he or she is likely to be persuaded by such an argument.

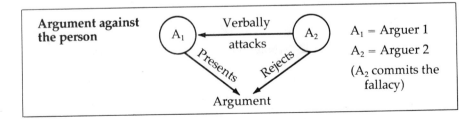

A CONCISE INTRODUCTION TO LOGIC

An especially important point to keep in mind about the *ad hominem* fallacy is that the fallacy always involves two *arguers* (at least implicitly). Consider the following arguments:

> Libyan dictator Moammar Kadafi has argued that Western nations have been reckless in their sale of arms to Israel. This argument is sheer nonsense. Kadafi is a lunatic who supports terrorists all over the world. Furthermore, he has territorial ambitions that extend to half the countries in Africa.

> Libyan dictator Moammar Kadafi is a lunatic who supports terrorists all over the world. Furthermore, he has territorial ambitions that extend to half the countries in Africa. Kadafi is therefore a wicked, irresponsible leader.

The first argument involves two arguers: Kadafi and the person attacking him. The argument commits an *ad hominem* abusive because the second arguer ignores Kadafi's argument and directs his attention instead to Kadafi himself. The second argument, however, involves only a single arguer, the person attacking Kadafi. No *ad hominem* is committed. If the premises are true, the argument is a good one.

The various forms of the argument against the person should not be confused with the appeal to force. In the appeal to force only one person need present an argument, and that person *threatens* the listener or reader in an effort to make him or her accept the conclusion. In the argument against the person two people must present arguments (the first person at least by implication), and the second person attempts to discredit the first's argument by verbally abusing him, by citing circumstances that affect him, or by shifting the burden of guilt onto him.

5. Accident

The fallacy of **accident** is committed when a general rule is applied wrongly to a specific case. Typically, the general rule is cited (either directly or implicitly) in the premises and then wrongly applied to the specific case mentioned in the conclusion. Because of the "accidental" features of the specific case, the general rule does not fit. Two examples:

> Freedom of speech is a constitutionally guaranteed right. Therefore, John Q. Radical should not be arrested for his speech that incited that riot last week.

> Property should be returned to its rightful owner. That drunken sailor who is starting a fight with his opponents at the pool table lent you his .45-caliber pistol, and now he wants it back. Therefore, you should return it to him now.

The right of freedom of speech has its limits, as does the rule that property be returned to its rightful owner. These rules are obviously misapplied in the above circumstances. The arguments therefore commit the fallacy of accident.

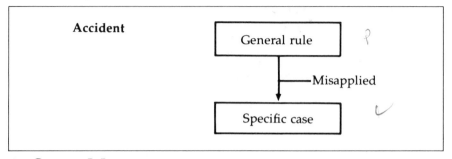

6. Straw Man

The **straw man** fallacy is committed when an arguer distorts an opponent's argument for the purpose of more easily attacking it, demolishes the distorted argument, and then concludes that the opponent's real argument has been demolished. By so doing, the arguer is said to have set up a straw man and knocked it down, only to conclude that the real man (opposing argument) has been knocked down as well. Example:

> Mr. Goldberg has argued against prayer in the public schools.
> Obviously Mr. Goldberg advocates atheism. But atheism is
> what they have in Russia. Atheism leads to the suppression of
> all religions and the replacement of God by an omnipotent
> state. Is that what we want for this country? I hardly think so.
> Clearly Mr. Goldberg's argument is nonsense.

Like the argument against the person fallacy, the straw man fallacy involves two arguers. Mr. Goldberg, who is the first arguer, has presented an argument against prayer in the public schools. The second arguer then attacks Goldberg's argument by equating it with an argument for atheism. He then attacks atheism and concludes that Goldberg's argument is nonsense. Since Goldberg's argument had nothing to do with atheism, the second argument commits the straw man fallacy.

As this example illustrates, the kind of distortion the second arguer resorts to is often an attempt to exaggerate the first person's argument or make it look more extreme than it really is. Here are two more examples:

> The garment workers have signed a petition arguing for better
> ventilation on the work premises. Unfortunately, air condition-
> ing is expensive. Air ducts would have to be run throughout
> the factory, and a massive heat exchange unit installed on the
> roof. Also, the cost of operating such a system during the
> summer would be astronomical. In view of these considera-
> tions the petition must be rejected.

> The student status committee has presented us with an argu-
> ment favoring alcohol privileges on campus. What do the stu-

dents want? Is it their intention to stay boozed up from the day they enter as freshmen till the day they graduate? Do they expect us to open a bar for them? Or maybe a chain of bars all over campus? Such a proposal is ridiculous!

In the first argument, the petition is merely for better ventilation in the factory—maybe a fan in the window during the summer. The arguer exaggerates this request to mean an elaborate air conditioning system installed throughout the building. He then points out that this is too expensive and concludes by rejecting the petition. A similar strategy is used in the second argument. The arguer distorts the request for alcohol privileges to mean a chain of bars all over campus. Such an idea is so patently outlandish that no further argument is necessary.

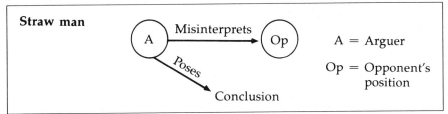

7. Missing the Point (*Ignoratio Elenchi*)

All the fallacies we have discussed thus far have been instances of cases where the conclusion of an argument is irrelevant to the premises. **Missing the point** illustrates a special form of irrelevance. This fallacy occurs when the premises of an argument appear to lead up to one particular conclusion, but then a completely different conclusion is drawn. Whenever one suspects that such a fallacy is being committed, he or she should be able to identify the *correct* conclusion, the conclusion that the premises *logically* imply. This conclusion must be completely different from the conclusion that is actually drawn. Examples:

> Crimes of theft and robbery have been increasing at an alarming rate lately. The conclusion is obvious: we must reinstate the death penalty immediately.

> Abuse of the welfare system is rampant nowadays. Our only alternative is to abolish the system altogether.

At least two correct conclusions are entailed by the premise of the first argument: either "We should provide increased police protection in vulnerable neighborhoods" or "We should initiate programs to eliminate the causes of the crimes." Reinstating the death penalty is not a logical conclusion at all. Among other things, theft and robbery are not capital crimes. In the second argument the premises logically suggest some systematic effort to eliminate the cheaters rather than eliminating the system altogether.

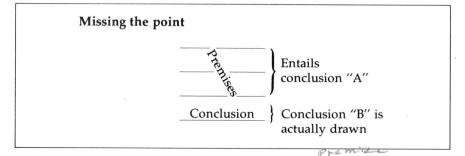

Missing the point

Premises ——————— } Entails conclusion "A"

Conclusion ————— } Conclusion "B" is actually drawn

Ignoratio elenchi means "ignorance of the proof." The arguer is ignorant of the logical implications of his or her own premises and, as a result, draws a conclusion that misses the point entirely. The fallacy has a distinct structure all its own, but in some ways it serves as a catchall for arguments that are not clear instances of one or more of the other fallacies.

8. Red Herring *(2 arguers, 1 at least implied)*

This fallacy is closely associated with missing the point (*ignoratio elenchi*). The **red herring** fallacy is committed when the arguer diverts the attention of the reader or listener by changing the subject to some totally different issue. He or she then finishes by either drawing a conclusion about this different issue or by merely presuming that some conclusion has been established. By so doing, the arguer purports to have won the argument. The fallacy gets its name from a procedure used to train hunting dogs to follow a scent. A red herring (or bag of them) is dragged across the trail with the aim of leading the animal astray. Since red herrings have an especially potent scent (caused in part by the smoking process used to preserve them), only the best dogs will follow the original scent. Here is an example of the fallacy:

> Environmentalists are continually harping about the dangers of nuclear power. Unfortunately, electricity is dangerous no matter where it comes from. Every year hundreds of people are electrocuted by accident. Since most of these accidents are caused by carelessness, they could be avoided if people would just exercise greater caution.

The original issue is whether nuclear power is dangerous. The arguer changes the subject to the danger of electrocution and concludes by stating that electrocution can be avoided by exercising caution. Obviously the danger of electrocution is totally different from the danger of a nuclear power plant blowing up or melting down. But the fact that both issues deal with electricity facilitates the arguer's intention to lead the reader or listener off the track. The structure of the fallacy is, "I have succeeded in drawing you off the track; therefore, I have won the argument."

Here are two more examples of the fallacy:

> People accuse the Alpha General Corporation of contributing to acid rain. But Alpha General is the lifeblood of this community. Alpha employs thousands of people and pays millions of dollars in property taxes. These taxes support our schools and pay the salaries of our police. Apparently the critics ignore these facts.

> There's a good deal of talk these days about the need to clamp down on welfare cheaters. But God loves the poor. "The poor you will have with you always," Jesus said. Not everyone in this world is blessed with material riches, but in the eyes of God the poor are on an equal standing with princes and kings.

Both arguments commit the red herring fallacy. In the first, the original issue is whether Alpha General contributes to acid rain. The arguer changes the subject to the contributions Alpha General makes to the community and concludes that the critics should pay more attention to the facts. The original issue in the second argument is whether action should be taken against welfare cheaters. The arguer changes the subject to the issue of whether God loves the poor. No conclusion is drawn about the new subject, but by simply leading the listener or reader off the track, the arguer purports to have won the argument. In both cases the slight connection between the original issue and the new one assists the arguer in accomplishing his or her purpose.

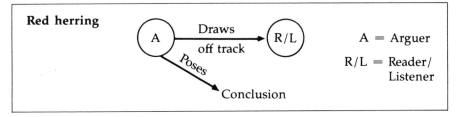

The red herring fallacy can be confused with the straw man fallacy because both have the effect of drawing the reader/listener off the track. This confusion can usually be avoided by remembering the unique ways in which they accomplish this purpose. In the straw man, the arguer begins by distorting an opponent's argument and concludes by knocking down the distorted argument. In the red herring, on the other hand, the arguer ignores the opponent's argument (if there is one) and subtly changes the subject. Thus, to distinguish the two fallacies, one should attempt to determine whether the arguer has distorted something or simply changed the subject.

Both red herring and straw man are susceptible of being confused with missing the point because all three involve a similar kind of irrelevancy. To avoid this confusion, one should realize that both red herring and straw man proceed by generating a new set of premises, whereas missing the point does not. Straw man draws a conclusion from new premises that are obtained by distorting an earlier argument, and red herring, if it draws any conclusion at all, draws one from new premises obtained by changing the subject. Missing the point, however, draws a conclusion from original premises. Also, in the red herring and straw man, the conclusion, if there is one, is *relevant* to the premises from which it is drawn; but in missing the point, the conclusion is *irrelevant* to the premises from which it is drawn.

EXERCISE 3.2

I. Identify the fallacies of relevance committed by the following arguments. If no fallacy is committed, write "no fallacy."

★1. The position open in the accounting department should be given to Frank Thompson. Frank has six hungry children to feed, and his wife desperately needs an operation to save her eyesight.

2. Los Angeles police chief Daryl Gates has argued against the decriminalization of drugs such as cocaine and heroin. But it is obvious why Gates takes this position. If these drugs were legalized, then most of Gates's officers would have nobody to arrest. Half the force would have to be released. Thus, no one should take Gates's argument seriously.

3. We hear a lot these days about the growing problem of alcoholism. But most alcoholics did not choose their affliction. Many are genetically predisposed to it; and then many others are simply trying to escape the psychological trauma of having been abused as children. Alcoholics deserve our sympathy and understanding rather than our vilification and condemnation.

★4. Whoever thrusts a knife into another person should be arrested. But surgeons do precisely this when operating. Therefore, surgeons should be arrested.

5. You should read Irving Stone's latest novel right away. It's sold over a million copies, and practically everyone in the Manhattan cocktail circuit is talking about it.

6. Friederich Nietzsche's philosophy is not worth the paper it's printed on. Nietzsche was an immoral reprobate who went completely insane from syphilis before he died.

★7. It is financially advisable for you to join our protective organization. Think of all the money you will lose in broken windows, overturned trucks, and damaged merchandise in the event of your not joining.

8. Senator Barrow advocates increased social security benefits for the poor. It is regrettable that the senator finds it necessary to advocate socialism. Socialism has been tried for over seventy years in Russia, and it has been a miserable failure. A capitalistic free market has always been more efficient and productive and, without question, will continue to be so.

9. Something is seriously wrong with high school education these days. After ten years of decline, SAT scores are still extremely low, and high school graduates are practically incapable of reading and writing. The obvious conclusion is that we should close the schools.

★10. The editors of the *Daily Register* have accused our company of being one of the city's worst water polluters. But the *Daily Register* is responsible for much more pollution than we are. After all, they own the Western Paper Company, and that company discharges tons of chemical residue into the city's river every day.

11. If 20 percent of adult Americans are functionally illiterate, then it's no wonder that morons get elected to public office. In fact, 20 percent of adult Americans *are* functionally illiterate. Therefore, it's no wonder that morons get elected to public office.

12. Ladies and gentlemen, today the lines of battle have been drawn. When the din of clashing armor has finally died away, the Republican party will emerge victorious! We are the true party of the American people! We embody the values that all real Americans hold sacred! We cherish and protect our founding fathers' vision that gave birth to the Constitution! We stand for decency and righteousness; for self-determination and the liberty to conduct our affairs as each of us freely chooses! In the face of our standard bearing the American eagle of freedom, our muddle-headed, weak-kneed opponents with their collectivist mentalities and their deluded programs for social reform will buckle and collapse! Victory will be ours, so help us God!

★13. We've all heard the argument that too much television is the reason our students can't read and write. Yet, many of today's TV shows are excellent. "L.A. Law" provides a genuine insight into the workings of the big city law firm, "Cheers" is an inspired human interest program, and "The Bill Cosby Show" engages the whole family. Today's TV is just great!

14. Surely you will not hold architect Norris responsible for the collapse of the Central Bank Tower. Norris has had nothing but trouble lately. His daughter eloped with a child molester, his son committed suicide, and his alcoholic wife recently left for Las Vegas with his retirement savings.

15. The First Amendment to the Constitution prevents the government from interfering with the free exercise of religion. The liturgical practice of the Religion of Internal Enlightenment involves the use of opium. Therefore, it would be wrong for the government to interfere with this religious practice.

★16. Senator Proxmire has argued persuasively in favor of price supports for dairy products. However, since Proxmire represents a state with a huge dairy industry, he would be expected to advocate price supports. Therefore, we should discount Proxmire's argument.

17. Professor Pearson's arguments in favor of the theory of evolution should be discounted. Pearson is a cocaine-snorting sex pervert and, according to some reports, a member of the Communist party.

18. Rudolf Hoess, commandant of the Auschwitz concentration camp, confessed to having exterminated one million people, most of whom were Jews, in the Auschwitz gas chamber. We can only conclude that Hoess was either insane or an extremely evil person.

★19. Dr. Redding has argued in favor of high IQ sperm banks to allow women who so choose to increase the chance of giving birth to a highly intelligent baby by being artificially inseminated. Obviously Dr. Redding advocates racism. Racism has no place in a civilized society. The racist eugenic theories of Adolf Hitler were rejected by the entire civilized world. Dr. Redding's proposal should be treated accordingly.

20. I know that some of you oppose the appointment of David Cole as the new sales manager. Upon further consideration, however, I am confident you will change your minds. If Cole is not appointed, it may become necessary to make severe personnel cutbacks in your department.

21. The social reformers are always arguing for an increase in the minimum wage. But many Third World nations don't even have a minimum wage. Instead of giving these countries aid in the form of guns and planes, we should be concerned about the plight of their faceless populations. Medicine, food, and clothing are what these people need so desperately. We certainly have the means to respond to that need. We should lose no time in doing so.

★22. Of course you want to buy a pair of Slinky fashion jeans. Slinky jeans really show off your figure, and all the Hollywood starlets down on the Strip can be seen wearing them these days.

23. Without even the slightest shred of evidence to support his position, Senator Arlen Specter of Pennsylvania has announced the need for tariffs and quotas on imported steel. Obviously the senator wants to protect the industry of his home state. He cares nothing for the increased construction cost that such a policy would cause. Senator Specter's idea should be rejected forthright.

24. Dr. Morrison has argued that smoking is responsible for the majority of health problems in this country and that every smoker who has even the slightest concern for his or her health should quit. Unfortunately, however, we must consign Dr. Morrison's argument to the trash bin. Only yesterday I saw none other than Dr. Morrison himself smoking a cigar.

★25. Mr. Rhodes is suffering from amnesia and has no recollection whatever of the events of the past two weeks. We can only conclude that he did not commit the crime of murdering his wife a week ago, as he has been accused of doing.

II. Answer "true" or "false" to the following statements:

1. In the appeal to force, the arguer physically attacks the listener.

2. In the direct variety of the appeal to the people, the arguer attempts to create a kind of mob mentality.

3. In the indirect variety of the appeal to the people, the arguer need not address more than a single individual.

4. The argument against the person (*argumentum ad hominem*) always involves two arguers.

5. In the *argumentum ad hominem* circumstantial, the circumstances cited by the second arguer are intended precisely to malign the character of the first arguer.

6. In the *tu quoque* fallacy, the arguer threatens the reader or listener.

7. In the fallacy of accident, a general rule is applied to a specific case where it does not fit.

8. In the straw man fallacy, an arguer often distorts another person's argument by making it look more extreme than it really is.

9. Whenever one suspects that a missing the point fallacy is being committed, one should be able to state the conclusion that is logically implied by the premises.

10. In the red herring fallacy, the arguer attempts to lead the reader or listener off the track.

3.3 FALLACIES OF WEAK INDUCTION

The **fallacies of weak induction** occur not because the premises are logically irrelevant to the conclusion, as is the case with the eight fallacies of relevance, but because the connection between premises and conclusion is not strong enough to support the conclusion. In each of the following fallacies, the premises provide at least a shred of evidence in support of the conclusion, but the evidence is not nearly good enough to cause a reasonable person to believe the conclusion. Like the fallacies of relevance, however, the fallacies of weak induction often involve emotional grounds for believing the conclusion.

9. Appeal to Authority (*Argumentum ad Verecundiam*)

We saw in Chapter 1 that an argument from authority is an inductive argument in which an arguer cites the authority or testimony of another person in support of some conclusion. The **appeal to authority** fallacy is a variety of the argument from authority and occurs when the cited authority or witness is not qualified or there is reason to believe that the person is mistaken, biased, or lying. For example:

> Dr. Bradshaw, our family physician, has stated that the creation of muonic atoms of deuterium and tritium hold the key to producing a sustained nuclear fusion reaction at room temper-

ature. In view of Dr. Bradshaw's expertise as a physician, we conclude that this is indeed true.

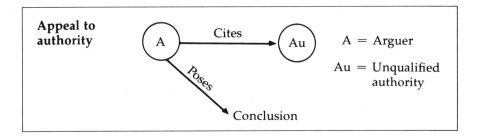

The conclusion of this argument deals with nuclear physics. Because it is highly improbable that a family physician should be an expert in nuclear physics, the argument commits an appeal to authority.

In deciding whether someone is a qualified authority, there are three important points to keep in mind. First, someone might be an authority in more than one field, and second, someone who is an authority in relation to one group of people might not be so in relation to another group. For example, a woman might be an authority in both chemistry and medicine, but this same woman, while she might be an authority in relation to any number of nonphysicians, might not be an authority in relation to her colleagues within the medical profession.

The third point to keep in mind is that there are some areas of argumentation where it often happens that practically no one can be considered an authority. Such areas include politics, morals, and religion. For example, if someone were to argue that abortion is immoral because a certain philosopher or religious leader has said so, the argument would be weak regardless of the authority's qualifications. Many questions in these areas are so hotly contested that there is no conventional wisdom an authority can depend on.

We stated earlier that appeals to authority can also involve witnesses. Here are two examples.

> Mob leader Gino Gambino has testified under oath that he clearly saw his rival Franco Frattiano murder the victim in cold blood with a sawed-off shotgun. Therefore, members of the jury, your only alternative is to find Frattiano guilty of murder.

> Paula Robertson, who has an excellent reputation for telling the truth, has testified under oath that she saw Micky ("Quick Fingers") Hogan pick Tom Ryan's pocket while she observed them from a distance of 100 yards. Therefore, even though Robertson is blind in one eye and has cataracts in the other, we must conclude that Micky is guilty as charged.

The credibility of a witness depends on various factors, including whether the witness has the capacity to perceive, remember, and communicate what he or she claims to have seen or heard, and whether the witness has some motive to lie. In the first argument, the witness, who probably lacks a reputation for truthfulness, testified that he saw his *rival* murder someone. Since the witness would probably be interested in sending such a rival to jail, the testimony is virtually worthless, and the argument is therefore fallacious.

In the second argument, the fact that the witness has a reputation for truthfulness has little relevance. Since the witness is practically blind, she could hardly have seen the crime from a distance of 100 yards. Thus, the argument based on her testimony is fallacious.

Now let us suppose someone attempts to discredit an argument involving an appeal to authority by discrediting the authority or witness appealed to. Does such an argument commit an argument against the person fallacy? The answer is no, because the argument against the person always involves an attack on an arguer, and mere statements by an authority or witness are not arguments. For example, suppose that Frattiano's attorney were to respond to the argument above with the following argument:

> Members of the jury, Gino Gambino is a notorious liar, and he has every reason to want the defendant, Franco Frattiano, sent to prison for the rest of his life. Therefore, his testimony is worthless, and you must find the defendant not guilty.

This argument commits no fallacy because the person attacked (Gambino) is not an arguer. Gambino's testimony does not consist of arguments but rather statements about what he claims to have seen and heard. For an *ad hominem* to be committed, the person attacked must be an *arguer*.

10. Appeal to Ignorance (*Argumentum ad Ignorantiam*)

When the premises of an argument state that nothing has been proved one way or the other about something, and the conclusion then makes a definite assertion about that thing, the argument commits an **appeal to ignorance.** The issue usually involves something that is incapable of being proved or something that has not yet been proved. Example:

> People have been trying for centuries to provide conclusive evidence for the claims of astrology, and no one has ever succeeded. Therefore, we must conclude that astrology is a lot of nonsense.

Conversely, the following argument commits the same fallacy.

People have been trying for centuries to disprove the claims of astrology, and no one has ever succeeded. Therefore, we must conclude that the claims of astrology are true.

The premises of an argument are supposed to provide positive evidence for the conclusion. The premises of these arguments, however, tell us nothing about astrology; rather, they tell us about what certain unnamed and unidentified people have tried unsuccessfully to do. This evidence may provide some slight reason for believing the conclusion, but certainly not sufficient reason.

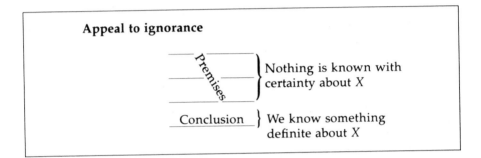

Appeal to ignorance

Premises } Nothing is known with certainty about X

Conclusion } We know something definite about X

These examples do, however, lead us to the first of two important exceptions to the appeal to ignorance. The first stems from the fact that if qualified researchers investigate a certain phenomenon within their range of expertise and fail to turn up any evidence that the phenomenon exists, this fruitless search by itself constitutes positive evidence about the question. Consider, for example, the following argument:

Teams of scientists attempted over a number of decades to detect the existence of the luminiferous aether, and all failed to do so. Therefore, the luminiferous aether does not exist.

The premises of this argument are true. Given the circumstances, it is likely that the scientists in question would have detected the aether if in fact it did exist. Since they did not detect it, it probably does not exist. Thus, we can say that the above argument is inductively strong (but not deductively valid).

As for the two arguments about astrology, if the attempts to prove or disprove the astrological claims had been done in a systematic way by qualified experts, it is more likely that the arguments would be good. Exactly what is required to qualify someone to investigate astrological claims is, of course, difficult to say. But as these arguments stand, the premises state nothing about the qualifications of the investigators, and so the arguments remain fallacious.

It is not *always* necessary, however, that the investigators have *special*

A CONCISE INTRODUCTION TO LOGIC

qualifications. The kinds of qualifications needed depend on the situation. Sometimes the mere ability to see and report what one sees is sufficient. Example:

> No one has ever seen Mr. Andrews drink a glass of wine, beer, or any other alcoholic beverage. Probably Mr. Andrews is a nondrinker.

Because it is highly probable that if Mr. Andrews were a drinker, somebody would have seen him drinking, this argument is inductively strong. No special qualifications are needed to be able to see someone take a drink.

The second exception to the appeal to ignorance relates to courtroom procedure. In the United States and Canada, among other countries, a person is presumed innocent until proven guilty. If the prosecutor in a criminal trial fails to prove the guilt of the defendant beyond reasonable doubt, counsel for the defense may justifiably argue that his or her client is not guilty. Example:

> Members of the jury, you have heard the prosecution present its case against the defendant. Nothing, however, has been proved beyond a reasonable doubt. Therefore, under the law, the defendant is not guilty.

This argument commits no fallacy because "not guilty" means, in the legal sense, that guilt beyond a reasonable doubt has not been proved. The defendant may indeed have committed the crime of which he or she is accused, but if the prosecutor fails to prove guilt beyond a reasonable doubt, the defendant is considered "not guilty".

11. Hasty Generalization (Converse Accident)

Hasty generalization is a fallacy that affects inductive generalizations. In Chapter 1 we saw that an inductive generalization is an argument that draws a conclusion about all members of a group from evidence that pertains to a selected sample. The fallacy occurs when there is a likelihood that the sample is not representative of the group. Such a likelihood may arise if the sample is either too small or not randomly selected. Here are two examples:

> After only one year the alternator went out in Mr. O'Grady's new Chevrolet. Mrs. Dodson's Oldsmobile developed a transmission problem after six months. The conclusion is obvious that cars made by General Motors are just a pile of junk these days.

Two weeks ago the Ajax Pharmacy was robbed and the suspect is a black man. Yesterday a black teenager snatched an old lady's purse while she was waiting at the corner bus stop. Clearly, blacks are nothing but a pack of criminals.

In these arguments a conclusion about a whole group is drawn from premises that mention only two instances. Because such small, atypical samples are not sufficient to support a general conclusion, each argument commits a hasty generalization. The second example indicates how hasty generalization plays a role in racial (and religious) prejudice.

The mere fact that a sample may be small, however, does not necessarily entail that it is atypical. Sometimes other factors intervene that cause the argument to be strong in spite of the fact that the sample may be small. Examples:

Ten milligrams of substance Z was fed to four mice, and within two minutes all four went into shock and died. Probably substance Z, in this amount, is fatal to the average mouse.

On three separate occasions I drank a bottle of Figowitz beer and found it flat and bitter. Probably I would find every bottle of Figowitz beer flat and bitter.

Neither of these arguments commits the fallacy of hasty generalization because in neither case is there any likelihood that the sample is atypical of the group. In the first argument the fact that the mice died in only two minutes suggests the existence of a causal connection between eating substance Z and death. If there is such a connection, it would hold for other mice as well. In the second example the fact that the taste of beer typically remains constant from bottle to bottle causes the argument to be strong, even though only three bottles were sampled.

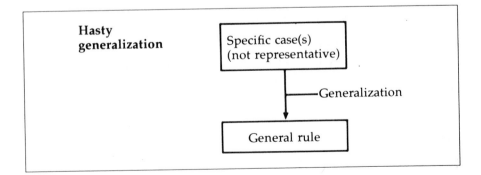

Hasty generalization is otherwise called "converse accident" because it proceeds in a direction opposite to that of accident. Whereas accident proceeds from the general to the particular, converse accident moves

A CONCISE INTRODUCTION TO LOGIC

from the particular to the general. The premises cite some characteristic affecting one or more atypical instances of a certain class, and the conclusion then applies that characteristic to all members of the class.

12. False Cause

[handwritten annotation: post hoc ergo procter hoc (temporal) / non cause pro cause]

The fallacy of **false cause** occurs whenever the link between premises and conclusion depends on some imagined causal connection that probably does not exist. Whenever an argument is suspected of committing the false cause fallacy, the reader or listener should be able to say that the conclusion depends on the supposition that X causes Y, whereas X probaby does not cause Y at all. Examples:

> During the past two months, every time that the cheerleaders have worn blue ribbons in their hair, the basketball team has been defeated. Therefore, to prevent defeats in the future, the cheerleaders should get rid of those blue ribbons.

> Successful business executives are paid salaries in excess of $50,000. Therefore, the best way to insure that Ferguson will become a successful executive is to raise his salary to at least $50,000.

> There are more laws on the books today than ever before, and more crimes are being committed than ever before. Therefore, to reduce crime we must eliminate the laws.

The first argument depends on the supposition that the blue ribbons caused the defeats, the second on the supposition that a high salary causes success, and the third on the supposition that laws cause crime. In no case is it likely that any causal connection exists.

The first argument illustrates a variety of the false cause fallacy called *post hoc ergo propter hoc* ("after this, therefore on account of this"). This variety of the fallacy presupposes that just because one event precedes another event the first event causes the second. Obviously, mere temporal succession is not sufficient to establish a causal connection. Nevertheless, this kind of reasoning is quite common and lies behind most forms of superstition. (Example: "A black cat crossed my path and later I tripped and sprained my ankle. It must be that black cats really are bad luck.")

The second and third arguments illustrate a variety of the false cause fallacy called *non causa pro causa* ("not the cause for the cause"). This variety is committed when what is taken to be the cause of something is not really the cause at all and the mistake is based on something other than mere temporal succession. In reference to the second argument, success as an executive causes increases in salary—not the other way around—so the argument mistakes the cause for the effect. In reference to the third argument, the increase in crime is, for the most part, only coincidental with the increase in the number of laws. Obviously, the mere fact that one event is coincidental with another is not sufficient reason to think that one caused the other.

The false cause fallacy is often convincing because it is sometimes difficult to determine whether two phenomena are causally related; and even when they are related, it is sometimes difficult to tell which is the cause and which the effect. One point that should be kept in mind when attempting to settle these issues is that statistical correlations by themselves often reveal little about what is actually going on. For example, if all that we knew about smoking and lung cancer is that the two frequently occur together, we might conclude any number of things. We might conclude that both have a common cause, such as a genetic predisposition, or we might conclude that lung cancer is a disease contracted early in life and that it manifests itself in its early stages by a strong desire for tobacco. Fortunately, in the case of smoking and lung cancer there is more evidence than a mere statistical correlation. This additional evidence inclines us to believe that the smoking is a cause of the cancer.

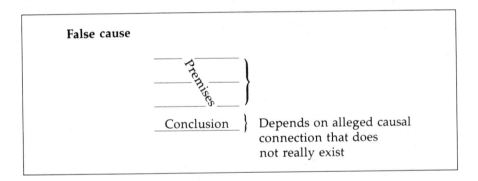

13. Slippery Slope

The fallacy of **slippery slope** is a variety of the false cause fallacy. It occurs when the conclusion of an argument rests upon the claim that a certain event will set off a chain reaction, leading in the end to some undesirable consequence, yet there is not sufficient reason to think that the chain reaction will actually take place. Here is an example:

> Immediate steps should be taken to outlaw pornography once and for all. The continued manufacture and sale of pornographic material will almost certainly lead to an increase in sex-related crimes such as rape and incest. This in turn will gradually erode the moral fabric of society and result in an increase in crimes of all sorts. Eventually a complete disintegration of

law and order will occur, leading in the end to the total collapse of civilization.

Because there is no good reason to think that the mere failure to outlaw pornography will result in all these dire consequences, this argument is fallacious. An equally fallacious counterargument is as follows:

> Attempts to outlaw pornography threaten basic civil rights and should be summarily abandoned. If pornography is outlawed, censorship of newspapers and news magazines is only a short step away. After that there will be censorship of textbooks, political speeches, and the content of lectures delivered by university professors. Complete mind control by the central government will be the inevitable result.

Both arguments attempt to persuade the reader or listener that the welfare of society rests on a "slippery slope" and that a single step in the wrong direction will result in an inevitable slide all the way to the bottom.

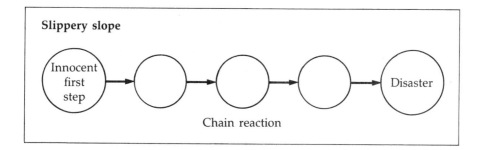

Deciding whether a slippery slope fallacy is or is not committed can be difficult when there is uncertainty whether the alleged chain reaction will or will not occur. This question is discussed in Section 3.5. But many slippery slopes rest on a mere emotional conviction on the part of the arguer that a certain action or policy is bad, and the arguer attempts to trump up support for his or her position by citing all sorts of dire consequences that will result if the action is taken or the policy followed. In such cases there is usually little problem in identifying the argument as a slippery slope.

14. Weak Analogy "False"

This fallacy affects inductive arguments from analogy. As we saw in Chapter 1, an argument from analogy is an argument in which the conclusion depends on the existence of an analogy, or similarity, between two things or situations. The fallacy of **weak analogy** is committed when the analogy is not strong enough to support the conclusion that is drawn. Example:

> Harper's new car is bright blue, has leather upholstery, and gets excellent gas mileage. Crowley's new car is also bright blue and has leather upholstery. Therefore, it probably gets excellent gas mileage, too.

Because the color of a car and the choice of upholstery have nothing to do with gasoline consumption, this argument is fallacious.

The basic structure of an argument from analogy is as follows:

> Entity A has attributes $a, b, c,$ and z.
> Entity B has attributes a, b, c.
> Therefore, entity B probably has attribute z also.

Evaluating an argument having this form requires a two-step procedure: (1) Identify the attributes $a, b, c, \ldots$ that the two entities A and B share in common, and (2) determine how the attribute z, mentioned in the conclusion, relates to the attributes $a, b, c, \ldots$ If some causal or systematic relation exists between z and $a, b,$ or c, the argument is strong; otherwise it is weak. In the argument above, the two entities share the attributes of being cars, the attributes entailed by being a car, such as having four wheels, and the attributes of color and upholstery material. Because none of these attributes is systematically or causally related to good gas mileage, the argument is fallacious.

As an illustration of when the requisite systematic or causal relation does and does not exist, consider the following arguments:

> The flow of electricity through a wire is similar to the flow of water through a pipe. Obviously a small-diameter pipe will carry a lesser flow of water than a pipe of large diameter. For analogous reasons, therefore, we should expect a small-diameter wire to carry a lesser flow of electricity than a large-diameter wire.

> The flow of electricity through a wire is similar to the flow of water through a pipe. When water runs downhill through a pipe, the pressure at the bottom of the hill is greater than it is at the top. Thus, when electricity flows downhill through a wire, we would expect the voltage to be greater at the bottom of the hill than at the top.

The first argument is good and the second is fallacious. Both arguments depend on the similarity between water molecules flowing through a pipe and electrons flowing through a wire. In both cases there is a systematic relation between the diameter of the pipe/wire and the amount of flow. In the first argument this systematic relation provides

A CONCISE INTRODUCTION TO LOGIC

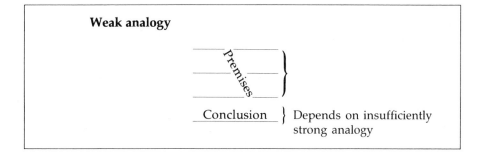

Weak analogy

Premises

Conclusion } Depends on insufficiently strong analogy

a strong link between premises and conclusion, and so the argument is a good one. But in the second argument a causal connection exists between difference in elevation and increase in pressure that holds for water but not for electricity. Water molecules flowing through a pipe are affected by gravity, but electrons flowing through a wire are not. Thus, the second argument is fallacious.

The theory and evaluation of arguments from analogy is one of the most complex and elusive subjects in all of logic. No complete treatment of the subject is attempted in this text, but a few of the problems that arise in this connection are taken up in Section 3.5.

EXERCISE 3.3

I. Identify the fallacies of weak induction committed by the following arguments. If no fallacy is committed, write "no fallacy."

★1. The *Daily News* carried an article this morning about three local teenagers who were arrested on charges of drug possession. Teenagers these days are nothing but a bunch of junkies.

2. If an automobile breaks down on the highway, no one expects a passing mechanic to be obligated to render emergency road service. For similar reasons, physicians should never be expected to render emergency medical assistance.

3. There must be something to psychical research. Three famous physicists, Oliver Lodge, James Jeans, and Arthur Stanley Eddington, took it seriously.

★4. The secretaries have asked us to provide lounge areas where they can spend their coffee breaks. This request will have to be refused. If we give them lounge areas, next they'll be asking for spas and swimming pools. Then it will be racquetball courts, tennis courts, and fitness centers. Expenditures for these facilities will drive us into bankruptcy.

5. The accumulation of pressure in a society is similar to the build-up of pressure in a boiler. If the pressure in a boiler increases beyond a critical point, the boiler will explode. Accordingly, if a government represses its people beyond a certain point, the people will rise up in revolt.

6. A few minutes after Governor Harrison finished his speech on television, a devastating earthquake struck southern Alaska. For the safety of the people up there, it is imperative that Governor Harrison make no more speeches.

★7. No one has ever been able to prove the existence of extrasensory perception. We must therefore conclude that extrasensory perception is a myth.

8. Lester Brown, universally respected author of the yearly *State of the World* report, has said that cutting down tropical rain forests is one of the ten most serious worldwide problems. Thus, it must be the case that this is indeed a very serious problem.

9. Governor Turner is prejudiced against Catholics. During his first week in office, he appointed three people to important offices, and all three were Protestants.

★10. Pianist Ray Charles says that Sinclair paints are groovy. We can only conclude that Sinclair paints are very groovy indeed.

11. Probably no life exists on Venus. Teams of scientists have conducted exhaustive studies of the planet's surface and atmosphere, and no living organisms have been found.

12. We don't dare let the animal rights activists get their foot in the door. If they sell us on the idea that dogs, cats, and dolphins have rights, next it will be chickens and cows. That means no more chicken Kiev or prime rib. Next it will be worms and insects. This will lead to the decimation of our agricultural industry. The starvation of the human race will follow close behind.

★13. No one would buy a pair of shoes without trying them on. Why should anyone be expected to get married without premarital sex?

14. No one has proved conclusively that America's nuclear power plants constitute a danger to people living in their immediate vicinity. Therefore, it is perfectly safe to continue to build nuclear power plants near large metropolitan centers.

15. There are more churches in New York City than in any other city in the nation, and more crimes are committed in New York City than anywhere else. So, if we are to eliminate crime, we must abolish the churches.

II. Answer "true" or "false" to the following statements:

1. If an arguer cites a statement by a qualified authority in support of a conclusion, the arguer commits the appeal to authority fallacy.
   F

2. If an attorney argues that testimony should be ignored because the witness has a reputation for being a liar, the attorney commits an *ad hominem* abusive.
   F

3. In the appeal to ignorance, the arguer accuses the reader or listener of being ignorant.
   F

A CONCISE INTRODUCTION TO LOGIC

4. If an attorney for the defense in an American or Canadian criminal trial argues that the prosecution has proved nothing beyond a reasonable doubt about the guilt of the defendant, then the attorney commits an appeal to ignorance.

5. Hasty generalization always proceeds from the particular to the general.

6. The *post hoc ergo propter hoc* variety of the false cause fallacy presupposes that X causes Y merely because X happens before Y.

7. If an argument presupposes that X causes Y when in fact Y causes X, the argument commits the *non causa pro causa* variety of the false cause fallacy.

8. If the conclusion of an argument depends on the occurrence of a chain reaction of events, and there is good reason to believe that the chain reaction will actually occur, the argument commits a slippery slope fallacy.

9. The fallacy of weak analogy always depends on an alleged similarity between two things or situations.

10. If an argument from analogy depends on a causal or systematic relationship between certain attributes, and there is good reason to believe that this relationship exists, then the argument commits no fallacy.

III. Identify the fallacies of relevance and weak induction committed by the following arguments. If no fallacy is committed, write "no fallacy."

★1. On our first date, George had his hands all over me, and I found it nearly impossible to keep him in his place. A week ago Tom gave me that stupid line about how, in order to prove my love, I had to spend the night with him. Men are all alike. All any of them want is sex.

2. When a machine breaks down, mechanics dismantle it and replace the broken parts. Similarly, when the human body breaks down, it makes good sense to replace diseased organs with new ones—either from a donor or artificially manufactured.

3. Senator Alan Cranston has argued at length in favor of the B-1 bomber. But the B-1 is to be manufactured in California, which is the state Cranston represents. Therefore, Cranston's argument is nonsense.

★4. Witness Taylor testified that she heard defendant Williams conspire with codefendant Pierson while the two were sitting in the next room with the door closed. Thus, we must conclude that Williams is guilty of conspiracy, even though Taylor is very hard of hearing and her hearing aid was shut off at the time.

5. What the farmer sows in the spring he reaps in the fall. In the spring he sows $8-per-bushel soybeans. Therefore, in the fall he will reap $8-per-bushel soybeans.

6. Physicist Edward Teller has stated that the Strategic Defense Initiative (Star Wars) could be defeated by Soviet missiles at one-tenth the cost of deploying it. In view of the fact that Teller would ordinarily be expected to support Star Wars, we must conclude that deployment is not justified.

★7. Animals and humans are similar in many ways. Both experience sensations, desires, fears, pleasures, and pains. Humans have a right not to be subjected to needless pain. Does it not follow that animals have a right not to be subjected to needless pain?

8. Johnny, I know you'll lend me your bicycle for the afternoon. After all, I'm sure you wouldn't want your mother to find out that you played hooky today.

9. As a businessperson you certainly want to subscribe to *Forbes* magazine. Virtually all the successful business executives in the country subscribe to it.

★10. Ellen Quinn has argued that logic is not the most important thing in life. Apparently Ellen advocates irrationality. It has taken two million years for the human race to achieve the position that it has, and Ellen would throw the whole thing into the garbage. What utter nonsense!

11. When water is poured on the top of a pile of rocks, it always trickles down to the rocks on the bottom. Similarly, when rich people make lots of money, we can expect this money to trickle down to the poor.

12. Extensive laboratory tests have failed to prove any deleterious side effects of the new pain killer lexaprine. We conclude that lexaprine is safe for human consumption.

★13. City officials have argued recently about the need for government aid to the homeless. But unfortunately, high-density public housing projects have been tried in the past and have failed. In no time such projects turn into ghettos with astronomical rates of crime and delinquency. Chicago's Cabrini-Green is a prime example. No sane urban planner would ever consider such projects today.

14. Mr. Scott's arguments in favor of increasing teacher salaries are totally worthless. Scott, as you all know, has a criminal record as long as my arm, and only a week ago he was released from the state prison after having served a two-year term for car theft.

15. The operation of a camera is similar in many ways to the operation of an eye. If we are to see anything in a darkened room, the pupils of your eyes must first dilate. Accordingly, if we are to take a photograph (without flash) in a darkened room, the aperature of the camera lens must first be opened.

★16. Certainly Miss Malone will be a capable and efficient manager. She has a great figure, a gorgeous face, and tremendous poise, and she dresses very fashionably.

17. Actor Martin Sheen has said that we should stop nuclear testing immediately. Therefore, it certainly follows that we should do this.

18. The internationally respected organization Amnesty International stated in its annual report that the systematic torture of political prisoners by right-wing paramilitary squads is widespread in Chile. Therefore, it is probably true that such torture is widespread in Chile.

★19. To prevent dangerous weapons from being carried aboard airliners, those seeking to board must pass through a magnetometer and submit to a possible pat-down search. Therefore, to prevent alcohol and drugs from being carried into rock concerts, it is appropriate that those entering submit to similar search procedures.

20. Mr. Flemming's arguments against the rent control initiative on the September ballot should be taken with a grain of salt. As a landlord he would naturally be expected to oppose the initiative.

21. India recently suffered a serious drought, thousands of children are dying of starvation in their mothers' arms, and homeless beggars line the streets of the major cities. Surely these poor downtrodden people should be given the chance of bettering their condition in America, the land of wealth and opportunity.

★22. Members of the jury, you have heard Shirley Gaines testify that she observed the entire scene and that at no time did the defendant offer to perform acts of prostitution for the undercover police officer. But Gaines is a known prostitute herself and a close friend of the defendant. Also, only a year ago she was convicted of twelve counts of perjury. Therefore, you should certainly discount Gaines's testimony.

23. It is ridiculous to hear that man from Peru complaining about America's poverty. Peru has twice as much poverty as America has ever had.

24. The secular humanists say that science comes closer to the truth than religion. But what kind of science is secular humanism? What kind of experiments does it conduct? Are its predictions fulfilled by subsequent discoveries? Is there a Nobel Prize awarded in the field of secular humanism? Clearly, the answer to all these questions is "no." We can only conclude that the secular humanists are preaching nonsense.

★25. No one has ever proved that massive federal deficits are actually harmful to the economy. We can only conclude that such deficits pose no real danger.

26. Freedom of speech is guaranteed by the First Amendment. Therefore, your friend was acting within his rights when he shouted "Fire! Fire!" in that crowded theater, even though it was only a joke.

27. No one, upon encountering a watch lying on a forest trail, would expect that it had simply appeared there without having been made by someone. For the same reason, no one should expect that the universe simply appeared without having been made by some being.

★28. On Monday I drank ten rum and Cokes, and the next morning I woke up with a headache. On Wednesday I drank eight gin and Cokes, and the next morning I woke up with a headache. On Friday I drank nine Bourbon and Cokes, and the next morning I woke up with a headache. Obviously, to prevent further headaches I must give up Coke.

29. The U.S. Committee for Nuclear Awareness says that nuclear power is safe and that it holds the answer for America's energy needs in the

years ahead. We can only conclude that the best policy is to push forward with nuclear power.

★30. Some of the parents in our school district have asked that we provide bilingual education in Spanish. This request will have to be denied. If we provide this service, then someone will ask for bilingual education in Greek. Then it will be German, French, and Hungarian. Polish, Russian, Chinese, Japanese, and Korean will follow close behind. We certainly can't accommodate all of them.

3.4 FALLACIES OF PRESUMPTION, AMBIGUITY, AND GRAMMATICAL ANALOGY

The **fallacies of presumption** include begging the question, complex question, false dichotomy, and suppressed evidence. These fallacies arise not because the premises are irrelevant to the conclusion or provide insufficient reason for believing the conclusion, but because the premises presume what they purport to prove. Begging the question attempts to hide the fact that a certain premise may not be true, and complex question attempts to trick the respondent into making some statement that will establish the truth of the presumption hidden in the question. The third fallacy of presumption, false dichotomy, presumes that an "either . . . or" statement presents mutually exhaustive alternatives.

The **fallacies of ambiguity** include equivocation and amphiboly. These fallacies arise from the occurrence of some form of ambiguity in either the premise or the conclusion (or both). In Chapter 2 we distinguished ambiguity from vagueness. We said that a term is vague if its meaning is blurred so that one cannot tell with any degree of precision whether or not it applies to a given situation. A term is ambiguous, on the other hand, if it is susceptible to different interpretations in a given context. Terms such as "light," "bank," and "race" lend themselves to ambiguous interpretations, while "love," "conservative," and "happiness" are often vague. As we will see in this section, ambiguity can affect not only terms but whole statements. When the conclusion of an argument depends on a certain interpretation being given to an ambiguous term or statement, the argument commits a fallacy of ambiguity.

The **fallacies of grammatical analogy** include composition and division. Arguments that commit these fallacies are grammatically analogous to other arguments that are good in every respect. Because of this similarity in linguistic structure, such fallacious arguments may appear good yet be bad.

15. Begging the Question (*Petitio Principii*)

Begging the question occurs when an arguer uses some form of phraseology that tends to conceal the questionably true character of a key premise. If the reader or listener is deceived into thinking that the key premise is true, he or she will accept the argument as sound, when in fact it may not be. Two requirements must be met for this fallacy to occur:

1. The argument must be valid.

2. Some form of phraseology must be used to conceal the questionably true character of a key premise.

The kind of phraseology used varies from argument to argument, but it often involves using the conclusion to support the questionable premise. One way of accomplishing this is to phrase the argument so that the premise and conclusion say the same thing in two slightly different ways. Example:

> Capital punishment is justified for the crimes of murder and kidnapping because it is quite legitimate and appropriate that someone be put to death for having committed such hateful and inhuman acts.

To say that capital punishment is "justified" means the same thing as to say that it is "legitimate and appropriate." Because premise and conclusion mean the same thing, it is obvious that if the premise is true, the conclusion is also true; so the argument is valid. The only question that remains is whether the premise is true. When read apart from the context of the argument, the premise is questionable, at best. But when it is preceded by the conclusion, as it is here, the alleged truth is strengthened. This strengthening is caused by the psychological illusion that results from saying the same thing in two slightly different ways. When a single proposition is repeated in two or more ways without the repetition becoming obvious, the suggested truth of the proposition is reinforced.

Another form of begging the question affects chains of arguments. Example: *Circular reasoning*

> Ford Motor Company clearly produces the finest cars in the United States. We know they produce the finest cars because they have the best design engineers. The reason why they have the best design engineers is because they can afford to pay them more than other manufacturers. Obviously, they can afford to pay them more because they make the finest cars in the United States.

In this chain of arguments the final conclusion is stated first. The truth of this conclusion depends on each link in the chain, and ultimately on the first premise (stated last), which asserts the same thing as the final conclusion (stated first). This example illustrates why begging the question is frequently called circular reasoning. The artifice used in arguments such as this depends on the fact that several statements intervene between the final conclusion and the first premise. The reader or listener tends to get lost in the maze of arguments, and since every statement appears to be supported by some other statement, he or she can be fooled into thinking that the final conclusion is necessarily true. What the reader or listener may fail to recognize is that the truth of the final conclusion is really supported only by itself, and therefore by nothing at all.

A third form of begging the question occurs when a questionably true premise, which is needed to make the argument valid, is completely ignored. Example:

> Murder is morally wrong. This being the case, it follows that
> abortion is morally wrong.

The questionable premise that is ignored is, "Abortion is a form of murder." The argument begs the question, "How do you know that abortion is a form of murder?" The premise that is stated, of course, is undisputably true, and the phrase "This being the case" makes it appear that the stated premise is all that is needed. If the reader or listener concentrates on the truth of the stated premise and overlooks the fact that a highly questionable premise is needed to complete the argument, he or she is liable to accept the argument as immediately sound.

An essential characteristic of begging the question is that some form of phraseology be used that tends to conceal the questionably true character of a key premise. If this premise is obviously true, then no such concealment is relevant, and the fallacy cannot occur. Consider the following argument:

> Snow is white
> Therefore, snow is white.

This argument is valid and the premise is true. The argument is therefore sound and contains no fallacies. Many logic texts consider arguments such as this to be instances of begging the question, but according to the position taken here, these views are mistaken. Obviously, the argument is trivial, but mere triviality is not a fallacy.

Here is another example:

> Snow is black.
> Therefore, snow is black.

This argument is valid but has a false premise. Accordingly, the argument is unsound, but it commits no fallacy. Although the premise is false, there is no phraseology that tends to hide this fact, and so begging the question is not committed.

Literally, *petitio principii* means "postulation of the beginning." In other words, what the argument sets out to do in the beginning is postulated instead of proven. "Begging the question" means the same thing. The argument begs the question at issue; it asks that the statement to be proved be granted beforehand.

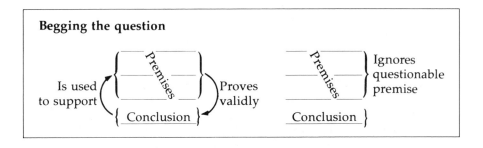

16. Complex Question   *Presumptive.*

The fallacy of **complex question** is committed when a single question that is really two (or more) questions is asked and the single answer is then applied to both questions. Every complex question presumes the existence of a certain condition. When the respondent's answer is added to the complex question, an argument emerges that establishes the presumed condition. Thus, although not an argument as such, a complex question involves an implicit argument. This argument is usually intended to trap the respondent into acknowledging something that he or she might otherwise not want to acknowledge. Examples:

> Have you stopped cheating on exams?
> Where did you hide the cookies you stole?

Let us suppose the respondent answers "yes" to the first question and "under the bed" to the second. The following arguments emerge:

> You were asked whether you have stopped cheating on exams. You answered "yes." Therefore, it follows that you have cheated in the past.

> You were asked where you hid the cookies you stole. You replied "under the bed." It follows that you did in fact steal the cookies.

On the other hand, let us suppose that the respondent answers "no" to the first question and "nowhere" to the second. We then have the following arguments:

You were asked whether you have stopped cheating on exams. You answered "no." Therefore, you continue to cheat.

You were asked where you hid the cookies you stole. You answered "nowhere." It follows that you must have stolen them and eaten them.

Obviously, each of the above questions is really two questions:

Did you cheat on exams in the past? If you did cheat in the past, have you stopped now?

Did you steal the cookies? If you did steal them, where did you hide them?

If respondents are not sophisticated enough to identify a complex question when one is put to them, they may answer quite innocently and be trapped by a conclusion that is supported by no evidence at all; or, they may be tricked into providing the evidence themselves. The correct response lies in resolving the complex question into its component questions and answering each separately.

The fallacy of complex question should be distinguished from another kind of question known in law as a leading question. A *leading*

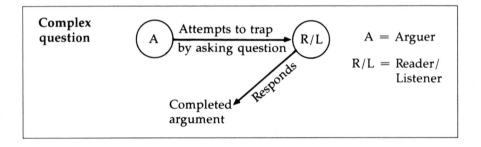

question is one in which the answer is in some way suggested in the question. Whether or not a question is a leading one is important in the direct examination of a witness by counsel. Example:

Tell us, on April 9, did you
see the defendant shoot the
deceased?   (leading question)

Tell us, what did you see on
April 9?   (straight question)

Leading questions differ from complex questions in that they involve no logical fallacies; that is, they do not attempt to trick the respondent into admitting something he or she does not want to admit. To

A CONCISE INTRODUCTION TO LOGIC

distinguish the two, however, it is sometimes necessary to know whether prior questions have been asked. Here are some additional examples of complex questions:

> Are you going to be a good little boy and eat your hamburger?
> Is George Hendrix still smoking marijuana?
> How long must I put up with your snotty behavior?
> When are you going to stop talking nonsense?

17. False Dichotomy

The fallacy of **false dichotomy** (otherwise called "false bifurcation" and the "either-or fallacy") is committed when one premise of an argument is an "either . . . or" (disjunctive) statement that presents two alternatives as if they were jointly exhaustive (i.e., as if no third alternative were possible). One of these alternatives is usually preferred by the arguer. When the arguer then proceeds to eliminate the undesirable alternative, the desirable one is left as the conclusion. Such an argument is clearly valid; but since the disjunctive premise is usually false, the argument is almost always unsound. Of course, not all unsound arguments are fallacious. The fallacious nature of false dichotomy lies in the attempt by the arguer to delude the reader or listener into thinking that the disjunctive premise presents jointly exhaustive alternatives and is therefore true by necessity. The fallacy is commonly committed by children and adolescents when arguing with their parents, by advertisers, and by adults generally. Here are some examples:

> Either you let me attend the Neil Diamond concert or I'll be miserable for the rest of my life. I know you don't want me to be miserable for the rest of my life, so it follows that you'll let me attend the concert.

> Either you use Ultra Guard deodorant or you risk the chance of perspiration odor. Surely you don't want to risk the chance of perspiration odor. Therefore, you will want to use Ultra Guard deodorant.

> Either you buy only American-made products or you don't deserve to be called a loyal American. Yesterday you bought a new Toyota. It's therefore clear that you don't deserve to be called a loyal American.

None of the disjunctive premises in these arguments presents alternatives that are jointly exhaustive. Yet in each case the arguer wants to make it appear that it does. For example, in the first argument the arguer wants to convey the illusion that either he or she goes to the concert or faces a lifetime of misery, and no other alternatives are possible. Clearly, however, such is not the case.

False dichotomy is classified as a fallacy of presumption because the soundness of the argument depends on the presumption that the two alternatives presented are the only ones that exist. If they are not the only ones that exist, the "either . . . or" statement is false, and the argument is unsound.

Most instances of false dichotomy are not presented as complete arguments. Only the disjunctive premise is expressed, and the arguer leaves it to the reader or listener to supply the missing parts:

> Either you buy me a new mink coat, or I'll freeze to death when winter comes.

> Either I continue smoking, or I'll get fat and you'll hate to be seen with me.

The missing premise and conclusion are easily introduced.

18. Suppressed Evidence   presumptive

The fallacy of **suppressed evidence** is committed when an arguer ignores evidence that would tend to undermine the premises of an otherwise good argument, causing it to be unsound or uncogent. Suppressed evidence is a fallacy of presumption and is closely related to begging the question. As such, its occurrence does not affect the relationship between premises and conclusion but rather the alleged truth of the premises. The fallacy consists in passing off what are at best half-truths as if they were the whole truth, thus making what is actually a defective argument appear to be good. The fallacy is especially common among arguers who have a vested interest in the situation to which the argument pertains. Consider, for example, the following argument dealing with the sale of a used car:

> *Used car salesman to buyer:* Mrs. Webb, I have just the car you
> need. This 1978 Chevrolet was recently traded in by a little old
> lady who kept it in the garage most of the time. The odometer
> reads low mileage, and the engine was recently tuned up. If you
> buy this car, it will give you trouble-free service for years.

Mrs. Webb accepts the salesman's argument and buys the car, only to have it fall apart two months later. Unfortunately, the salesman had failed to tell her that whenever the car was not in the garage the little old lady was driving it cross-country, that the odometer had rolled around twice, and that even though the engine was recently tuned up, it had two cracked pistons and a burned valve. By suppressing this evidence, the salesman made it appear that Mrs. Webb was getting a good deal, whereas in fact she was getting a pile of junk for her money.

Another form of suppressed evidence is committed by arguers who quote passages out of context from sources such as the Bible, the Constitution, and the Bill of Rights to support a conclusion that the passage was not intended to support. Consider, for example, the following argument against gun control:

> The Second Amendment to the Constitution states that the right of the people to keep and bear arms shall not be infringed. But a law controlling handguns would infringe on the right to keep and bear arms. Therefore, a law controlling handguns would be unconstitutional.

In fact, the Second Amendment reads, "A well regulated militia, being necessary to the security of a free state, the right of the people to keep and bear arms, shall not be infringed." In other words, the amendment states that the right to bear arms shall not be infringed when the arms are necessary for the preservation of a militia. Because a law controlling handguns (pistols) would have little effect on the preservation of a militia, it is unlikely that such a law would be unconstitutional. By ignoring the militia qualification, the first premise of the above argument makes it appear that *any* law controlling guns would be unconstitutional, which is clearly not the case. In fact, the Supreme Court has upheld a federal law banning the interstate shipment of sawed-off shotguns because these arms are unrelated to the preservation of a militia.

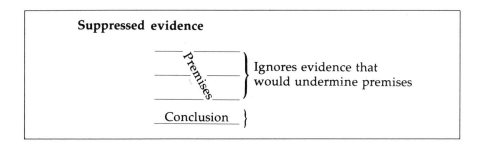

To detect the fallacy of suppressed evidence, the reader or listener must be cautious that the arguer is not ignoring evidence that has a bearing on the premises. This, in turn, requires a general knowledge of the topic to which the argument pertains and a familiarity with the devices used by unscrupulous individuals to pass off half-truths as the whole truth.

143

19. Equivocation

The fallacy of **equivocation** occurs when the conclusion of an argument depends on the fact that one or more words are used, either explicitly or implicitly, in two different senses in the argument. Either such arguments are invalid or a premise is false and the argument is unsound. Examples:

> Some triangles are obtuse. Whatever is obtuse is ignorant. Therefore, some triangles are ignorant.
>
> Any law can be repealed by the legislative authority. But the law of gravity is a law. Therefore, the law of gravity can be repealed by the legislative authority.
>
> We have a duty to do what is right. We have the right to speak out as we choose. Therefore, we have a duty to speak out as we choose.
>
> A mouse is an animal. Therefore, a large mouse is a large animal.

In the first argument "obtuse" is used in two different senses. In the first premise it describes a certain kind of angle, while in the second it means dull or stupid. The second argument equivocates on the word "law." In the first premise it means statutory law, and in the second it means law of nature. The third argument uses "right" in two senses. In the first premise "right" means morally correct, but in the second it means a just claim or power. The fourth argument illustrates the ambiguous use of a relative term. The word "large" means different things depending on the context. Other relative terms that are susceptible to this same kind of ambiguity include "small," "good," "bad," "light," "heavy," "difficult," "easy," "tall," "short," and so on.

For an argument that commits an equivocation to be convincing, it is essential that the equivocal term be used in two ways that are subtly related. For this reason the triangle argument would probably not convince anyone. It takes but a moment for the reader or listener to realize that something is wrong with this argument and only a few additional seconds to see that the problem stems from the equivocal use of a word. For the same reason, few would be fooled by the second example either; but there are some who might be taken in by the third. In the third example, both senses of the word "right" pertain to ethics, and the conclusion, if not true, is at least plausible. If the reader or listener fails to distinguish the two meanings of "right," he or she is liable to think that the conclusion follows from the premises, when in fact it does not.

Most actual occurrences of the fallacy of equivocation do not, however, occur in succinct, straightforward arguments such as those above. Rather, they occur in protracted, drawn out arguments of the sort found in political speeches. If a certain word gradually shifts in meaning throughout the duration of a lengthy speech, and different conclusions are drawn from the different meanings, detection of the fallacy becomes more difficult. Terms that lend themselves to this kind of meaning shift include "disarmament," "equal opportunity," "gun control," "national security," "balanced budget," and "environmental protection."

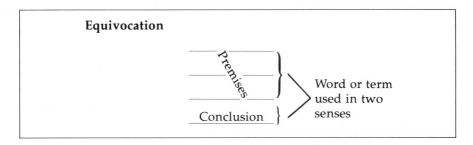

Another strategy used by speechmakers is to use a certain word in one sense when addressing one group of people and in quite another sense when addressing an opposing group. Depending on the specific usage, completely different conclusions may be drawn. For example, a speech-maker addressing a group of defense contractors might argue in favor of disarmament, but the context of the speech would make it clear that by "disarmament" he or she means the limitation of only a narrow range of weaponry. Such an interpretation would certainly please those in attendance. That same speechmaker, later addressing a group of antiwar militants, might again argue in favor of disarmament, but this time meaning the curtailment of all forms of weaponry. To detect the fallacy the listener would have to compare the two speeches.

20. Amphiboly   ambiguous

The fallacy of **amphiboly** occurs when the arguer misinterprets a statement that is ambiguous owing to some structural defect and proceeds to draw a conclusion based on this faulty interpretation. The original statement is usually asserted by someone other than the arguer, and the structural defect is usually a mistake in grammar or punctuation—a missing comma, a dangling modifier, an ambiguous antecedent of a pronoun, or some other careless arrangement of words. Because of this defect, the statement may be understood in two clearly distinguishable ways. The arguer typically selects the unintended interpretation and proceeds to draw a conclusion based upon it. Here are some examples:

> The tour guide said that standing in Greenwich Village, the Empire State Building could easily be seen. It follows that the Empire State Building is in Greenwich Village.

John told Henry that he had made a mistake. It follows that John has at least the courage to admit his own mistakes.

Professor Johnson said that he will give a lecture about heart failure in the biology lecture hall. It must be the case that a number of heart failures have occurred there recently.

The premise of the first argument contains a dangling modifier. Is it the observer or the Empire State Building that is supposed to be standing in Greenwich Village? The correct interpretation is the former. In the second argument the pronoun "he" has an ambiguous antecedent; it can refer either to John or to Henry. Perhaps John told Henry that *Henry* had made a mistake. In the third argument the ambiguity concerns what takes place in the biology lecture hall; is it the lecture or the heart failures? The correct interpretation is probably the former. The ambiguity can be eliminated by inserting commas ("Professor Johnson said that he will give a lecture, about heart failure, in the biology lecture hall") or by moving the ambiguous modifier ("Professor Johnson said that he will give a lecture in the biology lecture hall about heart failure").

Amphiboly differs from equivocation in two important ways. First, equivocation is always traced to an ambiguity in the meaning of one or more *words*, whereas amphiboly involves a structural defect in a *statement*. The second difference is that amphiboly usually involves a mistake made by the arguer in interpreting an ambiguous statement made by someone else, whereas the ambiguity in equivocation is typically the arguer's own creation. If these distinctions are kept in mind, it is usually easy to distinguish amphiboly from equivocation. Occasionally, however, the two fallacies occur together, as the following example illustrates:

> The *Great Western Cookbook* recommends that we serve the oysters when thoroughly stewed. Apparently the delicate flavor is enhanced by the intoxicated condition of the diners.

First, it is unclear whether "stewed" refers to the oysters or to the diners, and so the argument commits an amphiboly. But if "stewed" refers to the oysters it means "cooked," and if it refers to the diners it means "intoxicated." Thus, the argument also involves an equivocation.

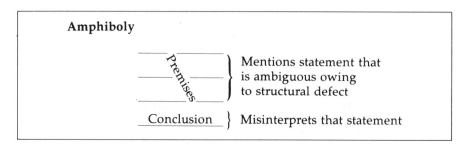

Amphiboly

Premises } Mentions statement that is ambiguous owing to structural defect

Conclusion } Misinterprets that statement

21. Composition

The fallacy of **composition** is committed when the conclusion of an argument depends on the erroneous transference of a characteristic from the parts of something onto the whole. In other words, the fallacy occurs when it is argued that because the parts have a certain characteristic, it follows that the whole has that characteristic, too, and the situation is such that the characteristic in question cannot be legitimately transferred from parts to whole. Examples:

> Maria likes anchovies. She also likes chocolate ice cream. Therefore, it is certain that she would like a chocolate sundae topped with anchovies.

> Each player on this basketball team is an excellent athlete. Therefore, the team as a whole is excellent.

> Each atom in this piece of chalk is invisible. Therefore, the chalk is invisible.

> Sodium and chlorine, the atomic components of salt, are both deadly poisons. Therefore, salt is a deadly poison.

In these arguments the characteristics that are transferred from the parts onto the whole are designated by the words "Maria likes," "excellent," "invisible," and "deadly poison," respectively. In each case the transference is illegitimate, and so the argument is fallacious.

Not every such transference is illegitimate, however. Consider the following arguments:

> Every atom in this piece of chalk has mass. Therefore, the piece of chalk has mass.

> Every picket in this picket fence is white. Therefore, the whole fence is white.

In each case a characteristic (having mass, being white) is transferred from the parts onto the whole, but these transferences are quite legitimate. Indeed, the fact that the atoms have mass is the very reason *why* the chalk has mass. The same reasoning extends to the fence. Thus, the validity of these arguments is attributable, at least in part, to the *legitimate* transference of a characteristic from parts onto whole.

These examples illustrate the fact that the fallacy of composition is indeed an informal fallacy. It cannot be discovered by a mere inspection of the form of an argument; that is, by the mere observation that a characteristic is being transferred from parts onto whole. In addition, detecting this fallacy requires a general knowledge of the situation and of the nature of the characteristic being transferred. The critic must be certain that, given the situation, the transference of this particular characteristic is not allowed.

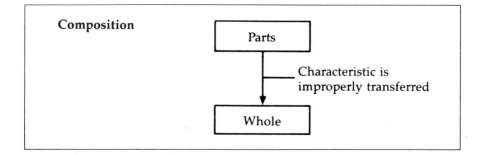

Composition

Parts

Characteristic is
improperly transferred

Whole

Further caution is required by the fact that composition is sometimes confused with hasty generalization. The only time this confusion is possible is when the "whole" is a class (such as the class of people in a city or the class of trees in a forest), and the "parts" are the members of the class. In such a case composition proceeds from the members of the class to the class itself. Hasty generalization, on the other hand, proceeds from the specific to the general. Because it is sometimes easy to mistake a statement about a class for a general statement, composition can be mistaken for hasty generalization. Such a mistake can be avoided if one is careful to keep in mind the distinction between a general statement and a class statement. This distinction falls back on the difference between the **collective** and the **distributive** predication of an attribute. Consider the following statements:

> Fleas are small.
> Fleas are numerous.

The first statement is a general statement. The attribute of being small is predicated distributively; that is, it is assigned (or distributed) to each and every flea in the class. Each and every flea in the class is said to be small. The second statement, on the other hand, is a class statement. The attribute of being numerous is predicated collectively; in other words, it is assigned not to the individual fleas but to the *class* of fleas. The meaning of the statement is not that each and every flea is numerous but that the class of fleas is large.

To distinguish composition from hasty generalization, therefore, the following procedure should be followed. Examine the conclusion of the argument. If the conclusion is a general statement, that is, a statement in which an attribute is predicated distributively to each and every member of a class, the fallacy committed is hasty generalization. But if the conclusion is a class statement, that is, a statement in which an attribute is predicated collectively to a class as a whole, the fallacy is composition. Example:

Less gasoline is consumed by a car than by a truck. Therefore, less gasoline is consumed in the United States by cars than by trucks.

At first sight this argument might appear to proceed from the specific to the general and, consequently, to commit a hasty generalization. But in fact the conclusion is not a general statement at all but a class statement. The conclusion states that the whole class of cars uses less gas than does the whole class of trucks (which is false, because there are many more cars than trucks). Since the attribute of using less gasoline is predicated collectively, the fallacy committed is composition.

22. Division   *grammatical*

The fallacy of **division** is the exact reverse of composition. As composition goes from parts to whole, division goes from whole to parts. The fallacy is committed when the conclusion of an argument depends on the erroneous transference of a characteristic from a whole (or a class) onto its parts (or members). Examples:

Salt is a nonpoisonous compound. Therefore, its component elements, sodium and chlorine, are nonpoisonous.

This jigsaw puzzle, when assembled, is circular in shape. Therefore, each piece is circular in shape.

The Royal Society is over 300 years old. Professor Thompson is a member of the Royal Society. Therefore, Professor Thompson is over 300 years old.

In each case a characteristic, designated respectively by the terms "nonpoisonous," "circular in shape," and "over 300 years old," is illegitimately transferred from the whole or class onto the parts or members. As with the fallacy of composition, however, this kind of transference is not always illegitimate. The following arguments are valid:

This piece of chalk has mass. Therefore, the atoms that compose this piece of chalk have mass.

This field of poppies is uniformly orange in color. Therefore, the individual poppies are orange in color.

Obviously, one must be acquainted with the situation and the nature of the characteristic being transferred to decide whether the fallacy of division is actually committed.

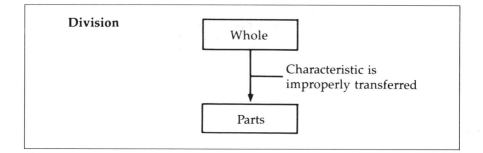

Division

Whole

Characteristic is improperly transferred

Parts

Just as composition is sometimes prone to being confused with hasty generalization (converse accident), division is sometimes prone to being confused with accident. As with composition, this confusion can occur only when the "whole" is a class. In such a case, division proceeds from the class to the members, while accident proceeds from the general to the specific. Thus, if a class statement is mistaken for a general statement, division may be mistaken for accident. To avoid such a mistake, one should analyze the premises of the argument. If the premises contain a general statement, the fallacy committed is accident; but if they contain a class statement, the fallacy is division. Example:

> Stanley Steamers have almost disappeared.
> This car is a Stanley Steamer.
> Therefore, this car has almost disappeared.

The first premise is not a general statement but a class statement. The attribute of having almost disappeared is predicated collectively. Accordingly, the fallacy committed is division, not accident. Sometimes, however, it is more difficult to decide whether a certain statement is a general or a class statement. Consider the following argument:

> The average American family has 2.5 children.
> The Jones family is an average American family.
> Therefore, the Jones family has 2.5 children.

Is the statement "The average American family has 2.5 children" a general statement or a class statement? While at first glance it might appear to make an assertion about each and every family, the sense of the statement is clearly *not* that each and every family has 2.5 children. In other words, the attribute of having 2.5 children is not predicated distributively, so the statement is not a general statement. Upon further analysis we see that saying that the *average* family has 2.5 children is equivalent to saying that the *class* of families is reducible to 55% children and 45% adults. In other words, the first premise is really a class statement, and so, once again, the fallacy is division, not accident.

A CONCISE INTRODUCTION TO LOGIC

In the foregoing account of composition and division, we have presented examples of arguments that commit these fallacies in conjunction with other, structurally similar arguments that do not. Because of the structural similarity between arguments that do and do not commit these fallacies, composition and division are classified as fallacies of grammatical analogy.

EXERCISE 3.4

I. Identify the fallacies of presumption, ambiguity, and grammatical analogy committed by the following arguments. If no fallacy is committed, write "no fallacy."

★1. Either we commit ourselves to massive increases in defense spending, or we will fall behind the Soviets in the ever-accelerating arms race. We certainly cannot afford to fall behind the Soviets. Therefore, we must commit ourselves to massive increases in defense spending.

2. Every sentence in this paragraph is well written. Therefore, the paragraph is well written.

3. A salesman is a human being. Therefore, a good salesman is a good human being.

★4. James said that he saw a picture of a beautiful girl stashed in Stephen's locker. We can only conclude that Stephen has broken the rules, because girls are not allowed in the lockerroom.

5. Why is it so difficult for you to reach a decision?

6. Water will quench one's thirst. Water is composed of hydrogen and oxygen. Therefore, hydrogen and oxygen will quench one's thirst.

★7. Philosophers are highly intelligent individuals, because if they weren't highly intelligent they wouldn't be philosophers.

8. Hydrogen is combustible. Therefore, it burns.

9. Homosexuals of both sexes should never be given high-level security clearances, because these persons are always subject to being blackmailed.

★10. If Thomas gives Marie a ring, then Thomas and Marie will be engaged. Thomas did give Marie a ring. In fact, he phoned her just the other night. Therefore, Thomas and Marie are engaged.

11. Why did you lie on the witness stand?

12. Johnson is employed by the General Services Administration, and everyone knows that the GSA is the most inefficient branch of the government. Therefore, Johnson must be an inefficient worker.

★13. All men are mortal. Therefore, some day man will disappear from the earth.

14. Each and every cell in this carrot is 90 percent water. Therefore, the entire carrot is 90 percent water.

15. George said that he was interviewing for a job drilling oil wells in the supervisor's office. We can only conclude that the supervisor must have an awfully dirty office.

★16. The American National 30-year whole-life insurance policy incorporates a wonderful savings feature: It builds up a cash value, just like a savings account. During the life of the policy, you are guaranteed a 3 percent interest rate on the cash balance, and if you ever need to borrow money from the policy, you can do so at an interest rate of only 10 percent. Clearly, this policy offers an excellent investment opportunity.

17. Either you marry me right now or I'll be forced to leave you and never speak to you again. I'm sure you wouldn't want me to leave you and never speak to you again. Therefore, you'll marry me right now.

18. Either the new American one-cent coins are made of pure copper, or they are mostly zinc. The new American one-cent coins are not made of pure copper. Therefore, they are mostly zinc.

★19. Switzerland is 48 percent Protestant. Heidi Gilsing is a Swiss. Therefore, Heidi Gilsing is 48 percent Protestant.

20. Picasso is the greatest artist of the twentieth century. We know that this is so because art critics have described him in these terms. These art critics are correct in their assessment because they have a more keenly developed sense of appreciation than the average person. This is true because it takes a more keenly developed sense of appreciation to realize that Picasso is the greatest artist of the twentieth century.

21. An atomic bomb causes more damage than a conventional bomb. Therefore, during World War II more damage was done by atomic bombs than by conventional bombs.

★22. Are you still drinking excessively?

23. The author warns about numerous computational errors in his accounting text. Therefore, he must have written it very carelessly.

24. Emeralds are seldom found in this country, so you should be careful not to misplace your emerald ring.

★25. Of course abortion is permissible. After all, a woman has a right to do as she pleases with her own body.

II. Answer "true" or "false" to the following statements:

1. Arguments that commit the fallacy of begging the question have conclusions that genuinely follow from the premises.

2. The effect of begging the question is to hide the fact that a premise may not be true.

3. The correct way of responding to a complex question is to divide the question into its component questions and answer each separately.

4. False dichotomy always involves an "either . . . or" statement, at least implicitly.

5. The fallacy of equivocation arises from a structural defect in a statement.

6. The fallacy of amphiboly usually involves the ambiguous use of a single word.

7. Amphiboly usually arises from the arguer's misinterpreting a statement made by someone else.

8. The fallacy of composition always proceeds from whole to parts.

9. The fallacy of division always proceeds from parts to whole.

10. A general statement makes an assertion about each and every member of a class.

11. A class statement makes an assertion about a class as a whole.

12. In the statement "Divorces are increasing," an attribute is predicated distributively.

13. In the statement "Waistlines are increasing," an attribute is predicated distributively.

14. In the fallacy of begging the question, the conclusion is irrelevant to the premises.

15. Equivocation and amphiboly are classified as fallacies of ambiguity.

III. Identify the fallacies of relevance, weak induction, presumption, ambiguity, and grammatical analogy committed by the following arguments. If no fallacy is committed, write "no fallacy."

★1. Jeffrey Noland's *History of the American Civil War* cannot be trusted. As a historian from Alabama, Noland could not possibly present an accurate account.

2. Mr. Wilson said that on July 4 he went out on the veranda and watched the fireworks go up in his pajamas. We conclude that Mr. Wilson must have had an exciting evening.

3. Evangelist Oral Roberts said that he spoke directly with Jesus for seven hours, that Jesus charged him with finding a cure for cancer, and that he requested that each of Roberts's followers send $240 to complete the Tower of Faith research center in Tulsa. In view of this evidence, we must conclude that Jesus really did want these contributions to be sent.

★4. A crust of bread is better than nothing. Nothing is better than true love. Therefore, a crust of bread is better than true love.

5. Every member of the Delta Club is over 70 years old. Therefore, the Delta Club must be over 70 years old.

6. Of course you should eat Wheaties. Wheaties is the breakfast of champions, you know.

★7. On Friday I took Virginia out to dinner. She told me that if I wasn't interested in a serious relationship, I should forget about dating her.

On Saturday I took Margie to a film. When we discussed it afterward over a drink, she couldn't understand why I wasn't interested in babies. Women are all alike. All they want is a secure marriage.

8. The twenty-story Carson Building is constructed of concrete blocks. Each and every concrete block in the structure can withstand an earthquake of 9.5 on the Richter scale. Therefore, the building can withstand an earthquake of 9.5 on the Richter scale.

9. No one has ever proved that the human fetus is not completely human. Therefore, abortion is morally wrong.

★10. California condors are practically extinct. This bird is a California condor. Therefore, this bird is practically extinct.

11. When a car breaks down so often that repairs become pointless, the car is thrown on the junk heap. Similarly, when a person becomes old and diseased, he or she should be mercifully put to death.

12. Judge Adams is going soft on dope peddlers. The other day he gave a suspended sentence to a 15-year-old girl after he heard that the girl's father had forced her to sell marijuana.

★13. During the time that General Grant was winning battles in the West, President Lincoln received numerous complaints about Grant's being a drunkard. When a delegation told him that Grant was hopelessly addicted to whiskey, Lincoln is reported to have replied, "I wish General Grant would send a barrel of his whiskey to each of my other generals."

14. This administration is not anti-German, as it has been alleged. Germany is a great country. It has contributed immensely to the world's artistic treasury. Goethe and Schiller made magnificent contributions to literature, and Bach, Beethoven, Wagner, and Brahms did the same in music.

15. How long have you been dealing in drugs?

★16. Pope John Paul II has stated that artificial insemination of women is immoral. We can only conclude that this practice is indeed immoral.

17. Senator Bradshaw's arguments in favor of legislation to create jobs for the poor should be ignored. Bradshaw is a hypocrite who supports this kind of legislation only to get his name in the newspapers.

18. Professor Andrews, surely you can find it in your heart to give me a "B" in logic. I know I deserve an "F," but if you give me that, I will lose my scholarship. That will force me to drop out of school, and my poor, aged parents, who yearn to see me graduate, will be grief-stricken for the rest of their lives.

★19. Molecules are in constant random motion. The Statue of Liberty is composed of molecules. Therefore, the Statue of Liberty is in constant random motion.

20. Either the government solicits oil leases in federally protected wilderness areas, or our country will remain subject to the whims of the Arab

oil cartel. Certainly we don't want to remain subject to the whims of the Arab oil cartel. Therefore, the government must solicit oil leases in federally protected wilderness areas.

21. White sheep eat more than black sheep (because there are more of them). Therefore, this white sheep eats more than that black sheep.

★22. If someone rents a piece of land and plants crops on it, the landlord is never permitted to come and take those crops for himself when harvest time arrives. Similarly, if couples enlist the services of a surrogate mother to provide them with a baby, the mother should never be allowed to welch on the deal and keep the baby for herself once it is born.

23. Motives and desires exert forces on people, causing them to choose one thing over another. But force is a physical quantity, governed by the laws of physics. Therefore, human choices are governed by the laws of physics.

24. Each and every brick in the Wainright Building has a reddish brown color. Therefore, the Wainright Building has a reddish brown color.

★25. Professor Janet King has argued in favor of computing the grades for our class on a curve. This would mean that all of us would be competing for grades. It's distressing to see an otherwise intelligent woman advocate Social Darwinism. For humans, the theory of the survival of the fittest was discarded years ago. It's disgusting to see such an immoral theory rearing its ugly head in our own classroom.

26. Pauline said that after she had removed her new mink coat from the shipping carton she threw it into the trash. We conclude that Pauline has no appreciation for fine furs.

27. We know that induction will provide dependable results in the future because it has always worked in the past. Whatever has consistently worked in the past will continue to work in the future, and we know that this is true because it has been established by induction.

★28. What goes up must come down. The price of gold has been going up for months. Therefore, it will surely come down soon.

29. Mr. Prime Minister, I am certain you will want to release the members of our National Liberation Group whom you currently hold in prison. After all, I'm sure you will want to avoid having car bombs go off in the centers of your most heavily populated cities.

30. Are you in favor of the ruinous economic policy of the Democratic Platform Committee?

★31. The nuclear freeze people argue in favor of an immediate halt to nuclear arms production. But the point is that we have always had wars. Even those most civilized of peoples, the ancient Greeks, fought wars. Why, the Peloponnesian War raged for a period of 27 years. Unfortunately, civilization will never be entirely free of war. Clearly, the nuclear freeze people are deluding themselves.

32. The Russians are constantly arguing that we should keep our noses out

of the internal affairs of Central American nations. What hypocrisy! A few years ago the Russians crushed a popular revolution in Hungary, and they nearly did the same thing in Poland. More recently they've waged an all-out war in Afghanistan.

33. The farmers of our state have asked that we introduce legislation to provide subsidies for soybeans. Unfortunately, we will have to turn down their request. If we give subsidies to the soybean farmers, then the corn and wheat growers will ask for the same thing. Then it will be the cotton growers, citrus growers, truck farmers, and cattle raisers. In the end, the cost will be astronomical.

★34. The travel brochure states that walking up O'Connell Street, the statue of Parnell comes into view. Apparently that statue has no trouble getting around.

35. A line is composed of points. Points have no length. Therefore, a line has no length.

36. Professor Glazebrooks' theory about the origin of the Martian craters is undoubtedly true. Rudolph Orkin, the great concert pianist, announced his support of the theory in this morning's newspaper.

★37. Mrs. Ford, you've just witnessed the demonstration I performed with the new Electrolux vacuum cleaner. After vacuuming the carpet with your Hoover, I placed a special filter on the new Electrolux and vacuumed the same area over again. The filter then showed how much dirt the Electrolux got out that the Hoover had left in the rug. This proves that the Electrolux is a superior vacuum.

38. Raising a child is like growing a tree. Sometimes violent things, such as cutting off branches, have to be done to force the tree to grow straight. Similarly, corporal punishment must sometimes be inflicted on children to force them to develop properly.

39. Good steaks are rare these days, so don't order yours well done.

★40. The Book of Mormon is true because it was written by Joseph Smith. Joseph Smith wrote the truth because he was divinely inspired. We know that Joseph Smith was divinely inspired because the Book of Mormon says that he was, and the Book of Mormon is true.

41. The students attending Bradford College come from every one of the fifty states. Michelle attends Bradford College. Therefore, Michelle comes from every one of the fifty states.

42. Rhubarb pie is a dessert. Therefore, whoever eats rhubarb pie eats a dessert.

★43. Welfare cheating is rampant these days. People feigning poverty are ripping the government off for millions. The obvious conclusion is to abolish the entire welfare system.

44. Either you support the nuclear freeze or you advocate nuclear war. Since no sane person advocates nuclear war, you will want to support the freeze.

45. No one has ever proved that taking vitamins actually improves a person's health. Therefore, we can conclude that vitamins are simply a waste of money.

3.5 DETECTING FALLACIES IN ORDINARY LANGUAGE

Most of the informal fallacies that we have seen thus far have been clear-cut, easily recognizable instances of a specific mistake. When fallacies occur in ordinary usage, however, they are often neither clear-cut nor easily recognizable. The reason is that there are innumerable ways of making mistakes in arguing, and variations inevitably occur that may not be exact instances of any specifically named fallacy. In addition, one fallacious mode of arguing may be mixed together with one or more others, and the strands of reasoning may have to be disentangled before the fallacies can be named. Yet another problem arises from the fact that arguments in ordinary language are rarely presented in complete form. It often happens that a premise or conclusion is left unexpressed, which may obscure the nature of the evidence that is presented or the strength of the link between premises and conclusion.

Consider, for example, the following letter that appeared in a newspaper:

> God, I am sick of "women's rights"! Every time one turns on the news we hear about some form of discrimination against some poor female who wants to be a fireman—or some "remark" that suggests or implies women are inferior to men.
>
> I, for one, do not want to be rescued by a "woman fireman," especially if I am a 6-foot-2 male and she is a 5-foot-6 female.
>
> Why is it that women find their "role" so degrading? What is wrong with being a wife and mother, staying home while the male goes out and "hunts for food" and brings it home to his family?
>
> I don't think women have proven themselves to be as inventive, as capable (on the average) of world leadership, as physically capable, or as "courageous" as men. They have yet to fight a war (the average American woman) and let's face it ladies, who wants to?
>
> Whether a person is female, black, white, handicapped— whatever—*ability* is what counts in the final analysis. Women cannot demand "equality"—no one can—unless it is earned.
>
> When push comes to shove and a damsel is in distress, she is hard-pressed to protect herself and usually has to be rescued by a man. Until I can move a piano, beat off a potential robber or rapist, or fight a war, I am quite content to be a woman, thank you.

This letter can be interpreted as committing a number of fallacies. The phrase "poor female who wants to be a fireman" suggests a mild *ad hominem* abusive, and the equating of women's rights in general with the right to be a fireman suggests a straw man. The second paragraph commits another straw man fallacy by supposing that the job of fireman inevitably entails such activities as climbing up ladders and rescuing people. Surely there are many male firemen who cannot do this. The same paragraph also can be interpreted as begging the question: Do women who want to be firemen want the specific job of rescuing tall men?

The third paragraph throws out a red herring. The issue is whether women have the right to be considered for a job of their choice and whether they must be paid as much as a man in the same situation. Whether there is something wrong with being a wife and mother is quite a different issue. Also, the reference to men hunting for food suggests a possible begging of the question: Are we still locked into a "hunter-gatherer" social structure?

The paragraph about whether women have proved themselves to be as inventive, capable, and courageous as men begs yet another question: Assuming, for the sake of argument, that this is true, have women been allowed to occupy roles in society where such inventiveness, capability, and courageousness can be demonstrated? Furthermore, this paragraph commits a red herring fallacy and/or misses the point: Even if women have not proved this, what does that have to do with the issue? Most jobs do not require any high degree of inventiveness or courage or a capacity for world leadership.

The paragraph about ability begs yet another question: Is it in fact the case that women have less ability? I am not aware that anything of the sort has ever been proved. Finally, the last paragraph throws out another red herring. What does moving pianos (bare handed?) and beating off rapists have to do with most jobs or the question of equal pay for equal work?

Some of the more difficult arguments to evaluate are those involving analogies. Consider the following example:

> When an individual is diagnosed as having cancer, every effort is made to kill the cancerous growth, whether by surgery, radiation treatment, or chemotherapy. But murderers and kidnappers are cancerous growths on society. Therefore, when these criminals are apprehended and convicted, they should be treated like any other cancer and eliminated by capital punishment.

This argument may be analyzed in two different ways. One way is to interpret it as depending on the analogy between the individual and society. These two entities share the attribute of having an interest in self-preservation, and there is a systematic relation between this attribute and the elimination of life-threatening factors. Thus, as so analyzed the argument does not appear to commit the fallacy of weak analogy. But it does commit the fallacy of equivocation. "Cancerous growth" is used in a literal sense when referring to the disease and in a highly metaphorical sense when referring to murderers and kidnappers. The latter are not cancers in the former sense at all.

Analyzed from another angle, the argument may be seen to depend on the analogy between cancer and criminals. These two entities share the attribute of being life-threatening, but there is only a rather loose connection between this attribute and that of deserving to die. Automobiles can be life-threatening, but in no sense do automobiles deserve to die. Cancerous tumors are killed by surgery because there is neither the capacity nor the good reason to allow them to live. Criminals, on the other hand, are human beings, and there is good reason to allow human beings to live. Thus, from this standpoint, the argument commits the fallacy of weak analogy.

Another example:

> After ingesting one milligram of substance alpha per day for 90 days, white mice developed genetic abnormalities. Since white mice are similar in many ways to humans, it follows that substance alpha probably produces genetic abnormalities in humans.

White mice share a number of attributes with humans and, given the truth of the premise, there is most likely a causal connection between ingesting substance alpha and certain attributes possessed by white mice that results in genetic damage. The question is whether these attributes are among those that white mice share with humans. If these attributes are not shared by humans, it might be the case that substance alpha is completely harmless to humans even though it causes genetic damage in white mice. Since it is not known whether this causal connection pertains to the *shared* attributes, we must evaluate this argument as having *undecided* strength. A great many arguments in ordinary language are of this kind. Because of the complexity of the subject matter, it may be impossible to determine with any precision the attributes between which the causal relationships lie.

Slippery slope is another fallacy that is sometimes difficult to evaluate. When the alleged chain reaction of events stretches the imagination, there is usually no problem. A problem arises when there is some likelihood that the chain reaction will actually occur. For example:

> It has been argued that euthanasia (mercy killing) should be permissible in cases where the party concerned has signed a document stating his or her desire to be given a lethal injection if afflicted by terminal cancer, crippling stroke, or irreversible brain damage. Let us suppose that such a policy were made law.

In cases where no document had been signed it would then be argued that the afflicted party *would* have signed one if the opportunity had arisen. This would open the door to such decisions by proxy. Should this be allowed, little imagination is required to envision grown children and other interested parties doing away with their aged parents or grandparents when the latter became a burden. A gradual deterioration in respect for human life would result, and in the end, all undesired persons might be put out of their misery, including mental defectives in state hospitals, convicted criminals, and unwanted children. The conclusion is obvious that euthanasia must never be permitted.

This argument is more difficult to evaluate. If some form of limited euthanasia were allowed by law, it is quite possible that some such chain of events would occur. Deciding the question more definitely would require a close study of society's commitment to the value of human life.

A potential slippery slope argument that was used with some measure of success during the early days of the Vietnam War was expressed in the so-called "domino theory." It was argued that if South Vietnam were allowed to go Communist, Laos and Cambodia would follow, then Thailand, Burma, and the rest of Southeast Asia. Heated debate continued for several years over whether this would actually happen. Events since the end of the war suggest that claims for the chain reaction were ill founded.

Another fallacy that is difficult to detect is suppressed evidence. For this fallacy to occur, the evidence that is ignored must be the kind that would undermine the premises. Many arguments ignore evidence that would support an opposing conclusion, but because the evidence is not the sort that would undermine the premises, the fallacy is not committed. Consider, for example, the following pair of arguments that reach opposite conclusions:

Heroin addicts steal millions of dollars every year to support their habits, and thousands of addicts die every year from overdose. Methadone is a legal drug that relieves the craving for heroin, and its strength and quality can be precisely controlled. If methadone were supplied to heroin addicts, it would eliminate the constant need to steal and reduce the number of deaths from overdose. Therefore, methadone treatment centers should be set up for heroin addicts.

Methadone is just as addictive as heroin, and its distribution to heroin addicts would only result in one form of addiction being replaced by another. Such a solution would undercut any effort to treat the psychological causes of the addiction. Furthermore, methadone programs would almost certainly be abused. Persons pretending to be addicts would obtain methadone for the illicit purpose of selling it on the streets. Therefore, methadone treatment centers should not be set up for heroin addicts.

Neither of these arguments commits the fallacy of suppressed evidence because the evidence that each argument ignores is not the sort that would undermine the premises. The fact that methadone is addictive and that it might be misused does not cause the premises of the first argument to be any less true. Conversely, the fact that heroin addicts steal millions of dollars annually to support their habits and die by the thousands from overdose does not cause the premises of the second argument to be any less true.

EXERCISE 3.5

I. Most of the following selections were taken from letters to the editor of newspapers and magazines. Evaluate the arguments in light of the material presented in this chapter. Some of the arguments may be good ones.

★1. I think we should nominate the woman who killed one of her [unborn] twins because it had Down's Syndrome for the "Mother of the Year" award. She can be an inspiration to mothers everywhere and we can honor her for her bravery in the handling of a crisis situation.

Maybe we should take what she did one step further and allow mothers who do not approve of their grown children's lifestyles to kill them also—the children who abuse sex and drugs, thus causing more damage to their minds and bodies than a birth defect could. Surely these children cause their mothers more anguish for more years than a Mongoloid child ever could.

There are so many problems that could be eliminated by killing the problem-person that we may have the "solution of the '80s."

(Sharon Jarrett)

2. When will these upper-crust intellectuals realize that the masses of working people are not in cozy, cushy, interesting, challenging, well-paying jobs, professions and businesses? My husband is now 51; for most of the last 33 years he has worked in the same factory job, and only the thought of retiring at 62 has sustained him. When he reaches that age in 11 years, who will tell him that his aging and physically wracked body must keep going another two years? My heart cries out for all the poor souls who man the assembly lines, ride the trucks or work in the fields or mines, or in the poorly ventilated, hot-in-summer, cold-in-winter factories and garages. Many cannot afford to retire at 62, 65, or even later. Never, never let them extend the retirement age. It's a matter of survival to so many.

(Isabel Fierman)

3. My 16-year-old daughter is traveling to Ireland this fall and needed my signature to get a passport. According to the Supreme Court, she could

have gotten an abortion the same day without my knowledge or permission. When are we going to get our priorities straight?

(Mary Louise Wallace)

★4. In his syndicated column, Dr. Walt Menninger stated that heart disease caused nearly 730,000 deaths and is the No. 1 killer in the U.S., according to the latest available (1978) complete figures.

Wrong! The No. 1 killer in the U.S. in 1978 according to federal statistics from the Center for Disease Control was abortion.

Over 1.33 million lost their lives that year in the ongoing holocaust.

(Art Little)

5. The American Civil Liberties Union did a study that found that in the last 80 years it believes 25 innocent people have been executed in the United States. This is unfortunate. But, there are innocent people who die each year in highway accidents. Out of 40,000 deaths, how many deaths are related to driving while intoxicated? How many more thousands are injured and incur financial ruin or are invalids and handicapped for the remainder of their lives?

(Mahlon R. Braden)

6. Mexico's President Lopez Portillo expresses legitimate concern when he questions supplying oil to Americans who are unwilling to apply "discipline" in oil consumption. In view of the fact that his country's population is expected to double in only 22 years, isn't it legitimate for us to ask when Mexicans will apply the discipline necessary to control population growth and quit dumping their excess millions over our borders?

(Wayne R. Bartz)

★7. There has been a recent and long overdue concern about the population growth of our country, which contributes to many of our social problems. There is one solution that would help to solve the population growth as well as relieve a portion of the tax burden.

We should instigate a ruling that welfare will pay support for only two children of families on welfare. This does not prohibit them from having a larger family; however, it does put them in the same position as the working family, whether or not they can afford more children.

It seems unfair and discriminatory to place the taxpayer in the position of having to limit his family while the government continues to reward the welfare family with increased monthly payments and additional benefits for each child.

(Elizabeth Thomas)

8. How would you feel to see your children starving, and have all doors slammed in your face? Isn't it time that all of us who believe in freedom and human rights stop thinking in terms of color and national boundaries? We should open our arms and hearts to those less fortunate and remember that a time could come when we might be in a similar situation.

(Lorna Doyle)

9. There is no way our government can get out of the red until we elect a Republican House of Representatives to fire at least 500,000 of the 2.1

million federal bureaucrats. All spending and tax bills originate in the House, which has been controlled by the Democrats for most of the past 49 years.

(Frank C. Worbs)

★10. After reading "Homosexuals in the Churches," I'd like to point out that I don't know any serious, capable exegetes who stumble over Saint Paul's denunciation of homosexuality. Only a fool (and there seem to be more and more these days) can fail to understand the plain words of Romans, Chapter one. God did not make anyone "gay." Paul tells us in Romans 1 that homosexuals become that way because of their own lusts. God loves homosexuals, drunkards, thieves, and so on, but sin is sin. Only those who ask forgiveness and change receive it. But the wonderful thing is that the homosexual can change. The Apostle says so in I Corinthians 6:9–11. It still works—there are homosexuals who are being delivered from this sin and are living changed, happy lives. Why don't you interview some who have been set free?

(LeRoy J. Hopper)

11. When will they ever learn—that the Republican Party is not for the people who voted for it?

(Alton L. Stafford)

12. Before I came to the United States in July, 1922, I was in Berlin where I visited the famous zoo. In one of the large cages were a lion and a tiger. Both respected each other's strength. It occurred to me that it was a good illustration of "balance of power." Each beast followed the other and watched each other's moves. When one moved, the other did. When one stopped, the other stopped.

In today's world, big powers or groups of powers are trying to maintain the status quo, trying to be as strong as or stronger than the other. They realize a conflict may result in mutual destruction. As long as the countries believe there is a balance of power we may hope for peace. But when Iraq thought it had a preponderance of power over Iran, it started a war.

(Emilie Lackow)

★13. Doctors say the birth of a baby is a high point of being a doctor. Yet a medical survey shows one out of every nine obstetricians in America has stopped delivering babies.

Expectant mothers have had to find new doctors. In some rural areas, women have had to travel elsewhere to give birth.

How did this happen? It's part of the price of the lawsuit crisis.

The number of lawsuits Americans file each year is on the rise. Obstetricians are among the hardest hit—almost three out of four have faced a malpractice claim. Many have decided it isn't worth the risk.

(Magazine ad by the Insurance Information Institute)

14. The conservative diatribe found in campus journalism comes from the mouths of a handful of affluent brats who were spoon-fed through the '70s. Put them on an ethnically more diverse campus, rather than a Princeton or a Dartmouth, and then let us see how long their newspapers survive.

(David Simons)

15. I see that our courts are being asked to rule on the propriety of outlawing video games as a "waste of time and money."

It seems that we may be on to something here. A favorable ruling would open the door to new laws eliminating show business, spectator sports, cocktail lounges, the state of Nevada, public education and, of course, the entire federal bureaucracy.

(A. G. Dobrin)

★16. The death penalty is the punishment for murder. Just as we have long jail terms for armed robbery, assault and battery, fraud, contempt of court, fines for speeding, reckless driving and other numerous traffic violations, so must we have a punishment for murder. Yes, the death penalty will not deter murders any more than a speeding ticket will deter violating speed laws again, but it is the punishment for such violation!

(Lawrence J. Barstow)

17. Would you rather invest in our nation's children or Pentagon waste? The choice is yours.

(Political ad)

18. My gun has protected me, and my son's gun taught him safety and responsibility long before he got hold of a far more lethal weapon—the family car. Cigarettes kill many times more people yearly than guns and, unlike guns, have absolutely no redeeming qualities. If John Lennon had died a long, painful and expensive death from lung cancer, would you have devoted a page to a harangue against the product of some of your biggest advertisers—the cigarette companies?

(Silvia A. DeFreitas)

★19. If the advocates of prayers in public schools win on this issue, just where will it end? Perhaps next they will ask for prayers on public transportation? Prayers by government workers before they start their job each day? Or maybe, mandatory prayers in public restaurants before starting each meal might be a good idea.

(Leonard Mendelson)

20. On the basis of religious faith, most people who believe that God is the Creator can draw the reasonable and evident conclusion that there is a relationship between the scourge of AIDS and the infringement of God's laws.

(Rev. Maurice Fitzgerald)

21. Pigeons are forced to leave our city to battle for life. Their struggle is an endless search for food. What manner of person would watch these hungry creatures suffer from want of food and deny them their survival? These helpless birds are too often ignored by the people of our city, with not the least bit of compassion shown to them. Pigeons are God's creatures just as the so-called human race is. They need help.

(Leslie Ann Price)

★22. You take half of the American population every night and set them down in front of a box watching people getting stabbed, shot and blown away. And then you expect them to go out into the streets hugging each other?

(Mark Hustad)

23. So you think that putting the worst type of criminal out of his misery is wrong. How about the Americans who were sent to Korea, to Vietnam, to Beirut, to Central America? Thousands of good men were sacrificed supposedly for the good of our country. At the same time we were saving and protecting Charles Manson, Sirhan Sirhan [Robert Kennedy's murderer], and a whole raft of others too numerous to mention.

(George M. Purvis)

24. If Castro had any regard for the Cubans, he would throw the Soviets and their bankrupt economics out and welcome Western capitalism. But no; the macho image prevails: the cigar, the beard, the fatigues, the whole clown act. Can one person's egotism lead to the creation of such monumental economic and historical illiteracy? Apparently so.

(Edward R. Wall)

★25. Countries where prostitution is almost nonexistent have a rate of unemployment approaching zero. The present U.S. unemployment rate is ten times the present Swiss rate [where prostitution is virtually unknown] and twice what the Swiss rate was even in the depth of the Great Depression. So there is a neat way to solve the problem of prostitution without licensing it: namely, enforcement of the Federal Full Employment Act of 1946, providing decent, productive employment for all.

(John H. Randolph)

26. According to the most recent data, there are now 4.7 billion human beings on this planet. Malthusianism will be vindicated unless the governments of the nations of the world take immediate action.

Because abortion is a mortal sin (murder) I know of only one rational and moral solution: After a woman has her second child, government must require her to undergo forced sterilization.

(Steven Dale Ahern)

27. If a woman is careless and has an unwanted pregnancy, she must suffer nine months of waiting and the pain of giving up her baby. I work at a hospital and see many children and adults suffering for more than nine months with cancers, renal diseases, etc., through no act of their own or their parents'. In this light it doesn't seem so bad to expect a woman to suffer nine months for a freely committed act. Birth control information is available to everyone. No one has to raise an unwanted child. There are many who want to adopt. I know because we have an adopted daughter. I shudder when I think her natural mother might have killed her by abortion.

(Leah J. Clark)

★28. The suggestion by Gorbachev that SDI "could easily be an offensive weapon" is ludicrous. Any atmospheric physicist will tell you that the proposed space-based particle beams could not dent hardened missile silos, and the threat to space-based satellites comes long after the U.S.S.R. has tested its own "killer satellites."

(Joel W. West III)

29. We've often heard the saying, "Far better to let 100 guilty men go free

than to condemn one innocent man." What happens then if we apply the logic of this argument to the question, "Is a fetus an unborn human being?" Then is it not better to let 100 fetuses be born rather than to mistakenly kill one unborn human being? This line of reasoning is a strictly humanist argument against abortion.

(James Sebastian)

30. Tom Hayden honored our fair city on May 20 (again) with a speech to a grand total of 100 people in Clairemont. You reported the event with a four-column headline and a photo.

By any stretch of the imagination, Hayden is not an expert or an authority. He holds no degrees in economics or political science. He's never held (for any length of time) a traditional job. And he has never been elected to a political office.

He tours the West speaking to a few misguided liberals and impressionable, young students only because his foolish wife pays his expenses from her movie career earnings.

Anyway you slice it, Tom Hayden is not news—and should be ignored accordingly.

(W. J. Gabriel)

★31. I say "bravo" and "right on!" Now we have some real-life humane heroes to look up to! These brave people [a group of animal liberators] went up against the insensitive bureaucratic technology, and won, saving former pet animals from senseless torture.

It should be a felony crime to use any dog or pet animal that has been lost and put in a pound for research experiments. These animals have known only love and gentle care, and because of some unscrupulous research lab, pet animals in shelters are procured for useless, horrendous experiments.

If researchers want to experiment, let them use computers, or themselves—but not former pet animals! I know it's bad enough they use monkeys and rats, but if those animals are bred knowing nothing else but these Frankensteins abusing them it's different (but not better) than dogs or cats that have been loved and petted all their lives to suddenly be tortured and mutilated in the name of science. End all animal research! Free all research animals!

Right on animal liberators!

(Linda Magee)

32. Europe paid a fearful price for ignoring the danger of Hitler. We would eventually pay an equally high price if we permit Russia to get established in Nicaragua. It will be much cheaper to give the contras everything they need to force the change in Nicaragua to a democratic government.

(S. Mayer)

33. Castro does great violence to the intelligence of the world. His extreme criticism of the U.S. for not sending aid to the hungry and shoeless children cannot be countenanced. What is Cuba's record? Castro's dictatorship exports armies, hate and killing on command of the Kremlin. Where in

the world does Communism feed and clothe little children without demanding their bodies and souls in payment?

(Will W. Orr)

★34. People of the Philippines, I have returned! The hour of your redemption is here! Rally to me! Let the indomitable spirit of Bataan and Corregidor lead on! As the lines of battle roll forward to bring you within the zone of operations, rise and strike! For future generations of your sons and daughters, strike! Let no heart be faint! Let every arm be steeled! The guidance of divine God points the way! Follow in his name to the Holy Grail of righteous victory!

(General Douglas MacArthur)

35. As the oldest of eleven children (all married), I'd like to point out our combined family numbers more than 100 who vote only for pro-life candidates. Pro-lifers have children, pro-choicers do not.

(Mrs. Kitty Reickenback)

36. Do health officials actually expect an individual with AIDS to observe his moral duty and warn sexual partners they have been put at risk? It was the immorality of the AIDS victim that got him into this fix in the first place.

(Francis Collins)

★37. As corporate farms continue to gobble up smaller family farms, they control a larger percentage of the grain and produce raised in the United States. Some have already reached a point in size where, if they should decide to withhold their grain and produce from the marketplace, spot shortages could occur and higher prices would result. The choice is to pay us family farmers now or pay the corporations later.

(Delwin Yost)

38. If you buy our airline ticket now you can save 60%, and that means 60% more vacation for you.

(Radio ad)

39. Why all the flap about atomic bombs? The potential for death is always with us. Of course, if you just want something to worry about, go ahead. Franklin D. Roosevelt said it: "The only thing we have to fear is fear itself."

(Lee Flemming Reese)

★40. September 17 marked the 193rd anniversary of the signing of the U.S. Constitution. How well have we, the people, protected our rights? Consider what has happened to our private-property rights.

"Property has divine rights, and the moment the idea is admitted into society that property is not as sacred as the laws of God, anarchy and tyranny begin." John Quincy Adams, 1767–1848, Sixth President of the United States.

Taxes and regulations are the two-edged sword which gravely threatens the fabric of our capitalistic republic. The tyranny of which Adams speaks is with us today in the form of government regulators and regulations which have all but destroyed the right to own property. Can anarchy be far behind?

(Timothy R. Binder)

41. The arguments of activists favoring an immediate bilateral freeze on nuclear weapons are superficial and unconvincing.

These people evidently derive most of their information from doomsday novels or from the deluded ravings of those who have made professional idiocy their lifework (such as Jane Fonda and husband Tom, Ted Kennedy, Dr. Helen Caldicott, Dan Rather and so on ad nauseam). Even when these people are factually correct, they distort the facts or use them selectively in ways that misinform rather than inform.

The American people are justifiably concerned about the threat of nuclear war, but the quality of the debate over how to prevent it is hardly enhanced by fairy tales.

(James C. Goff)

42. Poland has gun control.

(Bumpersticker)

★43. If a car or truck kills a person, do politicians call for car control or truck control? And call in all cars/trucks?

If a child burns down a house do we have match control or child control and call in all of each?

Gun control and confiscation is equally as pathetic a thought process in an age of supposed intelligence.

(Pete Hawes)

44. I was incensed to read in your article about the return of anti-Semitism that New York City Moral Majority Leader Rev. Dan C. Fore actually said that "Jews have a God-given ability to make money, almost a supernatural ability. . ." I find it incredibly ironic that he and other Moral Majority types conveniently overlook the fact that they, too, pack away a pretty tidy sum themselves through their fund-raising efforts. It is sad that anti-Semitism exists, but to have this prejudice voiced by leaders of religious organizations is deplorable. These people are in for quite a surprise come Judgment Day.

(John R. Murks)

45. Most Americans don't realize the extent of military power—both offensive and defensive—that the Soviet Union commands. If they did, they wouldn't be so strongly against building up defense in America.

(Mark Tobino)

★46. So! After 40 years, the Japanese-American who was interned, not only for the nation's security, but for his own safety, decides to sue the United States! Why, if he was so abused by this country, didn't he go to the land of his ancestors [after being released]? During that 40 years, didn't he make a free living in this nation, coming and going as he pleased?

By the same token, do the families of Pearl Harbor victims have the same privilege of suing the Japanese empire for the dead and injured of that beastly action? Of course, considering Washington's opinion of the American citizens' rights these days, that question answers itself.

(Patricia Kay)

47. What's wrong with kids today? Answer: nothing, for the majority of them. They are great.

Witness the action of two San Diego teenage boys recently, when the Normal Heights fire was at it worst. They took a garden hose to the roof of a threatened house—a house belonging to four elderly sisters, people they didn't even know. They saved the house, while neighboring houses burned to the ground.

In the Baldwin Hills fire, two teenage girls rescued a blind, retired Navy man from sure death when they braved the flames to find him, confused, outside his burning house. He would probably have perished if they hadn't run a distance to rescue him.

(Theodore H. Wickham)

48. Now that Big Brother has decided that I must wear a seat belt when I ride in a car, how long will it take before I have to wear an inner tube when I swim in my pool, a safety harness when I climb a ladder, and shoes with steel-reinforced toecaps when I carry out the garbage?

(G. R. Turgeon)

★49. Dear Ann: I was disappointed in your response to the girl whose mother used the strap on her. The gym teacher noticed the bruises on her legs and backside and called it "child abuse." Why are you against strapping a child when the Bible tells us in plain language that this is what parents should do?

The Book of Proverbs mentions many times that the rod must be used. Proverbs 23:13 says: "Withhold not correction from the child for if thou beatest him with the rod he shall not die." Proverbs 23:14 says: "Thou shalt beat him with the rod and shalt deliver his soul from death."

There is no substitute for a good whipping. I have seen the results of trying to reason with kids. They are arrogant, disrespectful and mouthy. Parents may wish for a more "humane" way, but there is none. Beating children is God's way of getting parents to gain control over their children.

(Davisville, W.VA.)

50. The Fourth Amendment guarantees our right to freedom from unreasonable search and seizure. It does not prohibit *reasonable* search and seizure. The matter of sobriety roadblocks to stop drunk drivers boils down to this: Are such roadblocks reasonable or unreasonable? The majority of people answer: "Reasonable." Therefore, sobriety roadblocks should not be considered to be unconstitutional.

(Haskell Collier)

II. The following essay, titled "There Goes the Sun," which has been condensed slightly, appeared in *Newsweek* magazine ("My Turn," December 3, 1979, copyright 1979 by Newsweek, Inc. All rights reserved. Reprinted by permission). The author is associate editor of *London Oil Reports*. Analyze the argument in terms of the material presented in this section.

Solar energy is potentially the most polluting and ecologically threatening form of commercial power being proposed in the world today.

You saw that right. Solar energy can be dangerous to everybody's health and the time has come for its advocates to stop strumming their amplified guitars in its behalf and start listening to some quiet truths.

I am not discussing solar in terms of wind, hydropower or agriculture, for to paraphrase Keynes, in the long run we are all solar. For the purpose of this essay, solar energy is sunlight converted directly to electricity or to commercially usable heat.

Arriving free of charge, leaving no residue and making no smoke, this energy nonetheless may turn out to be more hazardous than nuclear, more polluting than coal, and more costly to the consuming public than petroleum.

Laws: Some elementary facts on the physical world in which we live, compiled recently by Resources for the Future under Ford Foundation sponsorship, are pertinent. Remember, now, we are dealing with the laws of nature and not of society, and we can neither repeal nor amend them.

Here is Fact One: Sunlight reaches the ground at a global average of 160 watts per square meter. The most optimistic engineers say that by the time we allow for variations in cloud and atmospheric cover, the natural resistance of materials, and the need to convert the electricity to alternating current, we are not likely to exceed a recovery efficiency of 5 to 10 percent.

That computes to an average power output of about 25 megawatts per square mile. Thus the entire estimated U.S. power requirement for the year 2000 could be met by covering an area equivalent to that of the state of Oregon with solar collectors. Or, less extreme, all existing and projected nuclear power plants for the year 2000 could be replaced by solar collectors covering a much smaller area—approximately that of West Virginia.

Here is Fact Two: The sun will not give up its energy for nothing. As we have shown, we are going to have an area equivalent to that of Oregon or West Virginia with solar conversion cells. Whether of the sunlight-to-electricity or sunlight-to-commercial-heat type, these cells will not be made out of guitar picks.

Direct-conversion photovoltaic units will contain larger—truly large—tonnages of cadmium, silicon, germanium, selenium, gallium, copper, arsenic, sulfur, and/or other conducting, semiconducting and nonconducting materials of varying availability on world markets. Thermal-conversion units will be made of thousands of tons of glass, plastics and rubber, and will house uncommonly great volumes of ethylene glycol, liquid metals, Freon and/or other heat movers.

Exotic materials: If we settle on cadmium-sulfide cells for direct photovoltaic conversion, for instance, it would require the entire 1978 world production of cadmium to produce only 180,000 megawatts of installed capacity, or about 10 percent of the capacity the world had in place last year.

On the other hand, if we opt for solar-heat transfer, from where will the medium come? I'm not referring to the few ounces of Freon in your refrigerator, or the four gallons of coolant in your car radiator. I'm referring to millions of tons of a toxic material coursing through miles of complicated plumbing out there in the hinterlands.

Now we are ready for the first set of serious questions: How much energy will it require to manufacture enough solar cells—either photovoltaic or heat-transfer—to cover an area the size of Oregon or West Virginia? How much oil or coal must we burn in the process? How much pollution will be belched into the atmosphere as a result? How much silicate matter? How much sulfur? How much arsenic?

Hazards: And now for the second set of serious questions: What will be the ecological price of covering an area the size of Oregon or West Virginia with solar cells? What will be the effect on land where sunlight has shone un-impeded but for clouds and eclipses for uncounted trillions of days? What of its wildlife? Its flora? What will be the effect on neighboring lands? What are the hazards of a massive ethylene glycol spill?

There is a third set of serious questions: Of what real value is a source of energy that operates only in the daytime and whose output is subject to unpredictable deterioration by the vagaries of weather and season? What kind of buffer and storage systems must we develop to accommodate such variations in output? Can we really devise a battery-powered assembly line to provide work for the night shift?

Which leads us to the polemical coda of this essay. Please answer for me the following questions:

Why do so many of the people who fear the effect of drugstore deodorant-spray cans on the ozone layer rush to risk a massive Freon spill on earth?

Why are so many of those who tremble in terror over the Three Mile Island accident, which killed nobody, ecstatic about the prospect of putting tons of silicate particles into the air we breathe?

Why are those so quick to protect the wilderness from a single pipeline so anxious to smother it with solar cells?

I don't have the answers. But it is clear that in energy as in life itself there is no free lunch. Our access to commercial solar power is only slightly more promising than the Ancient Mariner's to potable water. And the shrill, facile sun worship to which we are increasingly subjected had better give way to more serious reflection on the energy mess in which we find ourselves.

Donald C. Winston

III. The following guest editorial appeared in the *San Diego Tribune* (May 21, 1981). The author is associate editor of *American Firearms Industry News.* Analyze the argument in terms of the material presented in this section.

It's about time that people in the news media stop their self-righteous preaching and grandstanding, speaking as though they reflect the views of the entire population.

The anti-firearms cause sounds good, looks good in print and seems the honorable course to take, but it is mostly the view of media personnel, not the view of the majority of U.S. citizens. It's fairly easy to blame the National Rifle Association for all of our country's crime and firearm incidents, and easier yet to focus on firearms themselves. But behind all their breast-beating and cries for "gun control," the media thrive on the misuse of firearms.

The week after John Lennon's death, every major newspaper and magazine, along with the major broadcasting networks, produced Lennon tributes. Everybody got their buck's worth. Very few major news publications devoted entire sections to Lennon after the Beatles' breakup, but they all had their special sections on the presses the day after his death. Yet, for all their articles and columns on gun control, the news publications are not dealing with the real Lennon story: the assailant, Mark David Chapman. If he's convicted, it's likely to be only second-degree murder—another way of saying he'll be walking the streets in a few years.

In a recent column in the Chicago *Sun-Times,* journalist Michael J. McManus mentioned an incident from his childhood: He found his father's revolver, pulled out the clip and pulled the trigger, firing a shot. To correct him: A revolver does not have a clip but a cylinder, which contains the cartridges. It's evident McManus knows nothing about firearms, yet he insists on instructing his readers on the use and misuse of them. I must agree, though, that anyone who leaves firearms loaded and unlocked should not have them around. Even as a youngster, in a house full of firearms, I was never stupid enough to place one in my mouth, as McManus claims to have done.

Probably the most important consideration for any firearms problem does not lie in new laws or regulations, but in mandatory enforcement of existing laws. We in the American firearms industry do not sanction the free-for-all sale of firearms, nor do we argue against fair and reasonable firearms laws aimed at seriously restricting the criminal and his use of firearms to pursue his trade. But very few people charged with crimes in connection with firearms are prosecuted for violating existing firearms laws; the federal Bureau of Alcohol, Tobacco and Firearms will confirm this. Regardless of what FBI statistics show or what law enforcement officials claim, you can get away with murder.

Firearms homicides are tolerated by the courts. Examples of such limpid justice are the cases of Sirhan Sirhan and David Berkowitz, the Son of Sam. Both murderers live a fairly comfortable life in prison, without regrets. Sirhan is eligible for parole in another year and Berkowitz collects Social Security benefits. Were their horrible crimes adequately punished? I think not. The Puerto Rican terrorists who killed a security guard in an attempted assassination of President Truman were pardoned by President Carter. They expressed no regrets for their action and hinted they would be willing to do it again. Not much of a deterrent, is it?

I suggest we concentrate on crime control instead of so-called gun control. The courts should be forced to impose mandatory jail terms for firearms offenses, without exception. Capital punishment should be mandatory for any firearm homicide in connection with a crime and for multiple crimes connected with firearms, without exception.

There are not too many people in the firearms business who would complain about a workable computer system that would record serial numbers of firearms. Any Chicago area dealer will tell you he gets very little support from police in using the National Crime Information Center to trace serial numbers on suspected stolen firearms.

We at the National Association of Federally Licensed Firearms Dealers have written to the federal Bureau of Alcohol, Tobacco and Firearms many times concerning this problem and the lack of support for dealers who try to run an honest business.

As for Sen. Edward M. Kennedy's anti-firearm propaganda and "ban all guns" philosophy, forget it. He was born very wealthy, never had to work to support his family, travels with heavily armed bodyguards and lives in the closed society of the super-rich that most Americans only dream about.

A man who has never struggled to earn a living, never lived in the real world of violence and crime and never experienced the blue-collar way of life has no right to impose his anti-firearm vendetta on all America. He talks a good line, but has never encountered life in Harlem or inner-city Chicago.

Kennedy cannot speak for the common man because he has never walked in his shoes.

R. A. Lesmeister

IV. Turn to the editorial pages of a newspaper and find an instance of a fallacious argument in the editorials or letters to the editor. Identify the premises and conclusion of the argument and write an analysis at least one paragraph in length stating why the argument is fallacious and identifying the fallacy or fallacies committed.

4

CATEGORICAL PROPOSITIONS

4.1 THE COMPONENTS OF CATEGORICAL PROPOSITIONS

In Chapter 1 we saw that a proposition (or statement—here we are ignoring the distinction) is a sentence that is either true or false. A proposition that relates two classes, or categories, is called a **categorical proposition.** The classes in question are denoted respectively by the **subject term** and the **predicate term,** and the proposition asserts that either all or part of the class denoted by the subject term is included in or excluded from the class denoted by the predicate term. Here are some examples of categorical propositions:

> Light rays travel at a fixed speed.
> Radical ideologues do not find it easy to compromise.
> Sea lions inhabit the coast of California.
> Not all convicted murderers get the death penalty.
> Cinnabar always contains mercury.
> Ernest Rutherford worked at the Cavendish Laboratory.

The first statement asserts that the entire class of light rays is included in the class of things that travel at a fixed speed, the second that the entire class of radical ideologues is excluded from the class of persons who find it easy to compromise, and the third that part of the class of sea lions is included in the class of things that inhabit the coast of California. The fourth statement asserts that part of the class of con-

A CONCISE INTRODUCTION TO LOGIC

victed murderers is excluded from the class of persons who get the death penalty, and the fifth asserts that the entire class of things consisting of cinnabar is included in the class of things that contain mercury. The last example asserts that the single individual denoted by the name "Ernest Rutherford" is included in the class of persons who worked at the Cavendish Laboratory.

Since any categorical proposition asserts that either all or part of the class denoted by the subject term is included in or excluded from the class denoted by the predicate term, it follows that there are exactly four types of categorical propositions: (1) those that assert that the whole subject class is included in the predicate class, (2) those that assert that part of the subject class is included in the predicate class, (3) those that assert that the whole subject class is excluded from the predicate class, and (4) those that assert that part of the subject class is excluded from the predicate class. A categorical proposition that expresses these relations with complete clarity is one that is in **standard form.** A categorical proposition is in standard form if and only if it is a substitution instance of one of the following four forms:

> All S are P.
> No S are P.
> Some S are P.
> Some S are not P.

Many categorical propositions, of course, are not in standard form because, among other things, they do not begin with the words "all," "no," or "some." In the final section of this chapter we will develop techniques for translating categorical propositions into standard form, but for now we may restrict our attention to those that are already in standard form.

The words "all," "no," and "some" are called **quantifiers** because they specify how much of the subject class is included in or excluded from the predicate class. The first form above asserts that the whole subject class is included in the predicate class, the second that the whole subject class is excluded from the predicate class, and so on. (Incidentally, in formal deductive logic the word "some" always means at least one.) The letters "S" and "P" stand respectively for the subject and predicate terms, and the words "are" and "are not" are called the **copula** because they link the subject term with the predicate term.

Consider the following example:

> All members of the American Medical Association are persons holding degrees from recognized academic institutions.

This standard-form categorical proposition is analyzed as follows:

> *quantifier:*   all
> *subject term:*   members of the American Medical Association
> *copula:*   are

predicate term: persons holding degrees from recognized academic institutions

In resolving standard-form categorical propositions into their four components, one must keep these components separate. They do not overlap each other. In this regard it should be noted that "subject term" and "predicate term" do not mean the same thing in logic that "subject" and "predicate" mean in grammar. The *subject* of the above statement includes the quantifier "all," but the *subject term* does not. Similarly, the *predicate* includes the copula "are," but the *predicate term* does not.

Two additional points should be noted about standard-form categorical propositions. The first is that the form "All S are not P" is *not* a standard form. This form is ambiguous and can be rendered as either "No S are P" or "some S are not P," depending on the content. The second point is that there are exactly three forms of quantifiers and two forms of copulas. Other texts allow the various forms of the verb "to be" (such as "is," "is not," "will," and "will not") to serve as the copula. For the sake of uniformity, this book restricts the copula to "are" and "are not." The last section of this chapter describes techniques for translating these alternate forms into the two accepted ones.

EXERCISE 4.1

In the following categorical propositions identify the quantifier, subject term, copula, and predicate term.

★1. Some college students are avid devotees of soap operas.

2. No persons who live near airports are persons who appreciate the noise of jets.

3. All oil-based paints are products that contribute significantly to photochemical smog.

★4. Some preachers who are intolerant of others' beliefs are not television evangelists.

5. All trials in which a coerced confession is read to the jury are trials in which a guilty verdict can be reversed.

6. Some artificial hearts are mechanisms that are prone to failure.

★7. No sex education courses that are taught competently are programs that are currently eroding public morals.

8. Some universities that emphasize research are not institutions that neglect undergraduate education.

4.2 QUALITY, QUANTITY, AND DISTRIBUTION

Quality and quantity are attributes of categorical propositions. In order to see how these attributes pertain, it is useful to rephrase the meaning of categorical propositions in class terminology:

Proposition	Meaning in Class Notation
All *S* are *P*.	Every member of the *S* class is a member of the *P* class; that is, the *S* class is included in the *P* class.
No *S* are *P*.	No member of the *S* class is a member of the *P* class; that is, the *S* class is excluded from the *P* class.
Some *S* are *P*.	At least one member of the *S* class is a member of the *P* class.
Some *S* are not P.	At least one member of the *S* class is not a member of the *P* class.

The **quality** of a categorical proposition is either affirmative or negative depending on whether it affirms or denies class membership. Accordingly, "All *S* are *P*" and "Some *S* are *P*" have **affirmative** quality, and "No *S* are *P*" and "Some *S* are not *P*" have **negative** quality.

The **quantity** of a categorical proposition is either universal or particular depending on whether the statement makes a claim about *every* member or just *some* member of the class denoted by the subject term. "All *S* are *P*" and "No *S* are *P*" each assert something about every member of the *S* class and thus are **universal.** "Some *S* are *P*" and "Some *S* are not *P*" assert something about one or more members of the *S* class and hence are **particular.**

Note that the quantity of a categorical proposition may be determined through mere inspection of the quantifier. "All" and "no" immediately imply universal quantity, while "some" implies particular. But categorical propositions have no "qualifier." In universal propositions the quality is determined by the quantifier, and in particular propositions it is determined by the copula.

It should also be noted that particular propositions mean no more and no less than the meaning assigned to them in class notation. The statement "Some *S* are *P*" does *not* imply that some *S* are not *P*, and the statement "Some *S* are not *P*" does *not* imply that some *S* are *P*. It often *happens*, of course, that substitution instances of these statement forms are both true. For example, "Some apples are red" is true, as is "Some apples are not red." But the fact that one is true does not *necessitate* that the other be true. "Some zebras are animals" is true (because at least one zebra is an animal), but "Some zebras are not animals" is false. Similarly, "Some turkeys are not fish" is true, but "Some turkeys are fish" is false. Thus, the fact that one of these statement forms is true does not *logically imply* that the other is true, as these substitution instances clearly prove.

Since the early Middle Ages the four kinds of categorical propositions have commonly been designated by letter names corresponding to the first four vowels of the Roman alphabet: **A, E, I, O.** The universal affirmative is called an **A** proposition, the universal negative an **E** proposition, the particular affirmative an **I** proposition, and the particular negative an **O** proposition. Tradition has it that these letters were derived from the first two vowels in the Latin words *affirmo* ("I affirm") and *nego* ("I deny"), thus:

	Universal			**Particular**				
	A	f	f	I	r	m	o	(affirmative)
n	E		g	O				(negative)

The material presented thus far in this section may be summarized as follows:

Proposition	Letter name	Quantity	Quality
All *S* are *P*.	A	universal	affirmative
No *S* are *P*.	E	universal	negative
Some *S* are *P*.	I	particular	affirmative
Some *S* are not *P*.	O	particular	negative

Unlike quality and quantity, which are attributes of *propositions*, **distribution** is an attribute of the *terms* (subject and predicate) of propositions. A term is said to be distributed if the proposition makes an assertion about every member of the class denoted by the term; otherwise, it is undistributed. Stated another way, a term is distributed if and only if the statement assigns (or distributes) an attribute to every member of the class denoted by the term. Thus, if a statement asserts something about every member of the *S* class, then *S* is distributed; if it asserts something about every member of the *P* class, then *P* is distributed; otherwise *S* and *P* are undistributed.

Let us imagine that the members of the classes denoted by the subject and predicate terms of a categorical proposition are contained respectively in circles marked with the letters "*S*" and "*P*." The meaning of the statement "All *S* are *P*" may then be represented by the following diagram:

The *S* circle is contained in the *P* circle, which represents the fact that every member of S is a member of P. (Of course, should S and P represent terms denoting identical classes, the two circles would overlap exactly.) Through reference to the diagram, it is clear that "All S are P" makes a claim about every member of the S class, since the statement says that every member of S is in the P class. But the statement does not make a claim about every member of the P class, since there may be some members of P that are outside of S. Thus, by the definition of "distributed term" given above, S is distributed and P is not. In other words, for any universal affirmative (**A**) proposition, the subject term, whatever it may be, is distributed, and the predicate term is undistributed.

Let us now consider the universal negative (**E**) proposition. "No S are P" states that the S and P classes are separate, which may be represented as follows:

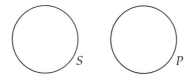

This statement makes a claim about every member of S and every member of P. It asserts that every member of S is separate from every member of P, and also that every member of P is separate from every member of S. Accordingly, by the definition above, both the subject and predicate terms of universal negative (**E**) propositions are distributed.

The particular affirmative (**I**) proposition states that at least one member of S is a member of P. If we represent this one member of S that we are certain about by an asterisk, the resulting diagram looks like this:

Since the asterisk is inside the P class, it represents something that is simultaneously an S and a P; in other words, it represents a member of the S class that is also a member of the P class. Thus, the statement "Some S are P" makes a claim about one member (at least) of S and also one member (at least) of P, but not about all members of either class. Hence, by the definition of distribution, neither S nor P is distributed.

The particular negative (**O**) proposition asserts that at least one member of S is not a member of P. If we once again represent this one member of S by an asterisk, the resulting diagram is as follows:

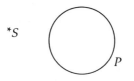

*S

P

Since the other members of S may or may not be outside of P, it is clear that the statement "Some S are not P" does not make a claim about every member of S, so S is not distributed. But, as may be seen from the diagram, the statement does assert that the entire P class is separated from this one member of S that is outside; that is, it does make a claim about every member of P. Thus, in the particular negative (**O**) proposition, P is distributed and S is undistributed.

At this point the notion of distribution may be somewhat vague and elusive. Unfortunately, there is no simple and easy way to make the idea graphically clear. The best that can be done is to repeat some of the things that have already been said. First of all, distribution is an attribute or quality that the subject and predicate terms of a categorical proposition may or may not possess, depending on the kind of proposition. If the proposition in question is an **A** type, then the subject term, whatever it may be, is distributed. If it is an **E** type, then both terms are distributed; if an **I** type, then neither; and if an **O** type, then the predicate. If a certain term is *distributed* in a proposition, this simply means that the proposition says something about every member of the class that the term denotes. If a term is *undistributed*, the proposition does not say something about every member of the class. The attribute of distribution, while not particularly important in relation to subsequent developments in this chapter, is essential to the evaluation of syllogisms in the next chapter.

The material of this section may now be summarized as follows:

Proposition	Letter name	Quantity	Quality	Terms distributed
All S are P.	A	universal	affirmative	S
No S are P.	E	universal	negative	S and P
Some S are P.	I	particular	affirmative	none
Some S are not P.	O	particular	negative	P

EXERCISE 4.2

I. For each of the following categorical propositions identify the letter name, quantity, and quality. Then state whether the subject and predicate terms are distributed or undistributed.

★1. No mobsters are persons who make good Labor Secretaries.

2. All governments that bargain with terrorists are governments that encourage terrorism.

3. Some symphony orchestras are organizations on the brink of bank-ruptcy.

★4. Some Soviet leaders are not thoroughgoing opponents of capitalist eco-nomics.

5. All human contacts with benzene are potential causes of cancer.

6. No labor strikes are events welcomed by management.

★7. Some hospitals are organizations that overcharge the Medicare program.

8. Some affirmative action plans are not programs that result in reverse dis-crimination.

II. Change the quality but not the quantity of the following statements:

★1. All drunk drivers are threats to others on the highway.

2. No wildlife refuges are locations suitable for condominium develop-ments.

3. Some slumlords are persons who eventually wind up in jail.

★4. Some CIA operatives are not champions of human rights.

III. Change the quantity but not the quality of the following statements:

★1. All owners of pit bull terriers are persons who can expect expensive law-suits.

2. No tax proposals that favor the rich are fair proposals.

3. Some grade school administrators are persons who choke the educa-tional process.

★4. Some residents of Manhattan are not people who can afford to live there.

IV. Change both the quality and the quantity of the following statements:

★1. All oil spills are events catastrophic to the environment.

2. No alcoholics are persons with a healthy diet.

3. Some Mexican vacations are episodes that end with Montezuma's re-venge.

★4. Some corporate lawyers are not persons with a social conscience.

4.3 THE TRADITIONAL SQUARE OF OPPOSITION

The **traditional square of opposition,** in essence originated by Aristotle more than 2,000 years ago, is a pattern of lines that illustrates logically necessary relationships among the four kinds of categorical proposi-tions. These relationships provide for valid inferences between one statement and another that hold as a result of the form of the statement and regardless of the subject matter. For example, if the nonsensical statement "All adlers are bobkins" is given as true, we can use the square to compute the truth value of the three corresponding propositions, "No adlers are bobkins," "Some adlers are bobkins," and "Some adlers are not bobkins." The traditional square of opposition is represented as follows:

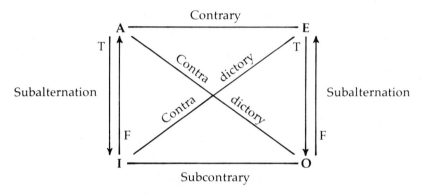

The four different categorical propositions are related to one another in terms of four different inferential relations. Here are the definitions of three of these relations (the fourth will be defined shortly):

> **contradictory** = opposite truth value
> **contrary** = at least one is false (not both true)
> **subcontrary** = at least one is true (not both false)

Returning to our nonsensical statement, "All adlers are bobkins," and supposing this statement is true, we can use the square of opposition to compute the truth value of the three corresponding propositions. The given proposition is an **A** proposition. By the *contradictory* relation we know immediately that the **O** proposition, "Some adlers are not bobkins," has the opposite truth value and is therefore false. By the *contrary* relation either the **A** or the **E** is false. Since we know that the **A** is true, it follows that the **E** proposition, "No adlers are bobkins," is false. Finally, since the **E** is false, it follows via the contradictory relation that the **I** proposition, "Some adlers are bobkins," is true. The truth value of the **I** proposition could also have been determined via the subcontrary relation: because the **O** was found to be false, and because either the **O** or the **I** is true, it follows that the **I** is true. Thus, from the supposition that "All adlers are bobkins" is true, we have determined the truth value of the other three corresponding propositions.

Let us take a closer look at the contrary and subcontrary relations. Contrary means "at least one is false," so if either the **A** or the **E** proposition is given as true, the other must be false. But what happens when one of these is given as false? In this case the other proposition could be *either* true or false without violating the "at least one is false" rule. That is, if **A** is given as false, **E** could be true and at least one of the **A**–**E** pair would be false, or **E** could be false and at least one of the **A**–**E** pair would be false. In such a case the **E** proposition is said to have **undetermined** truth value. This means that the **E** proposition is not *necessarily* either true or false. To determine its actual truth value one would have to use some method other than the inferences provided by the square of opposition.

Analogous reasoning extends to the subcontrary relation. Subcontrary means "at least one is true," so if either the **I** or the **O** proposition is given as false, the other is true. But if either the **I** or the **O** is given as true, the other proposition could be either true or false without violating the "at least one is true" rule. So, if either the **I** or the **O** proposition is given as true, the other proposition has undetermined truth value. In summary, in order to obtain determined results from the contrary relation, we must first be told that either the **A** or the **E** proposition is *true,* and in order to obtain determined results from the subcontrary relation, we must first be told that either the **I** or the **O** proposition is *false.*

We can illustrate these results by returning to the nonsensical proposition "All adlers are bobkins." If we suppose this proposition is false, we can tell by the contradictory relation that the **O** proposition, "Some adlers are not bobkins," is true. But by the contrary relation, the **E** proposition, "No adlers are bobkins," is undetermined. Similarly, by the subcontrary relation, the **I** proposition, "Some adlers are bobkins," is also undetermined.

Up until now we have used the square of opposition quite successfully without at any time depending on the relation of **subalternation.** This relation is needed only if one wishes to make immediate inferences between the **A** and **I** propositions or between the **E** and **O** propositions. Of course, it also serves as a useful supplement to the other three relations. Note that the subalternation relation is represented by two arrows, the downward arrow marked with the letter "T" (true) and the upward one with "F" (false). These arrows may be thought of as pipelines through which truth values "flow." The downward arrow transmits only truth, the upward arrow only falsity. Thus, if the **A** proposition is given as true, we may conclude that the **I** proposition is also true; conversely, if the **I** is given as false, we may conclude that the **A** proposition is also false. But if the **A** proposition is given as false, the downward arrow, which transmits only truth, is useless and, of course, the upward arrow goes in the wrong direction. So in this case we conclude that the **I** proposition has undetermined truth value. Similarly, if the **I** proposition is given as true, the **A** proposition has undetermined truth value. Analogous reasoning prevails for the subalternation relation between the **E** and **O** propositions.

Rather than attempt a rigorous proof of the four inferential relations involved in the square of opposition, let us settle for a less rigorous illustration of their correctness. For reasons that will become apparent in Section 4.5, it is important that the categorical propositions to which the traditional square of opposition is applied have subject terms that denote actually existing things. But this hardly constitutes a severe restriction on its use. Let us first consider the statement "All tigers are mammals." This statement is in fact true, and the results given by the square of opposition are quite expected: "Some tigers are mammals" (subalternation) is true, "Some tigers are not mammals" (contradictory) is false, and "No tigers are mammals" (contrary) is false. Next, consider the statement "Some apples are red." This statement is actually true. Accordingly, it is hardly unexpected that "No apples are red" (contradiction) should be false. By the other three relations, contrary, subcontrary, and subalternation, the corresponding **A** and **O** propositions are undetermined. This means that the square of opposition alone will not tell us the truth value of these statements. But, of course, we know from having actually experienced green apples that "All apples are red" is false, and "Some apples are not red" is true. Thus, we have a case where the **A** and **E** propositions are both false and the **I** and **O** propositions both true: a result quite consistent with the square of opposition.

Because the square of opposition illustrates *necessary* relationships between statements, it can be used to test arguments for validity. Example:

> All supernovas are things that emit neutrinos.
> Therefore, it is false that no supernovas are things that emit neutrinos.

We begin by assuming the premise to be true and then determine whether the conclusion follows necessarily from that assumption. Since the premise is an **A** statement, by the contrary relation the corresponding **E** statement is false. Thus, the conclusion is true, and the argument is valid.

Here is another example:

> Some viruses are structures that attack T cells.
> Therefore, some viruses are not structures that attack T cells.

Here the relation in question is subcontrary. By that relation, if the premise is assumed true, the conclusion has undetermined truth value, and so the argument is invalid. The argument commits the formal fallacy of **illicit subcontrary.** Analogously, arguments that depend on an incorrect application of the contrary relation commit the formal fallacy of **illicit contrary,** and those that depend on an incorrect application of subalternation commit an **illicit subalternation.**

When the square of opposition is used in the capacity of a single relationship only, as when evaluating an argument, no special precautions are necessary. But when one relationship is used in conjunction with another, the contradictory relation should always be used first. If, for example, a certain **A** proposition is given as true and we wish to determine the truth value of the corresponding **O** proposition, one possible procedure is to infer that the **E** statement is false, and from there proceed to the **O** statement. But subalternation from a false **E** statement yields undetermined results, and we might therefore be persuaded that the truth value of the **O** statement is undetermined. The relation of contradiction, however, tells us immediately that the **O** statement is false. This example illustrates the fact that the relation of contradiction is stronger than the others and gives determined results when the combination of two other relations does not.

Another point that should be kept in mind is that when undetermined truth values do turn up, they always do so in pairs across the diagonal of the square. This is only natural, of course. For if we were to say that a certain **E** statement, for example, has undetermined truth value, and that the corresponding **I** statement is, let us say, true, we could then conclude via contradiction that the **E** statement is really false. Such an inference would necessarily involve some prior mistake in the use of the square.

The following table may be used to check results when using the square of opposition:

> If **A** is given as true, then: **E** is false, **I** is true, **O** is false.
> If **E** is given as true, then: **A** is false, **I** is false, **O** is true.
> If **I** is given as true, then: **E** is false, **A** is undetermined, **O** is undetermined.
> If **O** is given as true, then: **A** is false, **E** is undetermined, **I** is undetermined.
>
> If **A** is given as false, then: **E** is undetermined, **I** is undetermined, **O** is true.
> If **E** is given as false, then: **A** is undetermined, **I** is true, **O** is undetermined.
> If **I** is given as false, then: **A** is false, **E** is true, **O** is true.
> If **O** is given as false, then: **A** is true, **E** is false, **I** is true.

EXERCISE 4.3

I. Use the traditional square of opposition to find the answers to these problems.

★1. If "All fashion fads are products of commercial brainwashing" is true, what is the truth value of the following statements:
   a. No fashion fads are products of commercial brainwashing.
   b. Some fashion fads are products of commercial brainwashing.
   c. Some fashion fads are not products of commercial brainwashing.

2. If "All fashion fads are products of commercial brainwashing" is false, what is the truth value of the following statements:
   a. No fashion fads are products of commercial brainwashing.
   b. Some fashion fads are products of commercial brainwashing.
   c. Some fashion fads are not products of commercial brainwashing.

3. If "No sting operations are cases of entrapment" is true, what is the truth value of the following statements:
   a. All sting operations are cases of entrapment.
   b. Some sting operations are cases of entrapment.
   c. Some sting operations are not cases of entrapment.

★4. If "No sting operations are cases of entrapment" is false, what is the truth value of the following statements:
   a. All sting operations are cases of entrapment.
   b. Some sting operations are cases of entrapment.
   c. Some sting operations are not cases of entrapment.

5. If "Some assassinations are morally justifiable actions" is true, what is the truth value of the following statements:
   a. All assassinations are morally justifiable actions.
   b. No assassinations are morally justifiable actions.
   c. Some assassinations are not morally justifiable actions.

6. If "Some assassinations are morally justifiable actions" is false, what is the truth value of the following statements:
   a. All assassinations are morally justifiable actions.
   b. No assassinations are morally justifiable actions.
   c. Some assassinations are not morally justifiable actions.

★7. If "Some obsessive-compulsive behaviors are not curable diseases" is true, what is the truth value of the following statements:
   a. All obsessive-compulsive behaviors are curable diseases.
   b. No obsessive-compulsive behaviors are curable diseases.
   c. Some obsessive-compulsive behaviors are curable diseases.

8. If "Some obsessive-compulsive behaviors are not curable diseases" is false, what is the truth value of the following statements:
   a. All obsessive-compulsive behaviors are curable diseases.
   b. No obsessive-compulsive behaviors are curable diseases.
   c. Some obsessive-compulsive behaviors are curable diseases.

II. Use the traditional square of opposition to determine whether the following arguments are valid or invalid. Name any fallacies that are committed.

★1. All advocates of school prayer are individuals who insist on imposing their views on others.
   Therefore, some advocates of school prayer are individuals who insist on imposing their views on others.

2. It is false that no papers in the Sigmund Freud archives are documents complimentary to their author.
   Therefore, some papers in the Sigmund Freud archives are not documents complimentary to their author.

3. All Holocaust survivors are people committed to sustaining the memory.
Therefore, it is false that no Holocaust survivors are people committed to sustaining the memory.

★4. Some campus romances are episodes plagued by violence.
Therefore, some campus romances are not episodes plagued by violence.

5. Some pornographic publications are materials protected by the First Amendment.
Therefore, it is false that no pornographic publications are materials protected by the First Amendment.

6. It is false that some forms of human creativity are activities amenable to mathematical analysis.
Therefore, it is false that all forms of human creativity are activities amenable to mathematical analysis.

★7. It is false that all mainstream conservatives are persons who support free legal services for the poor.
Therefore, no mainstream conservatives are persons who support free legal services for the poor.

8. It is false that some orthodox psychoanalysts are not individuals driven by a religious fervor.
Therefore, it is false that some orthodox psychoanalysts are individuals driven by a religious fervor.

9. Some product safety standards are not measures that can be implemented on a state by state basis.
Therefore, all product safety standards are measures that can be implemented on a state by state basis.

★10. It is false that some school officials who censure *The Diary of Anne Frank* are not persons who threaten the groundwork of civilization.
Therefore, some school officials who censure *The Diary of Anne Frank* are persons who threaten the groundwork of civilization.

III. Use the traditional square of opposition to determine whether the following arguments are valid or invalid. Then determine whether they are sound or unsound. Name any fallacies that are committed.

★1. Some Middle Eastern nations are anxious exporters of religious fanaticism.
Therefore, some Middle Eastern nations are not anxious exporters of religious fanaticism.

2. All needy college students are persons who qualify for federally guaranteed student loans.
Therefore, it is false that no needy college students are persons who qualify for federally guaranteed student loans.

3. It is false that no African nations are countries with an AIDS epidemic.
Therefore, some African nations are countries with an AIDS epidemic.

★4. Some cases of sex discrimination are violations of the 1964 Civil Rights Act.
Therefore, all cases of sex discrimination are violations of the 1964 Civil Rights Act.

5. It is false that some human cells are not entities that contain DNA.
Therefore, all human cells are entities that contain DNA.

6. It is true that some CD players are not machines that contain lasers.
Therefore, some CD players are machines that contain lasers.

★7. No Vietnam veterans are persons who were brutalized by the enemy.
Therefore, some Vietnam veterans are not persons who were brutalized by the enemy.

8. No quartz watches are timepieces that will operate without a battery.
Therefore, it is false that all quartz watches are timepieces that will operate without a battery.

9. It is false that some airplanes are craft that have circled the globe without refueling.
Therefore, it is false that all airplanes are craft that have circled the globe without refueling.

★10. It is false that some forms of slavery are not assaults on human dignity.
Therefore, all forms of slavery are assaults on human dignity.

4.4 CONVERSION, OBVERSION, AND CONTRAPOSITION

Many statements expressed in ordinary English contain negated terms that sometimes obscure the meaning of the statements involved. Consider the following example:

> Some employees who are not currently on the payroll are not ineligible for workers' benefits.

As it stands, this statement is rather complicated, and its meaning may not be immediately clear; but it may be shown to be equivalent to the much simpler statement:

> Some of those eligible for workers' benefits are not currently on the payroll.

To justify this equivalence, and others like it, we need the operations of conversion, obversion, and contraposition.

Conversion, the simplest of the three, consists in switching the subject term with the predicate term. For example, if the E statement "No foxes are hedgehogs" is converted, the resulting statement is "No hedgehogs are foxes." This new statement is called the converse of the given statement and has the same truth value as the given statement. Similarly, converting the **I** statement "Some women are lawyers" gives us "Some lawyers are women," which has the same truth value as the given statement. Generalizing these results we obtain the following rule: *Converting an **E** or **I** statement gives a new statement that is logically equivalent to the given statement.* Two statements are said to be **logically equivalent** when they *necessarily* have the same truth value. Thus, converting an **E** or **I** statement gives a new statement that always has the same truth value as the original statement.

When we convert an **A** or **O** statement, on the other hand, the resulting statement does not necessarily have the same truth value as the given statement. For example, converting the true **A** statement "All carnations are flowers" gives the false statement "All flowers are carnations," and converting the true **O** statement "Some birds are not robins"

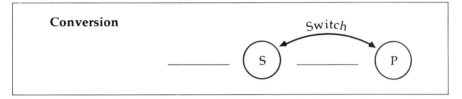

Conversion

Switch

S P

gives the false statement "Some robins are not birds." But converting the true **A** statement "All bachelors are unmarried men" gives the *true* statement "All unmarried men are bachelors," and converting the true **O** statement "Some apples are not oranges" gives the *true* statement "Some oranges are not apples." Thus, as these examples illustrate, the truth value of the converse of an **A** or **O** statement depends on the terms in the statement. In some cases the converse may happen to have the same truth value as the original statement and in other cases not. Since logic alone cannot decide which is the case, from the standpoint of logic the converse of an **A** or **O** statement has *undetermined* truth value.*

Conversion may be used to provide the link between the premise and conclusion of an argument. The following argument forms are valid:†

> No *A* are *B*.
> Therefore, no *B* are *A*.
>
> Some *A* are *B*.
> Therefore, some *B* are *A*.

---

*Some textbooks include treatment of an operation called "conversion by limitation," by which a true **A** statement entails a true **I** statement. Because this operation is merely a synthesis of ordinary conversion and subalternation, no special treatment is given it in this text. For analogous reasons, no special treatment is given to a similar operation called "contraposition by limitation."

†Some texts interpret arguments such as these as instances of begging the question. This text does not. See Section 3.4.

Since the premise of each argument form necessarily has the same truth value as the conclusion, if the premise is assumed true, the conclusion is necessarily true. On the other hand, the next two argument forms are invalid. Each commits the fallacy of **illicit conversion:**

All *A* are *B.*
Therefore, all *B* are *A.*

Some *A* are not *B.*
Therefore, some *B* are not *A.*

Obversion is more complicated than conversion and involves a two-step process: (1) changing the quality (without changing the quantity),

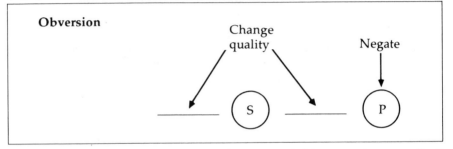

and (2) negating the predicate. The first part of this operation was dealt with in the exercise at the end of Section 4.2. For example, the following pairs of propositions have different quality but the same quantity:

All horses are animals.	No horses are animals.
Some trees are maples.	Some trees are not maples.

The second step involves negating the predicate. For simple predicates this is usually done by affixing the prefix "non-" to the predicate. When the two operations are performed together, the given proposition is said to be obverted, and the resulting proposition is called the "obverse" of the given proposition. Examples:

Given statement	**Obverse**
All horses are animals.	No horses are non-animals
No cats are dogs.	All cats are non-dogs.
Some trees are maples.	Some trees are not non-maples.
Some birds are not robins.	Some birds are non-robins.

Each of these statements (**A, E, I, O**) has the same truth value as its obverse. To see this it helps to be familiar with the concept of class complement. The **complement** of a class is the group consisting of all things that are *not* members of the class—in other words, everything *outside* the class. For example, the complement of the class of turtles includes everything that is not a turtle—houses, battleships, oak trees, and so on. Relating this concept to negation, if a term denotes a certain class, the negation of that term denotes the complement of that class.

If we use this concept of class complement to interpret the four obverted statements above, the obverse of the first statement asserts that the class of horses is *excluded* from the complement of the class of animals. This is simply another way of saying that the class of horses is *included* in the class of animals. Similarly, the obverse of the second statement asserts that the class of cats is included in the complement of the class of dogs. This is just another way of saying that the class of cats is excluded from the class of dogs. Similar remarks pertain to the other two statements. These results may be generalized to obtain this rule: *The obverse of an A, E, I, or O statement is logically equivalent to, and therefore necessarily has the same truth value as, the given statement.*

If a proposition is obverted and then obverted again, the predicate will have been negated twice. Example:

All horses are animals.
No horses are non-animals.   (obverse)
All horses are non-non-animals.   (obverse of the obverse)

The prefix "non-non" is called double negation and may be deleted. The obverse of the obverse thus yields a statement identical in all respects to the given statement (as does the converse of the converse and the contrapositive of the contrapositive). However, while "non-non" may be deleted, the phrase "are not non-" should be left as it is. The word "not" is part of the copula, and "non-" is part of the predicate. These two components of categorical propositions must be kept separate.

As was noted earlier, when the predicate is a simple term, negating it can usually be accomplished by simply adding the prefix "non-." When the predicate is complex, more ingenuity is required. For example, if we want to obvert the statement "All returnable beverage containers are things that do not collect along highways," it would hardly do to write "No returnable beverage containers are non-things that do not collect along highways." It would be much better to write "No returnable beverage containers are things that collect along highways." Of course, the term "Things that collect along highways" is not technically the negation of "Things that do not collect along highways," but if we imagine the scope of discourse to be restricted to the subject of tangible things, then such a procedure is justified.

The legitimacy of this procedure can be clearly seen by appealing once again to the concept of class complement. The complement of the class consisting of Persian carpets, for example, is the class consisting of everything that is not a Persian carpet—ripe tomatoes, china teacups, gold rings, and so on. But if we restrict the scope of discourse to carpets, the complement of this class is the class consisting of carpets that are not Persian. Thus, under this restriction, the negation of the term "carpets that were made in Persia" is simply "carpets that were not made in Persia."

As is the case with conversion, obversion may be used to supply the link between premise and conclusion in deductive arguments. The following argument forms are valid:

All *A* are *B*.
Therefore, no *A* are non-*B*.
No *A* are *B*.
Therefore, all *A* are non-*B*.
Some *A* are *B*.
Therefore, some *A* are not non-*B*.
Some *A* are not *B*.
Therefore, some *A* are non-*B*.

The premise of each argument form has the same truth value as the conclusion; accordingly, if the premise is assumed true, the conclusion must necessarily be true.

Contraposition also involves a two-step process: (1) switching subject and predicate terms, and (2) negating subject and predicate terms. When a given statement is contraposed, the resulting statement is called the "contrapositive" of the given statement. Examples:

Given statement	Contrapositive
All goats are animals.	All non-animals are non-goats.
Some birds are not parrots.	Some non-parrots are not non-birds.

The contrapositive of the first statement asserts that the complement of the class of animals is included in the complement of the class of goats, which is just another way of saying that the class of goats is included in the class of animals. The contrapositive of the second statement asserts that part of the complement of the class of parrots (that is, sparrows) is excluded from the complement of the class of birds (that is, it is *included* in the class of birds), which is simply another way of saying that some birds (sparrows) are not parrots. These results may be generalized to obtain this rule: *The contrapositive of an A or O statement is logically equivalent to, and therefore necessarily has the same truth value as, the given statement.*

When we contrapose an **E** or **I** statement, on the other hand, the contrapositive does not necessarily have the same truth value as the given statement. For example, the truth value of the contrapositives of the following statements is different from that of the given statements:

Given statement	Contrapositive
No dogs are cats.	No non-cats are non-dogs.
Some birds are non-parrots.	Some parrots are non-birds.

In each case the given statement is true and the contrapositive is false. For example, an instance of both a non-cat and a non-dog is a pig. Thus the statement "No non-cats are non-dogs" implies that "no pigs are pigs"—which is clearly false. As for the second pair of statements, "Some parrots are non-birds" is also clearly false because it implies that some parrot is not a bird.

On the other hand, contraposing the true **E** statement "No fish are non-fish" gives the *true* (and identical) statement "No fish are non-fish," and contraposing the true **I** statement "Some apples are red things" gives the *true* statement "Some non-red things are non-apples." Thus, the truth value of the contrapositive of an **E** or **I** statement, as with the converse of an **A** or **O** statement, depends on the terms in the statement. In other words, the contrapositive of an **E** or **I** statement is not logically equivalent to the given statement, and so from the standpoint of logic, it has *undetermined* truth value.

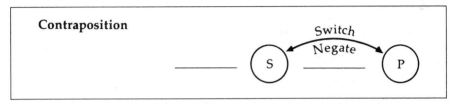

As with conversion and obversion, contraposition may provide the link between the premise and the conclusion of an argument. The following argument forms are valid:

>All *A* are *B*.
>Therefore, all non-*B* are non-*A*.
>
>Some *A* are not *B*.
>Therefore, some non-*B* are not non-*A*.

On the other hand, the following argument forms are invalid. Each commits the fallacy of **illicit contraposition:**

>Some *A* are *B*.
>Therefore, some non-*B* are non-*A*.
>
>No *A* are *B*.
>Therefore, no non-*B* are non-*A*.

Both illicit contraposition and illicit conversion are formal fallacies; that is, they can be detected through mere examination of the form of an argument.

Conversion, obversion, and contraposition may be used in conjunction with the traditional square of opposition to establish the validity of certain arguments. Consider the following:

>All non-*A* are *B*.
>Therefore, some *B* are not *A*.

Proving this argument valid requires three steps. Each step is derived from the one preceding it, and the justification for each is written to the immediate right:

>All non-*A* are *B*.
>Some non-*A* are *B*.   subalt.
>Some *B* are non-*A*.   conv.
>Some *B* are not *A*.   obv.

Various strategies may be used to obtain the conclusion of arguments such as this, but one procedure is to concentrate first on obtaining the individual terms as they appear in the conclusion. The order of the terms may be attended to next, and finally the square of opposition may be used to adjust the quality and quantity. As the above proof illustrates, however, variations on this procedure are sometimes necessary. The conclusion of the above argument requires that the "non-*A*" in the premise be negated, thus suggesting obversion. But to use obversion to accomplish this, the "non-*A*" must be moved into the predicate position via conversion. The latter operation, however, is valid only on **E** and **I** statements. The fact that the conclusion is a particular statement suggests subalternation as an intermediate step, thus yielding an **I** statement that can be converted.

The results of this section are summarized in the following table:

Conversion: Switch subject and predicate terms.

Given statement	Converse	Truth value
E: No *S* are *P*. **I:** Some *S* are *P*.	No *P* are *S*. Some *P* are *S*.	Same truth value as given statement
A: All *S* are *P*. **O:** Some *S* are not *P*.	All *P* are *S*. Some *P* are not *S*.	Undetermined truth value

Obversion: Change quality, negate predicate term.

Given statement	Obverse	Truth value
A: All *S* are *P*. **E:** No *S* are *P*. **I:** Some *S* are *P*. **O:** Some *S* are not *P*.	No *S* are non-*P*. All *S* are non-*P*. Some *S* are not non-*P*. Some *S* are non-*P*.	Same truth value as given statement

Contraposition: Switch and negate subject and predicate terms.

Given statement	Contrapositive	Truth value
A: All *S* are *P*. **O:** Some *S* are not *P*.	All non-*P* are non-*S*. Some non-*P* are not non-*S*.	Same truth value as given statement
E: No *S* are *P*. **I:** Some *S* are *P*.	No non-*P* are non-*S*. Some non-*P* are non-*S*.	Undetermined truth value

EXERCISE 4.4

I. Perform the operations of conversion, obversion, and contraposition as indicated.

1. Convert the following propositions and state whether the converse is logically equivalent or not logically equivalent to the given proposition.
   ★a. All homes contaminated by radon gas are potential causes of lung cancer.

b. No sex-change operations are completely successful events.

c. Some murals by Diego Rivera are works that celebrate the revolution-ary spirit.

d. Some forms of carbon are not substances with a crystalline structure.

2. Obvert the following propositions and state whether the obverse is logi-cally equivalent or not logically equivalent to the given proposition.

★a. All radically egalitarian societies are societies that do not preserve in-dividual liberties.

b. No cult leaders are people who fail to brainwash their followers.

c. Some college football coaches are persons who do not slip money to their players.

d. Some budgetary cutbacks are not actions fair to the poor.

3. Contrapose the following propositions and state whether the contraposi-tive is logically equivalent or not logically equivalent to the given proposi-tion.

★a. All physicians whose licenses have been revoked are physicians ineli-gible to practice.

b. No gases are incompressible substances.

c. Some Congressmen who recommend overhauling the Pentagon are persons unpopular with the administration.

d. Some people who decline to support mandatory busing are not those who fail to advocate integrated schools.

II. Use conversion, obversion, and contraposition to determine whether the following arguments are valid or invalid. For those that are invalid, name the fallacy committed.

★1. All commodity traders are gamblers who risk sudden disaster. Therefore, all gamblers who risk sudden disaster are commodity trad-ers.

2. No child abusers are persons who belong in day-care centers. Therefore, all child abusers are persons who do not belong in day-care centers.

3. Some states having limited powers are not slave states. Therefore, some free states are not states having unlimited powers.

★4. Some insane people are illogical people. Therefore, some logical people are sane people.

5. Some organ transplants are not sensible operations. Therefore, some organ transplants are senseless operations.

6. No refugees from El Salvador are persons given political asylum. Therefore, no persons given political asylum are refugees from El Salva-dor.

★7. All periods when interest rates are high are times businesses tend not to expand. Therefore, all times businesses tend to expand are periods when interest rates are low.

8. Some swimsuits are not garments intended for the water.
Therefore, some garments intended for the water are not swimsuits.

9. No promises made under duress are enforceable contracts.
Therefore, no unenforceable contracts are promises made in the absence of duress.

★10. All ladies of the night are individuals with low self-esteem.
Therefore, no ladies of the night are individuals with high self-esteem.

III. In 1 through 10 you are given a statement, its truth value in parentheses, and an operation to be performed on that statement. You must supply the new statement and the truth value of the new statement. In 11 through 20 you are given a statement, its truth value in parentheses, and a new statement. You must determine how the new statement was derived from the given statement and supply the truth value of the new statement. Some of these exercises involve the traditional square of opposition.

Given statement	Operation	New statement	Truth value
★1. All non-*A* are *B*. (T)	contrap.	_____	_____
2. Some *A* are non-*B*. (F)	subalt.	_____	_____
3. No *A* are non-*B*. (T)	obv.	_____	_____
★4. Some non-*A* are not *B*. (T)	subcon.	_____	_____
5. No *A* are non-*B*. (F)	contradic.	_____	_____
6. No *A* are *B*. (T)	contrap.	_____	_____
★7. All non-*A* are *B*. (T)	contrary	_____	_____
8. Some *A* are not non-*B*. (F)	obv.	_____	_____
9. No *A* are non-*B*. (F)	conv.	_____	_____
★10. Some non-*A* are non-*B*. (F)	subcon.	_____	_____
11. Some non-*A* are not *B*. (T)	_____	All non-*A* are *B*.	_____
12. Some *A* are non-*B*. (T)	_____	Some non-*B* are *A*.	_____
★13. All non-*A* are *B*. (F)	_____	No non-*A* are non-*B*.	_____
14. Some non-*A* are not *B*. (T)	_____	No non-*A* are *B*.	_____
15. All *A* are non-*B*. (F)	_____	All non-*B* are *A*.	_____
★16. Some non-*A* are non-*B*. (F)	_____	No non-*A* are non-*B*.	_____
17. Some *A* are not non-*B*. (T)	_____	Some *B* are not non-*A*.	_____
18. No non-*A* are *B*. (T)	_____	Some non-*A* are not *B*.	_____
★19. No *A* are non-*B*. (F)	_____	All *A* are non-*B*.	_____
20. Some non-*A* are *B*. (F)	_____	Some non-*A* are not *B*.	_____

IV. Use conversion, obversion, contraposition, and the traditional square of opposition to prove that the following arguments are valid. Show each intermediate step in the deduction.

★1. All insurance policies are cryptically written documents.
Therefore, some cryptically written documents are insurance policies.

2. No gemstones that do not contain chromium are emeralds.
Therefore, some gemstones that are not emeralds are not gemstones that contain chromium.

3. It is false that some ficus benjaminas are untemperamental house plants.
Therefore, all ficus benjaminas are temperamental house plants.

★4. All exogenous morphines are addictive subtances.
Therefore, it is false that all addictive substances are endogenous morphines.

5. No persons who advocate free-enterprise economics are fundamentalist Christians.
Therefore, it is false that some fundamentalist Christians are not persons who advocate free enterprise economics.

6. It is false that some Gothic cathedrals are buildings that do not feature pointed arches.
Therefore, some buildings that feature pointed arches are Gothic cathedrals.

★7. Some persons who recognize paranormal events are not non-scientists.
Therefore, it is false that no scientists are persons who recognize paranormal events.

8. It is false that no unhealthy things to ingest are food additives.
Therefore, some food additives are not healthy things to ingest.

9. It is false that some illegal searches are not sobriety checkpoints.
Therefore, some sobriety checkpoints are not legal searches.

★10. It is false that some feminists are not advocates of equal pay for equal work.
Therefore, it is false that all advocates of equal pay for equal work are non-feminists.

4.5 THE MODERN SQUARE OF OPPOSITION AND THE EXISTENTIAL FALLACY

As was suggested in Section 4.3, a problem arises if the traditional square of opposition is used in connection with statements that make assertions about things that do not actually exist. Consider, for example, the statement "All unicorns are one-horned animals." If this statement is considered to be false (because there are no unicorns), the traditional square of opposition, via the relation of contradiction, tells us that "Some unicorns are not one-horned" is true. But this latter statement asserts that at least one unicorn is not one-horned—which is false, because no unicorns exist. And if "All unicorns are one-horned animals" is considered to be true (because if there were any unicorns, by definition they would be one-horned), the relation of subalternation tells us that "Some unicorns are one-horned animals" is true. But once again, because no unicorns exist, this statement is false. Thus, as this example illustrates, the traditional square of opposition simply cannot be used in conjunction with statements that make assertions about things that do not exist. In these cases we must use what is called the **modern square of opposition**.

The modern square of opposition is based on an interpretation of categorical statements introduced by the nineteenth-century logician George Boole. According to this interpretation, universal statements have the following meaning:

All S are P. = No members of S are outside P.
No S are P. = No members of S are inside P.

These interpretations of the **A** and **E** statements tell us where members of S do *not* exist. They say nothing about where they do exist, or, for that matter, whether they exist at all. In other words, from the Boolean standpoint, universal statements are neutral about existence.

Particular statements, on the other hand, make a positive assertion about existence. They mean the same thing from the Boolean standpoint as they do from the standpoint of the traditional square of opposition:

Some S are P. = At least one S exists, and that S is a P.
Some S are not P. = At least one S exists, and that S is not a P.

The square of opposition that results from the Boolean interpretation of categorical statements—that is, the modern square of opposition—is presented in this way:

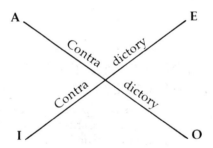

The only relation that exists in the modern square of opposition is the contradictory relation—the relations of contrary, subcontrary, and sub-alternation do not apply. Thus, the modern square of opposition provides for fewer inferences than the traditional square—which is only natural, since it makes fewer assumptions.

Let us now apply the modern square of opposition to the statement "All unicorns are one-horned animals." According to the Boolean interpretation of universal propositions, this statement means "No unicorns are outside the class of one-horned animals"—which is true, because there are no unicorns at all. By the contradictory relation, therefore, "Some unicorns are not one-horned animals" is false—which is exactly what we would expect it to be. No additional inferences are possible.

Now that we have two squares of opposition, the traditional and the modern, the question naturally arises of when to use one and when to use the other. The answer is that although the modern square may be used on all categorical propositions, it is preferable to use the traditional square on categorical propositions that make assertions about actually existing things, because it provides for more inferences. On categorical propositions that make assertions about things that do not actually exist (such as unicorns or leprechauns), the traditional square cannot be used; only the modern square may be used.

The **existential fallacy** is a formal fallacy that occurs when the traditional square of opposition is used in conjunction with propositions that make assertions about things that do not actually exist. In other words, it occurs when the relations of contrary, subcontrary, and subalternation are used (in a manner that would normally yield a determinate truth value) to draw inferences from propositions whose subject terms denote empty classes. Under these conditions, as I have pointed out, only the modern square of opposition may be used, and the modern square does not include these relations. The existential fallacy is a formal fallacy in that, once the Boolean standpoint has been adopted, it may be detected through mere inspection of the form of an argument. The following arguments commit the existential fallacy:

> All witches that fly on broomsticks are fearless women.
> Therefore, some witches that fly on broomsticks are fearless women.
>
> No wizards with magical powers are malevolent creatures.
> Therefore, it is false that all wizards with magical powers are malevolent creatures.

The first argument depends on the subalternation relation, the second on the contrary relation.

EXERCISE 4.5

Use the traditional and modern squares of opposition to determine whether the following arguments are valid or invalid. For those that are invalid, name any fallacies that are committed.

★1. All teenage smokers are persons who jeopardize their health.
   Therefore, some teenage smokers are persons who jeopardize their health.

2. No werewolves are creatures that lurk about in the daytime.
   Therefore, some werewolves are not creatures that lurk about in the daytime.

3. It is false that some cities in Japan are high crime areas.
   Therefore, some cities in Japan are not high crime areas.

★4. All current residents of Atlantis are people with gills.
Therefore, it is false that some current residents of Atlantis are not people with gills.

5. Some Miami policemen are not officers involved in drug trafficking.
Therefore, no Miami policemen are officers involved in drug trafficking.

6. No vampires are avid connoisseurs of garlic bread.
Therefore, it is false that some vampires are avid connoisseurs of garlic bread.

★7. It is false that some lung cancer vaccines are readily obtainable inoculations.
Therefore, some lung cancer vaccines are not readily obtainable inoculations.

8. It is false that all opponents of school prayer are people who object to a moment of silence.
Therefore, no opponents of school prayer are people who object to a moment of silence.

9. No palm trees indigenous to the arctic are natural habitats for rodents.
Therefore, it is false that all palm trees indigenous to the arctic are natural habitats for rodents.

★10. It is false that some juvenile killers are not criminals who deserve to be tried as adults.
Therefore, it is false that no juvenile killers are criminals who deserve to be tried as adults.

4.6 VENN DIAGRAMS

The nineteenth-century logician John Venn, following the interpretation of universal statements introduced earlier by George Boole, developed a system of diagrams to represent the information contained in categorical propositions. These diagrams have come to be known as **Venn diagrams.**

A Venn diagram is an arrangement of overlapping circles. Each circle represents the class denoted by a term in a categorical proposition. Since each categorical proposition has exactly two terms, the Venn diagram consists of two circles. Once the circles are drawn, they are labeled with letters corresponding to the terms in the statement. The left-hand circle is usually selected to represent the subject term, and the right-hand circle, the predicate term, but the exact order is not important. The first letter in each term is usually selected for labeling the circles, but if two terms begin with the same letter, this convention is modified.

A CONCISE INTRODUCTION TO LOGIC

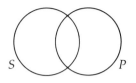

The members of the class denoted by the subject term (if any such members exist) are conceived as being located in the S circle, and the members of the class denoted by the predicate term (if any such members exist) are conceived as being located in the P circle. The members of the S class may all be located in the part of the S circle that is outside the P circle, or in the part that the P circle overlaps, or in both; and the members of the P class may all be located in the part of the P circle that is outside the S circle, or in the part that the S circle overlaps, or in both.

Conversely, if an entity is inside the S circle, it is a member of the S class, and if it is inside the P circle, it is a member of the P class. Obviously, if something is in the central area where the S and P circles overlap, it is a member of both the S and P classes. For example, in the diagram below, if the letter "A" represents the term "Americans" and "F" the term "farmers," then anything in the area marked "1" is an American but not a farmer, anything in the area marked "2" is both an American and a farmer, and anything in the area marked "3" is a farmer but not an American. The area marked "4" is the area outside both circles—anything in this area is neither a farmer nor an American.

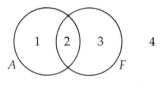

Unless an exception is made to the contrary, categorical propositions represented in Venn diagrams are given the Boolean interpretation:

All S are P. = No members of S are outside P.
No S are P. = No members of S are inside P.
Some S are P. = At least one S exists, and that S is a P.
Some S are not P. = At least one S exists, and that S is not a P.

Each proposition is represented by making a single mark in a pair of overlapping circles. Two kinds of marks are allowed: shading an area and placing an "X" in an area. Shading an area means that the shaded area is empty, and placing an "X" in an area means that at least one thing exists in that area.* The "X" may be thought of as representing that one thing. If no mark appears in a certain area, nothing is known about that area; it may contain members or it may be empty. Shading is

---

*In many mathematics texts shading an area of a Venn diagram indicates that the area is *not* empty. The significance of shading in logic is exactly the opposite.

always used in connection with universal propositions, and placing an "X" is used in connection with particular propositions. The content of the four kinds of categorical propositions is represented as follows:

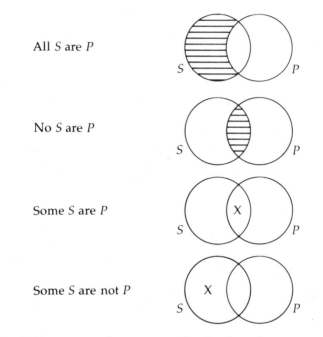

All S are P

No S are P

Some S are P

Some S are not P

These four diagrams exactly represent the Boolean interpretations of the four propositions. The first diagram states that the portion of the S circle that is outside the P circle is empty; in other words, no members of S are outside P. The second diagram states that the area where the S and P circles overlap is empty; in other words, no members of S are inside P. The third diagram states that there is at least one thing that is both an S and a P, and the fourth diagram states that at least one thing exists in the S circle that is not a P.

It should be noted that the diagrams that represent the universal propositions state nothing about existence. For example, the one that represents the **A** proposition states that the portion of S that is outside P is empty; but it does not say that the part of S that is inside P is not empty. Because no marks are made in these areas, we know nothing of their contents. They may be empty or they may have members. All of this is in conformity with the nonexistential character of the Boolean interpretation. Similarly, it should be noted that the diagrams that represent the particular propositions tell us that something exists in one single area. For example, the diagram that represents the **I** proposition tells us that something exists in the central area; but since no marks appear in either of the other two areas, we know nothing about their possible content.

EXERCISE 4.6

Draw Venn diagrams for the following propositions:

★1. No life decisions are happenings based solely on logic.

2. All electric motors are machines that depend on magnetism.

3. Some political campaigns are mere attempts to discredit opponents.

★4. Some rock music lovers are not fans of Madonna.

5. All redistricting plans are sources of controversy.

6. No tax audits are pleasant experiences for cheaters.

★7. Some housing developments are complexes that exclude children.

8. Some victims of Altzheimer's disease are not persons with damaged optic nerves.

4.7 USING VENN DIAGRAMS TO PROVE LOGICAL RELATIONSHIPS

Venn diagrams provide a convenient illustration of, and proof for, the inferences involved in both the traditional and the modern squares of opposition, as well as the operations of conversion, obversion, and contraposition. Let us first consider the modern square of opposition, shown on page 198.

The meaning of the contradictory relation is clearly illustrated by the diagrams. The diagram for the **A** statement says that the left-hand part of the *S* circle is empty, and the diagram for the **O** statement says that it is not empty. This is the strictest form of opposition. Similarly, the diagram for the **E** statement says that the central area is empty, while the diagram for the **I** statement says that it is not empty.

The relations of contrary, subcontrary, and subalternation do not hold in this diagram. This may be illustrated through the (quite legitimate) supposition that the *S* class is empty. If this is so, then we may imagine the entire *S* circle as shaded, in which case the diagrams for both the **A** and the **E** statements make a true assertion. This violates the definition of contrary. Continuing, if the entire *S* circle is empty, then the diagrams for both the **I** and **O** statements (which claim that some portion

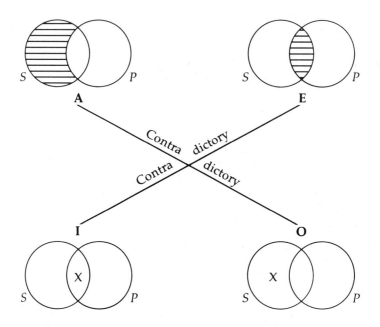

of the S circle is not empty) are false. This violates the definition of sub-contrary. Finally, if the **A** and **E** statements are both true, and the **I** and **O** statements both false, the definition of subalternation is violated.

Now let us turn to the traditional square of opposition. What distinguishes the traditional square from the modern one is the supposition that the universal statements to which it is applied make an assertion about things that actually exist. In other words, it is assumed that the classes denoted by the subject terms of these statements are not empty. In the diagram representing the **A** statement, this means that since the left-hand portion of the S circle is empty, the right-hand portion is not empty. This fact is represented by placing an "X" in the right-hand portion of the S circle. In addition, a small circle may be placed around this "X" to indicate that it comes not from the statement as such but from the special assumption peculiar to the traditional square of opposition. By similar reasoning, in the diagram that represents the **E** statement, a circled "X" is placed in the left-hand portion of the S circle.

Now, by inspecting the diagrams, we see that the **A** and **E** statements cannot both be true, because one says that an area is empty while the other says that that same area is not empty. Thus, the contrary relation prevails. Turning to subalternation, if the **A** statement is true, then the right-hand portion of the S circle has at least one member, making the **I** statement true. By similar reasoning, if the **E** statement is true, then the **O** statement is also true. Conversely, if the **I** statement is false, then the right-hand portion of the S circle is empty, making the **A** statement false; and if the **O** statement is false, then the left-hand portion of the S

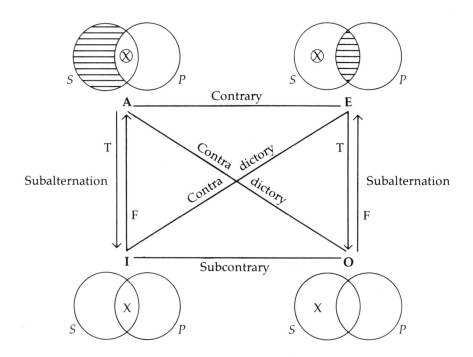

circle is empty, making the **E** statement false. Finally, turning to sub-contrary, if the **I** statement is false, the right-hand portion of the *S* circle is empty, and (since the entire *S* circle has at least one thing in it) this means that the left-hand portion of the *S* circle is not empty, making the **O** statement true. By similar reasoning, if the **O** statement is false, the right-hand portion of the *S* circle is not empty, making the **I** statement true. Thus, the relation of subcontrary prevails.

The diagrams for the traditional square show how contrary, subcon-trary, and subalternation come back into the picture when the assump-tion is made that at least one *S* exists. Unfortunately, these diagrams obscure the meaning of contradiction; but since contradiction is estab-lished by the diagrams for the modern square, which make no existen-tial assumptions, contradiction remains valid when existential assump-tions are made. This same line of thinking underlies the use of Venn diagrams to prove the operations of conversion, obversion, and con-traposition. Since these operations hold from the modern standpoint, proving them from this standpoint is sufficient to prove that they hold from the traditional standpoint as well.

Let us begin with conversion. The diagram for "No *S* are *P*" is clearly identical to that for "No *P* are *S*," and the diagram for "Some *S* are *P*" is clearly identical to that for "Some *P* are *S*." The operation of conversion thus yields equivalent results for **E** and **I** statements. But the diagram for "All *S* are *P*" is clearly different from that for "All *P* are *S*," and the diagram for "Some *S* are not *P*" is clearly different from that for "Some *P* are not *S*." Thus, in general, conversion does not yield equivalent results for **A** and **O** statements.

Conversion

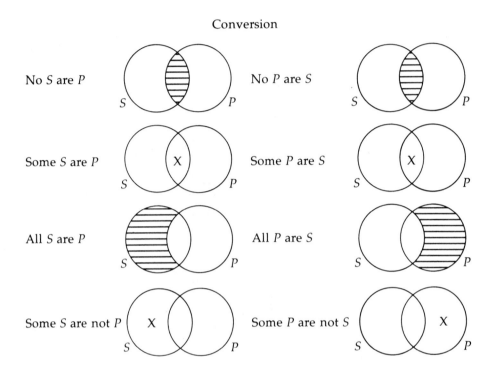

These diagrams also show that conversion yields logically equivalent results for **E** and **I** statements regardless of whether the terms denote actually existing things. Thus, "No unicorns are griffins" is logically equivalent to "No griffins are unicorns." The same is true for obversion and contraposition. All three operations yield the results that they do regardless of existence.

In the case of obversion, the diagrams are identical for all four kinds of categorical propositions. When drawing these diagrams, keep in mind that "non-*P*" designates the complement of *P*, which is the area outside the *P* circle. The statement "No *S* are non-*P*" therefore asserts that the area where *S* overlaps the complement of *P* is empty, which is represented by shading the left-hand part of the *S* circle. The statement "All *S* are non-*P*" asserts that all members of *S* (if there are any) are in the complement of *P*, which is represented by shading the part of *S* that is inside *P*. "Some *S* are not non-*P*" asserts that at least one member of *S* is not in the complement of *P*; that is, at least one member of *S* is *inside P*. Finally, "Some *S* are non-*P*" asserts that at least one member of *S* is in the complement of *P*.

Turning to the diagrams for contraposition, "All non-P are non-S" asserts that all the members of the complement of P are in the complement of S. In other words, no members of the complement of P are in S, which is represented by shading the left-hand part of the S circle. Contraposition is illustrated only as it applies to the **A** statement; diagrams for the **E**, **I**, and **O** statements are left to an exercise.

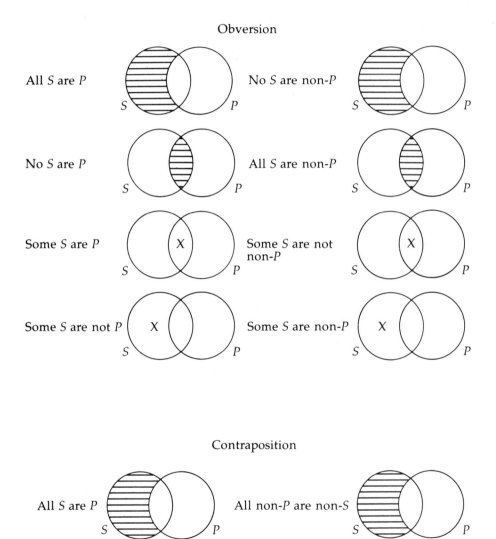

Obversion

Contraposition

Now that we have seen how Venn diagrams are used to prove the relations of the square of opposition and those of conversion, obversion, and contraposition, we turn to the use of these diagrams to check single-premise arguments for validity. Here is an example:

> All alcohols are substances derived from water.
> Therefore, some alcohols are not substances that are not derived
> from water.

We begin by drawing diagrams for the premise and conclusion. Note that the two diagrams are labeled identically.

All *A* are *S*.

Some *A* are not non-*S*.

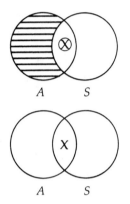

Since the premise is an **A** statement, we shade the left-hand portion of the *A* circle. Then, since alcohols exist, we represent this fact by placing a circled "X" in the remaining portion of the *A* circle. The diagram for the conclusion asserts that something exists in the area where the two circles overlap. Since this fact is implied by the premise, the argument is valid.

Here is another example:

> All superpowers are nonemergent nations.
> Therefore, it is false that some emergent nations are superpowers.

All *S* are non-*E*.

It is false that
some *E* are *S*.

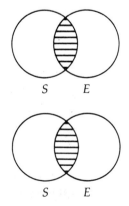

The premise states that all members of S (if there are any) are outside E. Thus, we shade the part of S that is inside E. In diagramming the conclusion, note that the statement "Some E are S" states that there is an "X" in the area where the two circles overlap. Thus, the negation of that statement is represented by *shading* that area. Shading an area is the negation of placing an "X" in that area. Since the diagram for the conclusion is implied by the diagram for the premise, the argument is valid.

Another example:

> Some wind generators are machines that are not cost-effective. Therefore, it is false that some machines that are cost-effective are not wind generators.

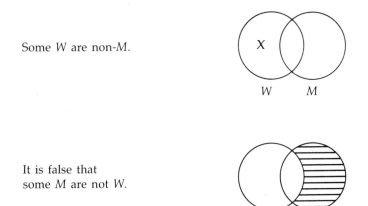

Some W are non-M.

It is false that
some M are not W.

Since the diagram for the conclusion is not implied by the diagram for the premise, the argument is invalid.

EXERCISE 4.7

I. Use Venn diagrams to show that contraposition yields logically equivalent results for **O** propositions and that it does not yield logically equivalent results for **I** and **E** propositions. For the diagrams corresponding to statements that include negated terms, supply a written explanation.

II. Use Venn diagrams to determine whether the following arguments are valid or invalid. In some cases, validity depends on whether the existential standpoint can be taken.

★1. All inflationary spirals are transitory phenomena.
Therefore, some transitory phenomena are inflationary spirals.

2. Some economists are followers of Ayn Rand.
Therefore, some followers of Ayn Rand are not economists.

3. No pet hamsters are animals that need much attention.
Therefore, all pet hamsters are animals that need little attention.

★4. Some genetically engineered drugs are medicines not approved by the FDA.
Therefore, some medicines approved by the FDA are drugs that are not genetically engineered.

5. All victims of dyslexia are persons who have trouble reading.
Therefore, it is false that no victims of dyslexia are persons who have trouble reading.

6. No sunspots are occurrences that fail to multiply every 11 years.
Therefore, all occurrences that multiply every 11 years are sunspots.

★7. It is false that some cases of whistle blowing are not actions disloyal to employers.
Therefore, some actions loyal to employers are cases that are not whistle blowing.

8. Some graffiti writers are persons relieving pent up frustrations.
Therefore, no persons who are not relieving pent up frustrations are graffiti writers.

9. Some opponents of abortion are not persons concerned about child welfare.
Therefore, it is false that no persons who are not concerned about child welfare are opponents of abortion.

★10. No fire-breathing dragons are lizards that flourish in soggy climates.
Therefore some lizards that languish in soggy climates are fire-breathing dragons.

11. It is false that no people who receive Social Security are people who cannot afford the necessities of life.
Therefore, some people who can afford the necessities of life are people who do not receive Social Security.

12. All computer designers are people who believe computers are incapable of genuine thought processes.
Therefore, it is false that some people who believe computers are capable of genuine thought processes are computer designers.

★13. It is false that some hired killers are not persons who deserve the death penalty.

Therefore, some persons who do not deserve the death penalty are hired killers.

14. It is false that some single parents are not persons who face special challenges raising children.
    Therefore, some persons who face special challenges raising children are married parents.

15. No fossil fuels are renewable energy sources.
    Therefore, it is false that no unrenewable energy sources are fossil fuels.

★16. Some substances that control cell growth are hormones.
    Therefore, it is false that all hormones are substances that do not control cell growth.

17. All physicians who prescribe pills for every malady are snake oil salesmen in disguise.
    Therefore, no snake oil salesmen in disguise are physicians who do not prescribe pills for every malady.

18. Some terminally ill patients are individuals who do not want to be attached to machines.
    Therefore, some recovering patients are individuals who want to be attached to machines.

★19. All tropical icebergs are objects that melt as they approach the equator.
    Therefore, it is false that all tropical icebergs are objects that do not melt as they approach the equator.

20. All stolen computer chips are difficult items to trace.
    Therefore, it is false that some easy items to trace are stolen computer chips.

21. It is false that some natural satellites of Venus are objects invisible to the naked eye.
    Therefore, it is false that some objects visible to the naked eye are natural satellites of Venus.

★22. No prescription drugs are medicines without adverse affects.
    Therefore, no nonprescription drugs are medicines with adverse affects.

23. It is false that no extramarital affairs are occurrences that do not destroy marriages.
    Therefore, some extramarital affairs are not occurrences that destroy marriages.

24. All Barbie dolls are toys that engender a false sense of values.
    Therefore, some Barbie dolls are not toys that engender a true sense of values.

★25. It is false that some meat-eating vegetarians are persons with a high carbohydrate diet.
    Therefore, some persons with a low carbohydrate diet are meat-eating vegetarians.

4.8 TRANSLATING ORDINARY LANGUAGE STATEMENTS INTO CATEGORICAL FORM

Although few statements that occur in ordinary written and oral expression are categorical propositions in standard form, many of them can be translated into standard form propositions. Two chief benefits are secured by such translation. The first is that the operations and inferences pertinent to standard form categorical propositions (contrary, subcontrary, etc.) become applicable to these statements. The second is that such statements, once translated, are completely clear and unambiguous as to their meaning. Many statements in ordinary language are susceptible to multiple interpretations, and each interpretation represents one possible mode of translation. The effort to translate such statements discloses the various interpretations and thus helps to prevent misunderstanding and confusion.

Translating statements into categorical form is like any other kind of translation in that no set of specific rules can be given that will cover every possible form of phraseology; yet one general rule always applies: Understand the *meaning* of the given statement, and then reexpress it in a new statement that has a quantifier, subject term, copula, and predicate term. Some of the forms of phraseology that are typically encountered are terms without nouns, nonstandard verbs, singular propositions, adverbs and pronouns, unexpressed and nonstandard quantifiers, conditional statements, exclusive propositions, "the only," and exceptive propositions.

1. Terms Without Nouns

The subject and predicate terms of a categorical proposition must contain either a noun or noun substitute that serves to denote the class indicated by the term. Nouns and noun substitutes denote classes, while adjectives (and participles) connote attributes. If a term consists of only an adjective, a noun or noun substitute should be introduced to make the term genuinely denotative. Examples:

Some roses are red.	Some roses are red *flowers.*
All tigers are carnivorous.	All tigers are carnivorous *animals.*

2. Nonstandard Verbs

According to the position adopted earlier in this chapter, the only copulas that are allowed in categorical propositions are "are" and "are not." Statements in ordinary usage often incorporate other forms of the verb "to be." Such statements may be corrected as the following examples illustrate:

Some persons who go to college will become educated.	Some persons who go to college *are persons who* will become educated.
Some dogs would rather bark than bite.	Some dogs *are animals that* would rather bark than bite.

In other statements no form of the verb "to be" occurs at all. These may be translated as the following examples indicate:

Some birds fly south during the winter.	Some birds *are animals that* fly south during the winter.
All ducks swim.	All ducks *are swimmers.*
	or
	All ducks *are animals that* swim.

3. Singular Propositions

A singular proposition is a proposition that makes an assertion about a specific person, place, thing, or time. Singular propositions are typically translated into universals by means of a parameter. A **parameter** is a phrase that, when introduced into a statement, affects the form but not the meaning. Some parameters that may be used to translate singular propositions are:

> persons identical to
> places identical to
> things identical to
> cases identical to
> times identical to

For example, the statement "Socrates is mortal" may be translated as "All persons identical to Socrates are persons who are mortal." Because only one person is identical to Socrates, namely Socrates himself, the term "persons identical to Socrates" denotes the class that has Socrates as its only member. In other words, it simply denotes Socrates. Note that the parameter "persons identical to" is *not* the same as "persons similar to" or "persons like." There may be many persons *like* Socrates, but there is only one person *identical* to Socrates. The same goes for the other parameters involving the word "identical." Here are some examples:

George went home.	All *persons identical to* George are *persons who* went home.

There is a radio in the back bedroom.	All *places identical to* the back bedroom are *places where* there is a radio.
The moon is full tonight.	All *things identical to* the moon are *things that* are full tonight.
	or
	All *times identical to* tonight are *times* the moon is full.
I hate gin.	All *persons identical to* me are *persons who* hate gin.
	or
	All *things identical to* gin are *things that* I hate.

One additional point to keep in mind about the use of these parameters is that they should *not* be used when the term in question already has a plural noun (or pronoun) that denotes the intended class. Such use is not wrong, technically, but it is redundant. Example:

| Diamonds are carbon allotropes. | *Correct:* All diamonds are carbon allotropes. |
| | *Redundant:* All things identical to diamonds are things identical to carbon allotropes. |

4. Adverbs and Pronouns

When a statement contains a spatial adverb such as "where," "wherever," "anywhere," "everywhere," or "nowhere," or a temporal adverb such as "when," "whenever," "anytime," "always," or "never," it may be translated in terms of "places" or "times," respectively. Statements containing pronouns such as "who," "whoever," "anyone," "what," "whatever," or "anything" may be translated in terms of "persons" or "things," respectively. Examples:

He always wears a suit to work.	All *times* he goes to work are *times* he wears a suit.
He is always clean shaven.	All *times* are *times* he is clean shaven.
She never brings her lunch to school.	No *times* she goes to school are *times* she brings her lunch.
	or
	No *times* are *times* she brings her lunch to school.

Nowhere are there any unicorns.	No *places* are *places* there are unicorns.
Whoever works hard will succeed.	All *persons* who work hard are *persons* who will succeed.
He glitters when he walks.	All *times* he walks are *times* he glitters.
She goes where she chooses.	All *places* she chooses to go are *places* she goes.
She does what she wants.	All *things* she wants to do are *things* she does.

Notice the order of the terms in the last three examples. When one of the aforenamed adverbs or pronouns occurs in the middle of a statement, the order of the terms must be reversed in the categorical form.

5. Unexpressed Quantifiers

Many statements in ordinary usage have quantifiers that are implied but not expressed. In introducing the quantifiers one must be guided by the most probable meaning of the statement. Examples:

Emeralds are green gems.	*All* emeralds are green gems.
There are lions in the zoo.	*Some* lions are animals in the zoo.
A tiger is a mammal.	*All* tigers are mammals.
A fish is not a mammal.	*No* fish are mammals.
A tiger roared.	*Some* tigers are animals that roared.
Children are human beings.	*All* children are human beings.
Children live next door.	*Some* children are persons who live next door.

6. Nonstandard Quantifiers

Sometimes the quantity of a statement is indicated by a word or words other than the three quantifiers that are allowed. Furthermore, statements having the form "All S are not P" are *not* in standard categorical form. Depending on the meaning, statements having this form must be rendered as either "No S are P" or "Some S are not P." Examples:

A few soldiers are heroes.	*Some* soldiers are heroes.

Anyone who votes is a citizen.	*All* voters are citizens.
Not everyone who votes is a Democrat.	*Some* voters are not Democrats.
Not a single dog is a cat.	*No* dogs are cats.
All race horses can't be winners.	*Some* race horses are not winners.
All goats are not sheep.	*No* goats are sheep.
Few sailors entered the regatta.	*Some* sailors are persons who entered the regatta *and some* sailors are not persons who entered the regatta.

Notice that statements beginning with "few" (and some statements beginning with "a few") cannot be translated as single categorical propositions. They must be translated as a compound arrangement of an **I** proposition and an **O** proposition. Statements beginning with "almost all" and "not quite all" must be handled in the same way. When these statements occur in arguments, the arguments must be treated in the same way as those containing exceptive propositions, which will be discussed shortly.

7. Conditional Statements

When the antecedent and consequent of a conditional statement talk about the same thing, the statement can usually be translated into categorical form. The Boolean interpretation of categorical propositions provides the key: such statements are always rendered as universals. Examples:

If it's a mouse, then it's a mammal.	All mice are mammals.
If an animal has four legs, then it is not a bird.	No four-legged animals are birds.
If Los Angeles is in California, then Los Angeles is a large city.	All California cities identical to Los Angeles are large cities.

Conditional statements such as "If Los Angeles is in California, then Houston is a large city" cannot be translated into categorical form.

When the word "if" occurs in the middle of a conditional statement, the statement must be restructured so that it occurs at the beginning. For example, "An animal is a fish if it has gills" means "If an animal has gills, then it is a fish." This is then translated, "All animals having gills are fish." Other examples:

A person will succeed if he perseveres.	All persons who persevere are persons who will succeed.
Jewelry is expensive if it is made of gold.	All pieces of jewelry made of gold are expensive things.

In translating conditional statements it is sometimes useful to employ a rule called **transposition**. According to this rule, the antecedent and consequent of a conditional statement may switch places if both are negated. For example, the statement "If something is not valuable, then it is not scarce" is logically equivalent to "If something is scarce, then it is valuable." This is then translated as "All scarce things are valuable things." Examples:

If it's not a mammal, then it's not a mouse.	All mice are mammals.
If a company is not well managed, then it is not a good investment.	All companies that are good investments are well-managed companies.

The word "unless" means "if . . . not." For example, the statement "A car will not run unless there is gas in the tank" means "A car will not run if there is not gas in the tank," which means, "If there is not gas in the tank, then a car will not run." By transposition, this means, "If a car runs, then there is gas in the tank," which is translated as "All cars that run are cars with gas in the tank." Although "unless" sometimes has the stronger sense of "if and only if . . . not," the weaker sense of "if . . . not" can always be depended upon. Here are some additional examples:

Tomatoes are edible unless they are spoiled.	All inedible tomatoes are spoiled tomatoes.
	or
	All unspoiled tomatoes are edible tomatoes.
Unless a boy misbehaves he will be treated decently.	All boys who do not misbehave are boys who will be treated decently.

8. Exclusive Propositions

Propositions that involve the words "only," "none but," "none except," and "no . . . except" are exclusive propositions. Efforts to translate them into categorical propositions frequently lead to confusion of the subject term with the predicate term. Such confusion can be avoided if the statement is phrased as a conditional statement first, then as a categorical statement. For example, the statement "Only executives can use the silver elevator" is equivalent to "If a person can use the silver elevator, he is an executive." The correct categorical proposition is "All persons who can use the silver elevator are executives." If the statement were translated "All executives are persons who can use the silver elevator," it would clearly be wrong. Thus, the occurrence of "only" and "none but" at the beginning of a statement indicates a reversal in the order of the terms when the statement is translated into categorical form. Examples:

Only elected officials will attend the convention.	All persons who will attend the convention are elected officials.
None but the brave deserve the fair.	All persons who deserve the fair are brave persons.
No birds except peacocks are proud of their tails.	All birds proud of their tails are peacocks.

When "only" and "none but" occur in the middle of a statement, the statement must first be restructured so that the term preceded by "only" or "none but" occurs first. Then the statement can be translated as those above. For example, the statement "Executives can use only the silver elevator" is equivalent to "Only the silver elevator can be used by executives." This, in turn, is equivalent to "If an elevator can be used by executives, then it is the silver elevator," which is translated: "All elevators that can be used by executives are elevators identical to the silver elevator." Other examples:

He owns only the shirt on his back.	All things owned by him are things identical to the shirt on his back.
She invited only wealthy socialites.	All persons invited by her are wealthy socialites.

Note that many English statements containing "only" are ambiguous owing to the fact that "only" can be interpreted as modifying one word and not another in the phrase that follows it. Thus, the last two examples might also be translated: "All shirts owned by him are shirts identical to the one on his back" and "All socialites invited by her are wealthy persons."

9. "The Only"

Statements beginning with the words "the only" are translated differently from those beginning with "only." For example, the statement "The only cars that are available are Chevrolets" means "If a car is available, then it is a Chevrolet." This, in turn, is translated as "All cars that are available are Chevrolets." In other words, "The only," when it occurs at the beginning of a statement, can simply be replaced with "all," and the order of the terms is *not* reversed in the translation.

When "the only" occurs in the middle of a statement, the statement must be restructured so that it occurs at the beginning. For example, "Romances are the only books he sells" is equivalent to "The only books he sells are romances." This is then translated as "All books that he sells are romances." Other examples:

The only animals that live in this canyon are skunks.	All animals that live in this canyon are skunks.
Accountants are the only ones who will be hired.	All those who will be hired are accountants.

10. Exceptive Propositions

Propositions of the form "All except *S* are *P*" and "All but *S* are *P*" are exceptive propositions. They must be translated not as single categorical propositions but as pairs of conjoined categorical propositions. Statements that include the phrase "none except," on the other hand, are exclusive (not exceptive) propositions. "None except" is synonymous with "none but." Some examples of exceptive propositions are:

All except students are invited.	No students are invited persons, and all nonstudents are invited persons.
All but managers must report to the President.	No managers are persons who must report to the president, and all nonmanagers are persons who must report to the president.

Because exceptive propositions cannot be translated into single categorical propositions, many of the simple inferences and operations pertinent to categorical propositions cannot be applied to them. Arguments that contain exceptive propositions as premises or conclusion can be evaluated only through the application of extended techniques. This topic is taken up in Section 5.5 of the next chapter.

Key word	Translation hint
whoever, wherever, always, anyone, never, etc.	use: "all" together with persons, places, times
a few	some
if . . . then	use: all *or* no
unless	if not
only, none but, none except, no . . . except	use: "all" and switch subject and predicate
the only	all
all but, all except, few	two statements required
not every, not all	some . . . are not

EXERCISE 4.8

I. Translate the following into standard form categorical propositions:

★1. Any bank that makes too many risky loans will fail.

2. Women military officers are not eligible for combat duty.

3. Terrorist attacks succeed whenever security measures are lax.

★4. Bromine is extractable from seawater.

5. Not all guilt feelings are psychological aberrations.

6. Every jazz fan admires Duke Ellington.

★7. If it's a halogen, then it isn't chemically inert.

8. A television show that depicts violence incites violence.

9. Manipulators do not make good marriage partners.

★10. None but 12-meter yachts are eligible for the America's Cup race.

11. Warmth always relieves pain.

12. Joseph J. Thomson discovered the electron.

★13. A few organic silicones are used as lubricants.

14. Only nuclear-powered vehicles are suitable for deep space exploration.

15. *Gone with the Wind* is the only novel Margaret Mitchell wrote.

★16. There is a giant star in the tarantula nebula.

17. If a pregnant woman drinks alcohol, she risks giving birth to a deformed child.

18. No element except titanium burns in nitrogen.

★19. Only those given to flights of fancy believe Noah's ark lies beneath the snows of Arrarat.

20. The electroscope is a device for detecting static electricity.

21. Occasionally there are concerts in Central Park.

★22. Berlin was the setting for the 1936 Olympic Games.

23. The Kentucky Derby is never run in January.

24. The only way to get rid of a temptation is to yield to it.

★25. Where there's smoke, there's fire.

26. Lunar eclipses do not occur unless the moon is full.

27. Radio transmissions are disrupted whenever sunspot activity increases.

★28. If an ore isn't radioactive, then it isn't pitchblende.

29. All but the rats left the sinking ship.

30. A pesticide is dangerous if it contains DDT.

★31. James Michener writes only historical novels.

32. He who hesitates is lost.

33. Modern corporations are all run in the interest of their managers.

★34. Unless the sun in shining, a rainbow cannot occur.

35. Whoever suffers allergic reactions has a weakened immune system.

36. All Western democracies except the United States have abolished capital punishment for ordinary offenses.

★37. Few corporate raiders are known for their integrity.

38. Monkeys are found in the jungles of Guatemala.

39. Monkeys are mammals.

★40. I like strawberries.

II. Correct the mistakes and redundancies in the following attempted translations.

★1. Some of the third-generation computers are things that are machines that take dictation.

2. All persons identical to Richard Nixon are the only American presidents who resigned from office.

3. All vertebrates except cartilaginous fishes are animals with a bony skeleton.

★4. No downhill skiers are effective competitors if they suffer from altitude sickness.

5. All substances like cobalt are things that are substances identical to ferromagnetic metals.

6. No persons identical to nuclear passivists are persons who believe a just war is possible.

★7. All persons who are victims of Huntington's disease are not persons helped by treatment.

8. All companies identical to IBM are facing growing competition in the personal computer market.

9. No toxic dumps are ecological catastrophes unless they leak.

★10. All crocodiles are things identical to dangerous animals when they are hungry.

5
CATEGORICAL SYLLOGISMS

5.1 STANDARD FORM, MOOD, AND FIGURE

In the general sense of the term, a **syllogism** is a deductive argument consisting of two premises and one conclusion. A **categorical syllogism** is a special type of syllogism in which all three statements are categorical propositions. In addition, these three propositions must contain a total of three different terms, each of which appears twice in distinct propositions. The following argument is a categorical syllogism:

> No wealthy individuals are paupers.
> All civic leaders are wealthy individuals.
> Therefore, no civic leaders are paupers.

The requirement that the premises and conclusion contain exactly three terms, each of which appears twice, needs two qualifications. The first is that an argument containing more than three terms qualifies as a categorical syllogism if it can be translated into an equivalent argument having exactly three terms. For example, if, in the argument above, the term "wealthy individuals" were changed in the second premise to "well-to-do individuals," the argument would have four terms. But since "well-to-do" is synonymous with "wealthy," the argument could easily be translated into the form above. Thus, the argument would still qualify as a categorical syllogism, even though, technically speaking, it had more than three terms. As we will see in Section 5.4, negated terms sometimes present similar problems, and techniques are developed in that section to reduce the number of terms when some of them are negated.

The second qualification is that each of the three terms must be used in the same sense throughout the argument. If a term is used in one sense in one statement and in a different sense in another statement, the argument really contains more than three terms. An argument containing the term "men," for example, might use the term in the sense of human beings in one statement and of male humans in another. Such an argument would commit the informal fallacy of equivocation and would therefore not qualify as a categorical syllogism.

It is not necessary that all three statements in an argument be standard-form categorical propositions for the argument to qualify as a categorical syllogism. If they are, however, the analysis is greatly simplified. Accordingly, all of the syllogisms presented in the next three sections of this chapter will consist of statements that are standard-form categorical propositions. In later sections, techniques will be developed for translating arguments involving nonstandard propositions into equivalent arguments composed of standard-form propositions.

The three terms in a categorical syllogism are given names depending on their role in the argument. The **major term,** by definition, is the predicate of the conclusion, and the **minor term** is the subject of the conclusion. The **middle term,** which provides the middle ground between the two premises, is the one that does not occur in the conclusion. For example, in the categorical syllogism

> All soldiers are patriots.
> No traitors are patriots.
> Therefore, no traitors are soldiers.

the major term is "soldiers," the minor term is "traitors," and the middle term is "patriots."

The premises of a categorical syllogism are also given names. The **major premise,** by definition, is the one that contains the major term, and the **minor premise** is the one that contains the minor term. This terminology enters into the definition of standard form. A categorical syllogism is said to be in **standard form** when the following three conditions are met:

1. All three statements are standard-form categorical propositions.
2. The two occurrences of each term are identical.
3. The major premise is listed first, the minor premise second, and the conclusion last.

The syllogism about soldiers is in standard form (as is the one about civic leaders at the beginning of this section). But consider this syllogism:

All watercolors are paintings.
Some watercolors are masterpieces.
Therefore, some paintings are masterpieces.

This syllogism is not in standard form because the premises are not listed in the right order. To conform with the third condition, the premise containing the predicate of the conclusion ("masterpieces") must be listed first, and the premise containing the subject of the conclusion ("paintings") must be listed second.

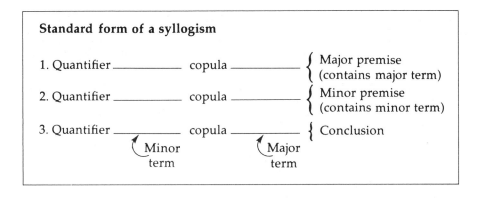

After a categorical syllogism has been put into standard form and checked for informal fallacies, its validity or invalidity may be determined through mere inspection of the form. The individual form of a syllogism consists of two factors: mood and figure. The **mood** of a categorical syllogism is determined by the kind of propositions (**A, E, I, O**) that make it up. For example, if the major premise is an **A** proposition, the minor premise an **O** proposition, and the conclusion an **E** proposition, the mood is **AOE**. To determine the mood of a categorical syllogism, one must first put the syllogism into standard form; the letter name of the statements may then be noted to the side of each. The mood of the syllogism is then designated by the order of these letters, reading the letter for the major premise first, the letter for the minor premise second, and the letter for the conclusion last.

The **figure** of a categorical syllogism is determined by the placement of the middle term. Four different arrangements are possible. If we let *S* represent the subject of the conclusion (minor term), *P* the predicate of the conclusion (major term), and *M* the middle term, the four possible arrangements may be illustrated as follows:

Figure 1	Figure 2	Figure 3	Figure 4
$-$ⓜ $-P$	$-P$ $-$ⓜ	$-$ⓜ $-P$	$-P$ $-$ⓜ
$-S$ $-$ⓜ	$-S$ $-$ⓜ	$-$ⓜ $-S$	$-$ⓜ $-S$
$-S$ $-P$	$-S$ $-P$	$-S$ $-P$	$-S$ $-P$

The blanks indicate the places for the quantifiers and copulas. In the first figure the middle term is top left, bottom right; in the second, top right, bottom right, and so on. Example:

> No painters are sculptors.
> Some sculptors are artists.
> Therefore, some artists are not painters.

This syllogism is in standard form. The mood is **EIO** and the figure is four. The form of the syllogism is therefore designated as **EIO-4**.

If you have difficulty remembering the correspondence between the arrangements of the middle term and the figure numbers, you may find the "shirt collar model" useful. To use this analogical device, you may imagine the arrangement of the middle term in the four figures as depicting the outline of a shirt collar:

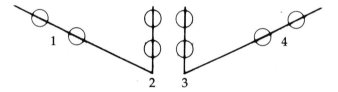

The only problem with this device is that it may lead you to confuse the second figure with the third. To avoid this confusion, keep in mind that for these two figures the S and P terms go on the same "collar flap" as the middle term. Thus, for the second figure, S and P are to the left of the middle term, and for the third figure they are to the right.

Since there are four kinds of categorical propositions and there are three categorical propositions in a categorical syllogism, there are 64 possible moods ($4 \times 4 \times 4 = 64$). And since there are four different figures, there are 256 different forms of categorical syllogisms ($4 \times 64 = 256$).

Because the validity of a syllogism is purely a function of the form, if the form is known, the validity of the syllogism can be determined. Two lists of valid syllogistic forms are presented below. The first list contains the fifteen forms that are valid from the Boolean standpoint—that is, valid without making any existential assumptions, or unconditionally valid. The second list contains an additional nine forms that are invalid from the Boolean standpoint but that become valid when a certain existential condition is fulfilled. The exact nature of the condition is indicated in the fifth column. Of course, the forms in the first list are valid regardless of whether these conditions are fulfilled.

Unconditionally valid

Figure 1	Figure 2	Figure 3	Figure 4
AAA	EAE	IAI	AEE
EAE	AEE	AII	IAI
AII	EIO	OAO	EIO
EIO	AOO	EIO	

Conditionally valid

Figure 1	Figure 2	Figure 3	Figure 4	Required condition
AAI	AEO		AEO	S exist
EAO	EAO			
		AAI	EAO	M exist
		EAO		
			AAI	P exist

For example, **AEO**-2 is invalid from the Boolean standpoint but becomes valid in the second list, if we assume that S (the subject of the conclusion, the minor term) denotes at least one existing thing. **AAI**-3 becomes valid if we assume that M (the middle term) denotes at least one existing thing, and so on. If these letters stand for a word such as "dogs" or "cats," the argument would be valid. But if they stand for a word such as "unicorns" or "leprechauns," the argument would be invalid.

It is interesting, from a historical perspective, to recall that logic students during the Middle Ages used to memorize a little poem that served as a rule of thumb for distinguishing valid from invalid syllogisms. The vowels in the words identified the mood, and the words "prioris," "secundae," and so on the figure.

> Barbara, Celarent, Darii, Ferioque prioris;
> Cesare, Camestres, Festino, Baroco secundae;
> Tertia, Darapti, Disamis, Datisi, Felapton,
> Bocardo, Ferison habet: quarta insuper addit
> Bramantip, Camenes, Dimaris, Fesapo, Fresison.

For example, the "Barbara" syllogism (this designation is still encountered today) is **AAA**-1, "Celarent" is **EAE**-1, and so on. This poem conforms substantially to the two lists above, except that five forms have been left out. The reason these forms were left out is that the logicians of that time considered them weak: They draw a particular conclusion from premises that would support a (stronger) universal conclusion. For example, the weaker **AAI**-1 is left out in favor of the stronger **AAA**-1. Needless to say, few students today depend on this poem to distinguish valid from invalid syllogisms.

We have seen how, given the syllogism, we can obtain the mood and figure. But sometimes we need to go in the reverse direction: from the mood and figure to the syllogistic form. Let us suppose we are given the form **EIO**-4. To reconstruct the syllogistic form is easy. First use the mood to determine the skeleton of the form:

E   No _____ are _____.
I   Some _____ are _____.
O   Some _____ are not _____.

Then use the figure to determine the arrangement of the middle terms:

E   No _____ are M.
I   Some M are _____.
O   Some _____ are not _____.

Finally, supply the major and minor terms, using the letters "S" and "P" to designate the subject and predicate of the conclusion. The predicate of the conclusion is always repeated in the first premise, and the subject of the conclusion in the second premise:

E   No P are M.
I   Some M are S.
O   Some S are not P.

EXERCISE 5.1

I. The following syllogisms are in standard form. Identify the major, minor, and middle terms, and the mood and figure of each. Then determine whether each is valid or invalid by checking the mood and figure against the two lists of valid syllogistic forms.

★1. All neutron stars are things that produce intense gravity.
All neutron stars are extremely dense objects.
Therefore, all extremely dense objects are things that produce intense gravity.

2. No insects that eat mosquitoes are insects that should be killed.
All dragonflies are insects that eat mosquitoes.
Therefore, no dragonflies are insects that should be killed.

3. No environmentally produced diseases are inherited afflictions.
   Some psychological disorders are not inherited afflictions.
   Therefore, some psychological disorders are environmentally produced diseases.

★4. No persons who mix fact with fantasy are good witnesses.
   Some hypnotized persons are persons who mix fact with fantasy.
   Therefore, some hypnotized persons are not good witnesses.

5. All ozone molecules are good absorbers of ultraviolet rays.
   All ozone molecules are things destroyed by chlorine.
   Therefore, some things destroyed by chlorine are good absorbers of ultraviolet rays.

II. Put the following syllogisms into standard form using letters to represent the terms, name the mood and figure, and determine whether each is valid or invalid by checking the mood and figure against the two lists of valid syllogistic forms.

★1. No Republicans are Democrats, so no Republicans are big spenders, since all big spenders are Democrats.

2. Some latchkey children are not kids who can stay out of trouble, for some youngsters prone to boredom are latchkey children, and no kids who can stay out of trouble are youngsters prone to boredom.

3. No rent control proposals are regulations welcomed by landlords, and all regulations welcomed by landlords are measures that allow a free hand in raising rents. Therefore, some rent control proposals are measures that allow a free hand in raising rents.

★4. Some insects that feed on milkweed are not foods suitable for birds, since no monarch butterflies are foods suitable for birds, and all monarch butterflies are insects that feed on milkweed.

5. No illegal aliens are persons who have a right to welfare payments, and some migrant workers are illegal aliens. Thus, some persons who have a right to welfare payments are migrant workers.

6. Some South American nations are not countries deserving military aid, for some South American nations are not upholders of human rights, and all countries deserving military aid are upholders of human rights.

★7. All pranksters are exasperating individuals, so some leprechauns are exasperating individuals, since all leprechauns are pranksters.

8. Some racists are not persons suited to be immigration officials, for some humanitarians are not persons suited to be immigration officials, and no humanitarians are racists.

9. No persons who respect human life are terrorists, and all airline hijackers are terrorists. Hence, no airline hijackers are persons who respect human life.

★10. Some silicates are crystalline substances, because all silicates are oxygen compounds, and some oxygen compounds are not crystalline substances.

III. Reconstruct the syllogistic forms from the following combinations of mood and figure.

★1. **OAE-3**

2. **EIA-4**

3. **AII-3**

★4. **IAE-1**

5. **AOO-2**

6. **EAO-4**

★7. **AAA-1**

8. **EAO-2**

9. **OEI-3**

★10. **OEA-4**

IV. Construct the following syllogisms:

★1. An **EIO**-2 syllogism with these terms: *major:* dogmatists; *minor:* theologians; *middle:* scholars who encourage free thinking.

2. A valid syllogism in the first figure with a particular affirmative conclusion and these terms: *major:* persons incapable of objectivity; *minor:* Supreme Court justices; *middle:* lock step ideologues.

3. A valid syllogism in the fourth figure having two universal premises and these terms: *major:* teenage suicides; *minor:* heroic episodes; *middle:* tragic occurrences.

★4. A valid syllogism having mood **OAO** and these terms: *major:* things capable of replicating by themselves; *minor:* structures that invade cells; *middle:* viruses.

5. A valid syllogism in the first figure having a universal negative conclusion and these terms: *major:* guarantees of marital happiness; *minor:* prenuptial agreements; *middle:* legally enforceable documents.

V. Answer "true" or "false" to the following statements:

1. Every syllogism is a categorical syllogism.

2. A categorical syllogism may contain a term that is used in two different senses.

3. The statements in a categorical syllogism need not be expressed in standard form.

4. The statements in a standard-form categorical syllogism need not be expressed in standard form.

5. In a standard-form categorical syllogism the two occurrences of each term must be identical.

6. The major premise of a standard-form categorical syllogism contains the subject of the conclusion.

7. To determine the mood and figure of a categorical syllogism, the syllogism must first be put into standard form.

8. In a standard-form syllogism having Figure 2, the middle terms are on the right.

9. The unconditionally valid syllogistic forms remain valid when existential conditions are fulfilled.

10. The conditionally valid syllogistic forms are invalid if no existential conditions are fulfilled.

5.2 VENN DIAGRAMS

Venn diagrams provide the most intuitively evident and, in the long run, easiest to remember technique for testing the validity of categorical syllogisms. The technique is basically an extension of the one developed in Chapter 4 to represent the information content of categorical propositions. Because syllogisms contain three terms, whereas propositions contain only two, the application of Venn diagrams to syllogisms requires three overlapping circles. These circles should be drawn so that seven areas are clearly distinguishable within the diagram. The second step is to label the circles, one for each term. The precise order of the labeling is not critical, but we will adopt the convention of always assigning the lower left circle to the subject of the conclusion, the lower right circle to the predicate of the conclusion, and the top circle to the middle term.

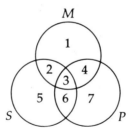

Anything in the area marked "1" is an M but neither an S nor a P, anything in the area marked "2" is both an S and an M but not a P, anything in the area marked "3" is a member of all three classes, and so on.

The test procedure consists in transferring the information content of the premises to the diagram and then inspecting the diagram to see whether it necessarily implies the truth of the conclusion. If the information in the diagram does do this, the argument is valid; otherwise it is invalid.

The use of Venn diagrams to evaluate syllogisms usually requires a little practice before it can be done with facility. Perhaps the best way of presenting the technique is through illustrative examples, but a few preliminary pointers are needed:

1. Marks (shading or placing an "X") are entered only for the premises. No marks are made for the conclusion.
2. If the argument contains one universal premise, this premise should be entered first in the diagram. If there are two universal premises, either one can be done first.
3. When entering the information contained in a premise, one should concentrate on the circles corresponding to the two terms in the statement. While the third circle cannot be ignored altogether, it should be given only minimal attention.
4. When inspecting a completed diagram to see whether it supports a particular conclusion, one should remember that particular statements assert two things. "Some S are P" means "At least one S exists *and* that S is a P"; "Some S are not P" means "At least one S exists *and* that S is not a P."
5. When shading an area, one must be careful to shade *all* of the area in question. Examples:

Right:

Wrong:

6. The area where an "X" goes is always initially divided into two parts. If one of these parts has already been shaded, the "X" goes in the unshaded part. Examples:

Right:

A CONCISE INTRODUCTION TO LOGIC

If one of the two parts is not shaded, the "X" goes on the line separating the two parts. Examples:

Right:

This means that the "X" may be in either (or both) of the two areas—but it is not known which one.

7. An "X" should never be placed in such a way that it dangles outside of the diagram altogether, and it should never be placed on the intersection of two lines.

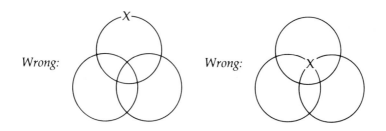

Wrong: *Wrong:*

Let us now consider some examples.

1. No *P* are *M.*   **EAE-2**
   All *S* are *M.*
   No *S* are *P.*

Since both premises are universal, it makes no difference which premise we enter first in the diagram. Beginning with the major premise, we have:

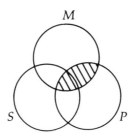

We may now complete the diagram by entering the information of the minor premise:

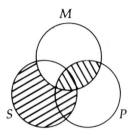

The conclusion states that the area where S and P overlap is empty. Inspection of the diagram reveals that this area is indeed empty, so the argument is valid.

2. No M are P.   **EAE-3**
   All M are S.
   No S are P.

Again, the conclusion states that the area where S and P overlap is empty. Inspection of the diagram reveals that only part of this area is empty, so the syllogism is invalid.

3. No M are P.   **EIO-1**
   Some S are M.
   Some S are not P.

The universal premise is entered first. The shaded part of the area where the S and M circles overlap leaves only a single area for the "X." The conclusion states that there is an "X" that is inside the S circle but outside the P circle. Inspection of the diagram reveals that this is indeed the case, so the syllogism is valid.

4. All M are P.   **AII-1**
   Some S are M.
   Some S are P.

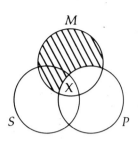

Again, only a single area is left for the "X." The conclusion states that there is an "X" in the S circle that is also in the P circle. There is such an "X," so the argument is valid.

5. Some M are P.   **IAI-1**
   All S are M.
   Some S are P.

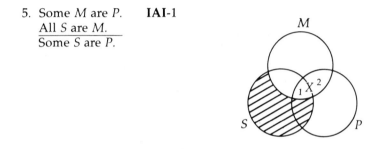

Even though the universal premise is entered first, there are still two possible areas for the "X" (the areas marked "1" and "2"). The "X" therefore goes on the line (the arc of the S circle) that separates the two parts. The conclusion states that there is an "X" that is in the S circle and also in the P circle. The one "X" in the diagram, however, is on the boundary of the S circle. We do not know whether it is in or out. Hence, the syllogism is invalid.

6. All M are P.   **AOO-1**
   Some S are not M.
   Some S are not P.

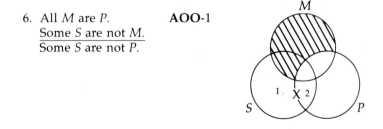

Again, there are two possible areas for the "X" (the areas marked "1" and "2"). The "X" goes on the line (arc of the P circle) separating the two areas. The conclusion states that there is an "X" in the S circle that is outside the P circle. There *is* an "X" in the S circle, but we do not know whether it is inside or outside the P circle. Hence, the argument is invalid.

7. All M are P.　**AAA-1**
   All S are M.
   All S are P.

This is the "Barbara" syllogism. The conclusion states that the part of the S circle that is outside the P circle is empty. Inspection of the diagram reveals that this area is indeed empty. Thus, the syllogism is valid.

8. Some M are not P.　**OIO-1**
   Some S are M.
   Some S are not P.

In this diagram no areas have been shaded, so there are two possible areas for each of the two "X"s. The "X" from the first premise goes on the line (arc of the S circle) separating areas 1 and 2, and the "X" from the second premise goes on the line (arc of the P circle) separating areas a and b. The conclusion states that there is an "X" in the S circle that is outside the P circle. We have no certainty that the "X" from the first premise is inside the S circle, and while the "X" from the second premise is inside the S circle, we have no certainty that it is outside the P circle. Hence, the argument is invalid.

We have yet to explain the rationale for placing the "X" on the boundary separating two areas when neither of the areas is shaded. Consider this argument:

No P are M.
Some S are not M.
Some S are P.

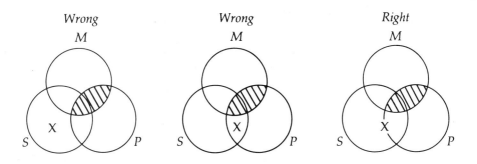

Wrong   *Wrong*   *Right*

In each of the three diagrams the content of the first premise is represented correctly. The problem concerns placing the "X" from the second premise. In the first diagram the "X" is placed inside the S circle but outside both the M circle and the P circle. This diagram asserts: "At least one S is not an M and it is also not a P." Clearly the diagram says more than the premise does, and so it is incorrect. In the second diagram the "X" is placed inside the S circle, outside the M circle, and inside the P circle. This diagram asserts: "At least one S is not an M, but it is a P." Again, the diagram says more than the premise says, and so it is incorrect. In the third diagram, which is done correctly, the "X" is placed on the boundary between the two areas. This diagram asserts: "At least one S is not an M, and it may or may not be a P." In other words, nothing at all is said about P, and so the diagram represents exactly the content of the second premise.

All of the examples of syllogisms that we have considered thus far have been unaffected by the existential standpoint; that is, it makes no difference to their validity whether or not we assume that the component propositions assert something about things that really exist. Of the 256 different syllogisms, there are nine that are so affected; namely, those that are included in the second list presented in Section 5.1. These syllogisms are invalid from the Boolean standpoint but become valid when the existential standpoint is adopted. Venn diagrams may be used in a special way to evaluate these nine syllogisms. Example:

No M are P.   **EAO-3**
All M are S.
Some S are not P.

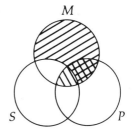

The conclusion asserts that there is an "X" that is inside the S circle and outside the P circle. Inspection of the diagram reveals no "X"s at all, so the syllogism is invalid from the Boolean standpoint. But let us now suppose that the universal statements in the syllogism (the two premises) make an assertion about really existing things; that is, let us assume that M denotes at least one existing thing. We may represent this one existing thing by placing an "X" in the one area of the M circle that is not shaded:

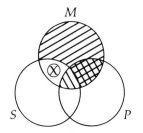

We place a small circle around this "X" to indicate that it comes from the assumption that the M class is not empty. We now have an "X" that is inside the S circle and outside the P circle, and so the syllogism is valid from the existential standpoint. Another example:

All M are P.   **AAI-1**
All S are M.
Some S are P.

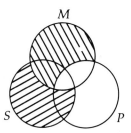

The conclusion asserts that there is an "X" in the S circle that is also in the P circle. The diagram contains no "X"s at all so the syllogism is invalid from the Boolean standpoint. But let us now assume that the subjects (S and M) of the universal premises denote at least one existing thing. If we consider the M circle first, we see that the "X" could go in either of two areas and should therefore be placed on the boundary between them. Since this "X" is not sufficient to make the syllogism valid, we turn to the S circle. Here only one unshaded area remains, and we place the "X" in that area:

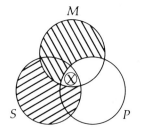

We now have an "X" that is inside the S circle and also inside the P circle, and so the syllogism is valid from the existential standpoint.

These two examples illustrate an important point about the use of Venn diagrams: If the premises of an argument are universal and the conclusion particular, and if after shading the diagram it turns out that one circle is completely shaded except for one area, then it should be determined whether placing an "X" in that one remaining area will provide support for the conclusion. If, after this addition, the conclusion is supported, the argument is one of those that is invalid from the Boolean standpoint but valid from the existential standpoint.

EXERCISE 5.2

I. Use Venn diagrams to determine whether the following standard-form categorical syllogisms are valid or invalid. Identify any that may be invalid from the Boolean standpoint but valid from the existential standpoint, and determine which standpoint is preferable. Determine the mood and figure, and cross-check your answers with the lists of valid forms found in Section 5.1.

★1. All corporations that overcharge their customers are unethical businesses.
Some unethical businesses are investor-owned utilities.
Therefore, some investor-owned utilities are corporations that overcharge their customers.

2. No AIDS victims are persons who pose an immediate threat to the lives of others.
Some kindergarten children are AIDS victims.
Therefore, some kindergarten children are not persons who pose an immediate threat to the lives of others.

3. No individuals truly concerned with the plight of suffering humanity are persons motivated primarily by self-interest.
All television evangelists are persons motivated primarily by self-interest.
Therefore, some television evangelists are not individuals truly concerned with the plight of suffering humanity.

★4. All high-fat diets are diets high in cholesterol.
Some diets high in cholesterol are not healthy food programs.
Therefore, some healthy food programs are not high-fat diets.

5. No concertos are symphonies.
No symphonies are string quartets.
Therefore, no string quartets are concertos.

6. All compounds that destroy the ozone layer are environmental hazards.
All chlorofluorocarbons are compounds that destroy the ozone layer.
Therefore, all chlorofluorocarbons are environmental hazards.

★7. No mere propaganda ploys are bona fide efforts to slow the arms race.
All nuclear test bans are bona fide efforts to slow the arms race.
Therefore, no nuclear test bans are mere propaganda ploys.

8. Some individuals prone to violence are not men who treat others humanely.
Some police officers are individuals prone to violence.
Therefore, some police officers are not men who treat others humanely.

9. Some automated teller machines are places criminals lurk.
All places criminals lurk are places to be avoided at night.
Therefore, some places to be avoided at night are automated teller machines.

★10. No corporations that defraud the government are organizations the government should deal with.
Some defense contractors are not organizations the government should deal with.
Therefore, some defense contractors are not corporations that defraud the government.

11. All circular triangles are plane figures.
All circular triangles are three-sided figures.
Therefore, some three-sided figures are plane figures.

12. All supernovas are objects that emit massive amounts of energy.
All quasars are objects that emit massive amounts of energy.
Therefore, all quasars are supernovas.

★13. No persons who profit from the illegality of their activities are persons who want their activities legalized.
All drug dealers are persons who profit from the illegality of their activities.
Therefore, no drug dealers are persons who want their activities legalized.

14. Some individuals who risk heart disease are persons who will die young.
Some smokers are individuals who risk heart disease.
Therefore, some smokers are persons who will die young.

15. Some measures that promote production are cases of free enterprise.
All measures that promote production are policies consistent with Marxist ideology.
Therefore, some policies consistent with Marxist ideology are cases of free enterprise.

★16. All presently living dinosaurs are giant reptiles.
All giant reptiles are ectothermic animals.
Therefore, some ectothermic animals are presently living dinosaurs.

17. All survivalists are persons who enjoy simulated war games.
No persons who enjoy simulated war games are soldiers who have tasted the agony of real war.
Therefore, all soldiers who have tasted the agony of real war are survivalists.

18. No persons majoring in greed are individuals concerned about the welfare of society.
Some college students are persons majoring in greed.
Therefore, some college students are not individuals concerned about the welfare of society.

★19. No occasions of economic crisis are times people can resist the desire to gamble.
All occasions of economic crisis are periods when money is short.
Therefore, some periods when money is short are not times people can resist the desire to gamble.

20. Some persons who employ surrogate mothers are not persons who have the right to keep the baby.
All persons who employ surrogate mothers are persons who invite custody battles.
Therefore, some persons who invite custody battles are not persons who have the right to keep the baby.

II. Use Venn diagrams to obtain the conclusion that is validly implied by each of the following sets of premises. If no conclusion can be validly drawn, write "no conclusion."

★1. No *P* are *M*.
All *S* are *M*.

2. Some *P* are not *M*.
Some *M* are *S*.

3. Some *M* are *P*.
All *S* are *M*.

★4. Some *M* are not *P*.
All *M* are *S*.

5. Some *P* are *M*.
All *M* are *S*.

6. No *M* are *P*.
Some *S* are not *M*.

★7. All *M* are *P*.
All *S* are *M*.

8. All *P* are *M*.
All *S* are *M*.

9. No *P* are *M*.
   Some *M* are *S*.

★10. No *P* are *M*.
   No *M* are *S*.

III. Answer "true" or "false" to the following statements:

1. In the use of Venn diagrams to test the validity of syllogisms, marks are sometimes entered in the diagram for the conclusion.
2. When an "X" is placed on the arc of a circle, it means that the "X" could be in either (or both) of the two areas that the arc separates.
3. If an "X" lies on the arc of a circle, the argument cannot be valid.
4. When representing a universal statement in a Venn diagram, one always shades two of the seven areas in the diagram (unless one of these areas is already shaded).
5. If a completed diagram contains two "X"s, the argument cannot be valid.
6. If the conclusion asserts that a certain area is shaded, and inspection of the diagram reveals that only half that area is shaded, the argument is valid.
7. If the conclusion asserts that a certain area contains an "X" and inspection of the diagram reveals that only half an "X" appears in that area, the argument is valid.
8. If the conclusion is in the form "All *S* are *P*," and inspection of the diagram reveals that the part of the *S* circle that is outside the *P* circle is shaded, then the argument is valid.
9. If, in a completed diagram, three areas of a single circle are shaded, and placing an "X" in the one remaining area would make the conclusion true, then the argument is valid from the existential standpoint but not from the Boolean standpoint.
10. If, in a completed diagram, three areas of a single circle are shaded, but the argument is not valid from the Boolean standpoint, then it must be valid from the existential standpoint.

5.3 RULES AND FALLACIES

The idea that valid syllogisms conform to certain rules was first expressed by Aristotle. Many such rules are discussed in Aristotle's own

A CONCISE INTRODUCTION TO LOGIC

account, but logicians of today generally settle on five or six.* If any one of these rules is violated, a specific formal fallacy is committed and, accordingly, the syllogism is invalid. These rules may be used as a convenient cross-check against the method of Venn diagrams. Of the five rules presented in this section, the first two depend on the concept of distribution, explained in Chapter 4, and the last three on the concepts of quality and quantity. In applying the first two rules, recall that the four categorical statements distribute their terms as follows.

Statement type	Terms distributed
A	subject
E	subject, predicate
I	none
O	predicate

Here is the first rule:

Rule 1:   *The middle term must be distributed at least once.*

Fallacy: **Undistributed middle.**

Example: All sharks are fish.
           All salmon are fish.
           All salmon are sharks.

In this standard-form categorical syllogism the middle term is "fish." In both premises "fish" occurs as the predicate of an **A** proposition and, therefore, by the rule developed in Chapter 4, is not distributed in either premise. (Only the subject term in an **A** proposition is distributed.) Thus, the syllogism commits the fallacy of undistributed middle and is invalid. If the major premise were rewritten to read "All fish are sharks," then "fish" would be distributed in that premise and the syllogism would be valid. But, of course, it would still be unsound because the rewritten premise would be false.

In applying this rule, note that from the Boolean standpoint the middle term must be distributed once and *only* once; but those arguments in which the middle term is distributed in both premises break some other rule.

The logic behind Rule 1 may be explained by recounting how the middle term accomplishes its intended purpose, which is to provide a common ground between the subject and predicate terms of the conclusion. Let us designate the minor, major, and middle terms by the

---

*Some texts include a rule stating that the three terms of a categorical syllogism must be used in the same sense throughout the argument. In this text this requirement is included as part of the definition of "categorical syllogism." See Section 5.1.

letters "S," "P," and "M," respectively, and let us suppose that M is distributed in the major premise. By definition, P is related to the *whole* of the M class. Then, when the M class is related either in whole or in part to S, S and P necessarily become related. But if M is undistributed in both premises, S and P may be related to *different parts* of the M class, in which case there is no common ground for relating S and P. This is exactly what happens in our fish example. The terms "salmon" and "sharks" are related to different parts of the fish class, so no common ground exists for relating them together.

Rule 2: *If a term is distributed in the conclusion, then it must be distributed in a premise.*

Fallacies: **Illicit major; illicit minor.**

Examples: All horses are animals.
Some dogs are not horses.
Some dogs are not animals.

All tigers are mammals.
All mammals are animals.
All animals are tigers.

In the first example the major term, "animals," is distributed in the conclusion but not in the major premise, so the syllogism commits the fallacy of illicit major, or, more precisely, "illicit process of the major term." In the second example the minor term, "animals," is distributed in the conclusion but not in the minor premise. The second example therefore commits the fallacy of illicit minor, or "illicit process of the minor term."

In applying this rule, one must always examine the conclusion first. If no terms are distributed in the conclusion, Rule 2 cannot be violated. If one or both terms in the conclusion are distributed, then the appropriate premise must be examined. If the term distributed in the conclusion is also distributed in the premise, then the rule is not violated. But, if the term is not distributed in the premise, the rule is violated and the syllogism is invalid. In applying Rule 2 (and also Rule 1), you may find it helpful to begin by marking all the distributed terms in the syllogism— either by circling them or by labeling them with a small letter "d."

The logic behind Rule 2 is easy to understand. Let us once again designate the minor, major, and middle terms by the letters "S," "P," and "M," respectively, and let us suppose that a certain syllogism commits the fallacy of illicit major. The conclusion of that syllogism then makes an assertion about every member of the P class, but the major premise makes an assertion about only some members of the P class. Because the minor premise, by itself, says nothing at all about the P class, the conclusion clearly contains information not contained in the premises, and the syllogism is therefore invalid. Analogous reasoning applies to the fallacy of illicit minor.

Rule 2 becomes intuitively plausible when it is recognized that distribution is a positive attribute. Granting this, an argument that has a term distributed in the conclusion but not in the premises has *more* in the conclusion than it does in the premises and is therefore invalid. Of course, it is always permissible to have more in a premise than appears in the conclusion, so it is perfectly all right for a term to be distributed in a premise but not in the conclusion.

Rule 3:   *Two negative premises are not allowed.*

Fallacy: **Exclusive premises.**

Example: No fish are mammals.
Some dogs are not fish.
Some dogs are not mammals.

This syllogism may be seen to be invalid because it has true premises and a false conclusion. The defect is attributable to the fact that it has two negative premises.

Upon reflection, Rule 3 should be fairly obvious. Let "*S*," "*P*," and "*M*" once again designate the minor, major, and middle terms. Now, if the *P* class and the *M* class are separate either wholly or partially, and the *S* class and the *M* class are separate either wholly or partially, nothing is said about the relation between the *S* class and the *P* class. These two classes may be either distinct or identical in whole or in part. Venn diagrams may be used effectively to illustrate the fact that no conclusion can be validly drawn from two negative premises.

Rule 4:   *A negative premise requires a negative conclusion, and a negative conclusion requires a negative premise.*

Fallacy: **Drawing an affirmative conclusion from a negative premise.**
or
Drawing a negative conclusion from affirmative premises.

Examples: All crows are birds.
Some wolves are not crows.
Some wolves are birds.

All triangles are three-angled polygons.
All three-angled polygons are three-sided polygons.
Some three-sided polygons are not triangles.

These arguments may be seen to be invalid because each has true premises and a false conclusion. The first draws an affirmative conclusion from a negative premise, and the second draws a negative conclusion from affirmative premises.

If "S," "P," and "M" once again designate the minor, major, and middle terms, an affirmative conclusion always states that the S class is contained either wholly or partially in the P class. The only way that such a conclusion can follow is if the S class is contained either wholly or partially in the M class, and the M class wholly in the P class. In other words, it follows only when both premises are affirmative. But if, for example, the S class is contained either wholly or partially in the M class, and the M class is separate either wholly or partially from the P class, such a conclusion will never follow. Thus, an affirmative conclusion cannot be drawn from negative premises.

Conversely, a negative conclusion asserts that the S class is separate either wholly or partially from the P class. But if both premises are affirmative, they assert class inclusion rather than separation. Thus, a negative conclusion cannot be drawn from affirmative premises.

Rule 5: *If both premises are universal, the conclusion cannot be particular.*

Fallacy: **Existential fallacy.**

Examples: All mammals are animals.
All unicorns are mammals.
Some unicorns are animals.

All mammals are animals.
All tigers are mammals.
Some tigers are animals.

If a categorical syllogism breaks only Rule 5, it is valid from the existential standpoint but not from the Boolean standpoint. The syllogistic forms that fall into this category are those that are included in the "conditionally valid" list in Section 5.1. In the first example above, if we make the assumption that one unicorn exists, the syllogism is valid. But since unicorns probably do not exist, it is preferable to adopt the Boolean standpoint and judge the syllogism invalid. It commits the existential fallacy. In the second example we must assume that one tiger exists for the syllogism to be valid. Since this assumption is justified, it is preferable in this case to adopt the existential standpoint and call the syllogism valid. From the existential standpoint there is no such thing as an existential fallacy, and the syllogism breaks no other rules.

The rationale behind Rule 5 is quite easy to understand. From the Boolean standpoint, universal statements make no assertions about existence, while particular statements do. Thus, if a syllogism is made up of universal premises and a particular conclusion, the conclusion asserts that something exists, while the premises do not. Thus the conclusion contains more information than the premises, and the syllogism is invalid. From the existential standpoint, on the other hand, the assumption is made that the subject term of a universal statement denotes at least one existing thing. Thus, under this assumption the mere fact that a syllogism has universal premises and a particular conclusion is not sufficient grounds for claiming that the conclusion contains more information than the premises. Provided that such a syllogism breaks no other rules, therefore, it is valid.

You may recall that the term "existential fallacy" first occurred in Section 4.5, where it was used in connection with the Boolean interpretation of the square of opposition. The existential fallacy that appears in connection with Rule 5 stems from the same idea, applied in this case to syllogisms.

EXERCISE 5.3

I. Reconstruct the following syllogistic forms and use the five rules for syllogisms to determine which are valid and which are invalid. For those that are invalid, name the fallacy or fallacies committed. Check your answers by constructing Venn diagrams. Finally, if any forms are invalid from the Boolean standpoint but valid from the existential standpoint, use the Venn diagrams to determine the existential assumption that must be made.

★1. AAA-3	11. AII-2
2. IAI-2	12. AIO-3
3. EIO-1	★13. AEE-4
★4. AAI-2	14. EAE-4
5. IEO-1	15. EAO-3
6. EOO-4	★16. EEE-1
★7. EAA-1	17. EAE-1
8. AII-3	18. OAI-3
9. AAI-4	★19. AOO-2
★10. IAO-3	20. EAO-1

II. Use the five rules to determine whether the following standard form syllogisms are valid or invalid. For those that are invalid, name the fallacy or fallacies committed. Check your answer by constructing a Venn diagram for each.

★1. Some nebulas are clouds of gas.
Some clouds of gas are objects invisible to the naked eye.
Therefore, some objects invisible to the naked eye are nebulas.

2. No individuals sensitive to the difference between right and wrong are people who measure talent and success in terms of wealth.
All corporate takeover experts are people who measure talent and success in terms of wealth.
Therefore, no corporate takeover experts are individuals sensitive to the difference between right and wrong.

3. No believers in fairy tales are good candidates for elected office.
All supporters of the Strategic Defense Initiative are believers in fairy tales.
Therefore, some supporters of the Strategic Defense Initiative are not good candidates for elected office.

★4. Some cases of affirmative action are not measures justified by past discrimination.
No cases of affirmative action are illegal practices.
Therefore, some illegal practices are not measures justified by past discrimination.

5. All transparent metals are good conductors of heat.
All transparent metals are good conductors of electricity.
Therefore, some good conductors of electricity are good conductors of heat.

6. All members of the National Rifle Association are persons opposed to gun control.
All members of the National Rifle Association are law-abiding citizens.
Therefore, all law-abiding citizens are persons opposed to gun control.

★7. No searches based on probable cause are violations of Fourth Amendment rights.
Some warrantless searches are violations of Fourth Amendment rights.
Therefore, some warrantless searches are not searches based on probable cause.

8. All war zones are places where abuse of discretion is rampant.
Some places where abuse of discretion is rampant are international borders.
Therefore, some international borders are war zones.

9. All inside traders are persons subject to prosecution.
Some executives with privileged information are not persons subject to prosecution.
Therefore, some executives with privileged information are inside traders.

★10. All successful flirts are masters at eye contact.
All masters at eye contact are persons genuinely interested in others.
Therefore, some persons genuinely interested in others are successful flirts.

III. Answer "true" or "false" to the following statements:

1. If an argument violates one of the first four rules, it may still be valid.

2. If a valid syllogism has an **E** statement as its conclusion, then both the major and minor terms must be distributed in the premises.

3. If a syllogism has two **I** statements as premises, then its middle term is undistributed.

4. If a syllogism has an **E** and an **O** statement as premises, then no conclusion follows validly.

A CONCISE INTRODUCTION TO LOGIC

5. If a syllogism has an **I** statement as its conclusion, then Rule 2 cannot be violated.

6. If a valid syllogism has an **O** statement as its conclusion, then its premises can be an **A** and an **I** statement.

7. If a valid syllogism has an **E** statement as a premise, then its conclusion can be an **A** statement.

8. If a syllogism breaks only Rule 5 and its three terms are "dogs," "cats," and "animals," then the syllogism is valid.

9. If a syllogism breaks only Rule 5 and its three terms are "elves," "trolls," and "gnomes," then the syllogism is valid.

10. Some syllogisms that are valid from the Boolean standpoint are not valid from the existential standpoint.

5.4 REDUCING THE NUMBER OF TERMS

Categorical syllogisms, as they occur in ordinary spoken and written expression, are seldom phrased according to the precise norms of the standard-form syllogism. Sometimes quantifiers, premises, or conclusions are left unexpressed, chains of syllogisms are strung together into single arguments, and terms are mixed together with their negations in a single argument. The final three sections of this chapter are concerned with developing techniques for reworking such arguments in order to render them testable by Venn diagrams or by the rules for syllogisms.

In this section we consider arguments that contain more than three terms but that can be modified to reduce the number of terms to three. Consider the following:

> All photographers are non-writers.
> Some editors are writers.
> Therefore, some non-photographers are not non-editors.

This syllogism is clearly not in standard form because it has six terms: "photographers," "editors," "writers," "non-photographers," "non-editors," and "non-writers." But because three of the terms are negations of the other three, the number of terms can be reduced to a total of three, each used twice in distinct propositions. To accomplish the reduction, we can use the three operations of conversion, obversion, and contraposition discussed in Chapter 4. But, of course, since the reworked syllogism must be equivalent in meaning to the original one, we must use these operations only on the kinds of statements for which they yield equivalent results. That is, we must use conversion only on **E** and **I** statements and contraposition only on **A** and **O** statements. Obversion yields equivalent results for all four kinds of categorical statements.

Let us rewrite our six-term argument using letters to represent the terms, and then obvert the first premise and contrapose the conclusion in order to eliminate the negated letters:

Symbolized argument	Reduced argument
All *P* are non-*W*.	No *P* are *W*.
Some *E* are *W*.	Some *E* are *W*.
Some non-*P* are not non-*E*.	Some *E* are not *P*.

Because the first premise of the original argument is an **A** statement and the conclusion an **O** statement, the reduced argument is equivalent in meaning to the original argument. The reduced argument is in standard syllogistic form and may be evaluated either with a Venn diagram or by the five rules for syllogisms. The application of these methods indicates that the reduced argument is valid. We conclude, therefore, that the original argument is also valid.

It is not necessary to eliminate the negated terms in order to reduce the number of terms. It is equally effective to convert certain non-negated terms into negated ones. Thus, instead of obverting the first premise of the above argument and contraposing the conclusion, we could have contraposed the first premise and converted and then obverted the second premise. The operation is performed as follows:

Symbolized argument	Reduced argument
All *P* are non-*W*.	All *W* are non-*P*.
Some *E* are *W*.	Some *W* are not non-*E*.
Some non-*P* are not non-*E*.	Some non-*P* are not non-*E*.

The reduced argument is once again equivalent to the original one, but now we must reverse the order of the premises to put the syllogism into standard form:

Some *W* are not non-*E*.
All *W* are non-*P*.
Some non-*P* are not non-*E*.

When tested with a Venn diagram or by means of the five rules, this argument will, of course, also be found valid, and so the original argument is valid. When using a Venn diagram no unusual method is needed; the diagram is simply lettered with the three terms "*W*," "non-*E*," and "non-*P*."

The most important point to remember in reducing the number of terms is that conversion and contraposition must never be used on statements for which they yield undetermined results. That is, conversion must never be used on **A** and **O** statements, and contraposition must never be used on **E** and **I** statements. The operations that are allowed are summarized as follows:

Conversion:	No *S* are *P*.	No *P* are *S*.
	Some *S* are *P*.	Some *P* are *S*.

Obversion:	All *S* are *P*.	No *S* are non-*P*.
	No *S* are *P*.	All *S* are non-*P*.
	Some *S* are *P*.	Some *S* are not non-*P*.
	Some *S* are not *P*.	Some *S* are non-*P*.

Contraposition:	All *S* are *P*.	All non-*P* are non-*S*.
	Some *S* are not *P*.	Some non-*P* are not non-*S*.

EXERCISE 5.4

Rewrite the following arguments using letters to represent the terms, reduce the number of terms, and put the arguments into standard form. Then test the new forms with Venn diagrams or by means of the five rules for syllogisms to determine the validity or invalidity of the original arguments.

★1. Some intelligible statements are true statements, because all unintelligible statements are meaningless statements and some false statements are meaningful statements.

2. Some persons who do not regret their crimes are convicted murderers, so some convicted murderers are persons insusceptible of being reformed, since all persons susceptible of being reformed are persons who regret their crimes.

3. All Peace Corps volunteers are persons who have witnessed poverty and desolation, and all persons insensitive to human need are persons who have failed to witness poverty and desolation. Thus, all Peace Corps volunteers are persons sensitive to human need.

★4. Some unintentional killings are not punishable offenses, inasmuch as all cases of self-defense are unpunishable offenses, and some intentional killings are cases of self-defense.

5. All recently constructed nuclear reactors are reactors other than the graphite-moderated type. Therefore, all unsafe sources of electricity are reactors that were not recently constructed, since all graphite-moderated reactors are unsafe sources of electricity.

6. No objects that sink in water are chunks of ice, and no objects that float in water are things at least as dense as water. Accordingly, all chunks of ice are things less dense than water.

★7. Some proposed flights to Mars are inexpensive ventures, because all unmanned space missions are inexpensive ventures, and some proposed flights to Mars are not manned space missions.

8. All institutions driven by careerism are institutions that do not emphasize liberal arts. It follows that some universities are not institutions
   that emphasize liberal arts, for some institutions that are not driven by
   careerism are universities.

9. No cases of AIDS are infections easily curable by drugs, since all diseases that infect the brain are infections not easily curable by drugs,
   and all diseases that do not infect the brain are cases other than AIDS.

★10. Some Soviet spies are persons without diplomatic immunity, so some
   persons invulnerable to arrest and prosecution are Soviet spies, because
   no persons with diplomatic immunity are persons vulnerable to arrest
   and prosecution.

5.5 ORDINARY LANGUAGE ARGUMENTS

Many categorical syllogisms that are not in standard form as written can
be translated into standard-form syllogisms. Such translation often involves making some of the corrective measures discussed in the last section of Chapter 4—namely, inserting quantifiers, modifying subject and
predicate terms, and correcting copulas. The goal, of course, is to produce an argument consisting of three standard-form categorical propositions that contain a total of three different terms, each of which is used
twice in distinct propositions. Since this task involves not only the
translation of the component statements into standard form but the ad-
justment of these statements one to another so that their terms occur in
matched pairs, a certain amount of practice is usually required before it
can be done with any facility. In reducing the terms to three matched
pairs it is often helpful to identify some factor common to two or all
three propositions and express this common factor through the strategic
use of parameters. Consider the following argument:

> Whenever people put off marriage until they are older, the di-
> vorce rate decreases. Today, people are putting off marriage
> until they are older. Therefore, the divorce rate is decreasing
> today.

The temporal adverbs "whenever" and "today" suggest that "times"
should be used as the common factor. Following this suggestion, we
have:

> All times people put off marriage until they are older are times
> the divorce rate decreases. All present times are times people
> put off marriage until they are older. Therefore, all present
> times are times the divorce rate decreases.

We now have a standard-form categorical syllogism. If we adopt the following convention

M = times people put off marriage until they are older

D = times the divorce rate decreases

P = present times

the syllogism may be symbolized as follows:

All M are D.
All P are M.
All P are D.

This is the so called "Barbara" syllogism and is, of course, valid. Here is another example:

McDonnell Douglas must be a manufacturer because it hires riveters, and anyone who hires riveters is a manufacturer.

For this argument the parameter "companies" suggests itself:

All companies identical to McDonnell Douglas are manufacturers, because all companies identical to McDonnell Douglas are companies that hire riveters, and all companies that hire riveters are manufacturers.

The first statement, of course, is the conclusion. When the syllogism is written in standard form, it will be seen that it has, like the previous syllogism, the form **AAA**-1.

Another example:

If a piece of evidence is trustworthy, then it should be admissible in court. Polygraph tests are not trustworthy. Therefore, they should not be admissible in court.

To translate this argument it is not necessary to use a single common factor:

All trustworthy pieces of evidence are pieces of evidence that should be admissible in court. No polygraph tests are trustworthy pieces of evidence. Therefore, no polygraph tests are pieces of evidence that should be admissible in court.

This syllogism commits the fallacy of illicit major and is therefore invalid.

As was mentioned in Section 4.8, arguments containing an exceptive proposition must be handled in a special way. Let us consider one that contains an exceptive proposition as a premise:

All European nations except Switzerland are members of the
U.N. Therefore, since Bulgaria is not the same nation as Switzerland, it must be a member.

The first premise is translated as two conjoined categorical propositions:
"No European nations identical to Switzerland are members of the U.N.
and all European nations not identical to Switzerland are members of
the U.N." These in turn give rise to two syllogisms:

> No European nations identical to Switzerland are members of
> the U.N.
> No nations identical to Bulgaria are European nations identical
> to Switzerland.
> Therefore, all nations identical to Bulgaria are members of the
> U.N.

> All European nations not identical to Switzerland are members
> of the U.N.
> No nations identical to Bulgaria are European nations identical
> to Switzerland.
> Therefore, all nations identical to Bulgaria are members of the
> U.N.

The first syllogism, which is in standard form, is invalid because it has
two negative premises. The second one, on the other hand, is not in
standard form, because it has four terms. If the second premise is obverted, so that it reads "All nations identical to Bulgaria are European
nations not identical to Switzerland," the syllogism becomes an **AAA-1**
standard form syllogism, which is valid.

Each of these two syllogisms may be viewed as a pathway in which
the conclusion of the original argument might follow necessarily from
the premises. Since it does follow via the second syllogism, the original
argument is valid. If both of the resulting syllogisms turned out to be
invalid, the original argument would be invalid.

If the conclusion of an argument is an exceptive proposition, and both
premises are categorical propositions, it is easy to see that the argument
is invalid because both of the categorical syllogisms would have to be
valid—and this is impossible. A more extended analysis can be used to
show that an argument having an exceptive proposition for its conclusion and for either or both of its premises is also invalid. Thus, any
argument having an exceptive proposition for its conclusion is invalid.

EXERCISE 5.5

Translate the following arguments into standard-form categorical syllogisms, then use Venn diagrams or the rules for syllogisms to determine

whether each is valid or invalid. See Section 4.8 for help with the translation.

★1. Inside traders are the only people who make lots of money on the stock market, and Ivan Boesky made millions. Thus, Ivan Boesky was an inside trader.

2. Whenever suicide rates decline, we can infer that people's lives are better adjusted. Accordingly, since suicide rates have been declining in recent years, we can infer that people's lives have been better adjusted in recent years.

3. People for the American Way supports only liberal candidates. Hence, Pat Robertson must not be a liberal, since People for the American Way does not support him.

★4. Whoever is a member of the British Conservative Party favors increased military spending, and Margaret Thatcher certainly favors that. Thus, Margaret Thatcher must be a member of the British Conservative Party.

5. There are public schools that teach secular humanism. Therefore, since secular humanism is a religion, there are public schools that teach religion.

6. Anyone who supports tobacco subsidies by the government supports tobacco-related health hazards. Therefore, Senator Jesse Helms must support tobacco-related health hazards, because he supports tobacco subsidies by the government.

★7. Kathleen Battle sings what she wants. Therefore, since Kathleen Battle sings Puccini arias, it follows that she must want to sing Puccini arias.

8. Not all interest expenses are tax-deductible. Home mortgage payments are interest expenses. Thus, they are not tax-deductible.

9. If a marriage is based on a meshing of neuroses, it allows little room for growth. If a marriage allows little room for growth, it is bound to fail. Therefore, if a marriage is based on a meshing of neuroses, it is bound to fail.

★10. Television viewers cannot receive scrambled signals unless they have a decoder. Whoever receives HBO receives scrambled signals. Therefore, whoever receives HBO has a decoder.

11. Wherever the national diet is rich in wheat bran, the incidence of colon cancer is low. The national diet in Canada is not rich in wheat bran. Thus, in Canada, the incidence of colon cancer is not low.

12. According to surveys, there are college students who think that Africa is in North America. But anyone who thinks that has no knowledge of geography. It follows that there are college students who have no knowledge of geography.

CATEGORICAL SYLLOGISMS

255

★13. Diseases carried by recessive genes can be inherited by offspring of two carriers. Thus, since cystic fibrosis is a disease carried by recessive genes, it can be inherited by offspring of two carriers.

14. All metals except mercury are solids at room temperature. Hence, cadmium is a solid at room temperature, because it is not the same metal as mercury.

★15. Autistic children are occasionally helped by aversive therapy. But aversive therapy is sometimes inhumane. Thus, autistic children are sometimes helped by inhumane therapy.

5.6 ENTHYMEMES

An **enthymeme** is an argument that is expressible as a categorical syllogism but that is missing a premise or a conclusion. Examples:

> The corporate income tax should be abolished; it encourages waste and high prices.

> Animals that are loved by someone should not be sold to a medical laboratory, and lost pets are certainly loved by someone.

The first enthymeme is missing the premise "Whatever encourages waste and high prices should be abolished," and the second is missing the conclusion "Lost pets should not be sold to a medical laboratory."

Enthymemes occur frequently in ordinary spoken and written English for a number of reasons. Sometimes it is simply boring to express every statement in an argument. The listener or reader's intelligence is called into play when he or she is required to supply a missing statement, and his or her interest is thereby sustained. On other occasions the arguer may want to slip an invalid or unsound argument past an unwary listener or reader, and this aim may be facilitated by leaving a premise or conclusion out of the picture.

Many enthymemes are easy to convert into syllogisms. The reader or listener must first determine what is missing, whether premise or conclusion, and then introduce the missing statement with the aim of converting the enthymeme into a good argument. Attention to indicator words will often provide the clue as to the nature of the missing statement, but a little practice can render this task virtually automatic. The missing statement need not be expressed in categorical form; expressing it in the general context of the other statements is sufficient and is often the easier alternative. Once this is done, the entire argument may be translated into categorical form and then tested with a Venn diagram or by the rules for syllogisms. Example:

Venus completes its orbit in less time than the Earth, because Venus is closer to the sun.

Missing premise: Any planet closer to the sun completes its orbit in less time than the Earth.

Translating this argument into categorical form, we have,

All planets closer to the sun are planets that complete their orbit in less time than the Earth.
All planets identical to Venus are planets closer to the sun.
All planets identical to Venus are planets that complete their orbit in less time than the Earth.

This syllogism is valid (and sound).

The kind of enthymemes that occur in letters to the editor of magazines and newspapers often require a bit more creativity to convert into syllogisms. Consider the following short letter:

It would behoove South Africa to remember that people who are not accorded their rights by reason will eventually take them by force.

(Gloria S. Ross)

This enthymeme consists of only a single statement. The implied conclusion is that people in South Africa will eventually take their rights by force, and the implied premise is that people in South Africa are not accorded their rights by reason. Having supplied the missing statements, we can now write the argument as a standard form syllogism:

All countries in which people are not accorded their rights by reason are countries in which people will eventually take their rights by force.
All countries identical to South Africa are countries in which people are not accorded their rights by reason.
Therefore, all countries identical to South Africa are countries in which people will eventually take their rights by force.

The argument is valid, and possibly sound. Here is another example:

I know several doctors who smoke. In a step toward my own health, I will no longer be their patient. It has occurred to me that if they care so little about their own health, how can they possibly care about mine?

(Joan Boyer)

In this argument the author draws three connections: the connection between doctors' smoking and doctors' caring about their own health, between doctors' caring about their own health and doctors' caring about the author's health, and between doctors' caring about the author's health and doctors who will have the author as a patient. Two arguments are needed to express these connections:

All doctors who smoke are doctors who do not care about their own health.

All doctors who do not care about their own health are doctors who do not care about my health.

Therefore, all doctors who smoke are doctors who do not care about my health.

And,

All doctors who smoke are doctors who do not care about my health.

All doctors who do not care about my health are doctors who will not have me as a patient.

Therefore, all doctors who smoke are doctors who will not have me as a patient.

Notice that the conclusion of the first argument becomes a premise in the second argument. To put these arguments into final standard form the order of the premises must be reversed. Both arguments are valid, but probably not sound.

The world of advertising is another fertile field for enthymemes. Consider the following ad for Honda cars.

Fasten your seat belt.

This ad is an enthymeme, and it persuades precisely by leaving the task of conversion to the subliminal consciousness of the prospective buyer. The ad might be converted into an argument as follows:

All cars in which you are urged to fasten your seat belt are fast and exciting cars.

All Honda cars are cars in which you are urged to fasten your seat belt.

Therefore, all Honda cars are fast and exciting cars.

Or, perhaps as follows:

All times one is requested to fasten one's seat belt are times one is about to take off (as in an airplane).

All times one drives a Honda are times one is requested to fasten one's seat belt.

Therefore, all times one drives a Honda are times one is about to take off (as in an airplane).

Both arguments are valid, but since the first premise in both is false, both arguments are unsound. Many ads, like this one, hide unsound or invalid arguments beneath the surface. People who take the trouble to make the arguments explicit are usually less prone to being duped by such ads.

EXERCISE 5.6

I. In the following enthymemes determine whether the missing statement is a premise or conclusion. Then supply the missing statement, attempting whenever possible to convert the enthymeme into a valid argument.

★1. Mechanistic materialists do not believe in free will because they think that everything is governed by deterministic laws.

2. Any organization that stands to gain by the expansion of the arms race supports that expansion, and Rockwell International certainly stands to gain.

3. Mikhail Gorbachev supports increased personal freedoms for the Soviet people, because anyone who advocates increased openness in government supports that.

★4. A few fraternities have dangerous initiation rites, and those that do have no legitimate role in campus life.

5. Only nonprofit organizations are exempt from paying taxes, so churches must be exempt.

6. All of the operas except Mozart's were well performed, and *Carmen* was not written by Mozart.

★7. Not all chardonnays are good wines, but all of them are expensive.

8. Higher life forms could not have evolved through merely random processes, because no organized beings could have evolved that way.

9. None but right-to-life advocates think that abortion is a form of murder, and Phyllis Schlaffly supports right to life.

★10. The humpback whale population has been decreasing in recent years because the humpback is being overhunted.

11. Wherever radioactive material is released into the atmosphere, increased incidence of cancer results. And radioactive material was released into the atmosphere at Chernobyl.

12. If a symphony orchestra has effective fund raisers, it will survive; and the Cleveland symphony has survived for years.

★13. Some police chiefs undermine the evenhanded enforcement of the law, because anyone who fixes parking tickets does that.

14. A contract to buy land is not enforceable unless it's in writing; but our client's contract to buy land *is* in writing.

★15. Whoever elevates the pride of a nation by succeeding in some extraordinary accomplishment deserves to be called a national hero. Dick Rutan and Jeana Yeager did precisely that.

(Diane Lynch)

II. Translate the enthymemes in Part I of this exercise into standard-form categorical syllogisms and test them for validity.

III. The following enthymemes were originally submitted as letters to the editor of magazines and newspapers. Convert them into valid standard-form syllogisms. In some cases two syllogisms may be required.

★1. If the Defense Department is so intent on fighting alcohol abuse, why does it make alcohol so readily available and acceptable? Alcohol is tax free at post liquor stores, and enlisted men's and officers' clubs make drinking almost a mandatory facet of military life. Indeed, people who don't drink and join the fun are looked upon as odd by most military personnel.

(Diane Lynch)

2. All aid to Israel should be stopped at once. Why should the American taxpayer be asked to send billions of dollars to Israel when every city in the United States is practically broke and millions of people are out of work?

(Bertha Grace)

3. Suicide is not immoral. If a person decides that life is impossible, it is his or her right to end it.

(Donald S. Farrar)

★4. The best way to get people to read a book is to ban it. The fundamentalist families in Church Hill, Tennessee, have just guaranteed sales of *Macbeth, The Diary of Anne Frank, The Wizard of Oz* and other stories.

(Paula Fleischer)

5. The budget deficit will not be brought under control because to do so would require our elected leaders in Washington to do the unthinkable—act courageously and responsibly.

(Bruce Crutcher)

6. The IRA must be as stupid as it is vicious. Does it think that the nation that stood up to a hail of bombs, night after night after night during World War II, will now succumb to isolated attacks?

(Alan Griffiths)

★7. College students of today are the higher-income taxpayers of tomorrow. Congress should consider financial aid as an investment in the financial future of our country.

(Carol A. Steimel)

8. Our genes and our environment control our destinies. The idea of conscious choice is ridiculous. Yes, prisons should be designed to protect society, but they should not punish the poor slobs who were headed for jail from birth.

(Paul R. Andrews)

9. The church has a right to be involved in disarmament because the nuclear-weapons issue is a moral question that must be faced. Who should be interested in such questions if not the clergy?

(Wendell Sherk)

★10. The U.S. surgeon general's latest report on cigarettes and cancer is an interesting example of natural selection in the late twentieth century. The intelligent members of our species will quit smoking, and survive. The dummies will continue to puff away.

(Kelly Kinnon)

IV. Convert the following advertisements into standard-form categorical syllogisms. In doing so, try to capture as closely as possible the emotional overtones of the ad.

★1. Lanvin Perfume: Dangerous but worth the risk.

2. Astra Sweaters: Definitely not the sweater for Aunt Nora (accompanied by a photo of a model in a sweater showing a prominent bust line).

3. Toyota Tercel: Stingy!

★4. Today's Florsheim shoe: 90 years in the making.

5. Players cigarettes: Players go places (accompanied by a picture of a party scene).

6. Ford cars: You'll love the security.

★7. Cruzan rum: Not many people have seen a bottle of Cruzan rum. Most of it disappears in the Virgin Islands.

8. Mazda cars: Please don't tell your mother you're going to buy one.

9. Waterford crystal: They cut diamonds by hand, don't they?

★10. Olympus cameras: When you have more to say than just smile.

5.7 SORITES

A **sorites** is a chain of categorical syllogisms in which the intermediate conclusions have been left out. The name is derived from the Greek word *soros*, meaning "heap," and is pronounced "sō rī tēz." The plural form is also "sorites." Here is an example:

> All bloodhounds are dogs.
> All dogs are mammals.
> No fish are mammals.
> Therefore, no fish are bloodhounds.

The first two premises validly imply the intermediate conclusion "All bloodhounds are mammals." If this intermediate conclusion is then treated as a premise and put together with the third premise, the final conclusion follows validly. The sorites is thus composed of two valid categorical syllogisms and is therefore valid. The rule in evaluating a sorites is based on the idea that a chain is only as strong as its weakest link. If any of the component syllogisms in a sorites is invalid, the entire sorites is invalid.

A sorites is in **standard form** when each of the component propositions is in standard form, when each term occurs twice, when the predicate of the conclusion is in the first premise, and when each successive premise has a term in common with the preceding one.* The sorites presented above, for example, is in standard form. Each of the propositions is in standard form, each term occurs twice, the predicate of the conclusion, "bloodhounds," is in the first premise, the other term in the first premise, "dogs," is in the second premise, and so on.

The procedure to be followed in evaluating a sorites is: (1) put the sorites into standard form, (2) introduce the intermediate conclusions, and (3) test each component syllogism for validity. If each component is valid, the sorites is valid. Consider the following sorites form:

> No B are C.
> Some E are A.
> All A are B.
> All D are C.
> Some E are not D.

To put the sorites form into standard form, the premises must be rearranged:

> All D are C.
> No B are C.
> All A are B.
> Some E are A.
> Some E are not D.

Next, the intermediate conclusions are drawn. Venn diagrams are useful in performing this step, and they serve simultaneously to check the validity of each component syllogism:

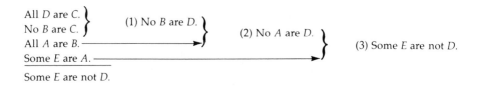

---

*Actually, there are two definitions of standard form: the Goclenian and the Aristotelian. The one given here is the Goclenian. In the Aristotelian version, the premises are arranged so that the *subject* of the conclusion occurs in the first premise.

A CONCISE INTRODUCTION TO LOGIC

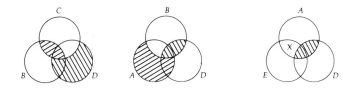

The first intermediate conclusion, "No *B* are *D*," is drawn from the first two premises. The second, "No *A* are *D*" is drawn from the first intermediate conclusion and the third premise. And the third conclusion, which is identical to the final conclusion, is drawn from the second intermediate conclusion and the fourth premise. Since all conclusions are drawn validly, the sorites is valid.

If, at any designated step in the procedure, no conclusion can be validly drawn, as, for example, if the first two premises are negative or contain undistributed middle terms, then the sorites is invalid. Sometimes immediate inspection will disclose that a certain sorites is invalid. For example, any sorites having two (or more) negative premises or two (or more) particular premises is invalid. Before any such inspection is attempted, however, one must be certain that the terms occur in pairs. Sometimes the operations of conversion, obversion, and contraposition must be used to reduce the number of terms in a sorites, and obversion, of course, affects the quality of the statements on which it is used.

EXERCISE 5.7

I. Rewrite the following sorites in standard form, reducing the number of terms when necessary. Then supply the intermediate conclusions and test with Venn diagrams.

★1. No *B* are *C*.
Some *D* are *C*.
All *A* are *B*.
_____
Some *D* are not *A*.

2. No *C* are *D*.
All *A* are *B*.
Some *C* are not *B*.
_____
Some *D* are not *A*.

3. No *S* are *M*.
All *F* are *S*.
Some *M* are *H*.
All *E* are *F*.
_____
Some *H* are not *E*.

★4. Some *T* are *K*.
No *K* are *N*.
Some *C* are *Q*.
All *T* are *C*.
_____
Some *Q* are not *N*.

5. No *A* are non-*B*.
No *C* are *B*.
All non-*A* are non-*D*.
_____
No *D* are *C*.

6. All *M* are non-*P*.
Some *M* are *S*.
All *K* are *P*.
_____
Some non-*K* are not non-*S*.

★7. All non-*U* are non-*V*.
No *U* are non-*W*.
All *V* are *Y*.
No *X* are *W*.
_____
All *Y* are non-*X*.

8. All *D* are non-*C*.
All non-*B* are non-*A*.
Some *E* are *D*.
All *B* are *C*.
_____
Some non-*A* are not non-*E*.

9. All non-*L* are non-*K*.
Some *K* are *M*.
All *P* are non-*L*.
No non-*N* are *M*.
No *Q* are non-*P*.
_____
Some *N* are not *Q*.

★10. All *R* are *S*.
No non-*V* are *T*.
No *Q* are non-*R*.
No non-*Q* are *P*.
All *T* are non-*S*.
_____
All *V* are non-*P*.

II. The following sorites are taken from Lewis Carroll's *Symbolic Logic*. All are valid. Rewrite each sorites in standard form, using letters to represent the terms and reducing the number of terms whenever necessary. Then use Venn diagrams to prove each one valid.

★1. No ducks waltz.
No officers ever decline to waltz.
All my poultry are ducks.
_____
My poultry are not officers.

2. No experienced person is incompetent.
Jenkins is always blundering.
No competent person is always blundering.
_____
Jenkins is inexperienced.

3. No terriers wander among the signs of the zodiac.
Nothing that does not wander among the signs
of the zodiac is a comet.
Nothing but a terrier has a curly tail.
_____
No comet has a curly tail.

★4. All hummingbirds are richly colored.
No large birds live on honey.
Birds that do not live on honey are dull in color.
_____
All hummingbirds are small.

5. All unripe fruit is unwholesome.
All these apples are wholesome.
No fruit grown in the shade is ripe.
_____
These apples were grown in the sun.

6. All my sons are slim.
No child of mine is healthy who takes no exercise.
All gluttons who are children of mine are fat.
No daughter of mine takes any exercise.
All gluttons who are children of mine are unhealthy.

★7. The only books in this library that I do not recommend for
reading are unhealthy in tone.
The bound books are all well-written.
All the romances are healthy in tone.
I do not recommend you to read any of the unbound books.
All the romances in this library are well-written.

8. No interesting poems are unpopular among people of real taste.
No modern poetry is free from affectation.
All your poems are on the subject of soap bubbles.
No affected poetry is popular among people of real taste.
No ancient poem is on the subject of soap bubbles.
All your poems are uninteresting.

9. All writers who understand human nature are clever.
No one is a true poet unless he can
stir the hearts of men.
Shakespeare wrote *Hamlet*.
No writer who does not understand human nature can
stir the hearts of men.
None but a true poet could have written *Hamlet*.
Shakespeare was clever.

★10. I trust every animal that belongs to me.
Dogs gnaw bones.
I admit no animals into my study unless they beg when told to do so.
All the animals in the yard are mine.
I admit every animal that I trust into my study.
The only animals that are really willing to beg when told to do so are
dogs.
All the animals in the yard gnaw bones.

6

PROPOSITIONAL LOGIC

6.1 SYMBOLS AND TRANSLATION

In earlier chapters we saw that the validity of a deductive argument is purely a function of its form. By knowing the specific form we can often tell immediately whether an argument is valid or invalid. Unfortunately, however, ordinary language usage frequently obscures the form of an argument. To correct for this, logic introduces various simplifying procedures that facilitate form recognition. In Chapter 5 letters were used to represent the terms in a syllogism, and techniques were developed to reduce syllogisms to what is called standard form. In this chapter form recognition is facilitated through the introduction of special symbols called **connectives.** When arguments are expressed in terms of these connectives, the determination of validity or invalidity often becomes a matter of mere visual inspection.

Propositional logic marks a break with the logic of the previous two chapters in that the fundamental elements are not terms, but whole statements (or propositions). Statements are represented by letters, and these letters are then combined with one another by means of the connectives to form more complex arrangements. To explain how this is done, it is necessary to distinguish between what are called simple, or "atomic," statements and compound, or "molecular," statements. A **simple** (atomic) **statement** is one that does not contain any other statement as a component. Here are some examples:

Butane is a hydrogen compound.
James Joyce wrote *Ulysses*.
Parakeets are colorful birds.
The monk seal is threatened with extinction.

Any convenient upper-case letter may be selected to represent each statement. Thus, *B* might be selected to represent the first, *J* the second, *P* the third, and *M* the fourth. As will be explained shortly, the lower-case letters are reserved for use as propositional variables.

A **compound** (molecular) **statement** is one that contains at least one atomic statement as a component. Here are some examples:

It is not the case that Emily Bronte wrote *Jane Eyre*.

If IBM introduces a new line, then Apple will also.

Either private air traffic will be restricted or mid-air collisions will continue.

The Boston Symphony will perform Mahler and the Cleveland Symphony will perform Mozart.

If the first letters in the atomic statements are selected to represent these statements, the molecular statements may be represented as follows:

It is not the case that *E*.
If *I*, then *A*.
Either *P* or *M*.
B and *C*.

The words "it is not the case that," "if . . . then," and so on, may be translated through the introduction of connective symbols. In all, five symbols are needed, and they are listed, together with their meanings, in the following table:

Connec-tive	Name	Meaning	Sample translations
~	negation	not	$\sim P$ = it is not the case that *P*
•	conjunction	and	$P \cdot Q = P$ and Q
v	disjunction	or	$P \text{ v } Q = P$ or Q
⊃	conditional or implication	if . . . then . . . or implies	$P \supset Q = \begin{cases} \text{if } P \text{ then } Q \\ or \\ P \text{ implies } Q \end{cases}$
≡	biconditional or equivalence	if and only if or is equivalent tc	$P \equiv Q = \begin{cases} P \text{ if and only if } Q \\ or \\ P \text{ is equivalent to } Q \end{cases}$

In the expression $P \cdot Q$ the propositions P and Q are called **conjuncts;** in $P \vee Q$ they are called **disjuncts;** and in $P \supset Q$ they are called the **antecedent** and **consequent,** respectively.

Let us now use these symbols to translate some typical statements found in ordinary English expression. In the examples that follow, the first letters in the atomic propositions are used to represent those propositions. The **negation sign** is used to translate any negated atomic proposition:

Braniff does not fly to Saint Louis:	$\sim B$
It is not the case that Braniff flies to Saint Louis:	$\sim B$
It is false that Braniff flies to Saint Louis:	$\sim B$

The **conjunction sign** is used equivalently to translate such conjunctions as "and," "however," "yet," "but," "also," "moreover," "although," "nevertheless," and "still":

Continental Flies to Houston and Delta flies to Dallas:	$C \cdot D$
Continental flies to Houston but Delta flies to Dallas:	$C \cdot D$
Continental flies to Houston; however, Delta flies to Dallas:	$C \cdot D$
Continental and United fly to Houston:	$C \cdot U$

Note that the last example is equivalent to the statement "Continental flies to Houston and United flies to Houston." To translate such a statement as a conjunction of two atomic statements, the original statement must be equivalent to a compound statement in English. For example, the statement "Blake and Clark are friends" is *not* equivalent to "Blake is a friend and Clark is a friend," so this statement *cannot* be translated as $B \cdot C$.

The word "or" in English has two meanings. "Or" is used *inclusively* when it means "one or the other and possibly both." It is used *exclusively* when it means "one or the other but not both." For example, "or" is used inclusively in the statement "Anyone who owns a car or a truck needs insurance" and exclusively in the statement "The Orient Express is on track one or track two." In the first statement it is intended that anyone who owns a car *and* a truck also needs insurance, but in the second it is *not* intended that the Orient Express should be on *both* tracks. In propositional logic the **disjunction sign** is given the *inclusive* meaning of "or." This is the weaker of the two meanings, and if ever the exclusive meaning is intended, it may be constructed from the inclusive meaning by simply adding the phrase "but not both."

Two other words that deserve some comment are "either" and "unless." In propositional logic the word "either" has primarily a punctuational meaning. As we will see shortly, the use of this word often tells us where parentheses or brackets should be introduced in the symbolic expression. If parentheses are not needed, "either" does not usually affect the translation.

The word "unless" is usually translated as "or." In an earlier chapter we saw that "unless" could be translated as "if not." This rule holds true in propositional logic as well; but as we will see, "if not" can be proven to be equivalent to "or." "Unless" gives rise to confusion because it often has the sense of *exclusive* "or." For example, the sense of the statement "It will snow unless the temperature goes up" is that it will either snow or the temperature will go up but it is not the case that both will happen. This, incidentally, is logically equivalent to "It will snow if and only if the temperature does not go up." If the stronger sense of unless is positively intended, it can be translated in the sense of exclusive "or" (or in the sense of "if and only if . . . not"). But translating it as inclusive "or" is usually not wrong; it is simply a weaker form of translation.

Cunard sails to Barbados or Princess sails to Nassau:	$C \lor P$
Either Cunard sails to Barbados or Princess sails to Nassau:	$C \lor P$
Cunard sails to Barbados unless Princess sails to Nassau:	$C \lor P \; or \; {\sim}P \supset C$
Unless Cunard sails to Barbados, Princess sails to Nassau:	$C \lor P \; or \; {\sim}C \supset P$

From the sense of these statements in English it should be clear that $A \cdot B$ is logically equivalent to $B \cdot A$. Similarly, $A \lor B$ is logically equivalent to $B \lor A$. Later in this chapter techniques will be developed for proving these equivalences.

The **conditional sign** is used to translate "if . . . then," "implies that," "entails that," and similar phrases indicating a conditional statement. When the word "if" occurs in the middle of a conditional statement, the statement should be mentally rearranged so that the proposition following the "if" (that is, the antecedent) occurs first. The phrases "in case," "provided that," "given that," and "on the condition that" are synonymous with "if." The phrases "only if" and "entails that" are synonymous with "implies that." As was mentioned earlier, "unless" may also be translated as "if not." Finally, it should be noted that the order of antecedent and consequent is essential in translating conditional statements. In other words, $A \supset B$ is not logically equivalent to $B \supset A$.

If SwissAir raises fares, then KLM will do the same:	$S \supset K$

SwissAir's raising fares implies that KLM will do the same:	$S \supset K$
Quantas will restrict seating if Pan American expands its routes:	$P \supset Q$
Quantas will restrict seating only if Pan American expands its routes:	$Q \supset P$
British Airways will improve service provided that Alitalia buys new aircraft:	$A \supset B$
British Airways will improve service on condition that Alitalia buys new aircraft:	$A \supset B$
TWA will reschedule flights unless Mexicana promotes vacation travel:	$T \lor M$ *or* $\sim M \supset T$

We saw earlier that "unless" sometimes has the stronger sense of exclusive disjunction (which is logically equivalent to "if and only if . . . not"). Analogous remarks apply to "only if." Sometimes people *say* "only if" but *mean* "if and only if." For example, the statement "It will snow only if the temperature stays below freezing" typically means if the temperature stays below freezing it will snow and if it snows the temperature will stay below freezing. As we will see shortly, this is logically equivalent to "It will snow if and only if the temperature stays below freezing." If the stronger sense of "only if" is positively intended, it can be translated as "if and only if"; but in general we will not expect this in the present text.

The conditional sign is also used to translate statements phrased in terms of sufficient conditions and necessary conditions. An event A is said to be a **sufficient condition** for an event B whenever the occurrence of A is all that is required for the occurrence of B. On the other hand, an event A is said to be a **necessary condition** for an event B whenever B cannot occur without the occurrence of A. For example, having the flu is a sufficient condition for feeling miserable, whereas having air to breathe is a necessary condition for survival. Other things besides having the flu might cause a person to feel miserable, but that by itself is sufficient; and other things besides having air to breathe are required for survival, but without air survival is impossible. In other words, air is necessary. To translate statements involving sufficient and necessary conditions into symbolic form, the statement that names the sufficient condition is placed in the antecedent of the conditional, and the statement that names the necessary condition is placed in the consequent*:

---

*The mnemonic device "SUN" may be conveniently used to keep this rule in mind: When the "U" is turned sideways we have $S \supset N$, where S and N designate sufficient and necessary conditions, respectively. Whatever is given as a sufficient condition goes in the place of the S, and whatever is given as a necessary condition goes in the place of the N.

Hertz's modernizing is a sufficient condition for Avis to advertise:	$H \supset A$
Hertz's modernizing is a necessary condition for Avis to advertise:	$A \supset H$

The **biconditional sign** is used to translate the phrases "is equivalent to," "if and only if," and "is a sufficient and necessary condition for":

Greyhound will expand if and only if Trailways reroutes:	$G \equiv T$
Greyhound's expanding is a sufficient and necessary condition for Trailways to reroute:	$G \equiv T$
"Greyhound will expand" is equivalent to "Trailways will reroute":	$G \equiv T$

In propositional logic, when one statement is said to be equivalent to another, as in the third example above, the meaning is that of **truth functional equivalence** (otherwise called "material equivalence"). As will be explained in the next section, such a statement asserts merely that the two component propositions have the same truth value—not that they have the same meaning.

Analysis of the first two examples reveals that $G \equiv T$ is logically equivalent to $(G \supset T) \cdot (T \supset G)$. Thus, for example, "Greyhound will expand only if Trailways reroutes" is translated $G \supset T$, and "Greyhound will expand if Trailways reroutes" is translated $T \supset G$. Putting the two English statements together, we have $(G \supset T) \cdot (T \supset G)$, which is otherwise translated as $G \equiv T$. Because the order of the two conjuncts may be reversed, $G \equiv T$ is logically equivalent to $T \equiv G$.

Do not confuse:	
A if B	$B \supset A$
A only if B	$A \supset B$
A if and only if B	$A \equiv B$

Whenever more than two letters appear in a translated statement, parentheses, brackets, or braces must be used to indicate the proper range of the connectives. The statement $A \cdot B \vee C$, for example, is ambiguous. When parentheses are introduced, this statement becomes either $(A \cdot B) \vee C$ or $A \cdot (B \vee C)$. These new statements have a distinct meaning, and they are not logically equivalent. Thus, with statements such as these, some clue must be found in the English statement that indicates the correct placement of the parentheses in the symbolic statement. Such clues are usually given by commas and semicolons, by such words as "either" and "both," and by the use of a single predicate in conjunction with two or more subjects. The following examples illustrate the correct placement of parentheses and brackets:

Admiral sails to Ensenada and Regency sails to Glacier Bay, or Carnival sails to Barbados:	$(A \cdot R) \vee C$
Admiral sails to Ensenada, and Regency sails to Glacier Bay or Carnival sails to Barbados:	$A \cdot (R \vee C)$
Either Admiral sails to Ensenada and Regency sails to Glacier Bay or Carnival sails to Barbados:	$(A \cdot R) \vee C$
Admiral sails to Ensenada and either Regency sails to Glacier Bay or Carnival sails to Barbados:	$A \cdot (R \vee C)$
Admiral sails to Ensenada or both Regency sails to Glacier Bay and Carnival sails to Barbados:	$A \vee (R \cdot C)$
Admiral sails to Ensenada or Premier and Carnival sail to Barbados:	$A \vee (P \cdot C)$
If TWA reduces fairs, then if British Airways curtails flights, then Lufthansa will expand routes:	$T \supset (B \supset L)$
If TWA's reducing fairs implies that British Airways curtails flights, then Lufthansa will expand routes:	$(T \supset B) \supset L$
If either TWA and SAS reduce fairs or British Airways curtails flights, then Lufthansa will expand routes:	$[(T \cdot S) \vee B] \supset L$

When a negation sign appears in a symbolic expression, by convention it is considered to affect only the unit that immediately follows it. Thus, for example, in the expression $\sim P \vee Q$ the negation sign affects only the P, while in the expression $\sim(P \vee Q)$ it affects the entire expression inside the parentheses. Analogously, the English expression "It is not the case that P or Q" is translated $\sim P \vee Q$—not as $\sim(P \vee Q)$, which is translated "Not either P or Q."

Expressions of the form "Not both P and Q" are translated alternately as $\sim(P \cdot Q)$ or $\sim P \vee \sim Q$, and those of the form "Not either P or Q" (i.e., "Neither P nor Q") are translated alternately as $\sim(P \vee Q)$ or $\sim P \cdot \sim Q$. A little reflection reveals that these alternate forms are equivalent to one another; in other words, $\sim(P \cdot Q)$ is equivalent to $\sim P \vee \sim Q$, and $\sim(P \vee Q)$ is equivalent to $\sim P \cdot \sim Q$. As will be seen in the next chapter,

A CONCISE INTRODUCTION TO LOGIC

these equivalences express an important rule, called DeMorgan's Rule. In this connection it is important to note that $\sim(P \cdot Q)$ is *not* equivalent to $\sim P \cdot \sim Q$ and $\sim(P \vee Q)$ is *not* equivalent to $\sim P \vee \sim Q$. As is indicated in the following examples, expressions of the form "Not both" are *not* the same as those of the form "Both ... not," and expressions of the form "Not either" are *not* the same as those of the form "Either ... not."

It is not the case that Dolphin sails to
Prince Rupert and Exploration sails to
Sitka: $\sim D \cdot E$

Not both Dolphin and Exploration sail to
Prince Rupert: $\sim(D \cdot E)$

Both Dolphin and Exploration do not sail
to Athens: $\sim D \cdot \sim E$

Not either Dolphin or Exploration sails to
Athens (Neither Dolphin nor Explora-
tion sails to Athens): $\sim(D \vee E)$

Either Dolphin or Exploration do not sail
to Martinique: $\sim D \vee \sim E$

The symbolic expressions that we have used throughout this section to translate meaningful, unambiguous English statements are called **well-formed formulas (WFFs).** A well-formed formula is a *syntactically correct* arrangement of symbols. In English, for example, the expression "there is a cat on the porch" is syntactically correct, but "Porch on the is cat a there" is not syntactically correct. Some examples of symbolic arrangements that are *not* well-formed formulas are "A $\supset \vee$ B," "A $\cdot$ B (v C)," and "$\sim \vee$ B $\equiv \supset$ C."

Summary	Symbol
not, it is not the case that, it is false that	$\sim$
and, yet, but, however, moreover, nevertheless, still, also, although, both	$\cdot$
or, unless	v
if, only if, implies that, entails that, provided that, on condition that, sufficient condition, necessary condition (Note: Do not confuse antecedent with consequent!)	$\supset$
if and only if, is equivalent to, sufficient and necessary condition	$\equiv$

EXERCISE 6.1

I. Translate the following English expressions into symbolic form:

★1. It is not the case that oxygen is chemically inert.

2. Cadmium is toxic but zinc is not.

3. Either iridium or osmium is the densest element.

★4. Both nickel and cobalt are ferromagnetic.

5. If lithium reacts violently with water, then so does sodium.

6. Lithium reacts violently with water if sodium does.

★7. Lithium reacts violently with water if and only if sodium does.

8. Lithium reacts violently with water only if sodium does.

9. Helium's being chemically inert implies that neon is, too.

★10. Zirconium does not absorb neutrons unless cadmium does.

11. Gallium's having a low melting point implies that indium and thallium do, too.

12. Sodium reacts with chlorine and either potassium reacts with iodine or calcium reacts with bromine.

★13. Either sodium reacts with chlorine and potassium reacts with iodine or calcium reacts with bromine.

14. It is not the case that both aluminum and magnesium burn in air.

15. Aluminum and magnesium both do not burn in air.

★16. Either platinum or aluminum does not dissolve in hydrochloric acid.

17. Not either platinum or aluminum dissolves in hydrochloric acid.

18. Neither platinum nor aluminum dissolves in hydrochloric acid.

★19. If actinium is radioactive, then if thorium is, then so is protactinium.

20. If actinium's being radioactive implies that thorium is, then so is protactinium.

21. Fluorine is highly reactive if and only if neither chlorine nor bromine is chemically inert.

★22. If strontium oxidizes readily, then either calcium or barium does, too.

23. Either sulfur is soluble in water or if bromine is soluble in water then iodine is soluble in alcohol.

24. If either helium or radon is the product of radioactive decay, then neither krypton nor xenon is chemically active.

★25. If both helium and radon are the product of radioactive decay, then both krypton and xenon are not chemically active.

26. Aluminum is present in rubies, and chromium is present in emeralds or manganese is present in amethyst.

27. Aluminum is present in rubies and chromium is present in emeralds, or manganese is present in amethyst.

★28. Silver and gold are good conductors of electricity unless antimony and bismuth are not.

29. If copper is a good conductor of heat, then so is gold; but sulfur is not.

30. Either copper or sulfur is a good conductor of electricity, but it is not the case that both of them are.

★31. Platinum dissolves in aqua regia; however, if gold also does, then either iron or cobalt dissolves in hydrochloric acid.

32. If platinum dissolves in aqua regia, then if gold also does, then both iron and cobalt dissolve in hydrochloric acid.

33. That osmium absorbs hydrogen is a sufficient condition for iridium to do so.

★34. That osmium absorbs hydrogen is a necessary condition for iridium to do so.

35. That osmium absorbs hydrogen is a sufficient and necessary condition for iridium to do so.

36. Chromium's resisting oxidation is a sufficient condition for nickel's doing so only if arsenic's tendency to oxidize is a necessary condition for phosphorus's tendency to oxidize.

★37. Germanium and silicon are semiconductors if and only if either arsenic or gallium is a doping agent.

38. Osmium has a very high melting point if rhenium has, provided that tungsten has a very high melting point.

39. If neon is useful for lasers, then argon is, too; moreover, xenon and kripton are used in strobe lights only if helium's being a product of radioactive decay is a sufficient condition for radon's being radioactive.

★40. If both lead's being a cumulative poison and tin's not being one is a sufficient and necessary condition for mercury's being one, then neither copper nor zinc is poisonous.

II. Determine which of the following are *not* well-formed formulas.

1. $(S \cdot \sim T) \vee (\sim U \cdot W)$

2. $\sim (K \vee L) \cdot (\supset G \vee H)$

3. $(E \sim F) \vee (W \equiv X)$

4. $(B \supset \sim T) \equiv \sim (\sim C \supset U)$

5. $(F \equiv \sim Q) \cdot (A \supset E \vee T)$

6. $\sim D \vee \sim [(P \supset Q) \cdot (T \supset R)]$

7. $[(D \cdot \vee Q) \supset (P \vee E)] \vee [A \supset (\cdot H)]$

8. $M(N \supset Q) \vee (\sim C \cdot D)$

9. $\sim (F \vee \sim G) \supset [(A \equiv E) \cdot \sim H]$

10. $(R \equiv S \cdot T) \supset \sim (\sim W \cdot \sim X)$

6.2 TRUTH FUNCTIONS

The truth value of a molecular proposition symbolized in terms of one or more connectives is said to be a **function** of the truth value of its atomic components. This means that the truth value of the molecular proposition is determined by the truth value of its components. To see how this happens, we will consider examples of statements involving each of the five connectives.

Let us first consider the negation $\sim p$. This statement form claims that p is false. If p is indeed false, then $\sim p$ is true. Conversely, if p is true, then $\sim p$ is false. For example, suppose $\sim S$ represents the statement "Shakespeare did not write *Huckleberry Finn*," where S designates the atomic statement "Shakespeare wrote *Huckleberry Finn*." The statement $\sim S$ claims that S is false. Since S is indeed false, $\sim S$ is true. On the other hand, if $\sim M$ represents the statement "Milton did not write *Paradise Lost*," then $\sim M$ is false, since M is true. This relationship between any statement p and its negation $\sim p$ is represented in the following table:

Negation	p	$\sim p$
	T	F
	F	T

In this table the lower-case letter p is called a **statement variable;** it can represent any statement we choose, either simple or compound. The expression $\sim p$, on the other hand, is called a **statement form,** and any

---

These statements are all **negations**

$\sim B$
$\sim (G \supset H)$
$\sim [(A \equiv F) \cdot (C \equiv G)]$

---

statement having this form is called a **substitution instance** of this form.

Let us next consider the conjunction $p \cdot q$. This statement form claims that both p and q are true. If they are indeed both true, then $p \cdot q$ is true; if not, then $p \cdot q$ is false. For example, if $L \cdot M$ represents the statement "London is the capital of England and Madrid is the capital of Spain, then $L \cdot M$ is true because both conjuncts L and M are true. On the other hand if $L \cdot P$ represents the statement "London is the capital of England and Paris is the capital of Spain," then $L \cdot P$ is false, because one of the conjuncts is false. Also, if $D \cdot P$ represents the statement "Dublin is the capital of England and Paris is the capital of Spain," then $D \cdot P$ is false because both conjuncts are false. This relationship between any conjunction $p \cdot q$ and its conjuncts p and q is represented in the following table:

Conjunction	p	q	$p \cdot q$
	T	T	T
	T	F	F
	F	T	F
	F	F	F

This table, like the previous one and the ones that follow, expresses the fact that truth functions, like validity and invalidity, are determined by the *form* of a statement. Regardless of what the content might be, once the truth values of the atomic components are known, the truth value of a molecular statement can be determined merely from a knowledge of its form.

These statements are all **conjunctions**

$K \cdot \sim L$

$(E \vee F) \cdot (G \vee H)$

$[(R \supset T) \vee (S \supset U)] \cdot [(W \equiv X) \vee (Y \equiv Z)]$

Turning now to disjunction, the statement form $p \vee q$ claims that at least one of the disjuncts p or q is true. If at least one is indeed true, then $p \vee q$ is true; otherwise it is false. Thus, if $T \vee A$ represents the statement "Thomas Jefferson was an American or Alexander Hamilton was a Frenchman," then $T \vee A$ is true because at least one of the disjuncts is true. Also, if $T \vee J$ represents the statement "Thomas Jefferson was an American or James Madison was an American," then again $T \vee J$ is true because at least one of the disjuncts is true. (Since "$\vee$" represents the inclusive sense of "or," it includes the possibility of both disjuncts being true.) But if $G \vee A$ represents the statement "George Washington was a German or Alexander Hamilton was a Frenchman," then $G \vee A$ is false, because both disjuncts are false. This relationship between any disjunction $p \vee q$ and its disjuncts p and q is represented in the following table:

Disjunction	p	q	$p \vee q$
	T	T	T
	T	F	T
	F	T	T
	F	F	F

These statements are all **disjunctions**

$\sim C \vee \sim D$

$(F \cdot H) \vee (\sim K \cdot \sim L)$

$[S \cdot (T \supset U)] \vee [X \cdot (Y \equiv Z)]$

The analysis of implication is more complicated than that of either conjunction or disjunction. For the moment we will settle for an intuitive illustration of this connective. Imagine that your logic instructor made the following statement: "If you get an 'A' on the final exam, you will get an 'A' for the course." Under what conditions would you say your instructor had lied to you? Clearly, if you got an "A" on the final exam but did not get an "A" for the course, you would say that your instructor had lied. In other words, if the antecedent of the conditional statement is true and the consequent false, the conditional

---

These statements are all **implications** (conditionals)

$H \supset {\sim}J$
$(A \vee C) \supset (D \cdot E)$
$[K \vee (S \cdot {\sim}T)] \supset [{\sim}F \vee (M \cdot O)]$

---

statement itself is false. On the other hand, if you got an "A" on the final exam and also an "A" for the course, you would say that your instructor had told the truth. In other words, if the antecedent is true and the consequent true, the conditional statement is true. But what if you failed to get an "A" on the final exam? Two alternatives are possible: Either you got an "A" for the course anyway, or you did not get an "A" for the course. In neither case, though, could you say that your instructor had lied to you. In other words, you would have to presume that he told the truth. Thus, if the antecedent is false, the conditional statement is true regardless of the truth value of the consequent. The following table generalizes these results. For a more complete analysis of implication, see the subsection titled "Implication Reexamined" at the end of this section.

	p	q	$p \supset q$
Implication	T	T	T
	T	F	F
	F	T	T
	F	F	T

Last, we consider equivalence. The statement form $p \equiv q$ claims that p and q have the same truth value. If indeed they do, then $p \equiv q$ is true; if not, then it is false. For example, if $B \equiv C$ symbolizes the statement "Boeing manufactures airplanes if and only if Chrysler manufactures cars," then $B \equiv C$ is true because B and C both have the same truth value. Similarly, if $L \equiv F$ represents "Lockheed manufactures cars if and only if Ford manufactures airplanes," the equivalence is true, because, once again, the two components have the same truth value, this time false. But if $B \equiv L$ represents "Boeing manufactures airplanes if and only if Lockheed manufactures cars," the statement is false because the two components have opposite truth values.

These statements are all **equivalences** (biconditionals)

$M \equiv \sim T$
$(B \lor D) \equiv (A \cdot C)$
$[K \lor (F \supset I)] \equiv [\sim L \cdot (G \lor H)]$

The same results can be reached through an alternate analysis. In Section 6.1 we saw that $p \equiv q$ is simply a shorter way of translating statements having the form $(p \supset q) \cdot (q \supset p)$. Now that we have a rule for implication we may use it together with the rule for conjunction to provide a rule for equivalence. If p and q are either both true or both false, then $p \supset q$ and $q \supset p$ are both true, making their conjunction true. But if p is true and q is false, then $p \supset q$ is false, making the conjunction false. Similarly, if p is false and q is true, then $q \supset p$ is false, making the conjunction false. Thus, $p \equiv q$ is true when p and q have the same truth value, and false when they have opposite truth values. This result is summarized in the following table:

Equivalence	p	q	$p \equiv q$
	T	T	T
	T	F	F
	F	T	F
	F	F	T

This table illustrates the difference between truth functional equivalence and equivalence of meaning. If two statements are equivalent in meaning, they literally mean the same thing. But if they are truth functionally equivalent, they need only have the same truth value; their meanings might be totally unrelated.

Let us now use the rules expressed in the tables for the five connectives to compute the truth value of more complex molecular propositions. The procedure to be followed is this: Enter the truth values of the atomic components directly beneath the letters. Then use these truth values to compute the truth values of the molecular components. The truth value of a molecular statement is written beneath the connective representing it. Let us suppose, for example, that we are told in advance that the atomic propositions A, B, and C are true, and D, E, and F are false. We may then compute the truth value of the following molecular proposition:

$$(A \ \lor \ D) \ \supset \ E$$

First we write the truth values of the atomic propositions immediately below the respective letters and bring the connectives and parentheses down:

$$(A \ \lor \ D) \ \supset \ E$$
$$(T \ \lor \ F) \ \supset \ F$$

Next we compute the truth value of the proposition in parentheses and write it beneath the connective to which it pertains:

$$(A \lor D) \supset E$$
$$(T \lor F) \supset F$$
$$T \qquad \supset F$$

Finally, we use the last-completed line to obtain the truth value of the conditional, which is the "main connective" in the proposition:

$$(A \lor D) \supset E$$
$$(T \lor F) \supset F$$
$$T \qquad \supset F$$
$$\textcircled{F}$$

The final answer is circled. This is the truth value of the molecular proposition given that A is true and D and E are false.

The general strategy is to build the truth values of the larger components from the truth values of the smaller ones. In general, the order to be followed in entering truth values is this:

1. Individual letters representing atomic propositions.
2. Negation signs immediately preceding individual letters.
3. Connectives joining letters or negated letters.
4. Negation signs immediately preceding parentheses.
5. Connectives joining parentheses or negated parentheses with letters, negated letters, parentheses, or negated parentheses.
6. Negation signs immediately preceding brackets.
7. And so on.

Here are some additional examples. As above, let A, B, and C be true, D, E, and F false. Note that the computed truth values are written beneath the connectives to which they pertain. The final answers, which are written beneath the main connectives, are circled.

1. $(B \cdot C) \supset (E \supset A)$
$(T \cdot T) \supset (F \supset T)$
$\quad T \quad \supset \quad\quad T$
$\quad\quad \textcircled{T}$

2. ~ (C v ~ A) ⊃ ~ B

   ~ (T v ~ T) ⊃ ~ T

   ~ (T v F)   ⊃ F

     ~   T   ⊃ F

    F   ⊃ F

          Ⓣ

3. [~(D v F)•(B v ~ A)] ⊃ ~(F ⊃ ~ C)

   [~(F v F)•(T v ~ T)] ⊃ ~(F ⊃ ~ T)

   [~(F v F)•(T v F)] ⊃ ~(F ⊃ F)

   [~   F •   T   ] ⊃ ~   T

   [T   •   T   ] ⊃ F

          T   ⊃ F

           Ⓕ

If preferred, the truth values of the molecular components may be entered directly beneath the connectives, without using the line by line approach illustrated in these examples. The following examples illustrate this second approach, which prepares for truth tables in the next section:

4. [(D ≡ ~ A) • ~ (C • ~ B)] ≡ ~ [(A ⊃ ~ D) v (C ≡ E)]
    F T FFT T T TFFT Ⓕ F TT T FTT T FF

5. ~ {[(C • ~ E) ⊃ ~ (A • ~ B)] ⊃ [~ (B v D) ≡ (~ C v E)]}
  Ⓕ T TT F T T T FFT T F TTF T F TFF

Implication Reexamined

The interpretation of implication given earlier was based on an analysis of the statement "If you get an 'A' on the final exam, you will get an 'A' for the course." In this analysis we saw that if the antecedent is true and the consequent false, the conditional statement is clearly false, whereas if the antecedent is true and the consequent true, the conditional is clearly true. The only possible question concerned what happens when the antecedent is false. In this case, we said we would have to presume that the instructor told the truth. But can we be *sure* of this? That is, can we know for certain that the conditional statement is true when the antecedent is false? The answer is that in many conditional statements this result is not strictly required (although in no sense does it violate the meaning of the statement). But in some cases it *is* required. So if we are to be consistent in all cases, we must adopt as a general rule that the conditional statement be true when the antecedent is false. Let us begin by considering some of the different kinds of relationships that can be expressed in terms of conditional statements.

1. If George brings flowers,
   then Marsha will be thrilled. (factual)
2. If the temperature rises above 32°F,
   then the ice in the lake will begin to melt. (nomological)
3. If figure A is a triangle,
   then figure A has three sides. (definitional)
4. If all *A* are *B* and all *B* are *C*,
   then all *A* are *C*. (logical)

The first statement is like the one about getting an "A" in the logic course and expresses the factual relationship between George's bringing flowers and Marsha's being thrilled. The second statement expresses a nomological relationship; that is, a relationship grounded in a physical law. The third expresses the fact that a triangle, by definition, has three sides, and the fourth states the relation between the premises and conclusion of a valid argument.

For the first statement, it is not strictly required that the statement be true when the antecedent is false. That is, if George does not bring flowers, there is as much reason to consider the statement false as there is to consider it true. But taking the statement to be true under these conditions in no sense violates the statement's meaning. The second statement, on the other hand, clearly remains true when the antecedent is false. This statement expresses a particular application of the physical law that states that ice melts above 32°F, and this law holds regardless of what the temperature might be at any particular moment. Thus, the statement remains true even though the temperature does not rise above 32°F. Similarly, the third statement remains true as long as the definition of "triangle" remains what it is. The mere fact that figure A might not be a triangle does not affect the fact that a triangle, by definition, has three sides. Finally, in the fourth statement, a proper selection of terms will render the antecedent false and (unlike the previous two statements) the consequent *either* true or false. Yet the statement itself remains true because the argument contained in the statement remains valid. In other words, regardless of what *A*, *B*, and *C* are, if all *A* are *B* and all *B* are *C*, it follows necessarily that all *A* are *C*.

These examples illustrate the fact that while most conditional statements that express factual relationships need not be considered true when their antecedents are false, many conditional statements that express other kinds of relationships do require this. Thus, for consistency, we adopt the rule that for all conditional statements, the conditional statement itself is true when the antecedent is false. Admittedly this rule leads to curious results in some situations (for example, the statement "If dogs are cats, then dogs are not cats" is true, because it has a false antecedent), but the rule will never result in any clearly false statement being called true.

As the four examples considered above illustrate, the rule that the conditional statement itself is true when the antecedent is false expresses the least common denominator of meaning for all conditional statements. Considered in this light, our treatment of conditional statements replicates that of disjunctive statements. We saw earlier that the inclusive meaning of "or" is part of the exclusive meaning. Thus, regardless of whether the intention in any particular disjunctive statement is inclusive or exclusive, the inclusive sense of "or" expresses the least common denominator of meaning.

EXERCISE 6.2

I. Identify the main connective in the following propositions:

★1. $\sim(A \lor M) \cdot \sim(C \supset E)$

 2. $(G \cdot \sim P) \supset \sim(H \lor \sim W)$

 3. $\sim[P \cdot (S \equiv K)]$

★4. $\sim(K \cdot \sim O) \equiv \sim(R \lor \sim B)$

 5. $(M \cdot B) \lor \sim[E \equiv \sim(C \lor I)]$

 6. $\sim[(P \cdot \sim R) \supset (\sim E \lor F)]$

★7. $\sim[(S \lor L) \cdot M] \supset (C \lor N)$

 8. $[\sim F \lor (N \cdot U)] \equiv \sim H$

 9. $E \cdot [(F \supset A) \equiv (\sim G \lor H)]$

★10. $\sim[(X \lor T) \cdot (N \lor F)] \lor (K \supset L)$

II. Write the following molecular statements in symbolic form, then use your knowledge of the historical events referred to by the atomic statements to determine the truth value of the molecular statements.

★1. It is not the case that Hitler ran the Third Reich.

 2. Nixon resigned the presidency and Lincoln wrote the Gettysburg Address.

 3. Caesar governed China or Lindbergh crossed the Atlantic.

★4. Hitler ran the Third Reich and Nixon did not resign the presidency.

 5. Edison invented the telephone or Magellan did not sail around the world.

6. Alexander the Great conquered America if Napoleon ruled France.

★7. Washington was assassinated only if Edison invented the telephone.

8. Lincoln wrote the Gettysburg Address if and only if Caesar governed China.

9. It is not the case that either Alexander the Great conquered America or Washington was assassinated.

★10. If Hitler ran the Third Reich, then either Magellan sailed around the world or Einstein discovered aspirin.

11. Either Lindbergh crossed the Atlantic and Edison invented the telephone or both Nixon resigned the presidency and it is false that Edison invented the telephone.

12. Lincoln's having written the Gettysburg Address is a sufficient condition for Alexander the Great's having conquered America if and only if Washington's being assassinated is a necessary condition for Magellan's having sailed around the world.

★13. Both Hitler ran the Third Reich and Lindbergh crossed the Atlantic if neither Einstein discovered aspirin nor Caesar governed China.

14. It is not the case that Magellan sailed around the world unless both Nixon resigned the presidency and Edison invented the telephone.

★15. Magellan sailed around the world, and Lincoln's having written the Gettysburg Address implies that either Washington was assassinated or Alexander the Great conquered America.

III. Determine the truth values of the following symbolized statements. Let A, B, and C be true; X, Y, and Z, false. Circle your answer.

★1. $A \cdot X$

2. $B \cdot \sim Y$

3. $X \vee \sim Y$

★4. $\sim C \vee Z$

5. $B \supset \sim Z$

6. $Y \supset \sim A$

★7. $\sim X \supset Z$

8. $B \equiv Y$

9. $\sim C \equiv Z$

★10. $\sim(A \cdot \sim Z)$

11. $\sim B \vee (Y \supset A)$

12. $A \supset \sim(Z \vee \sim Y)$

★13. $(A \cdot Y) \vee (\sim Z \cdot C)$

14. $\sim(X \vee \sim B) \cdot (\sim Y \vee A)$

15. $(Y \supset C) \cdot \sim(B \supset \sim X)$

★16. $(C \equiv \sim A) \vee (Y \equiv Z)$

17. $\sim(A \cdot \sim C) \supset (\sim X \supset B)$

18. $\sim[(B \vee \sim C) \cdot \sim(X \vee \sim Z)]$

★19. $\sim[\sim(X \supset C) \equiv \sim(B \supset Z)]$

20. $(X \supset Z) \supset [(B \equiv \sim X) \cdot \sim(C \vee \sim A)]$

21. $[(\sim X \vee Z) \supset (\sim C \vee B)] \cdot [(\sim X \cdot A) \supset (\sim Y \cdot Z)]$

★22. $\sim[(A \equiv X) \vee (Z \equiv Y)] \vee [(\sim Y \supset B) \cdot (Z \supset C)]$

23. $[(B \cdot \sim C) \vee (X \cdot \sim Y)] \supset \sim[(Y \cdot \sim X) \vee (A \cdot \sim Z)]$

24. $\sim\{\sim[(C \vee \sim B) \cdot (Z \vee \sim A)] \cdot \sim[\sim(B \vee Y) \cdot (\sim X \vee Z)]\}$

★25. $(Z \supset C) \supset \{[(\sim X \supset B) \supset (C \supset Y)] \equiv [(Z \supset X) \supset (\sim Y \supset Z)]\}$

IV. When possible, determine the truth values of the following symbolized statements. Let A and B be true, Y and Z false. P and Q have unknown truth value. If the truth value of the statement cannot be determined, write "undetermined."

★1. $A \vee P$

2. $Q \vee Z$

3. $Q \cdot Y$

★4. $Q \cdot A$

5. $P \supset B$

6. $Z \supset Q$

★7. $A \supset P$

8. $P \equiv \sim P$

9. $(P \supset A) \supset Z$

★10. $(P \supset A) \equiv (Q \supset B)$

11. $(Q \supset B) \supset (A \supset Y)$

12. $\sim(P \supset Y) \vee (Z \supset Q)$

★13. $\sim(Q \cdot Y) \equiv \sim(Q \vee A)$

14. $[(Z \supset P) \supset P] \supset P$

★15. $[Q \supset (A \vee P)] \equiv [(Q \supset B) \supset Y]$

6.3 TRUTH TABLES FOR PROPOSITIONS

A **truth table** is an arrangement of truth values that shows how the truth value of a molecular proposition varies depending on the truth value of its atomic components. In the previous section we showed how the truth value of a molecular proposition could be determined, given a *designated* truth value for each atomic component. A truth table gives the truth value of a molecular proposition for *every possible* truth value of its atomic components. Each line in the truth table represents one such possible arrangement of truth values.

In constructing a truth table the first factor that must be determined is the number of lines. Because each line represents one possible arrangement of truth values, the total number of lines is equal to the number of possible combinations of truth values for the atomic propositions. Where L designates the number of lines and n the number of *different* atomic propositions, the number of lines may be computed by the following formula:

$$L = 2^n$$

By means of this formula we obtain the following table:

Number of different atomic propositions	Number of lines in truth table
1	2
2	4
3	8
4	16
5	32
6	64

Let us now construct a truth table for a molecular proposition. We may begin with a fairly simple one:

$$(P \lor \sim Q) \supset Q$$

The number of different atomic propositions is two. Thus, the number of lines in the truth table is four. We draw these lines beneath the proposition as follows:

$$(P \lor \sim Q) \supset Q$$

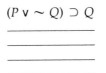

The next step is to divide the number of lines in half and assign "T" to the first half of the lines beneath P and "F" to the remaining half. Since the number of lines is four, we have two T's and two F's:

$$(P \lor \sim Q) \supset Q$$

T
T
F
F

A CONCISE INTRODUCTION TO LOGIC

Next we divide that number (two) in half and, since the result is one, write one T, one F, one T, and one F beneath Q.

$$(P \vee \sim Q) \supset Q$$

T	T
T	F
F	T
F	F

Inspection of the truth table at this stage reveals that every possible combination of truth and falsity has now been assigned to P and Q. In other words, the truth table exhausts the entire range of possibilities. The next step is to duplicate the Q column under the second Q.

$$(P \vee \sim Q) \supset Q$$

T	T	T
T	F	F
F	T	T
F	F	F

This much has been automatic. Now, using the principles developed in the previous section, we compute the remaining columns. First, the column under the negation sign is computed from the column under Q, and then the column under the disjunction sign is computed from the columns under P and the negation sign. Last, the column under the implication sign is computed from the columns under the disjunction sign and Q.

$(P$	$\vee$	$\sim$	$Q)$	$\supset$	Q
T	T	F	T	T	T
T	T	T	F	F	F
F	F	F	T	T	T
F	T	T	F	F	F

We outline the column under the main connective to indicate that it represents the entire molecular proposition. Inspecting the completed truth table, we see that the truth value of the molecular proposition is true when Q is true and false when Q is false, irrespective of the truth value of P.

Let us consider another example: $(P \cdot \sim Q) \supset R$. The number of different letters is three, so the number of lines is eight. Under P we make half this number true, half false (that is, four true, four false). Then, under Q, we make half *this* number true, half false, and so on (two true, two false, two true, two false). Finally, under R the truth value alternates on every line. The truth table thus exhausts every possible arrangement of truth values:

$$(P \cdot \sim Q) \supset R$$

P		Q	R
T	T	T
T	T	F
T	F	T
T	F	F
F	T	T
F	T	F
F	F	T
F	F	F

Now we compute the truth values for the remaining columns—first for the negation sign, then for the conjunction sign, and finally for the conditional sign:

$$(P \cdot \sim Q) \supset R$$

(P	·	~	Q)	⊃	R
T	F	F	T	**T**	T
T	F	F	T	**T**	F
T	T	T	F	**T**	T
T	T	T	F	**F**	F
F	F	F	T	**T**	T
F	F	F	T	**T**	F
F	F	T	F	**T**	T
F	F	T	F	**T**	F

Inspecting the completed truth table, we see that the molecular proposition is false only when P is true and Q and R are false.

Classifying Statements

Truth tables may be used to determine whether the truth value of a molecular statement depends solely upon its form or whether it also depends on the specific truth values of its components. A molecular statement is said to be **logically true** or **tautologous** if it is true regardless of the truth values of its components. It is said to be **logically false** or **self-contradictory** if it is false regardless of the truth value of its components. And it is said to be **contingent** if its truth value varies depending on the truth value of the components. By inspecting the column of truth values under the main connective, we can determine how the molecular proposition should be classified.

Statement classification	Column under main connective
tautologous (logically true)	all true
self-contradictory (logically false)	all false
contingent	at least one true, at least one false

As the truth table we developed indicates, $(P \cdot \sim Q) \supset R$ is a contingent proposition. The final column of the truth table contains at least one T and at least one F. In other words, the truth value of the molecular proposition is "contingent" upon the truth values of its components. Sometimes it is true, sometimes false, depending on the truth value of the components.

On the other hand, consider the following truth tables:

[(P	⊃	Q)	•	P]	⊃	Q
T	T	T	T	T	**T**	T
T	F	F	F	T	**T**	F
F	T	T	F	F	**T**	T
F	T	F	F	F	**T**	F

(P	v	Q)	≡	(~	P	•	~	Q)
T	T	T	**F**	F	T	F	F	T
T	T	F	**F**	F	T	F	T	F
F	T	T	**F**	T	F	F	F	T
F	F	F	**F**	T	F	T	T	F

The proposition on the left is tautologous (logically true or a tautology) because the column under the main connective is all true, and the one on the right is self-contradictory (logically false) because the main connective column is all false. In neither case is the truth value of the molecular proposition contingent upon the truth value of the components. The one on the left is true irrespective of the truth value of its components—in other words, *necessarily* true; and the one on the right is *necessarily* false.

If a proposition is either logically true or logically false, its truth value depends merely upon its form and has nothing to do with its content. As a result, such statements do not make any genuine assertions about things in the world. For example, the tautologous statement "It is either raining or it is not raining" provides no information about the weather. Similarly, the self-contradictory statement "It is raining and it is not raining" provide no information about the weather. On the other hand, the contingent statement "It is raining in the mountains" does provide information about the weather.

Comparing Statements

Truth tables may also be used to determine how two propositions are related to one another. Two propositions are said to be **logically equivalent** if they have the same truth value regardless of the truth values of their atomic components. They are **contradictory** if they have opposite truth values regardless of the truth values of their atomic components. And they are *neither* logically equivalent nor contradictory if they sometimes have the same truth value and sometimes opposite truth values, depending on the truth values of the components. By comparing the main connective columns in the respective truth tables one can determine which is the case:

Relation	Columns under main connectives
logically equivalent	same truth value on each line
contradictory	opposite truth value on each line
neither logically equivalent nor contradictory	same truth value on at least one line; opposite truth value on at least one line

For example, the following pair of propositions are logically equivalent. The main connective columns of their respective truth tables are identical. Note that for proper comparison the columns under P must be identical and the columns under Q must be identical:

```
P ⊃ Q                    ~  Q ⊃ ~  P
T  T  T                  F  T  T  F  T
T  F  F                  T  F  F  F  T
F  T  T                  F  T  T  T  F
F  T  F                  T  F  T  T  F
```

The next two propositions are mutually contradictory:

```
P ⊃ Q                    P  •  ~  Q
T  T  T                  T  F  F  T
T  F  F                  T  T  T  F
F  T  T                  F  F  F  T
F  T  F                  F  F  T  F
```

Finally, the next two propositions are neither logically equivalent nor contradictory. On two lines the truth values under the main connectives are the same but on the other two lines they are opposite:

```
P  v  Q                  P  •  Q
T  T  T                  T  T  T
T  T  F                  T  F  F
F  T  T                  F  F  T
F  F  F                  F  F  F
```

As these examples illustrate, there is a distinction between two statements merely having the same truth value and their being logically equivalent. For example, the statements "Water boils at 100°C" and "The current population of the United States is over 200 million" have the same truth value; they are both true. But they are not *logically* equivalent because their truth values are not *necessarily* the same. The truth value of the second one might change while the first remains constant. The same holds true, incidentally, for the distinction between two statements having opposite truth values and their being contradictory.

A CONCISE INTRODUCTION TO LOGIC

EXERCISE 6.3

I. Use truth tables to determine whether the following symbolized statements are tautologous, self-contradictory, or contingent:

★1. $A \supset (A \supset A)$

2. $(D \supset D) \supset D$

3. $(R \supset S) \cdot (R \cdot \sim S)$

★4. $[(E \supset F) \supset F] \supset E$

5. $(H \supset J) \equiv (H \cdot \sim J)$

6. $(N \supset P) \vee (P \supset N)$

★7. $[(X \supset Z) \cdot (X \vee Z)] \supset Z$

8. $[(C \supset D) \cdot \sim C] \supset \sim D$

9. $[F \supset (T \supset X)] \equiv [(F \supset T) \supset X]$

★10. $[G \supset (N \supset \sim G)] \cdot [(G \equiv N) \cdot (G \vee N)]$

11. $[(P \supset Q) \cdot (\sim P \supset R)] \cdot \sim (Q \vee R)$

12. $[(H \supset N) \cdot (T \supset N)] \supset [(H \vee T) \supset N]$

★13. $[S \cdot (T \vee U)] \equiv [(\sim S \vee \sim T) \cdot (\sim S \vee \sim U)]$

14. $\{[(G \cdot H) \supset N] \cdot [(G \supset N) \supset P]\} \supset (H \supset P)$

★15. $[(E \vee F) \cdot (G \vee H)] \equiv [(E \cdot G) \vee (F \cdot H)]$

II. Use truth tables to determine whether the following pairs of symbolized statements are logically equivalent, contradictory, or neither:

★1. $\sim D \vee T$ $\sim (D \cdot \sim T)$

2. $\sim K \supset L$ $K \supset \sim L$

3. $R \vee \sim S$ $S \cdot \sim R$

★4. $N \supset \sim P$ $N \cdot P$

5. $\sim A \equiv X$ $(X \cdot \sim A) \vee (\sim X \cdot A)$

6. $G \equiv \sim H$ $(H \cdot G) \vee (\sim G \cdot \sim H)$

★7. $(E \supset F) \supset G$ $E \supset (F \supset G)$

8. $J \supset (K \supset L)$ $(K \cdot J) \supset L$

9. $P \cdot (R \vee S)$ $(S \vee P) \cdot (R \vee P)$

★10. $H \cdot (J \vee K)$ $(J \cdot H) \vee (H \cdot K)$

III. Use truth tables to obtain the answers to the following exercises.

★1. Renowned economist Harold Carlson makes the following prediction: "The balance of payments will decrease if and only if interest rates remain steady; however, it is not the case that either interest rates will not remain steady or the balance of payments will decrease." What can we say about Carlson's prediction?

2. Dr. Bradshaw, professor of political science, stated in one of his lectures, "Either the Russians will not tear down the Berlin wall or East-West relations will be enhanced; furthermore, East-West relations will not be enhanced if and only if the Russians tear down the Berlin wall." Assuming Bradshaw is correct, what has he said about the Berlin wall and the future of East-West relations?

3. Christina and Thomas are having a discussion about their plans for the evening. Christina: "If you don't love me, then I'm certainly not going to have sex with you." Thomas: "Well, that means that If I do love you, then you will have sex with me, right?" Is Thomas correct?

★4. Two astronomers are discussing supernovas. Dr. Frank says, "Research has established that if a supernova occurs within 10 light years of the earth, then life on earth will be destroyed." Dr. Harris says, "Research has also established that either a supernova will not occur within 10 light years of the earth or life on earth will not be destroyed." Assuming both astronomers are correct, what can we determine about the occurrence of a supernova?

5. Antonia Martinez, who is running for the state senate, makes this statement: "Either a tax reduction is feasible only if both educational costs do not increase and the welfare program is abolished, or a tax reduction is feasible and either the welfare program will not be abolished or educational costs will increase." What has Martinez told us about a tax reduction?

6. Automotive expert Frank Goodbody has this to say about Japanese imports: "If Mitsubishi is the sportiest, then both Toyota is the most trouble-free and Isuzu is not the lowest priced; also, if Isuzu is the lowest priced, then both Toyota is not the most trouble-free and Mitsubishi is the sportiest." Assuming that Goodbody is correct in his assessment, what may we conclude about Mitsubishi, Toyota, and Isuzu?

★7. Alice and Cathy witnessed a murder. Alice testified that if Mackie killed the victim, then both Ratzo was an accomplice and Smilie was not involved. Cathy testified that Ratzo was not an accomplice and if Mackie did not kill the victim, then Smilie was involved. Assuming both witnesses told the truth, what can we conclude about Mackie, Ratzo, and Smilie?

8. Steven and Michael witnessed a burglary. Steven testified that Leftie pried open the window and that either Hank or Pinkie did not enter the building. Michael testified that Leftie did not pry open the window if and only if both Pinkie entered the building but Hank did not. Under cross examination it was revealed that Stephen told the truth but Mi-

chael lied. With this information, what can we conclude about Leftie, Hank, and Pinkie?

9. Ann, Herbert, and Kristin appeared before a congressional investigating committee. Ann testified that Morgan shredded the evidence if and only if either Parker did not bribe foreign officials or Wilson forged the documents. Herbert testified that if Wilson did not forge the documents, then both Morgan did not shred the evidence and Parker bribed foreign officials. Kristin testified that if Parker bribed foreign officials, then both Morgan shredded the evidence and Wilson did not forge the documents. Assuming that all three witnesses told the truth, what can we conclude about Morgan, Parker, and Wilson?

★10. Paul, Genelle, and Homer testified before a grand jury. Paul testified that Fisher did not embezzle funds only if both Laskey defrauded clients and Marshall did not receive stolen property. Genelle testified that Fisher embezzled funds and either Laskey did not defraud clients or Marshall received stolen property. Homer testified that Laskey did not defraud clients if and only if both Marshall received stolen property and Fisher embezzled funds. Based on this evidence, the grand jury indicted two people. Who were they? After the indictment was handed down, it was discovered that Genelle had lied. How does this affect the evidence?

6.4 ARGUMENT FORMS AND FALLACIES

Many of the arguments that occur in propositional logic have forms that bear specific names and can be immediately recognized as either valid or invalid. The first part of this section presents some of the more common ones and explains how they are recognized. The second part discusses ways of refuting two of these forms, constructive and destructive dilemmas.

Common Argument Forms

A **disjunctive syllogism** is an argument that consists of a disjunctive premise, a premise that denies one of the disjuncts, and a conclusion that affirms the other disjunct. Example:

Either Alan Ladd or Gary Cooper starred in *High Noon*.	$A \lor G$
Alan Ladd did not star in *High Noon*.	$\sim A$
Therefore, Gary Cooper starred in *High Noon*.	G

It is easy to see that this argument is valid. The first premise presents two alternatives, and the second premise eliminates one of them, leaving the other for the conclusion. This is the so-called "method of elimination" and is essential to the validity of a disjunctive syllogism. If the second premise were to affirm one of the disjuncts instead of denying it, the argument would be invalid. Example:

Either Humphrey Bogart or Ingrid Berg-man starred in *Casablanca*.	$H \lor I$
Humphrey Bogart starred in *Casablanca*.	H
Therefore, Ingrid Bergman did not star in *Casablanca*.	$\sim I$

Since both Bogart and Bergman starred in the film, the premises are true and the conclusion false.

Unless explicitly stated to the contrary, the word "or" is always understood in the inclusive sense that includes the possibility of both disjuncts being true. Thus, if one disjunct is not denied by the second premise, as in the above example, no conclusion follows.

In the broad sense of the term, each of the above arguments is a disjunctive syllogism in that the first premise of each is a disjunctive statement. This text, however, opts to use the term "disjunctive syllogism" only in the narrower sense of denoting the valid form of the argument. In accordance with this convention we may define "disjunctive syllogism" in terms of the following **argument form.** Any argument having this form—that is, any substitution instance—will be a valid argument:

disjunctive syllogism (DS):
$$\frac{p \lor q \quad\quad \sim p}{q}$$

Incidentally, the mere fact that this argument form is called a "syllogism" should not be cause for assuming it to be a categorical syllogism. As was noted in Chapter 5, the term "syllogism," in the broad sense, means simply an argument having two premises and one conclusion. If the premises and conclusion are categorical statements, then the argument is a categorical syllogism; if not, then it is some other kind of syllogism. Apart from the mere fact that both have two premises and one conclusion, there is little similarity between categorical syllogisms and disjunctive syllogisms. They are essentially different kinds of arguments, and different methods and principles are used to evaluate each.

Another kind of syllogism that occurs frequently in propositional logic and that consists of one or more conditional statements is called a **hypothetical syllogism.** If all three statements in the argument are conditional statements, the argument is a **pure hypothetical syllogism;** if only one is a conditional statement, the argument is a **mixed hypothetical syllogism.** Here is an example of a pure hypothetical syllogism:

If the Persian Gulf is closed, then the flow of oil will halt.	$P \supset F$
If the flow of oil halts, then Western economies will falter.	$F \supset W$
Therefore, if the Persian Gulf is closed, then Western economies will falter.	$P \supset W$

This argument is valid because the premises link together like a chain; the consequent of the first is identical to the antecedent of the second. Under such conditions the antecedent of the first implies the consequent of the second. If this order is mixed up, however, the resulting argument is invalid. Example:

$$
\begin{array}{ll}
\text{If aluminum is a metal, then it conducts} & \\
\quad \text{electricity.} & A \supset C \\
\text{If sulfur is a metal, then it conducts elec-} & \\
\quad \text{tricity.} & S \supset C \\
\text{Therefore, if aluminum is a metal, then} & \\
\quad \text{sulfur is a metal} & \overline{A \supset S}
\end{array}
$$

By the rule for conditional statements the premises are true and the conclusion false. The argument is therefore clearly invalid. The problem stems from the fact that the antecedent and consequent of the second premise are in the wrong order. If they were to be reversed, the argument would become valid.

In the broad sense of the term, both of these arguments are pure hypothetical syllogisms. As with "disjunctive syllogism," however, this text prefers to use "pure hypothetical syllogism" to designate only the valid form of the argument. In accord with this convention we define "pure hypothetical syllogism" in terms of the following argument form. Any substitution instance of this form is a valid argument:

$$
\text{pure hypothetical syllogism (HS):} \quad
\begin{array}{c}
p \supset q \\
q \supset r \\
\hline
p \supset r
\end{array}
$$

Mixed hypothetical syllogism comprises four forms, two of which are valid, two invalid. The two valid forms are called *modus ponens* ("asserting mode") and *modus tollens* ("denying mode"), and the two invalid forms are called affirming the consequent and denying the antecedent. These four forms are called "mixed" hypothetical syllogisms because only one of the premises is a conditional statement. Usually, however, the term "mixed hypothetical syllogism" is not used to name these forms; they are identified instead by their specific names. Here is an example of **modus ponens:**

$$
\begin{array}{ll}
\text{If manic depressive illness is genetically} & \\
\quad \text{caused, then it can be inherited.} & M \supset I \\
\text{Manic depressive illness is genetically} & \\
\quad \text{caused.} & M \\
\text{Therefore, it can be inherited.} & \overline{I}
\end{array}
$$

In *modus ponens* it is essential that the antecedent of the first premise be asserted in the second. The conclusion then asserts the consequent of the first premise. If, on the other hand, the consequent of the first premise is asserted in the second, the resulting argument is invalid, regardless of what the conclusion might be. It would commit the fallacy of **affirming the consequent.** The following example is clearly invalid:

If Napoleon was killed in a plane crash, then
    Napoleon is dead. $K \supset D$
Napoleon is dead. $\dfrac{D}{K}$
Therefore, Napoleon was killed in a plane crash.

In ***modus tollens,*** the consequent of the first premise is *denied* in the second premise, and the conclusion then denies the antecedent of the first premise. Example:

If a perpetual motion machine is possible,
    then the laws of thermodynamics can
    be broken. $P \supset L$
The laws of thermodynamics cannot be
    broken. $\sim L$
Therefore, a perpetual motion machine is
    not possible. $\overline{\sim P}$

Upon reflection this argument will be seen to be valid. If, on the other hand, the *antecedent* of the first premise is denied in the second, the resulting argument is invalid regardless of what the conclusion might be. Such an argument commits the fallacy of **denying the antecedent.** Example:

If Napoleon was killed in a plane crash, then
    Napoleon is dead. $K \supset D$
Napoleon was not killed in a plane crash. $\dfrac{\sim K}{\sim D}$
Therefore, Napoleon is not dead.

Modus ponens and *modus tollens* are defined in terms of the following argument forms. Any substitution instance of either of these forms is a valid argument:

modus ponens (MP): $p \supset q$
                       $\dfrac{p}{q}$

modus tollens (MT): $p \supset q$
                       $\dfrac{\sim q}{\sim p}$

The invalid forms are defined as follows. Any argument that is best interpreted as an instance of either of these forms is invalid.*

affirming the consequent (AC):
$$p \supset q$$
$$\underline{q}$$
$$p$$

denying the antecedent (DA):
$$p \supset q$$
$$\underline{\sim p}$$
$$\sim q$$

The substitution instances given above for affirming the consequent and denying the antecedent provide a convenient illustration of the difference between a sufficient and a necessary condition. In the statement "If Napoleon was killed in a plane crash, then Napoleon is dead," Napoleon's being killed in a plane crash is a *sufficient* condition for his being dead. The fallacy of denying the antecedent mistakenly converts this sufficient condition into a necessary condition, with the effect that Napoleon's not being killed in a plane crash supposedly entails his not being dead. Conversely, Napoleon's being dead is actually a *necessary* condition for his being killed in a plane crash. The fallacy of affirming the consequent mistakenly converts this necessary condition into a sufficient condition and concludes that because Napoleon is dead he was therefore killed in a plane crash. Obviously, converting sufficient conditions into necessary conditions, and vice versa, is not legitimate.

In a **constructive dilemma,** the first premise consists of two conjoined conditional statements, and the second premise asserts the truth of one of the antecedents. The conclusion, which follows logically via two *modus ponens* steps, asserts the truth of at least one of the consequents. Example:

If lawyers defend guilty clients, then they assist future crimes; but if they send them away, they jeopardize the defendant's right to a fair trial.	$(D \supset A) \cdot (S \supset J)$
Lawyers must either defend guilty clients or send them away.	$D \lor S$
Therefore, lawyers either assist future crimes or jeopardize the right to a fair trial.	$\overline{A \lor J}$

---

*Following the convention adopted in Section 1.5, we say that an argument is best interpreted as a substitution instance of an invalid form only if it is not susceptible to being interpreted as a substitution instance of a valid form. For example, the symbolized argument "$(A \equiv A) \supset B$; B; therefore, $A \equiv A$" is a substitution instance of affirming the consequent, but it is not best interpreted as a substitution instance of this form because it is susceptible to being interpreted as a substitution instance of the valid form "p; therefore, t," where t is any tautology.

The **destructive dilemma** is similar in form to the constructive dilemma, but the second premise, instead of asserting the truth of at least one of the antecedents, asserts the falsity of at least one of the consequents. The conclusion, which follows validly via two *modus tollens* steps, asserts the falsity of at least one of the antecedents. Example:

> If prosecutors are to obtain a conviction, then they must conceal exculpatory evidence; but if they want to ensure a fair trial, then they must disclose exculpatory evidence.
> $(O \supset C) \cdot (E \supset D)$
>
> Prosecutors must either disclose exculpatory evidence or conceal it.
> $\sim C \vee \sim D$
>
> Therefore, prosecutors will either not obtain a conviction or not ensure a fair trial.
> $\overline{\sim O \vee \sim E}$

In translating the second premise, note that disclosing is the negation of concealing, and concealing is the negation of disclosing.

The constructive and destructive dilemmas are defined in terms of the following argument forms. Any substitution instance of either of these forms is a valid argument:

constructive dilemma (CD): $(p \supset q) \cdot (r \supset s)$
$$\frac{p \vee r}{q \vee s}$$

destructive dilemma (DD): $(p \supset q) \cdot (r \supset s)$
$$\frac{\sim q \vee \sim s}{\sim p \vee \sim r}$$

In identifying substitution instances of the various argument forms one should use the following procedure. First, symbolize the argument using upper-case letters for the atomic propositions. Then see whether the symbolized argument fits the pattern of one of these forms. In doing so, one should keep four points in mind. The first is that the statement form $p \vee q$ is logically equivalent to $q \vee p$. (In the next chapter this equivalence will be expressed as a rule, but for now it may be assumed.) As a result, if an argument appears having the form

$$\frac{\begin{array}{c} A \vee B \\ \sim B \end{array}}{A}$$

it may be reexpressed in the form

$$\frac{\begin{array}{c} B \vee A \\ \sim B \end{array}}{A}$$

This second version is a substitution instance of disjunctive syllogism, and so the original argument may also be considered to be a substitution instance of disjunctive syllogism.

The second point is that negated letters, as well as non-negated letters, may be interpreted as substitution instances of the p, q, r, and s in the argument forms. Consider, for example, the following argument:

$$\begin{array}{l} \sim A \supset B \\ \underline{\sim A} \\ B \end{array}$$

When $\sim A$ is substituted in the place of p and B in the place of q, the above argument will be seen to be a substitution instance of *modus ponens*.

The third point to remember is that the simple statement form p is logically equivalent to $\sim\sim p$. Like the previous equivalence, this one will be expressed as a rule in the next chapter, but for now it may be assumed. In view of this equivalence, an argument having the form

$$\begin{array}{l} A \supset \sim B \\ \underline{B} \\ \sim A \end{array}$$

may be reexpressed as

$$\begin{array}{l} A \supset \sim B \\ \underline{\sim\sim B} \\ \sim A \end{array}$$

Now when A is substituted in place of p and $\sim B$ in place of q, this argument will be seen to be a substitution instance of *modus tollens*.

Finally, the fourth point is that the order of the premises does not affect the form of the argument. Consider the following arguments:

$$\begin{array}{ll} \sim A & B \supset C \\ \underline{B \supset A} & \underline{A \supset B} \\ \sim B & A \supset C \end{array}$$

The argument on the left is *modus tollens,* and the one on the right is pure hypothetical syllogism.

Here are some additional examples. In some cases the symbolized argument may have to be reexpressed, using one or more of these three logical equivalences, before it fits the pattern of the argument form indicated in parentheses:

$$\begin{array}{ll} \sim A \supset \sim B & A \supset \sim B \\ \underline{\sim B \supset C} \quad \text{(HS)} & \underline{B \supset \sim C} \quad \text{invalid} \\ \sim A \supset C & A \supset \sim C \end{array}$$

$$\begin{array}{l} \sim A \supset \sim B \\ \underline{B} \\ A \end{array} \quad \text{(MT)}$$

$$\begin{array}{l} \sim A \supset B \\ \underline{A} \\ \sim B \end{array} \quad \text{(DA)}$$

$$\begin{array}{l} \sim A \vee \sim B \\ \underline{A} \\ \sim B \end{array} \quad \text{(DS)}$$

$$\begin{array}{l} \sim A \vee B \\ \underline{\sim A} \\ \sim B \end{array} \quad \text{invalid}$$

$$\begin{array}{l} (A \supset \sim B) \cdot (\sim C \supset D) \\ \underline{A \vee \sim C} \\ \sim B \vee D \end{array} \quad \text{(CD)}$$

$$\begin{array}{l} (\sim A \supset B) \cdot (C \supset \sim D) \\ \underline{B \vee \sim D} \\ A \vee \sim C \end{array} \quad \text{invalid}$$

$$\begin{array}{l} A \vee \sim B \\ \underline{B} \\ A \end{array} \quad \text{(DS)}$$

$$\begin{array}{l} A \supset \sim B \\ \underline{\sim B} \\ A \end{array} \quad \text{(AC)}$$

$$\begin{array}{l} A \\ \underline{A \supset B} \\ B \end{array} \quad \text{(MP)}$$

$$\begin{array}{l} A \vee C \\ \underline{(A \supset B) \cdot (C \supset D)} \\ B \vee D \end{array} \quad \text{(CD)}$$

Refuting Constructive and Destructive Dilemmas

Now that we are familiar with a number of argument forms in propositional logic, we may return for a closer look at two of them, constructive and destructive dilemmas. Arguments having these forms occur frequently in public debate, where they may be used by an arguer to trap an opponent. Since both forms are intrinsically valid, the only direct mode of defense available to the opponent is to prove the dilemma unsound. This can be done by proving at least one of the premises false. If the first premise (the conjunctive premise—otherwise called the "horns of the dilemma") is proven false, the opponent is said to have "grasped the dilemma by the horns." This, of course, may be done by proving either one of the conditional statements false. If, on the other hand, the second (disjunctive) premise is proven false, the opponent is said to have "escaped between the horns of the dilemma." The latter strategy often involves finding a third alternative to the two that are given in the disjunctive premise. If a third alternative can be found, then neither of these disjuncts need be true. Consider the following constructive dilemma:

> If taxes increase, the economy will suffer, and if taxes decrease, needed governmental services will be curtailed. Since taxes must either increase or decrease, it follows that the economy will suffer or that needed governmental services will be curtailed.

It is easy to escape between the horns of this dilemma by arguing that taxes could be kept as they are, in which case they would neither increase nor decrease.

Some dilemmas, however, do not allow for the possibility of escaping between the horns. Consider the following constructive dilemma:

> If we encourage competition, we will have no peace, and if we do not encourage competition, we will make no progress. Since we must either encourage competition or not encourage it, we will either have no peace or make no progress.

Since the second premise of this dilemma is a tautology, it cannot be proven false. This leaves the strategy of grasping the dilemma by the horns, which may be done by proving either of the conditional statements in the first premise false. A debater with conservative inclinations might want to attack the first conditional and argue that competition and peace can coexist, while one with liberal inclinations might want to attack the second and argue that progress can be achieved through some means other than encouraging competition.

Grasping by the horns:
Prove the conjunctive
premise false by proving
either conjunct false

e.g.: $(p \supset q) \cdot (r \supset s)$
T F F Ⓕ

Escaping between the horns:
Prove the disjunctive
premise false

e.g.: $p \lor r$
F Ⓕ F

The strategy to be followed in refuting a dilemma is therefore this: Examine the disjunctive premise. If this premise is a tautology, attempt to grasp the dilemma by the horns by attacking one or the other of the conditional statements in the conjunctive premise. If the disjunctive premise is not a tautology, then either escape between the horns by, perhaps, finding a third alternative, or grasp the dilemma by the horns—whichever is easier.

A third, indirect strategy for refuting a dilemma involves constructing a counterdilemma. This is typically done by changing either the antecedents or the consequents of the conjunctive premise while leaving the disjunctive premise as it is, so as to obtain a different conclusion. If the dilemma in question is a constructive dilemma, the consequents of the conjunctive premise are changed. Here are possible counterdilemmas for the two dilemmas presented above:

> If taxes increase, needed governmental services will be extended, and if taxes decrease, the economy will improve. Since taxes must either increase or decrease, it follows that needed governmental services will be extended or the economy will improve.

> If we encourage competition, we will make progress, and if we do not encourage competition, we will have peace. Since we must either encourage competition or not encourage it, we will either make progress or have peace.

Constructing a counterdilemma does not accomplish a complete refutation of a given dilemma because it merely shows that a different approach can be taken to a certain problem. Nevertheless, this strategy is often quite effective because it testifies to the cleverness of the debater who can accomplish it successfully. In the heat of debate the attending audience is often persuaded that the original argument has been thoroughly demolished.

Summary and Application

Any argument that has one of the following forms is valid:

$p \lor q$ $\underline{\sim p}$ q	disjunctive syllogism (DS)	$p \supset q$ $\underline{q \supset r}$ $p \supset r$	pure hypothetical syllogism (HS)
$p \supset q$ $\underline{p}$ q	*modus ponens* (MP)	$p \supset q$ $\underline{\sim q}$ $\sim p$	*modus tollens* (MT)
$(p \supset q) \cdot (r \supset s)$ $\underline{p \lor r}$ $q \lor s$	constructive dilemma (CD)	$(p \supset q) \cdot (r \supset s)$ $\underline{\sim q \lor \sim s}$ $\sim p \lor \sim r$	destructive dilemma (DD)

Any argument that is best interpreted as an instance of either of the following forms is invalid.

$p \supset q$ $\underline{q}$ p	affirming the consequent (AC)	$p \supset q$ $\underline{\sim p}$ $\sim q$	denying the antecedent (DA)

Let us now see how these argument forms can be used to interpret the structure of some real-life arguments. Consider the following letter to the editor of a newspaper:

> I presume that those who believe that the United States can work with the Soviet Union to help the Third World also believe that the PTA can work with the Mafia to eliminate the drug problem.
>
> (Bill Rosenthall, *Los Angeles Times*)

This argument is enthematic; in other words, it is missing certain parts. The arguer's intention is that no one would expect the PTA to work with the Mafia to solve the drug problem, so no one should expect the United States to work with the Soviet Union to solve Third World problems. The argument can thus be structured as a *modus tollens*:

A CONCISE INTRODUCTION TO LOGIC

If the United States can work with the Soviet Union to help the Third World, then the PTA can work with the Mafia to eliminate the drug problem.

The PTA cannot work with the Mafia to eliminate the drug problem.

Therefore, the United States cannot work with the Soviet Union to help the Third World.

Here is another example:

In a time when an entire nation believes in Murphy's law (that if anything can go wrong, it surely will) and has witnessed serious accidents in the highly regulated, supposedly fail-safe nuclear industry, it's fascinating that people can persist in the fantasy that an error will not occur in the area of nuclear weaponry.

(Burk Gossom, *Newsweek*)

Although this argument allows for more than one analysis, it is clear that the arguer presents two main reasons why we can expect an accident in the area of nuclear weaponry: "Murphy's law" (which everyone believes to be true) dictates it, and accidents have occurred in the area of nuclear power (which is presumed fail-safe). Thus, at the very least, we can extract two *modus ponens* arguments from this selection:

If everyone believes Murphy's law, then we can expect accidents in nuclear weaponry.
Everyone believes Murphy's law.
Therefore, we can expect accidents in nuclear weaponry.

If accidents have occurred in nuclear power, then we can expect accidents in nuclear weaponry.
Accidents have occurred in nuclear power.
Therefore, we can expect accidents in nuclear weaponry.

Most arguments that we encounter in ordinary life can be interpreted as instances of valid argument forms. After being so interpreted, however, not all will turn out sound. The invalid forms (denying the antecedent and affirming the consequent) should be reserved for the relatively few arguments that are clearly invalid as originally expressed.

EXERCISE 6.4

I. Identify the forms of the following symbolized arguments. All of the ones without a specific name are invalid. For these, write "invalid form."

★1. $N \supset C$
$\underline{\sim C}$
$\sim N$

2. $S \supset F$
$\underline{F \supset \sim L}$
$S \supset \sim L$

3. $A \lor \sim Z$
   $\sim Z$
   ───
   A

★4. $(S \supset \sim P) \cdot (\sim S \supset D)$
   $S \lor \sim S$
   ─────────────
   $\sim P \lor D$

5. $\sim N$
   $\sim N \supset T$
   ───────
   T

6. $M \lor \sim B$
   $\sim M$
   ───
   $\sim B$

★7. $(E \supset N) \cdot (\sim L \supset \sim K)$
   $\sim N \lor K$
   ──────────────
   $\sim E \lor L$

8. $W \supset \sim M$
   $\sim M$
   ───
   W

9. $\sim B \supset \sim L$
   $G \supset \sim B$
   ─────────
   $G \supset \sim L$

★10. $F \supset O$
   $\sim F$
   ───
   $\sim O$

11. $(K \lor B) \cdot (N \lor Q)$
   $K \lor N$
   ─────────────
   $B \lor Q$

12. $X \supset \sim E$
   X
   ───
   $\sim E$

★13. $P \lor \sim S$
   S
   ───
   P

14. $B \cdot T$
   T
   ───
   $\sim B$

15. $\sim R \lor \sim Q$
   $(G \supset Q) \cdot (H \supset R)$
   ──────────────
   $\sim G \lor \sim H$

★16. $\sim G \supset H$
   H
   ───
   $\sim G$

17. $K \supset \sim C$
   C
   ───
   $\sim K$

18. $(I \supset M) \cdot (\sim O \supset A)$
   $\sim O \lor I$
   ─────────────
   $M \lor A$

★19. $X \supset \sim F$
   $W \supset \sim F$
   ─────────
   $W \supset X$

20. $\sim L \supset U$
   L
   ───
   $\sim U$

II. Identify the forms of the following arguments. All of the ones without a specific name are invalid. For these write "invalid form."

★1. Future presidents will be allowed to serve a third term only if the Twenty-second Amendment is repealed. The Twenty-second Amendment will not be repealed. Therefore, future presidents will not be allowed to serve a third term.

2. If the Japanese continue selling their semiconductors below actual cost, then the U.S. trade deficit will not improve. The U.S. trade deficit will not improve. Therefore, the Japanese will continue selling their semiconductors below actual cost.

3. If you enter the teaching profession, you will have no money for vacations; and if you do not enter the teaching profession, you will have no time for vacations. Since you must either enter or not enter the teaching profession, it follows that either you will have no money or no time for vacations.

★4. Either the wealthiest people are the happiest, or it is not the case that money can buy everything. The wealthiest people are not the happiest. Therefore, money cannot buy everything.

5. Either tortured political prisoners in El Salvador can openly complain of their mistreatment or El Salvador is not a democracy. Tortured political prisoners in El Salvador can openly complain of their mistreatment. Therefore, El Salvador is a democracy.

6. If the sun is a variable star, then its energy will drop drastically at some point in the future. If the sun's energy drops drastically at some point in the future, then the earth will become a giant iceball. Therefore, if the sun is a variable star, then the earth will become a giant iceball.

★7. Twenty percent of America's children have never seen a dentist. But if that is so, health care in America is not properly distributed. Therefore, health care in America is not properly distributed.

8. If people who are old enough to kill are old enough to die, then it is proper to execute juvenile killers. But it is not true that people who are old enough to kill are old enough to die. Therefore, it is not proper to execute juvenile killers.

9. If high school clinics are to stem the tide of teenage pregnancy, then they must dispense birth control devices; but if they want to discourage illicit sex, then they must not dispense these devices. Since high school clinics must either dispense or not dispense birth control devices, either they will not stem the tide of teenage pregnancy, or they will not discourage illicit sex.

★10. If limits are imposed on medical malpractice suits, then patients will not be adequately compensated for their injuries; but if the cost of malpractice insurance continues to rise, then physicians will be forced out of business. Limits will not be imposed, and the cost of malpractice insurance will not continue to rise. Therefore, patients will be adequately compensated and physicians will not be forced out of business.

11. If Prohibition succeeded in the 1920s, then the war on drugs will succeed in the 1980s and 1990s. But Prohibition did not succeed in the 1920s. Therefore, the war on drugs will not succeed in the 1980s and 1990s.

12. If life were always better than death, then people would not commit suicide. People do commit suicide. Therefore, life is not always better than death.

★13. If we want to prevent foreign subsidies and dumping, then we must have tariffs and quotas; but if we want to avoid an international trade war, then we must have no tariffs or quotas. Since we must either have tariffs and quotas or not have them, we will either have foreign subsidies and dumping or an international trade war.

14. Either industrial pollutants will be more stringently controlled, or acid rain will continue to fall. Industrial pollutants will be more stringently controlled. Therefore, acid rain will not continue to fall.

15. Insurance companies contribute millions of dollars to political campaigns. But if that is so, then meaningful insurance reform is impossible. Therefore, meaningful insurance reform is impossible.

★16. If Mexico does not get its population growth under control, then its unemployment problem will never be solved. Mexico's unemployment problem will never be solved. Therefore, Mexico will not get its population growth under control.

17. Either the dinosaurs were not cold-blooded or they were not the ancestors of modern birds. The dinosaurs were the ancestors of modern birds. Therefore, the dinosaurs were not cold-blooded.

18. If an orbiting space station is to be constructed, then a fifth shuttle must be added to the fleet. If a fifth shuttle is not added to the fleet, then numerous scientific experiments will have to be abandoned. Therefore, if an orbiting space station is not constructed, then numerous scientific experiments will have to be abandoned.

★19. If sea levels were to rise 20 feet worldwide, then coastal cities from New York to Sidney would be inundated. If the ice sheets on Antarctica were to slip into the sea, then sea levels would rise 20 feet worldwide. Therefore, if the ice sheets on Antarctica were to slip into the sea, then coastal cities from New York to Sidney would be inundated.

20. If tax credits are given for private education, then the government will be supporting religion; but if tax credits are not given for private education, then some parents will end up paying double tuition. Either tax credits will or will not be given for private education. Therefore, either the government will be supporting religion, or some parents will end up paying double tuition.

III. Identify the following dilemmas as either constructive or destructive. Then suggest a refutation for each by either escaping between the horns, grasping by the horns, or constructing a counterdilemma.

★1. If Melinda spends the night studying, she will miss the party; but if she does not spend the night studying, she will fail the test tomorrow. Melinda must either spend the night studying or not studying. Therefore, she will either miss the party or fail the test.

2. If we build our home in the valley, it will be struck by floods; and if we build it on the hilltop, it will be hit by lightning. Since we must either build it in the valley or on the hilltop, our home will either be struck by floods or hit by lightning.

3. If psychotherapists respect their clients' right to confidentiality, then they will not report child abusers to the authorities; but if they have any concern for the welfare of children, then they will report them. Psychotherapists must either report or not report child abusers to the authorities. Therefore, psychotherapists either have no respect for their clients' right to confidentiality or no concern for the welfare of children.

★4. If corporations are to remain competitive, then they must not spend money to neutralize their toxic waste; but if the environment is to be preserved, then corporations must spend money to neutralize their toxic waste. Corporations either will or will not spend money to neutralize their toxic waste. Therefore, either they will not remain competitive, or the environment will be destroyed.

5. If physicians pull the plug on terminally ill patients, then they risk being charged with murder; but if they do not pull the plug, they prolong their patients' pain and suffering. Since physicians with terminally ill patients must do one or the other, either they risk being charged with murder or they prolong their patients' pain and suffering.

6. If the Mitchels get a divorce, they will live separately in poverty; but if they stay married, they will live together in misery. Since they must either get a divorce or stay married, they will either live separately in poverty or together in misery.

★7. If college students want courses that are interesting and rewarding, then they must major in liberal arts; but if they want a job when they graduate, then they must major in business. College students will either not major in liberal arts, or they will not major in business. Therefore, either they will not take courses that are interesting and rewarding, or they will not have a job when they graduate.

8. If merchants arrest suspected shoplifters, then they risk false imprisonment; but if they do not arrest them, they risk loss of merchandise. Merchants must either arrest or not arrest suspected shoplifters. Therefore, they will either risk false imprisonment or loss of merchandise.

9. If women threatened with rape want to avoid being maimed or killed, then they must not resist their assaulter; but if they want to ensure successful prosecution of the assailant, they must resist him. Since women threatened with rape must do one or the other, either they will risk being maimed or killed or they will jeopardize successful prosecution of the assailant.

★10. If we prosecute suspected terrorists, then we risk retaliation by other terrorists; but if we release them, then we encourage terrorism. Since we must either prosecute or release suspected terrorists, we either risk retaliation by other terrorists or we encourage terrorism.

IV. The following selections were taken from letters to the editor of newspapers. Each contains one or more arguments, but the exact form of the argument may be hidden or ambiguous. Use the argument forms presented in this section to structure the selections as specifically named arguments.

★1. Anyone who is wondering how well Oral Roberts receives messages from God will be interested in our experience. Two weeks after my mother died, a letter came from Oral Roberts saying God had told him to write to her that day and ask for money! It makes one wonder.

(Hazel Woodsmall)

2. OK, I've tried it for a week again this year, but I still don't like daylight-saving time. My grass is brown enough already—it doesn't need another hour of daylight each day. Let's turn the clocks back to the way God intended—standard time.

(Jim Orr)

3. The religious right, in its impassioned fervor to correct our alleged moral wrongs and protect the rights of our unborn "children," may one day realize its ultimate goal of a constitutional amendment banning abortion. And what will the punishment be for those caught performing or receiving an abortion? The death penalty, of course.

(David Fisher)

★4. Where is it written that the number of bodies lined up at a polling booth is any measurement of democracy in a nation? If this concept had any validity, then surely Russia and the other Communist dictatorships, which regularly have a 99.99% voter turnout, should qualify as the world's outstanding democracies!

(Earl Carter)

5. If voluntary school prayer for our children is going to make them more moral, then just think what mandatory church attendance on Sunday could do for the rest of us.

(Roderick M. Boyes)

6. A country that replaces the diseased hearts of old white men but refuses to feed schoolchildren, pay women adequately, educate adolescents, or care for the elderly—that country is doomed. We are acting as if there is no tomorrow. Where is our shame?

(Robert Birch)

★7. We cannot afford to close the library at Central Juvenile Hall. These young people in particular need to have access to ideas, dreams, and alternative ways of living. It can make the difference for many students who might become interested in reading for the first time in their lives while in Juvenile Hall.

(Natalie S. Field)

8. If the death penalty deters one person from becoming a murderer, it is effective. There are also some other important reasons for having the death penalty. First, the families and friends of innocent victims have the right to see effective retribution. Second, terminating the life of a killer is more economical than keeping him in jail at the taxpayer's expense. Third, everyone will have greater respect for the judicial system when justice is carried out.

(Doug Kroker)

9. Regarding the bill to require parental consent for a minor's abortion, I would like to point out that the pious platitudes about parental authority quickly fall by the wayside when the minor wants to keep the baby and the parents say, "Don't be silly! You have an abortion and finish your education." If the parents can veto a minor's abortion, shouldn't they also be able to require one? Better the choice, either pro or con, be left to the girl/woman herself.

(Jane Roberts)

★10. So the President asked the reporters what they were doing on August 8, 1985. If I were manager of a company and I attended a management meeting where an important matter was being discussed, I would either (a) remember it, (b) make a note of it, or (c) dictate the results of the meeting afterwards to my secretary. Now, if the President does in fact remember it, then he is a liar. If he made a note of the meeting, then he is a liar. If after the meeting he had already forgotten and could not dictate to his secretary, then he is senile or irresponsible. In any case, he is either a liar, senile, or grossly irresponsible. This is no way to run a business, let alone a country.

(Janice Folick)

6.5 TRUTH TABLES FOR ARGUMENTS

Truth tables provide the standard technique for testing the validity of arguments in propositional logic. To construct a truth table for an argument, follow these steps:

1. Symbolize the argument, using letters to represent the atomic propositions.
2. Write out the symbolized argument, placing a single slash between the premises and a double slash between the last premise and the conclusion.
3. Draw a truth table for the symbolized argument as if it were a proposition broken into parts, outlining the columns representing the premises and conclusion.
4. Look for a line in which the premises are all true and the conclusion false. If such a line exists, the argument is invalid; if not, it is valid.

For example, let us test the following argument for validity:

If juvenile killers are as responsible for their crimes as adults, then execution is a justifiable punishment.
Juvenile killers are not as responsible for their crimes as adults.
Therefore, execution is not a justifiable punishment.

The first step is to symbolize the argument:

$$J \supset E$$
$$\frac{\sim J}{\sim E}$$

Now a truth table may be constructed. Since the symbolized argument contains two different letters, the truth table has four lines. Make sure that identical letters have identical columns beneath them. Here are the columns for the individual letters:

```
J ⊃ E  /  ~ J  //  ~ E
T   T         T          T
T   F         T          F
F   T         F          T
F   F         F          F
```

The truth table is now completed, and the columns representing the premises and conclusion are outlined:

```
J  ⊃  E  /  ~ J  //  ~ E
T [T] T    [F] T     [F] T
T [F] F    [F] T     [T] F
F (T) T    (T) F     (F) T
F [T] F    [T] F     [T] F
```

Inspection of the third line reveals that the premises are both true and the conclusion false. The argument is therefore invalid.

Another example:

> If insider trading continues, then investors will not trust the securities markets. If investors do not trust the securities markets, then business in general will suffer. Therefore, if insider trading continues, then business in general will suffer.

The completed truth table is:

```
C ⊃ ~ T  /  ~ T ⊃ B  //  C ⊃ B
T F  F T     F T T  T      T T T
T F  F T     F T T  F      T F F
T T  T F     T F T  T      T T T
T T  T F     T F F  F      T F F
F T  F T     F T T  T      F T T
F T  F T     F T T  F      F T F
F T  T F     T F T  T      F T T
F T  T F     T F F  F      F T F
```

Inspection of the truth table reveals that there is no line on which both premises are true and the conclusion false. The argument is therefore valid.

The logic behind the method of truth tables is easy to understand. By definition, a valid argument is one in which the conclusion follows necessarily from the premises. In other words, in a valid argument it is not possible for the premises to be true and the conclusion false. A truth table presents every possible combination of truth values that the components of an argument may have. Therefore, if no line exists on which the premises are true and the conclusion false, then it is not possible for the premises to be true and the conclusion false, in which case the argument is valid. Conversely, if there *is* a line on which the premises are true and the conclusion false, then it *is* possible for the premises to be true and the conclusion false, and the argument is invalid. We therefore have the following rules for testing arguments by truth tables:

> If there is no line on which all the premises are true and the conclusion false, the argument is valid.

> If there is at least one line on which all the premises are true and the conclusion false, the argument is invalid.

Truth tables provide a convenient illustration of the fact that any argument having contradictory premises is valid regardless of what its conclusion may be, and any argument having a tautologous conclusion is valid regardless of what its premises may be. Example:

The sky is blue.
The sky is not blue.
Therefore, Paris is the capital of France.

S	/	~	S	//	P
T		F	T		T
T		F	T		F
F		T	F		T
F		T	F		F

Since the premises of this argument are self-contradictory, there is no line on which the premises are both true. Accordingly, there is no line on which the premises are both true and the conclusion false, so the argument is valid. Of course, the argument is unsound, because it has a false premise. Another example:

Bern is the capital of Switzerland. Therefore, it is either raining or it is not raining.

B	//	R	v	~	R
T		T	T	F	T
T		F	T	T	F
F		T	T	F	T
F		F	T	T	F

The conclusion of this argument is a tautology. Accordingly, there is no line on which the premise is true and the conclusion false, and so the argument is valid. Incidentally, it is also sound, because the premise is true.

EXERCISE 6.5

I. Translate the following arguments into symbolic form. Then determine whether each is valid or invalid by constructing a truth table for each.

★1. If national elections deteriorate into TV popularity contests, then smooth-talking morons will get elected. Therefore, if national elections do not deteriorate into TV popularity contests, then smooth-talking morons will not get elected.

2. Brazil has a huge foreign debt. Therefore, either Brazil or Argentina has a huge foreign debt.

3. If fossil fuel combustion continues at its present rate, then a greenhouse effect will occur. If a greenhouse effect occurs, then world temperatures will rise. Therefore, if fossil fuel combustion continues at its present rate, then world temperatures will rise.

★4. If there are dried-up riverbeds on Mars, then water once flowed on the Martian surface. There are dried-up riverbeds on Mars. Therefore, water once flowed on the Martian surface.

5. If high school graduates are deficient in reading, they will not be able to compete in the modern world. If high school graduates are deficient in writing, they will not be able to compete in the modern world. Therefore, if high school graduates are deficient in reading, then they are deficient in writing.

6. The disparity between rich and poor is increasing. Therefore, political control over economic equality will be achieved only if restructuring the economic system along socialist lines implies that political control over economic equality will be achieved.

★7. Einstein won the Nobel Prize either for explaining the photoelectric effect or for the special theory of relativity. But he did win the Nobel Prize for explaining the photoelectric effect. Therefore, Einstein did not win the Nobel Prize for the special theory of relativity.

8. If chromosome mapping is successful, then the human genetic code will be deciphered. The human genetic code will not be deciphered and chromosome mapping will be successful. Therefore, new treatments will be developed for hereditary diseases.

9. Either the USS *Arizona* or the USS *Missouri* was not sunk in the attack on Pearl Harbor. Therefore, it is not the case that either the USS *Arizona* or the USS *Missouri* was sunk in the attack on Pearl Harbor.

★10. If racial quotas are adopted for promoting employees, then qualified employees will be passed over; but if racial quotas are not adopted, then prior discrimination will go unaddressed. Either racial quotas will or will not be adopted for promoting employees. Therefore, either qualified employees will be passed over or prior discrimination will go unaddressed.

II. Determine whether the following symbolized arguments are valid or invalid by constructing a truth table for each:

★1. $\dfrac{K \supset \sim K}{\sim K}$

2. $\dfrac{R \supset R}{R}$

3. $\dfrac{E \supset F}{E \supset (E \cdot F)}$

★4. $\dfrac{G \cdot (I \vee J)}{(G \cdot I) \vee (G \cdot J)}$

5. $\dfrac{\sim(K \cdot L)}{\sim K \cdot \sim L}$

6. $\dfrac{S}{(T \supset U) \equiv (\sim T \vee U)}$

★7. $\begin{array}{l} \sim W \vee X \\ \sim W \\ \hline X \end{array}$

8. $\begin{array}{l} C \equiv D \\ E \vee \sim D \\ \hline E \supset C \end{array}$

9. $\begin{array}{l} A \equiv (B \vee C) \\ \sim C \vee B \\ \hline A \supset B \end{array}$

★10. $\begin{array}{l} J \supset (K \supset L) \\ K \supset (J \supset L) \\ \hline (J \vee K) \supset L \end{array}$

11. $\dfrac{P \equiv Q}{(P \cdot \sim Q) \vee (Q \cdot \sim P)}$

12. $\begin{array}{l} E \supset (F \cdot G) \\ F \supset (G \supset H) \\ \hline E \supset H \end{array}$

★13. $\begin{array}{l} (A \vee B) \supset (A \cdot B) \\ \sim(A \vee B) \\ \hline \sim(A \cdot B) \end{array}$

14. $\begin{array}{l} (X \vee Y) \supset Z \\ Z \supset (X \cdot Y) \\ \hline (X \cdot Y) \supset (X \vee Y) \end{array}$

15. $\begin{array}{l} L \supset M \\ M \supset N \\ N \supset L \\ \hline L \vee N \end{array}$

★16. $\begin{array}{l} S \supset T \\ S \supset \sim T \\ \sim T \supset S \\ \hline S \vee \sim T \end{array}$

17. $\begin{array}{l} P \supset Q \\ R \supset S \\ \sim Q \vee \sim S \\ \hline \sim P \vee \sim R \end{array}$

18. $\begin{array}{l} A \supset B \\ (A \cdot B) \supset C \\ A \supset (C \supset D) \\ \hline A \supset D \end{array}$

★19. $\begin{array}{l} K \equiv (L \vee M) \\ L \supset M \\ M \supset K \\ K \vee L \\ \hline K \supset L \end{array}$

20. $\begin{array}{l} W \supset X \\ X \supset W \\ X \supset Y \\ Y \supset X \\ \hline W \equiv Y \end{array}$

6.6 INDIRECT TRUTH TABLES FOR ARGUMENTS

Indirect truth tables provide a shorter and faster method for testing the validity of arguments than that provided by ordinary truth tables. This method is especially applicable to arguments that contain a large number of different atomic propositions. For example, an argument containing five different atomic propositions would require an ordinary truth table having thirty-two lines. The indirect truth table for such an argument, on the other hand, would usually require only a single line and could be constructed in a fraction of the time required for the ordinary truth table.

To construct an indirect truth table for an argument, we begin by assuming that the argument is invalid. That is, we assume that it is possible for the premises to be true and the conclusion false. Truth values corresponding to true premises and false conclusion are entered beneath the symbols corresponding to the premises and conclusion. Then, working backward, the truth values of the separate components are derived. If no contradiction is obtained in the process, this means that it is indeed possible for the premises to be true and the conclusion false, as originally assumed, so the argument is therefore invalid. If, however, the attempt to make the premises true and the conclusion false leads to a contradiction, it is not possible for the premises to be true and the conclusion false, in which case the argument is valid. Consider the following symbolized argument:

$$\sim A \supset (B \lor C)$$
$$\underline{\sim B}$$
$$C \supset A$$

We begin as before by writing the symbolized argument on a single line, placing a single slash between the premises and a double slash between the last premise and the conclusion. Then we assign T to the premises and F to the conclusion, thus:

$$\sim A \supset (B \lor C) \quad / \quad \sim B \quad // \quad C \supset A$$
$$ T \quad T F$$

We can now obtain the truth values of B, C, and A, as follows:

$$\sim A \supset (B \lor C) \quad / \quad \sim B \quad // \quad C \supset A$$
$$ T \quad T \ F T \ F \ F$$

These truth values are now transferred to the first premise:

$$\sim A \supset (B \lor C) \quad / \quad \sim B \quad // \quad C \supset A$$
$$T \ F \ T \quad F \ T \ T \quad T \ F \quad T \ F \ F$$

We thus have a perfectly consistent assignment of truth values, which makes the premises true and the conclusion false. The argument is therefore invalid. If an ordinary truth table were constructed for this argument, it would be seen that the argument fails on the line on which A is false, B is false, and C is true. This is the exact arrangement presented in the indirect truth table above.

314   A CONCISE INTRODUCTION TO LOGIC

Here is another example. As always, we begin by assigning T to the premises and F to the conclusion:

$$A \supset (B \lor C) \quad / \quad B \supset D \quad / \quad A \quad // \quad \sim C \supset D$$
$$\text{T} \qquad\qquad\quad \text{T} \qquad\quad \text{T} \qquad\qquad \text{F}$$

From the conclusion we can now obtain the truth values of C and D, which are then transferred to the first two premises:

$$A \supset (B \lor C) \quad / \quad B \supset D \quad / \quad A \quad // \quad \sim C \supset D$$
$$\text{T} \quad\; \text{F} \qquad\quad \text{T F} \qquad\; \text{T} \qquad\quad \text{T F F F}$$

The truth value of B is now obtained from the second premise and transferred, together with the truth value of A, to the first premise:

$$A \supset (B \lor C) \quad / \quad B \supset D \quad / \quad A \quad // \quad \sim C \supset D$$
$$\boxed{\text{T T F F}}\,\text{F} \qquad\quad \text{F T F} \qquad\; \text{T} \qquad\quad \text{T F F F}$$

A contradiction now appears in the truth values assigned to the first premise. The inconsistent truth values are circled. These results show that it is impossible for the premises to be true and the conclusion false. The argument is therefore valid.

Sometimes a single row of truth values is not sufficient to prove an argument valid. Example:

$$\sim A \supset B \quad / \quad B \supset A \quad / \quad A \supset \sim B \quad // \quad A \cdot \sim B$$
$$\text{T} \qquad\qquad \text{T} \qquad\qquad \text{T} \qquad\qquad\quad \text{F}$$

Since a conditional statement can be true in any one of three ways, and a conjunctive statement can be false in any one of three ways, merely assigning truth to the premises and falsity to the conclusion of this argument is not sufficient to obtain the truth values of any of the component statements. When faced with a situation such as this, we must list all of the possible ways that one of the premises can be true or the conclusion false, and proceed from there. If we list all of the possible ways the conclusion may be false, we obtain the following:

$$\sim A \supset B \quad / \quad B \supset A \quad / \quad A \supset \sim B \quad // \quad A \cdot \sim B$$

$\sim A \supset B$	$B \supset A$	$A \supset \sim B$	$A \cdot \sim B$
T	T	T	T F F T
T	T	T	F F T F
T	T	T	F F F T

Extending the truth values of A and B to the premises, we obtain the following result:

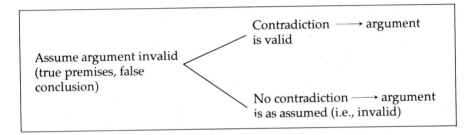

Since a contradiction is obtained on each line, the argument is valid. If a contradiction had not been obtained on every line, the argument would, of course, be invalid, because it would be possible for the premises to be true and the conclusion false. Note that in this argument it is not necessary to fill out all the truth values on any one line to be forced into a contradiction. On each line the contradiction is obtained within the context of a single premise.

Assume argument invalid (true premises, false conclusion)
Contradiction ⟶ argument is valid
No contradiction ⟶ argument is as assumed (i.e., invalid)

Two final reminders are in order about indirect truth tables. First, if a contradiction is obtained in the assignment of truth values, it is essential that every step leading to it be logically implied by some prior step. In other words, the contradiction must be unavoidable. If a contradiction is obtained after truth values are assigned haphazardly or by guessing, then nothing has been proved. The objective is not merely to reach a contradiction but to be *forced* into one.

For example, in the following indirect truth table a contradiction is apparent in the first premise:

$$A \supset B \quad / \quad C \supset B \quad // \quad A \supset C$$
$$\boxed{\text{T T F}} \qquad \text{F T F} \qquad \text{T F F}$$

Yet the argument is invalid. The contradiction that appears is not *required* by the assignment of truth to the premises and falsity to the conclusion. The following indirect truth table, which is done correctly, proves the argument invalid:

$$A \supset B \quad / \quad C \supset B \quad // \quad A \supset C$$
$$\text{T T T} \qquad \text{F T T} \qquad \text{T F F}$$

The second point to remember is that it is essential that identical letters be assigned identical truth values. For example, if the letter A

appears three times in a certain symbolized argument and the truth value T is assigned to it in one occurrence, then the same truth value must be assigned to it in the other occurrences as well. After the truth table has been completed, each letter should be rechecked to ensure that one and the same truth value has been assigned to its various occurrences.

EXERCISE 6.6

Use indirect truth tables to determine whether the following arguments are valid or invalid:

★1. $B \equiv C$
   $\overline{\sim C \supset \sim B}$

2. $\sim E \lor F$
   $\sim E$
   $\overline{\sim F}$

3. $P \supset (Q \supset R)$
   $\overline{(P \cdot Q) \supset R}$

★4. $\sim (I \equiv J)$
   $\overline{\sim (I \supset J)}$

5. $W \supset (X \supset Y)$
   $X \supset (Y \supset Z)$
   $\overline{W \supset (X \supset Z)}$

6. $A \supset (B \lor C)$
   $C \supset (D \cdot E)$
   $\sim B$
   $\overline{A \supset .\sim E}$

★7. $G \supset H$
   $H \supset I$
   $\sim J \supset G$
   $\sim I$
   $\overline{J}$

8. $J \supset (\sim L \supset \sim K)$
   $K \supset (\sim L \supset M)$
   $(L \lor M) \supset N$
   $\overline{J \supset N}$

9. $P \cdot (Q \lor R)$
   $(P \cdot R) \supset \sim (S \lor T)$
   $(\sim S \lor \sim T) \supset \sim (P \cdot Q)$
   $\overline{S \equiv T}$

★10. $(M \lor N) \supset O$
   $O \supset (N \lor P)$
   $M \supset (\sim Q \supset N)$
   $(Q \supset M) \supset \sim P$
   $\overline{N \equiv O}$

11. $(A \lor B) \supset (C \cdot D)$
   $(\sim A \lor \sim B) \supset E$
   $\overline{(\sim C \lor \sim D) \supset E}$

12. $F \supset G$
   $\sim H \lor I$
   $(G \lor I) \supset J$
   $\sim J$
   $\overline{\sim (F \lor H)}$

★13. $(A \lor B) \supset (C \cdot D)$
   $(X \lor \sim Y) \supset (\sim C \cdot \sim W)$
   $(X \lor Z) \supset (A \cdot E)$
   $\overline{\sim X}$

14. $\sim G \supset (\sim H \cdot \sim I)$
   $J \supset H$
   $K \supset (L \cdot M)$
   $K \lor J$
   $\overline{L \cdot G}$

★15. $N \lor \sim O$
   $P \lor O$
   $P \supset Q$
   $(N \lor Q) \supset (R \cdot S)$
   $S \supset (R \supset T)$
   $O \supset (T \supset U)$
   $\overline{U}$

7

NATURAL DEDUCTION IN PROPOSITIONAL LOGIC

7.1 RULES OF IMPLICATION I

Natural deduction is a method for establishing the validity of propositional type arguments that is both simpler and more enlightening than the method of truth tables. By means of this method, the conclusion of an argument is actually derived from the premises through a series of discrete steps. In this respect natural deduction resembles the method used in geometry to derive theorems relating to lines and figures; but whereas each step in a geometrical proof depends on some mathematical principle, each step in a logical proof depends on a **rule of inference.** Eighteen rules of inference will be set forth in this chapter. The first four should be familiar from the previous chapter:

1. *Modus ponens* (MP):

$$p \supset q$$
$$\underline{p}$$
$$q$$

2. *Modus tollens* (MT):

$$p \supset q$$
$$\underline{\sim q}$$
$$\sim p$$

3. Hypothetical syllogism (HS):

$$p \supset q$$
$$\underline{q \supset r}$$
$$p \supset r$$

4. Disjunctive syllogism (DS):

$$p \vee q$$
$$\underline{\sim p}$$
$$q$$

For an illustration of the use of three of these rules, consider the following argument:

> If the Astros win the playoff, then the Braves will lose the pennant. If the Astros do not win the playoff, then either Connolly or Davis will be fired. The Braves will not lose the pennant. Furthermore, Connolly will not be fired. Therefore, Davis will be fired.

The first step is to symbolize the argument, numbering the premises and writing the conclusion to the right of the last premise, separated by a slash mark:

1. $A \supset B$
2. $\sim A \supset (C \lor D)$
3. $\sim B$
4. $\sim C$ / D

The conclusion is now derived from the premises via steps 5 through 7. The justification for each line is written to the immediate right:

5. $\sim A$ 1, 3, MT
6. $C \lor D$ 2, 5, MP
7. D 4, 6, DS

Line 5 is obtained from lines 1 and 3 via *modus tollens*. In other words, when A and B in these lines are substituted respectively for the p and q of the *modus tollens* rule, line 5 follows as the conclusion. Then, when $\sim A$ and $C \lor D$ in lines 2 and 5 are substituted respectively for the p and q of the *modus ponens* rule, line 6 follows as the conclusion. Finally, when C and D in lines 4 and 6 are substituted respectively for the p and q of the disjunctive syllogism rule, line 7 follows as the final conclusion. These lines constitute a valid derivation of the conclusion from the premises because each line is a substitution instance of a valid argument form.

These arguments are all instances of ***modus ponens*** (MP)

$\sim F \supset (G \equiv H)$	$(A \lor B) \supset \sim (C \cdot D)$	$K \cdot L$
$\sim F$	$A \lor B$	$(K \cdot L) \supset [(R \supset S) \cdot (T \supset U)]$
$G \equiv H$	$\sim (C \cdot D)$	$(R \supset S) \cdot (T \supset U)$

Here is an example of another completed proof. The conclusion to be obtained is written to the right of the last premise (line 4). Lines 5 through 7 are used to derive the conclusion:

1. $F \supset G$
2. $F \lor H$
3. $\sim G$
4. $H \supset (G \supset I)$ $/ F \supset I$
5. $\sim F$ 1, 3, MT
6. H 2, 5, DS
7. $G \supset I$ 4, 6, MP
8. $F \supset I$ 1, 7, HS

When the letters in lines 1 and 3 are substituted into the *modus tollens* rule, line 5 is obtained. Then, when the letters in lines 2 and 5 are substituted into the disjunctive syllogism rule, line 6 is obtained. Line 7 is obtained by substituting H and $G \supset I$ from lines 4 and 6 into the *modus ponens* rule. Finally, line 8 is obtained by substituting the letters in lines 1 and 7 into the hypothetical syllogism rule. Notice that the conclusion, stated to the right of line 4, is not (and never is) part of the proof. It merely indicates what the proof is supposed to yield in the end.

These arguments are all instances of **modus tollens** (MT)

$(D \lor F) \supset K$	$\sim G \supset \sim (M \lor N)$	$\sim T$
$\sim K$	$\sim\sim (M \lor N)$	$[(H \lor K) \cdot (L \lor N)] \supset T$
$\sim (D \lor F)$	$\sim\sim G$	$\sim [(H \lor K) \cdot (L \lor N)]$

The successful use of natural deduction to derive a conclusion from one or more premises depends on the ability of the reasoner to visualize more or less complex arrangements of atomic propositions as instances of the basic rules of inference. Here is a slightly more complex example:

1. $\sim (A \cdot B) \lor [\sim (E \cdot F) \supset (C \supset D)]$
2. $\sim\sim (A \cdot B)$
3. $\sim (E \cdot F)$
4. $D \supset G$ $/ C \supset G$
5. $\sim (E \cdot F) \supset (C \supset D)$ 1, 2, DS
6. $C \supset D$ 3, 5, MP
7. $C \supset G$ 4, 6, HS

Line 4 is the last premise. To obtain line 5, $\sim (A \cdot B)$ and $[\sim (E \cdot F) \supset (C \supset D)]$ are substituted respectively for the p and q of the disjunctive syllogism rule, yielding $[\sim (E \cdot F) \supset (C \supset D)]$ as the conclusion. Next, $\sim (E \cdot F)$ and $C \supset D$ are substituted respectively for the p and q of *modus ponens*, yielding $C \supset D$ on line 6. Finally, lines 6 and 4 are combined to yield line 7 via the hypothetical syllogism rule.

The proofs that we have investigated thus far have been presented in ready-made form. We turn now to the question of how the various lines are obtained, leading in the end to the conclusion. What strategy is used in deriving these lines? While the answer is somewhat complex, there

These arguments are all instances of pure **hypothetical syllogism** (HS)

$A \supset (D \cdot F)$	$\sim M \supset (R \supset S)$	$(L \supset N) \supset [(S \vee T) \cdot K]$
$(D \cdot F) \supset \sim H$	$(C \vee K) \supset \sim M$	$(C \equiv F) \supset (L \supset N)$
$A \supset \sim H$	$(C \vee K) \supset (R \supset S)$	$(C \equiv F) \supset [(S \vee T) \cdot K]$

are a few basic rules of thumb that should be followed. Always begin by looking at the conclusion and by then attempting to locate the conclusion in the premises. Let us suppose that the conclusion is a single letter L. We begin by looking for L in the premises. Let us suppose we find it in a premise that reads:

$$K \supset L$$

Immediately we see that we can obtain L via *modus ponens* if we first obtain K. We now begin searching for K. Let us suppose that we find K in another premise that reads

$$J \vee K$$

From this we see that we could obtain K via disjunctive syllogism if we first obtain $\sim J$. The process continues until we isolate the required statement on a line by itself. Let us suppose that we find $\sim J$ on a line by itself. The thought process is then complete, and the various steps may be written out in the reverse order in which they were obtained mentally. The proof would look like this:

1. $\sim J$
2. $J \vee K$
3. $K \supset L$ $/ L$
4. K 1, 2, DS
5. L 3, 4, MP

These arguments are all instances of **disjunctive syllogism** (DS)

$U \vee \sim (W \cdot X)$	$\sim (E \vee F)$	$\sim B \vee [(H \supset M) \cdot (S \supset T)]$
$\sim U$	$(E \vee F) \vee (N \supset K)$	$\sim \sim B$
$\sim (W \cdot X)$	$N \supset K$	$(H \supset M) \cdot (S \supset T)$

Turning now to a different example, let us suppose that the conclusion is the conditional statement $R \supset U$. We begin by attempting to locate $R \supset U$ in the premises. If we cannot find it, we look for its separate components, R and U. Let us suppose we find R in the antecedent of the conditional statement

$$R \supset S$$

Furthermore, let us suppose we find U in the consequent of the conditional statement

$$T \supset U$$

We then see that we can obtain $R \supset U$ via a series of hypothetical syllogism steps if we first obtain $S \supset T$. Let us suppose that we find $S \supset T$ on a line by itself. The proof has now been completely thought through and may be written out as follows:

1. $S \supset T$
2. $T \supset U$
3. $R \supset S$ $/ R \supset U$
4. $R \supset T$ 1, 3, HS
5. $R \supset U$ 2, 4, HS

At this point a word of caution is in order about the meaning of a proposition being "obtained." Let us suppose that we are searching for E and we find it in a premise that reads $E \supset F$. The mere fact that we have located the letter E in this line does not mean that we have obtained E. $E \supset F$ means that *if* we have E, then we have F; it does *not* mean that we *have* either E or F. From such a line we could obtain F (via *modus ponens*) if we first obtain E, or, we could obtain $\sim E$ (via *modus tollens*) if we first obtain $\sim F$. $E \supset F$ by itself gives us nothing, and even if we combine it with other lines, there is no way that we could ever obtain E from such a line.

Here is a sample argument:

1. $A \vee B$
2. $\sim C \supset \sim A$
3. $C \supset D$
4. $\sim D$ $/ B$

We begin by searching for B in the premises. Finding it in line 1, we see that it can be obtained via disjunctive syllogism if we first obtain $\sim A$. This in turn can be gotten from line 2 via *modus ponens* if we first obtain $\sim C$, and this can be gotten from line 3 via *modus tollens* once $\sim D$ is obtained. Happily, the latter is stated by itself on line 4. The proof has now been completely thought through and can be written out as follows:

1. $A \vee B$
2. $\sim C \supset \sim A$
3. $C \supset D$
4. $\sim D$ $/ B$
5. $\sim C$ 3, 4, MT

6. $\sim A$ 2, 5, MP
7. B 1, 6, DS

Another example:

1. $E \supset (K \supset L)$
2. $F \supset (L \supset M)$
3. $G \lor E$
4. $\sim G$
5. F / $K \supset M$

We begin by searching for $K \supset M$ in the premises. Not finding it, we search for the separate components, K and M, and locate them in lines 1 and 2. The fact that K appears in the antecedent of a conditional statement, and M in the consequent of another, immediately suggests hypothetical syllogism. But first we must obtain these conditional statements on lines by themselves. We can obtain $K \supset L$ via *modus ponens* if we first obtain E. This, in turn, we can obtain from line 3 via disjunctive syllogism if we first obtain $\sim G$. Since $\sim G$ appears by itself on line 4, the first part of the thought process is now complete. The second part requires that we obtain $L \supset M$. This we can get from line 2 via *modus ponens* if we can get F, and we do have F by itself on line 5. All of the steps leading to the conclusion have now been thought through, and the proof can be written out:

1. $E \supset (K \supset L)$
2. $F \supset (L \supset M)$
3. $G \lor E$
4. $\sim G$
5. F / $K \supset M$
6. E 3, 4, DS
7. $K \supset L$ 1, 6, MP
8. $L \supset M$ 2, 5, MP
9. $K \supset M$ 7, 8, HS

The thought process behind these proofs illustrates an important point about the construction of proofs by natural deduction. As a rule, we should never write down a line in a proof unless we know why we are doing it and where it leads. Typically, good proofs are not produced haphazardly or by luck; rather, they are produced by organized logical thinking. Occasionally, of course, we may be baffled by an especially difficult proof, and random deductive steps noted on the side may be useful. But we should not commence the actual writing out of the proof until we have used logical thinking to discover the path leading to the conclusion.

EXERCISE 7.1

I. Supply the required justification for the derived steps in the following proofs. No justification, of course, is required for the premises. The last premise is always the line adjacent to the required conclusion.

★(1) 1. $J \supset (K \supset L)$
    2. $L \vee J$
    3. $\sim L$ / $\sim K$
    4. J _____
    5. $K \supset L$ _____
    6. $\sim K$ _____

(2) 1. $\sim(S \equiv T) \supset (\sim P \supset Q)$
    2. $(S \equiv T) \supset P$
    3. $\sim P$ / Q
    4. $\sim(S \equiv T)$ _____
    5. $\sim P \supset Q$ _____
    6. Q _____

(3) 1. $\sim A \supset (B \supset \sim C)$
    2. $\sim D \supset (\sim C \supset A)$
    3. $D \vee \sim A$
    4. $\sim D$ / $\sim B$
    5. $\sim A$ _____
    6. $B \supset \sim C$ _____
    7. $\sim C \supset A$ _____
    8. $B \supset A$ _____
    9. $\sim B$ _____

★(4) 1. $\sim G \supset [G \vee (S \supset G)]$
    2. $(S \vee L) \supset \sim G$
    3. $S \vee L$ / L
    4. $\sim G$ _____
    5. $G \vee (S \supset G)$ _____
    6. $S \supset G$ _____
    7. $\sim S$ _____
    8. L _____

(5) 1. $H \supset [\sim E \supset (C \supset \sim D)]$
    2. $\sim D \supset E$
    3. $E \vee H$
    4. $\sim E$ / $\sim C$
    5. H _____
    6. $\sim E \supset (C \supset \sim D)$ _____
    7. $C \supset \sim D$ _____
    8. $C \supset E$ _____
    9. $\sim C$ _____

                A CONCISE INTRODUCTION TO LOGIC

II. Use the first four rules of inference to derive the conclusions of the following symbolized arguments:

★(1) 1. $(G \equiv J) \vee (B \supset P)$
    2. $\sim(G \equiv J)$ / $B \supset P$

(2) 1. $(K \cdot O) \supset (N \vee T)$
    2. $K \cdot O$ / $N \vee T$

(3) 1. $(M \vee P) \supset \sim K$
    2. $D \supset (M \vee P)$ / $D \supset \sim K$

★(4) 1. $\sim\sim(R \vee W)$
    2. $S \supset \sim(R \vee W)$ / $\sim S$

(5) 1. $\sim C \supset (A \supset C)$
    2. $\sim C$ / $\sim A$

(6) 1. $F \vee (D \supset T)$
    2. $\sim F$
    3. D / T

★(7) 1. $(K \cdot B) \vee (L \supset E)$
    2. $\sim(K \cdot B)$
    3. $\sim E$ / $\sim L$

(8) 1. $P \supset (G \supset T)$
    2. $Q \supset (T \supset E)$
    3. P
    4. Q / $G \supset E$

(9) 1. $\sim W \supset [\sim W \supset (X \supset W)]$
    2. $\sim W$ / $\sim X$

★(10) 1. $\sim S \supset D$
    2. $\sim S \vee (\sim D \supset K)$
    3. $\sim D$ / K

(11) 1. $A \supset (E \supset \sim F)$
    2. $H \vee (\sim F \supset M)$
    3. A
    4. $\sim H$ / $E \supset M$

(12) 1. $N \supset (J \supset P)$
    2. $(J \supset P) \supset (N \supset J)$
    3. N / P

★(13) 1. $G \supset [\sim O \supset (G \supset D)]$
    2. $O \vee G$
    3. $\sim O$ / D

(14) 1. $\sim M \vee (B \vee \sim T)$
    2. $B \supset W$
    3. $\sim\sim M$
    4. $\sim W$ / $\sim T$

(15) 1. $(L \equiv N) \supset C$
    2. $(L \equiv N) \vee (P \supset \sim E)$
    3. $\sim E \supset C$
    4. $\sim C$ / $\sim P$

★(16) 1. $\sim J \supset [\sim A \supset (D \supset A)]$
    2. $J \vee \sim A$
    3. $\sim J$ / $\sim D$

(17) 1. $(B \supset \sim M) \supset (T \supset \sim S)$
    2. $B \supset K$
    3. $K \supset \sim M$
    4. $\sim S \supset N$ / $T \supset N$

(18) 1. $(R \supset F) \supset [(R \supset \sim G) \supset (S \supset Q)]$
    2. $(Q \supset F) \supset (R \supset Q)$
    3. $\sim G \supset F$
    4. $Q \supset \sim G$ / $S \supset F$

★(19) 1. $\sim A \supset [A \vee (T \supset R)]$
    2. $\sim R \supset [R \vee (A \supset R)]$
    3. $(T \vee D) \supset \sim R$
    4. $T \vee D$ / D

(20) 1. $\sim N \supset [(B \supset D) \supset (N \vee \sim E)]$
    2. $(B \supset E) \supset \sim N$
    3. $B \supset D$
    4. $D \supset E$ / $\sim D$

III. Translate the following arguments into symbolic form and use the first four rules of inference to derive the conclusion of each. The letters to be used for the atomic statements are given in parentheses after each exercise. Use these letters in the order in which they are listed.

★1. If the average child watches more than five hours of television per day, then either his power of imagination is improved or he becomes conditioned to expect constant excitement. The average child's power of imagination is not improved by watching television. Also, the average child does watch more than five hours of television per day. Therefore, the average child is conditioned to expect constant excitement. (*W, P, C*)

2. If a tenth planet exists, then its orbit is perpendicular to that of the other planets. Either a tenth planet is responsible for the death of the dinosaurs, or its orbit is not perpendicular to that of the other planets. A tenth planet is not responsible for the death of the dinosaurs. Therefore, a tenth planet does not exist. (*E, O, R*)

3. If imposing quotas on textile imports implies that jobs will not be lost, then the domestic textile industry will modernize only if the domestic textile industry is not destroyed. If quotas are imposed on textile imports, the domestic textile industry will modernize. The domestic textile industry will modernize only if jobs are not lost. Therefore, if quotas are imposed on textile imports, the domestic textile industry will not be destroyed. (*Q, J, M, D*)

★4. If teachers are allowed to conduct random drug searches on students only if teachers are acting *in loco parentis,* then if teachers are acting *in loco parentis,* then students have no Fourth Amendment protections. Either students have no Fourth Amendment protections or if teachers are allowed to conduct random drug searches on students, then teachers are acting *in loco parentis.* It is not the case that students have no Fourth Amendment protections. Therefore, teachers are not allowed to conduct random drug searches on students. (*R, L, F*)

5. Either funding for nuclear fusion will be cut or if sufficiently high temperatures are achieved in the laboratory, nuclear fusion will become a reality. Either the supply of hydrogen fuel is limited, or if nuclear fusion becomes a reality, the world's energy problems will be solved. Funding for nuclear fusion will not be cut. Furthermore, the supply of hydrogen fuel is not limited. Therefore, if sufficiently high temperatures are achieved in the laboratory, the world's energy problems will be solved. (*C, H, R, S, E*)

6. Either the continents are not subject to drift or if Antarctica was always located in the polar region, then it would contain no fossils of plants from a temperate climate. If the continents are not subject to drift, then Antarctica would contain no fossils of plants from a temperate climate. But it is not the case that Antarctica contains no fossils of plants from a temperate climate. Therefore, Antarctica was not always located in the polar region. (*D, L, F*)

★7. If terrorists take more hostages, then terrorist demands will be met if and only if the media give full coverage to terrorist acts. Either the media will voluntarily limit the flow of information or if the media will recognize they are being exploited by terrorists, they will voluntarily limit the flow of information. Either the media will recognize they are being exploited by terrorists or terrorists will take more hostages. The media will not voluntarily limit the flow of information. Therefore, terrorist demands will be met if and only if the media give full coverage to terrorist acts. (*H, D, A, V, R*)

8. Either the Soviets will delay developing a first-strike nuclear submarine, or they will be forced to launch their land-based missiles "on warning." If the Trident 2's ability to deliver nuclear warheads within 400 feet of targets implies that the Trident 2 is a first-strike weapon, then the Soviets will not delay developing a first-strike nuclear submarine. If Soviet land-based missiles are vulnerable to direct attack, then if the Trident 2 has the ability to deliver nuclear warheads within 400 feet of targets, then it can destroy Soviet land-based missiles. If the Trident 2 can destroy Soviet land-based missiles, then it is a first-strike weapon. Soviet land-based missiles are vulnerable to direct attack. Therefore, the Soviets will be forced to launch their land-based missiles "on warning." (S, F, T, W, V, D)

9. If strengthening the drug interdiction program implies that cocaine will become more readily available, then either the number of addicts is decreasing or the war on drugs is failing. If the drug interdiction program is strengthened, then smugglers will shift to more easily concealable drugs. If smugglers shift to more easily concealable drugs, then cocaine will become more readily available. Furthermore, the number of addicts is not decreasing. Therefore, the war on drugs is failing. (D, C, N, W, S)

★10. If the death penalty is not cruel and unusual punishment, then either it is cruel and unusual punishment or if society is justified in using it, then it will deter other criminals. If the death penalty is cruel and unusual punishment, then it is both cruel and unusual and its use degrades society as a whole. It is not the case that both the death penalty is cruel and unusual and its use degrades society as a whole. Furthermore, the death penalty will not deter other criminals. Therefore, society is not justified in using the death penalty. (C, J, D, U)

7.2 RULES OF IMPLICATION II

Four additional rules of inference are listed below. Constructive dilemma should be familiar from Chapter 6. The other three are new.*

5. Constructive dilemma (CD):

$$(p \supset q) \cdot (r \supset s)$$
$$\underline{p \lor r}$$
$$q \lor s$$

6. Simplification (Simp):

$$\underline{p \cdot q}$$
$$p$$

7. Conjunction (Conj):

$$p$$
$$\underline{q}$$
$$p \cdot q$$

8. Addition (Add):

$$\underline{p}$$
$$p \lor q$$

Like the previous four rules, these four are fairly easy to understand, but if there is any doubt about them their validity may be proven by means of a truth table.

---

*Some texts include a rule called "absorption" by which the statement form $p \supset (q \cdot p)$ is deduced from $p \supset q$. This rule is necessary only if conditional proof is not presented. This text opts in favor of conditional proof.

Constructive dilemma can be understood as involving two *modus ponens* steps. The first premise states that if we have *p* then we have *q*, and if we have *r* then we have *s*. But since, by the second premise, we do have either *p* or *r*, it follows by *modus ponens* that we have either *q* or *s*. Constructive dilemma is the only form of dilemma that will be included as a rule of inference. By the rule of transposition, which will

---

These arguments are both instances of **constructive dilemma** (CD)

$$\sim M \vee N$$
$$(\sim M \supset S) \cdot (N \supset \sim T)$$
$$\overline{S \vee \sim T}$$

$$[(K \supset T) \supset (A \cdot B)] \cdot [(H \supset P) \supset (A \cdot C)]$$
$$(K \supset T) \vee (H \supset P)$$
$$\overline{(A \cdot B) \vee (A \cdot C)}$$

---

be presented in Section 7.4, any argument that is a substitution instance of the destructive dilemma form can be easily converted into a substitution instance of constructive dilemma. Destructive dilemma, therefore, is not needed as a rule of inference.

Simplification states that if two propositions are given as true on a single line, then each of them is true separately. According to the strict interpretation of the simplification rule, only the left-hand conjunct may be stated in the conclusion. Once the commutativity rule for conjunction has been presented, however (see Section 7.3), we will be justified in replacing a statement such as *H* • *K* with *K* • *H*. Having done this, the *K* now appears on the left, and the appropriate conclusion is *K*.

These arguments are all instances of **simplification** (Simp)

$$\frac{\sim F \cdot (U \equiv E)}{\sim F}$$

$$\frac{(M \vee T) \cdot (S \supset R)}{(M \vee T)}$$

$$\frac{[(X \supset Z) \cdot M] \cdot (G \supset H)}{[(X \supset Z) \cdot M]}$$

Conjunction states that two propositions—for example, *H* and *K*—asserted separately on different lines may be conjoined on a single line. The two propositions may be conjoined in whatever order we choose (either *H* • *K* or *K* • *H*) without appeal to the commutativity rule for conjunction.

These arguments are all instances of **conjunction** (Conj)

$$\frac{\begin{array}{c}\sim E \\ \sim G\end{array}}{\sim E \cdot \sim G}$$

$$\frac{\begin{array}{c}C \supset M \\ D \supset N\end{array}}{(C \supset M) \cdot (D \supset N)}$$

$$\frac{\begin{array}{c}R \supset (H \cdot T) \\ K \supset (H \cdot O)\end{array}}{[R \supset (H \cdot T)] \cdot [K \supset (H \cdot O)]}$$

Addition states that whenever a proposition is asserted on a line by itself it may be joined disjunctively with any proposition we choose. In other words, if G is asserted to be true by itself, it follows that $G \vee H$ is true. This may appear somewhat puzzling at first, but once one realizes that $G \vee H$ is a much weaker statement than G by itself, the puzzlement should disappear. The new proposition must, of course, always be joined disjunctively (not conjunctively) to the given proposition. If G is

---

These arguments are all instances of **addition** (Add)

S	$C \cdot D$	$W \equiv Z$
$S \vee \sim T$	$(C \cdot D) \vee (K \cdot \sim P)$	$(W \equiv Z) \vee [A \supset (M \supset O)]$

---

stated on a line by itself, we are *not* justified in writing $G \cdot H$ as a consequence of addition.

The use of these four rules may now be illustrated. Consider the following argument form:

1. $A \supset B$
2. $(B \vee C) \supset (D \cdot E)$
3. A / D

As usual, we begin by looking for the conclusion in the premises. D appears in the consequent of the second premise, which we can obtain via simplification if we first obtain $B \vee C$. This expression as such does not appear in the premises, but from lines 1 and 3 we see that we can obtain B by itself via *modus ponens*. Having obtained B, we can get $B \vee C$ via addition. The proof has now been thought through, and can be written out as follows:

1. $A \supset B$
2. $(B \vee C) \supset (D \cdot E)$
3. A / D
4. B 1, 3, MP
5. $B \vee C$ 4, Add
6. $D \cdot E$ 2, 5, MP
7. D 6, Simp

Another example:

1. $K \supset L$
2. $(M \supset N) \cdot S$
3. $N \supset T$
4. $K \vee M$ / $L \vee T$

Seeing that $L \lor T$ does not appear as such in the premises, we look for the separate components. Finding L and T as the consequents of two distinct conditional statements causes us to think that the conclusion can be obtained via the constructive dilemma. If a constructive dilemma can be set up, it will need a disjunctive statement as its second premise, and such a statement appears on line 4. Furthermore, the components of this statement, K and M, each appear as the antecedent of a conditional statement, exactly as they should for a dilemma. The only statement that is missing now is $M \supset T$. Inspecting line 2 we see that we can obtain $M \supset N$ via simplification, and putting this together with line 3 gives us $M \supset T$ via hypothetical syllogism. The completed proof may now be written out.

> 1. $K \supset L$
> 2. $(M \supset N) \cdot S$
> 3. $N \supset T$
> 4. $K \lor M$ / $L \lor T$
> 5. $M \supset N$ 2, Simp
> 6. $M \supset T$ 3, 5, HS
> 7. $(K \supset L) \cdot (M \supset T)$ 1, 6, Conj
> 8. $L \lor T$ 4, 7, CD

Another example:

> 1. $\sim M \cdot N$
> 2. $P \supset M$
> 3. $Q \cdot R$
> 4. $(\sim P \cdot Q) \supset S$ / $S \lor T$

When we look for $S \lor T$ in the premises we find S in the consequent of line 4, but no T at all. This signals an important principle: Whenever the conclusion of an argument contains a letter not found in the premises, addition must be used to introduce the missing letter. Addition is the *only* rule of inference that can introduce new letters. To introduce T by addition, however, we must first obtain S on a line by itself. S can be obtained from line 4 via *modus ponens* if we first obtain $\sim P \cdot Q$. This, in turn, can be gotten via conjunction, but first $\sim P$ and Q must be obtained individually on separate lines. Q can be obtained from line 3 via simplication and $\sim P$ from line 2 via *modus tollens*, but the latter step requires that we first obtain $\sim M$ on a line by itself. Since this can be gotten from line 1 via simplification, the proof is now complete. It may be written out as follows:

> 1. $\sim M \cdot N$
> 2. $P \supset M$
> 3. $Q \cdot R$

4. $(\sim P \cdot Q) \supset S$ / $S \vee T$
5. $\sim M$ 1, Simp
6. $\sim P$ 2, 5, MT
7. Q 3, Simp
8. $\sim P \cdot Q$ 6, 7, Conj
9. S 4, 8, MP
10. $S \vee T$ 9, Add

Addition is used together with disjunctive syllogism to derive the conclusion of arguments having contradictory premises. As we saw in Chapter 6, such arguments are always valid. The procedure is illustrated as follows:

1. S
2. $\sim S$ / T
3. $S \vee T$ 1, Add
4. T 2, 3, DS

With arguments of this sort the conclusion is always introduced via addition and then separated via disjunctive syllogism. Since addition can be used to introduce any letter or arrangement of letters we choose, it should be clear from this example that inconsistent premises validly entail any conclusion whatever.

To complete this presentation of the eight rules of implication, let us consider some of the typical ways in which they are *misapplied*. Examples are as follows:

1. $A \supset (B \supset C)$
2. B
———————
3. C 1, 2, MP (invalid—$B \supset C$ must first be obtained on a line by itself)

1. $P \vee (S \cdot T)$
———————
2. S 1, Simp (invalid—$S \cdot T$ must first be obtained on a line by itself)

1. K
———————
2. $K \cdot L$ 1, Add (invalid—the correct form of addition is "$K \vee L$")

1. $M \vee N$
———————
2. M 1, Simp (invalid—simplification is possible only with conjunctive premise; line 1 is a disjunction)

1. $G \supset H$
———————
2. $G \supset (H \vee J)$ 1, Add (improper—J must be added to the whole line, not just to the consequent: $(G \supset H) \vee J$)

1. $(W \supset X) \supset Y$
2. $\sim X$
___
3. $\sim W$ 1, 2, MT (invalid—$W \supset X$ must first be obtained on a line by itself)

1. $L \supset M$
2. $L \supset N$
___
3. $M \cdot N$ 1, 2, Conj (invalid—M and N must first be obtained on lines by themselves)

1. $\sim(P \cdot Q)$
___
2. $\sim P$ 1, Simp (invalid—parentheses must be removed first)

1. $\sim(P \vee Q)$
2. $\sim P$
___
3. $\sim Q$ 1, 2, DS (improper—parentheses must be removed first)

Regarding the last two examples, a rule will be presented in the next section (DeMorgan's Rule) that will allow us to remove parentheses preceded by negation signs. But even after the parentheses have been removed from these examples, the inferences remain invalid.

EXERCISE 7.2

I. Supply the required justification for the derived steps in the following proofs:

★(1)   1. $(\sim M \cdot \sim N) \supset [(\sim M \vee H) \supset (K \cdot L)]$
     2. $\sim M \cdot (C \supset D)$
     3. $\sim N \cdot (F \equiv G)$ / $K \cdot \sim N$
     4. $\sim M$ _____
     5. $\sim N$ _____
     6. $\sim M \cdot \sim N$ _____
     7. $(\sim M \vee H) \supset (K \cdot L)$ _____
     8. $\sim M \vee H$ _____
     9. $K \cdot L$ _____
   10. K _____
   11. $K \cdot \sim N$ _____

(2) 1. $(P \lor S) \supset (E \supset F)$
2. $(P \lor T) \supset (G \supset H)$
3. $(P \lor U) \supset (E \lor G)$
4. P / $F \lor H$
5. $P \lor S$ _____
6. $E \supset F$ _____
7. $P \lor T$ _____
8. $G \supset H$ _____
9. $P \lor U$ _____
10. $E \lor G$ _____
11. $(E \supset F) \cdot (G \supset H)$ _____
12. $F \lor H$ _____

(3) 1. $(S \supset Q) \cdot (Q \supset \sim S)$
2. $S \lor Q$
3. $\sim Q$ / $P \cdot R$
4. $Q \lor \sim S$ _____
5. $\sim S$ _____
6. Q _____
7. $Q \lor (P \cdot R)$ _____
8. $P \cdot R$ _____

★(4) 1. $(D \supset B) \cdot (C \supset D)$
2. $(B \supset D) \cdot (E \supset C)$
3. $B \lor E$ / $D \lor B$
4. $D \lor C$ _____
5. $B \lor D$ _____
6. $B \supset D$ _____
7. $D \supset B$ _____
8. $(B \supset D) \cdot (D \supset B)$ _____
9. $D \lor B$ _____

(5) 1. $(R \supset H) \cdot (S \supset I)$
2. $(\sim H \cdot \sim L) \supset (R \lor S)$
3. $\sim H \cdot (K \supset T)$
4. $H \lor \sim L$ / $I \lor M$
5. $\sim H$ _____
6. $\sim L$ _____
7. $\sim H \cdot \sim L$ _____
8. $R \lor S$ _____
9. $H \lor I$ _____
10. I _____
11. $I \lor M$ _____

II. Use the first eight rules of inference to derive the conclusions of the following symbolized arguments:

★(1) 1. ~M ⊃ Q
2. R ⊃ ~T
3. ~M v R   / Q v ~T

(2) 1. E ⊃ (A • C)
2. A ⊃ (F • E)
3. E   / F

(3) 1. G ⊃ (S • T)
2. (S v T) ⊃ J
3. G   / J

★(4) 1. (L v T) ⊃ (B • G)
2. L • (K ≡ R)   / L • B

(5) 1. (~F v X) ⊃ (P v T)
2. F ⊃ P
3. ~P   / T

(6) 1. (N ⊃ B) • (O ⊃ C)
2. Q ⊃ (N v O)
3. Q   / B v C

★(7) 1. (U v W) ⊃ (T ⊃ R)
2. U • H
3. ~R • ~J   / U • ~T

(8) 1. (D v E) ⊃ (G • H)
2. G ⊃ ~D
3. D • F   / M

(9) 1. (B v F) ⊃ (A ⊃ G)
2. (B v E) ⊃ (G ⊃ K)
3. B • ~H   / A ⊃ K

★(10) 1. (P ⊃ R) ⊃ (M ⊃ P)
2. (P v M) ⊃ (P ⊃ R)
3. P v M   / R v P

(11) 1. (C ⊃ N) • E
2. D v (N ⊃ D)
3. ~D   / ~C v P

(12) 1. [A v (K • J)] ⊃ (~E • ~F)
2. M ⊃ [A • (P v R)]
3. M • U   / ~E • A

★(13) 1. ~H ⊃ (~T ⊃ R)
2. H v (E ⊃ F)
3. ~T v E
4. ~H • D   / R v F

(14) 1. (U • ~ ~P) ⊃ Q
2. ~O ⊃ U
3. ~P ⊃ O
4. ~O • T   / Q

(15) 1. (M v N) ⊃ (F ⊃ G)
2. D ⊃ ~C
3. ~C ⊃ B
4. M • H
5. D v F   / B v G

★(16) 1. (F • M) ⊃ (S v T)
2. (~S v A) ⊃ F
3. (~S v B) ⊃ M
4. ~S • G   / T

(17) 1. (~K • ~N) ⊃
    [(~P ⊃ K) • (~R ⊃ G)]
2. K ⊃ N
3. ~N • B
4. ~P v ~R   / G

(18) 1. (~A v D) ⊃ (B ⊃ F)
2. (B v C) ⊃ (A ⊃ E)
3. A v B
4. ~A   / E v F

★(19) 1. (J ⊃ K) • (~O ⊃ ~P)
2. (L ⊃ J) • (~M ⊃ ~O)
3. ~K ⊃ (L v ~M)
4. ~K • G   / ~P

(20) 1. (W • X) ⊃ (Q v R)
2. (S v F) ⊃ (Q v W)
3. (S v G) ⊃ (~Q ⊃ X)
4. Q v S
5. ~Q • H   / R

III. Translate the following arguments into symbolic form and use the first eight rules of inference to derive the conclusion of each. Use the letters in the order in which they are listed.

★1. If topaz is harder than quartz, then it will scratch quartz and also feldspar. Topaz is harder than quartz and it is also harder than calcite. Therefore, either topaz will scratch quartz or it will scratch corundum. (*T, Q, F, C, O*)

2. If TV viewers send money to evangelist Jimmy Lee Swaggart and the money does not go to the starving children in Africa, then either the money does go to the starving children in Africa or Swaggart will continue to live in opulence. TV viewers do send money to evangelist Jimmy Lee Swaggart. Also, the money does not go to the starving children in Africa. Therefore, Swaggart will continue to live in opulence. (*T, A, O*)

3. If the rate at which rubidium becomes strontium or the rate at which potassium becomes argon are accurate indicators of age, then rocks from Greenland are 3.8 billion years old or rocks from the moon are 4.6 billion years old. The rate at which rubidium becomes strontium and the rate at which uranium becomes lead are accurate indicators of age. If rocks from Greenland are 3.8 billion years old, then the earth was formed more than 3.8 billion years ago; also, if rocks from the moon are 4.6 billion years old, then the earth was formed 4.6 billion years ago. If either the earth was formed more than 3.8 billion years ago or 4.6 billion years ago, then the Creationists are wrong. Therefore, the Creationists are wrong. (*R, P, G, M, U, E, F, C*)

★4. Either animals are mere mechanisms or they feel pain. If either animals feel pain or they have souls, then they have a right not to be subjected to needless pain and humans have a duty not to inflict needless pain on them. It is not the case that animals are mere mechanisms. Therefore, animals have a right not to be subjected to needless pain. (*M, P, S, R, D*)

5. If a nuclear war would destroy civilization altogether, then if either the voters elect responsible leaders or those that are elected act responsibly, then nuclear disarmament will begin immediately. If either a nuclear war would destroy civilization altogether or the development and production of nuclear weapons is an extremely profitable business, then nuclear disarmament will not begin immediately. A nuclear war would destroy civilization altogether. Therefore, it is not the case that either the voters will elect responsible leaders or those that are elected will act responsibly. (*W, V, A, D, P*)

6. If either parents get involved in their children's education or the school year is lengthened, then if the children learn phonics, their reading will improve and if they are introduced to abstract concepts earlier, their math will improve. If either parents get involved in their children's education or nebulous subjects are dropped from the curriculum, then either the children will learn phonics or they will be introduced to abstract concepts earlier. Parents will get involved in their children's education, and writing lessons will be integrated with other subjects. Therefore, either the children's reading or math will improve. (*P, S, L, R, I, M, N, W*)

★7. If either manufacturers will not concentrate on producing a superior product or they will not market their product abroad, then if they will not concentrate on producing a superior product, then the trade deficit will worsen. Either manufacturers will concentrate on producing a superior product or the trade deficit will not worsen. Manufacturers will not concentrate on producing a superior product. Therefore, today's business managers lack imagination. (C, M, T, B)

8. If either American and Soviet space scientists engage in cooperative endeavors or a student exchange is implemented, then international tensions will abate and the threat of nuclear war will diminish. If American and Soviet space scientists can identify areas of mutual interest, then they will engage in cooperative endeavors. If ideological issues can be deemphasized, a student exchange will be implemented. Either American and Soviet space scientists can identify areas of mutual interest or ideological issues can be deemphasized, and also a summit meeting will be held to discuss these issues. Therefore, international tensions will abate. (E, I, A, N, M, D, S)

9. If we are less than certain the human fetus is a person, then we must give it the benefit of the doubt. If we are certain the human fetus is a person, then we must accord it the right to live. If either we must give the fetus the benefit of the doubt or accord it the right to live, then it is not the case that we are less than certain the fetus is human and it is not merely a part of the mother's body. Either we are less than certain the human fetus is a person or we are certain about it. If we are certain the human fetus is a person, then abortion is immoral. Therefore, abortion is immoral. (L, G, C, A, M, I)

★10. If the assassination of terrorist leaders violates civilized values and also would not be effective in the long run, then if it would prevent terrorist atrocities, then it would be effective in the long run. If the assassination of terrorist leaders violates civilized values, then it would not be effective in the long run. The assassination of terrorist leaders violates civilized values and is also illegal. If the assassination of terrorist leaders would not be effective in the long run, then either it would prevent terrorist atrocities or it would justify acts of revenge by terrorists. Therefore, the assassination of terrorist leaders would justify acts of revenge by terrorists and also would not be effective in the long run. (V, E, P, I, J)

7.3 RULES OF REPLACEMENT I

The ten rules of replacement are stated in the form of logical equivalences. Underlying their use is an **axiom of replacement,** which asserts that within the context of a proof, logically equivalent expressions may replace one another. The first five rules of replacement are as follows:

9. DeMorgan's Rule (DM):

$$\sim(p \cdot q) \equiv (\sim p \lor \sim q)$$
$$\sim(p \lor q) \equiv (\sim p \cdot \sim q)$$

10. Commutativity (Com):

$$(p \lor q) \equiv (q \lor p)$$
$$(p \cdot q) \equiv (q \cdot p)$$

11. Associativity (Assoc):

$$[p \lor (q \lor r)] \equiv [(p \lor q) \lor r]$$
$$[p \cdot (q \cdot r)] \equiv [(p \cdot q) \cdot r]$$

12. Distribution (Dist):

$$[p \cdot (q \lor r)] \equiv [(p \cdot q) \lor (p \cdot r)]$$
$$[p \lor (q \cdot r)] \equiv [(p \lor q) \cdot (p \lor r)]$$

13. Double negation (DN):

$$p \equiv \mathord{\sim}\mathord{\sim}p$$

DeMorgan's Rule (named after the nineteenth-century logician Augustus DeMorgan) was discussed in Section 6.1 in connection with translation. There it was pointed out that "Not both p and q" is equivalent to "Not p or not q," and that "Not either p or q" is equivalent to "Not p and not q." When applying DeMorgan's Rule, one should keep in mind that it holds only for conjunction and disjunction (not for implication or equivalence). The rule may be summarized as follows: When moving a negation sign inside or outside a set of parentheses, "and" switches to "or," and conversely.

The **commutativity** rule asserts that the meaning of a conjunction or disjunction is unaffected by the order in which the components are listed. In other words, the component statements may be commuted, or switched for one another, without affecting the meaning. The validity of this rule should be immediately apparent. You may recall from arithmetic that the commutativity rule also applies to addition and multiplication and asserts, for example, that $3 + 5$ equals $5 + 3$, and that 2×3 equals 3×2. However, it does *not* apply to division; $2 \div 4$ does not equal $4 \div 2$. A similar lesson applies in logic: The commutativity rule applies only to conjunction and disjunction; it does *not* apply to implication.

The **associativity** rule states that the meaning of a conjunction or disjunction is unaffected by the placement of parentheses when the same connective is used throughout. In other words, the way in which the component propositions are grouped, or associated with one another, can be changed without affecting the meaning. The validity of this rule is quite easy to see, but if there is any doubt about it, it may be readily checked by means of a truth table. You may recall that the associativity rule also applies to addition and multiplication and asserts, for example, that $3 + (5 + 7)$ equals $(3 + 5) + 7$, and that $2 \times (3 \times 4)$ equals $(2 \times 3) \times 4$. But it does *not* apply to division; $(8 \div 4) \div 2$ does not equal $8 \div (4 \div 2)$. Analogously, in logic, the associativity rule applies only to conjunction and disjunction; it does *not* apply to implication. Also note, when applying this rule, that the order of the letters remains unchanged; only the placement of the parentheses changes.

The **distribution** rule, like DeMorgan's Rule, pertains only to conjunction and disjunction. In the first form of the rule, a statement is distributed through a disjunction, and in the second form, through a conjunction. While the rule may not be immediately obvious, it is easy to remember: The connective that is at first outside the parentheses goes inside, and the connective that is at first inside the parentheses goes outside. Note also how distribution differs from commutativity and associativity. The latter two rules apply only when the *same* connective (either conjunction or disjunction) is used throughout a statement. Distribution applies when conjunction and disjunction appear *together* in a statement.

The **double negation** rule is fairly obvious and needs little explanation. The rule states simply that pairs of negation signs immediately adjacent to one another may be either deleted or introduced without affecting the meaning of the statement.

There is an important difference between the rules of implication, treated in the first two sections of this chapter, and the rules of replacement. The **rules of implication** derive their name from the fact that each is an atomic argument form in which the premises imply the conclusion. To be applicable in natural deduction, certain lines in a proof must be interpreted as substitution instances of the argument form in question. Stated another way, the rules of implication are applicable only to *whole lines* in a proof. For example, step 3 in the following proof is not a legitimate application of *modus ponens,* because the first premise in the *modus ponens* rule is applied to only a *part* of line 1.

> 1. $A \supset (B \supset C)$
> 2. B
> 3. C 1, 2 MP (incorrect)

The **rules of replacement,** on the other hand, are not rules of implication but rules of equivalence. Since, by the axiom of replacement, logically equivalent statement forms can always replace one another in a proof sequence, the rules of replacement can be applied either to a whole line or to any part of a line. Step 2 in the following proof is a quite legitimate application of DeMorgan's Rule, even though the rule is applied to only part of line 1:

> 1. $S \supset \sim(T \cdot U)$
> 2. $S \supset (\sim T \vee \sim U)$ 1, DM (valid)

Another way of viewing this distinction is that the rules of implication are "one way" rules, whereas the rules of replacement are "two way" rules. The rules of implication allow us to proceed only from the premise lines of a rule to the conclusion line, but the rules of replacement allow us to replace either side of an equivalence expression with the other side.

Application of the first five rules of replacement may now be illustrated. Consider the following argument:

1. $A \supset \sim(B \cdot C)$
2. $A \cdot C$ / $\sim B$

Examining the premises, we find B in the consequent of line 1. This leads us to suspect that the conclusion can be obtained via *modus ponens.* If this is correct, the negation sign would then have to be taken inside the parentheses via DeMorgan's Rule and the resulting $\sim C$ eliminated by disjunctive syllogism. The following completed proof indicates that this strategy yields the anticipated result:

1. $A \supset \sim(B \cdot C)$
2. $A \cdot C$ / $\sim B$
3. A 2, Simp
4. $\sim(B \cdot C)$ 1, 3, MP
5. $\sim B \lor \sim C$ 4, DM
6. $C \cdot A$ 2, Com
7. C 6, Simp
8. $\sim \sim C$ 7, DN
9. $\sim C \lor \sim B$ 5, Com
10. $\sim B$ 8, 9, DS

The rationale for line 6 is to get C on the left side so that it can be separated via simplification. Similarly, the rationale for line 9 is to get $\sim C$ on the left side so that it can be eliminated via disjunctive syllogism. Line 8 is required because, strictly speaking, the negation of $\sim C$ is $\sim \sim C$—not simply C. Thus, C must be replaced with $\sim \sim C$ to set up the disjunctive syllogism. For brevity, however, these steps may be combined together with other steps, as the following shortened proof illustrates:

1. $A \supset \sim(B \cdot C)$
2. $A \cdot C$ / $\sim B$
3. A 2, Simp
4. $\sim(B \cdot C)$ 1, 3, MP
5. $\sim B \lor \sim C$ 4, DM
6. C 2, Com, Simp
7. $\sim B$ 5, 6, Com, DN, DS

Another example:

1. $D \cdot (E \lor F)$
2. $\sim D \lor \sim F$ / $D \cdot E$

The conclusion requires that we get D and E together. Inspection of the first premise suggests distribution as the first step in achieving this. The completed proof is as follows:

1. $D \cdot (E \vee F)$
2. $\sim D \vee \sim F$ $/ D \cdot E$
3. $(D \cdot E) \vee (D \cdot F)$ 1, Dist
4. $\sim(D \cdot F)$ 2, DM
5. $D \cdot E$ 3, 4, Com, DS

Sometimes it is useful to use distribution in the reverse manner. Consider this argument:

1. $(G \cdot H) \vee (G \cdot J)$
2. $(G \vee K) \supset L$ $/ L$

The conclusion can be obtained from line 2 via *modus ponens* if we first obtain $G \vee K$ on a line by itself. Since K does not occur in the first premise at all, it must be introduced by addition. To do this requires in turn that we obtain G on a line by itself. Distribution applied to line 1 provides the solution:

1. $(G \cdot H) \vee (G \cdot J)$
2. $(G \vee K) \supset L$ $/ L$
3. $G \cdot (H \vee J)$ 1, Dist
4. G 3, Simp
5. $G \vee K$ 4, Add
6. L 2, 5, MP

Application of the associativity rule is illustrated in the next proof:

1. $M \vee (N \vee O)$
2. $\sim O$ $/ M \vee N$
3. $(M \vee N) \vee O$ 1, Assoc
4. $O \vee (M \vee N)$ 3, Com
5. $M \vee N$ 2, 4, DS

Before O can be eliminated via disjunctive syllogism from line 1, it must be moved over to the left side. Associativity and communtativity together accomplish this objective.

EXERCISE 7.3

I. Supply the required justifications for the derived steps in the following proofs:

★(1)　1. $(J \lor F) \lor M$
　　　　2. $(J \lor M) \supset \sim P$
　　　　3. $\sim F$　　　　　　　$/ \sim(F \lor P)$
　　　　4. $(F \lor J) \lor M$　　　＿＿＿＿
　　　　5. $F \lor (J \lor M)$　　　＿＿＿＿
　　　　6. $J \lor M$　　　　　　　＿＿＿＿
　　　　7. $\sim P$　　　　　　　　＿＿＿＿
　　　　8. $\sim F \cdot \sim P$　　　　＿＿＿＿
　　　　9. $\sim(F \lor P)$　　　　　＿＿＿＿

　(2)　1. $(K \cdot P) \lor (K \cdot Q)$
　　　　2. $P \supset \sim K$　　　　　$/ Q \lor T$
　　　　3. $K \cdot (P \lor Q)$　　　　＿＿＿＿
　　　　4. K　　　　　　　　　　＿＿＿＿
　　　　5. $\sim\sim K$　　　　　　　＿＿＿＿
　　　　6. $\sim P$　　　　　　　　＿＿＿＿
　　　　7. $(P \lor Q) \cdot K$　　　　＿＿＿＿
　　　　8. $P \lor Q$　　　　　　　＿＿＿＿
　　　　9. Q　　　　　　　　　　＿＿＿＿
　　　10. $Q \lor T$　　　　　　　＿＿＿＿

　(3)　1. $E \lor \sim(D \lor C)$
　　　　2. $(E \lor \sim D) \supset C$　　　$/ E$
　　　　3. $E \lor (\sim D \cdot \sim C)$　　＿＿＿＿
　　　　4. $(E \lor \sim D) \cdot (E \lor \sim C)$　＿＿＿＿
　　　　5. $E \lor \sim D$　　　　　　＿＿＿＿
　　　　6. C　　　　　　　　　　＿＿＿＿
　　　　7. $(E \lor \sim C) \cdot (E \lor \sim D)$　＿＿＿＿
　　　　8. $E \lor \sim C$　　　　　　＿＿＿＿
　　　　9. $\sim C \lor E$　　　　　　＿＿＿＿
　　　10. $\sim\sim C$　　　　　　　＿＿＿＿
　　　11. E　　　　　　　　　　＿＿＿＿

★(4)　1. $(T \lor R) \lor P$
　　　　2. $(T \lor P) \supset \sim S$
　　　　3. $\sim R$　　　　　　　　$/ \sim(R \lor S)$
　　　　4. $(R \lor T) \lor P$　　　＿＿＿＿
　　　　5. $R \lor (T \lor P)$　　　＿＿＿＿
　　　　6. $T \lor P$　　　　　　　＿＿＿＿
　　　　7. $\sim S$　　　　　　　　＿＿＿＿
　　　　8. $\sim R \cdot \sim S$　　　　＿＿＿＿
　　　　9. $\sim(R \lor S)$　　　　　＿＿＿＿

(5) 1. $A \cdot (F \cdot L)$
     2. $A \supset (U \vee W)$
     3. $F \supset (U \vee X)$ / $U \vee (W \cdot X)$
     4. $(A \cdot F) \cdot L$ _____
     5. $A \cdot F$ _____
     6. A _____
     7. $U \vee W$ _____
     8. $F \cdot A$ _____
     9. F _____
     10. $U \vee X$ _____
     11. $(U \vee W) \cdot (U \vee X)$ _____
     12. $U \vee (W \cdot X)$ _____

II. Use the first thirteen rules of inference to derive the conclusions of the following symbolized arguments:

★(1) 1. $(\sim M \supset P) \cdot (\sim N \supset Q)$
      2. $\sim(M \cdot N)$ / $P \vee Q$

(2) 1. $J \vee (K \cdot L)$
     2. $\sim K$ / J

(3) 1. $R \supset \sim B$
     2. $D \vee R$
     3. B / D

★(4) 1. $(O \vee M) \supset S$
      2. $\sim S$ / $\sim M$

(5) 1. $Q \vee (L \vee C)$
     2. $\sim C$ / $L \vee Q$

(6) 1. $\sim(\sim E \cdot \sim N) \supset T$
     2. $G \supset (N \vee E)$ / $G \supset T$

★(7) 1. $H \cdot (C \cdot T)$
      2. $\sim(\sim F \cdot T)$ / F

(8) 1. $(E \cdot I) \vee (M \cdot U)$
     2. $\sim E$ / M

(9) 1. $\sim(J \vee K)$
     2. $B \supset K$
     3. $S \supset B$ / $\sim S \cdot \sim J$

★(10) 1. $(G \cdot H) \vee (M \cdot G)$
       2. $G \supset (T \cdot A)$ / A

(11) 1. $(D \cdot S) \vee (C \cdot T)$
      2. $\sim T$ / S

(12) 1. $\sim(U \vee R)$
      2. $(\sim R \vee N) \supset (P \cdot H)$
      3. $Q \supset \sim H$ / $\sim Q$

★(13) 1. ∼(F · A)
     2. ∼(L v ∼A)
     3. D ⊃ (F v L)   / ∼D

(14) 1. [(I v M) v G] ⊃ ∼G
     2. M v G   / M

(15) 1. E ⊃ ∼B
     2. U ⊃ ∼C
     3. ∼(∼E · ∼U)   / ∼(B · C)

★(16) 1. ∼(K v F)
     2. ∼F ⊃ (K v C)
     3. (G v C) ⊃ ∼H   / ∼(K v H)

(17) 1. S v (I · ∼J)
     2. S ⊃ ∼R
     3. ∼J ⊃ ∼Q   / ∼(R · Q)

(18) 1. P v (I · L)
     2. (P v I) ⊃ ∼(L v C)
     3. (P · ∼C) ⊃ (E · F)   / F v D

★(19) 1. B v (S · N)
     2. B ⊃ ∼S
     3. S ⊃ ∼N   / B v W

(20) 1. (∼M v E) ⊃ (S ⊃ U)
     2. (∼Q v E) ⊃ (U ⊃ H)
     3. ∼(M v Q)   / S ⊃ H

(21) 1. (∼R v D) ⊃ ∼(F · G)
     2. (F · R) ⊃ S
     3. F · ∼S   / ∼(S v G)

★(22) 1. ∼Q ⊃ (C · B)
     2. ∼T ⊃ (B · H)
     3. ∼(Q · T)   / B

(23) 1. ∼(A · G)
     2. ∼(A · E)
     3. G v E   / ∼(A · F)

(24) 1. (M · N) v (O · P)
     2. (N v O) ⊃ ∼P   / N

★(25) 1. (T · K) v (C · E)
     2. K ⊃ ∼E
     3. E ⊃ ∼C   / T · K

III. Translate the following arguments into symbolic form and use the first thirteen rules of inference to derive the conclusion of each. Use the translation letters in the order in which they are listed.

★1. Either health care costs are skyrocketing and they are attributable to greedy doctors, or health care costs are skyrocketing and they are attributable to greedy hospitals. If health care costs are skyrocketing, then both the government should intercede and health care may have to be rationed. Therefore, health care costs are skyrocketing and health care may have to be rationed. (S, D, H, I, R)

2. Either the ancient Etruscans were experienced city planners and they invented the art of writing or they were highly skilled engineers and they invented the art of writing. If the ancient Etruscans were bloodthirsty numbskulls (as scholars once thought), they could not have invented the art of writing. Therefore, the ancient Etruscans were not bloodthirsty numbskulls (as scholars once thought). (C, I, H, B)

3. It is not the case that either the earth's molten core is stationary or that it contains no iron. If it is not the case that both the earth's molten core is stationary and has a regular topography, then either the earth's core contains no iron or the direction of the earth's magnetic field is subject to change. Therefore, the direction of the earth's magnetic field is subject to change. (S, C, R, D)

★4. Either mosquito genes can be cloned or mosquitoes will become resistant to all insecticides and the incidence of encephalitis will increase. If either mosquito genes can be cloned or the incidence of encephalitis increases, then mosquitoes will not become resistant to all insecticides. Therefore, either mosquito genes can be cloned or mosquitoes will multiply out of control. (G, R, E, M)

5. Protein engineering will prove to be as successful as genetic engineering, and new enzymes will be developed for producing food and breaking down industrial wastes. If protein engineering proves to be as successful as genetic engineering and new enzymes are developed for breaking down industrial wastes, then it is not the case that new enzymes will be developed for producing food but not medicines. Therefore, protein engineering will prove to be as successful as genetic engineering and new enzymes will be developed for producing medicines. (E, P, B, M)

6. If workers have a fundamental right to a job (as in the Soviet Union), then unemployment will be virtually nonexistent but job redundancy will become a problem. If workers have no fundamental right to a job (as in the United States) then production efficiency will be maximized but job security will be jeopardized. Workers either have or do not have a fundamental right to a job. Therefore, either unemployment will be virtually nonexistent (as in the Soviet Union) or production efficiency will be maximized (as in the United States). (F, U, R, P, S)

★7. If Japan is to reduce its huge trade surplus, then it must either convince its citizens to spend more or it must move its manufacturing facilities to other countries. It is not the case that Japan will either increase its imports or convince its citizens to spend more. Furthermore, it is not the case that Japan will either allow foreign construction companies to compete on an equal footing or move its manufacturing facilities to other countries. Therefore, Japan will not reduce its huge trade surplus. (R, C, M, I, A)

8. If women were incapable of thinking either logically or analytically, then there would be no women logicians. If men were incapable of either nurturing or caring for children, then there would be no preschool teachers who are men. But it is not the case that there are either no women logicians or no preschool teachers who are men. Therefore, it is not the case that either women are incapable of thinking analytically or men are incapable of caring for children. (*L, A, W, N, C, P*)

9. It is not the case that either the sun's interior rotates faster than its surface or Einstein's general theory of relativity is wrong. If the sun's interior does not rotate faster than its surface and eccentricities in the orbit of Mercury can be explained by solar gravitation, then Einstein's general theory of relativity is wrong. Therefore, eccentricities in the orbit of Mercury cannot be explained by solar gravitation. (*S, E, M, G*)

★10. Either school dropout programs are not as effective as they could be, or they provide basic thinking skills and psychological counseling to their students. Either school dropout programs are not as effective as they could be, or they adequately prepare their students for getting a job and working effectively with others. Either school dropout programs do not provide psychological counseling to their students or they do not provide adequate preparation for working effectively with others. Therefore, school dropout programs are not as effective as they could be. (*E, B, P, G, W*)

7.4 RULES OF REPLACEMENT II

The remaining five rules of replacement are as follows:

14. Transposition (Trans):

$$(p \supset q) \equiv (\sim q \supset \sim p)$$

15. Material implication (Impl):

$$(p \supset q) \equiv (\sim p \lor q)$$

16. Material equivalence (Equiv):

$$(p \equiv q) \equiv [(p \supset q) \cdot (q \supset p)]$$
$$(p \equiv q) \equiv [(p \cdot q) \lor (\sim p \cdot \sim q)]$$

17. Exportation (Exp):

$$[(p \cdot q) \supset r] \equiv [p \supset (q \supset r)]$$

18. Tautology (Taut):

$$p \equiv (p \lor p)$$
$$p \equiv (p \cdot p)$$

Transposition was first mentioned in Section 6.1, where it was introduced to assist in translation. The rule is fairly easy to understand and is provable via *modus tollens*. In applying the rule one need only remember that antecedent and consequent may switch places if and only if both are negated.

The rule of **material implication** is less obvious than transposition, but it can be illustrated by substituting actual statements in place of the letters. A little reflection should disclose that the statement "If you don't leave me alone, then I'll punch you in the nose" $(D \supset P)$ is logically equivalent to "Either you leave me alone or I'll punch you in the nose" $(\sim D \lor P)$. The rule states that an implication sign may be replaced by a disjunction sign if the left-hand component is negated, and the reverse replacement is allowed if a negation sign is deleted from the left-hand component.

The **material equivalence** rule has two formulations. The first is the same as the definition of material equivalence given in Section 6.1. The second formulation is easy to remember through recalling the two ways in which $p \equiv q$ may be true. Either p and q are both true or p and q are both false. This, of course, is the meaning of $[(p \cdot q) \lor (\sim p \cdot \sim q)]$.

The **exportation** rule is also fairly easy to understand. It asserts that the statement "If we have p, then if we have q we have r" is logically equivalent to "If we have both p and q, we have r." Upon consideration, this rule should appear reasonable.

The last rule, **tautology,** is obvious. Its effect is to eliminate redundancy in disjunctions and conjunctions.

The following proofs illustrate the use of these five rules.

1. $\sim A$ / $A \supset B$

In this argument the conclusion contains a letter not found in the premise. Obviously, addition must be used to introduce the B. The material implication rule completes the proof:

1. $\sim A$ / $A \supset B$
2. $\sim A \lor B$ 1, Add
3. $A \supset B$ 2, Impl

Here is another example:

1. $F \supset G$
2. $F \lor G$ / G

To derive the conclusion of this argument, some method must be found to link the two premises together and eliminate the F. Hypothetical syllogism provides the solution, but first the second premise must be converted into a conditional. Here is the proof:

1. $F \supset G$
2. $F \lor G$ / G
3. $\sim F \supset G$ 2, DN, Impl
4. $\sim G \supset F$ 3, Trans, DN
5. $\sim G \supset G$ 1, 4, HS
6. $G \lor G$ 5, Impl, DN
7. G 6, Taut

Another example:

    1. $J \supset (K \supset L)$ $/ K \supset (J \supset L)$

The conclusion can be obtained by simply rearranging the components of the single premise. Exportation provides the simplest method:

    1. $J \supset (K \supset L)$ $/ K \supset (J \supset L)$
    2. $(J \cdot K) \supset L$ 1, Exp
    3. $(K \cdot J) \supset L$ 2, Com
    4. $K \supset (J \supset L)$ 3, Exp

Another example:

    1. $M \supset N$
    2. $M \supset O$ $/ M \supset (N \cdot O)$

As with the second example above, some method must be found to link the two premises together. In this case, however, hypothetical syllogism will not work. The solution lies in setting up a distribution step:

    1. $M \supset N$
    2. $M \supset O$ $/ M \supset (N \cdot O)$
    3. $\sim M \lor N$ 1, Impl
    4. $\sim M \lor O$ 2, Impl
    5. $(\sim M \lor N) \cdot (\sim M \lor O)$ 3, 4, Conj
    6. $\sim M \lor (N \cdot O)$ 5, Dist
    7. $M \supset (N \cdot O)$ 6, Impl

Another example:

    1. $P \supset Q$
    2. $R \supset (S \cdot T)$
    3. $\sim R \supset \sim Q$
    4. $S \supset (T \supset P)$ $/ P \equiv R$

The conclusion is a biconditional, and there are only two ways that a biconditional can be obtained; namely, via the two formulations of the material equivalence rule. The fact that the premises are all conditional statements suggests the first formulation of this rule. Accordingly, we must try to obtain $P \supset R$ and $R \supset P$. Again, the fact that the premises are themselves conditionals suggests hypothetical syllogism to accomplish this. Premises 1 and 3 can be used to set up one hypothetical syllogism; premises 2 and 4 provide the other. Here is the proof:

    1. $P \supset Q$
    2. $R \supset (S \cdot T)$
    3. $\sim R \supset \sim Q$

4. $S \supset (T \supset P)$ $/ P \equiv R$
5. $Q \supset R$ 3, Trans
6. $P \supset R$ 1, 5, HS
7. $(S \cdot T) \supset P$ 4, Exp
8. $R \supset P$ 2, 7, HS
9. $(P \supset R) \cdot (R \supset P)$ 6, 8, Conj
10. $P \equiv R$ 9, Equiv

Occasionally, mere inspection of the premises of an argument provides little insight into how the conclusion should be derived. In such cases it often helps to apply the rules of replacement to the conclusion with the aim of bridging the gap between it and the premises. Once this is done, the strategy to be used for deriving the conclusion should become evident. Because the rules of replacement are biconditionals, the same rules applied to the conclusion may then be used in reverse order on the premises. For example, consider the following argument:

1. $K \supset M$
2. $L \supset M$ $/ (K \lor L) \supset M$

If it is not clear upon first inspection exactly how the conclusion of this argument should be derived, we may be able to obtain some insight by applying the rules of replacement to the conclusion and then attempting to work backward toward the premises. Beginning with the implication rule, we proceed as follows:

1. $(K \lor L) \supset M$
2. $\sim(K \lor L) \lor M$ 1, Impl
3. $(\sim K \cdot \sim L) \lor M$ 2, DM
4. $(\sim K \lor M) \cdot (\sim L \lor M)$ 3, Com, Dist, Com
5. $(K \supset M) \cdot (L \supset M)$ 4, Impl

Comparing line 5 with the original premises, it should now be completely clear how to proceed. The proof is as follows:

1. $K \supset M$
2. $L \supset M$ $/ (K \lor L) \supset M$
3. $(K \supset M) \cdot (L \supset M)$ 1, Conj
4. $(\sim K \lor M) \cdot (\sim L \lor M)$ 3, Impl
5. $(\sim K \cdot \sim L) \lor M$ 4, Com, Dist, Com
6. $\sim(K \lor L) \lor M$ 5, DM
7. $(K \lor L) \supset M$ 6, Impl

EXERCISE 7.4

I. Supply the required justifications for the derived steps in the following arguments.

★(1) 1. $K \equiv R$
      2. $K \supset (R \supset P)$
      3. $\sim P$ / $\sim R$
      4. $(K \cdot R) \vee (\sim K \cdot \sim R)$ _____
      5. $(K \cdot R) \supset P$ _____
      6. $\sim(K \cdot R)$ _____
      7. $\sim K \cdot \sim R$ _____
      8. $\sim R \cdot \sim K$ _____
      9. $\sim R$ _____

(2) 1. $C \supset (\sim L \supset Q)$
     2. $L \supset \sim C$
     3. $\sim Q$ / $\sim C$
     4. $(C \cdot \sim L) \supset Q$ _____
     5. $\sim(C \cdot \sim L)$ _____
     6. $\sim C \vee \sim \sim L$ _____
     7. $\sim C \vee L$ _____
     8. $C \supset L$ _____
     9. $C \supset \sim C$ _____
     10. $\sim C \vee \sim C$ _____
     11. $\sim C$ _____

(3) 1. $(E \supset A) \cdot (F \supset A)$
     2. $E \vee G$
     3. $F \vee \sim G$ / A
     4. $\sim E \supset G$ _____
     5. $\sim F \supset \sim G$ _____
     6. $G \supset F$ _____
     7. $\sim E \supset F$ _____
     8. $\sim \sim E \vee F$ _____
     9. $E \vee F$ _____
     10. $A \vee A$ _____
     11. A _____

★(4) 1. $(F \cdot H) \supset N$
      2. $F \vee S$
      3. H / $N \vee S$
      4. $(H \cdot F) \supset N$ _____
      5. $H \supset (F \supset N)$ _____
      6. $F \supset N$ _____
      7. $\sim N \supset \sim F$ _____
      8. $\sim F \supset S$ _____
      9. $\sim N \supset S$ _____
      10. $\sim \sim N \vee S$ _____
      11. $N \vee S$ _____

(5) 1. $T \supset (H \cdot J)$
     2. $(H \vee N) \supset T$ / $T \equiv H$
     3. $\sim T \vee (H \cdot J)$ _____
     4. $(\sim T \vee H) \cdot (\sim T \vee J)$ _____
     5. $\sim T \vee H$ _____

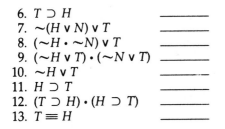

6. $T \supset H$ _____

7. $\sim(H \lor N) \lor T$ _____

8. $(\sim H \cdot \sim N) \lor T$ _____

9. $(\sim H \lor T) \cdot (\sim N \lor T)$ _____

10. $\sim H \lor T$ _____

11. $H \supset T$ _____

12. $(T \supset H) \cdot (H \supset T)$ _____

13. $T \equiv H$ _____

II. Use the eighteen rules of inference to derive the conclusions of the following symbolized arguments:

★(1) 1. $(J \cdot R) \supset H$
    2. $(R \supset H) \supset M$
    3. $\sim(P \lor \sim J)$ $/ M \cdot \sim P$

(2) 1. $(B \supset G) \cdot (F \supset N)$
    2. $\sim(G \cdot N)$ $/ \sim(B \cdot F)$

(3) 1. T $/ S \supset T$

★(4) 1. $\sim(U \cdot W) \supset X$
    2. $U \supset \sim U$ $/ \sim(U \lor \sim X)$

(5) 1. $(O \supset C) \cdot (\sim S \supset \sim D)$
    2. $(E \supset D) \cdot (\sim E \supset \sim C)$ $/ O \supset S$

(6) 1. $T \supset R$
    2. $T \supset \sim R$ $/ \sim T$

★(7) 1. $M \supset (U \supset H)$
    2. $(H \lor \sim U) \supset F$ $/ M \supset F$

(8) 1. $S \lor \sim N$
    2. $\sim S \lor Q$ $/ N \supset Q$

(9) 1. $\sim R \lor P$
    2. $R \lor \sim P$ $/ R \equiv P$

★(10) 1. $J \supset (G \supset L)$ $/ G \supset (J \supset L)$

(11) 1. $\sim B \supset H$
    2. $\sim D \supset H$
    3. $\sim(B \cdot D)$ $/ H$

(12) 1. $S \supset (L \cdot M)$
    2. $M \supset (L \supset R)$ $/ S \supset R$

★(13) 1. $(I \supset E) \supset C$
    2. $C \supset \sim C$ $/ I$

(14) 1. $F \supset (A \cdot K)$
    2. $G \supset (\sim A \cdot \sim K)$
    3. $F \lor G$ $/ A \equiv K$

(15) 1. $T \supset G$
    2. $S \supset G$ $/ (T \lor S) \supset G$

★(16) 1. $Q \supset (W \cdot D)$ / $Q \supset W$

(17) 1. $H \supset U$ / $H \supset (U \vee T)$

(18) 1. $P \supset (\sim E \supset B)$
2. $\sim(B \vee E)$ / $\sim P$

★(19) 1. $I \vee (N \cdot F)$
2. $I \supset F$ / F

(20) 1. $(G \supset J) \supset (H \supset Q)$
2. $J \cdot \sim Q$ / $\sim H$

(21) 1. $T \supset \sim(A \supset N)$
2. $T \vee N$ / $T \equiv \sim N$

★(22) 1. $(O \supset R) \supset S$
2. $(P \supset R) \supset \sim S$ / $\sim R$

(23) 1. $(D \supset E) \supset (E \supset D)$
2. $(D \equiv E) \supset \sim(G \cdot \sim H)$
3. $E \cdot G$ / $G \cdot H$

(24) 1. $(L \vee P) \supset U$
2. $(M \supset U) \supset I$
3. P / I

★(25) 1. $(S \vee T) \supset (S \supset \sim T)$
2. $(S \supset \sim T) \supset (T \supset K)$
3. $S \vee T$ / $S \vee K$

(26) 1. $A \equiv W$
2. $\sim A \vee \sim W$
3. $R \supset A$ / $\sim(W \vee R)$

(27) 1. $G \equiv M$
2. $G \vee M$
3. $G \supset (M \supset T)$ / T

★(28) 1. $H \equiv I$
2. $H \supset (I \supset F)$
3. $\sim(H \vee I) \supset F$ / F

(29) 1. $O \supset (Q \cdot N)$
2. $(N \vee E) \supset S$ / $O \supset S$

★(30) 1. $P \supset A$
2. $Q \supset B$ / $(P \vee Q) \supset (A \vee B)$

III. Translate the following arguments into symbolic form and use the eighteen rules of inference to derive the conclusion of each. Use the translation letters in the order in which they are listed.

★1. If sports shoe manufacturers decline to use kangaroo hides in their products, then Australian hunters will cease killing millions of kangaroos yearly. It is not the case that both Australian hunters will cease killing millions of kangaroos yearly and the kangaroo not be saved from extinction. Therefore, if sports shoe manufacturers decline to use kangaroo hides in their products, then the kangaroo will be saved from extinction. (D, C, S)

2. If there were a direct correlation between what a nation spends for health care and the health of its citizens, then America would have the lowest incidence of disease and the lowest mortality rates of any nation on earth. But America does not have the lowest mortality rates of any nation on earth. Therefore, there is not a direct correlation between what a nation spends for health care and the health of its citizens. (C, D, M)

3. It is not the case that strict controls exist on either the manufacture or the sale of handguns. Therefore, if strict controls existed on the sale of handguns, then the use of handguns in the commission of crimes would decrease. (M, S, U)

★4. If birth control devices are made available in high school clinics, then the incidence of teenage pregnancy will decrease. Therefore, if both birth control information and birth control devices are made available in high school clinics, then the incidence of teenage pregnancy will decrease. (D, P, I)

5. If Congress enacts a law that either establishes a religion or prohibits the free exercise of religion, then that law is unconstitutional. Therefore, if Congress enacts a law that establishes a religion, then that law is unconstitutional. (E, P, U)

6. If cigarette smokers are warned of the hazards of smoking and they continue to smoke, then they cannot sue tobacco companies for any resulting lung cancer or emphysema. Cigarette smokers are warned of the hazards of smoking. Therefore, if cigarette smokers continue to smoke, they cannot sue tobacco companies for any resulting lung cancer or emphysema. (W, C, S)

★7. If grade school children are assigned daily homework, then their achievement level will increase dramatically. But if grade school children are assigned daily homework, then their love for learning may be dampened. Therefore, if grade school children are assigned daily homework, then their achievement level will increase dramatically but their love for learning may be dampened. (G, A, L)

8. If a superconducting particle collider is built, then the data it could yield would benefit scientists of all nations and it deserves international funding. Either a superconducting particle collider will be built, or the ultimate nature of matter will remain hidden and the data it could yield would benefit scientists of all nations. Therefore, the data a superconducting particle collider could yield would benefit scientists of all nations. (S, D, I, U)

9. If parents are told that their unborn child has Tay-Sachs disease, then if they go ahead with the birth, then they are responsible for their child's pain and suffering. Therefore, if parents are not responsible for their child's pain and suffering, then if they go ahead with the birth, then they were not told that their unborn child had Tay-Sachs disease. (T, G, R)

★10. "Star Wars" provides protection against nuclear attack and should be deployed if and only if it can shoot down cruise missiles. But it is not the case that either "Star Wars" can shoot down cruise missiles or it does not provide protection against nuclear attack. Therefore, "Star Wars" should not be deployed. (*P, D, C*)

7.5 CONDITIONAL PROOF

Conditional proof is a method for obtaining a line in a proof sequence (either the conclusion or some intermediate line) that frequently offers the advantage of being both shorter and simpler to use than the conventional method. Moreover, there are a number of arguments having conclusions that cannot be derived by the conventional method, so some form of conditional proof must be used on them. While in theory the method of conditional proof can be used to derive any line in a proof sequence, in practice it is usually reserved for obtaining lines that are expressed in the form of conditional statements. The method consists in assuming the antecedent of the required conditional statement on one line, deriving the consequent on a subsequent line, and then "discharging" this sequence of lines in a conditional statement that exactly replicates the one that was to be obtained.

Any argument whose conclusion is a conditional statement is an immediate candidate for conditional proof. Consider the following example:

1. $A \supset (B \cdot C)$
2. $(B \lor D) \supset E$ / $A \supset E$

Using the conventional method to derive the conclusion of this argument would require a proof having at least twelve lines, and the precise strategy to be followed in constructing it might not be immediately obvious. Nevertheless, we need only give cursory inspection to the argument to see that the conclusion does indeed follow from the premises. The conclusion states that if we have A, we then have E. Let us suppose, for a moment, that we do have A. We could then obtain $B \cdot C$ from the first premise via *modus ponens*. Simplifying this expression we could obtain B, and from this we could get $B \lor D$ via addition. E would then follow from the second premise via *modus ponens*. In other words, if we assume that we have A, we can get E. But this is exactly what the conclusion says; in other words, we have just proved that the conclusion follows from the premises.

The method of conditional proof consists of incorporating this simple thought process into the body of a proof sequence. A conditional proof for this argument requires only eight lines and is substantially simpler than a proof constructed by the conventional method:

1. $A \supset (B \cdot C)$

$$2. \ (B \lor D) \supset E \qquad / \ A \supset E$$

3. A	ACP
4. $B \cdot C$	1, 3, MP
5. B	4, Simp
6. $B \lor D$	5, Add
7. E	2, 6, MP

$$8. \ A \supset E \qquad\qquad 3\text{-}7, \text{CP}$$

Lines 3 through 7 are indented to indicate their hypothetical character: they all depend on the assumption introduced in line 3 via "Assump." These lines, which constitute the conditional proof sequence, tell us that if we assume A (line 3), we can obtain E (line 7). In line 8 the conditional sequence is discharged in the conditional statement $A \supset E$, which simply reiterates the result of the conditional sequence. Since line 8 is not hypothetical, it is written adjacent to the original margin, under lines 1 and 2. A vertical line is added to the conditional sequence to emphasize the indentation.

The first step in constructing a conditional proof is to decide what should be assumed on the first line of the conditional sequence. While any statement whatsoever *can* be assumed on this line, only the right statement will lead to the desired result. The clue is always provided by the conditional statement to be obtained in the end. The antecedent of this statement is what must be assumed. For example, if the statement to be obtained is $(K \cdot L) \supset M$, then $K \cdot L$ should be assumed on the first line. This line is always indented and tagged with the designation "Assump." Once the initial assumption has been made, the second step is to obtain the consequent of the desired conditional statement at the end of the conditional sequence. To do this, we simply apply the ordinary rules of inference to any previous line in the proof (including the assumed line), writing the result directly below the assumed line. The third and final step is to discharge the conditional sequence in a conditional statement. The antecedent of this conditional statement is whatever appears on the first line of the conditional sequence, and the consequent is whatever appears on the last line. For example, if $A \lor B$ is on the first line and $C \cdot D$ is on the last, the sequence is discharged by $(A \lor B) \supset (C \cdot D)$. This discharging line is always written adjacent to the original margin and is tagged with the designation "CP" (conditional proof) together with the numerals corresponding to the first and last lines of the sequence.

I suggested earlier that conditional proof can be used to obtain a line other than the conclusion of an argument. The following proof, which illustrates this fact, incorporates two conditional sequences, one after the other, within the scope of a single conventional proof:

1. $G \supset (H \cdot I)$	
2. $J \supset (K \cdot L)$	
3. $G \lor J$	/ $H \lor K$
4. G	ACP

	5. $H \cdot I$	1, 4, MP
	6. H	5, Simp
7. $G \supset H$		4–6, CP
	8. J	ACP
	9. $K \cdot L$	2, 8, MP
	10. K	9, Simp
11. $J \supset K$		8–10, CP
12. $(G \supset H) \cdot (J \supset K)$		7, 11, Conj
13. $H \vee K$		3, 12, CD

The first conditional proof sequence gives us $G \supset H$, and the second $J \supset K$. These two lines are then conjoined and used together with line 3 to set up a constructive dilemma, from which the conclusion is obtained.

This proof sequence provides a convenient opportunity to introduce an important rule governing conditional proof. The rule states that after a conditional proof sequence has been discharged, no line in the sequence may be used as a reason for a subsequent line in the proof. If, for example, line 5 in the above proof were used as a reason in support of line 9 or line 12, this rule would be violated, and the corresponding inference would be invalid. Once the conditional sequence is discharged, it is sealed off from the remaining part of the proof. The logic behind this rule is easy to understand. The lines in a conditional sequence are hypothetical in that they depend on the assumption stated in the first line. Because no mere assumption can provide any genuine support for anything, neither can any line that depends on such an assumption. When a conditional sequence is discharged, the assumption upon which it rests is expressed as the antecedent of a conditional statement. This conditional statement *can* be used to support subsequent lines because it makes no claim that its antecedent is true. The conditional statement merely asserts that *if* its antecedent is true, then its consequent is true, and this, of course, is what has been established by the conditional sequence from which it is obtained.

Just as a conditional sequence can be used within the scope of a conventional proof to obtain a desired statement form, one conditional sequence can be used within the scope of another to obtain a desired statement form. The following proof provides an example:

1. $L \supset [M \supset (N \vee O)]$	
2. $M \supset \sim N$	/ $L \supset (\sim M \vee O)$
3. L	ACP
4. $M \supset (N \vee O)$	1, 3, MP
5. M	ACP
6. $N \vee O$	4, 5, MP
7. $\sim N$	2, 5, MP
8. O	6, 7, DS
9. $M \supset O$	5–8, CP
10. $\sim M \vee O$	9, Impl
11. $L \supset (\sim M \vee O)$	3–10, CP

The rule introduced in connection with the previous example applies unchanged to examples of this sort. No line in the sequence 5–8 could be used to support any line subsequent to line 9, and no line in the sequence 3–10 could be used to support any line subsequent to line 11. Line 3 or 4 could, of course, be used to support any line in the sequence 5–8.

One final reminder regarding conditional proof is that every conditional proof must be discharged. It is absolutely improper to end a proof on an indented line. If this rule is ignored, any conclusion one chooses can be derived from any set of premises. The following invalid proof illustrates this mistake:

1. P $/ Q \supset R$
2. $\sim Q$ ACP
3. $\sim Q \vee R$ 2, Add
4. $Q \supset R$ 2, Impl

EXERCISE 7.5

I. Use conditional proof and the eighteen rules of inference to derive the conclusions of the following symbolized arguments. Having done so, attempt to derive the conclusions without using conditional proof.

★(1) 1. $N \supset O$
     2. $N \supset P$ $/ N \supset (O \cdot P)$

(2) 1. $F \supset E$
     2. $(F \cdot E) \supset R$ $/ F \supset R$

(3) 1. $G \supset T$
     2. $(T \vee S) \supset K$ $/ G \supset K$

★(4) 1. $(G \vee H) \supset (S \cdot T)$
     2. $(T \vee U) \supset (C \cdot D)$ $/ G \supset C$

(5) 1. $A \supset \sim(A \vee E)$ $/ A \supset F$

(6) 1. $J \supset (K \supset L)$
     2. $J \supset (M \supset L)$
     3. $\sim L$ $/ J \supset \sim(K \vee M)$

★(7) 1. $M \vee (N \cdot O)$ $/ \sim N \supset M$

(8) 1. $P \supset (Q \vee R)$
     2. $(P \supset R) \supset (S \cdot T)$
     $\sim \supset R$ $/ T$

(9) 1. $H \supset (I \supset N)$
     2. $(H \supset \sim I) \supset (M \vee N)$
     3. $\sim N$ $/ M$

★(10) 1. $C \supset (A \cdot D)$
     2. $B \supset (A \cdot E)$ $/ (C \vee B) \supset A$

(11) 1. $M \supset (K \supset L)$
    2. $(L \lor N) \supset J$ / $M \supset (K \supset J)$

(12) 1. $F \supset (G \cdot H)$ / $(A \supset F) \supset (A \supset H)$

★(13) 1. $R \supset B$
    2. $R \supset (B \supset F)$
    3. $B \supset (F \supset H)$ / $R \supset H$

(14) 1. $(F \cdot G) \equiv H$
    2. $F \supset G$ / $F \equiv H$

(15) 1. $C \supset (D \lor \sim E)$
    2. $E \supset (D \supset F)$ / $C \supset (E \supset F)$

★(16) 1. $Q \supset (R \supset S)$
    2. $Q \supset (T \supset \sim U)$
    3. $U \supset (R \lor T)$ / $Q \supset (U \supset S)$

(17) 1. $N \supset (O \cdot P)$
    2. $Q \supset (R \cdot S)$ / $(P \supset Q) \supset (N \supset S)$

(18) 1. $E \supset (F \supset G)$
    2. $H \supset (G \supset I)$
    3. $(F \supset I) \supset (J \lor \sim H)$ / $(E \cdot H) \supset J$

★(19) 1. $P \supset [(L \lor M) \supset (N \cdot O)]$
    2. $(O \lor T) \supset W$ / $P \supset (M \supset W)$

(20) 1. $A \supset [B \supset (C \cdot \sim D)]$
    2. $(B \lor E) \supset (D \lor E)$ / $(A \cdot B) \supset (C \cdot E)$

II. Translate the following arguments into symbolic form, using the letters in the order in which they are listed. Then use conditional proof and the eighteen rules of inference to derive the conclusion of each. Having done so, attempt to derive the conclusion without using conditional proof.

★1. If high-tech products are exported to the Soviet Union, then domestic industries will benefit. If the Soviets can effectively utilize high-tech products, then their standard of living will improve. Therefore, if high-tech products are exported to the Soviet Union and the Soviets can effectively utilize them, then their standard of living will improve and domestic industries will benefit. (*H, D, U, S*)

2. If the police take you into custody, then if they inform you that you have the right to remain silent, then whatever you say will be used against you. If the police inform you that you have the right to remain silent, then if whatever you say will be used against you, then you should not say anything. Therefore, if the police take you into custody, then if they inform you that you have the right to remain silent, then you should not say anything. (*P, I, W, S*)

3. A doctor must disconnect a dying patient from a respirator if and only if the fact that patients are self-determining implies that the doctor must follow the patient's orders. If a dying patient refuses treatment, then the doctor must disconnect the patient from a respirator and the patient will

die peacefully. Patients are self-determining. Therefore, if a dying patient refuses treatment, then the doctor must follow the patient's orders. (*D, S, F, R, P*)

★4. If jails are overcrowded, then dangerous suspects will be released on their own recognizance. If jails are overcrowded and dangerous suspects are released on their own recognizance, then crime will increase. If no new jails are built and crime increases, then innocent victims will pay the price of crime. Therefore, if jails are overcrowded, then if no new jails are built, then innocent victims will pay the price of crime. (*J, D, C, N, I*)

5. If astronauts attempt interplanetary space travel, then heavy shielding will be required to protect them from solar radiation. If massive amounts of either fuel or water must be carried, then the space craft will have to be very large. Therefore, if the fact that heavy shielding will be required to protect the astronauts from solar radiation implies that massive amounts of fuel must be carried, then if astronauts attempt interplanetary space travel, then the space craft must be very large. (*A, H, F, W, L*)

7.6 INDIRECT PROOF

Indirect proof is a variety of conditional proof that can be used on any argument to derive either the conclusion or some intermediate line leading to the conclusion. It consists in assuming the negation of the statement form to be obtained, using this assumption to derive a contradiction, and then concluding that the original assumption is false. This last step, of course, establishes the truth of the statement form to be obtained. The following proof sequence uses indirect proof to derive the conclusion:

$$
\begin{array}{lll}
1. & (A \lor B) \supset (C \cdot D) & \\
2. & C \supset {\sim}D & / \sim A \\
& \quad 3. \; A & \text{AIP} \\
& \quad 4. \; A \lor B & \text{3, Add} \\
& \quad 5. \; C \cdot D & \text{1, 4, MP} \\
& \quad 6. \; C & \text{5, Simp} \\
& \quad 7. \; {\sim}D & \text{2, 6, MP} \\
& \quad 8. \; D & \text{5, Com, Simp} \\
& \quad 9. \; D \cdot {\sim}D & \text{7, 8, Conj} \\
10. & \quad {\sim}A & \text{3-9, IP}
\end{array}
$$

The indirect proof sequence (lines 3-9) begins by assuming the negation of the conclusion. This assumption, which is tagged "AIP" (assumption for indirect proof), leads to a contradiction in line 9. Since any assumption that leads to a contradiction is false, the indirect sequence is discharged (line 10) by asserting the negation of the assumption made in line 3. This line is then tagged with the designation "IP" (indirect proof) together with the numerals indicating the scope of the indirect sequence from which it is obtained.

Indirect proof can also be used to derive an intermediate line leading to the conclusion. Example:

1. $E \supset [(F \lor G) \supset (H \cdot J)]$
2. $E \cdot \sim(J \lor K)$ / $\sim(F \lor K)$
3. E 2, Simp
4. $(F \lor G) \supset (H \cdot J)$ 1, 3, MP
5. $\sim(J \lor K)$ 2, Com, Simp
6. $\sim J \cdot \sim K$ 5, DM
      | 7. F AIP
      | 8. $F \lor G$ 7, Add
      | 9. $H \cdot J$ 4, 8, MP
      | 10. J 9, Com, Simp
      | 11. $\sim J$ 6, Simp
      | 12. $J \cdot \sim J$ 10, 11, Conj
13. $\sim F$ 7–12, IP
14. $\sim K$ 6, Com, Simp
15. $\sim F \cdot \sim K$ 13, 14, Conj
16. $\sim(F \lor K)$ 15, DM

The indirect proof sequence begins with the assumption of F (line 7), leads to a contradiction (line 12), and is discharged (line 13) by asserting the negation of the assumption.

As with conditional proof, when an indirect proof sequence is discharged, no line in the sequence may be used as a justification for a subsequent line in the proof. In reference to the above proof, this means that none of the lines 7–12 could be used as a justification for any of the lines 14–16. Occasionally, this rule requires certain priorities in the derivation of lines. For example, for the purpose of deriving the contradiction, lines 5 and 6 could have been included as part of the indirect sequence. But this would not have been advisable because line 6 is needed as a justification for line 14, which lies outside the indirect sequence. If lines 5 and 6 had been included within the indirect sequence, they would have had to be repeated after the sequence had been discharged to allow $\sim K$ to be obtained on a line outside the sequence.

Just as a conditional sequence may be constructed within the scope of another conditional sequence, so a conditional sequence can be constructed within the scope of an indirect sequence, and, conversely, an indirect sequence may be constructed within the scope of either a conditional sequence or another indirect sequence. The next example illustrates the use of an indirect sequence within the scope of a conditional sequence:

1. $L \supset [\sim M \supset (N \cdot O)]$
2. $\sim N \cdot P$ $/ L \supset (M \cdot P)$
    3. L ACP
    4. $\sim M \supset (N \cdot O)$ 1, 3, MP
       5. $\sim M$ AIP
       6. $N \cdot O$ 4, 5, MP
       7. N 6, Simp
       8. $\sim N$ 2, Simp
       9. $N \cdot \sim N$ 7, 8, Conj
    10. $\sim \sim M$ 5–9, IP
    11. M 10, DN
    12. P 2, Com, Simp
    13. $M \cdot P$ 11, 12, Conj
14. $L \supset (M \cdot P)$ 3–13, CP

The indirect sequence (lines 5–9) is discharged (line 10) by asserting the negation of the assumption made in line 5. Technically, the double negation step (line 11) is required, but it could be incorporated into line 10. The conditional sequence (lines 3–13) is discharged (line 14) in the conditional statement that has the first line of the sequence as its antecedent and the last line as its consequent.

Indirect proof provides a convenient way for proving the validity of an argument having a tautology for its conclusion. In fact, the only way in which the conclusion of such an argument can be derived (assuming the premises of the argument are not self-contradictory) is through either conditional or indirect proof.

For the following argument, indirect proof is the easier of the two:

1. S $/ T \vee \sim T$
    2. $\sim (T \vee \sim T)$ AIP
    3. $\sim T \cdot \sim \sim T$ 2, DM
4. $\sim \sim (T \vee \sim T)$ 2–3, IP
5. $T \vee \sim T$ 4, DN

Here is another example of an argument having a tautology as its conclusion. In this case, since the conclusion is a conditional statement, conditional proof is the easier alternative:

1. S $/ T \supset T$
    2. T ACP
    3. $T \vee T$ 2, Add
    4. T 3, Taut
5. $T \supset T$ 2–4, CP

I mentioned earlier that indirect proof is really a variety of conditional proof. This fact may be illustrated by returning to the first example presented in this section. In the proof that follows, conditional proof—not indirect proof—is used to obtain the conclusion:

```
 1. (A v B) ⊃ (C · D)
 2. C ⊃ ~D              / ~A
      3. A              ACP
      4. A v B          3, Add
      5. C · D          1, 4, MP
      6. C              5, Simp
      7. ~D             2, 6, MP
      8. D              5, Com, Simp
      9. D v ~A         8, Add
     10. ~A             7, 9, DS
11. A ⊃ ~A              3–10, CP
12. ~A v ~A             11, Impl
13.  ~A                 12, Taut
```

This example illustrates how a conditional proof can be used to derive the conclusion of *any* argument, whether or not the conclusion is a conditional statement. Simply begin by assuming the negation of the conclusion, derive contradictory statements on separate lines, and use these lines to set up a disjunctive syllogism yielding the negation of the assumption as the last line of the conditional sequence. Then, discharge the sequence and use tautology to obtain the negation of the assumption outside the sequence.

Indirect proof is a variety of conditional proof in that it amounts to a modification of the way in which the indented sequence is discharged, resulting in an overall shortening of the proof for many arguments. The indirect proof for the argument above is repeated below, with the requisite changes noted in the margin:

```
 1. (A v B) ⊃ (C · D)
 2. C ⊃ ~D              / ~A
      3. A              AIP
      4. A v B          3, Add
      5. C · D          1, 4, MP
      6. C              5, Simp
      7. ~D             2, 6, MP
      8. D              5, Com, Simp
      9. D · ~D         7, 8, Conj  ⎫
10.  ~A                 3–9, IP     ⎬——changed
                                    ⎭
```

The reminder at the end of the previous section regarding conditional proof pertains to indirect proof as well: It is essential that every indirect proof be discharged. No proof can be ended on an indented line. If this rule is ignored, indirect proof, like conditional proof, can produce any conclusion whatsoever. The following invalid proof illustrates such a mistake:

```
    1. P              / Q
      | 2. Q          AIP
      | 3. Q v Q      2, Add
      | 4. Q          3, Taut
```

EXERCISE 7.6

I. Use either indirect proof or conditional proof (or both) and the eighteen rules of inference to derive the conclusions of the following symbolized arguments. Having done so, attempt to derive the conclusions without using indirect proof or conditional proof.

★(1) 1. $(S \lor T) \supset \sim S$ / $\sim S$

 (2) 1. $(K \supset K) \supset R$
      2. $(R \lor M) \supset N$ / N

 (3) 1. $(C \cdot D) \supset E$
      2. $(D \cdot E) \supset F$ / $(C \cdot D) \supset F$

★(4) 1. $H \supset (L \supset K)$
      2. $L \supset (K \supset \sim L)$ / $\sim H \lor \sim L$

 (5) 1. $S \supset (T \lor \sim U)$
      2. $U \supset (\sim T \lor R)$
      3. $(S \cdot U) \supset \sim R$ / $\sim S \lor \sim U$

 (6) 1. $\sim A \supset (B \cdot C)$
      2. $D \supset \sim C$ / $D \supset A$

★(7) 1. $(E \lor F) \supset (C \cdot D)$
      2. $(D \lor G) \supset H$
      3. $E \lor G$ / H

 (8) 1. $\sim M \supset (N \cdot O)$
      2. $N \supset P$
      3. $O \supset \sim P$ / M

 (9) 1. $(R \lor S) \supset T$
      2. $(P \lor Q) \supset T$
      3. $R \lor P$ / T

★(10) 1. K / $S \supset (T \supset S)$

 (11) 1. $(A \lor B) \supset C$
      2. $(\sim A \lor D) \supset E$ / $C \lor E$

 (12) 1. $(K \lor L) \supset (M \cdot N)$
      2. $(N \lor O) \supset (P \cdot \sim K)$ / $\sim K$

★(13) 1. $[C \supset (D \supset C)] \supset E$ / E

 (14) 1. F / $(G \supset H) \lor (\sim G \supset J)$

 (15) 1. $B \supset (K \cdot M)$
      2. $(B \cdot M) \supset (P \equiv \sim P)$ / $\sim B$

★(16) 1. $(N \lor O) \supset (C \cdot D)$
    2. $(D \lor K) \supset (P \lor \sim C)$
    3. $(P \lor G) \supset \sim(N \cdot D)$ $/ \sim N$

(17) 1. $(R \cdot S) \equiv (G \cdot H)$
    2. $R \supset S$
    3. $H \supset G$ $/ R \equiv H$

(18) 1. $K \supset [(M \lor N) \supset (P \cdot Q)]$
    2. $L \supset [(Q \lor R) \supset (S \cdot \sim N)]$ $/ (K \cdot L) \supset \sim N$

★(19) 1. $A \supset [(N \lor \sim N) \supset (S \lor T)]$
    2. $T \supset \sim(F \lor \sim F)$ $/ A \supset S$

(20) 1. $F \supset [(C \supset C) \supset G]$
    2. $G \supset \{[H \supset (E \supset H)] \supset (K \cdot \sim K)\}$ $/ \sim F$

II. Translate the following arguments into symbolic form, using the letters in the order in which they are listed. Then use indirect proof and the eighteen rules of inference to derive the conclusion of each. Having done so, attempt to derive the conclusion without using indirect proof.

★1. If government deficits continue at their present rate and a recession sets in, then interest on the national debt will become unbearable and the government will default on its loans. If a recession sets in, then the government will not default on its loans. Therefore, either government deficits will not continue at their present rate or a recession will not set in. (C, R, I, D)

2. If either the sea turtle population continues to decrease or rescue efforts are commenced to save the sea turtle from extinction, then nesting sanctuaries will be created and the indiscriminate slaughter of these animals will be halted. If either nesting sanctuaries are created or poachers are arrested, then if the indiscriminate slaughter of these animals is halted, then the sea turtle population will not continue to decrease. Therefore, the sea turtle population will not continue to decrease. (C, R, N, I, P)

3. If asbestos workers sue their employers, then if punitive damages are awarded, then their employers will declare bankruptcy. If asbestos workers sue their employers, then punitive damages will be awarded. If asbestos workers contract asbestosis, then either they will sue their employers or their employers will declare bankruptcy. Therefore, either asbestos workers will not contract asbestosis or their employers will declare bankruptcy. (S, P, B, C)

★4. If the fact that astronauts spend long periods in zero gravity implies that calcium is resorbed in their bodies, then astronauts on a Mars voyage will arrive with brittle bones. If the fact that astronauts attempt a voyage to Mars implies that they spend long periods in zero gravity, then astronauts on a Mars voyage will arrive with brittle bones. Therefore, astronauts on a Mars voyage will arrive with brittle bones. (Z, C, B, V)

5. Either deposits should be required on beer and soft drink containers, or these containers will be discarded along highways and the countryside

will look like a dump. If these containers will be discarded either in parks or along highways, then deposits should be required on soft drink containers. Therefore, deposits should be required on soft drink containers. (B, S, H, C, P)

7.7 PROVING LOGICAL TRUTHS

Both conditional and indirect proof can be used to establish the truth of a tautology (logical truth). Tautological statements can be treated as if they were the conclusions of arguments having no premises. Such a procedure is suggested by the fact that any argument having a tautology for its conclusion is valid regardless of what its premises are. As we saw in the previous section, the proof for such an argument does not use the premises at all but derives the conclusion as the exclusive consequence of either a conditional or indirect sequence. Using this strategy for logical truths, we write the statement to be proved as if it were the conclusion of an argument, and we indent the first line in the proof and tag it as being the beginning of either a conditional or indirect sequence. In the end, this sequence is appropriately discharged to yield the desired statement form.

Tautologies expressed in the form of conditional statements are most easily proved via a conditional sequence. The following example utilizes two such sequences, one within the scope of the other:

$$/ P \supset (Q \supset P)$$

1. P	ACP
2. Q	ACP
3. $P \lor P$	1, Add
4. P	3, Taut
5. $Q \supset P$	2-4, CP
6. $P \supset (Q \supset P)$	1-5, CP

Notice that line 6 restores the proof to the original margin—the first line is indented.

Here is a proof of the same statement using an indirect proof. The indirect sequence begins, as usual, with the negation of the statement to be proved:

$$/ P \supset (Q \supset P)$$

1. $\sim[P \supset (Q \supset P)]$	AIP
2. $\sim[\sim P \lor (\sim Q \lor P)]$	1, Impl
3. $P \cdot \sim(\sim Q \lor P)$	2, DM, DN
4. $P \cdot (Q \cdot \sim P)$	3, DM, DN
5. $(P \cdot \sim P) \cdot Q$	4, Com, Assoc
6. $P \cdot \sim P$	5, Simp
7. $\sim\sim[P \supset (Q \supset P)]$	1-6, IP
8. $P \supset (Q \supset P)$	7, DN

More complex conditional statements are proved by merely extending the technique used in the first proof above. In the proof that follows, notice how each conditional sequence begins by asserting the antecedent of the conditional statement to be obtained:

/ [P ⊃ (Q ⊃ R)] ⊃ [(P ⊃ Q) ⊃ (P ⊃ R)]

1. P ⊃ (Q ⊃ R)		ACP
2. P ⊃ Q		ACP
3. P		ACP
4. Q ⊃ R		1, 3, MP
5. Q		2, 3, MP
6. R		4, 5, MP
7. P ⊃ R		3-6, CP
8. (P ⊃ Q) ⊃ (P ⊃ R)		2-7, CP
9. [P ⊃ (Q ⊃ R)] ⊃ [(P ⊃ Q) ⊃ (P ⊃ R)]		1-8, CP

Tautologies expressed as equivalences are usually proved using two conditional sequences, one after the other. Example:

/ P ≡ [P · (Q ⊃ P)]

1. P	ACP
2. P v ~Q	1, Add
3. ~Q v P	2, Com
4. Q ⊃ P	3, Impl
5. P · (Q ⊃ P)	1, 4, Conj
6. P ⊃ [P · (Q ⊃ P)]	1-5, CP
7. P · (Q ⊃ P)	ACP
8. P	7, Simp
9. [P · (Q ⊃ P)] ⊃ P	7-8, CP
10. P ≡ [P · (Q ⊃ P)]	6, 9, Conj, Equiv

EXERCISE 7.7
Use conditional proof or indirect proof and the eighteen rules of inference to establish the truth of the following tautologies:

★1. P ⊃ [(P ⊃ Q) ⊃ Q]

2. (~P ⊃ Q) v (P ⊃ R)

3. P ≡ [P v (Q · P)]

★4. (P ⊃ Q) ⊃ [(P · R) ⊃ (Q · R)]

5. (P v ~Q) ⊃ [(~P v R) ⊃ (Q ⊃ R)]

6. P ≡ [P · (Q v ~Q)]

★7. (P ⊃ Q) v (~Q ⊃ P)

8. (P ⊃ Q) ≡ [P ⊃ (P · Q)]

9. [(P ⊃ Q) · (P ⊃ R)] ⊃ [P ⊃ (Q · R)]

★10. $[\sim(P \cdot \sim Q) \cdot \sim Q] \supset \sim P$

11. $(P \supset Q) \vee (Q \supset P)$

12. $[P \supset (Q \supset R)] \equiv [Q \supset (P \supset R)]$

★13. $(P \supset Q) \supset [(P \supset \sim Q) \supset \sim P]$

14. $[(P \supset Q) \supset R] \supset [(R \supset \sim R) \supset P]$

15. $(\sim P \vee Q) \supset [(P \vee \sim Q) \supset (P \equiv Q)]$

★16. $\sim[(P \supset \sim P) \cdot (\sim P \supset P)]$

17. $P \supset [(Q \cdot \sim Q) \supset R]$

18. $[(P \cdot Q) \vee R] \supset [(\sim R \vee Q) \supset (P \supset Q)]$

★19. $P \equiv [P \vee (Q \cdot \sim Q)]$

20. $P \supset [Q \equiv (P \supset Q)]$

A CONCISE INTRODUCTION TO LOGIC

8

PREDICATE LOGIC

8.1 SYMBOLS AND TRANSLATION

Techniques were developed in earlier chapters for evaluating two basically different kinds of arguments. The chapter on categorical syllogisms dealt with arguments such as the following:

> All plays by Ibsen are serious dramas.
> No serious dramas are light-hearted comedies.
> Therefore, no plays by Ibsen are light-hearted comedies.

In such arguments the fundamental components are *terms,* and the validity of the argument depends on the arrangement of the terms within the premises and conclusion.

The chapter on propositional logic, on the other hand, dealt with arguments such as this:

> If the control rods fail, then the reactor will run wild and the
> core will melt. If the core melts, radiation will be released
> into the atmosphere. Therefore, if the control rods fail, radia-
> tion will be released into the atmosphere.

In such arguments the fundamental components are not terms but *statements.* The validity of these arguments depends not on the arrangement of the terms within the statements but on the arrangement of the statements themselves as atomic units.

Not all arguments, however, can be assigned to one or the other of these two groups. There is a third type that is a kind of hybrid, sharing features with both categorical syllogisms and propositional arguments. Consider, for example, the following:

Morgan Fairchild is rich and beautiful.
If a woman is either rich or famous, she is happy.
Therefore, Morgan Fairchild is happy.

The validity of this argument depends both on the arrangement of the terms and on the arrangement of the statements. Accordingly, neither syllogistic logic nor propositional logic alone is sufficient to establish its validity. What is needed is a third kind of logic that combines the distinctive features of syllogistic logic and propositional logic. This third kind is called **predicate logic.**

The fundamental component in predicate logic is the **predicate,** symbolized by upper-case letters (A, B, C, . . . X, Y, Z). Here are some examples of bare predicates:

English predicate	Symbolic predicate
——is a rabbit	R__
——is gigantic	G__
——is a doctor	D__
——is helpless	H__

The blank space immediately following the predicate letter is not part of the predicate; rather, it indicates the place for some lower-case letter that will represent the subject of the statement. Depending on what lower-case letter is used, and on the additional symbolism involved, symbolic predicates may be used to translate three distinct kinds of statements: singular statements, universal statements, and particular statements.

A **singular statement,** you may recall from Section 4.8, is a statement that makes an assertion about a specifically named person, place, thing, or time. Translating a singular statement involves writing a lower-case letter corresponding to the subject of the statement to the immediate right of the upper-case letter corresponding to the predicate. The letters that are allocated to serve as names of individuals are the first twenty-three letters of the alphabet (a, b, c, . . . u, v, w). These letters are called **individual constants.** Here are some examples of translated statements:

Statement	Symbolic translation
Socrates is mortal.	Ms
Tokyo is populous.	Pt
The *Sun-Times* is a newspaper.	Ns
King Lear is not a fairytale.	$\sim Fk$
Berlioz was not a German.	$\sim Gb$

Compound arrangements of singular statements may be translated by using the familiar connectives of propositional logic. Here are some examples:

Statement	Symbolic translation
If Paris is beautiful, then Andre told the truth.	$Bp \supset Ta$
Irene is either a doctor or a lawyer.	$Di \lor Li$
Senator Wilkins will be elected only if he campaigns.	$Ew \supset Cw$
General Motors will prosper if either Ford is crippled by a strike or Chrysler declares bankruptcy.	$(Cf \lor Dc) \supset Pg$
Indianapolis gets rain if and only if Chicago and Milwaukee get snow.	$Ri \equiv (Sc \cdot Sm)$

A **universal statement** is a statement that makes an assertion about every member of its subject class. Such statements are either affirmative or negative, depending on whether the statement affirms or denies that the members of the subject class are members of the predicate class. The key to translating universal statements is provided by the Boolean interpretation of these statements (see Section 4.5):

Statement form	Boolean interpretation
All S are P.	If anything is an S, then it is a P.
No S are P.	If anything is an S, then it is not a P.

According to the Boolean interpretation, universal statements are translated as conditionals. Now that we have a symbol (the horseshoe " $\supset$ ") to translate conditional statements, we may use it to translate universal statements. What is still needed, however, is a symbol to indicate that universal statements make an assertion about *every* member of the S class. This symbol, which we introduce now, is called the **universal quantifier** and is formed by placing a lower-case letter in parentheses, thus: (x), which is translated as "for any x." The letters that are allocated for forming the universal quantifier are the last three letters of the alphabet (x, y, z). These letters are called **individual variables.**

The symbol for implication and the universal quantifier are combined to translate universal statements as follows:

Statement form	Symbolic translation	Verbal meaning
All S are P.	$(x)(Sx \supset Px)$	For any x, if x is an S, then x is a P.
No S are P.	$(x)(Sx \supset {\sim}Px)$	For any x, if x is an S, then x is not a P.

An individual variable differs from an individual constant in that it can stand for any item at random in the universe. Accordingly, the expression $(x)(Sx \supset Px)$ means "If anything is an S, then it is a P," and (x) $(Sx \supset {\sim}Px)$ means "If anything is an S, then it is not a P." The fact that these expressions are equivalent to the Boolean interpretation of universal statements may be seen by recalling how the Boolean interpretation is represented by Venn diagrams (see Section 4.6). The Venn diagrams corresponding to the two universal statement forms are as follows:

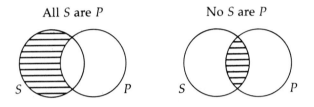

Where shading designates emptiness, the diagram on the left asserts that if anything is in the S circle, it is also in the P circle, and the one on the right asserts that if anything is in the S circle, it is not in the P circle. This is exactly what is asserted by the symbolic expressions above. These symbolic expressions may therefore be taken as being exactly synonymous with the Boolean interpretation of universal statements.

A possible source of confusion at this point concerns the fact that both S and P in the symbolic expressions are predicates, whereas in the original statement forms S is the subject and P is the predicate. Any problem in this regard vanishes, however, once one understands what happens when universal statements are converted into conditionals. When so converted, S becomes the predicate of the antecedent and P becomes the predicate of the consequent. In other words, in the conditional "If anything is an S, then it is a P," both S and P are predicates. Thus, using predicate symbolism to translate universal statements leads to no difficulties. When translating these statements, the point to remember is simply this: The subject of the original statement is represented by a capital letter in the antecedent, and the predicate by a capital letter in the consequent. Here are some examples:

Statement	Symbolic translation
All skyscrapers are tall.	$(x)(Sx \supset Tx)$
No frogs are birds.	$(x)(Fx \supset {\sim}Bx)$
All ambassadors are statesmen.	$(x)(Ax \supset Sx)$
No diamonds are rubies.	$(x)(Dx \supset {\sim}Rx)$

In these examples, the expressions $Sx \supset Tx$, $Fx \supset {\sim}Bx$, and so on are called **statement functions**. The first one may be read "If *it* is an S, then *it* is a T," where "it" designates any random item in the universe. Similarly, the second one may be read, "if *it* is an *F*, then *it* is not a *B*." Statement functions, by themselves, are mere patterns for statements. They differ from complete statements in that they make no definite assertion about any item in the universe. Accordingly, they have no truth value. The variables that occur in statement functions are called **free variables** because they are not bound by any quantifier. In contrast, the variables that occur in statements are called **bound variables.**

In using quantifiers to translate statements, we adopt a convention similar to the one adopted for the negation symbol. That is: the quantifier governs only the expression immediately following it. For example, in the statement $(x)(Ax \supset Bx)$ the universal quantifier governs the entire statement function in parentheses—namely, $Ax \supset Bx$. But in the expression $(x) Ax \supset Bx$, the universal quantifier governs only the statement function Ax. The same convention is adopted for the existential quantifier, which will be introduced presently.

Particular statements are statements that make an assertion about one or more unnamed members of the subject class. As with universal statements, particular statements are either affirmative or negative, depending on whether the statement affirms or denies that members of the subject class are members of the predicate class. Also, as with universal statements, the key to translating particular statements is provided by the Boolean interpretation:

Statement form	Boolean interpretation
Some *S* are *P*.	At least one thing is an *S* and it is also a *P*.
Some *S* are not *P*.	At least one thing is an *S* and it is not a *P*.

In other words, particular statements are translated as conjunctions. Since we are already familiar with the symbol for conjunction (the dot), the only additional symbol that we need in order to translate these statements is a symbol for existence. This is provided by the **existential quantifier,** formed by placing a variable to the right of a backward "E" in parentheses, thus: $(\exists x)$. This expression is translated "there exists an *x* such that." The existential quantifier is combined with the symbol for conjunction to translate particular statements as follows:

Statement form	Symbolic translation	Verbal meaning
Some *S* are *P*.	$(\exists x)(Sx \cdot Px)$	There exists an *x* such that *x* is an *S* and *x* is a *P*.
Some *S* are not *P*.	$(\exists x)(Sx \cdot \sim Px)$	There exists an *x* such that *x* is an *S* and *x* is not a *P*.

As in the symbolic expression of universal statements, the letter x is an individual variable, which can stand for any item in the universe. Accordingly, the expression $(\exists x)(Sx \cdot Px)$ means "Something exists that is both an S and a P," and $(\exists x)(Sx \cdot \sim Px)$ means "Something exists that is an S and not a P." To see the equivalence of these expressions with the Boolean interpretation of particular statements, it is again useful to recall how these statements are represented by Venn diagrams:

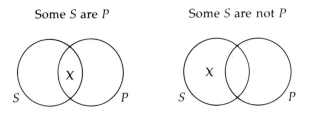

Some S are P Some S are not P

Where the "X" designates at least one existing item, the diagram on the left asserts that something exists that is both an S and a P, and the one on the right asserts that something exists that is an S and not a P. In other words, these diagrams assert exactly the same thing as the symbolic expressions above. These symbolic expressions, therefore, exactly express the Boolean interpretation of particular statements. Here are some examples:

Statement	Symbolic translation
Some men are paupers.	$(\exists x)(Mx \cdot Px)$
Some diseases are not contagious.	$(\exists x)(Dx \cdot \sim Cx)$
Some jobs are boring.	$(\exists x)(Jx \cdot Bx)$
Some vehicles are not motorcycles.	$(\exists x)(Vx \cdot \sim Mx)$

The general rule to follow in translating statements in predicate logic is always to make an effort to understand the meaning of the statement to be translated. If the statement makes an assertion about every member of its subject class, a universal quantifier should be used to translate it; but if it makes an assertion about only one or more members of this class, an existential quantifier should be used.

Many of the principles developed in syllogistic logic (see Section 4.8) may be carried over into predicate logic. Specifically, it should be understood that statements beginning with the words *only* and *none but* are exclusive propositions. When these statements are translated, the term occurring first in the original statement becomes the consequent in the symbolic expression, and the term occurring second becomes the antecedent. One of the few differences in this respect between predicate logic and syllogistic logic concerns singular statements. In syllogistic logic singular statements are translated as universals, while in predicate logic, as we have seen, they are translated in a unique way. Here are some examples of a variety of statements:

Statement	Symbolic translation
Sea lions are mammals.	$(x)(Sx \supset Mx)$
Sea lions live in these caves.	$(\exists x)(Sx \cdot Lx)$
Egomaniacs are not pleasant companions.	$(x)(Ex \supset \sim Px)$
A few egomaniacs did not arrive on time.	$(\exists x)(Ex \cdot \sim Ax)$
Only close friends were invited to the wedding.	$(x)(Ix \supset Cx)$
None but citizens are eligible to vote.	$(x)(Ex \supset Cx)$
It is not the case that every Girl Scout sells cookies.	$\sim(x)(Gx \supset Sx)$ or $(\exists x)(Gx \cdot \sim Sx)$
Not a single psychologist attended the convention.	$\sim(\exists x)(Px \cdot Ax)$ or $(x)(Px \supset \sim Ax)$

The last two examples illustrate the fact that a particular statement is equivalent to a negated universal, and vice versa. The first of these is equivalent to "Some Girl Scouts do not sell cookies" and the second to "No psychologists attended the convention." Actually, any quantified statement can be translated using either a universal or existential quantifier, provided that one of them is negated. The equivalence of these two forms of expression will be analyzed further in Section 8.3.

More complex statements may be translated by following the basic rules just presented. Examples:

Statement	Symbolic translation
1. Only snakes and lizards thrive in the desert.	$(x)[Tx \supset (Sx \vee Lx)]$
2. Oranges and lemons are citrus fruits.	$(x)[(Ox \vee Lx) \supset Cx]$
3. Ripe apples are crunchy and delicious.	$(x)[(Rx \cdot Ax) \supset (Cx \cdot Dx)]$
4. Azaleas bloom if and only if they are fertilized.	$(x)[Ax \supset (Bx \equiv Fx)]$

5. Peaches are edible unless $(x)[Px \supset (\sim Rx \supset Ex)]$
they are rotten.   or
                        $(x)[Px \supset (Ex \lor Rx)]$

6. Cats and dogs bite if they $(x)\{(Cx \lor Dx) \supset [(Fx \lor Hx) \supset Bx]\}$
are frightened or harassed.

Notice that the first example is translated in terms of the disjunction $Sx \lor Lx$ even though the English statement reads "snakes *and* lizards." If the translation were rendered as $(x)[Tx \supset (Sx \cdot Lx)]$ it would mean that anything that thrives in the desert is both a snake and a lizard (at the same time). And this is surely *not* what is meant. For the same reason, the second example is translated in terms of the disjunction $Ox \lor Lx$ even though the English reads "oranges *and* lemons." If the statement were translated $(x)[(Ox \cdot Lx) \supset Cx]$, it would mean that anything that is simultaneously an orange and a lemon (and there are none of these) is a citrus fruit. The same principle is used in translating the sixth example, which, incidentally, reads "If anything is a cat or a dog, then if it is frightened or harassed, it bites." The third example employs the conjunction $Rx \cdot Ax$ to translate ripe apples. This, of course, is correct, because such a thing is both ripe and an apple at the same time. The fifth example illustrates the fact that "unless" may be translated as either "if not" or "or."

The connectives of propositional logic can be used to form compound arrangements of universal and particular statements, just as they can be used to form compound arrangements of singular statements. Here are some examples:

Statement

If Elizabeth is a historian, then some women are historians.

If some cellists are music directors, then some orchestras are properly led.

Either everything is alive or Bergson's theory is not correct.

All novels are interesting if and only if some Steinbeck novels are not romances.

Green avocados are never purchased unless all the ripe ones are expensive.

Symbolic translation

$He \supset (\exists x)(Wx \cdot Hx)$

$(\exists x)(Cx \cdot Mx) \supset (\exists x)(Ox \cdot Px)$

$(x)Ax \lor \sim Cb$

$(x)(Nx \supset Ix) \equiv (\exists x)[(Nx \cdot Sx) \cdot \sim Rx]$

$(x)[(Gx \cdot Ax) \supset \sim Px] \lor (x)[(Rx \cdot Ax) \supset Ex]$

In translating statements into the symbolism of predicate logic, the usual procedure is to translate universal statements as conditionals preceded by a universal quantifier and to translate particular statements as conjunctions preceded by an existential quantifier. There are exceptions to this procedure, however. Whenever a statement is made about literally everything in the universe, the statement is translated in terms of a single predicate preceded by a universal quantifier. For example, the statement "Everything is made of matter" is translated $(x)Mx$, where Mx means "x is made of matter." Similarly, whenever it is asserted that a certain thing simply exists, the statement is translated in terms of a single predicate preceded by an existential quantifier. For example, the statement "An acorn exists" is translated $(\exists x)Ax$.

It is interesting to note what happens to ordinary universal and particular statements when they are translated using the wrong quantifier. Let us consider the false statement "No cats are animals." This is correctly translated $(x)(Cx \supset \sim Ax)$. If, however, it were translated $(\exists x)(Cx \supset \sim Ax)$, the symbolic statement would turn out to be true. This may be seen as follows. $(\exists x)(Cx \supset \sim Ax)$ is equivalent via material implication to $(\exists x)(\sim Cx \lor \sim Ax)$, which in turn is equivalent via DeMorgan's Rule to $(\exists x)\sim(Cx \cdot Ax)$. The latter statement, however, merely asserts that something exists that is not both a cat and an animal—for example, a dog—which is true. Again, consider the true statement "Some cats are animals." This is correctly translated $(\exists x)(Cx \cdot Ax)$. If, however, it were translated $(x)(Cx \cdot Ax)$, the symbolic statement would assert that everything in the universe is both a cat and an animal, which is clearly false. Thus, as these examples illustrate, it is imperative that the two quantifiers not be confused with each other.

One final observation needs to be made. It was mentioned earlier that the letters x, y, and z are reserved for use as variables for translating universal and particular statements. In accord with this convention, the other twenty-three lower-case letters (a, b, c, ... u, v, w) may be used as names for translating singular statements. Thus, for example, "Albert is a scientist" is translated Sa. But a question naturally arises with statements such as "Xerxes was a king." Should this statement be translated Kx? The answer is no. Some other letter, for example the second letter in the name, should be selected instead of x. Maintaining this alphabetical convention will help us avoid mistakes in the next section when we use natural deduction to derive the conclusions of arguments.

EXERCISE 8.1

Translate the following statements into symbolic form. Avoid negation signs preceding quantifiers. The predicate letters are given in parentheses.

★1. Elaine is a chemist. (C)

2. All maples are trees. (M, T)

3. Some grapes are sour. (G, S)

★4. No novels are biographies. (N, B)

5. Some holidays are not relaxing. (H, R)

6. If Gertrude is correct, then the Taj Mahal is made of marble. (C, M)

★7. Gertrude is not correct only if the Taj Mahal is made of granite. (C, G)

8. A thoroughbred is a horse. (T, H)

9. A thoroughbred won the race. (T, W)

★10. Not all mushrooms are edible. (M, E)

11. Not any horsechestnuts are edible. (H, E)

12. A few guests arrived late. (G, A)

★13. None but gentlemen prefer blondes. (G, P)

14. The only musicians that are available are trombonists. (M, A, T)

15. Only talented musicians perform in the symphony. (T, M, P)

★16. Any well-made car runs smoothly. (W, C, R)

17. Not every foreign car runs smoothly. (F, C, R)

18. A good violin is rare and expensive. (G, V, R, E)

★19. Violins and cellos are stringed instruments. (V, C, S, I)

20. A room with a view is available. (R, V, A)

21. A room with a view is expensive. (R, V, E)

★22. Some French restaurants are exclusive. (F, R, E)

23. Some French cafes are not recommended. (F, C, R)

24. Taylor is guilty if and only if all the witnesses committed perjury. (G, W, C)

★25. If any witnesses told the truth, then either Parsons or Harris is guilty. (W, T, G)

26. If all mysteries are interesting, then *Rebecca* is interesting. (M, I)

27. If there are any interesting mysteries, then *Rebecca* is interesting. (M, I)

★28. Skaters and dancers are energetic individuals. (S, D, E, I)

29. Swiss watches are not expensive unless they are made of gold. (S, W, E, M)

30. If all the buildings in Manhattan are skyscrapers, then the Chrysler building is a skyscraper. (B, M, S)

★31. Experienced mechanics are well paid only if all the inexperienced ones are lazy. (E, M, W, L)

32. Balcony seats are never chosen unless all the orchestra seats are taken. (B, S, C, O, T)

33. Some employees will get raises if and only if some managers are overly generous. (E, R, M, O)

★34. The physicists and astronomers at the symposium are listed in the program if they either chair a meeting or read a paper. (P, A, S, L, C, R)

35. If the scientists and technicians are conscientious and exacting, then some of the mission directors will be either pleased or delighted. (S, T, C, E, M, P, D)

8.2 REMOVING AND INTRODUCING QUANTIFIERS

The chief reason for using truth functional connectives (implication, conjunction, and so on) in translating statements into the symbolism of predicate logic is to allow for the application of the eighteen rules of inference to derive the conclusion of arguments via natural deduction. Since, however, the first eight of these rules are applicable only to whole lines in an argument, as long as the quantifier is attached to a line these rules of inference cannot be applied. To provide for their application, four additional rules are required to remove quantifiers at the beginning of a proof sequence and to introduce them, when needed, at the end of the sequence. These four rules are called universal instantiation, universal generalization, existential instantiation, and existential generalization. The first two are used to remove and introduce universal quantifiers, respectively, and the second two to remove and introduce existential quantifiers.

Let us first consider **universal instantiation.** As an illustration of the need for this rule, consider the following argument:

All economists are social scientists.
Milton Friedman is an economist.
Therefore, Milton Friedman is a social scientist.

This argument, which is clearly valid, is symbolized as follows:

1. $(x)(Ex \supset Sx)$
2. Em / Sm

As the argument now stands, none of the first eight rules of inference can be applied; as a result, there is no way in which the two premises can be combined to obtain the conclusion. However, if the first premise could be used to obtain a line that reads $Em \supset Sm$, this statement could be combined with the second premise to yield the conclusion via *modus ponens*. Universal instantiation serves exactly this purpose.

The first premise states that for any item x in the universe, if that item is an E, then it is an S. But since Milton Friedman is himself an item in the universe, the first premise implies that if Milton Friedman is an E, then Milton Friedman is an S. A line stating exactly this can be obtained by universal instantiation (UI). In other words, universal instantiation provides us with an *instance* of the universal statement $(x)(Ex \supset Sx)$. In the completed proof, which follows, the m in line 3 is called the **instantial letter**:

    1. $(x)(Ex \supset Sx)$
    2. Em / Sm
    3. $Em \supset Sm$ 1, UI
    4. Sm 2, 3, MP

At this point the question might arise as to why *modus ponens* is applicable to lines 2 and 3. In Chapter 7 we applied *modus ponens* to lines of the form $p \supset q$, but are we justified in applying it to a line that reads $Em \supset Sm$? The answer is yes, because Em and Sm are simply alternate ways of symbolizing atomic statements. As so understood, these symbols do not differ in any material way from the p and q of propositional logic.

Let us now consider **universal generalization.** The need for this rule may be illustrated through reference to the following argument:

    All psychiatrists are doctors.
    All doctors are college graduates.
    Therefore, all psychiatrists are college graduates.

This valid argument is symbolized as follows:

    1. $(x)(Px \supset Dx)$
    2. $(x)(Dx \supset Cx)$ / $(x)(Px \supset Cx)$

Once universal instantiation is applied to the two premises, we will have lines that can be used to set up a hypothetical syllogism. But then we will have to reintroduce a universal quantifier to obtain the conclusion as written. This final step is obtained by universal generalization (UG). The justification for such a step lies in the fact that both premises are universal statements. The first states that if *anything* is a P, then it is a D, and the second states that if *anything* is a D, then it is a C. We may therefore conclude that if *anything* is a P, then it is a C. But because of the complete generality of this reasoning process, there is a special way in which we must perform the universal instantiation step. Instead of selecting a *specifically named* instance, as we did in the previous example, we must select a *variable* that can range over every instance in the universe. The variables at our disposal, you may recall from the previous section, are x, y, and z. Let us select y. The completed proof is as follows:

1. $(x)(Px \supset Dx)$
2. $(x)(Dx \supset Cx)$ / $(x)(Px \supset Cx)$
3. $Py \supset Dy$ 1, UI
4. $Dy \supset Cy$ 2, UI
5. $Py \supset Cy$ 3, 4, HS
6. $(x)(Px \supset Cx)$ 5, UG

As was noted earlier, the expression $Py \supset Dy$ in line 3 is called a *statement function*. It may be read, "If *it* is a P, then *it* is a D." Similarly, line 4 may be read, "If *it* is a D, then *it* is a C." In these lines "it" can stand for any item at random in the universe. Accordingly, line 5 may be read, "If any item in the universe is a P, then that item is a C." Line 6 is simply another way of expressing line 5.

As the two previous examples illustrate, we have two ways of performing universal instantiation. On the one hand, we may instantiate with respect to a *constant*, such as a or b, and on the other, with respect to a *variable*, such as x or y. The exact way in which this operation is to be performed depends on the kind of result intended. If we want some part of a universal statement to match a singular statement on another line, as in the first example, we instantiate with respect to a constant. But if, at the end of the proof, we want to perform universal generalization over some part of the statement we are instantiating, then we *must* instantiate by using a variable. This latter point leads to an important restriction governing universal generalization, namely, that we cannot perform this operation when the instantial letter is a constant. Consider the following *erroneous* proof sequence:

1. Ta
2. $(x)Tx$ 1, UG (invalid)

If Ta means "Albert is a thief," then on the basis of this information, we have concluded (line 2) that everything in the universe is a thief. Clearly, such an inference is invalid. This illustrates the fact that universal generalization can be performed only when the instantial letter (in this case a) is a variable.

The need for **existential generalization** can be illustrated through the following argument:

> All chemists are scientists.
> Linus Pauling is a chemist.
> Therefore, there is at least one scientist.

This argument is symbolized as follows:

1. $(x)(Cx \supset Sx)$
2. Cp / $(\exists x)Sx$

If we instantiate the first line with respect to p, we can obtain Sp via *modus ponens*. But if it is true that Linus Pauling is a scientist, then it certainly follows that there is at least one scientist (namely, Pauling). This last step is accomplished by existential generalization (EG). The proof is as follows:

1. $(x)(Cx \supset Sx)$
2. Cp / $(\exists x)Sx$
3. $Cp \supset Sp$ 1, UI
4. Sp 2, 3, MP
5. $(\exists x)Sx$ 4, EG

There are no restrictions on existential generalization, and the operation can be performed when the instantial letter is either a constant (as above) or a variable. As an instance of the latter, consider the following sequence:

1. $(x)(Px \supset Qx)$
2. $(x) Px$ / $(\exists x)Qx$
3. $Py \supset Qy$ 1, UI
4. Py 2, UI
5. Qy 3, 4, MP
6. $(\exists x) Qx$ 5, EG

Line 5 states in effect that everything in the universe is a Q. From this, the much weaker conclusion follows (line 6) that *something* is a Q. If you should wonder how an existential conclusion can be drawn from universal premises, the answer is that predicate logic assumes that at least one thing exists in the universe. Hence, line 2, which asserts that everything in the universe is a P, entails that at least one thing is a P. Without this assumption, universal instantiation in line 4 would not be possible.

The need for **existential instantiation** can be illustrated through the following argument:

> All attorneys are college graduates.
> Some attorneys are golfers.
> Therefore, some golfers are college graduates.

The symbolic formulation is as follows:

1. $(x)(Ax \supset Cx)$
2. $(\exists x)(Ax \cdot Gx)$ / $(\exists x)(Gx \cdot Cx)$

If both quantifiers can be removed, the conclusion can be obtained via simplification, *modus ponens,* and conjunction. The universal quantifier can be removed by universal instantiation, but to remove the existential quantifier we need existential instantiation (EI). Line 2 states that there is *something* that is both an *A* and a *G*. Existential instantiation consists in giving this something a *name,* for example, "David." We will call this name an "existential name" because it is obtained through existential instantiation. The completed proof is as follows:

1. $(x)(Ax \supset Cx)$
2. $(\exists x)(Ax \cdot Gx)$ / $(\exists x)(Gx \cdot Cx)$
3. $Ad \cdot Gd$ 2, EI
4. $Ad \supset Cd$ 1, UI
5. Ad 3, Simp
6. Cd 4, 5, MP
7. Gd 3, Com, Simp
8. $Gd \cdot Cd$ 6, 7, Conj
9. $(\exists x)(Gx \cdot Cx)$ 8, EG

Examination of this proof reveals an immediate restriction that must be placed on existential instantiation. The name that we have assigned to the particular something in line 2 that is both an *A* and a *G* is a hypothetical name. It would be a mistake to conclude that this something really has that name. Accordingly, we must introduce a restriction that prevents us from ending the proof with some line that includes the letter *d*. If, for example, the proof were ended at line 8, we would be concluding that the something that is a *G* and a *C* really does have the name *d*. This, of course, would not be legitimate, because *d* is an arbitrary name introduced into the proof for mere convenience. To prevent such a mistake, we require that the name selected for existential instantiation not appear to the right of the slanted line adjacent to the last premise that indicates the conclusion to be obtained. Since the last line in the proof must be identical to this line, such a restriction prevents us from ending the proof with a line that contains the existential name.

Further examination of this proof indicates another important restriction on existential instantiation. Notice that the line involving existential instantiation is listed before the line involving universal instantiation. There is a reason for this. If the order were reversed, the existential instantiation step would rest upon the illicit assumption that the something that is both an *A* and a *G* has the *same* name as the name used in the earlier universal instantiation step. In other words, it would involve the assumption that the something that is both an *A* and a *G* is the very same something named in the line $Ad \supset Cd$. Of course, no such assumption is legitimate. To keep this mistake from happening, we introduce the restriction that the name introduced by existential instantiation be a new name not occurring earlier in the proof sequence.

The following defective proof illustrates what can happen if this restriction is violated:

1. $(\exists x)(Fx \cdot Ax)$
2. $(\exists x)(Fx \cdot Ox)$ / $(\exists x)(Ax \cdot Ox)$
3. $Fb \cdot Ab$ 1, EI
4. $Fb \cdot Ob$ 2, EI (invalid)
5. Ab 3, Com, Simp
6. Ob 4, Com, Simp
7. $Ab \cdot Ob$ 5, 6, Conj
8. $(\exists x)(Ax \cdot Ox)$ 7, EG

To see that this proof is indeed defective, let F stand for fruits, A for apples, and O for oranges. The argument that results is:

Some fruits are apples.
Some fruits are oranges.
Therefore, some apples are oranges.

Since the premises are true and the conclusion false, the argument is clearly invalid. The defect in the proof occurs on line 4. This line asserts that the something that is both an F and an O is the very same something that is both an F and an A. In other words, the restriction that the name introduced by existential instantiation be a new name not occurring earlier in the proof is violated.

The first restriction on existential instantiation requires that the existential name not occur in the line that indicates the conclusion to be obtained, and the second restriction requires that this name be a new name that has not occurred earlier in the proof. These two restrictions can easily be combined into a single restriction that requires that the name introduced by existential instantiation be a new name that has not occurred *anywhere* in the proof, including the line adjacent to the last premise that indicates the conclusion to be obtained.

One further restriction that affects all four of these rules of inference requires that the rules be applied only to *whole lines* in a proof. The following sequence illustrates a violation of this restriction:

1. $(x)Px \supset (x)Qx$
2. $Py \supset Qy$ 1, UI (invalid)

In line 2 universal instantiation is applied to both the antecedent and consequent of the first line. To obtain line 2 validly the first line would have to read $(x)(Px \supset Qx)$. With this final restriction in mind, the four new rules of inference may now be summarized. In the formulation that follows, the symbol $\mathcal{F} x$ represents any **statement function**—that is, any symbolic arrangement containing individual variables, such as $Ax \supset Bx$, $Cy \supset (Dy \vee Ey)$, or $Gz \cdot Hz$. And the symbol $\mathcal{F} a$ represents any **statement;** that is, any symbolic arrangement containing individual constants (or names), such as $Ac \supset Bc$, $Cm \supset (Dm \lor Em)$, or $Gw \cdot Hw$:

1. Universal instantiation (UI):

$$\frac{(x)\mathfrak{F}x}{\mathfrak{F}y} \qquad \frac{(x)\mathfrak{F}x}{\mathfrak{F}a}$$

2. Universal generalization (UG):

$$\frac{\mathfrak{F}y}{(x)\mathfrak{F}x} \qquad \text{not allowed:} \qquad \frac{\mathfrak{F}a}{(x)\mathfrak{F}x}$$

3. Existential instantiation (EI):

$$\frac{(\exists x)\mathfrak{F}x}{\mathfrak{F}a} \qquad \text{not allowed:} \qquad \frac{(\exists x)\mathfrak{F}x}{\mathfrak{F}y}$$

Restriction: The existential name a must be a new name that has not occurred earlier in the proof.

4. Existential generalization (EG):

$$\frac{\mathfrak{F}a}{(\exists x)\mathfrak{F}x} \qquad \frac{\mathfrak{F}y}{(\exists x)\mathfrak{F}x}$$

The *not allowed* version of universal generalization recalls the already familiar fact that generalization is not possible when the instantial letter is a constant. In other words, the mere fact that the individual a is an $\mathfrak{F}$ is not sufficient to allow us to conclude that everything in the universe is an $\mathfrak{F}$. At present this is the only restriction needed for universal generalization. In Sections 8.4 and 8.6, however, two additional restrictions will be introduced. The *not allowed* version of existential instantiation merely recalls the fact that this operation is a naming process. Because variables (x, y, and z) are not names, they cannot be used as instantial letters in existential instantiation.

Let us now investigate some applications of these rules. Consider the following proof:

1. $(x)(Hx \supset Ix)$
2. $(x)(Ix \supset Hx)$ / $(x)(Hx \equiv Ix)$
3. $Hx \supset Ix$ 1, UI
4. $Ix \supset Hx$ 2, UI
5. $(Hx \supset Ix) \cdot (Ix \supset Hx)$ 3, 4, Conj
6. $Hx \equiv Ix$ 5, Equiv
7. $(x)(Hx \equiv Ix)$ 6, UG

Because we want to perform universal generalization on the last line of the proof, we instantiate in lines 3 and 4 using a variable, not a constant. Notice that the variable selected is the same letter that occurs in lines 1 and 2. While a new letter (y or z) *could* have been selected, this is never necessary in such a step. It *is* necessary, however, since we want to combine lines 3 and 4, that the *same* variable be selected in obtaining these lines. Another example:

1. $(x)[(Ax \lor Bx) \supset Cx]$
2. $(\exists x)Ax$ / $(\exists x)Cx$
3. Am 2, EI
4. $(Am \lor Bm) \supset Cm$ 1, UI
5. $Am \lor Bm$ 3, Add
6. Cm 4, 5, MP
7. $(\exists x)Cx$ 6, EG

In conformity with the restriction on existential instantiation, the EI step is performed *before* the UI step. The same letter is then selected in the UI step as was used in the EI step. In line 5, Bm is joined disjunctively via addition to Am. This rule applies in predicate logic in basically the same way that it does in propositional logic. Any statement or statement function we choose can be joined disjunctively to a given line.

Another example:

1. $(\exists x)Kx \supset (x)(Lx \supset Mx)$
2. $Kc \cdot Lc$ / Mc
3. Kc 2, Simp
4. $(\exists x)Kx$ 3, EG
5. $(x)(Lx \supset Mx)$ 1, 4, MP
6. $Lc \supset Mc$ 5, UI
7. Lc 2, Com, Simp
8. Mc 6, 7, MP

Since the instantiation (and generalization) rules must be applied to whole lines, it is impossible to instantiate line 1. The only strategy that can be followed is to use some other line to obtain the antecedent of this line and then obtain the consequent via *modus ponens*. Once the consequent is obtained (line 5), it is instantiated using the same letter that appears in line 2. The following example incorporates all four of the instantiation and generalization rules:

1. $(x)(Px \supset Qx) \supset (\exists x)(Rx \cdot Sx)$
2. $(x)(Px \supset Sx) \cdot (x)(Sx \supset Qx)$ / $(\exists x)Sx$
3. $(x)(Px \supset Sx)$ 2, Simp
4. $(x)(Sx \supset Qx)$ 2, Com, Simp
5. $Py \supset Sy$ 3, UI
6. $Sy \supset Qy$ 4, UI
7. $Py \supset Qy$ 5, 6, HS
8. $(x)(Px \supset Qx)$ 7, UG
9. $(\exists x)(Rx \cdot Sx)$ 1, 8 MP
10. $Ra \cdot Sa$ 9, EI
11. Sa 10, Com, Simp
12. $(\exists x)Sx$ 11, EG

As with the previous example, line 1 cannot be instantiated. To instantiate the two conjuncts in line 2, they must first be separated (lines 3 and 4). Because UG is to be used in line 8, lines 3 and 4 are instantiated using a variable. On the other hand, a constant is used to instantiate line 9 because the statement in question is a particular statement.

Another example:

1. $[(\exists x)Ax \cdot (\exists x)Bx] \supset Cj$
2. $(\exists x)(Ax \cdot Dx)$
3. $(\exists x)(Bx \cdot Ex)$ / Cj
4. $Am \cdot Dm$ 2, EI
5. $Bn \cdot En$ 3, EI
6. Am 4, Simp
7. Bn 5, Simp
8. $(\exists x)Ax$ 6, EG
9. $(\exists x)Bx$ 7, EG
10. $(\exists x)Ax \cdot (\exists x)Bx$ 8, 9, Conj
11. Cj 1, 10, MP

When line 2 is instantiated (line 4), a letter other than j, which appears in line 1, is selected. Then, when line 3 is instantiated (line 5), another new letter is selected. The conclusion is obtained, as in earlier examples, via *modus ponens* by obtaining the antecedent of line 1.

The following examples illustrate *invalid* or *improper* applications of the instantiation and generalization rules:

1. $Fb \cdot Gb$
2. $\overline{(\exists x)(Fx \cdot Gb)}$ 1, EG   (improper—every instance of b must be replaced with x)

1. $(x)Fx \supset Ga$
2. $\overline{Fx \supset Ga}$ 1, UI   (invalid—instantiation can be applied only to whole lines)

1. $(x)Fx \supset (x)Gx$
2. $\overline{Fx \supset Gx}$ 1, UI   (invalid—instantiation can be applied only to whole lines)

1. Fc
2. $(\exists x)Gx$
3. $\overline{Gc}$ 2, EI   (invalid—c appears in line 1)

1. $Fm \supset Gm$
2. $\overline{(x)(Fx \supset Gx)}$ 1, UG   (invalid—the instantial letter must be a variable; m is a constant.)

1. $(\exists x) Fx$
2. $(\exists x) Gx$
3. $\overline{Fe}$ 1, EI
4. Ge 2, EI   (invalid—e appears in line 3)

1. $Fs \cdot Gs$
2. $(\exists x) Fx \cdot Gs$ 1, EG   (improper—generalization can be applied only to whole lines)

1. $\sim(x)Fx$
2. $\sim Fy$ 1, UI   (invalid—lines involving negated quantifiers cannot be instantiated; see Section 8.3)

EXERCISE 8.2

I. Use the eighteen rules of inference to derive the conclusions of the following symbolized arguments. Do not use either conditional proof or indirect proof.

★(1)   1. $(x)(Ax \supset Bx)$
      2. $(x)(Bx \supset Cx)$ / $(x)(Ax \supset Cx)$

(2)   1. $(x)(Bx \supset Cx)$
      2. $(\exists x)(Ax \cdot Bx)$ / $(\exists x)(Ax \cdot Cx)$

(3)   1. $(x)(Ax \supset Bx)$
      2. $\sim Bm$ / $(\exists x)\sim Ax$

★(4)   1. $(x)[Ax \supset (Bx \lor Cx)]$
      2. $Ag \cdot \sim Bg$ / Cg

(5)   1. $(x)[(Ax \lor Bx) \supset Cx]$
      2. $(\exists y)(Ay \cdot Dy)$ / $(\exists y)\, Cy$

(6)   1. $(x)[Jx \supset (Kx \cdot Lx)]$
      2. $(\exists y)\sim Ky$ / $(\exists z)\sim Jz$

★(7)   1. $(x)[Ax \supset (Bx \lor Cx)]$
      2. $(\exists x)(Ax \cdot \sim Cx)$ / $(\exists x)\, Bx$

(8)   1. $(x)(Ax \supset Bx)$
      2. $Am \cdot An$ / $Bm \cdot Bn$

(9)   1. $(x)(Ax \supset Bx)$
      2. $Am \lor An$ / $Bm \lor Bn$

★(10)   1. $(x)(Bx \lor Ax)$
       2. $(x)(Bx \supset Ax)$ / $(x)\, Ax$

(11)   1. $(x)[(Ax \cdot Bx) \supset Cx]$
       2. $(\exists x)(Bx \cdot \sim Cx)$ / $(\exists x)\sim Ax$

(12)   1. $(\exists x)\, Ax \supset (x)(Bx \supset Cx)$
       2. $Am \cdot Bm$ / Cm

★(13)   1. $(\exists x)\, Ax \supset (x)\, Bx$
       2. $(\exists x)\, Cx \supset (\exists x)\, Dx$
       3. $An \cdot Cn$ / $(\exists x)(Bx \cdot Dx)$

(14) 1. $(\exists x) Ax \supset (x)(Cx \supset Bx)$
    2. $(\exists x)(Ax \lor Bx)$
    3. $(x)(Bx \supset Ax)$ / $(x)(Cx \supset Ax)$

★(15) 1. $(\exists x) Ax \supset (x)(Bx \supset Cx)$
    2. $(\exists x) Dx \supset (\exists x) \sim Cx$
    3. $(\exists x)(Ax \cdot Dx)$ / $(\exists x) \sim Bx$

II. Translate the following arguments into symbolic form. Then use the eighteen rules of inference to derive the conclusion of each. Do not use conditional or indirect proof.

★1. Oranges are sweet. Also, oranges are fragrant. Therefore, oranges are sweet and fragrant, (O, S, F)

  2. Tomatoes are vegetables. Therefore, the tomatoes in the garden are vegetables. (T, V, G)

  3. Apples and pears grow on trees. Therefore, apples grow on trees. (A, P, G)

★4. Carrots are vegetables and peaches are fruit. Furthermore, there are carrots and peaches in the garden. Therefore, there are vegetables and fruit in the garden. (C, V, P, F, G)

  5. Beans and peas are legumes. There are no legumes in the garden. Therefore, there are no beans in the garden. (B, P, L, G)

  6. There are some cucumbers in the garden. If there are any cucumbers, there are some pumpkins in the garden. All pumpkins are vegetables. Therefore, there are some vegetables in the garden. (C, G, P, V)

★7. All gardeners are industrious. Furthermore, anyone industrious is respected. Therefore, since Arthur and Catherine are gardeners, it follows that they are respected. (G, I, R)

  8. Some huckleberries are ripe. Furthermore, some boysenberries are sweet. If there are any huckleberries, then the boysenberries are edible if they are sweet. Therefore, some boysenberries are edible. (H, R, B, S, E)

  9. If there are any ripe watermelons, then the caretakers performed well. Furthermore, if there are any large watermelons, then whoever performed well will get a bonus. There are some large, ripe watermelons. Therefore, the caretakers will get a bonus. (R, W, C, P, L, B)

★10. If the artichokes in the kitchen are ripe, then the guests will be surprised. Furthermore, if the artichokes in the kitchen are flavorful, then the guests will be pleased. The artichokes in the kitchen are ripe and flavorful. Therefore, the guests will be surprised and pleased. (A, K, R, G, S, F, P)

8.3 CHANGE OF QUANTIFIER RULES

The rules of inference developed thus far are not sufficient to derive the conclusion of every argument in predicate logic. For instance, consider the following:

$$\sim(\exists x)(Px \cdot \sim Qx)$$
$$\frac{\sim(x)(\sim Rx \lor Qx)}{(\exists x)\sim Px}$$

Both premises have negation signs preceding the quantifiers. As long as these negation signs remain, neither statement can be instantiated; and if these statements cannot be instantiated, the conclusion cannot be derived. What is needed is a set of rules that will allow us to remove the negation signs. These rules, which we will proceed to develop now, are called **change of quantifier rules.**

For the purpose of introducing these rules, it is convenient to use the square of opposition in modern logic (see Sections 4.5 and 4.7):

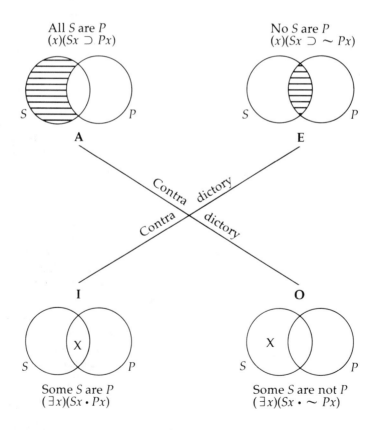

A CONCISE INTRODUCTION TO LOGIC

The four types of statements—universal affirmative, universal negative, particular affirmative, and particular negative—are identified respectively by the letters **A, E, I,** and **O** (see Section 4.2). The Venn diagrams illustrate the contradictory relationship prevailing between **A** and **O** on the one hand and between **I** and **E** on the other.

In these diagrams, shading an area indicates that the area in question is empty, and placing an "X" in an area indicates that the area contains at least one member. For the **A** statement, the left-hand portion of the S circle is empty, and for the **O** statement the corresponding area is not empty. Clearly, these two statements contradict each other. Similarly, for the **E** statement the overlapping portion of the diagram is empty, and for the **I** statement it is not empty.

Now, since any statement is logically equivalent to the negation of its contradictory, it follows that the **A** statement is logically equivalent to the negation of the **O**, the **I** is logically equivalent to the negation of the **E**, and so on. Let us consider the first of these equivalences:

$$(x)(Sx \supset Px) \quad \equiv \quad \sim(\exists x)(Sx \cdot \sim Px)$$
$$\equiv \quad \sim(\exists x)\sim(\sim Sx \vee Px) \text{ by DN \& DM}$$
$$\equiv \quad \sim(\exists x)\sim(Sx \supset Px) \text{ by Impl}$$

We begin by setting the **A** statement equivalent to the negation of the **O** statement and then proceed to rearrange the components of the **O** statement using double negation, DeMorgan's Rule, and the rule of material implication. Such a procedure is quite legitimate because these rules are rules of equivalence; they apply to parts of lines as well as to whole lines. It is therefore not necessary to remove the existential quantifiers to perform these operations. In the end we arrive at the equivalence

$$(x)(Sx \supset Px) \equiv \sim(\exists x)\sim(Sx \supset Px)$$

Notice that the statement functions in these expressions are identical. This fact allows us to conclude that a universal quantifier may be replaced by an existential quantifier if and only if a negation sign is introduced immediately before and after the new quantifier.

Similar results are obtained by setting the negation of the **A** statement equivalent to the **O** statement:

$$\sim(x)(Sx \supset Px) \quad \equiv \quad (\exists x)(Sx \cdot \sim Px)$$
$$\equiv \quad (\exists x)\sim(\sim Sx \vee Px) \text{ by DN \& DM}$$
$$\equiv \quad (\exists x)\sim(Sx \supset Px) \text{ by Impl}$$

By setting the **I** statement equivalent to the negation of the **E** statement we obtain:

$$(\exists x)(Sx \cdot Px) \equiv \sim(x)(Sx \supset \sim Px)$$
$$\equiv \sim(x)(\sim Sx \vee \sim Px) \text{ by Impl}$$
$$\equiv \sim(x)\sim(Sx \cdot Px) \text{ by DM}$$

And finally, by setting the negation of the **I** statement equivalent to the **E** statement, we have:

$$\sim(\exists x)(Sx \cdot Px) \equiv (x)(Sx \supset \sim Px)$$
$$\equiv (x)(\sim Sx \vee \sim Px) \text{ by Impl}$$
$$\equiv (x)\sim(Sx \cdot Px) \text{ by DM}$$

These equivalences demonstrate that negated and non-negated quantifiers may be replaced by their correlative if and only if negation signs are appropriately introduced or deleted before and after the new quantifier. If we let $\mathfrak{F}x$ represent any statement function, we may abbreviate these results as follows:

$$(x)\mathfrak{F}x \equiv \sim(\exists x)\sim\mathfrak{F}x$$
$$\sim(x)\mathfrak{F}x \equiv (\exists x) \sim \mathfrak{F}x$$
$$(\exists x)\mathfrak{F}x \equiv \sim(x)\sim\mathfrak{F}x$$
$$\sim(\exists x)\mathfrak{F}x \equiv (x)\sim\mathfrak{F}x$$

These are the change of quantifier rules (CQ). Since they are stated as logical equivalences, they apply to parts of lines as well as to whole lines. They can be summarized into a single rule that reads:

> One type of quantifier can be replaced by the other type if and only if immediately before and after the new quantifier:
> 1. Negation signs that were present earlier are deleted.
> 2. Negation signs that were not present earlier are introduced.

At this point we might question whether statements of the form $(x)Px$ and $(\exists x)Qx$ fall under this rule, since they are not in the same form as the more typical universal and particular statements. The answer is that they do indeed fall under this rule. The statement that everything in the universe is a P, symbolized $(x)Px$, is simply a shortened form of $(x)(Ux \supset Px)$, where Ux means "x is in the universe," and the statement that something in the universe is a Q, symbolized $(\exists x)Qx$, is simply another way of writing $(\exists x)(Ux \cdot Qx)$. Since everything whatsoever is a thing in the universe, the expression Ux is always true. As a result, $(x)(Ux \supset Px)$ reduces to $(x)Px$, and $(\exists x)(Ux \cdot Qx)$ reduces to $(\exists x)Qx$.

Let us now turn to some applications of the change of quantifier rule. Consider first the argument mentioned at the beginning of this section. The proof is as follows:

1. $\sim(\exists x)(Px \cdot \sim Qx)$
2. $\sim(x)(\sim Rx \vee Qx)$ / $(\exists x)\sim Px$
3. $(x)\sim(Px \cdot \sim Qx)$ 1, CQ
4. $(\exists x)\sim(\sim Rx \vee Qx)$ 2, CQ
5. $\sim(\sim Ra \vee Qa)$ 4, EI
6. $\sim(Pa \cdot \sim Qa)$ 3, UI
7. $Ra \cdot \sim Qa$ 5, DM, DN
8. $\sim Pa \vee Qa$ 6, DM, DN
9. $\sim Qa$ 7, Com, Simp
10. $\sim Pa$ 8, 9, Com, DS
11. $(\exists x)\sim Px$ 10, EG

Before either line 1 or line 2 can be instantiated, the negation signs preceding the quantifiers must be removed. In accordance with the change of quantifier rule, negation signs are introduced immediately after the new quantifiers in the expressions on lines 3 and 4.

Another example:

1. $(\exists x)(Hx \cdot Gx) \supset (x)Ix$
2. $\sim Im$ / $(x)(Hx \supset \sim Gx)$
3. $(\exists x)\sim Ix$ 2, EG
4. $\sim(x)Ix$ 3, CQ
5. $\sim(\exists x)(Hx \cdot Gx)$ 1, 4, MT
6. $(x)\sim(Hx \cdot Gx)$ 5, CQ
7. $(x)(\sim Hx \vee \sim Gx)$ 6, DM
8. $(x)(Hx \supset \sim Gx)$ 7, Impl

The statement that m is not an I (line 2) intuitively implies that not everything is an I (line 4); but existential generalization and change of quantifier are needed to get the desired result. Notice that lines 7 and 8 are obtained via DeMorgan's rule and the rule of material implication, even though the quantifier is still attached. Since these rules are rules of logical equivalence, they apply to parts of lines as well as to whole lines. The following example illustrates the same point with respect to the change of quantifier rules:

1. $(\exists x)Jx \supset \sim(\exists x)Kx$
2. $(x)\sim Kx \supset (x)\sim Lx$ / $(\exists x)Jx \supset \sim(\exists x)Lx$
3. $(\exists x)Jx \supset (x)\sim Kx$ 1, CQ
4. $(\exists x)Jx \supset (x)\sim Lx$ 2, 3, HS
5. $(\exists x)Jx \supset \sim(\exists x)Lx$ 4, CQ

The change of quantifier rule is applied to only the consequent of line 1, yielding line 3. Similarly, the change of quantifier rule is then applied to only the consequent of line 4, yielding line 5.

EXERCISE 8.3

I. Use the change of quantifier rule together with the eighteen rules of inference to derive the conclusions of the following symbolized arguments. Do not use either conditional proof or indirect proof.

★(1) 1. $(x)Ax \supset (\exists x)Bx$
    2. $(x){\sim}Bx$ / $(\exists x){\sim}Ax$

(2) 1. $(\exists x){\sim}Ax \lor (\exists x){\sim}Bx$
    2. $(x)Bx$ / ${\sim}(x)Ax$

(3) 1. ${\sim}(\exists x)Ax$ / $(x)(Ax \supset Bx)$

★(4) 1. $(\exists x)Ax \lor (\exists x)(Bx \cdot Cx)$
    2. ${\sim}(\exists x)Bx$ / $(\exists x)Ax$

(5) 1. $(x)(Ax \cdot Bx) \lor (x)(Cx \cdot Dx)$
    2. ${\sim}(x)Dx$ / $(x)Bx$

(6) 1. $(\exists x){\sim}Ax \supset (x)(Bx \supset Cx)$
    2. ${\sim}(x)(Ax \lor Cx)$ / ${\sim}(x)Bx$

★(7) 1. $(x)(Ax \supset Bx)$
    2. ${\sim}(x)Cx \lor (x)Ax$
    3. ${\sim}(x)Bx$ / $(\exists x){\sim}Cx$

(8) 1. $(x)Ax \supset (\exists x){\sim}Bx$
    2. ${\sim}(x)Bx \supset (\exists x){\sim}Cx$ / $(x)Cx \supset (\exists x){\sim}Ax$

(9) 1. $(\exists x)(Ax \lor Bx) \supset (x)Cx$
    2. $(\exists x){\sim}Cx$ / ${\sim}(\exists x)Ax$

★(10) 1. ${\sim}(\exists x)(Ax \cdot {\sim}Bx)$
    2. ${\sim}(\exists x)(Bx \cdot {\sim}Cx)$ / $(x)(Ax \supset Cx)$

(11) 1. ${\sim}(\exists x)(Ax \cdot {\sim}Bx)$
    2. ${\sim}(\exists x)(Ax \cdot {\sim}Cx)$ / $(x)[Ax \supset (Bx \cdot Cx)]$

(12) 1. $(x)[(Ax \cdot Bx) \supset Cx]$
    2. ${\sim}(x)(Ax \supset Cx)$ / ${\sim}(x)Bx$

★(13) 1. $(x)(Ax \cdot {\sim}Bx) \supset (\exists x)Cx$
    2. ${\sim}(\exists x)(Cx \lor Bx)$ / ${\sim}(x)Ax$

(14) 1. $(\exists x){\sim}Ax \supset (x){\sim}Bx$
    2. $(\exists x){\sim}Ax \supset (\exists x)Bx$
    3. $(x)(Ax \supset Cx)$ / $(x)Cx$

★(15) 1. ${\sim}(\exists x)(Ax \lor Bx)$
    2. $(\exists x)Cx \supset (\exists x)Ax$
    3. $(\exists x)Dx \supset (\exists x)Bx$ / ${\sim}(\exists x)(Cx \lor Dx)$

II. Translate the following arguments into symbolic form. Then use the change of quantifier rule and the eighteen rules of inference to derive the conclusion of each. Do not use either conditional proof or indirect proof.

★1. If all the physicians are either hematologists or neurologists, then there are no cardiologists. But Dr. Frank is a cardiologist. Therefore, some physicians are not neurologists. (*P*, *H*, *N*, *C*)

2. Either Dr. Adams is an internist or all the pathologists are internists. But it is not the case that there are any internists. Therefore, Dr. Adams is not a pathologist. (*I*, *P*)

3. If some surgeons are allergists, then some psychiatrists are radiologists. But no psychiatrists are radiologists. Therefore, no surgeons are allergists. (*S*, *A*, *P*, *R*)

★4. Either some general practitioners are pediatricians or some surgeons are endocrinologists. But it is not the case that there are any endocrinologists. Therefore, there are some pediatricians. (*G*, *P*, *S*, *E*)

5. All physicians who did not attend medical school are incompetent. It is not the case, however, that some physicians are incompetent. Therefore, all physicians have attended medical school. (*P*, *A*, *I*)

6. It is not the case that some internists are not physicians. Furthermore, it is not the case that some physicians are not doctors of medicine. Therefore, all internists are doctors of medicine. (*I*, *P*, *D*)

★7. All pathologists are specialists and all internists are generalists. Therefore, since it is not the case that some specialists are generalists, it is not the case that some pathologists are internists. (*P*, *S*, *I*, *G*)

8. If some obstetricians are not gynecologists, then some hematologists are radiologists. But it is not the case that there are any hematologists or gynecologists. Therefore, it is not the case that there are any obstetricians. (*O*, *G*, *H*, *R*)

9. All poorly trained allergists and dermatologists are untrustworthy specialists. It is not the case, however, that some specialists are untrustworthy. Therefore, it is not the case that some dermatologists are poorly trained. (*P*, *A*, *D*, *U*, *S*)

★10. It is not the case that some physicians are either on the golf course or in the hospital. All of the neurologists are physicians in the hospital. Either some physicians are cardiologists or some physicians are neurologists. Therefore, some cardiologists are not on the golf course. (*P*, *G*, *H*, *N*, *C*)

8.4 CONDITIONAL AND INDIRECT PROOF

Many arguments with conclusions that are either difficult or impossible to derive by the conventional method can be handled with ease by using either conditional or indirect proof. The use of these techniques on arguments in predicate logic is basically the same as it is on arguments in propositional logic. Arguments having conclusions expressed in the form of conditional statements or disjunctions (which can be converted into conditional statements) are immediate candidates for conditional proof. For these arguments, the usual strategy is to assume the antecedent of the conditional statement to be obtained as the first line of an indented sequence, to derive the consequent as the last line, and to discharge the conditional sequence in a conditional statement that exactly matches the one to be obtained. Here is an example of such a proof:

1. $(x)(Hx \supset Ix)$ / $(\exists x)Hx \supset (\exists x)Ix$
    2. $(\exists x)Hx$ ACP
    3. Ha 2, EI
    4. $Ha \supset Ia$ 1, UI
    5. Ia 3, 4, MP
    6. $(\exists x)Ix$ 5, EG
7. $(\exists x)Hx \supset (\exists x)Ix$ 2–6, CP

In this argument the antecedent of the conclusion is a complete statement consisting of a statement function, Hx, preceded by a quantifier. This complete statement is assumed as the first line in the conditional sequence. The instantiation and generalization rules are used within an indented sequence (both conditional and indirect) in basically the same way as they are in a conventional sequence. When the consequent of the conclusion is obtained, the conditional sequence is completed, and it is then discharged in a conditional statement having the first line of the sequence as its antecedent and the last line as its consequent.

The next example differs from the previous one in that the antecedent of the conclusion is a statement function, not a complete statement. With arguments such as this, only the statement function is assumed as the first line in the conditional sequence. The quantifier is added after the sequence is discharged.

1. $(x)[(Ax \lor Bx) \supset Cx]$ / $(x)(Ax \supset Cx)$
    2. Ax ACP
    3. $Ax \lor Bx$ 2, Add
    4. $(Ax \lor Bx) \supset Cx$ 1, UI
    5. Cx 3, 4, MP
6. $Ax \supset Cx$ 2–5, CP
7. $(x)(Ax \supset Cx)$ 6, UG

This example leads to an important restriction on the use of universal generalization. You may recall that the x in line 2 of this proof is called a *free variable* because it is not governed by any quantifier. (In contrast, the x's in lines 1 and 7 are called *bound variables*.) The restriction is as follows:

UG: $\dfrac{\mathfrak{F}y}{(x)\mathfrak{F}x}$ *Restriction:*   UG must not be used within the scope of an indented sequence if the instantial variable occurs free in the first line of that sequence.

The above proof does not violate this restriction because UG is not used within the scope of the indented sequence at all. It is used only after the sequence has been discharged, which is perfectly acceptable. If, on the other hand, UG had been applied to line 5 to produce a statement reading $(x)Cx$, the restriction would have been violated because the instantial variable x occurs free in the first line of the sequence.

To understand why this restriction is necessary, consider the following *defective* proof:

1. $(x)Rx \supset (x)Sx$	/ $(x)(Rx \supset Sx)$
2. Rx	ACP
3. $(x)Rx$	2, UG (invalid)
4. $(x)Sx$	1, 3, MP
5. Sx	4, UI
6. $Rx \supset Sx$	2–5, CP
7. $(x)(Rx \supset Sx)$	6, UG

If Rx means "x is a rabbit" and Sx means "x is a snake," then the premise translates "If everything in the universe is a rabbit, then everything in the universe is a snake." This statement is *true* because the antecedent is false; that is, it is *not* the case that everything in the universe is a rabbit. The conclusion, on the other hand, is *false*, because it asserts that all rabbits are snakes. The argument is therefore invalid. If the restriction on UG had been obeyed, UG would not have been used on line 3 and, as a result, the illicit conclusion would not have been obtained.

It is interesting to see what happens when the premise and the conclusion of this defective argument are switched. The proof, which is perfectly legitimate, is as follows:

1. $(x)(Rx \supset Sx)$	/ $(x)Rx \supset (x)Sx$
2. $(x)Rx$	ACP
3. Rx	2, UI
4. $Rx \supset Sx$	1, UI
5. Sx	3, 4, MP
6. $(x)Sx$	5, UG
7. $(x)Rx \supset (x)Sx$	2–6, CP

Notice in this proof that UG *is* used within the scope of a conditional sequence, but the restriction is not violated because the instantial variable x is not free on the first line of the sequence.

Let us now consider some examples of *indirect* proof. We begin an indirect sequence by assuming the negation of the statement to be obtained. When a contradiction is derived, the indirect sequence is discharged by asserting the denial of the original assumption. In the examples that follow, the negation of the conclusion is assumed as the first line of the sequence, and the change of quantifier rule is then used to eliminate the negation sign. When the resulting statement is then instantiated, a new letter, m, is selected that has not appeared anywhere in a previous line. The same letter is then selected for the universal instantiation of line 1:

1. $(x)[(Px \supset Px) \supset (Qx \supset Rx)]$	/ $(x)(Qx \supset Rx)$
2. $\sim (x)(Qx \supset Rx)$	AIP
3. $(\exists x)\sim(Qx \supset Rx)$	2, CQ
4. $\sim(Qm \supset Rm)$	3, EI
5. $(Pm \supset Pm) \supset (Qm \supset Rm)$	1, UI
6. $\sim(Pm \supset Pm)$	4, 5, MT
7. $\sim(\sim Pm \vee Pm)$	6, Impl
8. $Pm \cdot \sim Pm$	7, DM, DN
9. $\sim\sim(x)(Qx \supset Rx)$	2–8, IP
10. $(x)(Qx \supset Rx)$	9, DN

The next example has a particular statement for its conclusion:

1. $(\exists x)Ax \vee (\exists x)Fx$	
2. $(x)(Ax \supset Fx)$	/ $(\exists x)Fx$
3. $\sim(\exists x)Fx$	AIP
4. $(\exists x)Ax$	1, 3, Com, DS
5. Ac	4, EI
6. $Ac \supset Fc$	2, UI
7. Fc	5, 6, MP
8. $(x)\sim Fx$	3, CQ
9. $\sim Fc$	8, UI
10. $Fc \cdot \sim Fc$	7, 9, Conj
11. $(\exists x)Fx$	3–10, IP, DN

Since indirect proof sequences are indented, they are subject to the same restriction on universal generalization as conditional sequences. The following proof, which is similar to the previous one, violates this restriction because the instantial variable x is free in the first line of the sequence. The violation (line 4) allows a universal statement to be drawn for the conclusion, whereas only a particular statement (as above) is legitimate:

1. $(\exists x)Ax \vee (\exists x)Fx$	
2. $(x)(Ax \supset Fx)$	/ $(x)Fx$
3. $\sim Fx$	AIP
4. $(x)\sim Fx$	3, UG (invalid)
5. $\sim(\exists x)Fx$	4, CQ
6. $(\exists x)Ax$	1, 5, Com, DS
7. Ac	6, EI

A CONCISE INTRODUCTION TO LOGIC

8. $Ac \supset Fc$	2, UI
9. Fc	7, 8, MP
10. $\sim Fc$	4, UI
11. $Fc \cdot \sim Fc$	9, 10, Conj
12. Fx	3–11, IP, DN
13. $(x)Fx$	12, UG

To see that this argument is indeed invalid, let Ax stand for "x is an apple" and Fx for "x is a fruit." The first premise then reads "Either an apple exists or a fruit exists" (which is true), and the second premise reads "All apples are fruits" (which is also true). The conclusion, however, reads "Everything in the universe is a fruit"; and this, of course, is false.

As in propositional logic, conditional and indirect sequences in predicate logic may include each other. The following proof uses an indirect sequence within the scope of a conditional sequence.

1. $(x)[(Px \lor Qx) \supset (Rx \cdot Sx)]$	/ $(\exists x)(Px \lor Sx) \supset (\exists x)Sx$
2. $(\exists x)(Px \lor Sx)$	ACP
3. $\sim(\exists x)Sx$	AIP
4. $(x)\sim Sx$	3, CQ
5. $Pa \lor Sa$	2, EI
6. $\sim Sa$	4, UI
7. Pa	5, 6, Com, DS
8. $Pa \lor Qa$	7, Add
9. $(Pa \lor Qa) \supset (Ra \cdot Sa)$	1, UI
10. $Ra \cdot Sa$	8, 9, MP
11. Sa	10, Com, Simp
12. $Sa \cdot \sim Sa$	6, 11, Conj
13. $(\exists x)Sx$	3–12, IP, DN
14. $(\exists x)(Px \lor Sx) \supset (\exists x)Sx$	2–13, CP

The conditional sequence begins, as usual, by assuming the antecedent of the conditional statement to be obtained. The objective, then, is to obtain the consequent. This is accomplished by the indirect sequence, which begins with the negation of the consequent and ends (line 12) with a contradiction.

EXERCISE 8.4

I. Use either indirect proof or conditional proof to derive the conclusions of the following symbolized arguments:

★(1) 1. $(x)(Ax \supset Bx)$
 2. $(x)(Ax \supset Cx)$ / $(x)[Ax \supset (Bx \cdot Cx)]$

(2) 1. $(\exists x)Ax \supset (\exists x)(Bx \cdot Cx)$
 2. $(\exists x)(Cx \lor Dx) \supset (x)Ex$ / $(x)(Ax \supset Ex)$

(3) 1. $(\exists x)Ax \supset (\exists x)(Bx \cdot Cx)$
    2. $\sim(\exists x)Cx$ / $(x)\sim Ax$

★(4) 1. $(x)(Ax \supset Cx)$
     2. $(\exists x)Cx \supset (\exists x)(Bx \cdot Dx)$ / $(\exists x)Ax \supset (\exists x)Bx$

(5) 1. $(x)(Ax \supset Bx)$
    2. $(x)[(Ax \cdot Bx) \supset Cx]$ / $(x)(Ax \supset Cx)$

(6) 1. $(\exists x)Ax \supset (x)Bx$
    2. $An \supset \sim Bn$ / $\sim An$

★(7) 1. $(x)[(Ax \vee Bx) \supset Cx]$
     2. $(x)[(Cx \vee Dx) \supset Ex]$ / $(x)(Ax \supset Ex)$

(8) 1. $(\exists x)(Ax \vee Bx) \supset \sim(\exists x)Ax$ / $(x)\sim Ax$

(9) 1. $(x)(Ax \supset Bx)$
    2. $(x)(Cx \supset Dx)$ / $(\exists x)(Ax \vee Cx) \supset (\exists x)(Bx \vee Dx)$

★(10) 1. $(x)(Ax \supset Bx)$
      2. $Am \vee An$ / $(\exists x)Bx$

(11) 1. $(x)[(Ax \vee Bx) \supset Cx]$
     2. $(x)[(Cx \vee Dx) \supset \sim Ax]$ / $(x)\sim Ax$

(12) 1. $(\exists x)Ax \supset (x)(Bx \supset Cx)$
     2. $(\exists x)Dx \supset (x)\sim Cx$ / $(x)[(Ax \cdot Dx) \supset \sim Bx]$

★(13) 1. $(\exists x)Ax \supset (x)(Bx \supset Cx)$
      2. $(\exists x)Dx \supset (\exists x)Bx$ / $(\exists x)(Ax \cdot Dx) \supset (\exists x)Cx$

(14) 1. $(\exists x)Ax \vee (\exists x)(Bx \cdot Cx)$
     2. $(x)(Ax \supset Cx)$ / $(\exists x)Cx$

(15) 1. $(\exists x)Ax \supset (\exists x)(Bx \cdot Cx)$
     2. $(\exists x)Cx \supset (x)(Dx \cdot Ex)$ / $(x)(Ax \supset Ex)$

★(16) 1. $(x)[(Ax \vee Bx) \supset Cx]$
      2. $(\exists x)(\sim Ax \vee Dx) \supset (x)Ex$ / $(x)Cx \vee (x)Ex$

(17) 1. $(x)Ax \equiv (\exists x)(Bx \cdot Cx)$
     2. $(x)(Cx \supset Bx)$ / $(x)Ax \equiv (\exists x)Cx$

(18) 1. $(x)(Ax \equiv Bx)$
     2. $(x)[Ax \supset (Bx \supset Cx)]$
     3. $(\exists x)Ax \vee (\exists x)Bx$ / $(\exists x)Cx$

★(19) 1. $(x)[Bx \supset (Cx \cdot Dx)]$ / $(x)(Ax \supset Bx) \supset (x)(Ax \supset Dx)$

(20) 1. $(x)[Ax \supset (Bx \cdot Cx)]$
     2. $(x)[Dx \supset (Ex \cdot Fx)]$ / $(x)(Cx \supset Dx) \supset (x)(Ax \supset Fx)$

(21) 1. $(\exists x)(Ax \vee Bx)$
     2. $(\exists x)Ax \supset (x)(Cx \supset Bx)$
     3. $(\exists x)Cx$ / $(\exists x)Bx$

II. Translate the following arguments into symbolic form. Then use conditional or indirect proof to derive the conclusion of each.

★1. All ambassadors are wealthy. Furthermore, all Republicans are clever. Therefore, all Republican ambassadors are clever and wealthy. (*A*, *W*, *R*, *C*)

2. All senators are well liked. Also, if there are any well-liked senators, then O'Brien is a voter. Therefore, if there are any senators, then O'Brien is a voter. (*S*, *W*, *V*)

3. If all judges are wise, then some attorneys are rewarded. Furthermore, if there are any judges who are not wise, then some attorneys are rewarded. Therefore, some attorneys are rewarded. (*J*, *W*, *A*, *R*)

★4. All secretaries and undersecretaries are intelligent and cautious. All those who are cautious or vigilant are restrained and austere. Therefore, all secretaries are austere. (*S*, *U*, *I*, *C*, *V*, *R*, *A*)

5. All ambassadors are diplomats. Furthermore, all experienced ambassadors are cautious, and all cautious diplomats have foresight. Therefore, all experienced ambassadors have foresight. (*A*, *D*, *E*, *C*, *F*)

6. If there are any senators, then some employees are well paid. If there is anyone who is either an employee or a volunteer, then there are some legislative assistants. Either there are some volunteers or there are some senators. Therefore, there are some legislative assistants. (*S*, *E*, *W*, *V*, *L*)

★7. If there are any counsels, then all ambassadors are satisfied diplomats. If no counsels are ambassadors, then some diplomats are satisfied. Therefore, some diplomats are satisfied. (*C*, *A*, *S*, *D*)

8. If there are any voters, then all politicians are astute. If there are any politicians, then whoever is astute is clever. Therefore, if there are any voters, then all politicians are clever. (*V*, *P*, *A*, *C*)

9. Either no senators are present or no representatives are present. Furthermore, either some senators are present or no women are present. Therefore, none of the representatives who are present are women. (*S*, *P*, *R*, *W*)

★10. Either some governors are present or some ambassadors are present. If anyone is present, then some ambassadors are clever diplomats. Therefore, some diplomats are clever. (*G*, *P*, *A*, *C*, *D*)

8.5 PROVING INVALIDITY

In a valid deductive argument the conclusion follows *necessarily* from the premises. This means that for such an argument the link between premises and conclusion is independent of the actual arrangement of things in the world. If an argument is valid, it remains valid irrespective of whether the sun rises in the east or whether World War III starts tomorrow. Accordingly, if the premises of a valid argument are assumed true, the conclusion must be true, no matter what happens. Conversely, if, under a certain assumption, the premises of an argument are true and the conclusion false, the argument is invalid. In other words, if we can imagine an arrangement of things in the world that causes the premises to be true and the conclusion false, the argument is invalid. The method that we are about to describe for proving the invalidity of arguments in predicate logic rests upon this basic insight.

To see how this method works, it is important to understand what happens to the meaning of universal and particular statements when we imagine the universe to be changed in certain ways. To this end, let us imagine that the universe contains only one thing instead of the billions of things that it actually contains. Let us name that one thing "Abigail." The statement "Everything in the universe is perfect" is then equivalent to "Abigail is perfect" (because Abigail is all that there is), and the statement "Something in the universe is perfect" is also equivalent to "Abigail is perfect" (because Abigail is that "something"). In symbols, we have:

$$(x)Px \equiv Pa$$
$$(\exists x)Px \equiv Pa$$

Proceeding, if we imagine that the universe contains exactly two things—let us name them "Abigail" and "Beatrice"—the statement "Everything in the universe is perfect" is equivalent to "Abigail is perfect *and* Beatrice is perfect." Conversely, the statement "Something in the universe is perfect" is equivalent to "Abigail is perfect *or* Beatrice is perfect" (because *some* means *at least one*). In other words, the universal statement is equivalent to a *conjunction* of singular statements, and the particular statement is equivalent to a *disjunction* of singular statements. In symbols:

$$(x)Px \equiv (Pa \cdot Pb)$$
$$(\exists x)Px \equiv (Pa \lor Pb)$$

If the universe is increased to three—let us call the new member "Charmaine"—we have:

$$(x)Px \equiv (Pa \cdot Pb \cdot Pc)$$
$$(\exists x)Px \equiv (Pa \lor Pb \lor Pc)$$

This equivalence continues indefinitely as more and more members are added to the universe.

Extending this treatment to the more typical kinds of universal and particular statements, we have, for a universe of three:

$$(x)(Px \supset Qx) \equiv [(Pa \supset Qa) \cdot (Pb \supset Qb) \cdot (Pc \supset Qc)]$$
$$(\exists x)(Px \cdot Qx) \equiv [(Pa \cdot Qa) \lor (Pb \cdot Qb) \lor (Pc \cdot Qc)]$$

For expressions involving combinations of quantified statements, each of the component statements is translated separately and the resulting statement groups are linked together by means of the connective appearing in the original statement. Here are two examples for a universe of three:

$$[(x)Px \supset (\exists x)Qx] \equiv [(Pa \cdot Pb \cdot Pc) \supset (Qa \lor Qb \lor Qc)]$$
$$[(x)(Px \supset Qx) \lor (\exists x)(Rx \cdot Sx)] \equiv \{[(Pa \supset Qa) \cdot (Pb \supset Qb) \cdot (Pc \supset Qc)]$$
$$\lor [(Ra \cdot Sa) \lor (Rb \cdot Sb) \lor (Rc \cdot Sc)]\}$$

The method for proving an argument invalid consists in translating the premises and conclusion into singular statements, as per the above examples, and then testing the result with an indirect truth table (see Section 6.6). First a universe of one is tried. If it is possible for the premises to be true and the conclusion false in this universe, the argument is immediately identified as invalid. If, on the other hand, a contradiction results from this assumption, a universe of two is then tried. If, in this second universe, it is possible for the premises to be true and the conclusion false, the argument is invalid. If not, a universe of three is tried, and so on.

Consider the following argument:

$$(x)(Gx \supset Hx)$$
$$(\exists x)Hx \qquad / \ (\exists x)Gx$$

For a universe having one member—call this member "Abigail"—the argument translates into:

$$Ga \supset Ha$$
$$Ha \qquad / \ Ga$$

Testing with an indirect truth table, we have

$Ga \supset Ha$	/	Ha	//	Ga
F T T		T		F

Because it is possible for the premises to be true and the conclusion false, the argument is invalid. Another example:

$$(x)\,(Jx \supset Kx)$$
$$(\exists x)Jx \qquad / \ (x)Kx$$

For a universe having one member, the indirect truth table is as follows:

$Ja \supset Ka$	/	Ja	//	Ka
T T F		T		F

Since it is impossible for the premises to be true and the conclusion false for this universe, we try a universe having two members, *a* and *b*:

$$(Ja \supset Ka) \cdot (Jb \supset Kb) \quad / \quad Ja \lor Jb \quad // \quad Ka \cdot Kb$$
$$\text{T T} \quad \text{T T F T} \quad \text{F} \qquad \text{T T F} \qquad \text{T F F}$$

Since it is possible for the premises to be true and the conclusion false for this universe, the argument is invalid.

Here is an example involving compound statements:

$$(\exists x)Hx \supset (x)(Fx \supset Gx)$$
$$(\exists x)Fx \quad / (\exists x)Hx \supset (x)Gx$$

The indirect truth table for a universe having one member is as follows:

$$Ha \supset (Fa \supset Ga) \quad / \quad Fa \quad // \quad Ha \supset Ga$$
$$\boxed{\text{T T} \quad \text{T F}} \;\text{F} \qquad \text{T} \qquad \text{T F F}$$

A contradiction results, so we try a universe having two members. The resulting indirect truth table, which follows, proves the argument invalid:

$$(Ha \lor Hb) \supset [(Fa \supset Ga) \cdot (Fb \supset Gb)] / Fa \lor Fb // (Ha \lor Hb) \supset (Ga \cdot Gb)$$
$$\text{T} \quad \text{T} \quad \text{T T T T F T} \quad \text{F} \qquad \text{T T F} \qquad \text{T} \quad \text{F T F F}$$

The next example involves singular statements:

$$(\exists x)Mx \cdot (\exists x)Nx$$
$$Md \quad /Nd$$

The second premise asserts that something named *d* is an *M*. For this argument, the assumption that the universe contains only one member entails that this one member is named *d*. Here is the indirect truth table for such a universe:

$$Md \cdot Nd \quad / \quad Md \quad // \quad Nd$$
$$\boxed{\text{T T F}} \qquad \text{T} \qquad \text{F}$$

When the universe is expanded to include two members, we are free to give any name we wish to the second member. Let us call it *e*. The resulting indirect truth table, which follows, shows that the argument is invalid. Notice that the second premise and the conclusion remain the same:

$$(Md \lor Me) \cdot (Nd \lor Ne) \quad / \quad Md \quad // \quad Nd$$
$$\text{T T} \quad \text{T F T T} \qquad \text{T} \qquad \text{F}$$

The basic concept behind this method of proving invalidity rests on the fact that a valid argument is valid in all possible universes. Consequently, if an argument fails in a universe consisting of one, two, or any number of members, it is invalid.

While this method is primarily intended for proving arguments invalid, theoretically it can also be used to prove arguments valid. Several years ago a theorem was proved to the effect that an argument that does not fail in a universe of 2^n members, where n designates the number of different predicates, is valid.* According to this theorem, establishing the validity of an argument containing two different predicates requires a universe having four members, establishing the validity of an argument containing three different predicates requires a universe having eight members, and so on. For most arguments, however, a universe having four members is unwieldy at best, and a universe having eight members approaches the impossible (although a computer could handle it easily). Thus, while this method is usually quite convenient for proving invalidity, its usefulness in establishing validity is impeded by certain practical limitations.

EXERCISE 8.5

I. Prove that the following symbolized arguments are invalid:

★(1) 1. $(x)(Ax \supset Bx)$
    2. $(x)(Ax \supset Cx)$ / $(x)(Bx \supset Cx)$

(2) 1. $(x)(Ax \lor Bx)$
    2. $\sim An$ / $(x)Bx$

(3) 1. $(\exists x)Ax \lor (\exists x)Bx$
    2. $(\exists x)Ax$ / $(\exists x)Bx$

★(4) 1. $(x)(Ax \supset Bx)$
    2. $(\exists x)Ax$ / $(x)Bx$

(5) 1. $(x)[Ax \supset (Bx \lor Cx)]$
    2. $(\exists x)Ax$ / $(\exists x)Bx$

(6) 1. $(\exists x)Ax$
    2. $(\exists x)Bx$ / $(\exists x)(Ax \cdot Bx)$

★(7) 1. $(x)(Ax \supset Bx)$
    2. $(\exists x)Bx \supset (\exists x)Cx$ / $(x)(Ax \supset Cx)$

---

*See Wilhelm Ackermann, *Solvable Cases of the Decision Problem* (Amsterdam: North-Holland Publishing Co., 1954), Chapter 4. This theorem, incidentally, holds only for monadic predicates.

(8) 1. $(\exists x)(Ax \cdot Bx) \equiv (\exists x)Cx$
    2. $(x)(Ax \supset Bx)$ / $(x)Ax \equiv (\exists x)Cx$

(9) 1. $(\exists x)(Ax \cdot {\sim}Bx)$
    2. $(\exists x)(Bx \cdot {\sim}Ax)$ / $(x)(Ax \lor Bx)$

★(10) 1. $(\exists x)(Ax \cdot Bx)$
      2. $(\exists x)({\sim}Ax \cdot {\sim}Bx)$ / $(x)(Ax \equiv Bx)$

II. Translate the following arguments into symbolic form. Then prove that each is invalid.

★1. Violinists who play well are accomplished musicians. There are some violinists in the orchestra. Therefore, some musicians are accomplished. (*V, P, A, M, O*)

2. Pianists and harpsichordists are meticulous. Rudoff Serkin is a pianist. Therefore, everyone is meticulous. (*P, H, M*)

3. If there are any oboists, there are some bassoonists. If there are any clarinetists, there are some flutists. Amelia is both an oboist and a clarinetist. Therefore, some bassoonists are flutists. (*O, B, C, F*)

★4. All tympanists are haughty. If some tympanists are haughty, then some percussionists are overbearing. Therefore, all tympanists are overbearing. (*T, H, P, O*)

5. All cellists and violinists are members of the string section. Some violinists are not cellists. Also, some cellists are not violinists. Therefore, everyone is a member of the string section. (*C, V, M*)

8.6 RELATIONAL PREDICATES AND OVERLAPPING QUANTIFIERS

Even the logical machinery developed thus far is not adequate for deriving the conclusions of a number of arguments. Consider, for example, the following:

> All dogs are animals. Therefore, whoever owns a dog owns an animal.

> If there are any butterflies, then if all butterflies are free, they are free. There are butterflies in the garden. Therefore, if all butterflies are free, something in the garden is free.

The first argument involves a relation—the relation of ownership—and we have yet to see how relations can be dealt with. The second argument, while not involving any relations, involves a quantifier that overlaps another quantifier. In this section the apparatus of predicate logic will be extended to cover examples such as these.

Relations (that is **relational predicates**) come in varying degrees of complexity, depending on the number of individuals related. The simplest, called *binary* (or *dyadic*) relations, establish a connection between two individuals. Some examples are the relation of being taller than, as expressed in the statement "Steve is taller than David," and the relation of being a friend, as expressed in "Sylvia is a friend of Olivia." *Trinary* (or *triadic*) relations establish a connection between three individuals. For example, the relation of being between, as in "St. Louis is between Chicago and New Orleans," and the relation of reading something to someone, as in "George read *Othello* to Madeline." *Quaternary* (or *tetradic*) relations link four individuals together—for example, the relation of reading something to someone at a certain time, as in "George read *Othello* to Madeline on Thursday." The complexity increases until we have what are called *n-ary* (or *n-adic*) relations, which link *n* things together. In this section we will restrict our attention to binary relations.

Relations are symbolized like other predicates except that two lower-case letters, representing the two related individuals, are written to the immediate right of the upper-case letter representing the relation. Here are some examples of relational statements involving specifically named individuals:

Statement	Symbolic translation
Anthony is married to Cynthia.	*Mac*
Deborah loves physics.	*Ldp*
The Sears Tower is taller than the Empire State Building.	*Tse*
Donald is the father of Jim.	*Fdj*

Notice that the order in which the lower-case letters are listed often makes a difference. If the third statement were translated *Tes*, the symbolic statement would read "The Empire State Building is taller than the Sears Tower," which is false. Quantifiers are attached to relational predicates in the same way they are to ordinary predicates. Some examples of relational statements involving quantifiers are as follows:

Statement	Symbolic translation
Thomas knows everything.	$(x)Ktx$
Thomas knows something.	$(\exists x)Ktx$
Everything is different from everything.	$(x)(y)Dxy$

Something is different from something.	$(\exists x)(\exists y)Dxy$
Everything is different from something (or other).	$(x)(\exists y)Dxy$
Something is different from everything.	$(\exists x)(y)Dxy$

The last four statements involve **overlapping quantifiers.** We may read these symbols as follows:

$(x)(y)$	For all x and for all y . . .
$(\exists x)(\exists y)$	There exists an x such that there exists a y such that . . .
$(x)(\exists y)$	For all x there exists a y such that . . .
$(\exists x)(y)$	There exists an x such that for all y . . .

Applying this phraseology to the last statement above, for example, we have "There exists an x such that for all y, x is different from y"—which is simply another way of saying "Something is different from everything."

When two quantifiers of the same sort appear adjacent to each other, the order in which they are listed is not significant. In other words, the statement $(x)(y)Dxy$ is logically equivalent to $(y)(x)Dxy$, and $(\exists x)(\exists y)Dxy$ is logically equivalent to $(\exists y)(\exists x)Dxy$. A little reflection on the meaning of these statements should justify this equivalence. But when different quantifiers appear adjacent to each other, the order *does* make a difference, sometimes even when the statement function is nonrelational. Accordingly, $(x)(\exists y)Dxy$ is not logically equivalent to $(\exists y)(x)Dxy$. This fact can be seen more clearly in terms of a different example. If Lxy means "x loves y" and we imagine the universe restricted to persons, then $(x)(\exists y)Lxy$ means "Everyone loves someone (or other)," while $(\exists y)(x)Lxy$ means "There is someone whom everyone loves." Clearly these two statements are not equivalent.

Relational predicates can be combined with ordinary predicates to translate statements having varying degrees of complexity. In the examples that follow, Px means "x is a person." The meaning of the other predicates should be clear from the context:

1. Any heavyweight can defeat any lightweight.
   $(x)[Hx \supset (y)(Ly \supset Dxy)]$

2. Some heavyweights can defeat any lightweight.
   $(\exists x)[Hx \cdot (y)(Ly \supset Dxy)]$

3. No heavyweight can defeat every lightweight.
$(x)[Hx \supset (\exists y)(Ly \cdot \sim Dxy)]$
   or
$\sim(\exists x)[Hx \cdot (y)(Ly \supset Dxy)]$

4. Everyone cares for someone (or other).
$(x)[Px \supset (\exists y)(Py \cdot Cxy)]$

5. Someone does not care for anyone.
$(\exists x)[Px \cdot (y)(Py \supset \sim Cxy)]$

6. Anyone who cares for someone is cared for himself.
$(x)\{[Px \cdot (\exists y)(Py \cdot Cxy)] \supset (\exists z)(Pz \cdot Czx)\}$

7. Not everyone respects himself.
$(\exists x)(Px \cdot \sim Rxx)$
   or
$\sim(x)(Px \supset Rxx)$

8. Anyone who does not respect himself is not respected by anyone.
$(x)[(Px \cdot \sim Rxx) \supset (y)(Py \supset \sim Ryx)]$

The same general rule applies in translating these statements as applies in translating any other statement in predicate logic: Universal quantifiers go with implications and existential quantifiers go with conjunctions. Every one of the symbolic expressions above follows this rule. For example, in the first statement, both quantifiers are universal and both connectives are implications. In the second statement, the main quantifier is existential and the subordinate quantifier universal; accordingly, the main connective is a conjunction and the subordinate connective is an implication. Among these statements, number 6 is the most complex. The symbolic translation of this statement reads, "For all x, if x is a person and there exists a y such that y is a person and x cares for y, then there exists a z such that z is a person and z cares for x." Upon reflection it should be clear that this is simply another way of expressing the original English statement.

Another important rule to keep in mind when translating statements of this kind is that every variable must be bound by some quantifier. If a variable is left dangling outside the scope of its intended quantifier, the translation is meaningless. For example, if the second statement were translated $(\exists x)Hx \cdot (y)(Ly \supset Dxy)$, then the x in Dxy would not be bound by the existential quantifier. As a result, the translation would be meaningless. To correct it, brackets must be inserted that provide for the existential quantifier to range over Dxy.

The same techniques used to translate these eight statements are also used to translate certain statements involving ordinary predicates throughout. Consider the following:

If anything is good and all good things are safe, then it is safe.

$$(x)\{[Gx \cdot (y)(Gy \supset Sy)] \supset Sx\}$$

If anything is good and some good things are dangerous, then it is dangerous.

$$(x)\{[Gx \cdot (\exists y)(Gy \cdot Dy)] \supset Dx\}$$

Since the "it" at the end of these statements refers to one of the "good" things mentioned at the beginning, the quantifier that binds the x in Gx must also bind the x in Sx and Dx. The set of braces in the symbolic expressions ensures this.

Another point to notice regarding statements such as these is that the quantified expression inside the brackets is expressed in terms of a *new* variable. This procedure is essential to avoid ambiguity. If instead of y, x had been used, the variable in this expression would be bound by two different quantifiers at the same time.

In other statements, the one or more individuals mentioned at the end are *not* necessarily the same ones mentioned at the beginning. In such cases the quantifier that binds the individuals at the beginning should *not* bind those at the end. Compare the next pair of statements with those we have just considered.

If anything is good and all good things are safe, then something is safe.

$$[(\exists x)Gx \cdot (y)(Gy \supset Sy)] \supset (\exists z)Sz$$

If anything is good and some good things are dangerous, then something is dangerous.

$$[(\exists x)Gx \cdot (\exists y)(Gy \cdot Dy)] \supset (\exists z)Dz$$

In these cases the "something" at the end is not necessarily one of the "good" things mentioned at the beginning. Accordingly, the quantifier that binds the x in Gx does *not* range all the way to the end of the statement. Furthermore, the quantifier in question is now an *existential* quantifier. In the previous pair of statements the quantifier had to be universal because it ranged over the main connective, which was an implication. In the new pair, however, no quantifier ranges over the implication symbol. As a result, the sense of these statements has shifted to mean "If *something* is good . . ."

I should point out here that although a different variable is used to express each of the three different components in the pair of statements above, this is not required. Because no quantifier ranges over any other quantifier, it would be perfectly appropriate to use the same variable throughout.

The next pair of statements involve relational predicates. Like the previous pair, no single quantifier ranges over the entire statement because the individuals mentioned at the end are not necessarily the same ones mentioned at the beginning:

If everyone helps himself, then everyone will be helped.

$$(x)(Px \supset Hxx) \supset (x)[(Px \supset (\exists y)Hyx)]$$

If someone helps himself, then someone will be helped.

$$(\exists x)(Px \cdot Hxx) \supset (\exists x)(\exists y)(Px \cdot Hyx)$$

Let us now see how the various quantifier rules apply to overlapping quantifiers. The change of quantifier rule is applied in basically the same way as it is with single quantifiers. The following short sequence illustrates its application:

1. $\sim(x)(\exists y)Pxy$
2. $(\exists x)\sim(\exists y)Pxy$ 1, CQ
3. $(\exists x)(y)\sim Pxy$ 2, CQ

As the negation sign is moved past a quantifier, the quantifier in question is switched for its correlative. With the exception of a restriction on universal generalization, which we will introduce presently, the instantiation and generalization rules are also used in basically the same way as they are with single quantifiers. Example:

1. $(\exists x)(\exists y)Pxy$
2. $(\exists y)Pay$ 1, EI
3. Pab 2, EI
4. $(\exists x)Pxb$ 3, EG
5. $(\exists y)(\exists x)Pxy$ 4, EG

With each successive instantiation the outermost quantifier drops off. Generalization restores the quantifiers in the reverse order.

This proof demonstrates our earlier observation that the order of the quantifiers is not significant when the same kind of quantifier is used throughout. We also observed that the order does make a difference when different quantifiers appear together. Accordingly, the statement $(x)(\exists y)Pxy$ is not logically equivalent to $(\exists y)(x)Pxy$. As the instantiation and generalization rules now stand, however, it is quite possible, with a proof similar to the one above, to establish the logical equivalence of these two expressions. Therefore, to keep this from happening we now introduce a new restriction on universal generalization:

UG: $\dfrac{\mathscr{F}y}{(x)\mathscr{F}x}$ *Restriction:*   UG must not be used if $\mathscr{F}y$ contains an existential name and y is free in the line where that name is introduced.

To see how this restriction applies, let us attempt to deduce $(\exists y)(x)Pxy$ from $(x)(\exists y)Pxy$:

    1. $(x)(\exists y)Pxy$
    2. $(\exists y)Pxy$ 1, UI
    3. Pxa 2, EI
    4. $(x)Pxa$ 3, UG (invalid)
    5. $(\exists y)(x)Pxy$ 4, EG

The proof fails on line 4 because $\exists y$ (that is, Pxa) contains a name introduced by existential instantiation (namely, a), and x is free in line 3 where that name is introduced. Our new restriction is required precisely to prevent this kind of proof sequence from occurring. The reasonableness of the restriction may be seen once it is realized what happens in this proof. Line 1 asserts that for every x in the universe there exists some y that has relation P to it. This does not mean that there is one *single* thing that is so related to every x but that each x has, perhaps, a *different* thing so related to it. On line 2 we select one of these x's at random, and on line 3 we give the name a to the thing so related to it. Then on line 4 we draw the conclusion that everything in the universe has relation P to a. But this, as we just saw, is precisely what line 1 does *not* say. Line 4, therefore, is fallacious.

In summary, we now have two restrictions on universal generalization. The first concerns only conditional and indirect sequences and prevents UG from occurring within the scope of such a sequence when the instantial variable is free in the first line. The second restriction concerns only arguments involving overlapping quantifiers. With these two restrictions in hand, we may now proceed to illustrate the use of natural deduction in arguments involving relational predicates and overlapping quantifiers. The example that follows does not include any relational predicates, but it does involve overlapping quantifiers.:

    1. $(\exists x)Ax \supset (\exists x)Bx$ / $(\exists y)(x)(Ax \supset By)$
      | 2. Ax ACP
      | 3. $(\exists x)Ax$ 2, EG
      | 4. $(\exists x)Bx$ 1, 3, MP
      | 5. Bc 4, EI
    6. $Ax \supset Bc$ 2-5, CP
    7. $(x)(Ax \supset Bc)$ 6, UG
    8. $(\exists y)(x)(Ax \supset By)$ 7, EG

Conditional and indirect proof are used in the same way with relational predicates and overlapping quantifiers as they are with ordinary predicates and nonoverlapping quantifiers. The conditional proof above begins, as usual, by assuming the antecedent of the conclusion. When line 7 is reached, we must be careful that neither of the restrictions against universal generalization is violated. While the instantial variable x is free in the first line of the conditional sequence, line 7 does not lie within that sequence, so the first restriction is obeyed. And while line 7 does include the existential name c, x is not free in line 5 where that name is introduced. Thus, the second restriction is obeyed as well.

The next proof involves a relational predicate. The proof shows that while $(x)(\exists y)Dxy$ is not *equivalent* to $(\exists y)(x)Dxy$, it can be deduced from that statement:

1. $(\exists y)(x)Dxy$ / $(x)(\exists y)Dxy$
2. $(x)Dxm$ 1, EI
3. Dxm 2, UI
4. $(\exists y)Dxy$ 3, EG
5. $(x)(\exists y)Dxy$ 4, UG

The next example concludes with a line in which an individual is related to itself. Since there are no restrictions on universal instantiation, the procedure leading up to this line is perfectly legitimate. Notice in line 4 that tautology is used with relational predicates in the same way that it is with ordinary predicates:

1. $(\exists y)(x)(Exy \lor Eyx)$ / $(\exists z)Ezz$
2. $(x)(Exa \lor Eax)$ 1, EI
3. $Eaa \lor Eaa$ 2, UI
4. Eaa 3, Taut
5. $(\exists z)Ezz$ 4, EG

Sometimes the order in which instantiation steps are performed is critical. The following proof provides an example:

1. $(x)(\exists y)(Fxy \supset Gxy)$
2. $(\exists x)(y)Fxy$ / $(\exists x)(\exists y)Gxy$
3. $(y)Fmy$ 2, EI
4. $(\exists y)(Fmy \supset Gmy)$ 1, UI
5. $Fmo \supset Gmo$ 4, EI
6. Fmo 3, UI
7. Gmo 5, 6, MP
8. $(\exists y)Gmy$ 7, EG
9. $(\exists x)(\exists y)Gxy$ 8, EG

Line 2 must be instantiated before line 1 because the step introduces a new existential name. For the same reason, line 4 must be instantiated before line 3.

The next proof involves an indirect sequence. Such sequences often make use of the change of quantifier rule, as this proof illustrates:

1. $(\exists x)(\exists y)(Jxy \lor Kxy) \supset (\exists x)Lx$	
2. $(x)(y)(Lx \supset {\sim}Ly)$	$/\ (x)(y){\sim}Jxy$
3. ${\sim}(x)(y){\sim}Jxy$	AIP
4. $(\exists x){\sim}(y){\sim}Jxy$	3, CQ
5. $(\exists x)(\exists y)Jxy$	3, CQ, DN
6. $(\exists y)Jmy$	5, EI
7. Jmn	6, EI
8. $Jmn \lor Kmn$	7, Add
9. $(\exists y)(Jmy \lor Kmy)$	8, EG
10. $(\exists x)(\exists y)(Jxy \lor Kxy)$	9, EG
11. $(\exists x)Lx$	1, 10, MP
12. Lo	11, EI
13. $(y)(Lo \supset {\sim}Ly)$	2, UI
14. $Lo \supset {\sim}Lo$	13, UI
15. ${\sim}Lo$	12, 14, MP
16. $Lo \cdot {\sim}Lo$	12, 15, Conj
17. $(x)(y){\sim}Jxy$	3–16, IP, DN

Because line 1 cannot be instantiated, the only strategy is to obtain the antecedent of the conditional with the aim of obtaining the consequent via *modus ponens*. This is accomplished on line 10 via indirect proof. Notice on line 8 that addition is used with relational predicates in the same way that it is with ordinary predicates.

A final word of caution is called for regarding universal instantiation and the two generalization rules. First, when UI is used to introduce variables into a proof, it is important that these variables end up free and that they not be captured in the process by other quantifiers. The following examples illustrate both correct and incorrect applications of this rule:

1. $(x)(\exists y)Pxy$		
2. $\overline{(\exists y)Pyy}$	1, UI	(invalid—the instantial variable y has been captured by the existential quantifier)

1. $(x)(\exists y)Pxy$		
2. $\overline{(\exists y)Pxy}$	1, UI	(valid—the instantial variable x is free)

1. $(x)(\exists y)Pxy$		
2. $\overline{(\exists y)Pzy}$	1, UI	(valid—the instantial variable z is free)

An analogous caution applies to the two generalization rules. When either UG or EG is used to introduce quantifiers, it is important that the quantifiers capture only the variables they are intended to capture. They

        A CONCISE INTRODUCTION TO LOGIC

must not capture variables that are already bound by other quantifiers, and they must not capture other free variables in the statement function. The following examples illustrate both correct and incorrect applications of these rules:

1. $(\exists x)Pxy$
2. $(x)(\exists x)Pxx$ 1, UG (invalid—the variable x is now bound by two quantifiers)

1. $(\exists x)Pxy$
2. $(\exists x)(\exists x)Pxx$ 1, EG (invalid—the variable x is now bound by two quantifiers)

1. $(\exists x)Pxy$
2. $(\exists y)(\exists x)Pxy$ 1, EG (valid)

1. $(x)(\exists y)Lxy$
2. $(\exists y)Lxy$ 1, UI
3. Lxa 2, EI
4. $(\exists x)Lxx$ 3, EG (invalid—the quantifier has captured the x immediately adjacent to the L)

1. $(x)(\exists y)Lxy$
2. $(\exists y)Lxy$ 1, UI
3. Lxa 2, EI
4. $(\exists z)Lxz$ 3, EG (valid—the x remains free)

1. $(x)(y)Kxy$
2 $(y)Kxy$ 1, UI
3. Kxx 2, UI
4. $(x)Kxx$ 3, UG (valid)

To see that the fourth example is indeed invalid, let Lxy stand for "x is larger than y," and let the variables range over the real numbers. The statement $(x)(\exists y)Lxy$ then means that there is no smallest number—which is true. But the statement $(\exists x)Lxx$ means that there is a number that is larger than itself—which is false.

EXERCISE 8.6

I. Translate the following statements into symbolic form:

★1. Charmaine read *Paradise Lost*. (Rxy: x read y)

2. Whoever reads *Paradise Lost* is educated. (Rxy: x reads y; Ex: x is educated)

3. James is a friend of either Ellen or Connie. (Fxy: x is a friend of y)

★4. If James has any friends, then Marlene is one of them. (Fxy: x is a friend of y)

5. Dr. Jordan teaches only geniuses. (*Txy*: *x* teaches *y*; *Gx*: *x* is a genius)

6. Dr. Nelson teaches a few morons. (*Txy*: *x* teaches *y*; *Mx*: *x* is a moron)

★7. Every person can sell something or other. (*Px*: *x* is a person; *Sxy*: *x* can sell *y*)

8. Some people cannot sell anything.

9. No person can sell everything.

★10. Some people can sell anything.

11. The Royal Hotel serves only good drinks. (*Sxy*: *x* serves *y*; *Gx*: *x* is good; *Dx*: *x* is a drink)

12. The Clark Corporation advertises everything it produces. (*Axy*: *x* advertises *y*; *Pxy*: *x* produces *y*)

★13. Peterson can drive some of the cars in the lot. (*Dxy*: *x* can drive *y*; *Cx*: *x* is a car; *Lx*: *x* is in the lot)

14. Jones can drive any car in the lot.

15. Sylvia invited only her friends. (*Ixy*: *x* invited *y*; *Fxy*: *x* is a friend of *y*)

★16. Christopher invited some of his friends.

17. Some people break everything they touch. (*Px*: *x* is a person; *Bxy*: *x* breaks *y*; *Txy*: *x* touches *y*)

18. Some people speak to whoever speaks to them. (*Px*: *x* is a person; *Sxy*: *x* speaks to *y*)

★19. Every person admires some people he or she meets. (*Px*: *x* is a person; *Axy*: *x* admires *y*; *Mxy*: *x* meets *y*)

20. Some people admire every person they meet.

21. Some policemen arrest only traffic violators. (*Px*: *x* is a policeman; *Axy*: *x* arrests *y*; *Tx*: *x* is a traffic violator)

★22. Some policemen arrest every traffic violator they see. (*Px*: *x* is a policeman; *Axy*: *x* arrests *y*; *Tx*: *x* is a traffic violator; *Sxy*: *x* sees *y*)

23. If there are any cheaters, then some cheaters will be punished. (*Cx*: *x* is a cheater; *Px*: *x* will be punished)

24. If there are any cheaters, then if all the referees are vigilant they will be punished. (*Cx*: *x* is a cheater; *Rx*: *x* is a referee; *Vx*: *x* is vigilant; *Px*: *x* will be punished)

★25. Every lawyer will represent a wealthy client. (*Lx*: *x* is a lawyer; *Rxy*: *x* will represent *y*; *Wx*: *x* is wealthy; *Cx*: *x* is a client)

26. Some lawyers will represent any person who will not represent himself. (*Lx*: *x* is a lawyer; *Px*: *x* is a person; *Rxy*: *x* represents *y*)

27. Some children in the third grade can read any of the books in the library. (*Cx*: *x* is a child; *Tx*: *x* is in the third grade; *Rxy*: *x* can read *y*; *Bx*: *x* is a book; *Lx*: *x* is in the library)

★28. All children in the fourth grade can read any of the books in the library.

29. If there are any safe drivers, then if none of the trucks break down they will be hired. (*Sx*: *x* is safe; *Dx*: *x* is a driver; *Tx*: *x* is a truck; *Bx*: *x* breaks down; *Hx*: *x* will be hired)

★30. If there are any safe drivers, then some safe drivers will be hired.

II. Derive the conclusion of the following symbolized arguments. Use conditional proof or indirect proof as needed.

★(1) 1. (*x*)[*Ax* ⊃ (*y*)*Bxy*]
　　2. *Am*　　/ (*y*)*Bmy*

(2) 1. (*x*)[*Ax* ⊃ (*y*)(*By* ⊃ *Cxy*)]
　　2. *Am* • *Bn*　　/*Cmn*

(3) 1. (∃*x*)[*Ax* • (*y*)(*By* ⊃ *Cxy*)]
　　2. (∃*x*)*Ax* ⊃ *Bj*　　/ (∃*x*)*Cxj*

★(4) 1. (*x*)(∃*y*)(*Ax* ⊃ *By*)　　/ (*x*)*Ax* ⊃ (∃*y*)*By*

(5) 1. (∃*x*)*Ax* ⊃ (∃*y*)*By*　　/ (∃*y*)(*x*)(*Ax* ⊃ *By*)

(6) 1. (*x*)(*y*)(*Ax* ⊃ *By*)
　　2. (*x*)(∃*y*)(*Ax* ⊃ *Cy*)　　/ (*x*)(∃*y*)[*Ax* ⊃ (*By* • *Cy*)]

★(7) 1. (∃*x*)[*Ax* • (*y*)(*Ay* ⊃ *Bxy*)]　　/ (∃*x*)*Bxx*

(8) 1. (∃*x*)[*Ax* • (*y*)(*By* ⊃ *Cxy*)]
　　2. (*x*)(∃*y*)(*Ax* ⊃ *By*)　　/ (∃*x*)(∃*y*)*Cxy*

(9) 1. (∃*x*)(*y*)(*Axy* ⊃ *Bxy*)
　　2. (*x*)(∃*y*)~*Bxy*　　/ ~(*x*)(*y*)*Axy*

★(10) 1. (*x*)(∃*y*)*Axy* ⊃ (*x*)(∃*y*)*Bxy*
　　2. (∃*x*)(*y*)~*Bxy*　　/ (∃*x*)(*y*)~*Axy*

(11) 1. (∃*x*){*Ax* • [(∃*y*)*By* ⊃ *Cx*]}
　　2. (*x*)(*Ax* ⊃ *Bx*)　　/ (∃*x*)*Cx*

(12) 1. (∃*x*)(*y*)[(*Ay* • *By*) ⊃ *Cxy*]
　　2. (*y*)(*Ay* ⊃ *By*)　　/ (*y*)[*Ay* ⊃ (∃*x*)*Cxy*]

★(13) 1. (∃*x*){*Ax* • (*y*)[(*By* v *Cy*) ⊃ *Dxy*]}
　　2. (∃*x*)*Ax* ⊃ (∃*y*)*By*　　/ (∃*x*)(∃*y*)*Dxy*

(14) 1. (*x*){*Ax* ⊃ [(∃*y*)(*By* • *Cy*) ⊃ *Dx*]}
　　2. (*x*)(*Bx* ⊃ *Cx*)　　/ (*x*)[*Ax* ⊃ (*Bx* ⊃ *Dx*)]

(15) 1. (∃*x*)(*y*)(*Ayx* ⊃ ~*Axy*)　　/ ~(*x*)*Axx*

★(16) 1. $(x)(\exists y)(Ax \cdot By)$ / $(\exists y)(x)(Ax \cdot By)$

(17) 1. $(x)(\exists y)(Ax \lor By)$ / $(\exists y)(x)(Ax \lor By)$

(18) 1. $(x)[Ax \supset (\exists y)(By \cdot Cxy)]$
    2. $(\exists x)[Ax \cdot (y)(By \supset Dxy)]$ / $(\exists x)(\exists y)(Cxy \cdot Dxy)$

★(19) 1. $(x)(\exists y)Axy \lor (x)(y)Bxy$
    2. $(x)(\exists y)(Cx \supset \sim Bxy)$ / $(x)(\exists y)(Cx \supset Axy)$

(20) 1. $(x)(y)[Axy \supset (Bx \cdot Cy)]$
    2. $(x)(y)[(Bx \lor Dy) \supset \sim Axy]$ / $\sim(\exists x)(\exists y)Axy$

III. Translate the following arguments into symbolic form. Then derive the conclusion of each, using conditional proof or indirect proof when needed.

★1. Any professional can outplay any amateur. Jones is a professional but he cannot outplay Meyers. Therefore, Meyers is not an amateur. (Px: x is a professional; Ax: x is an amateur; Oxy: x can outplay y)

2. Whoever is a friend of either Michael or Paul will receive a gift. If Michael has any friends, then Eileen is one of them. Therefore, if Ann is a friend of Michael, then Eileen will receive a gift. (Fxy: x is a friend of y; Rx: x will receive a gift)

3. A horse is an animal. Therefore, whoever owns a horse owns an animal. (Hx: x is a horse; Ax: x is an animal; Oxy: x owns y)

★4. O'Brien is a person. Furthermore, O'Brien is smarter than any person in the class. Since no person is smarter than himself, it follows that O'Brien is not in the class. (Px: x is a person; Sxy: x is smarter than y; Cx: x is in the class)

5. If there are any honest politicians, then if all the ballots are counted they will be reelected. Some honest politicans will not be reelected. Therefore, some ballots will not be counted. (Hx: x is honest; Px: x is a politician; Bx: x is a ballot; Cx: x is counted; Rx: x will be reelected)

6. Dr. Rogers can cure any person who cannot cure himself. Dr. Rogers is a person. Therefore, Dr. Rogers can cure himself. (Px: x is a person; Cxy: x can cure y)

★7. Some people are friends of every person they know. Every person knows someone (or other). Therefore, at least one person is a friend of someone. (Px: x is a person; Fxy: x is a friend of y; Kxy: x knows y)

8. If there are any policemen, then if there are any robbers, then they will arrest them. If any robbers are arrested by policemen, they will go to jail. There are some policemen and Macky is a robber. Therefore, Macky will go to jail. (Px: x is a policeman; Rx: x is a robber; Axy: x arrests y; Jx: x will go to jail)

9. If anything is missing, then some person stole it. If anything is damaged, then some person broke it. Something is either missing or damaged. Therefore, some person either stole something or broke

something. (*Mx*: *x* is missing; *Px*: *x* is a person; *Sxy*: *x* stole *y*; *Dx*: *x* is damaged; *Bxy*: *x* broke *y*)

★10. If there are any instructors, then if at least one classroom is available they will be effective. If there are either any textbooks or workbooks, there will be instructors and classrooms. Furthermore, if there are any classrooms, they will be available. Therefore, if there are any textbooks, then some instructors will be effective. (*Ix*: *x* is an instructor; *Cx*: *x* is a classroom; *Ax*: *x* is available; *Ex*: *x* is effective; *Tx*: *x* is a textbook; *Wx*: *x* is a workbook)

9
INDUCTION

Unlike deductive logic, the logic of induction offers no neat, harmonious system of ideas agreed upon by all logicians. Rather, it consists of several independently developed areas of thought about which there is little agreement. The sections in this chapter touch upon four such areas. The first section deals with causality and John Stuart Mill's methods for discovering causal connections, the second with probability, the third with statistical methods of reasoning, and the fourth with hypotheses. Because these four sections are basically independent of one another, they can be read in any order. Furthermore, the material presented is only slightly dependent on ideas developed earlier in this book. In addition to material from Chapter 1, which is presupposed by all four sections, Sections 9.1 and 9.2 presuppose only a few ideas from Chapter 6, and Section 9.3 extends the material developed in Chapter 3.

9.1 CAUSALITY AND MILL'S METHODS

A knowledge of causal connections plays a prominent role in our effort to control the environment in which we live. We insulate our homes because we know insulation will prevent heat loss, we vaccinate our children because we know vaccination will protect them from smallpox and diphtheria, we practice the piano and violin because we know that by doing so we may become proficient on these instruments, and we cook our meat and fish because we know that doing so will make them edible.

When the word "cause" is used in ordinary English, however, it is seriously affected by ambiguity. For example, when we say that sprinkling water on the flowers will cause them to grow, we mean that water is required for growth, not that water alone will do the job—sunshine and the proper temperature are also required. On the other hand, when we say that taking a swim on a hot summer day will cause us to cool off, we mean that the dip by itself *will* do the job; but we understand that other things will work just as well, such as taking a cold shower, entering an air-conditioned room, and so on.

To clear up this ambiguity affecting the meaning of "cause," it is useful to adopt the language of sufficient and necessary conditions. When we say that electrocution is a cause of death, we mean "cause" in the sense of *sufficient* condition. Electrocution is sufficient to produce death; but there are other methods equally effective, such as poisoning, drowning, and shooting. On the other hand, when we say that the presence of clouds is a cause of rain, we mean "cause" in the sense of *necessary* condition. Without clouds, rain cannot occur, but clouds alone are not sufficient. Certain combinations of pressure and temperature are also required.

Sometimes "cause" is used in the sense of necessary *and* sufficient condition, as when we say that the action of a force causes a body to accelerate or that an increase in voltage causes an increase in electrical current. For a body to accelerate, nothing more and nothing less is required than for it to be acted on by a net force; and for an electrical current to increase through a resistive circuit, nothing more and nothing less is required than an increase in voltage.

Thus, as these examples illustrate, the word "cause" can have any one of three different meanings:

1. Sufficient condition.
2. Necessary condition.
3. Sufficient and necessary condition.

Sometimes the context provides an immediate clue to the sense in which "cause" is being used. If we are trying to *prevent* a certain phenomenon from happening, we usually search for a cause that is a necessary condition, and if we are trying to *produce* a certain phenomenon we usually search for a cause that is a sufficient condition. For example, in attempting to prevent the occurrence of smog around cities, scientists try to isolate a necessary condition or group of necessary conditions that, if removed, will eliminate the smog. And in their effort to produce an abundant harvest, farmers search for a sufficient condition that, given sunshine and rainfall, will increase crop growth.

Another point that should be understood is that whenever an event occurs, at least *one* sufficient condition is present and *all* the necessary conditions are present. The conjunction of the necessary conditions *is* the sufficient condition that actually produces the event. For example, the necessary conditions for lighting a match are heat (produced by striking) and oxygen. Combining these two necessary conditions gives the sufficient condition. In other words, striking the match in the presence of oxygen is sufficient to ignite it. In cases where the sufficient condition is also a necessary condition, there is only one necessary condition, which is identical with the sufficient condition.

In Chapter 1 we saw that statements expressed in terms of sufficient and necessary conditions could be translated as conditional statements:

A is a sufficient condition for B: If A occurs, then B must occur.
A is a necessary condition for B: If B occurs, then A must occur.

From these translations we see that if A is a sufficient condition for B, then B is a necessary condition for A; conversely, if A is a necessary condition for B, then B is a sufficient condition for A. In addition, by the transposition rule for conditional statements, we see that the following pairs of statements are equivalent:

The absence of A is a sufficient condition for the absence of B ≡
B is a sufficient condition for A

The absence of A is a necessary condition for the absence of B ≡
B is a necessary condition for A

Finally, using the rule that a conditional statement is false if and only if the antecedent is true and the consequent false, we obtain the following:

A is not a sufficient condition for B if A occurs without B.

A is not a necessary condition for B if B occurs without A.

These concepts will be useful in understanding and applying Mill's methods for induction, to which we now turn.

In his *System of Logic*, the nineteenth-century philosopher John Stuart

Mill compiled five methods for identifying causal connections between events. These he called the method of agreement, the method of difference, the joint method of agreement and difference, the method of residues, and the method of concomitant variation. In the years that have elapsed since the publication of this work, the five methods have received a good deal of philosophical criticism. Today most logicians agree that the methods fall short of the claims made for them by Mill, but the fact nevertheless remains that the methods function implicitly in many of the inductive inferences we make in everyday life. The presentation that follows differs from Mill's in that Mill did not distinguish the various senses of "cause" to which the methods pertain. When "cause" in the sense of necessary condition is distinguished from "cause" in the sense of sufficient condition, the method of agreement breaks down into two methods, here called the direct method of agreement and the inverse method of agreement. Combining these two methods yields a third method, the double method of agreement. Additional variations are possible, but I have chosen to ignore them in this text.

Direct Method of Agreement

The **direct method of agreement** is a method for identifying a causal connection between an effect and a necessary condition. The method consists in recognizing some single factor that is present in a number of different occurrences in which the effect is also present. This single factor, which is the one way that all the occurrences agree, is taken to be the cause. Here is an example:

> After eating lunch at the same restaurant, five individuals became ill with hepatitis. Inspectors from the Health Department learned that while the five individuals had eaten different foods, they all had had tomatoes in their salad. Furthermore, this was the only food that all five had eaten. The inspectors concluded that the disease had been transmitted by the tomatoes.

To see how the argument contained in this example identifies a cause in the sense of a necessary condition, it is helpful to present the evidence in the form of a table. Where $A, B, C, \ldots G$ designate the various foods eaten, with B standing for tomatoes, and the five occurrences designate the five individuals, the table is as follows (an asterisk means that a certain condition is present and a dash means it is absent:

Table 1

Occurrence	Possible necessary condition							Phenomenon (hepatitis)
	A	*B*	*C*	*D*	*E*	*F*	*G*	
1	*	*	–	*	*	–	*	*
2	*	*	*	–	*	*	–	*
3	*	*	*	*	–	*	*	*
4	–	*	*	*	*	–	*	*
5	*	*	–	*	*	*	–	*

Occurrence 1 asserts that the designated individual ate the foods represented by the letters *A*, *B*, *D*, *E*, and *G* and avoided foods *C* and *F*. Occurrence 2 asserts that the designated individual ate foods *A*, *B*, *C*, *E*, and *F* and avoided *D* and *G*, and so on. The application of the direct method of agreement consists in systematically eliminating as many of the possible necessary conditions as the evidence allows, leaving in the end (it is hoped) only a single candidate as the cause of the phenomenon. The principle used in accomplishing this elimination was stated earlier:

> *X* is not a necessary condition for *Y* if *X* is absent when *Y* is present.

Beginning with occurrence 1 we eliminate *C* and *F*. These conditions are absent when the phenomenon is present, so they are not necessary for the occurrence of the phenomenon. Occurrence 2 eliminates *D* and *G*, occurrence 3 eliminates *E*, occurrence 4 eliminates *A* and *F* (again), and occurrence 5 eliminates *C* (again) and *G* (again). This leaves only *B* as a possible necessary condition. The conclusion is therefore warranted that the tomatoes (condition *B*) were the cause of the hepatitis.

This conclusion follows only probably, for two reasons. First, it is quite possible that some important condition was overlooked. For example, if the eating utensils were contaminated, the hepatitis might have been transmitted through them and not through the tomatoes. Second, if *more than one* of the foods had been contaminated, the disease might have been transmitted through a combination of foods, in which case, once again, the tomatoes might not have been involved. Thus, the strength of the argument depends on the nonoccurrence of these two possibilities.

Another important point to understand is that the conclusion applies directly to only the five occurrences listed and not to everyone who ate in the restaurant. The conclusion does not say that all patrons who did not eat tomatoes would not get hepatitis. It is quite possible that some food other than those listed was also contaminated, in which case only if they did not eat *that* food as well as the tomatoes could the other patrons be assured that they would not become ill. But if, among all the foods in the restaurant, only the tomatoes were contaminated, the conclusion would extend to the other patrons as well. This point serves to illustrate the fact that a conclusion derived via the method of agreement has limited generality. The conclusion applies directly to only those occurrences listed, and only indirectly, through a second inductive inference, to others. Obviously, the more occasions listed and the larger the number of possible conditions, the more general the conclusion.

Basically, what the conclusion says is that condition *B*, the tomatoes, is a highly suspect factor and that if investigators want to track down the source of the hepatitis, this is where they should begin. It does not say that the tomatoes were the only source of the disease for all those who ate in the restaurant or, least of all, for those who ate in other restaurants. And certainly it does not say that anyone who had eaten the tomatoes would have contracted the disease. Many people are relatively immune to hepatitis and do not get the disease even if they eat contaminated food.

An example of an actual use of the direct method of agreement is provided by the discovery of the beneficial effects of fluoride on teeth. It was noticed several years ago that people in certain communities were favored with especially healthy teeth. In researching the various factors these communities shared in common, scientists discovered that all had a high level of natural fluoride in their water supply. The scientists concluded from this evidence that fluoride causes teeth to be healthy and free of cavities.

Inverse Method of Agreement

Whereas the direct method of agreement identifies a connection between an effect and a *necessary* condition, the **inverse method of agreement** identifies a connection between an effect and a *sufficient* condition. The method consists in recognizing some single factor that is absent from a number of occurrences in which the effect is also absent. This factor is taken to be the cause of the phenomenon. Here is an example:

> After conducting a study on the work force at a certain factory, industrial engineers found that five workers performed their tasks with less efficiency than others doing the same kind of work. A list was made of the various factors that were present and absent in the employment conditions of these five employees. It was discovered that among eight likely candidates, only one factor was missing for all five: participation in a profit sharing program. The conclusion was therefore drawn that profit sharing causes workers to be efficient.

The conclusion of the argument asserts, in regard to the five workers, that profit sharing is a sufficient condition for efficiency. In other words, if these five workers began to participate in profit sharing, they would be expected to become efficient. To see how this conclusion follows, we may represent the evidence in a table similar to the one used previously. The letters $A, B, C, \ldots H$ designate the eight likely candidates for a sufficient condition, with B standing for profit sharing, and the five occurrences designate the five individuals. Notice in Table 2 that the phenomenon is absent in every occurrence, whereas in Table 1 it was present:

Table 2

Occurrence	Possible sufficient conditions								Phenomenon (efficiency)
	A	B	C	D	E	F	G	H	
1	–	–	–	–	*	–	*	–	–
2	*	–	–	–	–	*	–	–	–
3	–	–	*	–	–	–	–	–	–
4	*	–	–	–	–	–	–	*	–
5	–	–	–	*	–	–	*	–	–

As with the direct method of agreement, we begin by attempting to eliminate as many of the possible conditions as the evidence allows; but here we use the rule for *sufficient* conditions:

> X is not a sufficient condition for Y if X is present when Y is absent.

Occurrence 1 eliminates conditions E and G. They are present when the phenomenon is absent, so they cannot be sufficient to produce the phenomenon. Similarly, occurrence 2 eliminates A and F, occurrence 3 eliminates C, occurrence 4 eliminates A (again) and H, and occurrence 5 eliminates D and G (again). Condition B (profit sharing) is the only candidate that remains, and so it is taken to be the cause of the phenomenon.

As with our first example, this conclusion follows only probably, for two reasons. First, there is no assurance that all the important conditions have been identified, and second, there is no assurance that the phenomenon is not caused by two or more factors acting in conjunction. If, for example, a sixth worker had turned up who was inefficient at doing the same task but who did participate in profit sharing, then candidate B would be eliminated, and the engineers would have to renew their search for relevant conditions. And if, for example, the combined occurrence of conditions A and C provided a sufficient condition for the phenomenon, this combination of conditions could be the sought-after cause, and not B at all.

A CONCISE INTRODUCTION TO LOGIC

As with the example treated in the direct method, the conclusion of this argument pertains directly only to the five people mentioned in the occurrences and only indirectly to others. Getting the five workers to participate in profit sharing might well stimulate efficiency, but it is less likely that it would work for everyone in the factory, and less likely still that it would work for all employees in all factories. As additional occurrences are added to the picture, an increasing number of possible conditions must be taken into account. These additional conditions may have a significant impact on the conclusion drawn in the end.

The sense of the conclusion drawn in this example is that the engineers should give paramount consideration to the factor of profit sharing if they want to increase the efficiency of the five workers. But the conclusion does not state that profit sharing is the only thing that might work. Condition B is identified as a sufficient, not a necessary condition. Thus, other solutions, such as higher pay or more frequent coffee breaks, might accomplish the same purpose.

Double Method of Agreement

The direct method of agreement may be combined with the inverse method to obtain the **double method of agreement.** This method may be used to identify causes that are both necessary and sufficient conditions. Researchers often use this method to determine the effectiveness of drugs on groups of people or animals. Example:

> Eight inhabitants of a South Pacific island contracted a rare form of plague. Hearing about it, a doctor flew to the island with a serum that was thought to be a cure. When the doctor arrived, only four of the infected inhabitants would accept the serum, but all eight had previously been treated with various native remedies. After a short time the four who received the serum recovered while the other four did not. Among those who recovered, no single native remedy had been given to all; and among those who did not recover, every native remedy had been given to at least one. The doctor concluded that the serum was a cure for the disease.

To see that this evidence suggests that the serum is a cure in the sense of a necessary and sufficient condition, we may once again present it in the form of a table. Conditions A, B, C, D, and E stand for the native remedies, and condition F for the serum. The eight occurrences stand for the infected inhabitants, with the first four designating those who recovered and the second four, those who did not. Table 3 reflects the doctor's findings regarding the remedies given to each native:

Table 3

Occurrence	Possible sufficient or necessary conditions						Phenomenon (cure)
	A	*B*	*C*	*D*	*E*	*F*	
1	*	*	–	*	*	*	*
2	*	–	*	*	–	*	*
3	–	*	–	*	*	*	*
4	*	–	*	–	*	*	*
5	–	*	–	*	–	–	–
6	–	*	–	*	*	–	–
7	*	–	–	–	–	–	–
8	–	–	*	–	*	–	–

To evaluate these findings we combine the techniques of the direct and inverse methods of agreement. When the phenomenon is present, we attempt to eliminate possible necessary conditions; when it is absent, we attempt to eliminate possible sufficient conditions. Occurrences 1, 2, 3, and 4 eliminate *A, B, C, D,* and *E* as necessary conditions, because they are absent when the phenomenon is present, and occurrences 5, 6, 7, and 8 eliminate *A, B, C, D,* and *E* as sufficient conditions because they are present when the phenomenon is absent. This leaves condition *F* as the sole candidate for either a necessary or sufficient condition. Thus, the conclusion is warranted that *F* is the cause of the phenomenon in the sense of a necessary and sufficient condition.

This conclusion should be interpreted as applying directly to the natives on the island and to hold for others only through a subsequent inductive generalization. While it is highly probable that the serum cured the natives on the island, it is somewhat less probable that it would cure *anyone* having that disease. But even as restricted to the natives, the conclusion is at best probable. As with the direct and inverse methods of agreement, it is quite possible that some relevant condition was overlooked (such as something mistakenly injected along with the serum), or that more than one of the candidates listed is a sufficient condition and that a combination of these candidates provides a necessary condition. The strength of the argument depends on the nonoccurrence of these possibilities.

Method of Difference

The **method of difference** identifies a sufficient condition among the possible candidates present in a specific occurrence. The method consists in finding one single factor that is present in that specific occurrence but absent in a similar occurrence in which the phenomenon is absent. This single factor, which is the one way in which the two occurrences differ, is taken to be the cause of the phenomenon. The method of difference is sometimes called the laboratory method because it is used by researchers to discover causal connections under carefully controlled conditions. Here is an example:

> Two identical white mice in a controlled experiment were given identical amounts of four different foods. In addition, one of the mice was fed a certain drug. A short time later the mouse that was fed the drug became nervous and agitated. The researchers concluded that the drug caused the nervousness.

The conclusion rests upon the supposition that the only relevant differentiating factor between the two mice is the drug. As with the previous methods, the procedure depends upon the elimination of the other factors as possible sufficient conditions. In Table 4, A, B, C, and D stand for the different foods, and E for the drug. Occurrence 1 represents the mouse that was given the drug:

Table 4

Occurrence	Possible sufficient conditions					Phenomenon (nervousness)
	A	B	C	D	E	
1	*	*	*	*	*	*
2	*	*	*	*	−	−

Occurrence 2 eliminates A, B, C, and D as possible sufficient conditions because they are present when the phenomenon is absent. This leaves E as the one remaining candidate.

The method of difference differs from the inverse method of agreement, which also identifies sufficient conditions, in that the conclusion yielded by the method of difference is less general. In this method the conclusion applies directly only to the specific occurrence in which the phenomenon is present, whereas in the inverse method of agreement it applies to all the occurrences listed. However, the conclusion yielded by the method of difference may often be extended to cover other occurrences as well. The white mice used in biological experiments are, for all practical purposes, genetically identical. Thus, what produces nervousness in one will probably produce nervousness in the others. But without some such basis of similarity, generalizing the results of this method to cover additional occurrences would not be legitimate.

The conclusion yielded by the method of difference is probabilistic, however, even for the one occurrence to which it directly pertains. The problem is that it is impossible for two occurrences to be literally identical in every respect but one. The mere fact that the two occurrences occupy different regions of space, that one is closer to the wall than the other, amounts to a difference. Such differences may be insignificant, but therein lies the possibility for error. It is not at all obvious how insignificant differences should be distinguished from significant ones. Furthermore, it is impossible to make an exhaustive list of all the possible conditions; but without such a list there is no assurance that significant conditions have not been overlooked.

The objective of the method of difference is to identify a sufficient condition among those that are *present* in a specific occurrence. Sometimes, however, the absence of a factor may count as something positive that must be taken into account. Here is an example:

> Two identical white mice in a controlled experiment were fed identical diets. In addition, both were given vitamins A, B, and C. One of the mice was also given vitamin D while the other was not. The mouse that was not fed vitamin D developed rickets, but the other one did not. The researchers concluded that the lack of vitamin D caused the rickets.

To represent these findings adequately in a table we must include the negations of the conditions as well as their affirmative expressions. Then the absence of condition *D* (vitamin D) can be represented by the presence of $\sim D$:

Table 5

Occurrence	Possible sufficient conditions								Phenomenon (rickets)
	A	*B*	*C*	*D*	$\sim A$	$\sim B$	$\sim C$	$\sim D$	
1	*	*	*	–	–	–	–	*	*
2	*	*	*	*	–	–	–	–	–

Now, since the method of difference is concerned with identifying a sufficient condition among those possible conditions that are *present* in occurrence 1, *D*, $\sim A$, $\sim B$, and $\sim C$ are immediately eliminated. Among those that remain, occurrence 2 eliminates *A*, *B*, and *C*, because they are present when the phenomenon is absent. This leaves $\sim D$ as the sole remaining candidate. In other words, the absence of vitamin D is the cause of the rickets in occurrence 1. This may otherwise be expressed by saying that the *presence* of vitamin D is a *necessary* condition for health in occurrence 1.

The method of difference may also be used, for example, by a farmer who fertilizes part of a field of corn but does not fertilize the other part. If the fertilized part turns out to be noticeably fuller and healthier, the farmer may conclude that the improvement has been caused by the fertilizer. Another situation in which this method can be used is in cooking. A cook may leave some ingredient out of one batch of biscuits to test the results. If that batch turns out hard and crunchy, the cook may attribute the difference to the absence of that ingredient.

Joint Method of Agreement and Difference

The **joint method** results from combining the method of difference with the direct method of agreement. Because the method of difference identifies a sufficient condition that is present in one specific occurrence, and the direct method of agreement identifies a necessary condition, the joint method can be used to identify a sufficient and necessary condition that is present in one specific occurrence. Here is an example:

> George, who exercised regularly, took vitamins, and got plenty of rest, contracted a rare disease. Doctors administered an antibiotic and the disease cleared up. Convinced that the cure was caused by either the exercise, the vitamins, the rest, or the antibiotics, the doctors searched for analogous cases. Of the two that were found, one got no exercise, took no vitamins, and got little rest. He was given the same antibiotic and was cured. The other person, who did the same things George did, was given no antibiotic and was not cured. The doctors concluded that George was cured by the antibiotic.

The conclusion suggests that the antibiotic caused the cure in the sense of a necessary and sufficient condition. This is illustrated in Table 6, where A, B, C, and D stand for exercise, vitamins, rest, and the antibiotic, respectively. Occurrence 1 represents George; occurrences 2 and 3 represent the analogous cases.

Table 6

Occurrence	Possible conditions				Phenomenon (cure)
	A	B	C	D	
1	*	*	*	*	*
2	–	–	–	*	*
3	*	*	*	–	–

The direct method of agreement is applied to occurrence 2, eliminating A, B, and C as necessary conditions because they are absent when the phenomenon is present. Then the method of difference is applied to occurrence 3, eliminating A, B, and C as sufficient conditions because they are present when the phenomenon is absent. The one remaining condition, D, is thus the sufficient and necessary condition for the phenomenon.

The joint method is similar to the double method of agreement in that it identifies conditions that are both necessary and sufficient. But the conclusion provided by the double method is more general in that it pertains directly to all the occurrences listed. The joint method, like the method of difference, yields a conclusion that pertains directly only to the one specific occurrence. In the above argument the conclusion asserts that the antibiotic is what cured *George;* the question is open as to whether it would cure others as well. But given some basis of similarity between George and other individuals, the conclusion might be extended by a subsequent inductive generalization.

The joint method differs from the method of difference in that it is sometimes simpler to apply. The method of difference requires strict controls to ensure that the two occurrences are identical in every important respect except one. In the joint method this need for strict control is relaxed in favor of additional occurrences that identify the sufficient condition as also being necessary.

The conclusion yielded by the joint method is only probable because, as with the method of difference, a relevant condition may have been overlooked. If, for example, George had taken some other medicine together with the antibiotic, the conclusion that the antibiotic cured him would be less probable.

Before turning to the last two methods, let us reiterate the pair of principles that have provided the basis for the five methods we have seen thus far:

1. X is not a necessary condition for Y if X is absent when Y is present.
2. X is not a sufficient condition for Y if X is present when Y is absent.

Understanding the use of these two principles is more important than remembering the peculiarities of the various methods to which they pertain.

Method of Residues

This method and the one that follows are used to identify a causal connection between two conditions without regard for the specific kind of connection. Both methods may be used to identify conditions that are sufficient, necessary, or both sufficient and necessary. The **method of residues** consists in separating from a group of causally connected conditions and phenomena those strands of causal connection that are already known, leaving the required causal connection as the "residue." The method may be diagramed as follows:

(A B C) causes (a b c.)
    A causes a.
    B causes b.
   Therefore, C causes c.

When the facts that A causes a and B causes b are subtracted from the compound causal connection, the fact that C causes c remains as the residue. Here is an example:

> After occupying his new house Mr. Smith found it drafty. He traced the source of the draft to three conditions: a broken window in the garage, a crack under the front door, and a broken damper in the fireplace. When the window was replaced he noticed an improvement, and a further improvement when weather stripping was installed on the door. He concluded that the draft that remained was caused by the broken damper in the fireplace.

The conclusion follows only probably because it is quite possible that a fourth source of the draft was overlooked. Here is another example:

> After realizing a loss of $100,000 a department store's chief accountant could suggest only three causes: an excessive number of clerks, increases in utility rates, and damage to merchandise caused by a flood. These expenses were estimated at $25,000, $30,000, and $10,000, respectively. Since no other ordinary sources could be found, the accountant attributed the remaining $35,000 to shoplifting.

Because the estimates might have been incorrect and because additional sources of financial loss might have been overlooked, the conclusion is only probable.

Some procedures that, at least on the face of it, appear to utilize the method of residues come closer to being deductive than inductive. A case in point is the procedure used to determine the weight of the cargo carried by a truck. First, the empty truck is put on a scale and the weight recorded. Then the truck is loaded and the truck together with the cargo is put on the same scale. The weight of the cargo is the difference between the two weights. If, to this procedure, we add the rather unproblematic assumptions that weight is an additive property, that the scale is accurate, that the scale operator reads the indicator properly, that the truck is not altered in the loading process, and a few others, the conclusion about the weight of the cargo follows deductively.

To distinguish deductive from inductive uses of the method of residues, one must take the intention of the arguer into account. If the intent is to argue necessarily, the use made of this method is deductive; but if the intent is to argue probabilistically, the use is inductive.

Method of Concomitant Variation

The **method of concomitant variation** identifies a causal connection between two conditions by matching variations in one condition with variations in another. According to one formulation, increases are matched with increases and decreases with decreases. Where plus and minus signs indicate increase and decrease, this formulation of the method may be diagramed as follows:

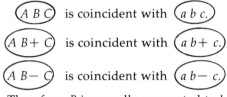

Therefore, B is causally connected to b.

The second formulation of the method matches increases with decreases and decreases with increases. It may be diagramed as follows:

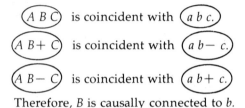

Therefore, B is causally connected to b.

In both cases the conclusion asserts that either B causes b, b causes B, or B and b have a common cause. If B happens before b, then, of course, the second alternative is eliminated, and if b happens before B, then the first alternative is eliminated.

The method of concomitant variation is useful when it is impossible for a condition to be either wholly present or wholly absent, as was required for the use of the first five methods. Many conditions are of this sort—for example, the temperature of the ocean, the price of gold, the incidence of crime, the size of a mountain glacier, a person's blood pressure, and so on. If some kind of correlation can be detected between variations in conditions such as these, the method of concomitant variation asserts that the two are causally connected. Example:

> In attempting to diagnose Mrs. Thompson's high blood pressure, doctors discovered a correlation between fluctuations in blood pressure and certain brain waves. As the blood pressure increased and decreased, so did the intensity of the brain waves. The doctors concluded that the two conditions were causally related.

Whether the changes in blood pressure caused the changes in the intensity of the brain waves or vice versa, or whether the two had a common cause, would have to be determined by further investigation. But the fact that the two were causally connected in some way follows with a high degree of probability. The conclusion is not absolutely certain, however, because the fluctuations could have been merely coincidental.

The blood pressure example illustrates the first formulation of the method. Here is an example of the second formulation:

> Researchers have discovered a correlation between changes in the national divorce rate and fluctuations in the gross national product. As the GNP increases, the divorce rate decreases, and when the GNP sags, the divorce rate goes up. The researchers have concluded that the two phenomena are causally connected.

In this case an even stronger conclusion could probably be drawn—namely, that decreases in the GNP cause increases in the divorce rate, and not conversely. That changes in economic prosperity should affect the divorce rate is quite plausible, but the converse is less so.

At this point we should note that the existence of a mere correlation between two phenomena is never sufficient to identify a causal connection. In addition, the causal connection suggested by the correlation must at least make sense. Consider the following example:

> After an in-depth study researchers discovered a correlation between the price of pork belly futures on the Chicago Mercantile Exchange and earthquake activity in Japan. As the number and intensity of the quakes increased, the future prices also increased, and vice versa. The researchers concluded that the two phenomena were causally connected.

The argument is clearly weak. Because it is virtually inconceivable that either phenomenon could cause a change in the other, or that changes in both could have a common cause, it is most likely that the correlation is purely coincidental.

When used correctly, the method of concomitant variation can yield conclusions that are highly probable. It has been used successfully in the past to help establish the existence of causal connections between such phenomena as smoking and lung cancer, nuclear radiation and leukemia, and alcohol consumption and cirrhosis of the liver.

EXERCISE 9.1

I. Identify the kind of causality intended by the following statements. Is the cause a sufficient condition, necessary condition, or both sufficient and necessary condition?

★1. Throwing a brick through a window will cause the window to break.

2. Heating an iron rod causes it to expand.

3. Slashing an inflated automobile tire with a knife will cause it to go flat.

★4. Releasing the shutter of a camera causes an image to appear on the film.

5. Pulling the trigger of a gun causes it to fire.

6. Wetting litmus paper with an acid causes it to turn red.

★7. Pouring water on a wood fire will cause it to be extinguished.

8. Eating contaminated food will cause one to become ill.

9. Stretching a spring causes it to exert an opposing force.

★10. Flipping the wall switch to the "up" position causes the overhead lights to go on.

II. Identify the method of reasoning used and the kind of causality intended in the following reports of argumentation:

★1. To determine the effectiveness of an oil additive, a testing firm purchased two identical automobiles and drove each a distance of 30,000 miles, using the same kind of gasoline, the same kind of oil, and the same driver. The oil in one engine included the additive, whereas the oil in the other did not. At the end of the test the engines of both cars were dismantled, and it was found that the engine that used the additive had less wear. The testing firm concluded that the oil additive caused the reduced wear.

2. An eighth-grade teacher had six pupils who read very poorly. These pupils came from different sized families, had different social and economic backgrounds, and attended different schools in the primary grades. The single factor they shared in common was the lack of any phonics instruction in the first grade. The teacher concluded that phonics causes children to be good readers.

3. An administrator for the Internal Revenue Service noticed that tax revenues for a certain year were substantially less than anticipated. Part of the deficiency could be attributed to the fact that productivity was down as a result of a recession, and another part to spiraling interest rates that led to higher than usual write-offs. Unable to account for the remaining deficiency, the administrator attributed it to increased cheating by the taxpayers.

★4. The repair manager for a manufacturer of home computers noticed that a large number of units were being returned for repairs. These units had been produced in different years and were sold in different cities to different kinds of customers. The only noticeable common factor was the fact that all of the units had been shipped from coastal areas. Since coastal areas have a higher salt content in the air, the repair manager concluded that salty air from the sea caused the breakdowns.

5. A manufacturer of fishing lures conducted a test on a new bass plug it had developed. The plug was given to four of a group of eight fishermen, and these fishermen then tried their luck in different locations in a lake using different kinds of poles, reels, lures, and techniques. At the end of the day, all of the fishermen who had used the new plug had caught fish, whereas none of those who had used other lures had caught anything. The manufacturer concluded that the new bass plug caused the fish to bite.

6. During the first storm of the season, Mrs. Johnson's telephone stopped working. After the weather dried up the phone began working again. Since no one at the phone company had been alerted to the problem, Mrs. Johnson concluded that the breakdown was caused by dampness in the lines.

★7. From a comparison of statistics a criminologist detected a correlation between fluctuations in the employment rate and crimes of theft. As the employment rate increased, the theft rate decreased, and vice versa. The criminologist concluded that unemployment causes an increase in crimes of theft.

8. A patient developed an allergic reaction to an unknown substance. Doctors instructed the patient to eliminate certain foods from her diet; after she had done so, the reaction disappeared. She was then told to gradually add the foods back into her diet. When the patient began to use milk products, the allergic reaction reappeared. The doctors concluded that the reaction was caused by milk products.

9. A psychiatrist had six adult women patients who were unable to sustain meaningful relationships with men. The patients came from different walks of life, were of varying ages, and had different religious and economic backgrounds. The only factor they shared in common was the lack of a male parent figure during their early childhood. The psychiatrist concluded that the presence of a male parent figure causes the ability in women to sustain meaningful relationships with men.

★10. A metallurgist added six different substances in various combinations to ten samples of molten aluminum for the purpose of producing aluminum alloys. Later she found that the five samples that contained silicon were resistant to corrosion, whereas the five that contained no silicon were not resistant. The metallurgist concluded that silicon causes aluminum to be resistant to corrosion.

11. A doctor had five patients suffering from an unusual form of cancer. The only factor common to all five was the fact that all were employed by a chemical company that produced a certain defoliant for use by the military. The doctor concluded that the defoliant chemical caused the cancer.

12. After moving to a new home in a distant city, a housewife noticed that her clothes came out of the washing machine noticeably cleaner

than before. Part of the cleaning she attributed to the soap and part to the machine, both of which were the same as she had used in her previous home. Unable to identify any other factor, she decided that the improvement must be because the water in the new location was softer than it was in the old location.

★13. A television set got an excellent picture in the front room of a home, but when the set was moved to other rooms, the picture greatly deteriorated. Since everything except the location appeared to be the same, the homeowner concluded that the location of the front room was the cause of the superior picture.

14. A health worker discovered a correlation between the weekly suicide rate and the index levels of the major stock exchanges. As stock prices increased, the suicide rate decreased, and as stock prices fell, the suicide rate increased. The health worker concluded that the price of stocks is a factor in why people commit suicide.

★15. Two of Mr. Andrews' rose bushes became infested with aphids. Mr. Andrews proceeded to spray one of the bushes with malathion but left the other bush untouched. Within three days the aphids disappeared from the bush that was sprayed, but they continued to thrive on the other bush. Mr. Andrews concluded that malathion killed the aphids on the bush that was sprayed.

III. Identify the cause suggested by the information presented in the following tables. Is the cause a sufficient condition, a necessary condition, or both a sufficient and necessary condition? What method is used?

★1.

Occurrence	Possible conditions					Phenomenon
	A	B	C	D	E	
1	−	*	−	−	*	−
2	−	−	*	−	−	−
3	−	*	*	−	−	−
4	−	−	−	−	*	−
5	−	*	−	*	−	−

2.

Occurrence	Possible conditions					Phenomenon
	A	B	C	D	E	
1	*	−	*	*	*	*
2	*	*	*	*	−	*
3	*	−	*	*	*	*
4	*	*	−	*	*	*
5	−	*	*	*	−	*

3.

Occurrence	Possible conditions					Phenomenon
	A	B	C	D	E	
1	*	*	*	*	*	*
2	*	–	*	*	*	–

★4.

Occurrence	Possible conditions						Phenomenon
	A	B	C	D	E	F	
1	*	–	–	*	–	–	–
2	–	*	*	*	–	–	*
3	*	–	*	*	*	–	*
4	–	*	–	–	–	*	–
5	*	–	–	–	*	–	–
6	*	*	*	–	*	–	*

5.

Occurrence	Possible conditions					Phenomenon
	A	B	C	D	E	
1	*	*	*	*	*	*
2	–	*	*	*	*	–
3	*	–	–	–	–	*

6.

Occurrence	Possible conditions					Phenomenon
	A	B	C	~A	~B	~C	
1	*	*	–	–	–	*	*
2	–	*	*	*	–	–	–
3	*	–	*	–	*	–	–

★7.

Occurrence	Possible conditions					Phenomenon
	A	B	C	D	E	
1	*	*	*	*	–	*
2	–	–	*	–	*	*
3	*	–	–	–	*	–
4	–	*	–	*	*	*
5	*	*	–	–	–	–
6	–	*	*	–	–	–

8.

Occurrence	Possible conditions					Phenomenon
	A	B	C	D	E	
1	−	−	*	−	*	−
2	−	*	*	−	*	*
3	*	*	−	*	*	*
4	−	*	−	−	*	−
5	*	−	*	*	−	−
6	*	*	*	−	−	*

IV. Prepare tables for arguments 1, 2, 4, 5, and 8 in Part II. Use your imagination to supplement the information given on the possible conditions.

9.2 PROBABILITY

Probability is a topic that is central to the question of induction, but like causality, it has different meanings. Consider the following statements:

> The probability of picking a spade from a full deck of cards is one-fourth.
>
> The probability that a 20-year-old man will live to age 75 is .63.
>
> There is a high probability that Margaret and Peter will get married.

In each statement the word "probability" is used in a different sense. This difference stems from the fact that a different procedure is used in each case to determine or estimate the probability. To determine the probability of picking a spade from a deck of cards, a purely mathematical procedure is used. Given that there are fifty-two cards in a deck and thirteen are spades, 13 is divided by 52 to obtain one-fourth. A different procedure is used to determine the probability that a 20-year-old man will live to age 75. For this, one must sample a large number of 20-year-old men and count the number that live 55 more years. Yet a different procedure is used to determine the probability that Margaret and Peter will get married. This probability can only be estimated roughly, and doing so requires that we become acquainted with Margaret and Peter and with how they feel toward each other and toward marriage. These three procedures give rise to three distinct theories about probability: the classical theory, the relative frequency theory, and the subjectivist theory.

The **classical theory** traces its origin to the work of the seventeenth-century mathematicians Blaise Pascal and Pierre de Fermat in determining the betting odds for a game of chance. The theory is otherwise called the *a priori* theory of probability because the computations are made independently of any sensory observation of actual events. According to the classical theory, the probability of an event A is given by the formula

$$P(A) = \frac{f}{n}$$

where f is the number of favorable outcomes and n is the number of possible outcomes. For example, in computing the probability of drawing an ace from a poker deck, the number of favorable outcomes is four (because there are four aces) and the number of possible outcomes is fifty-two (because there are fifty-two cards in the deck). Thus, the probability of that event is 4/52 or 1/13 (or .077).

Two assumptions are involved in computing probabilities according to the classical theory: (1) that all possible outcomes are taken into account, and (2) that all possible outcomes are equally probable. In the card example the first assumption entails that only the fifty-two ordinary outcomes are possible. In other words, it is assumed that the cards will not suddenly self-destruct or reproduce, that the printing will not suddenly vanish, and so on. The second assumption, which is otherwise called the **principle of indifference,** entails that there is an equal likelihood of selecting any card. In other words, it is assumed that the cards are stacked evenly, that none are glued together, and so on.

Whenever these two assumptions can be made about the occurrence of an event, the classical theory can be used to compute its probability. Here are some additional examples:

P(a fair coin turning up heads) $= 1/2$
P(drawing a face card) $= 12/52 = 3/13$
P(a single die coming up "3") $= 1/6$
P(a single die coming up "even") $= 3/6 = 1/2$

Strictly speaking, of course, the two assumptions underlying the classical theory are never perfectly reflected in any actual situation. Every coin is slightly off balance, as is every pair of dice. As a result, the probabilities of the various outcomes are never exactly equal. Similarly, the outcomes are never strictly confined to the normal ones entailed by the first assumption. When tossing a coin, there is always the possibility that the coin will land on edge, and in rolling dice there is the analogous possibility that one of them might break in half. These outcomes may not be possible in the *practical* sense, but they are *logically* possible in that they do not involve any contradiction. Because these outcomes are so unusual, however, it is reasonable to think that for all practical purposes the two assumptions hold and that therefore the classical theory is applicable.

There are many events, however, for which the two assumptions required by the classical theory obviously do not hold. For example, in attempting to determine the probability of a 60-year-old woman dying of a heart attack within ten years, it would be virtually impossible to take account of all the possible outcomes. She might die of cancer, pneumonia, or an especially virulent case of the flu. She might be incapacitated by a car accident, or she might move to Florida and buy a house on the beach. Furthermore, none of these outcomes is equally probable in comparison with the others. To compute the probability of events such as these we need the relative frequency theory of probability.

The **relative frequency theory** originated with the use of mortality tables by life insurance companies in the eighteenth century. In contrast with the classical theory, which rests upon a priori computations, the relative frequency theory depends on actual observations of the frequency with which certain events happen. The probability of an event A is given by the formula

$$P(A) = \frac{f_O}{n_O}$$

where f_O is the number of *observed* favorable outcomes and n_O is the total number of *observed* outcomes. For example, to determine the probability that a 50-year-old man will live five more years, a sample of 1,000 50-year-old men could be observed. If 968 were alive five years later, the probability that the man in question will live an additional five years is 968/1000 or .968.

Similarly, if one wanted to determine the probability that a certain irregularly shaped pyramid with different colored sides would, when rolled, come to rest with the green side down, the pyramid could be rolled 1,000 times. If it came to rest with its green side down 327 times, the probability of this event happening would be computed to be .327.

The relative frequency method can also be used to compute the probability of the kinds of events that conform to the requirements of the classical theory. For example, the probability of a coin coming up heads could be determined by tossing the coin 100 times and counting the heads. If, after this many tosses, 46 heads have been recorded, one might assign a probability of .46 to this event. This leads us to an important point about the relative frequency theory: the results hold true only in the long run. It might be necessary to toss the coin 1,000 or even 10,000 times to get a close approximation. After 10,000 tosses one would expect to count close to 5,000 heads. If in fact only 4,623 heads have been recorded, one would probably be justified in concluding that the coin is off balance or that something was irregular in the way it had been tossed.

Strictly speaking, neither the classical method nor the relative frequency method can assign a probability to individual events. From the standpoint of these approaches only certain *kinds* or *classes* of events have probabilities. But many events in the actual world are unique, one-of-a-kind happenings—for example, Margaret's marrying Peter or Native Prancer's winning the fourth race at Churchill Downs. To interpret the probability of these events we turn to the subjectivist theory.

The **subjectivist theory** interprets the meaning of probability in terms of the beliefs of individual people. Although such beliefs are vague and nebulous, they may be given quantitative interpretation through the odds that a person would accept on a bet. For example, if a person believes that a certain horse will win a race and he or she is willing to give 7 to 4 odds on that event happening, this means that he or she has assigned a probability of $7/(7+4)$ or $7/11$ to that event. This procedure is unproblematic as long as the person is consistent in giving odds on the same event *not* happening. If, for example, 7 to 4 odds are given that an event will happen and 5 to 4 odds that it will not happen, the individual who gives these odds will inevitably lose. If 7 to 4 odds are given that an event *will* happen, no better than 4 to 7 odds can be given that the same event will *not* happen.

One of the difficulties surrounding the subjectivist theory is that one and the same event can be said to have different probabilities, depending on the willingness of different people to give different odds. If probabilities are taken to be genuine attributes of events, this would seem to be a serious problem. The problem might be avoided, though, either by interpreting probabilities as attributes of beliefs or by taking the average of the various individual probabilities as *the* probability of the event.

The three theories discussed thus far, the classical theory, the relative frequency theory, and the subjectivist theory, provide separate procedures for assigning a probability to an event (or class of events). Sometimes one theory is more readily applicable, sometimes another. But once individual events have been given a probability, the groundwork has been laid for computing the probabilities of compound arrangements of events. This is done by means of what is called the **probability calculus.** In this respect the probability calculus functions analogously to the set of truth functional rules in propositional logic. Just as the truth functional rules allow us to compute the truth values of molecular propositions from the individual truth values of the atomic components, the rules of the probability calculus allow us to compute the probability of compound events from the individual probabilities of the events.

Two preliminary rules of the probability calculus are (1) the probability of an event that must necessarily happen is taken to be 1, and (2) the probability of an event that necessarily cannot happen is taken to be 0. For example, the event consisting of it either raining or not raining (at the same time and place) has probability 1, and the event consisting of it both raining and not raining (at the same time and place) has proba-

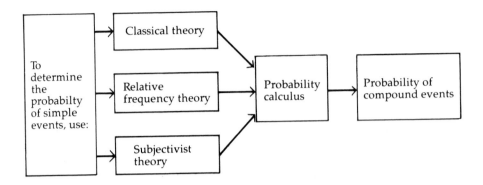

bility 0. These events correspond to statements that are tautological and self-contradictory, respectively. Contingent events, on the other hand, have probabilities greater than 0 but less than 1. For example, the probability that the Dow Jones Industrial Averages will end a certain week at least five points higher than the previous week would usually be around 1/2, the probability that the polar ice cap will melt next year is very close to 0, and the probability that a traffic accident will occur somewhere tomorrow is very close to 1. Let us now consider five additional rules of the probability calculus.

1. Restricted Conjunction Rule

The **restricted conjunction rule** is used to compute the probability of two events occurring together when the events are *independent* of one another. Events are said to be independent when the occurrence of one has no effect on the occurrence of the other. Examples include tossing two coins, drawing two cards from a deck when the first is replaced before the second is drawn, and playing two sequential games of poker or roulette. The probability of two such events A and B occurring together is given by the formula

$$P(A \text{ and } B) = P(A) \times P(B)$$

For example, the probability of tossing two heads on a single throw of two coins is

$$P(H_1 \text{ and } H_2) = 1/2 \times 1/2 = 1/4$$

This result may be checked very easily by listing all the possible outcomes and comparing that number with the number of favorable outcomes:

Coin 1	Coin 2
H	H
H	T
T	H
T	T

Only one of the four possible outcomes shows both coins turning up heads.

Similarly, we may compute the probability of rolling two sixes with a pair of dice:

$$P(S_1 \text{ and } S_2) = 1/6 \times 1/6 = 1/36$$

Again, we may check the results by listing all the possible outcomes:

1-1	2-1	3-1	4-1	5-1	6-1
1-2	2-2	3-2	4-2	5-2	6-2
1-3	2-3	3-3	4-3	5-3	6-3
1-4	2-4	3-4	4-4	5-4	6-4
1-5	2-5	3-5	4-5	5-5	6-5
1-6	2-6	3-6	4-6	5-6	6-6

Since only one of the thirty-six possible outcomes shows two sixes together, the probability of this event is 1/36.

2. General Conjunction Rule

The **general conjunction rule** is used to compute the probability of two events occurring together whether or not the events are independent. When the events are independent, the general conjunction rule reduces to the restricted conjunction rule. Some examples of events that are not independent (that is, that are *dependent*) are drawing two cards from a deck when the first card drawn is not replaced, and selecting two or more seats on an airplane. After the first card is drawn, the number of cards available for the second draw is reduced, and after one of the seats is taken on the plane, the number of seats remaining for subsequent choices is reduced. In other words, in both cases the second event is dependent on the first. The formula for computing the probability of two such events occurring together is

$$P(A \text{ and } B) = P(A) \times P(B \text{ given } A)$$

The expression $P(B \text{ given } A)$ is the probability that B will occur on the assumption that A has already occurred. Let us suppose, for example, that A and B designate the events of drawing two kings from a deck when the first card is not replaced before the second is drawn. If event A

occurs, then only three kings remain, and the deck is also reduced to fifty-one cards. Thus, $P(B$ given $A)$ is 3/51. Since the probability of event A is 4/52, the probability of both events happening is the product of these two fractions, or 12/2652 ($= 1/221$).

For another illustration, consider an urn containing five red balls, six green balls, and seven yellow balls. The probability of drawing two red balls (without replacement) is computed as follows:

$$P(R_1 \text{ and } R_2) = 5/18 \times 4/17 = 20/306 = 10/153$$

If a red ball is selected on the first draw, this leaves four red balls from a total of seventeen. Thus, the probability of drawing a second red ball if one has already been drawn is 4/17.

For another example, consider the same urn with the same contents, but let us compute the probability of drawing first a green ball and then a yellow ball (without replacement):

$$P(G \text{ and } Y) = 6/18 \times 7/17 = 42/306 = 7/51$$

If a green ball is selected on the first draw, this affects the selection of a yellow ball on the second draw only to the extent of reducing the total number of balls to seventeen.

3. Restricted Disjunction Rule

The **restricted disjunction rule** is used to compute the probability of either of two events occurring when the events are *mutually exclusive*—that is, when they cannot both occur. Examples of such events include picking either an ace or a king from a deck of cards on a single draw or rolling either a six or a one on a single roll of a die. The probability is given by the formula

$$P(A \text{ or } B) = P(A) + P(B)$$

For example, the probability of drawing either a king or a queen (of any suit) from a deck of cards on a single draw is

$$P(K \text{ or } Q) = 4/52 + 4/52 = 8/52 = 2/13$$

For another example, consider an urn containing six black balls, four white balls, and two red balls. The probability of selecting either a black or red ball on a single draw is

$$P(B \text{ or } R) = 6/12 + 2/12 = 8/12 = 2/3$$

When the event in question is one that must *necessarily* occur, the probability is, of course, 1. Thus, the probability of obtaining either heads or tails on a single toss of a coin is

$$P(H \text{ or } T) = 1/2 + 1/2 = 1$$

The restricted disjunction rule may be combined with the restricted conjunction rule to compute the probability of getting either a five or a six on each of two consecutive rolls of a single die:

$$
\begin{aligned}
P[(F \text{ or } S)_1 \text{ and } (F \text{ or } S)_2] &= P(F \text{ or } S)_1 \times P(F \text{ or } S)_2 \\
&= (1/6 + 1/6) \times (1/6 + 1/6) \\
&= 1/3 \times 1/3 \\
&= 1/9
\end{aligned}
$$

Since getting a five and getting a six on a single die are mutually exclusive events, $P(F \text{ or } S)_1$ is evaluated using the restricted disjunction rule. The same is true of $P(F \text{ or } S)_2$. Then, since rolling a die is an independent event, the conjunction of the two disjunctive events is evaluated by the restricted conjunction rule.

4. General Disjunction Rule

The **general disjunction rule** is used to compute the probability of either of two events whether or not they are mutually exclusive. The rule holds for any two events, but since its application is simplified when the events are independent, we will confine our attention to events of this kind. Examples of independent events that are not mutually exclusive include obtaining at least one head on two tosses of a coin, drawing at least one king from a deck on two draws when the first card is replaced before the second card is drawn, and getting at least one six when rolling a pair of dice. The formula for computing the probability of either of two such events is

$$P(A \text{ or } B) = P(A) + P(B) - P(A \text{ and } B)$$

If the events are independent, $P(A \text{ and } B)$ is computed using the restricted conjunction rule, and the general disjunction formula reduces to

$$P(A \text{ or } B) = P(A) + P(B) - [P(A) \times P(B)]$$

The general disjunction rule may be proved as follows. When A and B are nonexclusive, A occurs either with or without B, and B occurs either with or without A. Thus

$$
\begin{aligned}
P(A) &= P(A \text{ and } B) + P(A \text{ and not-}B) \\
P(B) &= P(B \text{ and } A) + P(B \text{ and not-}A)
\end{aligned}
$$

But A or B occurs in exactly three possible ways: A and not-B, B and not-A, and A and B. Thus

$$P(A \text{ or } B) = P(A \text{ and not-}B) + P(B \text{ and not-}A) + P(A \text{ and } B)$$

Thus, when $P(A \text{ and } B)$ is subtracted from $P(A) + P(B)$, the difference is equal to $P(A \text{ or } B)$. [Note: $P(A \text{ and } B) = P(B \text{ and } A)$.]

For an example of the use of the general disjunction rule let us consider the probability of getting heads on either of two tosses of a coin. We have

$$
\begin{aligned}
P(H_1 \text{ or } H_2) &= 1/2 + 1/2 - (1/2 \times 1/2) \\
&= 1 - 1/4 \\
&= 3/4
\end{aligned}
$$

For another example, consider the probability of getting at least one six when rolling a pair of dice. The computation is

$$
\begin{aligned}
P(S_1 \text{ or } S_2) &= 1/6 + 1/6 - (1/6 \times 1/6) \\
&= 2/6 - 1/36 \\
&= 11/36
\end{aligned}
$$

The general disjunction rule may be combined with the restricted disjunction rule to compute the probability of getting either a three or a five when rolling a pair of dice. This is the probability of getting either a three or a five on the first die or either a three or a five on the second:

$$
\begin{aligned}
P[(T \text{ or } F)_1 \text{ or } (T \text{ or } F)_2] &= P(T \text{ or } F)_1 + P(T \text{ or } F)_2 \\
&\quad -[P(T \text{ or } F)_1 \times P(T \text{ or } F)_2] \\
&= (1/6 + 1/6) + (1/6 + 1/6) \\
&\quad - [(1/6 + 1/6) \times (1/6 + 1/6)] \\
&= 2/6 + 2/6 - 4/36 \\
&= 20/36 \\
&= 5/9
\end{aligned}
$$

Since getting a three or a five on a single throw is an exclusive event, $P(T \text{ or } F)_1$ is equal to the sum of the separate probabilities. The same is true for $P(T \text{ or } F)_2$.

The general disjunction rule may be combined with the general conjunction rule to compute the probability of drawing first a red ball and then a black ball on pairs of draws from either of two urns (without replacement). Suppose that the first urn contains two red balls, two black balls, and one green ball, and that the second urn contains three red balls, one black ball, and one white ball. The probability, giving two draws per urn, is

$$P[(R \text{ and } B)_1 \text{ or } (R \text{ and } B)_2]$$
$$= P(R \text{ and } B)_1 + P(R \text{ and } B)_2 - [P(R \text{ and } B)_1 \times P(R \text{ and } B)_2]$$
$$= (2/5 \times 2/4) + (3/5 \times 1/4) - [(2/5 \times 2/4) \times (3/5 \times 1/4)]$$
$$= 4/20 + 3/20 - (4/20 \times 3/20)$$
$$= 7/20 - 12/400$$
$$= 8/25$$

5. Negation Rule

The **negation rule** is useful for computing the probability of an event when the probability of the event *not* happening is either known or easily computed. The formula is as follows:

$$P(A) = 1 - P(\text{not-}A)$$

The formula can be proved very easily. By the restricted disjunction rule the probability of A or not-A is

$$P(A \text{ or not-}A) = P(A) + P(\text{not-}A)$$

But since A or not-A happens necessarily, $P(A \text{ or not-}A) = 1$. Thus

$$1 = P(A) + P(\text{not-}A)$$

Rearranging the terms in this equation gives us the negation rule. For an example of the use of this rule, consider the probability of getting heads at least once on two tosses of a coin. The probability of the event *not* happening, which is the probability of getting tails on both tosses, is immediately computed by the restricted conjunction rule to be $1/4$. Then, applying the negation rule

$$P(H_1 \text{ or } H_2) = 1 - 1/4$$
$$= 3/4$$

The negation rule may also be used to compute the probabilities of disjunctive events that are *dependent*. In presenting the general disjunction rule we confined our attention to *independent* events. Let us suppose we are given an urn containing two black balls and three white balls. To compute the probability of getting at least one black ball on two draws (without replacement), we first compute the probability of the event not happening. This event consists in drawing two white balls, which, by the general conjunction rule, has the probability

$$P(W_1 \text{ and } W_2) = 3/5 \times 2/4 = 6/20$$

Now, applying the negation rule, the probability of getting at least one black ball on two draws is

$$P(B_1 \text{ or } B_2) = 1 - 6/20$$
$$= 14/20$$
$$= 7/10$$

For an example that is only slightly more complex, consider an urn containing two white, two black, and two red balls. To compute the probability of getting either a white or black ball on two draws (without replacement) we first compute the probability of the event not happening. This is the probability of getting red balls on both draws, which is

$$P(R_1 \text{ and } R_2) = 2/6 \times 1/5 = 2/30 = 1/15$$

Now, by the negation rule the probability of drawing either a white or black ball is

$$P(W \text{ or } B) = 1 - 1/15$$
$$= 14/15$$

All of the examples considered thus far have used the classical theory to determine the probability of the component events. But as was mentioned earlier, the probability calculus can also be used in conjunction with the relative frequency theory and the subjectivist theory. If we apply the relative frequency theory to the mortality tables used by insurance companies, we find that the probability of a 25-year-old man living an additional 40 years is .82, and the probability of a 25-year-old woman living the same number of years is .88. To compute the probability of two such people living that long we use the restricted conjunction rule and obtain $.82 \times .88 = .72$. For the probability that either of these people would live that long, we use the general disjunction rule and obtain

$$.82 + .88 - (.82 \times .88) = .98$$

Let us suppose that these two people are married and both would give 9 to 1 odds on their staying married for 40 years. This translates into a probability of $9/(9+1)$ or .9. Using the restricted conjunction rule, the probability of this event happening is the product of the latter figure and the probability of their both living that long, or .65.

For an example involving the subjectivist theory, if the Dallas Cowboys are given 7 to 5 odds at winning the NFC championship, and the Pittsburgh Steelers are given 3 to 2 odds at winning the AFC championship, the probability that at least one of these teams will win is computed using the general disjunction rule. The odds translate respectively into probabilities of $7/12$ and $3/5$, and so the probability of the disjunction is $7/12 + 3/5 - (7/12 \times 3/5) = 5/6$. The probability that the two teams will meet in the Superbowl (that both will win their conference championship) is, by the restricted conjunction rule, $7/12 \times 3/5 =$

21/60, or 7/20. The probability that neither will play in the Superbowl is, by the negation rule, $1 - 5/6 = 1/6$.

The probability calculus can also be used to evaluate the strength of inductive arguments. Consider the following argument:

> The Dallas Cowboys are given 7 to 5 odds on winning the NFC championship. The Pittsburgh Steelers are given 3 to 2 odds on winning the AFC championship. Therefore, probably the Cowboys and the Steelers will meet in the Superbowl.

On the assumption that the premises are true, that is, on the assumption that the odds are reported correctly, the conclusion follows with a probability of 7/20 or .35. Thus, the argument is not particularly strong. But if the odds given in the premises should increase, the strength of the argument would increase proportionately. The premises of the following argument give different odds:

> The Dallas Cowboys are given 7 to 2 odds on winning the NFC championship. The Pittsburgh Steelers are given 8 to 3 odds on winning the AFC championship. Therefore, probably the Cowboys and the Steelers will meet in the Superbowl.

In this argument, if the premises are assumed true, the conclusion follows with probability $7/9 \times 8/11 = 56/99$, or .57. Thus, the argument is at least moderately strong.

Lest this procedure be misinterpreted, however, it is important to recall a point raised in Chapter 1. The strength of an inductive argument depends not merely upon whether the conclusion is probably true but upon whether the conclusion follows probably from the premises. As a result, to evaluate the strength of an inductive argument it is not sufficient merely to know the probability of the conclusion on the assumption that the premises are true. One must also know whether the probability of the conclusion rests upon the evidence given in the premises. If the probability of the conclusion does not rest on this evidence, the argument is weak regardless of whether the conclusion is probably true. The following argument is a case in point:

> All dogs are animals.
> Therefore, probably a traffic accident will occur somewhere tomorrow.

The conclusion of this argument is probably true independently of the premises, so the argument is weak.

In this connection the analogy between deductive and inductive arguments breaks down. As we saw in Chapter 6, any argument having a conclusion that is necessarily true is deductively valid regardless of the content of its premises. But any inductive argument having a probably true conclusion is not strong unless the probability of the conclusion rests upon the evidence given in the premises.

A final comment is in order about the material covered in this section. Probability is one of those subjects about which there is little agreement in philosophical circles. There are philosophers who defend each of the theories we have discussed as providing the only acceptable approach, and there are numerous views regarding the fine points of each. In addition, some philosophers argue that there are certain uses of "probability" that none of these theories can interpret. The statement "There is high probability that Einstein's theory of relativity is correct" may be a case in point. In any event, the various theories about the meaning of probability, as well as the details of the probability calculus, are highly complex subjects, and the brief account given here has done little more than scratch the surface.

EXERCISE 9.2

I. Simple events.

★1. What is the probability of rolling a five on a single roll of a die?

2. From a sample of 9,750 Ajax trucks, 273 developed transmission problems within the first two years of operation. What is the probability that an Ajax truck will develop transmission problems within the first two years?

3. If the standard odds are 8 to 5 that the Chargers will beat the Lions, what is the probability that this event will happen?

★4. From a sample of 7,335 75-year-old women, 6,260 lived an additional 5 years. What is the probability that a 75-year-old woman will live to age 80?

5. What is the probability of picking a black jack from a poker deck (without jokers) on a single draw?

6. If the standard odds are 6 to 11 that the Red Sox will beat the Tigers, what is the probability that this event will happen?

★7. Given an urn containing three red balls, four green balls, and five yellow balls, what is the probability of drawing a red ball on a single draw?

II. Compound events.

★1. What is the probability of getting either a six or a one from a single roll of a die?

2. What is the probability of getting heads on three successive tosses of a coin?

3. What is the probability of drawing either a king or a queen from a poker deck (no jokers) on a single draw?

★4. What is the probability of drawing two aces from a poker deck in two draws:
a. If the first card is replaced before the second is drawn?
b. If the first card is not replaced before the second is drawn?

5. What is the probability of drawing at least one ace from a poker deck on two draws if the first card is replaced before the second is drawn?

6. What is the probability of getting at least one head on three tosses of a coin?

★7. What is the probability of getting at least one six on three rolls of a die?

8. If a pair of dice are rolled, what is the probability that the points add up to:
a. 5?
b. 6?
c. 7?

9. Given two urns, one containing two red, three green, and four yellow balls, the other containing four red, two green, and three yellow balls, if a single ball is drawn from each urn, what is the probability that:
a. Both are red?
b. At least one is green?
c. One is red, the other yellow?
d. At least one is either red or yellow?
e. Both are the same color?

★10. Given an urn containing three red, four green, and five yellow balls, if two balls are drawn from the urn (without replacement), what is the probability that:
a. Both are red?
b. One is green, the other yellow?
c. One is either red or green?
d. At least one is green?
e. Both have the same color?

11. What is the probability of drawing either an ace or a king (or both) on three draws (without replacement) from a poker deck? (Hint: Use the negation rule.)

12. What is the probability of drawing an ace and a king on three draws (without replacement) from a poker deck? (Hint: Use the negation rule.)

★13. The probability of a 20-year-old man living to age 70 is .74, and the probability of a 20-year-old woman living to the same age is .82. If a recently married couple, both age 20, give 8 to 1 odds on their staying married for 50 years, what is the probability that:

a. At least one will live to age 70?

b. They will celebrate their golden wedding anniversary?

14. Assign a numerical value to the strength of the following argument: The odds are 5 to 3 that the Indians will win the American League pennant and 7 to 5 that the Cardinals will win the National League pennant. Therefore, the Indians and the Cardinals will probably meet in the World Series.

★15. Assign a numerical value to the strength of the following argument: The Wilson family has four children. Therefore, at least two of the children were probably born on the same day of the week.

9.3 STATISTICAL REASONING

In our day-to-day experience all of us encounter arguments that rest on statistical evidence. An especially prolific source of such arguments is the advertising industry. We are constantly told that we ought to smoke a certain brand of cigarettes because it has 20 percent less tar, buy a certain kind of car because it gets 5 percent better gas mileage, and use a certain cold remedy because it is recommended by four out of five physicians. But the advertising industry is not the only source. We often read in the newspapers that some union is asking an increase in pay because its members earn less than the average or that a certain region is threatened with floods because rainfall has been more than the average.

To evaluate such arguments, we must be able to interpret the statistics upon which they rest, but doing so is not always easy. Statements expressing averages and percentages are often ambiguous and can mean any number of things, depending on how the average or percentage is computed. These difficulties are compounded by the fact that statistics provide a highly convenient way for people to deceive one another. Such deceptions can be effective even though they fall short of being outright lies. Thus, to evaluate arguments based on statistics one must be familiar not only with the ambiguities that occur in the language but with the devices that unscrupulous individuals use to deceive others.

This section touches on five areas that are frequent sources of such ambiguity and deception: problems in sampling, the meaning of "average," the importance of dispersion in a sample, the use of graphs and pictograms, and the use of percentages for the purpose of comparison. By becoming acquainted with these topics and with some of the misuses that occur, we are better able to determine whether a conclusion follows probably from a set of statistical premises.

Samples

Much of the statistical evidence presented in support of inductively drawn conclusions is gathered from analyzing samples. When a sample is found to possess a certain characteristic, it is argued that the group as a whole (the population) possesses that characteristic. For example, if we wanted to know the opinion of the student body at a certain university about whether the Selective Service System should reinstate the draft, we could take a poll of 10 percent of the students. If the results of the poll showed that 80 percent of those sampled were opposed to the draft, we might draw the conclusion that 80 percent of the entire student body was opposed. Such an argument would be classified as an inductive generalization.

The problem that arises with the use of samples has to do with whether the sample is representative of the population. Samples that are not representative are said to be **biased.** Depending on what the population consists of, whether machine parts or human beings, different considerations enter into determining whether a sample is biased. These considerations include (1) whether the sample is randomly selected, (2) the size of the sample, and (3) psychological factors.

A sample is *random* if and only if every member of the population has an equal chance of being selected. The requirement that a sample be randomly selected applies to practically all samples, but sometimes it can be taken for granted. For example, when a physician draws a blood sample to test for blood sugar, there is no need to take a little bit from the finger, a little from the arm, and a little from the leg. Because blood is a circulating fluid, it can be assumed that it is homogenous in regard to blood sugar.

The randomness requirement must be given more attention when the population consists of discrete units. Suppose, for example, that a quality control engineer for a manufacturing firm needed to determine whether the components on a certain conveyor belt were within specifications. To do so, let us suppose the engineer removed every tenth component for measurement. The sample obtained by such a procedure would not be random if the components were not randomly arranged on the conveyor belt. As a result of some malfunction in the manufacturing process it is quite possible that every tenth component turned out perfect and the rest imperfect. If the engineer happened to select only the perfect ones, the sample would be biased. A selection procedure that would be more likely to insure a random sample would be to roll a pair of dice and remove every component corresponding to a roll of ten. Since the outcome of a roll of dice is a random event, the selection would also be random. Such a procedure would be more likely to include defective components that turn up at regular intervals.

The randomness requirement presents even greater problems when the population consists of human beings. Suppose, for example, that a public opinion poll is to be conducted on the question of excess corporate profits. It would hardly do to ask such a question randomly of the people encountered on Wall Street in New York City. Such a sample would almost certainly be biased in favor of the corporations. A less biased sample could be obtained by randomly selecting phone numbers from the telephone directory, but even this procedure would not yield a completely random sample. Among other things, the time of day in which a call is placed influences the kind of responses obtained. Most people who are employed full time are not available during the day, and even if calls are made at night, approximately 25 percent of the population have unlisted numbers.

A poll conducted by mail based on the addresses listed in the city directory would also yield a fairly random sample, but this method, too, has shortcomings. Many apartment dwellers are not listed, and others move before the directory is printed. Furthermore, none of those who live in rural areas are listed. In short, it is both difficult and expensive to conduct a large-scale public opinion poll that succeeds in obtaining responses from anything approximating a random sample of individuals.

A classic case of a poll that turned out to be biased in spite of a good deal of effort and expense was conducted by *Literary Digest* magazine to predict the outcome of the 1936 presidential election. The sample consisted of a large number of the magazine's subscribers together with a number of others selected from the telephone directory. Because four similar polls had picked the winner in previous years, the results of this poll were highly respected. As it turned out, however, the Republican candidate, Alf Landon, got a significant majority in the poll, but Franklin D. Roosevelt won the election by a landslide. The incorrect prediction is explained by the fact that 1936 occurred in the middle of the Depression, at a time when many people could afford neither a telephone nor a subscription to the *Digest*. These were the people who were overlooked in the poll, and they were also the ones who voted for Roosevelt.

Size is also an important factor in determining whether a sample is representative. Given that a sample is randomly selected, the larger the sample, the more closely it replicates the population. In statistics, this degree of closeness is expressed in terms of **sampling error.** The sampling error is the difference between the frequency with which some characteristic occurs in the sample and the frequency with which the same characteristic occurs in the population. If, for example, a poll were taken of a labor union and 60 percent of the members sampled expressed their intention to vote for Smith for president but in fact only 55 percent of the whole union intended to vote for Smith, the sampling error would be 5 percent. If a larger sample were taken, the error would be less.

Just how large a sample should be is a function of the size of the population and of the degree of sampling error that can be tolerated. For a sampling error of, say, 5 percent, a population of 10,000 would require a larger sample than would a population of 100. However, the ratio is not linear. The sample for the larger population need not be 100 times as large as the one for the smaller population to obtain the same precision. When the population is very large, the size of the sample needed to ensure a certain precision levels off to a constant figure. Studies based on the Gallup poll show that a random sample of 400 will yield results of plus or minus 6 percent whether the population is 100,000 or 100 million. Additional figures for large populations are given in Table 7[*]:

Table 7 Sample Size and Sampling Error

Numbers of interviews	Margin of error (in percentage points)
4,000	±2
1,500	±3
1,000	±4
750	±4
600	±5
400	±6
200	±8
100	±11

As the table indicates, reducing the sampling error below 5 percent requires rather substantial increases in the size of the sample. The cost of obtaining large samples may not justify an increase in precision. The table also points up the importance of randomness. The sample in the 1936 *Literary Digest* poll was based on 2 million responses, yet the sampling error was huge because the sample was not randomly selected.

Statements of sampling error are often conspicuously absent from surveys used to support advertising claims. Marketers of products such as patent medicines have been known to take a number of rather small samples until they obtain one that gives the "right" result. For example, twenty polls of twenty-five people might be taken inquiring about the preferred brand of aspirin. Even though the samples might be randomly selected, one will eventually be found in which twenty of the twenty-five respondents indicate their preference for alpha brand aspirin. Having found such a sample, the marketing firm proceeds to promote this brand as the one preferred by four out of five of those sampled. The results of the other samples are, of course, discarded, and no mention is made of sampling error.

Psychological factors can also have a bearing on whether the sample is representative. When the population consists of inanimate objects, such as cans of soup or machine parts, psychological factors are usually irrelevant, but they can play a significant role when the population consists of human beings. If the people composing the sample think that they

[*]From Charles W. Roll Jr. and Albert H. Cantril, *Polls: Their Use and Misuse in Politics* (New York: Basic Books, 1972), p. 72.

will gain or lose something by the kind of answer they give, it is to be expected that their involvement will affect the outcome. For example, if the residents of a neighborhood were to be surveyed for annual income with the purpose of determining whether the neighborhood should be ranked among the fashionable areas in the city, it would be expected that the residents would exaggerate their answers. But if the purpose of the study were to determine whether the neighborhood could afford a special levy that would increase property taxes, one might expect the incomes to be underestimated.

The kind of question asked can also have a psychological bearing. Questions such as "How often do you brush your teeth?" and "How many books do you read in a year?" can be expected to generate responses that overestimate the truth, while "How many times have you been intoxicated?" and "How many extramarital affairs have you had?" would probably receive answers that underestimate the truth. Similar exaggerations can result from the way a question is phrased. For example, "Do you favor a reduction in welfare benefits as a response to rampant cheating?" would be expected to receive more affirmative answers than simply "Do you favor a reduction in welfare benefits?"

Another source of psychological influence is the personal interaction between the surveyor and the respondent. Suppose, for example, that a door-to-door survey were taken to determine how many people believe in God or attend church on Sunday. If the survey were conducted by priests and ministers dressed in clerical garb, one might expect a larger number of affirmative answers than if the survey were taken by nonclerics. The simple fact is that many people like to give answers that please the questioner.

To prevent this kind of interaction from affecting the outcome, scientific studies are often conducted under "double blind" conditions in which neither the surveyor nor the respondent knows what the "right" answer is. For example, in a double blind study to determine the effectiveness of a drug, bottles containing the drug would be mixed with other bottles containing a placebo (sugar tablet). The contents of each bottle would be matched with a code number on the label, and neither the person distributing the bottles nor the person recording the responses would know what the code is. Under these conditions the persons conducting the study would not be able to influence, by some smile or gesture, the response of the persons to whom the drugs are given.

Most of the statistical evidence encountered in ordinary experience contains no reference to such factors as randomness, sampling error, or the conditions under which the sample was taken. In the absence of such information, the person faced with evaluating the evidence must use his or her best judgment. If either the organization conducting the study or the persons composing the sample have something to gain by the kind of answer that is given, the results of the survey should be regarded as suspect. And if the questions that are asked concern topics that would naturally elicit distorted answers, the results should probably be rejected. In either event, the mere fact that a study *appears* scientific or is expressed in mathematical language should never intimidate a person into accepting the results. Numbers and scientific terminology are no substitute for an unbiased sample.

The Meaning of "Average"

In statistics the word "average" is used in three different senses: mean, median, and mode. In evaluating arguments and inferences that rest upon averages, it is often important to know in precisely what sense the word is being used.

The **mean** value of a set of data is the arithmetical average. It is computed by dividing the sum of the individual values by the number of data in the set. Suppose, for example, that we are given Table 8 listing the ages of a group of people:

Table 8

Number of people	Age
1	16
4	17
1	18
2	19
3	23

To compute the mean age, we divide the sum of the individual ages by the number of people:

$$\text{mean age} = \frac{(1 \times 16) + (4 \times 17) + (1 \times 18) + (2 \times 19) + (3 \times 23)}{11}$$
$$= 19$$

The **median** of a set of data is the middle point when the data are arranged in ascending order. In other words, the median is the point at which there are an equal number of data above and below. In Table 8 the median age is 18 because there are five people above this age and five below.

The **mode** is the value that occurs with the greatest frequency. Here the mode is 17, because there are four people with that age and fewer people with any other age.

In this example, the mean, median, and mode, while different from one another, are all fairly close together. The problem for induction occurs when there is a great disparity between these values. This sometimes occurs in the case of salaries. Consider, for example, Table 9, which reports the salaries of a hypothetical architectural firm:

Table 9

Capacity	Number of personnel	Salary
president	1	$140,000
senior architect	2	80,000
junior architect	2	66,000
senior engineer	1	35,000←mean
junior engineer	4	32,000
senior draftsman	1	20,000←median
junior draftsman	10	12,000←mode

Since there are twenty-one employees and a total of $735,000 is paid in salaries, the mean salary is $735,000/21, or $35,000. The median salary is $20,000 because ten employees earn less than this and ten earn more, and the mode, which is the salary that occurs most frequently, is $12,000. Each of these figures represents the "average" salary of the firm, but in different senses. Depending on the purpose for which the average is used, different figures might be cited as the basis for an argument.

For example, if the senior engineer were to request a raise in salary, the president could respond that his or her salary is already well above the average (in the sense of median and mode) and that therefore that person does not deserve a raise. If the junior draftsmen were to make the same request, the president could respond that they are presently earning the firm's average salary (in the sense of mode), and that for draftsmen to be earning the average salary is excellent. Finally, if someone from outside the firm were to make the allegation that the firm pays subsistence-level wages, the president could respond that the average salary of the firm is a hefty $35,000. All of the president's responses would be true, but if the reader or listener is not sophisticated enough to distinguish the various senses of "average," he or she might be persuaded by the arguments.

In some situations, the mode is the most useful average. Suppose, for example, that you are in the market for a three-bedroom house. Suppose further that a real estate agent assures you that the houses in a certain complex have an average of three bedrooms and that therefore you will certainly want to see them. If the salesman has used "average" in the sense of mean, it is possible that half the houses in the complex are four-bedroom, the other half are two-bedroom, and there are no three-bedroom houses at all. A similar result is possible if the salesman has used average in the sense of median. The only sense of average that would be

A CONCISE INTRODUCTION TO LOGIC

useful for your purposes is mode: If the modal average is three bed-rooms, there are more three-bedroom houses than any other kind.

On other occasions a mean average is the most useful. Suppose, for example, that you have taken a job as a pilot on a plane that has nine passenger seats and a maximum carrying capacity of 1,350 pounds (in addition to yourself). Suppose further that you have arranged to fly a group of nine passengers over the Grand Canyon and that you must determine whether their combined weight is within the required limit. If a representative of the group tells you that the average weight of the passengers is 150 pounds, this by itself tells you nothing. If he means average in the sense of median, it could be the case that the four heavier passengers weigh 200 pounds and the four lighter ones weigh 145, for a combined weight of 1,530 pounds. Similarly, if the passenger represen-tative means average in the sense of mode, it could be that two pas-sengers weigh 150 pounds and that the others have varying weights in excess of 200 pounds, for a combined weight of over 1,700 pounds. Only if the representative means average in the sense of mean do you know that the combined weight of the passengers is 9 $\times$ 150 or 1,350 pounds.

Finally, sometimes a median average is the most meaningful. Sup-pose, for example, that you are a manufacturer of a product that appeals to an age group under 35. To increase sales you decide to run an ad in a national magazine, but you want some assurance that the ad will be read by the right age group. If the advertising director of a magazine tells you that the average age of the magazine's readers is 35, you know virtually nothing. If the director means average in the sense of mean, it could be that 90 percent of the readership is over 35 and that the re-maining 10 percent bring the average down to 35. Similarly, if the direc-tor means average in the sense of mode, it could be that 3 percent of the readership are exactly 35 and that the remaining 97 percent have ages ranging from 35 to 85. Only if the director means average in the sense of median do you know that half the readership is 35 or less.

As these examples illustrate, the sense of average used often makes an important difference. There is one group of data, however, for which the three senses always have identical values. This is the group of data that corresponds to random phenomena. Examples include the height of adult men or women, the velocity of the wind in a certain area, the useful life of a certain kind of light bulb or automobile tire, the weekly sales of a certain kind of toothpaste or shampoo, and the results of any random sample. Data that correspond to these phenomena usually con-form quite closely to what is called the **normal probability distribution,** whose curve has the shape of a bell (see Figure 1).

As the curve indicates, the number of instances tapers off to zero when the data reach maximum and minimum values, and it reaches a high point when the data have middle values. Mean, median, and mode occur together at the high point on the curve. This point indicates an

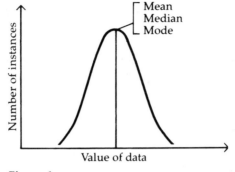

Figure 1

average in the sense of mode because it is the point at which the most instances are recorded. It is a median point because the data are random, so the number of instances greater than the high point equals the number of instances less than the high point. And this same point is a mean because the values of the data under the right-hand part exceed the median value to the same extent that the values under the left-hand part are less than the median value. An example of the use of this curve will be given in connection with dispersion.

Dispersion

The **dispersion** of a set of data refers to how spread out the data are in regard to numerical value. Suppose, for example, that wind velocity measurements are taken over a period of several months in the middle of the ocean. Suppose further that the wind blows constantly at this particular point, never dropping below 30 mph but never exceeding 60 mph. The dispersion of the data in this case would be rather slight, and, assuming that the data conform to the normal probability distribution, the curve would be relatively high and narrow, as in Figure 2:

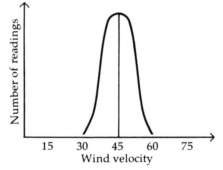

Figure 2

A CONCISE INTRODUCTION TO LOGIC

This curve indicates that all the velocity readings occur within the rather narrow range of 30 to 60 mph, for an average velocity of 45 mph.

If, on the other hand, the same number of velocity measurements are taken at a different point, where the wind occasionally stops completely but at other times reaches a maximum of 90 mph, the dispersion of the data would be much greater. Assuming that the data conform to the normal probability distribution, the curve would be flatter and lower, as in Figure 3:

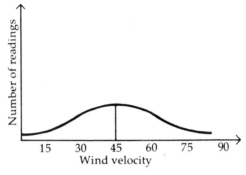

Figure 3

In both cases the average velocity in the sense of mean, median, and mode is 45 mph, but the difference in dispersion indicates that the situations are clearly different.

In statistics dispersion is expressed in terms of such parameters as range, variance, and standard deviation. The **range** of a set of data is the difference between the largest and the smallest values. Thus, in the first case the range is 30 and in the second case it is 90. The **variance** and **standard deviation,** on the other hand, measure how far the data vary or deviate from the mean value. (The standard deviation is defined as the square root of the variance.) In the two curves we have presented, the first has a relatively small variance and standard deviation in comparison with the second.

Information about the dispersion of a set of data is important in drawing inductive inferences because it supplements information about averages. Sometimes statements about averages are virtually useless without some additional statement about the dispersion, which, if ignored, can produce disastrous consequences. Suppose, for example, that after living for many years in an intemperate climate, you decide to relocate in an area that has a more ideal mean temperature. Upon discovering that the annual mean temperature of Oklahoma City is 60°F you decide to move there, only to find that you roast in the summer and freeze in the winter. Unfortunately, you had ignored the fact that Oklahoma City has a temperature *range* of 130°, extending from a record low of −17° to a record high of 113°. In contrast, San Nicholas Island, off the coast of

California, has a mean temperature of 61° but a range of only 40 degrees, extending from 47° in the winter to 87° in the summer. The temperature ranges for these two locations are approximated in Figure 4*:

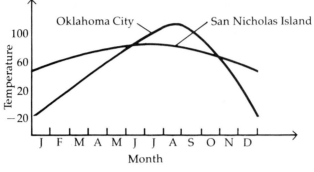

Figure 4

For another example, suppose that you are 25 years old and are planning an ocean cruise. Your primary concern in selecting a tour is that there be plenty of people on the ship within your age group. The manager of Holiday Tours sets your mind at rest when he assures you that the mean age of the voyagers departing on the Holiday Prince for a cruise of the Caribbean is 25. You select that cruise, and after departing you find to your dismay that the voyagers are primarily comprised of two groups, one ranging in age from 1 to 10, the other from 40 to 50. Together they balance out for a mean age of 25. This situation is depicted in Figure 5:

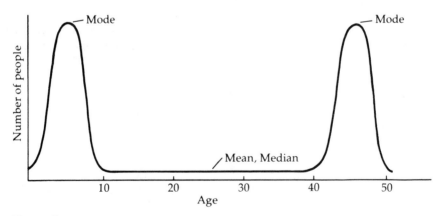

Figure 5

*This example is taken from Darrell Huff, *How To Lie with Statistics* (New York: W. W. Norton, 1954), p. 52.

A CONCISE INTRODUCTION TO LOGIC

The curve has two modes and is thus described as bimodal. In this case if you had known either the average age in the sense of mode or the dispersion, you would not have signed up for the cruise.

For a final example, suppose that you decide to put your life savings into a business that designs and manufactures women's clothing. As corporation president you decide to save money by restricting production to clothes that fit the average woman. Because the average size in the sense of mean, median, and mode is 12, you decide to make only size 12 clothing. Unfortunately, you later discover that while size 12 is indeed the average, 95 percent of women fall outside this range, as Figure 6 shows:

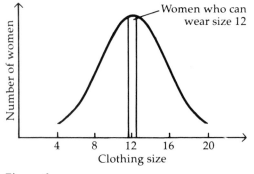

Figure 6

Again, if you had taken into account the dispersion of the data, you would not have made this mistake.

Graphs and Pictograms

Graphs provide a highly convenient and informative way to represent statistical data, but they are also susceptible to misuse and misinterpretation. Here we will confine our attention to some of the typical ways in which graphs are misused.

First of all, if a graph is to represent an actual situation, it is essential that both the vertical and horizontal axes be scaled. Suppose, for example, that the profit level of a corporation is represented by a graph such as Figure 7. Such a graph is practically meaningless because it fails to show how much the profits increased over what period of time. If the curve represents a 10 percent increase over 20 years, then, of course, the picture is not very bright. Although they convey practically no information, graphs of this kind are used quite often in advertising. A manufacturer of vitamins, for example, might print such a graph on the label of the bottle to suggest that a person's energy level is supposed to increase dramatically after taking the tablets. Such ads frequently make an impression because they look scientific, and the viewer rarely bothers to

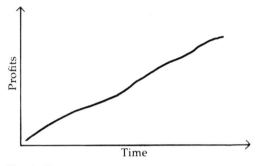

Figure 7

check whether the axes are scaled or precisely what the curve is supposed to signify.

A graph that more appropriately represents corporate profits is represented in Figure 8 (the corporation is fictitious):

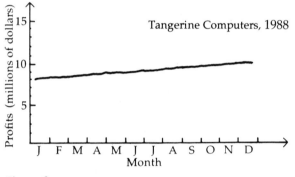

Figure 8

Inspection of the graph reveals that between January and December profits rose from $8 to $10 million, which represents a respectable 25 percent increase. This increase can be made to *appear* even more impressive by chopping off the bottom of the graph, as shown in Figure 9:

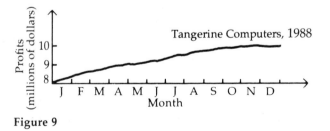

Figure 9

Strictly speaking, the new graph accurately represents the increase because the scale on the vertical axis indicates that the profits increased 25 percent. But the increase *looks* more impressive because the curve now stretches from the bottom of the graph to the top. This same effect can be exaggerated by altering the scale on the vertical axis while leaving the horizontal scale as is:

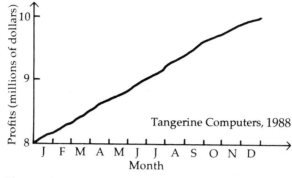

Figure 10

Again, strictly speaking, the graph accurately represents the facts, but if the viewer fails to notice what has been done to the vertical scale, he or she is liable to derive the impression that the profits have increased by something like a thousand percent.

The same strategy can be used with bar graphs. The graphs in Figure 11 compare sales volume for two consecutive years, but the one on the right conveys the message more dramatically:

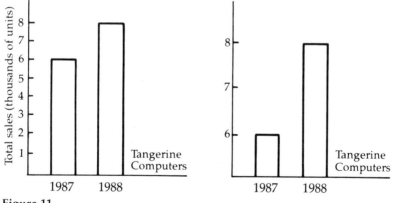

Figure 11

Of course, if the sales volume has decreased, the corporate directors would probably want to minimize the difference, in which case the design on the left is preferable.

An even greater illusion can be created with the use of pictograms. A **pictogram** is a diagram that compares two situations through drawings that differ either in size or in the number of entities depicted. Consider

Figure 12, which illustrates the increase in the amount of oil consumed in the United States between 1960 and 1978:

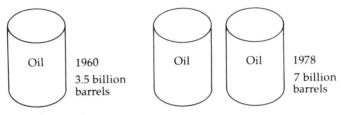

Figure 12

This pictogram accurately represents the facts because it unequivocally shows that the amount doubled between the years represented. But the effect is not especially dramatic. The increase in consumption can be exaggerated by representing the 1978 level with an oil barrel twice as tall:

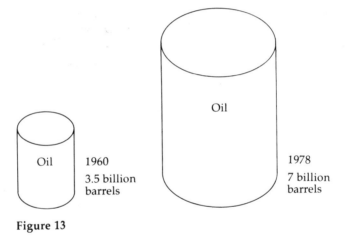

Figure 13

Even though the actual consumption is stated adjacent to each drawing, this pictogram creates the illusion that consumption has much more than doubled. While the drawing on the right is exactly twice as high as the one on the left, it is also twice as wide. Thus, it occupies four times as much room on the page. Furthermore, when the viewer's three-dimensional judgment is called into play, the barrel on the right is perceived as having eight times the volume of the one on the left. Thus, when the third dimension is taken into account, the increase in consumption is exaggerated by 400 percent.

Percentages

The use of percentages to compare two or more situations or quantities is another source of illusion in statistics. A favorite of advertisers is to make claims such as "Zesty Cola has 20 percent fewer calories" or "The price of the new Computrick computer has been reduced by 15 percent." These claims are virtually meaningless. The question is, 20 percent less than *what*, and 15 percent reduced from *what*? If the basis of the comparison or reduction is not mentioned, the claim tells us nothing. Yet such claims are often effective because they leave one with the impression that the product is in some way superior or less expensive.

Another strategy sometimes used by governments and businesses involves playing sleight-of-hand tricks with the base of the percentages. Suppose, for example, that you are a university president involved with a funding drive to increase the university's endowment. Suppose further that the endowment presently stands at $15 million and that the objective is to increase it to $20 million. To guarantee the success of the drive, you engage the services of a professional fund-raising organization. At the end of the alotted time the organization has increased the endowment to $16 million. They justify their effort by stating that, since $16 of the $20 million has been raised, the drive was 80 percent successful (16/20 × 100%).

In fact, of course, the drive was nowhere near that successful. The objective was not to raise $20 million, but only $5 million, and of that amount only $1 million has actually been raised. Thus, at best the drive was only 20 percent successful. Even this figure is probably exaggerated, though, because $1 million might have been raised without any special drive. The trick played by the fund-raising organization consisted in switching the numbers by which the percentage was to be computed.

This same trick, incidentally, was allegedly used by Joseph Stalin to justify the success of his first five-year plan.* Among other things, the original plan called for an increase in steel output from 4.2 million tons to 10.3 million. After five years the actual output rose to 5.9 million, whereupon Stalin announced that the plan was 57 percent successful (5.9/10.3 × 100%). The correct percentage, of course, is much less. The plan called for an increase of 6.1 million tons and the actual increase was only 1.7 million. Thus, at best, the plan was only 28 percent successful.

Similar devices have been used by employers on their unsuspecting employees. When business is bad, an employer may argue that salaries must be reduced by 20 percent. Later, when business improves, salaries will be raised by 20 percent, thus restoring them to their original level. Such an argument, of course, is fallacious. If a person earns $10 per hour and that person's salary is reduced by 20 percent, the adjusted salary is $8. If that figure is later increased by 20 percent, the final salary is $9.60.

---

*Stephen K. Campbell, *Flaws and Fallacies in Statistical Thinking* (Englewood Cliffs, N.J.: Prentice-Hall, 1974) p. 8. The original reference is to Eugene Lyons' *Workers' Paradise Lost*.

The problem, of course, stems from the fact that a different base is used for the two percentages. The fallacy committed by such arguments is a variety of equivocation. Percentages are relative terms, and they mean different things in different contexts.

A different kind of fallacy occurs when a person attempts to add percentages as if they were cardinal numbers. Suppose, for example, that a baker increases the price of a loaf of bread by 50 percent. To justify the increase the baker argues that it was necessitated by rising costs: the price of flour increased by 10 percent, the cost of labor by 20 percent, utility rates went up 10 percent, and the cost of the lease on the building increased 10 percent. This adds up to a 50 percent increase. Again, the argument is fallacious. If *everything* had increased by 20 percent, this would justify only a 20 percent increase in the price of bread. As it is, the justified increase is less than that. The fallacy committed by such arguments would probably be best classified as a case of missing the point (*ignoratio elenchi*). The arguer has failed to grasp the significance of his own premises.

Statistical variations of the suppressed evidence fallacy are also quite common. One variety consists in drawing a conclusion from a comparison of two different things or situations. For example, persons running for political office sometimes cite figures indicating that crime in the community has increased by, let us say, 20 percent during the past three or four years. What is needed, they conclude, is an all-out war on crime. But they fail to mention the fact that the population in the community has also increased by 20 percent during the same period. The number of crimes per capita, therefore, has not changed. Another example of the same fallacy is provided by the ridiculous argument that 90 percent more traffic accidents occur in clear weather than in foggy weather and that therefore it is 90 percent more dangerous to drive in clear than in foggy weather. The arguer ignores the fact that the vast percentage of vehicle miles are driven in clear weather, which accounts for the greater number of accidents.

A similar misuse of percentages is committed by businesses and corporations that, for whatever reason, want to make it appear that they have earned less profits than they actually have. The technique consists in expressing profits as a percentage of sales volume instead of as a percentage of investment. For example, during a certain year a corporation might have a total sales volume of $100 million, a total investment of $10 million, and a profit of $5 million. If profits are expressed as a percentage of investment, they amount to a hefty 50 percent; but as a percentage of sales they are only 5 percent. To appreciate the fallacy in this procedure, consider the case of the jewelry merchant who buys one piece of jewelry each morning for $9 and sells it in the evening for $10. At the end of the year the total sales volume is $3650, the total investment $9, and the total profit $365. Profits as a percentage of sales amount to only 10 percent, but as a percentage of investment they exceed 4000 percent.

EXERCISE 9.3

I. Criticize the following arguments in light of the material presented in this section:

★1. To test the algae content in a lake, a biologist took a sample of the water at one end. The algae in the sample registered 5 micrograms per liter. Therefore, the algae in the lake at that time registered 5 micrograms per liter.

2. To estimate public support for a new municipality-funded convention center, researchers surveyed 100 homeowners in one of the city's fashionable neighborhoods. They found that 89 percent of those sampled were enthusiastic about the project. Therefore, we may conclude that 89 percent of the city's residents favor the convention center.

3. A quality-control inspector for a food-processing firm needed assurance that the cans of fruit in a production run were filled to capacity. He opened every tenth box in the warehouse and removed the can in the left front corner of each box. He found that all of these cans were filled to capacity. Therefore, it is probable that all of the cans in the production run were filled to capacity.

★4. When a random sample of 600 voters was taken on the eve of the presidential election, it was found that 51 percent of those sampled intended to vote for the Democrat and 49 percent for the Republican. Therefore, the Democrat will probably win.

5. To determine the public's attitude toward TV soap operas, 1,000 people were contacted by telephone between 8 A.M. and 5 P.M. on week days. The numbers were selected randomly from the phone directories of cities across the nation. The researchers reported that 43 percent of the respondents said that they were avid viewers. From this we may conclude that 43 percent of the public watches TV soap operas.

6. To predict the results of a U.S. Senate race in New York State, two polls were taken. One was based on a random sample of 750 voters, the other on a random sample of 1,500 voters. Since the second sample was twice as large as the first, the results of the second poll were twice as accurate as the first.

★7. In a survey conducted by the manufacturers of Ultrasheen toothpaste, 65 percent of the dentists randomly sampled preferred that brand over all others. Clearly Ultrasheen is the brand preferred by most dentists.

8. To determine the percentage of adult Americans who have never read the U.S. Constitution, surveyors put this question to a random sample of 1,500 adults. Only 13 percent gave negative answers. Therefore, since the sampling error for such a sample is 3 percent, we may conclude that no more than 16 percent of American adults have not read the Constitution.

9. To determine the percentage of patients who follow the advice of their personal physician, researchers asked 200 randomly chosen physicians to put the question to their patients. Of the 4,000 patients surveyed, 98 percent replied that they did indeed follow their doctor's advice. We may therefore conclude that at least 95 percent of the patients across the nation follow the advice of their personal physician.

★10. Janet Ryan can afford to pay no more than $15 for a birthday gift for her 8-year-old daughter. Since the average price of a toy at General Toy Company is $15, Janet can expect to find an excellent selection of toys within her price range at that store.

11. Anthony Valardi, who owns a fish market, pays $2 per pound to fishermen for silver salmon. A certain fisherman certifies that the average size of the salmon in his catch of the day is 10 pounds, and that the catch numbers 100 salmon. Mr. Valardi is therefore justified in paying the fisherman $2,000 for the whole catch.

12. Pamela intends to go shopping for a new pair of shoes. She wears size 8. Since the average size of the shoes carried by the Bon Marche is size 8, Pamela can expect to find an excellent selection of shoes in her size at that store.

★13. Tim Cassidy, who works for a construction company, is told to load a pile of rocks onto a truck. The rocks are randomly sized, and the average piece weighs 50 pounds. Thus, Tim should have no trouble loading the rocks by hand.

14. The average IQ (in the sense of mean, median, and mode) of the students in Dr. Jacob's symbolic logic class is 120. Thus, none of the students should have any trouble mastering the subject matter.

15. An insecticide manufacturer prints the following graph on the side of its spray cans:

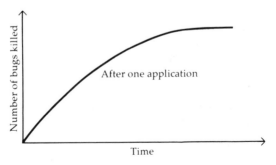

A CONCISE INTRODUCTION TO LOGIC

Obviously, the insecticide is highly effective at killing bugs, and it keeps working for a long time.

★16. A corporation's sales for two consecutive years are represented in a bar graph. Since the bar for the later year is twice as high as the one for the previous year, it follows that sales for the later year were double those for the previous year.

17. Forced to make cutbacks, the president of a manufacturing firm reduced certain costs as follows: Advertising by 4 percent, transportation by 5 percent, materials by 2 percent, and employee benefits by 3 percent. The president thus succeeded in reducing total costs by 14 percent.

18. During a certain year, a grocery store chain had total sales of $100 million, and profits of $10 million. The profits thus amounted to a modest 10 percent for that year.

★19. There were 40 percent more traffic accidents in 1980 than there were in 1950. Therefore, it was 40 percent more dangerous to drive a car in 1980 than it was in 1950.

20. An efficiency expert was hired to increase the productivity of a manufacturing firm and was given three months to accomplish the task. At the end of the period the productivity had increased from 1500 units per week to 1700. Since the goal was 2000 units per week, the effort of the efficiency expert was 85 percent successful (1700/2000).

II. Determine the average in the sense of mean, median, and mode for the following distributions of weight and salary:

★1.

Number of people	Weight
2	150
4	160
3	170
1	180
1	190
1	200
1	220
2	230

2.

Number of people	Salary
1	$95,000
2	85,000
1	70,000
3	40,000
1	30,000
2	20,000
5	15,000

III. Answer "true" or "false" to the following statements:

★1. If a sample is very large, it need not be randomly selected.

2. If a population is randomly arranged, a sample obtained by selecting every tenth member would be a random sample.

3. If a sample is randomly selected, the larger the sample is the more closely it replicates the population.

★4. To ensure the same precision, a population of 1 million would require a much larger random sample than would a population of 100,000.

5. In general, if sample A is twice as large as sample B, then the sampling error for A is one-half that for B.

6. When a sample consists of human beings, the purpose for which the sample is taken can affect the outcome.

★7. The personal interaction between a surveyor and a respondent can affect the outcome of a survey.

8. The mean value of a set of data is the value that occurs with the greatest frequency.

9. The median value of a set of data is the middle point when the data are arranged in ascending order.

★10. The modal value of a set of data is the arithmetical average.

11. If one needed to know whether a sizable portion of a group were above or below a certain level, the most useful sense of average would be mode.

12. Data reflecting the results of a random sample conform fairly closely to the normal probability distribution.

★13. If a set of data conform to the normal probability distribution, then the mean, median, and mode have the same value.

14. The range, variance, and standard deviation are measurements of dispersion.

15. Statements about averages often present an incomplete picture without information about the dispersion.

★16. Data reflecting the size of full-grown horses would exhibit greater dispersion than data reflecting the size of full-grown dogs.

17. The visual impression made by graphs can be exaggerated by changing one of the scales while leaving the other unchanged.

18. Data reflecting a 100 percent increase in housing construction could be accurately represented by a pictogram of two houses, one twice as high as the other.

★19. If a certain quantity is increased by 10 percent and later decreased by 10 percent, the quantity is restored to what it was originally.

20. Expressing profits as a percentage of sales volume presents an honest picture of the earnings of a corporation.

9.4 HYPOTHETICAL REASONING

All inductive arguments proceed from the known to the unknown. For example, we might see storm clouds gathering overhead and predict that it will rain, or we might drive past a signboard advertising a new bank in town and conclude that the town really does have a new bank. We can see the rain clouds and the signboard, and our reasoning leads us beyond these to the storm in the future and the bank in some distant part of town.

Sometimes, though, the available evidence does not immediately suggest what lies ahead, beyond, or beneath the surface. For example, if we should turn the key in the ignition of our car and hear the engine crank but fail to start, we might not be able to reason directly to the unknown cause. If we know anything at all about the workings of an automobile, we might begin to wonder: Could it be the spark plugs? The carburetor? The fuel pump? The ignition coil? The distributor? The evidence by itself, the fact that the engine cranks but does not start, is not sufficient to provide the answer. To fill the gap, our creative imagination supplements the evidence by suggesting possible approaches to the problem. These possible approaches are **hypotheses,** and the reasoning process used to produce them is **hypothetical reasoning.**

Hypothetical reasoning is used by nearly all of us in our day-to-day experience. The television repairman constructs hypotheses to determine why the picture appears unclear after all the ordinary solutions have been tried without success, the motorist on the freeway or turnpike reasons hypothetically to determine why the traffic is backed up bumper-to-bumper even though it is not yet rush hour, the physician hypothesizes about the cause of a disease prior to prescribing medicine, the teacher hypothesizes about the best way to present a complicated subject in the classroom, and the prosecuting attorney suggests hypotheses to the jury in arguing about the motive for a crime. In all of these cases the evidence is not sufficient to indicate exactly what is going on, what lies behind the scene, or what approach to take, so hypotheses are constructed to make sense of the situation and to direct future action.

Hypothetical reasoning is used most explicitly in philosophical and scientific inquiry. Every scientific theory can be viewed as a hypothesis for unifying and rationalizing events in nature. The Ptolemaic and Copernican theories about the sun and planets, Dalton's atomic theory, Darwin's theory of evolution, and Einstein's theory of relativity are all hypotheses for making sense of the data of observation. The problem for the scientist is that the underlying structure of nature is hidden from view, and the data of observation by themselves are not sufficient to reveal this structure. In response, the scientist constructs hypotheses that provide ways of conceptualizing the data and that suggest specific questions to be answered through the design of controlled experiments.

Analogously, every philosophical system can be viewed as a grand hypothesis for interpreting the content of experience. Plato's theory of forms, Aristotle's theory of substance, Leibniz's monads, and Kant's theory about the mind are all hypotheses aimed at illuminating various aspects of experience. Just as the structure of nature is hidden from the scientist, the meaning of experience is hidden from the philosopher, and ordinary common sense will not provide the answer. In response, the philosopher constructs hypotheses that can be used to shed light on the content of experience and to provide suggestions for further analysis.

Whether it is applied in philosophy, science, or ordinary life, the hypothetical method involves four basic stages:

1. Occurrence of a problem.
2. Formulating a hypothesis.
3. Drawing implications from the hypothesis.
4. Testing the implications.

These four stages may be illustrated through the procedure used by a detective in solving a crime. Suppose that a woman has been murdered in her apartment. Initially, everything in the apartment is a potential clue: the empty wine glasses in the sink, the small container of cocaine on the coffee table, the automobile key found on the carpet, the strand of blonde hair removed from the couch, and so on. To introduce an element of rationality into the situation, the detective formulates a hypothesis—let us say the hypothesis that the key found on the carpet fits the murderer's car.

From this hypothesis a number of implications can be drawn. Suppose that the key is the kind that fits only late-model Cadillacs. It follows that the murderer drives a late-model Cadillac. Furthermore, if the key is the only one the murderer owns, it follows that the car may be parked nearby. A third implication is that the murderer's name may be on record at the local Cadillac dealership. To test these implications, the detective conducts a search of the streets in the vicinity and contacts the local Cadillac dealer for the names of recent buyers.

This example illustrates three additional points about hypotheses. The first is that a hypothesis is not *derived* from the evidence to which it pertains but rather is *added* to the evidence by the investigator. A hypothesis is a free creation of the mind used to structure the evidence and unveil the pattern that lies beneath the surface. It may be that the detective's hypothesis is completely false. Perhaps the key fits a car that was lent to the victim for the weekend. Any number of other possibilities are conceivable.

The second point is that a hypothesis directs the search for evidence. Without a hypothesis for guidance, all facts are equally relevant. The mineral content of moon rocks and the temperature in the Sahara would be as relevant as the cars parked on the street outside the apartment. The hypothesis tells the investigator what to look for and what to ignore.

The third point concerns the proof of hypotheses. Let us suppose that the detective finds a late-model Cadillac parked outside the apartment building and that the key fits the ignition. Such a discovery might lend credibility to the hypothesis, but it would not in any sense prove it. Concluding that a hypothesis is proven true by the discovery that one of its implications is true amounts to committing the fallacy of affirming the consequent (see Section 6.4). Where H stands for a hypothesis and I for an implication, such an argument has the invalid form

$$\begin{array}{l} \text{If } H, \text{ then } I \\ \underline{I} \\ H \end{array}$$

Let us suppose, on the other hand, that the murderer turns himself or herself in to the police and that the only car the murderer owns or drives is a Ford. Such a fact would prove the hypothesis false because it would falsify the implication that the murderer drives a Cadillac. The argument form involved in such an inference is *modus tollens:*

$$\begin{array}{l} \text{If } H, \text{ then } I \\ \underline{\text{not } I} \\ \text{not } H \end{array}$$

For the hypothesis to be proved true, the car that the key fits would have to be found and the owner would have to confess to the crime.

Some of the clearest illustrations of the hypothetical method of reasoning can be found in scientific discoveries. Four examples are the discovery of radium by Pierre and Marie Curie; the discovery of the planet Neptune by Adams, Leverrier, and Galle; the discovery of atmospheric pressure by Torricelli; and Pasteur's research concerning the spontaneous generation of life. Following is a consideration of each of these examples with special attention to the four stages of hypothetical inquiry.

Radium

In 1896 the French physicist Henri Becquerel discovered that crystals containing uranium had the power to expose photographic plates. He found that when these crystals were placed on top of an unexposed plate and left for a certain time, dark blotches appeared in their place when the plate was developed. Becquerel concluded that the crystals emitted certain rays that penetrated the opaque covering of the plates and reacted with the photosensitive material underneath. Further investigation showed that these rays were not as strong as x-rays, which could be used to photograph bone structure, and so Becquerel's interest in them lapsed.

A year later Marie Curie revived the question when she adopted it as the topic of her doctoral research at the University of Paris. In place of Becquerel's photographic plates she substituted an electrometer, which was better suited to measuring the intensity of the rays, and she proceeded to conduct various experiments with pure uranium to determine the source of the rays that the metal emitted. When none of these experiments proved fruitful, she shifted her attention to the question of whether other metals or minerals emitted the same kind of rays as uranium. She tested hundreds of metals, compounds, and ores, but the only one that proved interesting was pitchblende, a certain ore of uranium. Because pitchblende contained uranium, she anticipated that it would emit rays; but because it also contained a number of impurities, she expected the rays to be weaker than they were for pure uranium. Instead, they turned out to be stronger. This problem caught Madame Curie's attention and provided the focus for her research in the months ahead.

In response to the problem, Madame Curie formulated the hypothesis that the impurities in the pitchblende somehow triggered the uranium to increase the emission of rays. One implication of this hypothesis was that mixing pure uranium with the kinds of impurities found in pitchblende would cause an increase in the emission of rays. To test this implication, Curie diluted pure uranium with various elements and measured the strength of the rays. The results were always the same: the emissions were always less than they were for pure uranium. Because of these results, she abandoned the hypothesis.

Madame Curie then formulated a second hypothesis: The intensified emissions were caused directly by some impurity in the pitchblende. The only other element besides uranium that was known to emit rays, however, was thorium, and the pitchblende that had been tested contained no thorium. Thus, an immediate implication of the hypothesis was that the increased rays were caused by an unknown element. A second implication was that this element could be separated from the pitchblende through a process of refinement. At this point Marie Curie was joined by her husband, Pierre, and they began a combined effort to isolate the unknown element.

Because the element was present in only the most minute quantities, separating a measurable amount from the other impurities required a great deal of effort. The Curies began by grinding up some pitchblende and dissolving it in acid. Finally, after numerous stages of filtration and the addition of other chemicals, they obtained a pinch of white powder. By weight, this material was found to be 900 times more radioactive than pure uranium, but since the primary component in the powder was barium, the unknown element still had not been isolated.

Rather than continue with additional stages of refinement, the Curies decided to attempt a spectographic analysis of the powder. Such analysis, they hoped, would reveal the characteristic spectrum line of the unknown element. This proposal, which amounted to a third implication of the hypothesis, was put to the test. When the powder was burned in a spectrometer, a line appeared in the ultraviolet range that was different from that for any other element. From the combined evidence of the spectrum line and the intense radiation the Curies announced in 1898 the discovery of a new element, which they called radium. After more processing and refinement, enough of the material was finally obtained to determine the atomic weight.

Neptune

In 1781 the planet Uranus was discovered by William Herschel, but the production of a table giving the motion of the new planet had to wait until the gravitational interaction between Uranus, Jupiter, and Saturn had been worked out mathematically. The latter task was accomplished by Pierre Laplace in his *Mechanique Celeste*, and in 1820 Alexis Bouvard used this work to construct tables for all three planets. These tables predicted the orbital motions of Jupiter and Saturn very accurately, but within a few years Uranus was found to have deviated from its predicted path. A problem thus emerged: Why did the tables work for Jupiter and Saturn but not for Uranus?

In response to this problem a number of astronomers entertained the hypothesis that an eighth planet existed beyond the orbit of Uranus and that the gravitational interaction between these two planets caused Uranus to deviate from its predicted position. It was not until 1843, however, that John Couch Adams, a recent graduate of Cambridge, undertook the task of working out the mathematical implications of this hypothesis. After two years' work Adams produced a table of motions and orbital elements that predicted the location of the hypothetical planet, and his computations were so accurate that if anyone with a telescope had bothered to look, they would have found the new planet within two degrees of its predicted position. Unfortunately, no one looked for it.

At about the same time that Adams completed his work on the problem, the French astronomer U. J. J. Leverrier, working independently of Adams, reported a similar set of motions and orbital elements to the French Academy of Science. The close agreement between Adams's and

Leverrier's predictions prompted a search for the planet; but because a rather broad section of sky was swept, the planet was missed.

Finally, Leverrier sent a copy of his figures to Johann Galle at the Berlin Observatory, where a set of star charts was being prepared. It was suggested that the region corresponding to Leverrier's computations be observed and the results matched against the charts. This was done, and a small starlike object was found that was not on the charts. The next night the same object was sighted, and it was found to have moved. The new planet was thus identified. It was named Neptune after most astronomers outside France objected to the original suggestion that it be called Leverrier.

Atmospheric Pressure

The principle that nature abhors a vacuum, originated by Aristotle, was used for centuries to explain the fact that in emptying a keg of wine an opening had to be made at the top as well as at the bottom. Because nature would not allow a vacuum to be created inside the keg, the wine would not drain from the bottom until air was let in at the top. It was thought that this principle held universally for all applications involving a vacuum, but in the sixteenth century it was found that suction pumps used to drain water from mine shafts would not work if the pump was situated over 30 feet above the water level. This caused people to wonder whether nature's abhorrence of a vacuum, while holding true for kegs of wine, had certain limits for pumps.

In 1630 Giovanni Baliani of Genoa discovered a similar limitation in regard to siphons. When he attempted to siphon water from a reservoir over a 60-foot hill, he found that the siphon would not work. When the siphon was completely filled with water and the stoppers were removed from both ends, a vacuum seemed to be created in the uppermost parts of the pipe.

These findings were communicated to Gasparo Berti in Rome, who, around 1641, attempted to determine more scientifically whether a vacuum could actually be created. Berti designed an apparatus consisting of a spherical glass vessel attached to a pipe about 40 feet long. The apparatus was affixed upright to the side of a tower, and after the valve at the lower end of the pipe was closed, water was poured through the upper opening in the glass vessel. When both the pipe and the glass vessel were completely filled, the opening in the vessel was sealed and the valve at the lower end of the pipe was opened. Immediately water rushed from the bottom of the pipe, creating a vacuum in the glass vessel. This experiment crystalized a problem that had been developing for a number of years: If nature abhorred a vacuum, how did it happen that it tolerated the creation of one in the glass vessel? Furthermore, why did it happen, when the experiment was repeated, that the water always descended to the same level in the pipe?

The results of Berti's experiment were communicated to Evangelista Torricelli in Florence, who was at that time Galileo's assistant. Galileo himself thought that the water was supported in the pipe by the power of the vacuum, but after Galileo's death in 1642, Torricelli formulated his own hypothesis: The water was supported in the pipe by the pressure of the atmosphere. Torricelli reasoned that we live "at the bottom of an ocean of air" and that the pressure of the air pushing against the bottom of the pipe supported the water at a certain height in the pipe. A point of equilibrium was reached, he thought, when the weight of the water remaining in the pipe equalled the weight of the air pushing down from above.

From this hypothesis Torricelli derived several implications. One was that the pressure of the atmosphere would support a column of mercury about 29 inches high in a tube sealed at the top. This followed from the fact that the atmosphere supports a column of water 33 feet high, that mercury is 13.6 times as dense as water, and that $33/13.6 \times 12$ inches = 29 inches. A second implication was that such a tube filled with mercury could be used to measure fluctuations in atmospheric pressure. This second implication won Torricelli the credit for formulating the theory of the barometer. Finally, Torricelli reasoned that if such a device were conveyed to a place where the air was more rarefied, such as on a mountaintop, the column of mercury would descend.

The first of these implications was tested by Torricelli's associate, Vincenzo Viviani. Viviani obtained a 4-foot section of glass tube sealed at one end, enough mercury to completely fill it, and a dish to hold more mercury. After pouring the mercury into the tube Viviani placed his thumb over the open end, inverted the tube, and placed the open end in the dish of mercury. After he released his thumb he watched the column of mercury descend to about 29 inches above the level of mercury in the dish. Thus was created the first barometer. Its successful use in measuring atmospheric pressure came later.

The test of Torricelli's third implication was taken up in 1647 by the French philosopher Blaise Pascal. Having received word of Torricelli's experiments with the barometer, Pascal constructed one for himself. He readily became convinced of the correctness of Torricelli's hypothesis, and to demonstrate its correctness in opposition to the vacuum principle, he requested that his brother-in-law, F. Perier, convey a barometer to the top of the Puy de Dôme, one of the highest mountains in Auvergne. A year later Perier was able to fulfill this request. He began the experiment by setting up two barometers in the monastery at the foot of the mountain. After noting that both columns of mercury rose to an identical height, he disassembled one of the barometers and instructed one of the friars to check the mercury level in the other throughout the day. Then Perier, accompanied by a group of witnesses, set off up the mountain with the other barometer. Upon reaching the summit, he assembled the second barometer and discovered to the amazement of all that the mercury level was more than 3 inches lower than it had been at the foot of the mountain. As a double check the barometer was taken apart and reassembled at five different spots on the summit. Each time the results were the same.

At the midpoint of his descent Perier reassembled the barometer once again. He found that the mercury level was about midway between where it was at the bottom and at the top of the mountain. Finally, upon returning to the monastery, the friar who had been watching the barometer there was questioned about what he had observed. He reported that the mercury level had not changed since early that morning when the group had departed. Pascal announced the results of this experiment to the educated world, and the announcement succeeded in abolishing the principle that nature abhors a vacuum.

Spontaneous Generation

The theory of spontaneous generation holds that living beings arise spontaneously from lifeless matter. The roots of the theory extend into ancient times. Aristotle held that worms, the larvae of bees and wasps, ticks, fireflies, and other insects developed continually from the morning dew and from dry wood and hair. He also held that crabs and various molluscs developed from moist soil and decaying slime. Extensions of this theory prevailed throughout the Middle Ages and well into modern times. In the seventeenth century it was widely held that frogs were produced from the slime of marshes and eels from river water, and the physician Van Helmont thought that mice were produced from the action of human sweat on kernels of wheat. All one needed to do, according to Van Helmont, was toss a dirty shirt into a container of wheat, and in 21 days the container would be teeming with mice. Even Descartes and Newton accepted the theory of spontaneous generation. Descartes held that various plants and insects originated in moist earth exposed to sunlight, and Newton thought that plants were produced from emanations from the tails of comets.

The first systematic effort to abolish the belief in spontaneous generation was made by the Italian physician Francesco Redi. In response to the commonly held idea that worms were spontaneously generated in rotting meat, Redi hypothesized that the worms were caused by flies. An immediate implication was that if flies were kept away from the meat, the worms would not develop. To test this hypothesis Redi cut up a piece of meat and put part of it in sealed glass flasks and the other part in flasks open to the air. Flies were attracted to the open flasks, and in a short time worms appeared; but no worms developed in the flasks that were sealed.

When Redi published his findings in 1668, they had an immediate impact on the theory of spontaneous generation. Within a few years, though, the microscope came into common use, and it was discovered that even though meat sealed in glass containers produced no worms, it did produce countless microorganisms. The theory of spontaneous generation was thus reawakened on the microbial level.

By the middle of the nineteenth century the theory had received considerable refinement. It was thought that spontaneous generation resulted from the direct action of oxygen on lifeless organic nutrients. Oxygen was thought to be essential to the process because the technique of canning fruits and vegetables had come into practice, and it was known that boiling fruits and vegetables and sealing them in the absence of oxygen would cause them to be preserved. If they were left exposed to the air, however, microbes would develop in a short time.

One of the defenders of spontaneous generation at that time was the Englishman John Needham, an amateur biologist. Needham conducted an experiment in which flagons containing oxygen and a vegetable solution were buried in hot coals. The coals would have been expected to kill any life in the solution, but several days later the flagons were opened and the contents were found to be alive with microbes. Needham concluded that the oxygen acting alone on the nutrient solution caused the generation of the microbes. In response to this experiment, Lazzaro Spallanzani, an Italian physiologist, conducted a similar experiment. To ensure that the nutrient solution was lifeless he boiled it for an hour. Later no microbes could be found. To this Needham objected that in boiling the solution for a full hour Spallanzani had destroyed its "vegetative force." In addition, Needham argued, he had polluted the small amount of oxygen in the containers by the fumes and heat. Thus, it was no wonder that microbes were not spontaneously generated.

To settle the issue once and for all, the French Academy of Science offered a prize for an experimental endeavor that would shed light on the question of spontaneous generation. This challenge succeeded in drawing Louis Pasteur into the controversy. Spontaneous generation presented a special problem for Pasteur because of his previous work with fermentation. He had discovered that fermentations, such as those involved in the production of wine and beer, required yeast; and yeast, as he also discovered, was a living organism. In view of these findings Pasteur adopted the hypothesis that life comes only from life. An immediate implication was that for life forms to develop in a sterile nutrient solution, they must first be introduced into the solution from the outside.

It was well known that life forms did indeed develop in sterile nutrient solutions exposed to the air. To account for this Pasteur adopted the second hypothesis that life forms are carried by dust particles in the air. To test this second hypothesis Pasteur took a wad of cotton and drew air through it, trapping dust particles in the fibers. Then he washed the cotton in a mixture of alcohol and examined drops of the fluid under a microscope. He discovered microbes in the fluid.

Returning to his first hypothesis, Pasteur prepared a nutrient solution and boiled it in a narrow-necked flask. As the solution boiled, the air in the neck of the flask was forced out by water vapor, and as it cooled the water vapor was slowly replaced by sterilized air drawn through a heated platinum tube. The neck of the flask was then closed off with a flame and blowpipe. The contents of the flask thus consisted of a sterilized nutrient solution and unpolluted sterilized air—all that was supposedly needed for the production of life. With the passage of time, however, no life developed in the flask. This experiment posed a serious threat to the theory of spontaneous generation.

Pasteur now posed the hypothesis that sterile nutrient solutions exposed to the air normally developed life forms precisely because these forms were deposited by dust particles. To test this third hypothesis Pasteur reopened the flask containing the nutrient solution, and, using a special arrangement of tubes that insured that only sterilized air would contact the solution, he deposited a piece of cotton in which dust particles had been trapped. The flask was then resealed, and in due course microbes developed in the solution. This experiment proved not only that dust particles were responsible for the life but that the "vegetative force" of the nutrient solution had not been destroyed by boiling, as Needham was prone to claim.

Pasteur anticipated one further objection from the proponents of spontaneous generation: Perhaps the capacity of oxygen to generate life was destroyed by drawing it through a heated tube. To dispel any such notions Pasteur devised yet another experiment. He boiled a nutrient solution in a flask with a long, narrow gooseneck. As the solution boiled, the air was forced out, and as it cooled, the air returned very slowly through the long neck, trapping the dust particles on the moist inside surface. No microbes developed in the solution. Then, after a prolonged wait, Pasteur sealed the flask and shook it vigorously, dislodging the particles that had settled in the neck. In a short time the solution was alive with microbes.

When Pasteur reported these experiments to the Academy of Science in 1860, he was awarded the prize that had been offered a year earlier. The experiments dealt a mortal blow to the theory of spontaneous generation, and although the theory was not abandoned immediately, by 1900 it had very little support.

The Proof of Hypotheses

The four instances of hypothetical reasoning in science that we have investigated illustrate the use of two different kinds of hypotheses. The hypotheses involved in the discovery of Neptune and radium are sometimes called **empirical hypotheses,** and those relating to atmospheric pressure and spontaneous generation are sometimes called **theoretical hypotheses.** Empirical hypotheses concern the production of some thing or the occurrence of some event that can be observed. When radium had finally been obtained as a pure metal it was something that could be seen directly, and when Neptune was finally sighted through the telescope, it, too, had been observed. Theoretical hypotheses, on the other hand, concern how something should be conceptualized. When Galileo observed the water level rising in a suction pump, he conceived it as being *sucked* up by the vacuum. When Torricelli observed it, however, he conceived it as being *pushed* up by the atmosphere. Similarly, when Needham observed life emerging in a sterile nutrient solution, he conceived it as being spontaneously generated by the action of oxygen. But when Pasteur observed it, he conceived it as being implanted there by dust particles in the air.

The distinction between empirical and theoretical hypotheses has certain difficulties, which we will turn to shortly, but it sheds some light on the problem of the verification or confirmation of hypotheses. Empirical hypotheses are for all practical purposes *proved* when the thing or event hypothesized is observed. Today practically all of us would agree that the hypotheses relating to radium and Neptune have been established. Theoretical hypotheses, on the other hand, are never proved but are only *confirmed* to varying degrees. The greater the number of implications that are found to be correct, the more certain we can be of the hypothesis. If an implication is found to be incorrect, however, a theoretical hypothesis can be *disproved.* For example, if it should happen some day that life is produced in a test tube from inorganic materials, Pasteur's hypothesis that life comes only from life might be considered to be disproved.

The problem with the distinction between empirical and theoretical hypotheses is that observation is theory-dependent. Consider, for example, a man and a woman watching a sunrise. The man happens to believe that the sun travels around the earth, as Ptolemy held, and the woman that the earth travels around the sun, as Copernicus and Galileo contended. As the sun rises, the man thinks that he sees the sun moving upward, while the woman thinks she sees the earth turning. The point is that all of us have a tendency to see what we think is out there to be seen. As a result, it is sometimes difficult to say when something has or has not been observed.

In regard to the discovery of Neptune, the unknown planet was observed two times in 1795 by J. J. Lalande, 51 years before it was "discovered" by Adams, Leverrier, and Galle. Lalande noted that his observations of the position of the small starlike object were discordant, so he rejected one as erroneous. But he thought he was observing a *star*, so he received no credit for discovering a *planet*. Analogous remarks extend to Galle's observations of the *planet* Neptune in 1846. If Leverrier's computations had been erroneous, Galle might have seen what was really a comet. Thus, if we can never be sure that we really see what we think we see, is it ever possible for a hypothesis to be actually proved? Perhaps it is better to interpret the proof of empirical hypotheses as a high degree of confirmation.

Conversely, with theoretical hypotheses, would we want to say that Torricelli's hypothesis relating to atmospheric pressure has *not* been proved? Granted, we cannot observe atmospheric pressure directly, but might we not say that we observe it *instrumentally?* If barometers can be regarded as extensions of our sense organs, Torricelli's hypothesis has been proved. Another example is provided by Copernicus' hypothesis that the earth and planets move around the sun, instead of the sun and planets around the earth, as Ptolemy hypothesized. Can we consider this theoretical hypothesis to be proved? If a motion picture camera were sent outside the solar system and pictures were taken supporting the Copernican hypothesis, would we say that these pictures constituted proof? We probably would. Thus, while the distinction between theoretical and empirical hypotheses is useful, it is more a distinction in degree than in kind.

The Tentative Acceptance of Hypotheses

A certain amount of time is required for a hypothesis to be proved or disproved. The hypotheses relating to the discovery of radium and Neptune required more than a year to prove. Theoretical hypotheses in science often take much longer, and theoretical hypotheses in philosophy may never be confirmed to the satisfaction of the majority of philosophers. During the period that intervenes between the proposal of a hypothesis and its proof, confirmation, or disproof, the question arises as to its tentative acceptability. Four criteria that bear upon this question are (1) adequacy, (2) internal coherence, (3) external consistency, and (4) fruitfulness.

A hypothesis is **adequate** to the extent that it fits the facts it is intended to unify or explain. A hypothesis is said to "fit" the facts when each fact can be interpreted as an instance of some idea or term in the hypothesis. For example, before the Neptune hypothesis was confirmed, every fluctuation in the position of Uranus could be interpreted as an instance of gravitational interaction with an unknown planet. Similarly, before Torricelli's hypothesis was confirmed, the fact that water would rise only 30 feet in suction pumps and siphons could be interpreted as an instance of equilibrium between the pressure of the water and the pressure of the atmosphere.

A hypothesis is inadequate to the extent that facts exist that the hypothesis cannot account for. The principle that nature abhors a vacuum was inadequate to explain the fact that water would rise no more than 30 feet in suction pumps and siphons. Nothing in the hypothesis could account for this fact. Similarly, Needham's hypothesis that life is generated by the direct action of oxygen on nutrient solutions was inadequate to account for the fact that life would not develop in Pasteur's flask containing a sterilized nutrient solution and sterilized oxygen.

In scientific hypotheses a second kind of adequacy is the *accuracy* with which a hypothesis accounts for the data. If one hypothesis accounts for a set of data with greater accuracy than another, then that hypothesis is more adequate than the other. For example, Kepler's hypothesis that the orbits of the planets were elipses rather than circles, as Copernicus had hypothesized, accounted for the position of the planets with greater accuracy than the Copernican hypothesis. Similarly, Einstein's theory of relativity accounted for the precise time of certain eclipses with greater accuracy than Newton's theory. For these reasons Kepler's and Einstein's theories were more adequate than the competing theories.

A hypothesis is **internally coherent** to the extent that its component ideas are rationally interconnected. The purpose of a hypothesis is to unify and interconnect a set of data and by so doing to *explain* the data. Obviously, if the hypothesis itself is not internally connected, there is no way that it can interconnect the data. After the mathematical details of the Neptune hypothesis had been worked out by Adams and Leverrier, it exhibited a great deal of internal coherence. The hypothesis showed how all the fluctuations in the position of Uranus could be rationally linked in terms of the gravitational interaction of an eighth planet. Similarly, Torricelli's hypothesis showed how the various fluid levels could be rationally interconnected in terms of the equilibrium of pressures. Internal coherence is responsible for the features of elegance and simplicity that often attract scientists to a hypothesis.

An example of incoherence in science is provided by the theoretical interpretation of light, electricity, and magnetism that prevailed during the first half of the nineteenth century. During that period each of these phenomena was understood separately, but the interconnections between them were unknown. Toward the end of the century the English physicist James Clerk Maxwell showed how these three phenomena were interconnected in terms of his theory of the electromagnetic field. Maxwell's theory was thus more coherent than the ones that preceded Similarly, in philosophy, Spinoza's metaphysical theory is more internally coherent than Descartes's. Descartes postulated the existence of two kinds of substance to account for the data of experience. He introduced extended, material substance to explain the data of the visible world, and nonextended, immaterial substance to explain the phenomena of the invisible world, including the existence and activity of the human soul. But Descartes failed to show how the two kinds of substance were interconnected. In the wake of this disconnection there arose the famous mind-body problem, according to which no account could be given of how the human body acted on the mind through the process of sensation or how the mind acted on the body through the exercise of free choice. Spinoza, on the other hand, postulated only one substance to account for everything. Spinoza's theory is thus more internally coherent than Descartes's.

A hypothesis is **externally consistent** when it does not disagree with other, well-confirmed hypotheses. Adams's and Leverrier's hypothesis of an eighth planet was perfectly consistent with the nineteenth-century theory of the solar system, and it was rendered even more attractive by the fact that the seventh planet, Uranus, had been discovered only a few years earlier. Similarly, Marie Curie's hypothesis of the existence of a new element was consistent with Mendeleev's periodic table and with the general hypothesis that elements could emit penetrating rays. In 1890 Mendeleev's table had certain gaps that were expected to be filled in by the discovery of new elements, and two ray-emitting elements, thorium and uranium, had already been discovered.

The fact that a hypothesis is inconsistent with other, well-confirmed hypotheses does not, however, immediately condemn it to obscurity. It often happens that a new hypothesis arises in the face of another, well-confirmed hypothesis and that the two hypotheses compete for acceptance in the future. Which hypothesis will win is determined by an appeal to the other three criteria. For example, Torricelli's hypothesis was inconsistent with the ancient hypothesis that nature abhors a vacuum, and Pasteur's hypothesis was inconsistent with the equally ancient hypothesis of spontaneous generation. In the end, the newer hypotheses won out because they were more adequate, coherent, or fruitful than their competitors. For the same reason the Copernican hypothesis eventually triumphed over the Ptolemaic, the theory of oxidation won out over the old phlogiston theory, and Einstein's theory of relativity won out over Newton's theory.

A hypothesis is **fruitful** to the extent that it suggests new ideas for future analysis and confirmation. Torricelli's hypothesis suggested the design of an instrument for measuring fluctuations in the pressure of the atmosphere. Similarly, Pasteur's hypothesis suggested changes in the procedures used to maintain sterile conditions in hospitals. After these changes were implemented, the death rate from surgical operations decreased dramatically. The procedure of pasteurization, used to preserve milk, was another outgrowth of the hypothesis that life comes only from life.

Newton's theory of universal gravitation is an example of a hypothesis that proved especially fruitful. It was originated to solve the problem of falling bodies, but it also explained such things as the ebb and flow of the tides, the orbital motion of the moon and planets, and the fluctuations in planetary motion caused by a planet's interaction with other planets. Einstein's theory of relativity is another example. It was originated to account for certain features of Maxwell's theory of electricity and magnetism, but it succeeded, 40 years later, in ushering in the atomic age.

The factors of coherence and fruitfulness together account for the overall rationality and explanatory power of a hypothesis. Suppose, for example, that someone formulated the hypothesis that the water level in suction devices is maintained by the action of demons instead of by atmospheric pressure. Such a hypothesis would be neither coherent nor fruitful. It would not be coherent because it would not explain why the maximum water level in these devices is consistently about 30 feet, why the mercury level in barometers is much less, and why the mercury level in a barometer decreases when the instrument is carried to the top of a mountain. Do the demons decide to maintain these levels by free choice or according to some plan? Because there is no answer to this question, the hypothesis exhibits internal disconnectedness, which leaves it open to the charge of being irrational. As for the fourth criterion, the demon hypothesis is unfruitful because it suggests no new ideas that experimenters can put to the test. The hypothesis that nature abhors a vacuum is hardly any more fruitful, which accounts in part for why it was so suddenly abandoned in favor of Torricelli's hypothesis—it simply did not lead anywhere.

In summary, for any hypothesis to receive tentative acceptance it must cover the facts it is intended to interpret and it must rationally interconnect these facts—in other words, it must be adequate and coherent. After that, it helps if the hypothesis does not conflict with other, well-confirmed hypotheses. Finally, it is important that a hypothesis capture the imagination of the community to which it is posed. This it does by being fruitful—by suggesting interesting ideas and experiments to which members of the community can direct their attention in the years ahead.

EXERCISE 9.4

I. For the four scientific discoveries presented in this section identify the problem, the hypotheses that were formulated, the implications that were drawn, and the test procedure that was used.

II. Write a short paper (3–5 pages) on one of the following scientific events. Discuss the problem, one or more hypotheses that were formulated, the implications that were drawn, and the test procedures that were used. Then evaluate the hypothesis in terms of adequacy, internal coherence, external consistency, and fruitfulness.

1. Isaac Newton: corpuscular theory of light.
2. Christian Huygens: wave theory of light.
3. Johannes Kepler: orbit of Mars.
4. Nicolaus Copernicus: theory of the solar system.
5. Count von Rumford: theory of heat.
6. Charles Darwin: theory of natural selection.
7. John Dalton: theory of atoms.
8. William Harvey: circulation of the blood.
9. Louis Pasteur: theory of vaccination.
10. J. J. Thomson: discovery of the electron.
11. Andre Marie Ampere: discovery of the electromagnet.
12. Niels Bohr: structure of the atom.
13. Alexander Fleming: discovery of penicillin.
14. Henri Becquerel: radioactivity of uranium.
15. Dmitri Mendeleev and Clemens Winkler: discovery of germanium.
16. Amedeo Avogadro: Avogadro's law.
17. Johann Balmer: theory of the spectograph.
18. Alfred Wegener: theory of continental drift.
19. James Watson and Francis Crick: structure of the DNA molecule.
20. John Bardeen: theory of superconductivity.
21. Albert Einstein: theory of Brownian motion.
22. Edwin Hubble: recession of the galaxies.
23. Jean Baptiste Lamarck: inheritance of acquired characteristics.

III. Write a short paper (2–3 pages) analyzing one or more of the hypotheses formulated by Sherlock Holmes in one of the stories by Arthur Conan Doyle. Include a discussion of the problem, the hypothesis, the implications that were drawn, and the test procedures.

IV. Answer "true" or "false" to the following statements:

★1. Hypothetical reasoning is useful when the evidence by itself does not provide the solution to the problem.

2. Hypotheses are derived directly from the evidence.

3. Hypotheses serve the purpose of directing the search for additional evidence.

★4. If the implications of a hypothesis are true, then we may conclude that the hypothesis is true.

5. If an implication of a hypothesis is false, then we may conclude that the hypothesis is false, at least in part.

6. In the episode pertaining to the discovery of radium, all of the hypotheses turned out to be true.

★7. In the Neptune episode, Adams and Leverrier deserve the credit for working out the implications of the hypothesis.

8. Torricelli's hypothesis was consistent with the hypothesis that nature abhors a vacuum.

9. In Pasteur's day, the theory of spontaneous generation held that life was produced by the direct action of oxygen on organic nutrients.

★10. The hypotheses relating to the discoveries of radium and Neptune may be classified as empirical hypotheses.

11. Torricelli's and Pasteur's hypotheses may be classified as theoretical hypotheses.

12. Theoretical hypotheses concern how something should be conceptualized.

★13. The problem with the distinction between empirical and theoretical hypotheses is that observation is dependent on theory.

14. The adequacy of a hypothesis has to do with how well the ideas or terms in the hypothesis are rationally interconnected.

15. The coherence of a hypothesis has to do with how well the hypothesis fits the facts.

★16. If a hypothesis is not externally consistent, then it must be discarded.

17. A hypothesis is fruitful to the extent that it suggests new ideas for future analysis and confirmation.

18. If a theory is incoherent, it is deficient in rationality.

★19. The theoretical interpretations of light, electricity, and magnetism during the first part of the nineteenth century illustrate a condition of inadequacy.

20. If a hypothesis gives rise to contradictory implications, it is incoherent.

ANSWERS TO SELECTED EXERCISES

Exercise 1.1

I.

1. P: Titanium combines readily with oxygen, nitrogen, and hydrogen, all of which have an adverse effect on its mechanical properties.
   C: Titanium must be processed in their absence.

4. P: When individuals voluntarily abandon property, they forfeit any expectation of privacy in it that they might have had.
   C: A warrantless search and seizure of abandoned property is not unreasonable under the Fourth Amendment.

7. P_1: For civil and for some scientific purposes, we want to know the time of day so that we can order events in sequence.
   P_2: In most scientific work, we want to know how long an event lasts.
   C: Any time standard must be able to answer the question "What time is it?" and the question "How long does it last?"

10. P_1: Punishment, when speedy and specific, may suppress undesirable behavior.
    P_2: Punishment cannot teach or encourage desirable alternatives.
    C: It is crucial to use positive techniques to model and reinforce appropriate behavior that the person can use in place of the unacceptable response that has to be suppressed.

13. P_1: To every existing thing God wills some good.
    P_2: To love any thing is to will good to that thing.
    C: It is manifest that God loves everything that exists.

16. P_1: Antipoverty programs provide jobs for middle-class professionals in social work, penology, and public health.
    P_2: Such workers' future advancement is tied to the continued growth of bureaucracies dependent on the existence of poverty.
    C: Poverty offers numerous benefits to the nonpoor.

19. P_1: At the close of the sixteenth century, Germany and Italy were patchworks of autocratic princely dominions.
    P_2: Spain was practically autocratic.
    P_3: The throne had never been so powerful in England.
    P_4: As the seventeenth century drew on, the French monarchy gradually became the grandest and most consolidated power in Europe.
    C: All over the world the close of the sixteenth century saw monarchy prevailing and tending toward absolutism.

22. P_1: Anyone familiar with our prison system knows that there are some inmates who behave little better than brute beasts.
    P_2: If the death penalty had been truly effective as a deterrent, such prisoners would long ago have vanished.
    C: The very fact that these prisoners exist is a telling argument against the efficacy of capital punishment as a deterrent.

25. P_1: World government means one central authority, a permanent standing world police force, and clearly defined conditions under which this force will go into action.
    P_2: A balance of power system has many sovereign authorities, each controlling its own army, combining only when they feel like it to control aggression.
    C: World government and the balance of power are in many ways opposites.

II.

1. Women should be members of the disarmament delegations of both the United States and the Soviet Union.

4. Business majors are robbing themselves of the true purpose of collegiate academics, a sacrifice that outweighs the future salary checks.

7. Today's college students should direct their extracurricular energies toward socially worthwhile goals.
10. The religious intolerance of television preachers must not be tolerated.

Exercise 1.2
I.
1. Explanation. 4. Illustration.
7. Argument (conclusion: If the earth's magnetic field disappears, then intense cosmic rays will bombard the earth).
10. Report. 13. Description. 16. Piece of advice.
19. Argument (conclusion: Behavior evoked by brain stimulation is sensitive to environmental changes, even in animals).
22. Argument (conclusion: Atoms can combine to form molecules, whose properties are generally very different from those of the constituent atoms).
25. Explanation.
28. Argument (conclusion: A person never becomes truly self-reliant).
31. This passage is probably best interpreted as an illustration. If it is interpreted as an argument, the conclusion is: Almost all living things act to free themselves from harmful contacts.
34. Report.

II.
1. Nonargument. 4. Nonargument.
7. Argument (conclusion: The poor quality of parenting and the lack in continuity of adult care provided to many U.S. children contribute to a passivity and a sense of helplessness that hobbles individuals for the remainder of their lives).
10. Nonargument.

Exercise 1.3
I.
1. Deductive (argument based on mathematics; also, conclusion follows necessarily from the premises).
4. Deductive (categorical syllogism; also, conclusion follows necessarily from the premises).
7. Inductive (causal inference; also, conclusion follows only probably from the premise).
10. Inductive (argument from analogy; also, conclusion follows only probably from the premise).
13. Inductive (argument from authority; also, conclusion follows only probably from the premise).
16. Deductive (conclusion follows necessarily from the premise).
19. Inductive (inductive indicator word; also, conclusion follows only probably from the premises).
22. Deductive (conclusion follows necessarily from the premise; this example might also be interpreted as an argument from definition—the definition of "refraction").
25. Inductive (causal inference: the dog's familiarity with the visitor caused the dog to be silent).
28. Inductive (conclusion follows only probably from the premise; also, "It is naturally to be expected" is a phrase that constitutes inductive indicator words).

Exercise 1.4
I.
1. Valid (false premises, false conclusion), unsound.
4. Invalid (false premises, true conclusion), unsound.
7. Valid (false premises, true conclusion), unsound.

II.
1. Weak (true premise, probably false conclusion), uncogent.
4. Strong (false premise, probably false conclusion), uncogent.
7. Weak (false premise, probably false conclusion), uncogent.

III.
1. Deductive, valid.	7. Inductive, weak.	13. Inductive, weak.
4. Deductive, valid.	10. Deductive, invalid.	16. Deductive, invalid.
		19. Inductive, strong.

Exercise 1.5

I.

1. All *G* are *S*.
   All *Q* are *S*.
   All *G* are *Q*.

   All cats are animals. (T)
   All dogs are animals. (T)
   All cats are dogs. (F)

4. No *I* are *P*.
   Some *I* are not *F*.
   Some *F* are not *P*.

   No fish are mammals. (T)
   Some fish are not cats. (T)
   Some cats are not mammals. (F)

7. No *A* are *S*.
   No *L* are *S*.
   No *A* are *L*.

   No dogs are fish. (T)
   No mammals are fish. (T)
   No dogs are mammals. (F)

10. Some *S* are not *O*.
    Some *G* are not *O*.
    Some *S* are not *G*.

    Some dogs are not fish. (T)
    Some animals are not fish. (T)
    Some dogs are not animals. (F)

II.

1. If *A* then *E*.
   Not *A*.
   Not *E*.

   If George Washington was assassinated, then
   George Washington is dead. (T)
   George Washington was not assassinated. (T)
   George Washington is not dead. (F)

4. Some *D* are *C*.
   Some *D* are *S*.
   Some *D* are *CS*.

   Some fruits are purple. (T)
   Some fruits are lemons. (T)
   Some fruits are purple lemons. (F)

Exercise 1.6

I.

1.

4.

7.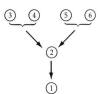

10.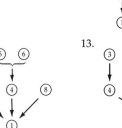

13.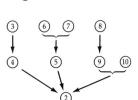

II.

1.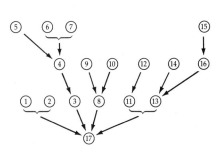

Exercise 2.1

II.

1. The creationists are incorrect in their attempt to have their factually unsupported views presented to others. They claim their efforts are justified by the "free exercise" clause of the First Amendment. This argument neglects the interests of most people, who want their children taught the theory commonly accepted by the scientific community—not the more traditional views of older societies.

III.

1. Clothing designed by Marithé and François Girbaud is perfectly contoured to fit your body, and you want to show it off. Therefore, you will want to buy clothing designed by Girbaud.

Exercise 2.2

I.

4a. Plant, tree, conifer, spruce, Sitka spruce.

Exercise 2.3

I.

1. Precising definition.	10. Theoretical definition.	19. Lexical definition.
4. Lexical definition.	13. Stipulative definition.	22. Precising definition.
7. Persuasive definition.	16. Persuasive definition.	25. Stipulative definition.

Exercise 2.4

I.

1. Definition by subclass.	16. Enumerative definition.
4. Enumerative definition.	19. Operational definition.
7. Demonstrative definition.	22. Synonymous definition.
10. Definition by genus and difference.	25. Operational definition.
13. Definition by subclass.	

II.

1a. "Skyscraper" means the Empire State Building, Chrysler Building, Sears Tower, and so on. Nonsynonymous term: building.

3a. "Animal" means a horse, bear, lion, and so on. Nonsynonymous term: mammal.

5a. "Intersection" means crossing.

6a. A person is a "genius" if and only if that person can earn a score of 140 on an IQ test.

7a. "Drake" means a male duck.

Exercise 2.5

1. Rule 3: too narrow; the definiens excludes images made of bronze, wood, plaster, and so on.
4. Rule 6: figurative language.
7. Rule 5: negative.
10. Rule 7: affective terminology.
13. Rule 1: improper grammar.
16. Rule 4: circular.
19. Rule 6: vague.
22. Rule 1: improper grammar; Rule 6: vague; Rule 3: too broad (the definiens also includes ketches, sloops, and yawls).
25. Rule 3: too broad (the definiens also describes violins, violas, and string basses).
28. Rule 2: fails to convey the essential meaning; the definition says nothing about the components of a camera or how a camera works.
31. Rule 7: affective terminology.
34. Rule 3: both too narrow and too broad; the definiens excludes instruments used for writing on canvas, glass, metal, plastic, and so on, and it includes pencils, crayons, and so on.

Exercise 3.1

1. Formal fallacy.	7. Informal fallacy.
4. Informal fallacy.	10. Formal fallacy.

Exercise 3.2

I.

1. Appeal to pity.
4. Accident.
7. Appeal to force.
10. *Tu quo que* (you, too).
13. Red herring.

16. *Ad hominem* (argument against the person) circumstantial.
19. Straw man.
22. Appeal to the people, indirect variety.
25. Missing the point.

Exercise 3.3

I.

1. Hasty generalization (converse accident).
4. Slippery slope.
7. Appeal to ignorance.

10. Appeal to authority.
13. Weak analogy.
15. False cause.

III.

1. Hasty generalization.
4. Appeal to authority.
7. No fallacy.
10. Straw man.
13. Red herring.
16. Missing the point.

19. Weak analogy.
22. No fallacy.
25. Appeal to ignorance.
28. False cause.
30. Slippery slope.

Exercise 3.4

I.

1. False dichotomy.
4. Amphiboly.
7. Begging the question.
10. Equivocation.
13. Composition.

16. Suppressed evidence.
19. Division.
22. Complex question.
25. Begging the question.

III.

1. *Ad hominem* (argument against the person) circumstantial.
4. Equivocation.
7. Hasty generalization (converse accident).
10. Division.
13. False cause.
16. Appeal to authority.
19. Composition.
22. Weak analogy.

25. Straw man.

28. Accident.
31. Red herring.

34. Amphiboly.
37. Suppressed evidence.
40. Begging the question.
43. Missing the point.
45. Appeal to ignorance.

Exercise 3.5

I.

1. Slippery slope.
4. Begging the question.
7. False cause? Suppressed evidence? Begging the question? No fallacy?
10. Appeal to authority. The statement "Only a fool . . ." involves an *ad hominem* abusive. The statement "There are homosexuals who are being delivered from this sin . . ." suggests begging the question.
13. False cause, suppressed evidence, begging the question. There is little or no evidence of any causal connection between malpractice suits and the decision of some obstetricians to leave the field. An unmentioned factor is the inconvenience of being on call twenty-four hours per day waiting for patients to deliver. There is also little or no evidence of any genuine "lawsuit crisis."
16. Begging the question? (Strange argument!)
19. Slippery slope.
22. False cause? No fallacy?
25. False cause? No fallacy?
28. Missing the point or begging the question. Gorbachev's point is that any weapon that could neutralize a nation's defenses is *ipso facto* an offensive weapon. The reference to killer satellites may involve a second case of missing the point.

31. Appeal to the people (direct variety). Also appeal to pity? Is there also a begging the question? Does the fact that former pets were once loved make any difference?
34. Appeal to the people (direct variety)?
37. False dichotomy? No fallacy?
40. Appeal to authority, slippery slope.
43. Several cases of weak analogy. Also, a possible case of *ad hominem* abusive.
46. At least three cases of begging the question. How is it relevant that the Japanese-American chose to stay? After being released, did the average Japanese-American have the wherewithal to leave? How is it relevant that Pearl Harbor victims cannot sue the Japanese government?
49. Appeal to authority. The last paragraph suggests a hasty generalization.

Exercise 4.1

1. *Quantifier:* some; *subject term:* college students; *copula:* are; *subject term:* avid devotees of soap operas.
4. *Quantifier:* some; *subject term:* preachers who are intolerant of others' beliefs; *copula:* are not; *predicate term:* television evangelists.
7. *Quantifier:* no; *subject term:* sex education courses that are taught competently; *copula:* are; *predicate term:* programs that are currently eroding public morals.

Exercise 4.2

I.

1. **E** proposition, universal, negative, subject and predicate terms are distributed.
4. **O** proposition, particular, negative, subject term undistributed, predicate term distributed.
7. **I** proposition, particular, affirmative, subject and predicate terms undistributed.

II.

1. No drunk drivers are threats to others on the highway.
4. Some CIA operatives are champions of human rights.

III.

1. Some owners of pit bull terriers are persons who can expect expensive lawsuits.
4. No residents of Manhattan are people who can afford to live there.

IV.

1. Some oil spills are not events catastrophic to the environment.
4. All corporate lawyers are persons with a social conscience.

Exercise 4.3

I.

1. (a) false, (b) true, (c) false.
4. (a) undetermined, (b) true, (c) undetermined.
7. (a) false, (b) undetermined, (c) undetermined.

II.

1. Valid.
4. Invalid (illicit subcontrary).
7. Invalid (illicit contrary).
10. Valid.

III.

1. Invalid (illicit subcontrary), unsound.
4. Invalid (illicit subalternation), unsound.
7. Valid, unsound.
10. Valid, sound.

Exercise 4.4

I.

1a. All potential causes of lung cancer are homes contaminated by radon gas. (not logically equivalent)
2a. No radically egalitarian societies are societies that preserve individual liberties. (logically equivalent)
3a. All physicians eligible to practice are physicians whose licenses are intact. (logically equivalent)

II.

1. Invalid (illicit conversion).
4. Invalid (illicit contraposition).
7. Valid.
10. Valid.

III.

1. All non-*B* are *A*. (true)
4. Some non-*A* are *B*. (undetermined)
7. No non-*A* are *B*. (false)
10. Some non-*A* are not non-*B*. (true)

13. Obversion. (false)
19. Contrary. (undetermined)

IV.

1. All *I* are *C*.
   Some *I* are *C*. (subalternation)
   Some *C* are *I*. (conversion)

7. Some *P* are not non-*S*.
   Some *P* are *S*. (obversion)
   Some *S* are *P*. (conversion)
   False: No *S* are *P*. (contradiction)

4. All *E* are *A*.
   False: No *E* are *A*. (contrary)
   False: No *A* are *E*. (conversion)
   False: All *A* are non-*E*. (obversion)

10. False: Some *F* are not *A*.
    False: No *F* are *A*. (subalternation)
    False: No *A* are *F*. (conversion)
    False: All *A* are non-*F*. (obversion)

Exercise 4.5
1. Valid.
7. Invalid (existential fallacy).

4. Valid
10. Valid

Exercise 4.6

1.
   L   H

4.
   X
   R   F

7.
   X
   H   C

Exercise 4.7
II.

1. All *I* are *T*.

   Some *T* are *I*.
   (valid)

4. Some *G* are non-*M*.

   Some *M* are non-*G*.
   (invalid)

7. False: Some *C*
   are not non-*A*.

   Some *A* are non-*C*.
   (valid)

10. No *F* are *L*.

    Some non-*L* are *F*.
    (invalid—existential
    fallacy)

13. False: Some *H* are
    not *P*.

    Some non-*P* are *H*.
    (invalid)

16. Some *S* are *H*.

    False: All *H* are
    non-*S*.
    (valid)

19. All *T* are *O*.

    False: All *T* are
    non-*O*.
    (invalid—
    existential fallacy)

22. No *P* are *M*.

    No non-*P* are
    non-*M*.
    (invalid)

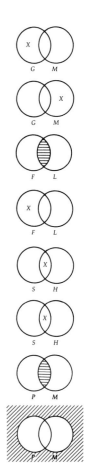

497

25. False: Some *M* are *P*.   Some non-*P* are *M*.
(invalid—existential fallacy)

M   P   M   P

Exercise 4.8

I.
1. All banks that make too many risky loans are banks that will fail.
4. All substances identical to bromine are substances extractable from seawater.
7. No halogens are chemically inert elements.
10. All yachts eligible for the America's Cup race are 12-meter yachts.
13. Some organic silicones are things used as lubricants.
16. Some giant stars are things in the tarantula nebula.
19. All persons who believe Noah's ark lies beneath the snows of Ararat are persons given to flights of fancy.
22. All cities identical to Berlin are cities that were the setting for the 1936 Olympic Games.
   Or All events identical to the 1936 Olympic Games are events that took place in Berlin.
25. All places there is smoke are places there is fire.
28. All ores identical to pitchblende are radioactive ores.
31. All novels written by James Michener are historical novels.
34. All times a rainbow occurs are times the sun is shining.
37. Some corporate raiders are persons known for their integrity, and some corporate raiders are not persons known for their integrity.
40. All persons identical to me are persons who like strawberries. *Or* All things identical to strawberries are things I like.

II.
1. Some third-generation computers are machines that take dictation.
4. No downhill skiers who suffer from altitude sickness are effective competitors.
7. No victims of Huntington's disease are persons helped by treatment.
10. All hungry crocodiles are dangerous animals.

Exercise 5.1

I.
1. *Major term:* things that produce intense gravity.
   Minor term: extremely dense objects.
   Middle term: neutron stars.
   Mood, figure: **AAA**-3; invalid.
4. *Major term:* good witnesses.
   Minor term: hypnotized persons.
   Middle term: persons who mix fact with fantasy.
   Mood, figure: **EIO**-1; valid.

II.

1. All *B* are *D*.
  No *R* are *D*.
  No *R* are *B*.
    AEE-2
    valid

4. No *M* are *F*.
  All *M* are *I*.
  Some *I* are not *F*.
    EAO-3
    valid

7. All *P* are *E*.
  All *L* are *P*.
  Some *L* are *E*.
    AAI-1
    invalid

10. Some *O* are not *C*.
  All *S* are *O*.
  Some *S* are *C*.
    OAI-1
    invalid

III.

1. Some *M* are not *P*.
  All *M* are *S*.
  No *S* are *P*.

4. Some *M* are *P*.
  All *S* are *M*.
  No *S* are *P*.

7. All *M* are *P*.
  All *S* are *M*.
  All *S* are *P*.

10. Some *P* are not *M*.
  No *M* are *S*.
  All *S* are *P*.

498

IV.

1. No dogmatists are scholars who encourage free thinking.
   Some theologians are scholars who encourage free thinking.
   Some theologians are not dogmatists.
4. Some viruses are not things capable of replicating by themselves.
   All viruses are structures that invade cells.
   Some structures that invade cells are not things capable of replicating by themselves.

Exercise 5.2

I.

1. All C are U.
   Some U are I.
   Some I are C.
   AII-4
   invalid

4. All H are D.
   Some D are not P.
   Some P are not H.
   AOO-4
   invalid

7. No M are B.
   All N are B.
   No N are M.
   EAE-2
   valid

10. No C are O.
    Some D are not O.
    Some D are not C.
    EOO-2
    invalid

13. No P are W.
    All D are P.
    No D are W.
    EAE-1
    valid

16. All P are G.
    All G are E.
    Some E are P.
    AAI-4
    invalid

19. No O are T.
    All O are P.
    Some P are not T.
    EAO-3
    valid

II.

1.

Conclusion: No S are P.

4.

Conclusion: Some S are not P.

7.

Conclusion: All S are P.

10.

Conclusion: None.

I.

1. All *M* are *P*.
   All *M* are *S*.
   All *S* are *P*.
   invalid;
   illicit minor

4. All *P* are *M*.
   All *S* are *M*.
   Some *S* are *P*.
   invalid;
   undistributed middle

7. No *M* are *P*.
   All *S* are *M*.
   All *S* are *P*.
   invalid;
   drawing affirmative
   conclusion from
   negative premise

10. Some *M* are *P*.
    All *M* are *S*.
    Some *S* are not *P*.
    invalid;
    illicit major;
    drawing negative
    conclusion from
    affirmative premises

13. All *P* are *M*.
    No *M* are *S*.
    No *S* are *P*.
    valid;
    no rules broken

16. No *M* are *P*.
    No *S* are *M*.
    No *S* are *P*.
    invalid;
    exclusive premises

19. All *P* are *M*.
    Some *S* are not *M*.
    Some *S* are not *P*.
    valid;
    no rules broken

II.

1. Some *N* are *C*.
   Some *C* are *O*.
   Some *O* are *N*.
   invalid;
   undistributed middle

4. Some *C* are not *M*.
   No *C* are *I*.
   Some *I* are not *M*.
   invalid;
   exclusive premises

7. No *S* are *V*.
   Some *W* are *V*.
   Some *W* are not *S*.
   valid;
   no rules broken

10. All *S* are *M*.
    All *M* are *P*.
    Some *P* are *S*.
    valid, since *S*
    exists

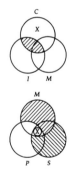

Exercise 5.4

1. Some non-*T* are *M*. (convert, obvert)
   All non-*I* are non-*M*. (contrapose)
   Some *I* are *T*.

   Some *M* are not *T*.
   All *M* are *I*.
   Some *I* are *T*.
   invalid; drawing affirmative conclusion
   from negative premise

4. Some *I* are *C*.
   All *C* are non-*P*.
   Some non-*I* are not *P*. (contrapose)

   Some *I* are *C*.
   All *C* are non-*P*.
   Some non-*P* are not *I*.
   invalid; illicit major

7. All non-*M* are non-*E*. (contrapose)
   Some *P* are not *M*.
   Some *P* are non-*E*. (obvert)

   All *E* are *M*.
   Some *P* are not *M*.
   Some *P* are not *E*.
   valid

10. Some *S* are non-*D*. (obvert)   Some *S* are not *D*.
    No *D* are *V*.   No *D* are *V*.
    ──────────────────   ──────────────────
    Some non-*V* are *S*. (convert, obvert)   Some *S* are not *V*.
                                         invalid; exclusive premises

Exercise 5.5

1. All people who made lots of money on the stock market are inside traders.
   All persons identical to Ivan Boesky are people who made lots of money on the stock market.
   ──
   All people identical to Ivan Boesky are inside traders.
   valid

4. All members of the British Conservative party are persons who favor increased military spending.
   All persons identical to Margaret Thatcher are persons who favor increased military spending.
   ──
   All persons identical to Margaret Thatcher are members of the British Conservative party.
   invalid, undistributed middle

7. Some songs Kathleen Battle sings are Puccini arias.
   All songs Kathleen Battle wants to sing are songs Kathleen Battle sings.
   ──
   Some songs Kathleen Battle wants to sing are Puccini arias.
   invalid, undistributed middle

10. All TV viewers who receive scrambled signals are viewers with a decoder.
    All persons who receive HBO are TV viewers who receive scrambled signals.
    ──
    All persons who receive HBO are persons with a decoder.
    valid

13. All diseases carried by recessive genes are diseases that can be inherited by offspring of two carriers.
    All diseases identical to cystic fibrosis are diseases carried by recessive genes.
    ──
    All diseases identical to cystic fibrosis are diseases that can be inherited by offspring of two carriers.
    valid

15. Some times are times aversive therapy is inhumane.
    Some times are times autistic children are helped by aversive therapy.
    ──
    Some times autistic children are helped by aversive therapy are times aversive therapy is inhumane.
    invalid, undistributed middle

Exercise 5.6

I.

1. Premise missing: No one who thinks that everything is governed by deterministic laws believes in free will.
4. Conclusion missing: A few fraternities have no legitimate role in campus life.
7. Conclusion missing: Some expensive wines are not good wines.
10. Premise missing: Whenever the humpback whale is overhunted, the humpback whale population decreases.
13. Premise missing: Some police chiefs fix parking tickets.
15. Conclusion missing: Dick Rutan and Jeana Yeager deserve to be called national heroes.

II.

1. No persons who think that everything is governed by deterministic laws are persons who believe in free will.

   All mechanistic materialists are persons who think everything is governed by deterministic laws.

   No mechanistic materialists are persons who believe in free will.
   valid

4. No groups that have dangerous initiation rites are groups that have a legitimate role in campus life.

   Some fraternities are groups that have dangerous initiation rites.

   Some fraternities are not groups that have a legitimate role in campus life.
   valid

7. Some chardonnays are not good wines.

   All chardonnays are expensive wines.

   Some expensive wines are not good wines.
   valid

10. All times the humpback whale is overhunted are times the humpback whale population decreases.

    All recent years are times the humpback whale is overhunted.

    All recent years are times the humpback whale population decreases.
    valid

13. All persons who fix parking tickets are persons who undermine the evenhanded enforcement of the law.

    Some police chiefs are persons who fix parking tickets.

    Some police chiefs are persons who undermine the evenhanded enforcement of the law.
    valid

15. All persons who elevated the pride of a nation by succeeding in an extraordinary accomplishment are persons who deserve to be called national heroes.

    All persons identical to either Dick Rutan or Jeana Yeager are persons who elevated the pride of a nation by succeeding in an extraordinary accomplishment.

    All persons identical to either Dick Rutan or Jeana Yeager are persons who deserve to be called national heroes.
    valid

III.

1. No organizations that make alcohol readily available and acceptable are organizations that are serious about fighting alcohol abuse.

   All organizations identical to the Defense Department are organizations that make alcohol readily available and acceptable.

   No organizations identical to the Defense Department are organizations that are serious about fighting alcohol abuse.

4. All efforts to ban books are efforts that ensure those books will be read.

   All efforts by the fundamentalist families in Church Hill, Tennessee to remove *Macbeth*, etc. from the libraries are efforts to ban books.

   All efforts by the fundamentalist families in Church Hill, Tennessee, to remove *Macbeth*, etc. from the libraries are efforts that ensure those books will be read.

7. All policies that promote more college graduates tomorrow are policies that result in higher tax revenues tomorrow.

   All policies that offer financial aid to college students today are policies that promote more college graduates tomorrow.

   All policies that offer financial aid to college students today are policies that result in higher tax revenues tomorrow.

and

All policies that result in higher tax revenues tomorrow are good investments in the the future.

All policies that offer financial aid to college students today are policies that result in higher tax revenues tomorrow.

All policies that offer financial aid to college students today are good investments in the future.

10. All people who act in ways that decrease their chances of survival are people who will die out through natural selection.

All smokers who continue smoking are people who act in ways that decrease their chances of survival.

All smokers who continue smoking are people who will die out through natural selection.

and

All people who act in ways that increase their chances of survival are people who will survive through natural selection.

All smokers who quit are people who act in ways that increase their chances of survival.

All smokers who quit are people who will survive through natural selection.

IV.

1. All women who dare to wear Lanvin perfume are women who will risk driving men wild.

All women identical to you are women who will risk driving men wild.

All women identical to you are women who dare to wear Lanvin perfume.

4. All shoes that have been perfected for over 90 years are shoes that are virtually perfect.

All shoes identical to today's Florsheim shoe are shoes that have been perfected for over 90 years.

All shoes identical to today's Florsheim shoe are shoes that are virtually perfect.

7. All products that are bought and consumed so rapidly in the country of their origin that practically nothing is left to export are very high quality products.

All Cruzan rums are products bought and consumed so rapidly in the country of their origin that practically nothing is left to export.

All Cruzan rums are very high quality products.

10. All people who have the ability to take professional-quality photographs are people who will select an Olympus.

All people identical to you are people who have the ability to take professional-quality photographs.

All people identical to you are people who will select an Olympus.

Exercise 5.7

I.

1. All *A* are *B*. ⎫
No *B* are *C*. ⎬   No *C* are *A*. ⎫
Some *D* are *C*. ——————————→ ⎬
Some *D* are not *A*.
   valid

4. No K are N.⎫
 Some T are K.⎭ Some T are not N.⎫
 All T are C. ────────────────⎬ Some C are not N. ⎫
 Some C are.Q. ──────────────────────────────⎬
 Some Q are not N.   ⎭
 invalid

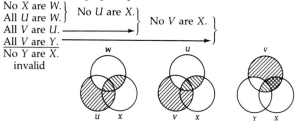

7. After contraposing the first premise, obverting the second premise and the conclusion, and rearranging the premises, we have:

 No X are W.⎫
 All U are W.⎭ No U are X.⎫
 All V are U. ──────────⎬ No V are X. ⎫
 All V are Y. ──────────────────────⎬
 No Y are X.   ⎭
 invalid

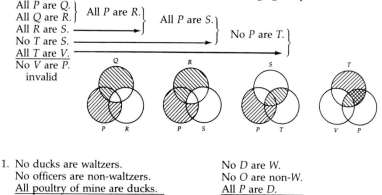

10. After converting and obverting the second and fourth premises, obverting the third and fifth premises and the conclusion, and rearranging the premises, we have:

 All P are Q. ⎫
 All Q are R. ⎭ All P are R.⎫
 All R are S. ──────────⎬ All P are S.⎫
 No T are S. ──────────────────⎬ No P are T.⎫
 All T are V. ──────────────────────────⎬
 No V are P.   ⎭
 invalid

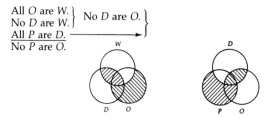

II.

1. No ducks are waltzers.   No D are W.
   No officers are non-waltzers.   No O are non-W.
   All poultry of mine are ducks.   All P are D.
   No poultry of mine are officers.   No P are O.

After obverting the second premise and rearranging the premises, we have:

 All O are W.⎫
 No D are W.⎭ No D are O.⎫
 All P are D. ──────────⎬
 No P are O.

504

4. All hummingbirds are richly colored birds.
   No large birds are birds that live on honey.
   All birds that do not live on honey are birds that are dull in
   __color.__
   All hummingbirds are small birds.

   All H are R.
   No L are O.

   All non-O are non-R.
   All H are non-L.

   After contraposing the third premise, obverting the conclusion, and rearranging the premises, we have:

   No L are O.⎫ No L are R.⎫
   All R are O.⎭
   __All H are R.__ ⟶ ⎭
   No H are L.

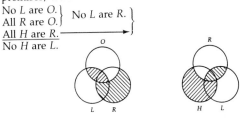

7. All books in this library that I do not recommend are books
      that are unhealthy in tone.
   All the bound books are well-written books.
   All the romances are books that are unhealthy in tone.
   All the unbound books are books in this library that I do
      __not recommend.__

   All the romances are well-written books.

   All non-R are non-H.
   All B are W.
   All O are H.

   All non-B are non-R.
   All O are W.

   After contraposing the first and fourth premises, we have:

   All B are W.⎫ All R are W.⎫
   All R are B.⎭
   All H are R. ⟶ ⎭ All H are W.⎫
   __All O are H.__ ⟶⟶⟶⟶⟶ ⎭
   All O are W.

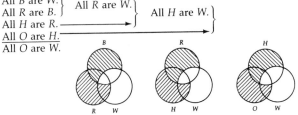

10. All animals that belong to me are animals I trust.
   All dogs are animals that gnaw bones.
   All animals I admit to my study are animals that beg when told to do
      so.
   All the animals in the yard are animals that belong to me.
   All animals I trust are animals I admit into my study.
   __All animals that are willing to beg when told to do so are dogs.__

   All the animals in the yard are animals that gnaw bones.

   All A are T.
   All D are G.

   All S are B.
   All Y are A.
   All T are S.
   __All B are D.__
   All Y are G.

   After rearranging the premises, we have:

   All D are G.⎫ All B are G.⎫
   All B are D.⎭
   All S are B. ⟶ ⎭ All S are G.⎫
   All T are S. ⟶⟶⟶ ⎭ All T are G.⎫
   All A are T. ⟶⟶⟶⟶⟶ ⎭ All A are G.⎫
   __All Y are A.__ ⟶⟶⟶⟶⟶⟶⟶ ⎭
   All Y are G.

Exercise 6.1
I.

1. ~O
4. N • C
7. L ≡ S
10. ~Z v C
13. (S • P) v C
16. ~P v ~A
19. A ⊃ (T ⊃ P)

22. S ⊃ (C v B)
25. (H • R) ⊃ (~K • ~X• ~X)
28. (S • G) v (~A • ~B)
31. P • [G ⊃ (I v C)]
34. I ⊃ O
37. (G • S) ≡ (A v G)
40. [(L • ~T) ≡ M] ⊃ ~(C v Z)

Exercise 6.2
I.

1. Conjunction. 4. Equivalence. 7. Implication. 10. Disjunction.

II.

1. ~ H
  Ⓕ T
4. H • ~ N
  T Ⓕ F T

7. W ⊃ E
  F Ⓣ F
10. H ⊃ (M v E)
  T Ⓣ T T F

13. ~ (E v C) ⊃ (H • L)
  T F F F Ⓣ T T T
15. M • [L ⊃ (W v A)
  T Ⓕ T F F F F

III.

1. A • X
  T Ⓕ F
4. ~ C v Z
  F T Ⓕ F
7. ~ X ⊃ Z
  T F Ⓕ F
19. ~[~ (X ⊃ C) ≡ ~ (B ⊃ Z)]
  Ⓣ F F T T F T T F F
22. ~ [(A ≡ X) v (Z ≡ Y)] v [(~ Y ⊃ B) • (Z ⊃ C)]
  F T F F T F T F Ⓣ T F T T T T F T T
25. (Z ⊃ C) ⊃ {[(~ X ⊃ B) ⊃ (C ⊃ Y)] ≡ [(Z ⊃ X) ⊃ (~ Y ⊃ Z)]}
  F T T Ⓣ T F T T T F T F F T F T F F T F F F

10. ~ (A • ~ Z)
  Ⓕ T T T F
13. (A • Y) v (~ Z • C)
  T F F Ⓣ T F T T
16. (C ≡ ~ A) v (Y ≡ Z)
  T F F T Ⓣ F T F

IV.

1. A v P
  T Ⓣ ?
4. Q • A
  ? Ⓠ T
7. A ⊃ P
  T Ⓠ ?

10. (P ⊃ A) ≡ (Q ⊃ B)
  ? T T Ⓣ ? T T
13. ~ (Q • Y) ≡ ~ (Q v A)
  T ? F F Ⓕ F ? T T
15. [Q ⊃ (A v P)] ≡ [(Q ⊃ B) ⊃ Y]
  ? T T T ? Ⓕ ? T T F F

Exercise 6.3
I.

1. A ⊃ (A ⊃ A)
  T | T | T T T
  F | T | F T F
  tautologous

4. [(E ⊃ F) ⊃ F] ⊃ E
  T T T T T | T | T
  T F F T F | T | T
  F T T T T | F | F
  F T F F F | T | F
  contingent

7. [(X ⊃ Z) • (X v Z)] ⊃ Z
  T T T T T T T | T | T
  T F F F T T F | T | F
  F T T T F T T | T | T
  F T F F F F F | T | F
  tautologous

10. [G ⊃ (N ⊃ ~ G] • [(G ≡ N) • (G v N)]
  T F T F F T | F | T T T T T T T
  T T F T F T | F | T F F F T T F
  F T T T T F | F | F F T F F T T
  F T F T T F | F | F T F F F F F
  self- contradictory

13. $[S \cdot (T \lor U)] \equiv [(\sim S \lor \sim T) \cdot (\sim S \lor \sim U)]$

S	T	T	v	U			(	~	S	v	~	T	)	(	~	S	v	~	U	)
T	T	T	T	T	F		F	T	F	F	T	F	F	T	F	F	T
T	T	T	T	F	F		F	T	F	F	T	F	F	T	T	T	F
T	T	F	T	T	F		F	T	T	T	F	F	F	T	F	F	T
T	F	F	F	F	F		F	T	T	T	F	T	T	T	T	T	F
F	F	T	T	T	F		T	F	T	F	T	T	T	F	T	F	T
F	F	T	T	F	F		T	F	T	F	T	T	T	F	T	T	F
F	F	F	T	T	F		T	F	T	T	F	T	T	F	T	F	T
F	F	F	F	F	F		T	F	T	T	F	T	T	F	T	T	F

self-contradictory

15. $[(E \lor F) \cdot (G \lor H)] \equiv [(E \cdot G) \lor (F \cdot H)]$

E	v	F	G	v	H			(	E	G	)	(	F	H	)
T	T	T	T	T	T		T	T	T	T	T	T	T	T
T	T	T	T	T	F		T	T	T	T	T	T	F	F
T	T	T	F	T	T		T	T	F	F	T	T	T	T
T	T	T	F	F	F		T	T	F	F	F	T	F	F
T	T	F	T	T	T		T	T	T	T	F	F	F	T
T	T	F	T	T	F		T	T	T	T	F	F	F	F
T	T	F	F	T	T		F	T	F	F	F	F	F	T
T	T	F	F	F	F		T	T	F	F	F	F	F	F
F	T	T	T	T	T		T	F	F	T	T	T	T	T
F	T	T	T	T	F		F	F	F	T	F	T	F	F
F	T	T	F	T	T		T	F	F	F	T	T	T	T
F	T	T	F	F	F		T	F	F	F	F	T	F	F
F	F	F	T	T	T		T	F	F	T	F	F	F	T
F	F	F	T	T	F		T	F	F	T	F	F	F	F
F	F	F	F	T	T		T	F	F	F	F	F	F	T
F	F	F	F	F	F		T	F	F	F	F	F	F	F

contingent

II.

1. $\sim D \lor T$

~	D	v	T
F	T	T	T
F	T	F	F
T	F	T	T
T	F	T	F

$\sim (D \cdot \sim T)$

~	(	D	~	T	)
T		T	F	F	T
F		T	T	T	F
T		F	F	F	T
T		F	F	T	F

logically equivalent

4. $N \supset \sim P$

N	⊃	~	P
T	F	F	T
T	T	T	F
F	T	F	T
F	T	T	F

$N \cdot P$

N	•	P
T	T	T
T	F	F
F	F	T
F	F	F

contradictory

7. $(E \supset F) \supset G$

(	E	⊃	F	)	⊃	G
	T	T	T		T	T
	T	T	T		F	F
	T	F	F		T	T
	T	F	F		T	F
	F	T	T		T	T
	F	T	T		F	F
	F	T	F		T	T
	F	T	F		F	F

$E \supset (F \supset G)$

E	⊃	(	F	⊃	G	)
T	T		T	T	T	
T	F		T	F	F	
T	T		F	T	T	
T	T		F	T	F	
F	T		T	T	T	
F	T		T	F	F	
F	T		F	T	T	
F	T		F	T	F	

neither

10. $H \cdot (J \lor K)$

H	•	(	J	v	K	)
T	T		T	T	T	
T	T		T	T	F	
T	T		F	T	T	
T	F		F	F	F	
F	F		T	T	T	
F	F		T	T	F	
F	F		F	T	T	
F	F		F	F	F	

$(J \cdot H) \lor (H \cdot K)$

(	J	•	H	)	v	(	H	•	K	)
	T	T	T		T		T	T	T	
	T	T	T		T		T	F	F	
	F	F	T		T		T	T	T	
	F	F	T		F		T	F	F	
	T	F	F		F		F	F	T	
	T	F	F		F		F	F	F	
	F	F	F		F		F	F	T	
	F	F	F		F		F	F	F	

logically equivalent

III.

1. Carlson's prediction is false (self-contradictory).
4. A supernova will not occur within 10 light-years of the earth. (Draw a truth table for each statement and examine the two lines on which both statements are true.)

7. Mackie did not kill the victim, Ratzo was not an accomplice, and Smilie was involved. (Draw a truth table for each statement and examine the one line on which both statements are true.)

10. Fisher and Morgan were indicted. Pending the discovery of Genelle's lie, the indictment should be quashed and Laskey should be indicted instead. (Construct a truth table for each statement and examine the one line on which all three statements are true. Then negate the column under the main connective in Genelle's statement and examine the two lines on which all three statements are true.)

Exercise 6.4

I.

1. MT.	7. DD.	13. DS.	19. Invalid form.
4. CD.	10. DA.	16. AC.	

II.

1. $F \supset T$
$\dfrac{\sim T}{\sim F}$ MT

4. $W \vee \sim M$
$\dfrac{\sim W}{\sim M}$ DS

7. T
$\dfrac{T \supset \sim H}{\sim H}$ MP

10. $(L \supset \sim A) \bullet (C \supset F)$
$\dfrac{\sim L \bullet \sim C}{A \bullet \sim F}$ invalid

13. $(P \supset T) \bullet (A \supset \sim T)$
$\dfrac{T \vee \sim T}{\sim P \vee \sim A}$ DD

16. $\sim M \supset U$
$\dfrac{U}{\sim M}$ AC

19. $S \supset C$
$I \supset S$
$\dfrac{}{I \supset C}$ HS

III.

1. $(S \supset M) \bullet (\sim S \supset F)$
$\dfrac{S \vee \sim S}{M \vee F}$ CD

Since the second premise is a tautology, it is impossible to escape between the horns. The two available strategies are therefore grasping by the horns and constructing a counterdilemma. Perhaps Melinda could take her books to the party and study there. Such an event would falsify the left-hand conjunct of the first premise, thus falsifying the entire premise. Here is a counterdilemma:

> If Melinda spends the night studying, she will pass the test tomorrow; and, if she doesn't spend the night studying, she will go to the party. She will either spend the night studying or not studying. Therefore, she will either pass the test or go to the party.

4. $(C \supset \sim S) \bullet (E \supset S)$
$\dfrac{S \vee \sim S}{\sim C \vee \sim E}$ DD

The second premise is a tautology, so it is impossible to escape between the horns. One could grasp the dilemma by the horns by arguing that corporations could share the cost of neutralizing toxic waste, thus preserving the competitive edge. Here is a constructive counterdilemma:

> If corporations spend money to neutralize their toxic waste, then the environment will be preserved; but if corporations do not spend money to neutralize their toxic waste, then they will remain competitive. Corporations will do one or the other. Therefore, either the environment will be preserved or corporations will remain competitive.

7. $(C \supset L) \bullet (J \supset B)$
$\dfrac{\sim L \vee \sim B}{\sim C \vee \sim J}$ DD

Here the second premise is not a tautology, so it is possible to escape between the horns. Perhaps students could take a double major in liberal arts and business. One could also grasp the dilemma by the horns by arguing that students could major in a liberal arts field where a job *would* be available upon graduation. Here is a constructive counterdilemma:

508

If students major in liberal arts, then they will take courses that are interesting and rewarding; but if they major in business, then they will have a job when they graduate. Students will either major in liberal arts or business. Therefore, either they will take courses that are interesting and rewarding or they will have a job when they graduate.

10. $(P \supset Ri) \cdot (Re \supset E)$
$\underline{P \vee Re}$
$Ri \vee E$ CD

The second premise is not a tautology, so it is at least possible to escape between the horns. If we instructed counter-terrorist squads to execute terrorists on the spot, we would neither prosecute them nor release them. Can you think of a way to grasp the dilemma by the horns? Here is a counterdilemma:

> If we prosecute suspected terrorists, then we discourage terrorism; but if we release them, then we avoid the risk of retaliation by other terrorists. We must either prosecute or release suspected terrorists. Therefore, either we will discourage terrorism or we will avoid the risk of retaliation by other terrorists.

IV.

1. If Oral Roberts actually receives messages from God, then he would not have sent the letter. Oral Roberts did send the letter. Therefore, he does not actually receive messages from God. (MT)

4. If voter turnout were a measure of democracy, then Communist countries would be the most democratic. Communist countries are not the most democratic. Therefore, voter turnout is not a measure of democracy. (MT)

7. If we close the library at Central Juvenile Hall, then delinquents will be deprived of an opportunity to read. If delinquents are deprived of an opportunity to read, then they will not have access to ideas, dreams, and alternative ways of living. Therefore, if we close the library at Central Juvenile Hall, then delinquents will not have access to ideas, dreams, and alternative ways of living. (HS)

> If we close the library at Central Juvenile Hall, then delinquents will not have access to ideas, dreams, and alternative ways of living. Delinquents must have access to ideas, dreams, and alternative ways of living. Therefore, we must not close the library at Central Juvenile Hall. (MT)

10. If the President remembers or made a note of what he was doing on August 8, 1985, then he is a liar; but if he forgot what he was doing before he could dictate it, then he is senile or grossly irresponsible. The President either remembers/made a note of what he was doing or he forgot what he was doing before he could dictate it. Therefore, the President is either a liar or senile/grossly irresponsible. (CD)

Exercise 6.5

I.

1.

N	⊃	S				∼	N	⊃	∼	S
T	**T**	T				F	T	**T**	F	T
T	**F**	F				F	T	**T**	T	F
F	**T**	T				T	F	**F**	F	T
F	**T**	F				T	F	**T**	T	F

invalid

4.

D	⊃	W			D			W
T	**T**	T			T			T
T	**F**	F			T			F
F	**T**	T			F			T
F	**T**	F			F			F

valid

7. Invalid (fails on first line).

10. Valid.

II.

1. Valid.
4. Valid.
7. Invalid (fails on fourth line).
10. Invalid (fails on fourth and sixth lines).
13. Valid.
16. Invalid (fails on third line).
19. Invalid (fails on third line).

Exercise 6.6

1. $B \equiv C$ // $\sim C \supset \sim B$

   ⟨T T F⟩ T F F F T

   valid

4. $\sim (I \equiv J)$ // $\sim (I \supset J)$

   T T F F   T T F F

   T F F T   ⟨F T F⟩ F

   T F F T   F F T T

   invalid

7. $G \supset H$ / $H \supset I$ / $\sim J \supset G$ / $\sim I$ // J

   T T T   T T T   T F T T   ⟨T T⟩   F

   valid

10. $(M \vee N) \supset O$ / $O \supset (N \vee P)$ / $M \supset (\sim Q \supset N)$ / $(Q \supset M) \supset \sim P$ // $N \equiv O$

    ⟨T T T F⟩ T   T   T   T T F

    T T   T T F T P   F T   T F F T F T   F F T

    invalid

13. $(A \vee B) \supset (C \cdot D)$ // $(X \vee \sim Y) \supset (\sim C \cdot \sim W)$ / $(X \vee Z) \supset (A \cdot E)$ // $\sim X$

    T ⟨T   T F F⟩   T T   T T F T T F   T T   T T T T   F T

    valid

15. $N \vee \sim O$ / $P \vee O$ / $P \supset Q$ / $(N \vee Q) \supset (R \cdot S)$ / $S \supset (R \supset T)$ / $O \supset (T \supset U)$ // U

    T T T F   T T F   T T T   T T T T T T   T T T T T   F T T F F   F

    T T F T   T   T   T T   T F F T T   T   F F

    F T T F   T   T   T   T   T   F

    invalid

Exercise 7.1

I.

(1) 4. 2, 3, DS
     5. 1, 4, MP
     6. 3, 5, MT

II.

(1) 1. $(G \equiv J) \vee (B \supset P)$
     2. $\sim(G \equiv J)$ / $B \supset P$
     3. $B \supset P$ 1, 2, DS

(4) 1. $\sim\sim(R \vee W)$
     2. $S \supset \sim(R \vee W)$ / $\sim S$
     3. $\sim S$ 1, 2, MT

(7) 1. $(K \cdot B) \vee (L \supset E)$
     2. $\sim(K \cdot B)$
     3. $\sim E$ / $\sim L$
     4. $L \supset E$ 1, 2, DS
     5. $\sim L$ 3, 4, MT

(10) 1. $\sim S \supset D$
     2. $\sim S \vee (\sim D \supset K)$
     3. $\sim D$ / K
     4. $\sim\sim S$ 1, 3, MT
     5. $\sim D \supset K$ 2, 4, DS
     6. K 3, 5, MP

(13) 1. $G \supset [\sim O \supset (G \supset D)]$
     2. $O \vee G$
     3. $\sim O$ / D
     4. G 2, 3, DS
     5. $\sim O \supset (G \supset D)$ 1, 4, MP
     6. $G \supset D$ 3, 5, MP
     7. D 4, 6, MP

(4) 4. 2, 3, MP
     5. 1, 4, MP
     6. 4, 5, DS
     7. 4, 6, MT
     8. 3, 7, DS

(16) 1. $\sim J \supset [\sim A \supset (D \supset A)]$
     2. $J \vee \sim A$
     3. $\sim J$ / $\sim D$
     4. $\sim A \supset (D \supset A)$ 1, 3, MP
     5. $\sim A$ 2, 3, DS
     6. $D \supset A$ 4, 5, MP
     7. $\sim D$ 5, 6, MT

(19) 1. $\sim A \supset [A \vee (T \supset R)]$
     2. $\sim R \supset [R \vee (A \supset R)]$
     3. $(T \vee D) \supset \sim R$
     4. $T \vee D$ / D
     5. $\sim R$ 3, 4, MP
     6. $R \vee (A \supset R)$ 2, 5, MP
     7. $A \supset R$ 5, 6, DS
     8. $\sim A$ 5, 7, MT
     9. $A \vee (T \supset R)$ 1, 8, MP
     10. $T \supset R$ 8, 9, DS
     11. $\sim T$ 5, 10, MT
     12. D 4, 11, DS

III.

(1) 1. $W \supset (P \vee C)$
     2. $\sim P$
     3. W / C
     4. $P \vee C$ 1, 3, MP
     5. C 2, 4, DS

(4) 1. $(R \supset L) \supset (L \supset \sim F)$
     2. $\sim F \vee (R \supset L)$
     3. $\sim\sim F$ / $\sim R$
     4. $R \supset L$ 2, 3, DS
     5. $L \supset \sim F$ 1, 4, MP
     6. $\sim L$ 3, 5, MT
     7. $\sim R$ 4, 6, MT

(7)   1. $H \supset (D \equiv A)$
      2. $V \vee (R \supset V)$
      3. $R \vee H$
      4. $\sim V$ / $D \equiv A$
      5. $R \supset V$ 2, 4, DS
      6. $\sim R$ 4, 5, MT
      7. H 3, 6, DS
      8. $D \equiv A$ 1, 7, MP

(10) 1. $\sim C \supset [C \vee (J \supset D)]$
      2. $C \supset (C \cdot U)$
      3. $\sim (C \cdot U)$
      4. $\sim D$ / $\sim J$
      5. $\sim C$ 2, 3, MT
      6. $C \vee (J \supset D)$ 1, 5, MP
      7. $J \supset D$ 5, 6, DS
      8. $\sim J$ 4, 7, MT

Exercise 7:2

I.

(1)   4. 2, Simp
      5. 3, Simp
      6. 4, 5, Conj
      7. 1, 6, MP
      8. 4, Add
      9. 7, 8, MP
      10. 9, Simp
      11. 5, 10, Conj

(4)   4. 2, 3, CD
      5. 1, 4, CD
      6. 2, Simp
      7. 1, Simp
      8. 6, 7, Conj
      9. 5, 8, CD

II.

(1)   1. $\sim M \supset Q$
      2. $R \supset \sim T$
      3. $\sim M \vee R$ / $Q \vee \sim T$
      4. $(\sim M \supset Q) \cdot (R \supset \sim T)$ 1, 2, Conj
      5. $Q \vee \sim T$ 3, 4, CD

(4)   1. $(L \vee T) \supset (B \cdot G)$
      2. $L \cdot (K \equiv R)$ / $L \cdot B$
      3. L 2, Simp
      4. $L \vee T$ 3, Add
      5. $B \cdot G$ 1, 4, MP
      6. B 5, Simp
      7. $L \cdot B$ 3, 6, Conj

(7)   1. $(U \vee W) \supset (T \supset R)$
      2. $U \cdot H$
      3. $\sim R \cdot \sim J$ / $U \cdot \sim T$
      4. U 2, Simp
      5. $U \vee W$ 4, Add
      6. $T \supset R$ 1, 5, MP
      7. $\sim R$ 3, Simp
      8. $\sim T$ 6, 7, MT
      9. $U \cdot \sim T$ 4, 8, Conj

(10) 1. $(P \supset R) \supset (M \supset P)$
      2. $(P \vee M) \supset (P \supset R)$
      3. $P \vee M$ / $R \vee P$
      4. $P \supset R$ 2, 3, MP
      5. $M \supset P$ 1, 4, MP
      6. $(P \supset R) \cdot (M \supset P)$ 4, 5, Conj
      7. $R \vee P$ 3, 6, CD

(13) 1. $\sim H \supset (\sim T \supset R)$
      2. $H \vee (E \supset F)$
      3. $\sim T \vee E$
      4. $\sim H \cdot D$ / $R \vee F$
      5. $\sim H$ 4, Simp
      6. $\sim T \supset R$ 1, 5, MP
      7. $E \supset F$ 2, 5, DS
      8. $(\sim T \supset R) \cdot (E \supset F)$ 6, 7, Conj
      9. $R \vee F$ 3, 8, CD

(16) 1. $(F \cdot M) \supset (S \vee T)$
      2. $(\sim S \vee A) \supset F$
      3. $(\sim S \vee B) \supset M$
      4. $\sim S \cdot G$ / T
      5. $\sim S$ 4, Simp
      6. $\sim S \vee A$ 5, Add
      7. F 2, 6, MP
      8. $\sim S \vee B$ 5, Add
      9. M 3, 8, MP
      10. $F \cdot M$ 7, 9, Conj
      11. $S \vee T$ 1, 10, MP
      12. T 5, 11, DS

(19) 1. $(J \supset K) \cdot (\sim O \supset \sim P)$
      2. $(L \supset J) \cdot (\sim M \supset \sim O)$
      3. $\sim K \supset (L \vee \sim M)$
      4. $\sim K \cdot G$ / $\sim P$
      5. $\sim K$ 4, Simp
      6. $L \vee \sim M$ 3, 5, MP
      7. $J \vee \sim O$ 2, 6, CD
      8. $K \vee \sim P$ 1, 7, CD
      9. $\sim P$ 5, 8, DS

III.

(1)　1. $T \supset (Q \cdot F)$
　　 2. $T \cdot C$ 　　　 / $Q \vee O$
　　 3. T 　　　　2, Simp
　　 4. $Q \cdot F$ 　　1, 3, MP
　　 5. Q 　　　　4, Simp
　　 6. $Q \vee O$ 　　5, Add

(4)　1. $M \vee P$
　　 2. $(P \vee S) \supset (R \cdot D)$
　　 3. $\sim M$ 　　　 / R
　　 4. P 　　　　1, 3, DS
　　 5. $P \vee S$ 　　4, Add
　　 6. $R \cdot D$ 　　2, 5, MP
　　 7. R 　　　　6, Simp

Exercise 7.3

I.

(1)　4. 1, Com
　　 5. 4, Assoc
　　 6. 3, 5, DS
　　 7. 2, 6, MP
　　 8. 3, 7, Conj
　　 9. 8, DM

(4)　4. 1, Com
　　 5. 4, Assoc
　　 6. 3, 5, DS
　　 7. 2, 6, MP
　　 8. 3, 7, Conj
　　 9. 8, DM

II.

(1)　1. $(\sim M \supset P) \cdot (\sim N \supset Q)$
　　 2. $\sim (M \cdot N)$ 　　 / $P \vee Q$
　　 3. $\sim M \vee \sim N$ 　　2, DM
　　 4. $P \vee Q$ 　　　　1, 3, CD

(4)　1. $(O \vee M) \supset S$
　　 2. $\sim S$ 　　　　 / $\sim M$
　　 3. $\sim (O \vee M)$ 　1, 2, MT
　　 4. $\sim O \cdot \sim M$ 　3, DM
　　 5. $\sim M \cdot \sim O$ 　4, Com
　　 6. $\sim M$ 　　　　5, Simp

(7)　1. $H \cdot (C \cdot T)$
　　 2. $\sim (\sim F \cdot T)$ 　/ F
　　 3. $\sim \sim F \vee \sim T$ 　2, DM
　　 4. $F \vee \sim T$ 　　3, DN
　　 5. $\sim T \vee F$ 　　4, Com
　　 6. $(H \cdot C) \cdot T$ 　1, Assoc
　　 7. $T \cdot (H \cdot C)$ 　6, Com
　　 8. T 　　　　7, Simp
　　 9. $\sim \sim T$ 　　8, DN
　　 10. F 　　　　5, 9, DS

(10)　1. $(G \cdot H) \vee (M \cdot G)$
　　 2. $G \supset (T \cdot A)$ 　/ A
　　 3. $(G \cdot H) \vee (G \cdot M)$ 　1, Com
　　 4. $G \cdot (H \vee M)$ 　3, Dist
　　 5. G 　　　　4, Simp
　　 6. $T \cdot A$ 　　2, 5, MP
　　 7. $A \cdot T$ 　　6, Com
　　 8. A 　　　　7, Simp

(7)　1. $(\sim C \vee \sim M) \supset (\sim C \supset T)$
　　 2. $C \vee \sim T$
　　 3. $\sim C$ 　　　　 / B
　　 4. $\sim C \vee \sim M$ 　3, Add
　　 5. $\sim C \supset T$ 　1, 4, MP
　　 6. T 　　　　3, 5, MP
　　 7. $T \vee B$ 　　6, Add
　　 8. $\sim T$ 　　　2, 3, DS
　　 9. B 　　　　7, 8, DS

(10)　1. $(V \cdot \sim E) \supset (P \supset E)$
　　 2. $V \supset \sim E$
　　 3. $V \cdot I$
　　 4. $\sim E \supset (P \vee J)$ 　/ $J \cdot \sim E$
　　 5. V 　　　　3, Simp
　　 6. $\sim E$ 　　　2, 5, MP
　　 7. $V \cdot \sim E$ 　　5, 6, Conj
　　 8. $P \supset E$ 　　1, 7, MP
　　 9. $\sim P$ 　　　6, 8, MT
　　 10. $P \vee J$ 　　4, 6, MP
　　 11. J 　　　　9, 10, DS
　　 12. $J \cdot \sim E$ 　　6, 11, Conj

(13)　1. $\sim (F \cdot A)$
　　 2. $\sim (L \vee \sim A)$
　　 3. $D \supset (F \vee L)$ 　/ $\sim D$
　　 4. $\sim L \cdot \sim \sim A$ 　2, DM
　　 5. $\sim \sim A \cdot \sim L$ 　4, Com
　　 6. $\sim \sim A$ 　　5, Simp
　　 7. $\sim F \vee \sim A$ 　1, DM
　　 8. $\sim A \vee \sim F$ 　7, Com
　　 9. $\sim F$ 　　　6, 8, DS
　　 10. $\sim L$ 　　　4, Simp
　　 11. $\sim F \cdot \sim L$ 　9, 10, Conj
　　 12. $\sim (F \vee L)$ 　11, DM
　　 13. $\sim D$ 　　　3, 12, MT

(16)　1. $\sim (K \vee F)$
　　 2. $\sim F \supset (K \vee C)$
　　 3. $(G \vee C) \supset \sim H$ 　/ $\sim (K \vee H)$
　　 4. $\sim K \cdot \sim F$ 　1, DM
　　 5. $\sim F \cdot \sim K$ 　4, Com
　　 6. $\sim F$ 　　　5, Simp
　　 7. $K \vee C$ 　　2, 6, MP
　　 8. $\sim K$ 　　　4, Simp
　　 9. C 　　　　7, 8, DS
　　 10. $C \vee G$ 　　9, Add
　　 11. $G \vee C$ 　　10, Com
　　 12. $\sim H$ 　　　3, 11, MP
　　 13. $\sim K \cdot \sim H$ 　8, 12, Conj
　　 14. $\sim (K \vee H)$ 　13, DM

(19)
1. $B \lor (S \cdot N)$
2. $B \supset \sim S$
3. $S \supset \sim N$ / $B \lor W$
4. $(B \lor S) \cdot (B \lor N)$ 1, Dist
5. $B \lor S$ 4, Simp
6. $(B \supset \sim S) \cdot (S \supset \sim N)$ 2, 3, Conj
7. $\sim S \lor \sim N$ 5, 6, CD
8. $\sim (S \cdot N)$ 7, DM
9. $(S \cdot N) \lor B$ 1, Com
10. B 8, 9, DS
11. $B \lor W$ 10, Add

(22)
1. $\sim Q \supset (C \cdot B)$
2. $\sim T \supset (B \cdot H)$
3. $\sim (Q \cdot T)$ / B
4. $\sim Q \lor \sim T$ 3, DM
5. $[\sim Q \supset (C \cdot B)] \cdot$ 1, 2, Conj
   $[\sim T \supset (B \cdot H)]$
6. $(C \cdot B) \lor (B \cdot H)$ 4, 5, CD
7. $(B \cdot C) \lor (B \cdot H)$ 6, Com
8. $B \cdot (C \lor H)$ 7, Dist
9. B 8, Simp

(25)
1. $(T \cdot K) \lor (C \cdot E)$
2. $K \supset \sim E$
3. $E \supset \sim C$ / $T \cdot K$
4. $[(T \cdot K) \lor C] \cdot [(T \cdot K) \lor E]$ 1, Dist
5. $[(T \lor C) \cdot (K \lor C)] \cdot [(T \lor E) \cdot (K \lor E)]$ 4, Com, Dist
6. $K \lor E$ 5, Com, Assoc, Simp
7. $(K \supset \sim E) \cdot (E \supset \sim C)$ 2, 3, Conj
8. $\sim E \lor \sim C$ 6, 7, CD
9. $\sim C \lor \sim E$ 8, Com
10. $\sim (C \cdot E)$ 9, DM
11. $(C \cdot E) \lor (T \cdot K)$ 1, Com
12. $T \cdot K$ 10, 11, DS

III.

(1)
1. $(S \cdot D) \lor (S \cdot H)$
2. $S \supset (I \cdot R)$ / $S \cdot R$
3. $S \cdot (D \lor H)$ 1, Dist
4. S 3, Simp
5. $I \cdot R$ 2, 4, MP
6. $R \cdot I$ 5, Com
7. R 6, Simp
8. $S \cdot R$ 4, 7, Conj

(4)
1. $G \lor (R \cdot E)$
2. $(G \lor E) \supset \sim R$ / $G \lor M$
3. $(G \lor R) \cdot (G \lor E)$ 1, Dist
4. $(G \lor E) \cdot (G \lor R)$ 3, Com
5. $G \lor E$ 4, Simp
6. $\sim R$ 2, 5, MP
7. $G \lor R$ 3, Simp
8. $R \lor G$ 7, Com
9. G 6, 8, DS
10. $G \lor M$ 9, Add

(7)
1. $R \supset (C \lor M)$
2. $\sim (I \lor C)$
3. $\sim (A \lor M)$ / $\sim R$
4. $\sim I \cdot \sim C$ 2, DM
5. $\sim A \cdot \sim M$ 3, DM
6. $\sim C \cdot \sim I$ 4, Com
7. $\sim C$ 6, Simp
8. $\sim M \cdot \sim A$ 5, Com
9. $\sim M$ 8, Simp
10. $\sim C \cdot \sim M$ 7, 9, Conj
11. $\sim (C \lor M)$ 10, DM
12. $\sim R$ 1, 11, MT

(10)
1. $\sim E \lor (B \cdot P)$
2. $\sim E \lor (G \cdot W)$
3. $\sim P \lor \sim W$ / $\sim E$
4. $(\sim E \lor B) \cdot (\sim E \lor P)$ 1, Dist
5. $(\sim E \lor P) \cdot (\sim E \lor B)$ 4, Com
6. $\sim E \lor P$ 5, Simp
7. $(\sim E \lor G) \cdot (\sim E \lor W)$ 2, Dist
8. $(\sim E \lor W) \cdot (\sim E \lor G)$ 7, Com
9. $\sim E \lor W$ 8, Simp
10. $(\sim E \lor P) \cdot (\sim E \lor W)$ 6, 9, Conj
11. $\sim E \lor (P \cdot W)$ 10, Dist
12. $(P \cdot W) \lor \sim E$ 11, Com
13. $\sim (P \cdot W)$ 3, DM
14. $\sim E$ 12, 13, DS

I.

(1) 4. 1, Equiv
    5. 2, Exp
    6. 3, 5, MT
    7. 4, 6, DS
    8. 7, Com
    9. 8, Simp

(4) 4. 1, Com
    5. 4, Exp
    6. 3, 5, MP
    7. 6, Trans
    8. 2, DN, Impl
    9. 7, 8, HS
    10. 9, Impl
    11. 10, DN

II.

(1)
1. $(J \cdot R) \supset H$
2. $(R \supset H) \supset M$
3. $\sim(P \vee \sim J)$ / $M \cdot \sim P$
4. $J \supset (R \supset H)$ 1, Exp
5. $J \supset M$ 2, 4, HS
6. $\sim P \cdot J$ 3, DM, DN
7. $\sim P$ 6, Simp
8. J 6, Com, Simp
9. M 5, 8, MP
10. $M \cdot \sim P$ 7, 9, Conj

(4)
1. $\sim(U \cdot W) \supset X$
2. $U \supset \sim U$ / $\sim(U \vee \sim X)$
3. $\sim U \vee \sim U$ 2, Impl
4. $\sim U$ 3, Taut
5. $\sim U \vee \sim W$ 4, Add
6. $\sim(U \cdot W)$ 5, DM
7. X 1, 6, MP
8. $\sim U \cdot X$ 4, 7, Conj
9. $\sim U \cdot \sim\sim X$ 8, DN
10. $\sim(U \vee \sim X)$ 9, DM

(7)
1. $M \supset (U \supset H)$
2. $(H \vee \sim U) \supset F$ / $M \supset F$
3. $(\sim U \vee H) \supset F$ 2, Com
4. $(U \supset H) \supset F$ 3, Impl
5. $M \supset F$ 1, 4, HS

(10)
1. $J \supset (G \supset L)$ / $G \supset (J \supset L)$
2. $(J \cdot G) \supset L$ 1, Exp
3. $(G \cdot J) \supset L$ 2, Com
4. $G \supset (J \supset L)$ 3, Exp

(22)
1. $(O \supset R) \supset S$
2. $(P \supset R) \supset \sim S$ / $\sim R$
3. $S \supset \sim(P \supset R)$ 2, Trans
4. $(O \supset R) \supset \sim(P \supset R)$ 1, 3, HS
5. $\sim(O \supset R) \vee \sim(P \supset R)$ 4, Impl
6. $\sim(\sim O \vee R) \vee \sim(\sim P \vee R)$ 5, Impl
7. $(O \cdot \sim R) \vee (P \cdot \sim R)$ 6, DM, DN
8. $(O \vee P) \cdot \sim R$ 7, Com, Dist, Com
9. $\sim R$ 8, Com, Simp

(25)
1. $(S \vee T) \supset (S \supset \sim T)$
2. $(S \supset \sim T) \supset (T \supset K)$
3. $S \vee T$ / $S \vee K$
4. $S \supset \sim T$ 1, 3, MP
5. $T \supset K$ 2, 4, MP
6. $\sim S \supset T$ 3, DN, Impl
7. $\sim S \supset K$ 5, 6, HS
8. $S \vee K$ 7, Impl, DN

(13)
1. $(I \supset E) \supset C$
2. $C \supset \sim C$ / I
3. $\sim C \vee \sim C$ 2, Impl
4. $\sim C$ 3, Taut
5. $\sim(I \supset E)$ 1, 4, MT
6. $\sim(\sim I \vee E)$ 5, Impl
7. $I \cdot \sim E$ 6, DM, DN
8. I 7, Simp

(16)
1. $Q \supset (W \cdot D)$ / $Q \supset W$
2. $\sim Q \vee (W \cdot D)$ 1, Impl
3. $(\sim Q \vee W) \cdot (\sim Q \vee D)$ 2, Dist
4. $\sim Q \vee W$ 3, Simp
5. $Q \supset W$ 4, Impl

(19)
1. $I \vee (N \cdot F)$
2. $I \supset F$ / F
3. $(I \vee N) \cdot (I \vee F)$ 1, Dist
4. $I \vee F$ 3, Com, Simp
5. $\sim I \supset F$ 4, Impl
6. $\sim F \supset \sim I$ 2, Trans
7. $\sim F \supset F$ 5, 6, HS
8. $F \vee F$ 7, Impl, DN
9. F 8, Taut

(28) 1. $H \equiv I$
2. $H \supset (I \supset F)$
3. $\sim(H \lor I) \supset F$ / F
4. $(H \cdot I) \lor (\sim H \cdot \sim I)$ 1, Equiv
5. $(H \cdot I) \supset F$ 2, Exp
6. $(\sim H \cdot \sim I) \supset F$ 3, DM
7. $[(H \cdot I) \supset F] \cdot [(\sim H \cdot \sim I) \supset F]$ 5, 6, Conj
8. $F \lor F$ 4, 7, CD
9. F 8, Taut

(30) 1. $P \supset A$
2. $Q \supset B$ / $(P \lor Q) \supset (A \lor B)$
3. $\sim P \lor A$ 1, Impl
4. $\sim Q \lor B$ 2, Impl
5. $(\sim P \lor A) \lor B$ 3, Add
6. $(\sim Q \lor B) \lor A$ 4, Add
7. $\sim P \lor (A \lor B)$ 5, Assoc
8. $\sim Q \lor (A \lor B)$ 6, Assoc, Com
9. $[\sim P \lor (A \lor B)] \cdot [\sim Q \lor (A \lor B)]$ 7, 8, Conj
10. $(\sim P \cdot \sim Q) \lor (A \lor B)$ 9, Com, Dist
11. $\sim(P \lor Q) \lor (A \lor B)$ 10, DM
12. $(P \lor Q) \supset (A \lor B)$ 11, Impl

III.

(1) 1. $D \supset C$
2. $\sim(C \cdot \sim S)$ / $D \supset S$
3. $\sim C \lor \sim\sim S$ 2, DM
4. $C \supset \sim\sim S$ 3, Impl
5. $C \supset S$ 4, DN
6. $D \supset S$ 1, 5, HS

(4) 1. $D \supset P$ / $(I \cdot D) \supset P$
2. $\sim D \lor P$ 1, Impl
3. $(\sim D \lor P) \lor \sim I$ 2, Add
4. $\sim I \lor (\sim D \lor P)$ 3, Com
5. $(\sim I \lor \sim D) \lor P$ 4, Assoc
6. $\sim(I \cdot D) \lor P$ 5, DM
7. $(I \cdot D) \supset P$ 6, Impl

(7) 1. $G \supset A$
2. $G \supset L$ / $G \supset (A \cdot L)$
3. $\sim G \lor A$ 1, Impl
4. $\sim G \lor L$ 2, Impl
5. $(\sim G \lor A) \cdot (\sim G \lor L)$ 3, 4, Conj
6. $\sim G \lor (A \cdot L)$ 5, Dist
7. $G \supset (A \cdot L)$ 6, Impl

(10) 1. $(P \cdot D) \equiv C$
2. $\sim(C \lor \sim P)$ / $\sim D$
3. $[(P \cdot D) \supset C] \cdot [C \supset (P \cdot D)]$ 1, Equiv
4. $(P \cdot D) \supset C$ 3, Simp
5. $\sim C \cdot \sim\sim P$ 2, DM
6. $\sim C$ 5, Simp
7. $\sim(P \cdot D)$ 4, 6, MT
8. $\sim P \lor \sim D$ 7, DM
9. $\sim\sim P \cdot \sim C$ 5, Com
10. $\sim\sim P$ 9, Simp
11. $\sim D$ 8, 10, DS

Exercise 7.5

I.

(1)
1. $N \supset O$
2. $N \supset P$ / $N \supset (O \cdot P)$
  | 3. N ACP
  | 4. O 1, 3, MP
  | 5. P 2, 3, MP
  | 6. $O \cdot P$ 4, 5, Conj
7. $N \supset (O \cdot P)$ 3–6, CP

(4)
1. $(G \vee H) \supset (S \cdot T)$
2. $(T \vee U) \supset (C \cdot D)$ / $G \supset C$
  | 3. G ACP
  | 4. $G \vee H$ 3, Add
  | 5. $S \cdot T$ 1, 4, MP
  | 6. T 5, Com, Simp
  | 7. $T \vee U$ 6, Add
  | 8. $C \cdot D$ 2, 7, MP
  | 9. C 8, Simp
10. $G \supset C$ 3–9, CP

(10)
1. $C \supset (A \cdot D)$
2. $B \supset (A \cdot E)$ / $(C \vee B) \supset A$
  | 3. $C \vee B$ ACP
  | 4. $[C \supset (A \cdot D)] \cdot [B \supset (A \cdot E)]$ 1, 2, Conj
  | 5. $(A \cdot D) \vee (A \cdot E)$ 3, 4, CD
  | 6. $A \cdot (D \vee E)$ 5, Dist
  | 7. A 6, Simp
8. $(C \vee B) \supset A$ 3–7, CP

(13)
1. $R \supset B$
2. $R \supset (B \supset F)$
3. $B \supset (F \supset H)$ / $R \supset H$
  | 4. R ACP
  | 5. B 1, 4, MP
  | 6. $B \supset F$ 2, 4, MP
  | 7. F 5, 6, MP
  | 8. $F \supset H$ 3, 5, MP
  | 9. H 7, 8, MP
10. $R \supset H$ 4–9, CP

(7)
1. $M \vee (N \cdot O)$ / $\sim N \supset M$
  | 2. $\sim M$ ACP
  | 3. $N \cdot O$ 1, 2, DS
  | 4. N 3, Simp
5. $\sim M \supset N$ 2, 4, CP
6. $\sim N \supset M$ 5, Trans, DN

(16)
1. $Q \supset (R \supset S)$
2. $Q \supset (T \supset \sim U)$
3. $U \supset (R \vee T)$ / $Q \supset (U \supset S)$
  | 4. Q ACP
  | | 5. U ACP
  | | 6. $R \supset S$ 1, 4, MP
  | | 7. $T \supset \sim U$ 2, 4, MP
  | | 8. $\sim T$ 5, 7, DN, MT
  | | 9. $R \vee T$ 3, 5, MP
  | | 10. R 8, 9, Com, DS
  | | 11. S 6, 10, MP
  | 12. $U \supset S$ 5–11, CP
13. $Q \supset (U \supset S)$ 4–12, CP

(19)
1. $P \supset [(L \vee M) \supset (N \cdot O)]$
2. $(O \vee T) \supset W$ / $P \supset (M \supset W)$
  | 3. P ACP
  | | 4. M ACP
  | | 5. $(L \vee M) \supset (N \cdot O)$ 1, 3, MP
  | | 6. $M \vee L$ 4, Add
  | | 7. $L \vee M$ 6, Com
  | | 8. $N \cdot O$ 5, 7, MP
  | | 9. O 8, Com, Simp
  | | 10. $O \vee T$ 9, Add
  | | 11. W 2, 10, MP
  | 12. $M \supset W$ 4–11, CP
13. $P \supset (M \supset W)$ 3–12, CP

II.

(1) 1. *H* ⊃ *D*
    2. *U* ⊃ *S*   / (*H* • *U*) ⊃ (*S* • *D*)
    | 3. *H* • *U*   ACP
    | 4. *H*   3, Simp
    | 5. *D*   1, 4, MP
    | 6. *U*   3, Com, Simp
    | 7. *S*   2, 6, MP
    | 8. *S* • *D*   5, 7, Conj
    9. (*H* • *U*) ⊃ (*S* • *D*)   3–8, CP

(4) 1. *J* ⊃ *D*
    2. (*J* • *D*) ⊃ *C*
    3. (*N* • *C*) ⊃ *I*   / *J* ⊃ (*N* ⊃ *I*)
    | | 4. *J*   ACP
    | | 5. *N*   ACP
    | | 6. *D*   1, 4, MP
    | | 7. *J* • *D*   4, 6, Conj
    | | 8. *C*   2, 7, MP
    | | 9. *N* • *C*   5, 8, Conj
    | | 10. *I*   3, 9, MP
    | 11. *N* ⊃ *I*   5–10, CP
    12. *J* ⊃ (*N* ⊃ *I*)   4–11, CP

Exercise 7.6
I.

(1) 1. (*S* ∨ *T*) ⊃ ~*S* / ~*S*
    | 2. *S*   AIP
    | 3. *S* ∨ *T*   2, Add
    | 4. ~*S*   1, 3, MP
    | 5. *S* • ~*S*   2, 4, Conj
    6. ~*S*   2–5, IP

(4) 1. *H* ⊃ (*L* ⊃ *K*)
    2. *L* ⊃ (*K* ⊃ ~*L*)   / ~*H* ∨ ~*L*
    | 3. *H* • *L*   AIP
    | 4. *H*   3, Simp
    | 5. *L* ⊃ *K*   1, 4, MP
    | 6. *L*   3, Com, Simp
    | 7. *K* ⊃ ~*L*   2, 6, MP
    | 8. *K*   5, 6, MP
    | 9. ~*L*   7, 8, MP
    | 10. *L* • ~*L*   6, 9, Conj
    11. ~(*H* • *L*)   3–10, IP
    12. ~*H* ∨ ~*L*   11, DM

(10) 1. *K*   / *S* ⊃ (*T* ⊃ *S*)
    | 2. *S*   ACP
    | 3. *S* ∨ ~*T*   2, Add
    | 4. ~*T* ∨ *S*   3, Com
    | 5. *T* ⊃ *S*   4, Impl
    6. *S* ⊃ (*T* ⊃ *S*)   2–5, CP

(13) 1. [*C* ⊃ (*D* ⊃ *C*)] ⊃ *E*   / *E*
    | 2. *C*   ACP
    | 3. *C* ∨ ~*D*   2, Add
    | 4. ~*D* ∨ *C*   3, Com
    | 5. *D* ⊃ *C*   4, Impl
    6. *C* ⊃ (*D* ⊃ *C*)   2–5, CP
    7. *E*   1, 6, MP

(7) 1. (*E* ∨ *F*) ⊃ (*C* • *D*)
    2. (*D* ∨ *G*) ⊃ *H*
    3. *E* ∨ *G*   / *H*
    | 4. ~*H*   AIP
    | 5. ~(*D* ∨ *G*)   2, 4, MT
    | 6. ~*D* • ~*G*   5, DM
    | 7. ~*D*   6, Simp
    | 8. ~*D* ∨ ~*C*   7, Add
    | 9. ~*C* ∨ ~*D*   8, Com
    | 10. ~(*C* • *D*)   9, DM
    | 11. ~(*E* ∨ *F*)   1, 10, MT
    | 12. ~*E* • ~*F*   11, DM
    | 13. ~*E*   12, Simp
    | 14. *G*   3, 13, DS
    | 15. ~*G*   6, Com, Simp
    | 16. *G* • ~*G*   14, 15, Conj
    17. *H*   4–16, IP, DN

(16) 1. $(N \lor O) \supset (C \cdot D)$
    2. $(D \lor K) \supset (P \lor \sim C)$
    3. $(P \lor G) \supset \sim (N \cdot D)$ / $\sim N$

4. N	AIP
5. $N \lor O$	4, Add
6. $C \cdot D$	1, 5, MP
7. D	6, Com, Simp
8. $D \lor K$	7, Add
9. $P \lor \sim C$	2, 8, MP
10. C	6, Simp
11. P	9, 10, Com, DN, DS
12. $P \lor G$	11, Add
13. $\sim (N \cdot D)$	3, 12, MP
14. $\sim N \lor \sim D$	13, DM
15. $\sim D$	4, 14, DN, DS
16. $D \cdot \sim D$	7, 15, Conj
17. $\sim N$	4–16, IP

(19) 1. $A \supset [(N \lor \sim N) \supset (S \lor T)]$
    2. $T \supset \sim (F \lor \sim F)$ / $A \supset S$

3. $A \cdot \sim S$	AIP
4. A	3, Simp
5. $(N \lor \sim N) \supset (S \lor T)$	1, 4, MP
6. N	ACP
7. $N \lor N$	6, Add
8. N	7, Taut
9. $N \supset N$	6–8, CP
10. $\sim N \lor N$	9, Impl
11. $N \lor \sim N$	10, Com
12. $S \lor T$	5, 11, MP
13. $\sim S$	3, Com, Simp
14. T	12, 13, DS
15. $\sim (F \lor \sim F)$	2, 14, MP
16. $\sim F \cdot F$	15, DM, DN
17. $\sim (A \cdot \sim S)$	3–16, IP
18. $\sim A \lor S$	17, DM, DN
19. $A \supset S$	18, Impl

II.

(1) 1. $(C \cdot R) \supset (I \cdot D)$
    2. $R \supset \sim D$ / $\sim C \lor \sim R$

3. $C \cdot R$	AIP
4. $I \cdot D$	1, 3, MP
5. $D \cdot I$	4, Com
6. D	5, Simp
7. $R \cdot C$	3, Com
8. R	7, Simp
9. $\sim D$	2, 8, MP
10. $D \cdot \sim D$	6, 9, Conj
11. $\sim (C \cdot R)$	3–10, IP
12. $\sim C \lor \sim R$	11, DM

(4) 1. $(Z \supset C) \supset B$
    2. $(V \supset Z) \supset B$ / B

3. $\sim B$	AIP
4. $\sim (Z \supset C)$	1, 3, MT
5. $\sim (\sim Z \lor C)$	4, Impl
6. $\sim \sim Z \cdot \sim C$	5, DM
7. $\sim \sim Z$	6, Simp
8. $\sim (V \supset Z)$	2, 3, MT
9. $\sim (\sim V \lor Z)$	8, Impl
10. $\sim \sim V \cdot \sim Z$	9, DM
11. $\sim Z \cdot \sim \sim V$	10, Com
12. $\sim Z$	11, Simp
13. $\sim Z \cdot \sim \sim Z$	7, 12, Conj
14. $\sim \sim B$	3–13, IP
15. B	14, DN

Exercise 7.7

(1) / $P \supset [(P \supset Q) \supset Q]$
    1. P ACP
       2. $P \supset Q$ ACP
       3. Q 1, 2, MP
    4. $(P \supset Q) \supset Q$ 2–3, CP
   5. $P \supset [(P \supset Q) \supset Q]$ 1–4, CP

(4) / $(P \supset Q) \supset [(P \cdot R) \supset (Q \cdot R)]$
    1. $P \supset Q$ ACP
       2. $P \cdot R$ ACP
       3. P 2, Simp
       4. Q 1, 3, MP
       5. R 2, Com, Simp
       6. $Q \cdot R$ 4, 5, Conj
    7. $(P \cdot R) \supset (Q \cdot R)$ 2–6, CP
   8. $(P \supset Q) \supset [(P \cdot R) \supset (Q \cdot R)]$ 1–7, CP

(7) / $(P \supset Q) \vee (\sim Q \supset P)$
    1. $\sim[(P \supset Q) \vee (\sim Q \supset P)]$ AIP
    2. $\sim(P \supset Q) \cdot \sim(\sim Q \supset P)$ 1, DM
    3. $\sim(\sim P \vee Q) \cdot \sim(Q \vee P)$ 2, Impl, DN
    4. $(P \cdot \sim Q) \cdot (\sim Q \cdot \sim P)$ 3, DM, DN
    5. $P \cdot \sim Q$ 4, Simp
    6. $\sim Q \cdot \sim P$ 4, Com, Simp
    7. P 5, Simp
    8. $\sim P$ 6, Com, Simp
    9. $P \cdot \sim P$ 7, 8, Conj
   10. $(P \supset Q) \vee (\sim Q \supset P)$ 1–9, IP, DN

(10) / $[\sim(P \cdot \sim Q) \cdot \sim Q] \supset \sim P$
    1. $\sim(P \cdot \sim Q) \cdot \sim Q$ ACP
    2. $\sim(P \cdot \sim Q)$ 1, Simp
    3. $\sim P \vee Q$ 2, DM, DN
    4. $\sim Q$ 1, Com, Simp
    5. $\sim P$ 3, 4, Com, DS
   6. $[\sim(P \cdot \sim Q) \cdot \sim Q] \supset \sim P$ 1–5, CP

(13) / $(P \supset Q) \supset [(P \supset \sim Q) \supset \sim P]$
    1. $P \supset Q$ ACP
       2. $P \supset \sim Q$ ACP
       3. $Q \supset \sim P$ 2, Trans, DN
       4. $P \supset \sim P$ 1, 3, HS
       5. $\sim P \vee \sim P$ 4, Impl
       6. $\sim P$ 5, Taut
    7. $(P \supset \sim Q) \supset \sim P$ 2–6, CP
   8. $(P \supset Q) \supset [(P \supset \sim Q) \supset \sim P]$ 1–7, CP

(16) / $\sim[(P \supset \sim P) \cdot (\sim P \supset P)]$
    1. $(P \supset \sim P) \cdot (\sim P \supset P)$ AIP
    2. $(\sim P \vee \sim P) \cdot (P \vee P)$ 1, Impl, DN
    3. $\sim P \cdot P$ 2, Taut
   4. $\sim[(P \supset \sim P) \cdot (\sim P \supset P)]$ 1–3, IP

(19) / $P \equiv [P \vee (Q \cdot \sim Q)]$
    1. P ACP
    2. $P \vee (Q \cdot \sim Q)$ 1, Add
   3. $P \supset [P \vee (Q \cdot \sim Q)]$ 1–2, CP
    4. $P \vee (Q \cdot \sim Q)$ ACP
       5. $\sim P$ AIP
       6. $Q \cdot \sim Q$ 4, 5, DS
    7. P 5–6, IP, DN
   8. $[P \vee (Q \cdot \sim Q)] \supset P$ 4–7, CP
   9. {line 3} $\cdot$ {line 8}   3, 8, Conj
   10. $P \equiv [P \vee (Q \cdot \sim Q]$ 9, Equiv

Exercise 8.1

1. *Ce*
4. (*x*)(*Nx* ⊃ ∼*Bx*)
7. ∼*Cq* ⊃ *Gt*
10. (∃*x*)(*Mx* • ∼*Ex*)
13. (*x*)(*Px* ⊃ *Gx*)

16. (*x*)[(*Wx* • *Cx*) ⊃ *Rx*]
19. (*x*)[(*Vx* ∨ *Cx*) ⊃ (*Sx* • *Ix*)]
22. (∃*x*)[(*Fx* • *Rx*) • *Ex*]
25. (∃*x*)(*Wx* • *Tx*) ⊃ (*Gp* ∨ *Gh*)
28. (*x*)[(*Sx* ∨ *Dx*) ⊃ (*Ix* • *Ex*)]

31. (*x*)[(*Ex* • *Mx*) ⊃ *Wx*] ⊃ (*x*)[(*Mx* • ∼*Ex*) ⊃ *Lx*]
34. (*x*){[(*Px* ∨ *Ax*) • *Sx*] ∨ [(*Cx* ∨ *Rx*) ⊃ *Lx*]}

Exercise 8.2

I.

(1)
1. (*x*)(*Ax* ⊃ *Bx*)
2. (*x*)(*Bx* ⊃ *Cx*)   / (*x*)(*Ax* ⊃ *Cx*)
3. *Ax* ⊃ *Bx*   1, UI
4. *Bx* ⊃ *Cx*   2, UI
5. *Ax* ⊃ *Cx*   3, 4, HS
6. (*x*)(*Ax* ⊃ *Cx*)   5, UG

(4)
1. (*x*)[*Ax* ⊃ (*Bx* ∨ *Cx*)]
2. *Ag* • ∼*Bg*   / *Cg*
3. *Ag* ⊃ (*Bg* ∨ *Cg*)   1, UI
4. *Ag*   2, Simp
5. *Bg* ∨ *Cg*   3, 4, MP
6. ∼*Bg*   2, Com, Simp
7. *Cg*   5, 6, DS

(7)
1. (*x*)[*Ax* ⊃ (*Bx* ∨ *Cx*)]
2. (∃*x*)(*Ax* • ∼*Cx*)   / (∃*x*)*Bx*
3. *Am* • ∼*Cm*   2, EI
4. *Am* ⊃ (*Bm* ∨ *Cm*)   1, UI
5. *Am*   3, Simp
6. *Bm* ∨ *Cm*   4, 5, MP
7. ∼*Cm*   3, Com, Simp
8. *Bm*   6, 7, Com, DS
9. (∃*x*)*Bx*   8, EG

(10)
1. (*x*)(*Bx* ∨ *Ax*)
2. (*x*)(*Bx* ⊃ *Ax*)   / (*x*)*Ax*
3. *Bx* ∨ *Ax*   1, UI
4. *Bx* ⊃ *Ax*   2, UI
5. *Ax* ∨ *Bx*   3, Com
6. ∼*Ax* ⊃ *Bx*   5, Impl
7. ∼*Ax* ⊃ *Ax*   4, 6, HS
8. *Ax* ∨ *Ax*   7, Impl, DN
9. *Ax*   8, Taut
10. (*x*)*Ax*   9, UG

(13)
1. (∃*x*)*Ax* ⊃ (*x*)*Bx*
2. (∃*x*)*Cx* ⊃ (∃*x*)*Dx*
3. *An* • *Cn*   / (∃*x*)(*Bx* • *Dx*)
4. *An*   3, Simp
5. (∃*x*)*Ax*   4, EG
6. (*x*)*Bx*   1, 5, MP
7. *Cn*   3, Com, Simp
8. (∃*x*)*Cx*   7, EG
9. (∃*x*)*Dx*   2, 8, MP
10. *Dm*   9, EI
11. *Bm*   6, UI
12. *Bm* • *Dm*   10, 11, Conj
13. (∃*x*)(*Bx* • *Dx*)   12, EG

(15)
1. (∃*x*)*Ax* ⊃ (*x*)(*Bx* ⊃ *Cx*)
2. (∃*x*)*Dx* ⊃ (∃*x*)∼*Cx*
3. (∃*x*)(*Ax* • *Dx*)   / (∃*x*)∼*Bx*
4. *Am* • *Dm*   3, EI
5. *Am*   4, Simp
6. *Dm*   4, Com, Simp
7. (∃*x*)*Ax*   5, EG
8. (∃*x*)*Dx*   6, EG
9. (*x*)(*Bx* ⊃ *Cx*)   1, 7, MP
10. (∃*x*)∼*Cx*   2, 8, MP
11. ∼*Cn*   10, EI
12. *Bn* ⊃ *Cn*   9, UI
13. ∼*Bn*   11, 12, MT
14. (∃*x*)∼*Bx*   13, EG

II.

(1)
1. (*x*)(*Ox* ⊃ *Sx*)
2. (*x*)(*Ox* ⊃ *Fx*)   / (*x*)[*Ox* ⊃ (*Sx* • *Fx*)]
3. *Ox* ⊃ *Sx*   1, UI
4. *Ox* ⊃ *Fx*   2, UI
5. ∼*Ox* ∨ *Sx*   3, Impl
6. ∼*Ox* ∨ *Fx*   4, Impl
7. (∼*Ox* ∨ *Sx*) • (∼*Ox* ∨ *Fx*)   5, 6, Conj
8. ∼*Ox* ∨ (*Sx* • *Fx*)   7, Dist
9. *Ox* ⊃ (*Sx* • *Fx*)   8, Impl
10. (*x*)[*Ox* ⊃ (*Sx* • *Fx*)]   9, UG

(4)
1. $(x)(Cx \supset Vx) \cdot (x)(Px \supset Fx)$
2. $(\exists x)(Cx \cdot Gx) \cdot (\exists x)(Px \cdot Gx)$ / $(\exists x)(Vx \cdot Gx) \cdot (\exists x)(Fx \cdot Gx)$
3. $(\exists x)(Cx \cdot Gx)$ 2, Simp
4. $Cm \cdot Gm$ 3, EI
5. $(\exists x)(Px \cdot Gx)$ 2, Com, Simp
6. $Pn \cdot Gn$ 5, EI
7. $(x)(Cx \supset Vx)$ 1, Simp
8. $Cm \supset Vm$ 7, UI
9. Cm 4, Simp
10. Vm 8, 9, MP
11. Gm 4, Com, Simp
12. $Vm \cdot Gm$ 10, 11, Conj
13. $(\exists x)(Vx \cdot Gx)$ 12, EG
14. $(x)(Px \supset Fx)$ 1, Com, Simp
15. $Pn \supset Fn$ 14, UI
16. Pn 6, Simp
17. Fn 15, 16, MP
18. Gn 6, Com, Simp
19. $Fn \cdot Gn$ 17, 18, Conj
20. $(\exists x)(Fx \cdot Gx)$ 19, EG
21. $(\exists x)(Vx \cdot Gx) \cdot (\exists x)(Fx \cdot Gx)$ 13, 20, Conj

(7)
1. $(x)[Gx \supset (Ix \cdot Px)]$
2. $(x)[(Ix \cdot Px) \supset Rx]$
3. $Ga \cdot Gc$ / $Ra \cdot Rc$
4. $Gx \supset (Ix \cdot Px)$ 1, UI
5. $(Ix \cdot Px) \supset Rx$ 2, UI
6. $Gx \supset Rx$ 4, 5, HS
7. $(x)(Gx \supset Rx)$ 6, UG
8. $Ga \supset Ra$ 7, UI
9. Ga 3, Simp
10. Ra 8, 9, MP
11. $Gc \supset Rc$ 7, UI
12. Gc 3, Com, Simp
13. Rc 11, 12, MP
14. $Ra \cdot Rc$ 10, 13, Conj

(10)
1. $(x)[(Ax \cdot Kx) \supset Rx] \supset (x)(Gx \supset Sx)$
2. $(x)[(Ax \cdot Kx) \supset Fx] \supset (x)(Gx \supset Px)$
3. $(x)[(Ax \cdot Kx) \supset (Rx \cdot Fx)]$ / $(x)[Gx \supset (Sx \cdot Px)]$
4. $(Ax \cdot Kx) \supset (Rx \cdot Fx)$ 3, UI
5. $\sim(Ax \cdot Kx) \vee (Rx \cdot Fx)$ 4, Impl
6. $[\sim(Ax \cdot Kx) \vee Rx] \cdot [\sim(Ax \cdot Kx) \vee Fx]$ 5, Dist
7. $\sim(Ax \cdot Kx) \vee Rx$ 6, Simp
8. $\sim(Ax \cdot Kx) \vee Fx$ 6, Com, Simp
9. $(Ax \cdot Kx) \supset Rx$ 7, Impl
10. $(Ax \cdot Kx) \supset Fx$ 8, Impl
11. $(x)[(Ax \cdot Kx) \supset Rx]$ 9, UG
12. $(x)[(Ax \cdot Kx) \supset Fx]$ 10, UG
13. $(x)(Gx \supset Sx)$ 1, 11, MP
14. $(x)(Gx \supset Px)$ 2, 12, MP
15. $Gx \supset Sx$ 13, UI
16. $Gx \supset Px$ 14, UI
17. $\sim Gx \vee Sx$ 15, Impl
18. $\sim Gx \vee Px$ 16, Impl
19. $(\sim Gx \vee Sx) \cdot (\sim Gx \vee Px)$ 17, 18, Conj
20. $\sim Gx \vee (Sx \cdot Px)$ 19, Dist
21. $Gx \supset (Sx \cdot Px)$ 20, Impl
22. $(x)[Gx \supset (Sx \cdot Px)]$ 21, UG

Exercise 8.3

I.

(1) 1. $(x)Ax \supset (\exists x)Bx$
     2. $(x)\sim Bx$ / $(\exists x)\sim Ax$
     3. $\sim(\exists x)Bx$ 2, CQ
     4. $\sim(x)Ax$ 1, 3, MT
     5. $(\exists x)\sim Ax$ 4, CQ

(4) 1. $(\exists x)Ax \lor (\exists x)(Bx \cdot Cx)$
     2. $\sim(\exists x)Bx$ / $(\exists x)Ax$
     3. $(x)\sim Bx$ 2, CQ
     4. $\sim Bx$ 3, UI
     5. $\sim Bx \lor \sim Cx$ 4, Add
     6. $\sim(Bx \cdot Cx)$ 5, DM
     7. $(x)\sim(Bx \cdot Cx)$ 6, UG
     8. $\sim(\exists x)(Bx \cdot Cx)$ 7, CQ
     9. $(\exists x)Ax$ 1, 8, Com, DS

(7) 1. $(x)(Ax \supset Bx)$
     2. $\sim(x)Cx \lor (x)Ax$
     3. $\sim(x)Bx$ / $(\exists x)\sim Cx$
     4. $(\exists x)\sim Bx$ 3, CQ
     5. $\sim Bm$ 4, EI
     6. $Am \supset Bm$ 1, UI
     7. $\sim Am$ 5, 6, MT
     8. $(\exists x)\sim Ax$ 7, EG
     9. $\sim(x)Ax$ 8, CQ
     10. $\sim(x)Cx$ 2, 9, Com, DS
     11. $(\exists x)\sim Cx$ 10, CQ

(10) 1. $\sim(\exists x)(Ax \cdot \sim Bx)$
      2. $\sim(\exists x)(Bx \cdot \sim Cx)$ / $(x)(Ax \supset Cx)$
      3. $(x)\sim(Ax \cdot \sim Bx)$ 1, CQ
      4. $(x)\sim(Bx \cdot \sim Cx)$ 2, CQ
      5. $\sim(Ax \cdot \sim Bx)$ 3, UI
      6. $\sim(Bx \cdot \sim Cx)$ 4, UI
      7. $\sim Ax \lor Bx$ 5, DM, DN
      8. $\sim Bx \lor Cx$ 6, DM, DN
      9. $Ax \supset Bx$ 7, Impl
      10. $Bx \supset Cx$ 8, Impl
      11. $Ax \supset Cx$ 9, 10, HS
      12. $(x)(Ax \supset Cx)$ 11, UG

(13) 1. $(x)(Ax \cdot \sim Bx) \supset (\exists x)Cx$
      2. $\sim(\exists x)(Cx \lor Bx)$ / $\sim(x)Ax$
      3. $(x)\sim(Cx \lor Bx)$ 2, CQ
      4. $\sim(Cx \lor Bx)$ 3, UI
      5. $\sim Cx \cdot \sim Bx$ 4, DM
      6. $\sim Cx$ 5, Simp
      7. $(x)\sim Cx$ 6, UG
      8. $\sim(\exists x)Cx$ 7, CQ
      9. $\sim(x)(Ax \cdot \sim Bx)$ 1, 8, MT
      10. $(\exists x)\sim(Ax \cdot \sim Bx)$ 9, CQ
      11. $\sim(Am \cdot \sim Bm)$ 10, EI
      12. $\sim Am \lor Bm$ 11, DM, DN
      13. $\sim Bx$ 5, Com, Simp
      14. $(x)\sim Bx$ 13, UG
      15. $\sim Bm$ 14, UI
      16. $\sim Am$ 12, 15, Com, DS
      17. $(\exists x)\sim Ax$ 16, EG
      18. $\sim(x)Ax$ 17, CQ

(15) 1. $\sim(\exists x)(Ax \lor Bx)$
      2. $(\exists x)Cx \supset (\exists x)Ax$
      3. $(\exists x)Dx \supset (\exists x)Bx$ / $\sim(\exists x)(Cx \lor Dx)$
      4. $(x)\sim(Ax \lor Bx)$ 1, CQ
      5. $\sim(Ax \lor Bx)$ 4, UI
      6. $\sim Ax \cdot \sim Bx$ 5, DM
      7. $\sim Ax$ 6, Simp
      8. $\sim Bx$ 6, Com, Simp
      9. $(x)\sim Ax$ 7, UG
      10. $(x)\sim Bx$ 8, UG
      11. $\sim(\exists x)Ax$ 9, CQ
      12. $\sim(\exists x)Bx$ 10, CQ

13. $\sim(\exists x)Cx$ 2, 11, MT
14. $\sim(\exists x)Dx$ 3, 12, MT
15. $(x)\sim Cx$ 13, CQ
16. $(x)\sim Dx$ 14, CQ
17. $\sim Cx$ 15, UI
18. $\sim Dx$ 16, UI
19. $\sim Cx \cdot \sim Dx$ 17, 18, Conj
20. $\sim(Cx \vee Dx)$ 19, DM
21. $(x)\sim(Cx \vee Dx)$ 20, UG
22. $\sim(\exists x)(Cx \vee Dx)$ 21, CQ

II.

(1)   1. $(x)[Px \supset (Hx \vee Nx)] \supset \sim(\exists x)Cx$
        2. Cf / $(\exists x)(Px \cdot \sim Nx)$
        3. $(\exists x)Cx$ 2, EG
        4. $\sim(x)[Px \supset (Hx \vee Nx)]$ 1, 3, DN, MT
        5. $(\exists x)\sim[Px \supset (Hx \vee Nx)]$ 4, CQ
        6. $\sim[Pm \supset (Hm \vee Nm)]$ 5, EI
        7. $\sim[\sim Pm \vee (Hm \vee Nm)]$ 6, Impl
        8. $Pm \cdot \sim(Hm \vee Nm)$ 7, DM, DN
        9. $Pm \cdot (\sim Hm \cdot \sim Nm)$ 8, DM
      10. Pm 9, Simp
      11. $\sim Hm \cdot \sim Nm$ 9, Com, Simp
      12. $\sim Nm$ 11, Com, Simp
      13. $Pm \cdot \sim Nm$ 10, 12, Conj
      14. $(\exists x)(Px \cdot \sim Nx)$ 13, EG

(4)   1. $(\exists x)(Gx \cdot Px) \vee (\exists x)(Sx \cdot Ex)$
        2. $\sim(\exists x)Ex$ / $(\exists x)Px$
        3. $(x)\sim Ex$ 2, CQ
        4. $\sim Ex$ 3, UI
        5. $\sim Ex \vee \sim Sx$ 4, Add
        6. $\sim Sx \vee \sim Ex$ 5, Com
        7. $\sim(Sx \cdot Ex)$ 6, DM
        8. $(x)\sim(Sx \cdot Ex)$ 7, UG
        9. $\sim(\exists x)(Sx \cdot Ex)$ 8, CQ
      10. $(\exists x)(Gx \cdot Px)$ 1, Com, DS
      11. $Gm \cdot Pm$ 10, EI
      12. Pm 11, Com, Simp
      13. $(\exists x)Px$ 12, EG

(7)   1. $(x)(Px \supset Sx) \cdot (x)(Ix \supset Gx)$
        2. $\sim(\exists x)(Sx \cdot Gx)$ / $\sim(\exists x)(Px \cdot Ix)$
        3. $(x)\sim(Sx \cdot Gx)$ 2, CQ
        4. $\sim(Sx \cdot Gx)$ 3, UI
        5. $\sim Sx \vee \sim Gx$ 4, DM
        6. $(x)(Px \supset Sx)$ 1, Simp
        7. $(x)(Ix \supset Gx)$ 1, Com, Simp
        8. $Px \supset Sx$ 6, UI
        9. $Ix \supset Gx$ 7, UI
      10. $\sim Sx \supset \sim Px$ 8, Trans
      11. $\sim Gx \supset \sim Ix$ 9, Trans
      12. $(\sim Sx \supset \sim Px) \cdot (\sim Gx \supset \sim Ix)$ 10, 11, Conj
      13. $\sim Px \vee \sim Ix$ 5, 12, CD
      14. $\sim(Px \cdot Ix)$ 13, DM
      15. $(x)\sim(Px \cdot Ix)$ 14, UG
      16. $\sim(\exists x)(Px \cdot Ix)$ 15, CQ

(10) 1. $\sim(\exists x)[Px \cdot (Gx \lor Hx)]$
      2. $(x)[Nx \supset (Px \cdot Hx)]$
      3. $(\exists x)(Px \cdot Cx) \lor (\exists x)(Px \cdot Nx)$ / $(\exists x)(Cx \cdot \sim Gx)$
      4. $(x)\sim[Px \cdot (Gx \lor Hx)]$ 1, CQ
      5. $\sim[Px \cdot (Gx \lor Hx)]$ 4, UI
      6. $\sim Px \lor \sim(Gx \lor Hx)$ 5, DM
      7. $\sim Px \lor (\sim Gx \cdot \sim Hx)$ 6, DM
      8. $(\sim Px \lor \sim Gx) \cdot (\sim Px \lor \sim Hx)$ 7, Dist
      9. $\sim Px \lor \sim Gx$ 8, Simp
     10. $\sim Px \lor \sim Hx$ 8, Com, Simp
     11. $\sim(Px \cdot Hx)$ 10, DM
     12. $Nx \supset (Px \cdot Hx)$ 2, UI
     13. $\sim Nx$ 11, 12, MT
     14. $\sim Nx \lor \sim Px$ 13, Add
     15. $\sim Px \lor \sim Nx$ 14, Com
     16. $\sim(Px \cdot Nx)$ 15, DM
     17. $(x)\sim(Px \cdot Nx)$ 16, UG
     18. $\sim(\exists x)(Px \cdot Nx)$ 17, CQ
     19. $(\exists x)(Px \cdot Cx)$ 3, 18, Com, DS
     20. $Pm \cdot Cm$ 19, EI
     21. $(x)(\sim Px \lor \sim Gx)$ 9, UG
     22. $\sim Pm \lor \sim Gm$ 21, UI
     23. Pm 20, Simp
     24. $\sim Gm$ 22, 23, DN, DS
     25. Cm 20, Com, Simp
     26. $Cm \cdot \sim Gm$ 24, 25, Conj
     27. $(\exists x)(Cx \cdot \sim Gx)$ 26, EG

Exercise 8.4
I.

(1) 1. $(x)(Ax \supset Bx)$
     2. $(x)(Ax \supset Cx)$ / $(x)[Ax \supset (Bx \cdot Cx)]$
     | 3. Ax ACP
     | 4. $Ax \supset Bx$ 1, UI
     | 5. $Ax \supset Cx$ 2, UI
     | 6. Bx 3, 4, MP
     | 7. Cx 3, 5, MP
     | 8. $Bx \cdot Cx$ 6, 7, Conj
     9. $Ax \supset (Bx \cdot Cx)$ 3–8, CP
    10. $(x)[Ax \supset (Bx \cdot Cx)]$ 9, UG

(4) 1. $(x)(Ax \supset Cx)$
     2. $(\exists x)Cx \supset (\exists x)(Bx \cdot Dx)$ / $(\exists x)Ax \supset (\exists x)Bx$
     | 3. $(\exists x)Ax$ ACP
     | 4. Am 3, EI
     | 5. $Am \supset Cm$ 1, UI
     | 6. Cm 4, 5, MP
     | 7. $(\exists x)Cx$ 6, EG
     | 8. $(\exists x)(Bx \cdot Dx)$ 2, 7, MP
     | 9. $Bn \cdot Dn$ 8, EI
     | 10. Bn 9, Simp
     | 11. $(\exists x)Bx$ 10, EG
    12. $(\exists x)Ax \supset (\exists x)Bx$ 3–11, CP

(7) 1. $(x)[(Ax \lor Bx) \supset Cx]$
    2. $(x)[(Cx \lor Dx) \supset Ex]$ / $(x)(Ax \supset Ex)$
	3. Ax	ACP
	4. $(Ax \lor Bx) \supset Cx$	1, UI
	5. $(Cx \lor Dx) \supset Ex$	2, UI
	6. $Ax \lor Bx$	3, Add
	7. Cx	4, 6, MP
	8. $Cx \lor Dx$	7, Add
	9. Ex	5, 8, MP
10. $Ax \supset Ex$		3–9, CP
11. $(x)(Ax \supset Ex)$		10, UG

(10) 1. $(x)(Ax \supset Bx)$
     2. $Am \lor An$ / $(\exists x)Bx$
	3. $\sim(\exists x)Bx$	AIP
	4. $(x)\sim Bx$	3, CQ
	5. $Am \supset Bm$	1, UI
	6. $An \supset Bn$	1, UI
	7. $(Am \supset Bm) \cdot (An \supset Bn)$	5, 6, Conj
	8. $Bm \lor Bn$	2, 7, CD
	9. $\sim Bm$	4, UI
	10. Bn	8, 9, DS
	11. $\sim Bn$	4, UI
	12. $Bn \cdot \sim Bn$	10, 11, Conj
13. $\sim\sim(\exists x)Bx$		3–12, IP
14. $(\exists x)Bx$		13, DN

(13) 1. $(\exists x)Ax \supset (x)(Bx \supset Cx)$
     2. $(\exists x)Dx \supset (\exists x)Bx$ / $(\exists x)(Ax \cdot Dx) \supset (\exists x)Cx$
	3. $(\exists x)(Ax \cdot Dx)$	ACP
	4. $Am \cdot Dm$	3, EI
	5. Am	4, Simp
	6. $(\exists x)Ax$	5, EG
	7 $(x)(Bx \supset Cx)$	1, 6, MP
	8. Dm	4, Com, Simp
	9. $(\exists x)Dx$	8, EG
	10. $(\exists x)Bx$	2, 9, MP
	11. Bn	10, EI
	12. $Bn \supset Cn$	7, UI
	13. Cn	11, 12, MP
	14. $(\exists x)Cx$	13, EG
15. $(\exists x)(Ax \cdot Dx) \supset (\exists x)Cx$		3–14, CP

(16) 1. $(x)[(Ax \lor Bx) \supset Cx]$
     2. $(\exists x)(\sim Ax \lor Dx) \supset (x)Ex$ / $(x)Cx \lor (x)Ex$
	3. $\sim[(x)Cx \lor (x)Ex]$	AIP
	4. $\sim(x)Cx \cdot \sim(x)Ex$	3, DM
	5. $\sim(x)Cx$	4, Simp
	6. $(\exists x)\sim Cx$	5, CQ
	7. $\sim Cm$	6, EI
	8. $(Am \lor Bm) \supset Cm$	1, UI
	9. $\sim(Am \lor Bm)$	7, 8, MT
	10. $\sim Am \cdot \sim Bm$	9, DM
	11. $\sim Am$	10, Simp
	12. $\sim Am \lor Dm$	11, Add
	13. $(\exists x)(\sim Ax \lor Dx)$	12, EG
	14. $(x)Ex$	2, 13, MP
	15. $\sim(x)Ex$	4, Com, Simp
	16. $(x)Ex \cdot \sim(x)Ex$	14, 15, Conj
17. $(x)Cx \lor (x)Ex$		3–16, IP, DN

(19) 1. $(x)[Bx \supset (Cx \cdot Dx)]$ / $(x)(Ax \supset Bx) \supset (x)(Ax \supset Dx)$

      2. $(x)(Ax \supset Bx)$ ACP

       3. Ax ACP

       4. $Ax \supset Bx$ 2, UI

       5. Bx 3, 4, MP

       6. $Bx \supset (Cx \cdot Dx)$ 1, UI

       7. $Cx \cdot Dx$ 5, 6, MP

       8. Dx 7, Com, Simp

      9. $Ax \supset Dx$ 3–8, CP

    10. $(x)(Ax \supset Dx)$ 9, UG

    11. $(x)(Ax \supset Bx) \supset (x)(Ax \supset Dx)$ 2–10, CP

II.

(1) 1. $(x)(Ax \supset Wx)$

     2. $(x)(Rx \supset Cx)$ / $(x)[(Rx \cdot Ax) \supset (Cx \cdot Wx)]$

       3. $Rx \cdot Ax$ ACP

       4. Rx 3, Simp

       5. Ax 3, Com, Simp

       6. $Ax \supset Wx$ 1, UI

       7. $Rx \supset Cx$ 2, UI

       8. Cx 4, 7, MP

       9. Wx 5, 6, MP

      10. $Cx \cdot Wx$ 8, 9, Conj

    11. $(Rx \cdot Ax) \supset (Cx \cdot Wx)$ 3–10, CP

    12. $(x)[(Rx \cdot Ax) \supset (Cx \cdot Wx)]$ 11, UG

(4) 1. $(x)[(Sx \lor Ux) \supset (Ix \cdot Cx)]$

     2. $(x)(Cx \lor Vx) \supset (Rx \cdot Ax)$ / $(x)(Sx \supset Ax)$

       3. Sx ACP

       4. $Sx \lor Ux$ 3, Add

       5. $(Sx \lor Ux) \supset (Ix \cdot Cx)$ 1, UI

       6. $Ix \cdot Cx$ 4, 5, MP

       7. Cx 6, Com, Simp

       8. $Cx \lor Vx$ 7, Add

       9. $(Cx \lor Vx) \supset (Rx \cdot Ax)$ 2, UI

      10. $Rx \cdot Ax$ 8, 9, MP

      11. Ax 10, Com, Simp

    12. $Sx \supset Ax$ 3–11, CP

    13. $(x)(Sx \supset Ax)$ 12, UG

(7) 1. $(\exists x)Cx \supset (x)[Ax \supset (Sx \cdot Dx)]$

     2. $(x)(Cx \supset \sim Ax) \supset (\exists x)(Dx \cdot Sx)$ / $(\exists x)(Dx \cdot Sx)$

       3. $\sim(\exists x)(Dx \cdot Sx)$ AIP

       4. $\sim(x)(Cx \supset \sim Ax)$ 2, 3, MT

       5. $(\exists x)\sim(Cx \supset \sim Ax)$ 4, CQ

       6. $\sim(Cm \supset \sim Am)$ 5, EI

       7. $\sim(\sim Cm \lor \sim Am)$ 6, Impl

       8. $Cm \cdot Am$ 7, DM, DN

       9. Cm 8, Simp

      10. $(\exists x)Cx$ 9, EG

      11. $(x)[Ax \supset (Sx \cdot Dx)]$ 1, 10, MP

      12. $Am \supset (Sm \cdot Dm)$ 11, UI

      13. Am 8, Com, Simp

      14. $Sm \cdot Dm$ 12, 13, MP

      15. $Dm \cdot Sm$ 14, Com

      16. $(\exists x)(Dx \cdot Sx)$ 15, EG

      17. $(\exists x)(Dx \cdot Sx) \cdot \sim(\exists x)(Dx \cdot Sx)$ 3, 16, Conj

    18. $(\exists x)(Dx \cdot Sx)$ 3–17, IP, DN

(10) 1. $(\exists x)(Gx \cdot Px) \lor (\exists x)(Ax \cdot Px)$
    2. $(\exists x)Px \supset (\exists x)[Ax \cdot (Cx \cdot Dx)]$ / $(\exists x)(Dx \cdot Cx)$
       3. $\sim(\exists x)Px$ AIP
       4. $(x) \sim Px$ 3, CQ
       5. $\sim Px$ 4, UI
       6. $\sim Px \lor \sim Gx$ 5, Add
       7. $\sim Gx \lor \sim Px$ 6, Com
       8. $\sim(Gx \cdot Px)$ 7, DM
       9. $(x) \sim(Gx \cdot Px)$ 8, UG
      10. $\sim(\exists x)(Gx \cdot Px)$ 9, CQ
      11. $(\exists x)(Ax \cdot Px)$ 1, 10, DS
      12. $Am \cdot Pm$ 11, EI
      13. Pm 12, Com, Simp
      14. $\sim Pm$ 4, UI
      15. $Pm \cdot \sim Pm$ 13, 14, Conj
    16. $\sim\sim(\exists x)Px$ 3–15, IP
    17. $(\exists x)Px$ 16, DN
    18. $(\exists x)[Ax \cdot (Cx \cdot Dx)]$ 2, 17, MP
    19. $An \cdot (Cn \cdot Dn)$ 18, EI
    20. $Cn \cdot Dn$ 19, Com, Simp
    21. $Dn \cdot Cn$ 20, Com
    22. $(\exists x)(Dx \cdot Cx)$ 21, EG

Exercise 8.5

I.

(1) 1. $(x)(Ax \supset Bx)$
    2. $(x)(Ax \supset Cx)$ / $(x)(Bx \supset Cx)$
For a universe consisting of one member, we have
$Aa \supset Ba$ / $Aa \supset Ca$ // $Ba \supset Ca$
 F T T   F T F   T F F

(4) 1. $(x)(Ax \supset Bx)$
    2. $(\exists x)Ax$ / $(x)Bx$
For a universe consisting of two members, we have
$(Aa \supset Ba) \cdot (Ab \supset Bb)$ / $Aa \lor Ab$ // $Ba \cdot Bb$
 T T T T F T F   T T F   T F F

(7) 1. $(x)(Ax \supset Bx)$
    2. $(\exists x)Bx \supset (\exists x)Cx$ / $(x)(Ax \supset Cx)$
For a universe consisting of two members, we have
$(Aa \supset Ba) \cdot (Ab \supset Bb)$ / $(Ba \lor Bb) \supset (Ca \lor Cb)$ // $(Aa \supset Ca) \cdot (Ab \supset Cb)$
 T T T T T T T   T T T T T T F   T T T F T F F

(10) 1. $(\exists x)(Ax \cdot Bx)$
    2. $(\exists x)(\sim Ax \cdot \sim Bx)$ / $(x)(Ax \equiv Bx)$
For a universe consisting of one member, we have
$Aa \cdot Ba$ / $\sim Aa \cdot \sim Ba$ // $Aa \equiv Ba$
 T T $\boxed{\text{F T T}}$ F

For a universe consisting of two members, we have
$(Aa \cdot Ba) \lor (Ab \cdot Bb)$ / $(\sim Aa \cdot \sim Ba) \lor (\sim Ab \cdot \sim Bb)$
 T T T T T F F   F T $\boxed{\text{F F T T F T F}}$ T F

      // $(Aa \equiv Ba) \cdot (Ab \equiv Bb)$
         T T T F T F F

For a universe consisting of three members, we have
$(Aa \cdot Ba) \lor [(Ab \cdot Bb) \lor (Ac \cdot Bc)]$ /
 T T T T   T F F T   F F F

      $(\sim Aa \cdot \sim Ba) \lor [(\sim Ab \cdot \sim Bb) \lor (\sim Ac \cdot \sim Bc)]$
       F T F F T   T   F T F T F   T   T F T T F

      // $(Aa \equiv Ba) \cdot [(Ab \equiv Bb) \cdot (Ac \equiv Bc)]$
         T T T F   T F F F   F T F

II.

(1) 1. $(x)[(Vx \cdot Px) \supset (Ax \cdot Mx)]$
   2. $(\exists x)(Vx \cdot Ox)$ / $(\exists x)(Mx \cdot Ax)$
   For a universe consisting of one member, we have
   $(Va \cdot Pa) \supset (Aa \cdot Ma)$ / $Va \cdot Oa$ / / $Ma \cdot Aa$
   T   F   F   T   F   F   F   T   T   T   F   F   F

(4) 1. $(x)(Tx \supset Hx)$
   2. $(\exists x)(Tx \cdot Hx) \supset (\exists x)(Px \cdot Ox)$ / $(x)(Tx \supset Ox)$
   For a universe consisting of two members, we have
   $(Ta \supset Ha) \cdot (Tb \supset Hb)$ / $[(Ta \cdot Ha) \vee (Tb \cdot Hb)] \supset [(Pa \cdot Oa) \vee (Pb \cdot Ob)]$
   T   T   T   T   T   T   T   T   T   T   T   T   T   T   F   F   F   T   T   T

          / / $(Ta \supset Oa) \cdot (Tb \supset Ob)$
               T   F   F   F   T   T   T

Exercise 8.6

I.

1. Rcp
4. $(\exists x)Fxj \supset Fmj$
7. $(x)[Px \supset (\exists y)Sxy]$
10. $(\exists x)[Px \cdot (y)Sxy]$
13. $(\exists x)[(Cx \cdot Lx) \cdot Dpx]$
16. $(\exists x)(Fxc \cdot Icx)$

19. $(x)\{Px \supset (\exists y)[Py \cdot (Mxy \supset Axy)]\}$
22. $(\exists x)\{Px \cdot (y)[(Ty \cdot Sxy) \supset Axy]\}$
25. $(x)\{Lx \supset (y)[(Wy \cdot Cy) \supset Rxy]\}$
28. $(x)\{(Cx \cdot Fx) \supset (y)[(By \cdot Ly) \supset Rxy]\}$
30. $(\exists x)(Sx \cdot Dx) \supset (\exists x)[(Sx \cdot Dx) \cdot Hx]$

II.

(1)   1. $(x)[Ax \supset (y)Bxy]$
      2. Am / $(y)Bmy$
      3. $Am \supset (y)Bmy$ 1, UI
      4. $(y)Bmy$ 2, 3, MP

(4)   1. $(x)(\exists y)(Ax \supset By)$ / $(x)Ax \supset (\exists y)By$
      | 2. $(x)Ax$ ACP
      | 3. Ax 2, UI
      | 4. $(\exists y)(Ax \supset By)$ 1, UI
      | 5. $Ax \supset Bm$ 4, EI
      | 6. Bm 3, 5, MP
      | 7. $(\exists y)By$ 6, EG
      8. $(x)Ax \supset (\exists y)By$ 2–7, CP

(7)   1. $(\exists x)[Ax \cdot (y)(Ay \supset Bxy)]$ / $(\exists x)Bxx$
      2. $Am \cdot (y)(Ay \supset Bmy)$ 1, EI
      3. Am 2, Simp
      4. $(y)(Ay \supset Bmy)$ 2, Com, Simp
      5. $Am \supset Bmm$ 4, UI
      6. Bmm 3, 5, MP
      7. $(\exists x)Bxx$ 6, EG

(10) 1. $(x)(\exists y)Axy \supset (x)(\exists y)Bxy$
      2. $(\exists x)(y)\sim Bxy$ / $(\exists x)(y)\sim Axy$
      3. $(\exists x)\sim(\exists y)Bxy$ 2, CQ
      4. $\sim(x)(\exists y)Bxy$ 3, CQ
      5. $\sim(x)(\exists y)Axy$ 1, 4, MT
      6. $(\exists x)\sim(\exists y)Axy$ 5, CQ
      7. $(\exists x)(y)\sim Axy$ 6, CQ

(13)   1. $(\exists x)Ax \cdot (y)[(By \vee Cy) \supset Dxy]$
    2. $(\exists x)\{Ax \supset (\exists y)By\}$ / $(\exists x)(\exists y)Dxy$
    3. $Am \cdot (y)[(By \vee Cy) \supset Dmy]$ 1, EI
    4. Am 3, Simp
    5. $(\exists x)Ax$ 4, EG
    6. $(\exists y)By$ 2, 5, MP
    7. Bn 6, EI
    8. $(y)[(By \vee Cy) \supset Dmy]$ 3, Com, Simp
    9. $(Bn \vee Cn) \supset Dmn$ 8, UI
   10. $Bn \vee Cn$ 7, Add
   11. Dmn 9, 10, MP
   12. $(\exists y)Dmy$ 11, EG
   13. $(\exists x)(\exists y)Dxy$ 12, EG

(16)   1. $(x)(\exists y)(Ax \cdot By)$ / $(\exists y)(x)(Ax \cdot By)$
    2. $\sim(\exists y)(x)(Ax \cdot By)$ AIP
    3. $(y)\sim(x)(Ax \cdot By)$ 2, CQ
    4. $(y)(\exists x)\sim(Ax \cdot By)$ 3, CQ
    5. $(\exists x)\sim(Ax \cdot By)$ 4, UI
    6. $\sim(Am \cdot By)$ 5, EI
    7. $(\exists y)(Am \cdot By)$ 1, UI
    8. $Am \cdot Bn$ 7, EI
    9. $\sim Am \vee \sim By$ 6, DM
   10. Am 8, Simp
   11. $\sim By$ 9, 10, DN, DS
   12. $(y)\sim By$ 11, UG
   13. $\sim Bn$ 12, UI
   14. Bn 8, Com, Simp
   15. $Bn \cdot \sim Bn$ 13, 14, Conj
   16. $(\exists y)(x)(Ax \cdot By)$ 2–15, IP, DN
(Note: Attempts to use direct proof on this argument violate the second restriction on UG.)

(19)   1. $(x)(\exists y)Axy \vee (x)(y)Bxy$
    2. $(x)(\exists y)(Cx \supset \sim Bxy)$ / $(x)(\exists y)(Cx \supset Axy)$
    3. Cx ACP
    4. $(\exists y)(Cx \supset \sim Bxy)$ 2, UI
    5. $Cx \supset \sim Bxm$ 4, EI
    6. $\sim Bxm$ 3, 5, MP
    7. $(\exists y)\sim Bxy$ 6, EG
    8. $(\exists x)(\exists y)\sim Bxy$ 7, EG
    9. $(\exists x)\sim(y)Bxy$ 8, CQ
   10. $\sim(x)(y)Bxy$ 9, CQ
   11. $(x)(\exists y)Axy$ 1, 10, Com, DS
   12. $(\exists y)Axy$ 11, UI
   13. Axn 12, EI
   14. $Cx \supset Axn$ 3–13, CP
   15. $(\exists y)(Cx \supset Axy)$ 14, EG
   16. $(x)(\exists y)(Cx \supset Axy)$ 15, UG

III.
(1)   1. $(x)[Px \supset (y)(Ay \supset Oxy)]$
    2. $Pj \cdot \sim Ojm$ / $\sim Am$
    3. $Pj \supset (y)(Ay \supset Ojy)$ 1, UI
    4. Pj 2, Simp
    5. $(y)(Ay \supset Ojy)$ 3, 4, MP
    6. $Am \supset Ojm$ 5, UI
    7. $\sim Ojm$ 2, Com, Simp
    8. $\sim Am$ 6, 7, MT

(4) 1. *Po*
     2. *(x)[(Px • Cx) ⊃ Sox]*
     3. *(x)(Px ⊃ ~Sxx)*   / ~Co
     | 4. *Co*   AIP
     | 5. *(Po • Co) ⊃ Soo*   2, UI
     | 6. *Po • Co*   1, 4, Conj
     | 7. *Soo*   5, 6, MP
     | 8. *Po ⊃ ~Soo*   3, UI
     | 9. *~Soo*   1, 8, MP
     |10. *Soo • ~Soo*   7, 9, Conj
     11. *~Co*   4–10, IP
 (7) 1. *(∃x){Px • (y)[(Py • Kxy) ⊃ Fxy]}*
      2. *(x) [Px ⊃ (∃y) (Py • Kxy)]*   / *(∃x) (∃y) [(Px • Py) • Fxy]*
      3. *Pm • (y)[(Py • Kmy) ⊃ Fmy]*   1, EI
      4. *Pm ⊃ (∃y)(Py • Kmy)*   2, UI
      5. *Pm*   3, Simp
      6. *(∃y)(Py • Kmy)*   4, 5, MP
      7. *Pn • Kmn*   6, EI
      8. *(y)[(Py • Kmy) ⊃ Fmy]*   3, Com, Simp
      9. *(Pn • Kmn) ⊃ Fmn*   8, UI
     10. *Fmn*   7, 9, MP
     11. *Pn*   7, Simp
     12. *Pm • Pn*   5, 11, Conj
     13. *(Pm • Pn) • Fmn*   10, 12, Conj
     14. *(∃y)[(Pm • Py) • Fmy]*   13, EG
     15. *(∃x)(∃y)[(Px • Py) • Fxy]*   14, EG
(10) 1. *(x){Ix ⊃ [(∃y)(Cy • Ay) ⊃ Ex]}*
      2. *[(∃x)Tx v (∃x)Wx] ⊃ [(∃x)Ix • (∃x)Cx]*
      3. *(x)(Cx ⊃ Ax)*   / *(∃x) Tx ⊃ (∃x) (Ix • Ex)*
      | 4. *(∃x)Tx*   ACP
      | 5. *(∃x)Tx v (∃x)Wx*   4, Add
      | 6. *(∃x)Ix • (∃x)Cx*   2, 5, MP
      | 7. *(∃x)Ix*   6, Simp
      | 8. *Im*   7, EI
      | 9. *Im ⊃ [(∃y)(Cy • Ay) ⊃ Em]*   1, UI
      |10. *(∃y)(Cy • Ay) ⊃ Em*   8, 9, MP
      |11. *(∃x)Cx*   6, Com, Simp
      |12. *Cn*   11, EI
      |13. *Cn ⊃ An*   3, UI
      |14. *An*   12, 13, MP
      |15. *Cn • An*   12, 14, Conj
      |16. *(∃y)(Cy • Ay)*   15, EG
      |17. *Em*   10, 16, MP
      |18. *Im • Em*   8, 17, Conj
      |19. *(∃x)(Ix • Ex)*   18, EG
     20. *(∃x)Tx ⊃ (∃x)(Ix • Ex)*   4–19, CP

Exercise 9.1

I.

  1. Sufficient condition. The window can also be broken by throwing a stone or baseball through it.

  4. Necessary condition. For an image to appear on the film the camera must also be loaded and focused and there must be sufficient light.

  7. Sufficient condition. The fire will also be extinguished if it is smothered.

 10. Necessary condition. Electricity must also be supplied from the main lines.

II.

  1. Method of difference—sufficient condition.

  4. Direct method of agreement—necessary condition.

  7. Method of concomitant variation—sufficient condition.

10. Double method of agreement—sufficient and necessary condition.
13. Joint method of agreement and difference—sufficient and necessary condition.
15. Method of difference—sufficient condition.

III.
1. By the inverse method of agreement, A is the cause in the sense of a sufficient condition.
4. By the double method of agreement, C is the cause in the sense of a sufficient and necessary condition.
7. By the inverse method of agreement, D is the cause in the sense of a sufficient condition.

Exercise 9.2

I.

1. 1/6   4. .853   7. 1/4 or .25

II.

1. $P(6 \text{ or } 1) = P(6) + P(1) = 1/6 = 1/6 = 2/6 = 1/3$

4a. $P(A_1 \text{ and } A_2) = P(A_1) \times P(A_2)$
$= 4/52 \times 4/52$
$= 1/169 = .0059$

4b. $P(A_1 \text{ and } A_2) = P(A_1) \times P(A_2 \text{ given } A_1)$
$= 4/52 \times 3/51$
$= 1/221 = .0045$

7. First compute the probability of getting no sixes:
$P(\text{no sixes}) = 5/6 \times 5/6 \times 5/6$
$= 125/216$
Then use the negation rule:
$P(\text{at least one six}) = 1 - P(\text{no sixes})$
$= 1 - 125/216$
$= 91/216 = .4213$

10. a. $P(R_1 \text{ and } R_2) = P(R_1) \times P(R_2 \text{ given } R_1)$
$= 3/12 \times 2/11$
$= 6/132 \times .045$

   b. $P(Y \text{ and } G) = P(Y_1 \text{ and } G_2) + P(G_1 \text{ and } Y_2)$
$= (5/12 \times 4/11) + (4/12 + 5/11)$
$= 20/132 + 20/132$
$= 10/33 = .303$

   c. $P(R \text{ or } G) = 1 - P(Y_1 \text{ and } Y_2)$
$= 1 - (5/12 \times 4/11)$
$= 1 - 20/132$
$= 28/33 = .848$

   d. $P(G_1 \text{ or } G_2) = 1 - P(\text{not } G)$
$= 1 - [P(R_1 \text{ and } R_2) + P(R_1 \text{ and } Y_2) + P(Y_1 \text{ and } R_2)$
$+ P(Y_1 \text{ and } Y_2)]$
$= 1 - [(3/12 \times 2/11) + (3/12 \times 5/11)$
$+ (5/12 \times 3/11) + (5/12 \times 4/11)]$
$= 1 - [6/132 + 15/132 + 15/132 + 20/132]$
$= 1 - 56/132$
$= 19/33 = .57$

   e. $P(\text{same color}) = P(R_1 \text{ and } R_2) + P(G_1 \text{ and } G_2) + P(Y_1 \text{ and } Y_2)$
$= (3/12 \times 2/11) + (4/12 \times 3/11) + (5/12 \times 4/11)$
$= 6/132 + 12/132 + 20/132$
$= 19/66 = .288$

13a. $P(M \text{ or } W) = P(M) + P(W) - P(M \text{ and } W)$
$= .74 + .82 - (.74 \times .82)$
$= .95$

13b. $P(M \text{ and } W \text{ and } S) = P(M) \times P(W) \times P(S)$
$= .74 \times .82 \times 8/9$
$= .54$

15. P(two on same day) $= 1 - P$(separate days)
$$= 1 - (7/7 \times 6/7 \times 5/7 \times 4/7)$$
$$= 1561/2401 = .65$$

Exercise 9.3

I.

1. Since the water in the lake might not be circulating, the algae content of the water at one end might not be representative of the whole lake. Thus, the sample might be biased.

4. According to Table 7, the margin of error for a random sample of 600 is $\pm$ 5 percent. Since the sample taken indicates a difference of only 2 percent, the results of the sample are inconclusive.

7. Since no mention is made of the size of the sample or of the expected sampling error, the sample might be biased. The manufacturer might have taken 25 separate samples consisting of ten dentists per sample and reported the results of only the most favorable one.

10. The problem concerns the meaning of "average." If the average is a mean, most of the toys could be over $15, and a few very cheap toys could bring the average down to $15. If the average is a mode, there might be a few toys priced at $15, and all the other toys might have varying prices exceeding $15. Only if the average is a median can one be assured that half the toys are $15 or less.

13. Since no mention is made of the dispersion, the argument is weak. The rock pile might consist of several pieces weighing 500 pounds and enough weighing only 4 or 5 pounds to bring the average down to 50 pounds. If the range were only 10 pounds or so, the conclusion would follow.

16. If the scale on the vertical axis does not begin at zero, the conclusion does not follow.

19. Since there were many more cars on the road in 1980 than there were in 1950, the comparison is faulty.

II.

1. mean $= 180$, median $= 170$, mode $= 160$

III.

1. False.	7. True.	13. True.	19. False.
4. False.	10. False.	16. False.	

Exercise 9.4

IV.

1. True.	7. True.	13. True.	19. False.
4. False.	10. True.	16. False.	

GLOSSARY/INDEX

A proposition: A categorical proposition having the form "All *S* are *P*," 178–180

Abelard, Peter, 6

Absorption, 327n

Accident: An informal fallacy that occurs when a general rule is wrongly applied to an atypical specific case, 113–114, 150

Ackermann, Wilhelm, 403n

Ad hominem abusive: A variety of the argument-against-the-person fallacy that occurs when an arguer verbally abuses a second arguer for the purpose of discrediting that person's argument, 111, 113, 123, 158

Ad hominem circumstantial: A variety of the argument-against-the-person fallacy that occurs when an arguer cites circumstances that affect a second arguer for the purpose of discrediting that person's argument, 111–112

Adams, John Couch, 475, 477, 484–485

Addition: A valid rule of inference: "*p* / / *p* or *q*," 327, 329, 331; with relational predicated, 412

Adequacy: The extent to which a hypothesis fits the facts it is intended to explain, 484

Adverbs, translation of, 214–215

Advertisements as enthymemes, 258

Advertising, language of, 68–69

Advice. *See* Piece of advice

Affective terminology and definitions, 100–101

Affirmative statement: A statement that asserts class membership, 177–178, 180

Affirming the consequent: An invalid argument form: "if *p* then *q* / *q* / / *p*," 296–297, 302, 475

"All except," "all but," 219

Ambiguity: Susceptibility to two or more clearly distinct meanings, 82, 136; fallacies of, 136, 144–146

Ambiguous definitions, 99–100

Amphiboly: An informal fallacy that occurs when the conclusion of an argument depends on the misinterpretation of a statement that is ambiguous owing to some structural defect, 145–146

Antecedent: The component of a conditional statement immediately following the word "if," 18, 268

Appeal to authority: An informal fallacy that occurs when an arguer cites the testimony of an unqualified authority in support of a conclusion, 121–123

Appeal to force: An informal fallacy that occurs when an arguer threatens a reader or listener for the purpose of getting him or her to accept a conclusion, 107–108

Appeal to ignorance: An informal fallacy that occurs when an arguer uses the fact that nothing has been proved about something as evidence in support of some conclusion about that thing, 123–125

Appeal to pity: An informal fallacy that occurs when an arguer attempts to evoke pity from a reader or listener for the purpose of getting him or her to accept a conclusion, 108–109

Appeal to snobbery: A variety of the appeal-to-the-people fallacy that occurs when the arguer plays upon the reader's or listener's need to feel superior, 110

Appeal to the people: An informal fallacy that occurs when an arguer plays upon certain psychological needs for the purpose of getting the reader or listener to accept a conclusion, 109–111

Appeal to vanity: A variety of the appeal-to-the-people fallacy that occurs when an arguer plays upon the vanity of the reader or listener, 110

Argument: A group of statements, one or more of which (the premises) are claimed to provide support for, or reasons to believe, one of the others (the conclusion), 1; cogent, 44–45; conditional statements and, 18–20; explanation and, 22–23; form of, 49–54, 293–300; recognition of, 14–23; sound, 42, 45; strong, 42, 45; valid, 40–42. *See also* Deductive argument; Inductive argument

Argument against the person: An informal fallacy that occurs when an arguer verbally attacks the person of a second arguer for the purpose of discrediting his or her argument, 111–113, 123, 158

Argument based on mathematics: A deductive argument in which the conclusion depends on some purely arithmetic or geometric computation or measurement, 31–32

Argument based on signs: An inductive argument that proceeds from the knowledge of a sign to a claim about the thing or situation that the sign symbolizes, 34

Argument form: The abstract structure of an argument, 49–54, 294

Argument from analogy: An inductive argument that depends on the existence of a similarity between two things or states of affairs, 33–34, 130–131, 158–159

Argument from authority: An inductive argument in which the conclusion rests upon a statement made by some presumed authority or witness, 33–34, 121–123

Argument from definition: A deductive argument in which the conclusion is claimed to depend merely upon the definition of some word or phrase used in the premise or conclusion, 32

Aristotelian sorites, 262

Aristotle, 6, 34–35, 106, 181, 242, 474, 480

Associativity: A valid rule of inference that allows for the relocation of parentheses in conjunctions and disjunctions, 337–338, 340

Atmospheric pressure, discovery of, 478–480

Atomic statement, 266–267

Average, meaning of, 457–460

Axiom of replacement: An axiom that states that

logically equivalent expressions may replace one another in a proof sequence, 336, 338

Baliani, Giovanni, 478
Bandwagon argument: A variety of the appeal-to-the-people fallacy that occurs when the arguer plays upon the reader's or listener's need to feel part of a group, 110
"Barbara" syllogism, 227
Barometer, invention of, 479–480
"Because," 4, 21–22
Becquerel, Henri, 475–476
Begging the question: An informal fallacy that occurs when the arguer uses some form of phraseology that tends to conceal the questionably true character of a key premise, 136–139, 142, 158
Begriffsschrift, 7
Berti, Gasparo, 478–479
Biased sample: A sample that is not representative of the population from which it was selected, 453–457
Biconditional sign: The symbol consisting of three short parallel lines that means "if and only if," 267, 271; truth functional interpretation of, 278–279
Biconditional statements, 271
Bimodal curves, 462–463
Boethius, 6
Bolzano, Bernard, 7
Boole, George, 7, 198, 200
Boolean standpoint/interpretation (modern standpoint), 198, 202, 226–227, 237–239, 243, 246–247; in predicate logic, 369–372
"Both . . . not," 273
Bound variable: A variable that is bound by a quantifier, 371
Bouvard, Alexis, 477
Braces, 271
Brackets, 271–272
Broad definitions, 98–99
Business, language of, 70–71

Campbell, Stephen K., 467n
Cantril, Albert H., 455n
Carroll, Lewis, 264
Categorical proposition: A proposition that relates two classes (or categories), 174–222; in class notation, 198; letter names of 178, 180; standard form of, 175
Categorical syllogism: A syllogism in which all three statements are categorical propositions, 32, 223–265; exceptive propositions in, 253–254; figure of, 225–226; form of, 226–227; mood of, 225–226; in ordinary language, 252–254; reconstruction of, from mood and figure, 228; reducing the number of terms in, 249–251; rules for, 242–247; standard form of, 224–225; Venn diagrams for, 231–239
Causal inference: An inductive inference that proceeds from knowledge of a cause to a claim about the effect, or from knowledge of an effect to a claim about the cause, 34
Causality, 418–433
Change of quantifier rule: A rule of inference that allows one kind of quantifier to be replaced by another, provided that certain negation signs are deleted or introduced, 388–391; with overlapping quantifiers, 412

Chrysippus, 6
Circular definitions, 99
Circular reasoning. *See* Begging the question
Class statement, 148–150
Classical theory of probability: The theory according to which probabilities are computed *a priori* by dividing the number of favorable outcomes by the number of possible outcomes, 438–448
Cogent argument: An inductive argument that is strong and has true premises, 44–45
Cognitive meaning, 67
Coherence. *See* Internal coherence
Collective predication: An attribute is predicated collectively when it is assigned to a class as a whole, 148–149
Common names, 74–75
Commutativity: A valid rule of inference that provides for the rearrangement of conjunctions and disjunctions, 337, 339–340
Complex question: An informal fallacy that occurs when a single question that is really *two* or more questions is asked, and a single answer is applied to both questions, 139–141
Composite pattern, 59
Composition: An informal fallacy that occurs when the conclusion of an argument depends on the erroneous transference of a characteristic from the parts of something onto the whole, 147–151
Compound statement: A statement that contains at least one atomic statement as a component, 267; truth values of, 276–281
Conclusion: The statement in an argument that is claimed to follow from the evidence presented in the premises, 2; tautologous, 311, 360
Conclusion indicator: A word that provides a clue to identifying a conclusion, 3, 14
Conditional proof, 353–356; incorrect use of, 356; indirect proof and, 359–361; in predicate logic, 393–395, 397, 410–411; to prove logical truths, 364–365
Conditional sign: The horseshoe symbol that means "if . . . then," 267, 271; truth functional interpretation of, 278, 281–283
Conditional statement: An "if . . . then" statement, 18–21; inferences and, 19; in propositional logic, 269–271; translating into categorical propositions, 216–217
Conjoint premises, 58–59
Conjunct: A component in a conjunctive statement, 268
Conjunction: A valid rule of inference: "$p \ / \ q \ / \ / \ p$ and q," 327–328, 330–331
Conjunction sign: The dot symbol that means "and," 267–268; truth functional interpretation of, 276–277
Conjunctive statements, 268, 277
Connectives: Symbols used to connect or negate atomic propositions in propositional logic, 266–271
Connotation: Intensional meaning or intension, 75–78
Connotative definition. *See* Intensional definition
Consequent: The component of a conditional statement immediately following the word "then"; the component of a conditional statement that is not the antecedent, 18, 268
Constant: *See* Individual constant

Constructive dilemma: A valid argument form/ rule of inference: "If *p* then *q*, and if *r* then *s* / *p* or *r* / / *q* or *s*," 297–298, 300–302, 327–328, 330

Context, definitions and, 101

Contingent statement: A statement that is neither necessarily true nor necessarily false, 288–289

Contradictory premises, 311, 331

Contradictory statements: Statements that necessarily have opposite truth values, 182–185, 198, 289–290

Contraposition: An operation that consists in switching and negating the subject and predicate terms in a standard form categorical proposition, 192–194; by limitation, 189n; proof of, 207; to reduce number of terms in a syllogism, 249–251

Contrapositive, 192–193

Contrary: The relation by which two statements are necessarily not both true, 182–185, 203–205

Conventional connotation: The intensional meaning conventionally agreed upon by the members of the community that speak the language in question, 76

Converse, 189, 194

Converse accident. *See* Hasty generalization

Conversion: An operation that consists in switching the subject and predicate terms in a standard form categorical proposition, 188–190, 193–194; by limitation, 189n; proof of, 205–206; to reduce number of terms in a syllogism, 249–251

Copernicus, Nicholas, 483–486

Copula: In standard form categorical propositions, the words "are" and "are not," 175–176

Counterdilemma, 301–302

Counterexample method: A method for proving invalidity that consists in constructing a substitution instance having true premises and false conclusion, 52–53

Curie, Marie, 475–477, 486

Curie, Pierre, 475–477

Decreasing extension: The order of decreasing class size, 77–78

Decreasing intension: The order of decreasing specificity or increasing generality, 77–78

Deduction. *See* Natural deduction

Deductive argument: An argument in which we expect the conclusion to follow necessarily from the premises, 30–31, 35; invalid, 40–42; sound, 42, 45; valid, 40–42

Definiendum: In a definition, the word or group of words that are proposed to be defined, 80

Definiens: In a definition, the words or group of words that do the defining, 80

Definition: A group of words that assigns a meaning to a word or group of words, 80; by genus and difference, 92–94; by subclass, 88–89; criteria for, 97–101; demonstrative (ostensive) 88–91; enumerative, 89; extensional (denotative), 88–91; intentional, 91–94; lexical, 82, 90, 94; operational, 91–92, 94; persuasive, 84–85, 90, 94; precising, 82–83, 90, 94; purposes of, 79–85; stipulative, 81–82, 90, 94; synonymous, 91, 94; theoretical, 83–84, 90, 94

Definition by genus and difference: A definition that assigns a meaning to a term by identifying a genus term and one or more difference words

that, when combined, convey the same meaning as the term being defined, 92–94

Definition by subclass: A definition that assigns a meaning to a term by naming subclasses of the class that the term denotes, 88–89

Definitional techniques, 88–94

Demonstrative definition: A definition that assigns a meaning to a word by pointing to members of the class that the word denotes, 88–91

DeMorgan, Augustus, 7

DeMorgan's rule: A valid rule of inference that allows negation signs to be moved inside and outside of parentheses, 273, 336–340

Denotation: Extensional meaning or extension, 75–78

Denotative definition. *See* Extensional definition

Denying the antecedent: An invalid argument form: "if *p* then *q* / not *p* / / *p*," 296–297, 302

Descartes, René, 480, 486

Description: A kind of nonargument consisting of one or more statements that cause a picture to appear in the mind of the reader or listener, 16

Descriptive phrases, 74–75

Destructive dilemma: A valid argument form/rule of inference: "If *p* then *q*, and if *r* then *s* / not *q* or not *s* / / not *p* or not *r*," 298, 300–302

Difference, 92–93

Dilemma. *See* Constructive dilemma; Destructive dilemma

Direct method of agreement: A method for identifying a causal connection between an effect and a necessary condition, 421–423, 425–426

Disjunct: A component in a disjunctive statement, 268

Disjunction sign: The vee symbol that means "or," 267–269; truth functional interpretation of, 277

Disjunctive statements, 269, 277

Disjunctive syllogism: A syllogism having a disjunctive statement for one or both of its premises, 32; a valid argument form/rule of inference: "*p* or *q* / not *p* / / *q*," 318–321

Dispersion: In statistics, an indicator of how spread out the data are in regard to numerical value, 460–463

Distribution: (1) an attribute possessed by a term in a categorical proposition if and only if the proposition makes a claim about all the members of the class denoted by the term, 178–180, 243; (2) A valid rule of inference that allows a conjunct/disjunct to be distributed through a disjunction/conjunction, 337–338, 340; (3) In statistics, the arrangement of a set of data, 459–463

Distributive predication: An attribute is predicated distributively when it is assigned to each and every member of a class, 148–149

Division: An informal fallacy that occurs when the conclusion of an argument depends on the erroneous transference of a characteristic from a whole (or class) onto its parts (or members), 149–151

Double blind studies, 456

Double method of agreement: A method for identifying a causal connection between an effect and a cause that is both sufficient and necessary, 425–426, 429

Double negation: A valid rule of inference that allows the introduction or deletion of pairs of negation signs, 337–339; in categorical propositions, 191

Drawing an affirmative/negative conclusion from negative/affirmative premises: A formal fallacy that occurs in a categorical syllogism when an affirmative conclusion is drawn from a negative premise or a negative conclusion is drawn from affirmative premises, 245–246

E proposition: A categorical proposition having the form "No S are P," 178–180

Einstein, Albert, 485, 487

Emotive meaning, 67

Empirical hypotheses: Hypotheses that concern the production of some thing or the occurrence of some event that can be observed, 483–484

Empty extension: The extension of a term that denotes something that does not exist; the null class, 76–77

Empty intension, 77

Enthymeme: A categorical syllogism that is missing a premise or conclusion, 256–258; an argument that is missing a premise or conclusion, 19, 302

Enumerative definition: A definition that assigns a meaning to a word by naming the members of the class that the word denotes, 89

Equivalence, 267, 271, 278–279. *See also* Biconditional sign; Biconditional statements; Logical equivalence; Material equivalence; Truth functional equivalence

Equivocation: An informal fallacy that occurs because some word or group of words is used either implicitly or explicitly in two different senses, 144–146, 468

Escaping between the horns of a dilemma, 300–301

Essential meaning, definitions and, 98

Exceptive propositions, 219, 253–254; syllogisms containing, 253–254

Exclusive disjunction, 268

Exclusive premises: A formal fallacy that occurs when both premises of a categorical syllogism are negative, 245

Exclusive propositions, 217–218; in predicate logic, 372–374

Existential fallacy: (1) A formal fallacy that occurs when the traditional square of opposition is used in conjunction with propositions that make assertions about nonexistent things, 199; (2) A formal fallacy that occurs when the premises of a categorical syllogism are universal and the conclusion is particular, 246–247

Existential generalization: A rule of inference that introduces existential quantifiers, 379–386; invalid applications of, 385–386, 413

Existential instantiation: A rule of inference that removes existential quantifiers, 380–385; invalid applications of, 385; restrictions on, 381–383

Existential names, 381–382

Existential quantifier: The quantifier used to translate particular statements in predicate logic, 371–372

Existential standpoint, 204–205, 237–239, 246–247

Explanandum: The component of an explanation that describes the event or phenomenon to be explained, 21

Explanans: The component of an explanation that

explains the event indicated by the explanandum, 21

Explanation: A statement or group of statements intended to shed light on some event, 21–23

Exportation: A valid rule of inference that allows conditional statements having conjunctive antecedents to be replaced with conditional statements having conditional consequents, and vice versa, 345–348

Expository passage: A kind of nonargument consisting of a topic sentence and one or more other sentences that expand or elaborate on the topic sentence, 17

Extended arguments, 56–59

Extensional definition: A definition that assigns a meaning to a term by indicating the members of the class that the term denotes, 88–91

Extensional meaning (extension): The members of the class that a term denotes, 75–78, 90–91

External consistency: The extent to which a hypothesis agrees with other, well-confirmed hypotheses, 486

Fallacies of ambiguity: A group of informal fallacies that occur because of an ambiguity in the premises or conclusion, 136, 144–146

Fallacies of grammatical analogy: A group of informal fallacies that occur because of a grammatical similarity to other arguments that are nonfallacious, 136, 147–151

Fallacies of presumption: A group of informal fallacies that occur when the premises of an argument presume what they purport to prove, 136–143

Fallacies of relevance: A group of informal fallacies that occur because the premises of an argument are irrelevant to the conclusion, 107–118

Fallacies of weak induction: A group of informal fallacies that occur because the connection between the premises and conclusion is not strong enough to support the conclusion, 121–131

Fallacy: A defect in an argument arising from some source other than merely false premises, 104–118. *See also* Formal fallacy; Informal fallacy

False cause: An informal fallacy that occurs when the conclusion of an argument depends on some imagined causal connection that does not really exist, 127–128

False dichotomy: An informal fallacy that is committed when an arguer presents two nonjointly exhaustive alternatives as if they were jointly exhaustive and then eliminates one, leaving the other as the conclusion, 141–142

"Few," "a few," 215–216

Figurative definitions, 99

Figure: An attribute of a categorical syllogism that specifies the location of the middle term, 225–226

"For this reason," 4

Form of a categorical syllogism, 226

Form of an argument, 49–54, 293–300

Formal fallacy: A fallacy that can be identified through mere inspection of the form or structure of an argument, 104–105. *See also* specific fallacies

Free variable: A variable that is not bound by a quantifier, 371

Frege, Gottlob, 7

Fruitfulness: The extent to which a hypothesis suggests new ideas for future analysis and confirmation, 486–487

Galen, 6
Galilei, Galileo, 479, 483
Galle, Johann, 475, 478, 484
Gallup poll, 455
General conjunction rule: In probability theory, a rule for computing the probability of two events occurring together whether or not the events are independent, 443–444
General disjunction rule: In probability theory, a rule for computing the probability of either of two events whether or not they are mutually exclusive, 445–447
General statement: A statement that makes a claim about all the members of a class, 35, 148–150
Generalization. *See* Existential generalization; Inductive generalization; Universal generalization
Genus, 92–93
Goclenian sorites, 262
Goedel, Kurt, 7–8
Grammar, definitions and, 97
Graphs, 463–465
Grasping a dilemma by the horns, 300–301

Hasty generalization: An informal fallacy that occurs when a general conclusion is drawn from atypical specific cases, 125–127, 148–149
Helmont, Jan Baptista Van, 480
Herschel, William, 477
History of logic, 6–8
Horizontal pattern, 57
Horns of a dilemma, 300
Huff, Darrell, 462n
Hypotheses: Conjectures offered as possible solutions to a problem, 473; empirical, 483–484; proof of, 483–484; tentative acceptance of, 484–487; theoretical, 483–484
Hypothetical reasoning: The reasoning process used to produce hypotheses, 473–487
Hypothetical syllogism: A syllogism having a conditional statement for one or both of its premises, 32, 294, 318. *See also* Mixed hypothetical syllogism; Pure hypothetical syllogism

I proposition: A categorical proposition having the form "some *S* are *P*," 178–180
Ignoratio elenchi. See Missing the point
Illicit contraposition: A formal fallacy that occurs when the conclusion of an argument depends on the contraposition of an **E** or **I** statement, 193
Illicit contrary: A formal fallacy that occurs when the conclusion of an argument depends on an incorrect application of the contrary relation, 184
Illicit conversion: A formal fallacy that occurs when the conclusion of an argument depends on the conversion of an **A** or **O** statement, 190, 193
Illicit major: A formal fallacy that occurs when the major term in a categorical syllogism is distributed in the conclusion but not in the premise, 244
Illicit minor: A formal fallacy that occurs when the minor term in a categorical syllogism is

distributed in the conclusion but not in the premise, 244
Illicit subalternation: A formal fallacy that occurs when the conclusion of an argument depends on an incorrect application of the subalternation relation, 184
Illicit subcontrary: A formal fallacy that occurs when the conclusion of an argument depends on an incorrect application of the subcontrary relation, 184
Illustration: A kind of nonargument composed of statements intended to show what something means or how something should be done, 17
Implication, 267, 278, 281–283; rules of, 318–332. *See also* Conditional sign; Conditional statement; Material implication
Inclusive disjunction, 268, 277
Increasing extension: The order of increasing class size, 77–78
Increasing intension: The order of increasing specificity, 77–78
Indirect proof, 358–362; incorrect use of, 361–362; in predicate logic, 393, 395–397, 410, 412; to prove logical truths, 364
Indirect truth tables, for arguments, 313–317
Individual constant: A lowercase letter (*a, b* . . . *u, v, w*) used to name individuals, 368–369
Individual variable: A lowercase letter (*x, y, z*) used to represent anything at random in the universe, 369–370
Inductive argument: An argument in which we expect the conclusion to follow only probably from the premises, 30, 33–35; cogency of, 44–45; strength of, 42–45, 449–450
Inductive generalization: An inductive argument that proceeds from the knowledge of a selected sample to some claim about the whole group, 33–34, 125
Inference: The reasoning process expressed by an argument, 5; conditional statements and, 19; rules of, 318ff
Informal fallacy: A fallacy that can be detected only through analysis of the content of an argument, 105–173. *See also* specific fallacies
Instantial letter: The letter (a variable or constant) introduced by universal instantiation or existential instantiation, 378
Instantiation. *See* Existential instantiation; Universal instantiation
Intensional definition: A definition that assigns a meaning to a word by indicating the qualities or attributes that the word connotes, 91–94
Intensional meaning (intension): The qualities or attributes that a term connotes, 75–78, 90–91
Internal coherence: The extent to which the ideas or terms in a hypothesis are rationally interconnected, 484–487
Invalid deductive argument: A deductive argument in which the conclusion does not follow necessarily from the premises, 40–42
Invalidity, alternate definition of, 51; proving, 52–54; proving in predicate logic, 399–403
Inverse method of agreement: A method for identifying a causal connection between an effect and a sufficient condition, 423–427

Jevons, William Stanley, 7
Joint method of agreement and difference: A method for identifying a causal connection be-

tween an effect and a sufficient and necessary condition present in a specific occurrence, 429–430

Kant, Immanuel, 474
Kepler, Johannes, 485

Lalande, J. J., 484
Laplace, Pierre, 477
Leading question, 140–141
Leibniz, Gottfried Wilhelm von, 7, 474
Letter names of categorical propositions, 178, 180
Leverrier, U. J. J., 475, 477–478, 484–485
Lexical definition: A definition intended to report the way a word is actually used in a language, 82, 85, 90, 94; criteria for, 97–101
Literary Digest poll, 455
Logic: The science that evaluates arguments, 1; history of, 6–8
Logically equivalent statements: Statements that necessarily have the same truth value, 189, 289–290
Logically false statement: A statement that is necessarily false, 288–289
Logically true statement: A statement that is necessarily true; a tautology, 288–289; proving, 364–365
Lyons, Eugene, 467n

Main connective, 280
Major premise: In a categorical syllogism, the premise that contains the major term, 224–225
Major term: In a standard form categorical syllogism, the predicate of the conclusion, 224–225
Material equivalence: (1) A valid rule of inference that allows an equivalence statement to be replaced by a conjunctive statement or a disjunctive statement, 345–348; (2) Having the same truth value, 271, 290
Material implication: A valid rule of inference that allows an implication sign to be replaced by a disjunction sign if and only if the antecedent is negated, 345–348
Maxwell, James Clerk, 485, 487
Mean: The arithmetical average, 457–460
Meaning: That which is symbolized by a word, 75; extensional, 75–78; intensional, 75–78
Median: The middle point where data are arranged in ascending order, 457–460
Mention of a word, 75
Method of agreement, 421. *See also* Direct method of agreement; Double method of agreement; Inverse method of agreement
Method of concomitant variation: A method for identifying a causal connection between two conditions by matching variations in one condition with variations in another, 431–433
Method of difference: A method for identifying a causal connection between an effect and a sufficient condition present in a specific occurrence, 426–430
Method of residues: A method of identifying a causal connection by subtracting strands of causal connection that are already known from a compound causal connection, 430–431
Middle term: In a standard form categorical syllogism, the term that occurs only in the premises, 224
Military terminology, 68

Mill, John Stuart, 7, 418, 420–421
Mill's methods of induction, 418, 420–433
Minor premise: In a categorical syllogism, the premise that contains the minor term, 224–225
Minor term: In a standard form categorical syllogism, the subject of the conclusion, 224–225
Missing the point: An informal fallacy that occurs when the premise of an argument entails one particular conclusion but a completely different conclusion is actually drawn, 115–118, 468
Mixed hypothetical syllogism: A syllogism containing a conditional statement for only one of its premises, 294–297
Mob mentality, 109
Modal logic: A kind of logic that deals with concepts such as possibility, necessity, belief, and doubt, 6–7
Mode: The value that occurs with the greatest frequency in a set of data, 457–460
Modern square of opposition: A restricted version of the traditional square of opposition that contains only the contradictory relation, 197–199, 203–204
Modus ponens: A valid argument form/rule of inference: "If p then q / p / / p," 295–296, 299, 302, 318–319
Modus tollens: A valid argument form/rule of inference: "If p then q / not q / / not p," 296, 299, 302, 318–320, 475
Molecular statement, 267; truth value of, 276–281
Mood: An attribute of a categorical syllogism that specifies the kind of statements (**A, E, I, O,**) that make it up, 225–226
Multiple conclusions, 58–59

Names, 74–75, 375; existential, 381–382
Narrow definitions, 98–99
Natural deduction: A procedure by which the conclusion of an argument is derived from the premises through the use of rules of inference, 318; in predicate logic, 377–417; in propositional logic, 318–366
Necessary condition: The condition represented by the consequent in a conditional statement, 20–21, 270–271; and causality, 419–423, 425–426, 429–430
Needham, John, 481, 483, 485
Negated statements, 268, 276, 299
Negation of terms, 190–191
Negation rule: A rule for computing the probability of an event from the probability of the event *not* happening, 447–449
Negation sign: The tilde symbol that means "not," 267–268; truth functional interpretation of, 276
Negative definitions, 99
Negative statement: A statement that denies class membership, 177–178, 180
"Neither . . . nor," 272–273
Neptune, discovery of, 477–478
Newton, Isaac, 480, 487
Non causa pro causa, 127–128
Nonarguments, typical kinds of, 15–23
"None but," 217–218, 372–374
"None except," 217–218
Nonstandard quantifiers, 215
Nonstandard verbs, translation of, 212–213
Normal probability distribution: A distribution of random phenomena having the shape of a bell, 459–461

"Not both," 272–273
"Not either," 272–273

O proposition: A categorical proposition having the form "Some *S* are not *P*," 178–180
Obscure definitions, 99–100
Obverse, 190–192
Obversion: An operation that consists of changing the quality and negating the predicate of a standard form categorical proposition, 190–194; proof of, 206–207; to reduce the number of terms in a syllogism, 249–251
Occam, William of, 6
"Only," 217–218, 372–374
"Only if," 269–270
Operational definition: A definition that assigns a meaning to a word by specifying experimental procedures that determine whether or not the word applies to a certain thing, 91–92, 94
Opinion, 15–16
Ostensive definition. *See* Demonstrative definition
Overlapping quantifiers: Quantifiers that lie within the scope of one another, 404–413

Parameter: A phrase that, when introduced into a statement, affects the form but not the meaning, 213–214
Parentheses, 271–272
Particular statement: A statement that makes a claim about one or more (but not all) members of a class, 35, 177–178, 180; in predicate logic, 371–372; in a restricted universe, 400
Pascal, Blaise, 479–480
Pasteur, Louis, 475, 481–483, 485–486
Percentages, 466–469
Perier, F., 479–480
Persuasive definition: A definition intended to engender a favorable or unfavorable attitude toward what is denoted by the definiendum, 84–85, 90, 94
Petitio principii. See Begging the question
Pictogram: A diagram that compares two situations through drawings that differ either in size or in number, 465–466
Piece of advice: A kind of nonargument composed of statements that recommend something to the reader or listener, 15
Plato, 79, 474
Politics, language of, 69–70
Post hoc ergo propter hoc, 127
Precising definition: A definition intended to reduce the vagueness of a word, 82–83, 90, 94
Predicate: An expression of the form "is a bird," "is a house," and "are fish," 176, 368
Predicate logic: A kind of logic that combines the symbolism of propositional logic with symbols used to translate predicates, 367–417
Predicate symbol: An uppercase letter used to translate a predicate, 368
Predicate term: In a standard form categorical proposition, the term that comes immediately after the copula, 174–176
Predication. *See* Collective predication; Distributive predication
Prediction: An inductive argument that proceeds from knowledge of some event in the relative past to a claim about some other event in the relative future, 33
Premise: A statement in an argument that sets

forth evidence, 2; contradictory, 311, 331; exclusive, 245
Premise indicator: A word that provides a clue to identifying a premise, 3–4, 14
Principia Mathematica, 7
Principle of indifference: In the classical theory of probability, the principle that the various possible outcomes are equally probable, 439–440
Probability calculus: A set of rules for computing the probability of compound events from the probabilities of simple events, 441–450
Probability of a necessary event, 441–442
Probability of an impossible event, 441–442
Pronouns, translation of, 214–215
Proper names, 74–75
Proposition: The information content of a statement, 5–6; exceptive, 219, 253–254; exclusive, 217–218, 372–374. *See also* Categorical proposition
Propositional logic: A kind of logic in which the fundamental components are whole statements or propositions, 266–366
Proving invalidity, 52–54; in predicate logic, 399–403
Psychological factors affecting a sample, 455–457
Ptolemy, 483–484, 486
Pure hypothetical syllogism: A valid argument form/rule of inference: "If *p* then *q* / If *q* then *r* / / If *p* then *r*," 294–295, 318–323

Quality: The attribute of a categorical proposition by which it is either affirmative or negative, 176–178, 180
Quantifier: In standard form categorical propositions, the words "all," "no," and "some," 175–176; existential, 371–372; nonstandard, 215; rule for change of, 388–391; unexpressed, 215; universal, 369–370
Quantity: The attribute of a categorical proposition by which it is either universal or particular, 176–178, 180

Radium, discovery of, 475–477
Randomness, of a sample, 453–455
Range: In statistics, the difference between the largest and smallest values in a set of data, 461–463
Red herring: A fallacy that occurs when the arguer diverts the attention of the reader or listener by addressing a number of extraneous issues and ends by presuming that some conclusion has been established, 116–118, 158
Redi, Francesco, 480–481
Relational predicate: A predicate that expresses a connection between two or more individuals, 404–413
Relations, 404–405
Relative frequency theory of probability: The theory according to which probabilities are computed by dividing the number of observed favorable events by the number of observed events, 440–442, 448, 450
Relevance, fallacies of. *See* Fallacies of relevance
Religion, language of, 71
Replacement, axiom of, 336, 338; rules of, 336–362
Report: A kind of nonargument consisting of one or more statements that convey information about some situation or event, 16

CONDITIONAL PROOF

$$
\begin{array}{ll}
\text{---} & \\
\text{---} & \\
\text{---} & \quad / \; q \supset r \\
\quad \big| \; q & \quad \text{ACP} \\
\quad \big| \; \text{---} & \\
\quad \big| \; \text{---} & \\
\quad \big| \; \text{---} & \\
\quad \big| \; r & \\
q \supset r & \quad \text{CP}
\end{array}
$$

INDIRECT PROOF

$$
\begin{array}{ll}
\text{---} & \\
\text{---} & \quad / \; q \\
\quad \big| \; {\sim}q & \quad \text{AIP} \\
\quad \big| \; \text{---} & \\
\quad \big| \; r & \\
\quad \big| \; {\sim}r & \\
\quad \big| \; r \cdot {\sim}r & \quad \text{Conj} \\
{\sim}{\sim}q & \quad \text{IP} \\
q & \quad \text{DN}
\end{array}
$$

RULES FOR REMOVING AND INTRODUCING QUANTIFIERS

(a, b, c, ... u, v, w = individual constants;
x, y, z = individual variables)

1. Universal instantiation (UI)

$$\frac{(x)\mathfrak{F}x}{\mathfrak{F}y} \qquad\qquad\qquad \frac{(x)\mathfrak{F}x}{\mathfrak{F}a}$$

2. Universal generalization (UG)

$$\frac{\mathfrak{F}y}{(x)\mathfrak{F}x} \qquad\qquad \text{not} \quad \frac{\mathfrak{F}a}{(x)\mathfrak{F}x}$$
$$\text{allowed:}$$

Restrictions: (conditional and indirect proof)

(1) UG must not be used within the scope of an indented sequence if the instantial variable occurs free in the first line of that sequence.

(overlapping quantifiers)

(2) UG must not be used if $\mathfrak{F}y$ contains an existential name and y is free in the line where that name is introduced.

3. Existential instantiation (EI)

$$\frac{(\exists x)\mathfrak{F}x}{\mathfrak{F}a} \qquad\qquad \text{not} \quad \frac{(\exists x)\mathfrak{F}x}{\mathfrak{F}y}$$
$$\text{allowed:}$$

Restriction: The existential name a must be a new name that has not occurred earlier in the proof.

4. Existential generalization (EG)

$$\frac{\mathfrak{F}a}{(\exists x)\mathfrak{F}x} \qquad\qquad\qquad \frac{\mathfrak{F}y}{(\exists x)\mathfrak{F}x}$$

CHANGE OF QUANTIFIER RULES

$$(x)\mathfrak{F}x \equiv {\sim}(\exists x){\sim}\mathfrak{F}x \qquad\qquad (\exists x)\mathfrak{F}x \equiv {\sim}(x){\sim}\mathfrak{F}x$$
$$ {\sim}(x)\mathfrak{F}x \equiv (\exists x){\sim}\mathfrak{F}x \qquad\qquad {\sim}(\exists x)\mathfrak{F}x \equiv (x){\sim}\mathfrak{F}x$$
